A

HISTORY OF NEW ENGLAND

WITH

Particular Reference to the Denomination of Christians

CALLED

BAPTISTS

ISAAC BACKUS
1724-1806

A

HISTORY OF NEW ENGLAND

WITH

Particular Reference to the Denomination of Christians

CALLED

BAPTISTS.

BY

ISAAC BACKUS.

Second Edition, with Notes.

BY

DAVID WESTON.

VOLUME I.

NEWTON, MASS.:
PUBLISHED BY THE BACKUS HISTORICAL SOCIETY. 1871

The Baptist Standard Bearer, Inc.
NUMBER ONE IRON OAKS DRIVE • PARIS, ARKANSAS 72855

Thou hast given a *standard* to them that fear thee;
that it may be displayed because of the truth.
-- Psalm 60:4

*Reprinted
by*

THE BAPTIST STANDARD BEARER, INC.
No. 1 Iron Oaks Drive
Paris, Arkansas 72855
(501) 963-3831

THE WALDENSIAN EMBLEM
lux lucet in tenebris
"The Light Shineth in the Darkness"

ISBN #1-57978-918-8

EDITOR'S PREFACE.

A historian who has been an actor in the events which he narrates, has peculiar advantages and disadvantages. He can write with more minuteness of detail, and with a fresher and more life-like coloring. He can write with more confidence, and, drawing from his own experience and observation, is in this respect more trustworthy. On the other hand, he is more liable to be warped by prejudice, to see only the excellences and none of the defects of those with whom he has been identified, and only the defects and none of the excellences of those to whom he has been opposed, to be a partizan rather than a judge, and to make his narration little more than the reflection of his personal opinions or his personal sympathy and affection, hostility and spite.

The Church History of Isaac Backus has all the above-named excellences. To a large extent he was an eye-witness of that which he describes; and where not an eye-witness, he placed himself in closest possible connection with it by personal acquaintance with the actors, and by immediate and most diligent and thorough examination of records and other evidence. While it may be too much to say that he absolutely avoided the defects above named, yet his sound judgment, his natural candor and honesty and his elevated Christian principle, have made him as nearly free from them as perhaps any author who has written in similar circumstances.

In the early history of the Baptists of New England, this work has always been justly regarded as the standard of authority. The single edition hitherto published was exhausted many years ago, and as the work became rare, the need of its republication was deeply felt. The Backus Historical Society, at a meeting in June, 1869, decided to undertake the task of republication; of which decision, the edition now presented to the public is the result.

This edition is a reproduction of the original work in full, and with only the following changes:—1. Grammatical errors and a few of the more prominent rhetorical errors have been corrected. These corrections have been made with the smallest possible variation from the text, and, for the most part, affect only some verbal form. 2. The author's errata of the first edition are corrected in the body of the work according to his direction. 3. The orthography of the work has been made to conform more nearly to the present standard. 4. The citations of the work have been collated with the originals, except in a few instances where the latter could not be found; and in many cases, more explicit references, or references to current editions, have been made in brackets. Such editorial references to Winthrop's Journal are to the New Edition by James Savage, Boston, 1853; those to Hubbard, are to Hubbard's History of New England, Massachusetts Historical Society, 1815; those to Mather's Magnalia are to the First American Edition, Hartford, 1820; those to Prince's Chronology and Prince's Annals are to the edition published in Boston, 1826; those to Morton's Memorial are to the edition of the Congregational Board of Publication, Boston, 1855. Where the author refers to Vol. I or Vol. II of "Massachusetts History," he means Hutchinson's History of Massachusetts, and the editorial references are to the edition published at Salem, 1795. By "Massachusetts History, Vol. III," the author means not the continuation of Hutchinson's work by his grandson, but the work commonly known as "Hutchinson's Collection of Original Papers." Differences between the originals and their citation by the author have been noted in brackets. In the letter of Robert Mascall, found in Vol. I, pages 311 to 313 of the present edition, Mr. Backus indicated such changes, in supplying or omitting words, &c., as he felt at liberty to make; and in the Preface to Vol. I, he said, "I have as strictly kept to the true sense in all my quotations as in that, yet I have not thought it necessary to continue such marks in all." That which is contained in brackets in the above-named letter is from the author; in all other places, from the editor. 5. Editorial foot-notes have been added, amounting in all to about a hundred pages. These are marked "ED."; and where an editorial note is appended to one by the author, they are distinguished by marking the latter "B." 6. A full Index to both volumes is appended to Vol. II, in place of the brief and very defective indices and tables of contents of the original work. 7. All the longer quotations are distinguished from the author's own words by change of type; topical headings are affixed to each alternate page, and necessary changes are made in the title pages.—Thus the only liberty taken with the original text has been to correct a few errors of language, while all other changes are so marked as to be clearly distinguished as such.

The circumstances in which the work is issued have not been favorable to typographical accuracy. The editor has been at a distance from the printers; and in order that sufficient care and labor might be expended in preparing the work for the press, and yet secure its completion without so much delay as to disappoint subscribers, it has been needful to urge it through the press with more haste than would have been otherwise desirable. It is believed however, that typographical errors will not be found to any unusual extent.

The editor would express his grateful acknowledgments to S. F. Haven, Esq., and E. M. Barton, Esq., librarians of the American Antiquarian Society, Worcester, Mass., for their kindness and courtesy in giving free access to the rare and extensive archæological library under their charge, and for the aid which they have been always ready to lend in consulting it; to his venerable relative, Rev. Silas Hall, of Raynham, Mass., who placed at his disposal a large, carefully prepared and most valuable collection of manuscripts relating to the history of New England Baptists,—a collection which has added much to the value of other historical works before this, and in which much valuable material still remains untouched;—to the Rhode Island Historical Society, for permission to use the Diary of John Comer; to Reuben A. Guild, Esq., librarian of Brown University, for permission to use the Diary of Hezekiah Smith, and for other assistance; to Rev. C. E. Barrows, of Newport, R. I., and to William E. Clarke, of Conneaut, Oo., for valuable material used in foot-notes; and to Alden A. Howe, Esq., of Worcester, Mass., for preparing the Index.

WORCESTER, MASS., December 5, 1870.

Sicut lilium inter spinas sic amica mea inter filias

On The Cover: We use the symbol of the "lily among the thorns" from Song of Solomon 2:2 to represent the Baptist History Series. The Latin, *Sicut lilium inter spinas sic amica mea inter filias*, translates, "As the lily among thorns, so is my love among the daughters."

AUTHOR'S PREFACE TO VOLUME I.

History has been so often written and improved, either for party purposes, or mere amusement, that some serious persons have been ready to treat it as a thing foreign to religion, and of little service to mankind. Yet the same persons will readily own, that nothing teaches like experience; and what is true history but the experiences of those who have gone before us? of which perhaps none have been more remarkable, since the affairs of Canaan, than those of this country. And as the present contests about liberty and government are very great, they call loudly for all the light therein that can be gained from every quarter.

Mr. Rollin, in his ancient history, says, "The powers that be are ordained of God; but neither every use that is made of this power, nor every means for the attainment of it, are from God, though every power be of him. And when we see these governments degenerating, sometimes to violence, factions, despotic sway and tyranny, 'tis wholly to the passions of mankind that we must ascribe those irregularities which are directly opposite to the primitive institution of states; and which a superior wisdom afterwards reduces to order, always making them contribute to the execution of his designs, full of equity and justice. This scene highly deserves our attention and admiration. It is with a view of making the reader attentive to this object, that I think it incumbent on me to add to the account of facts and events what regards the manners and customs of nations; because these shew their genius and character, which we may call, in some measure, the soul of history."

Now it may well be supposed, that men who are striving for more power over others than belongs to them, will not nor cannot set either their own or their opponents' "genius and character" in their just light. And if it should be found, that nearly all the histories of this country which are much known, have been written by persons who thought themselves invested with power to act as lawgivers and judges for their neighbors, under the name either of orthodoxy, or of immediate power from heaven, the inference will be strong, that our affairs have never been set in so clear light as they ought to be; and if this is not indeed the case I am greatly mistaken; of which the following account will enable the reader to judge for himself.

The greatest objection that I have heard against this design is, that we ought not to rake up the ashes of our good fathers, nor to rehearse those old controversies, which will tend to increase our present difficulties. But what is meant by this objection? To reveal secrets, or to repeat matters that have been well settled between persons or parties, is forbidden, and its effects are very pernicious; but what is that to a history of public facts, and an examination of the principles and conduct, both of oppressors, and of the oppressed?

Men who are still fond of arbitrary power may make the above objection; but a learned and ingenious pædobaptist that felt the effects of such power, lately said, "The Presbyterians, I confess, formerly copied too nearly the Episcopalians. The genuine principles of universal and impartial liberty were very little understood by any; and all parties were too much involved in the guilt of intolerance and persecution. The dissenters in our times freely acknowledge this, and condemn the narrow principles of many of their predecessors; having no objection to transmitting down to posterity, in their true colors, the acts of oppression and intolerance of which all sects have been guilty. Not indeed, as is sometimes done, with a view of encouraging such conduct in one party by the example of others; but of exposing it alike in all, and preventing it wholly, if possible, in time to come."[1] This is the great design of the ensuing work; and such a work seems essentially necessary to that end. For as every one is orthodox to himself, they who have oppressed others, have always denied it. After our Baptist fathers in Boston, had been greatly injured for fifteen years, they published a vindication of their character; but as to their sufferings, contented themselves with saying, "Some of us were oftentimes brought before councils and courts, threatened, fined, our estates taken away, imprisoned and banished." A noted minister called their vindication a fallacious narrative, and said, "Errors lie in generals, a particular account might have been more satisfying."[2] Here therefore are a great number of particulars with good vouchers to support them; which shew that oppression on religious accounts was not of the first principles of New England, but was an intruder that came in afterward.

When I was requested by several gentlemen of note and others, to undertake this work, two great objections presented themselves to my mind against it; namely, my great unfitness for it, and the difficulty of obtaining the necessary materials. But their importunity prevailed against the first, and divine providence has removed the other, by conveying into my hands a variety of authentic materials, much beyond what I conceived could have now been obtained in the world. Many of them I have taken

---

[1] Furneaux's letter to Blackstone, p. 74.   [2] Willard's *Ne sutor*, p. 10.

from the ancient records of the colonies of Plymouth, Massachusetts, Providence and Rhode Island, as well as the records of the United Colonies; though I regret the want of better acquaintance with the two latter, before the first two hundred pages of our history were printed off. Many other records have also been serviceable; and I would now return my public thanks to the several gentlemen who are keepers of them, for the candid and kind treatment they have shown on this occasion. A great variety of other manuscripts have been serviceable to me, whereof Mr. Hubbard's History, and extracts from Governor Winthrop's Journal are not the least. It is to be noted, that only the word "Hubbard" in the following quotations refers to that history, in distinction from another valuable collection, of which take the following account :—Mr. Samuel Hubbard came over to Salem in 1633, in his youth; joined to Watertown church in 1635; but went the same year up to Windsor, [Conn.] where he soon married a church member that removed from Dorchester, and they settled at Weathersfield; till in May, 1639, they removed to Springfield, and he was one of the five men who first joined in founding that church. It was constituted under Connecticut government, but falling afterward into the Massachusetts, he removed in 1647 to Fairfield. Though he says, "God having enlightened both, but mostly my wife, into his holy ordinance of baptizing only visible believers; and being zealous for it, she was mostly struck at, and answered twice publicly, where I was also said to be as bad as she, and threatened with imprisonment to Hartford goal, if we did not renounce it or remove. That Scripture came into our minds, If they persecute you in one place, flee to another." Whereupon they removed to Newport, and joined to Elder Clarke's church there on November 3, 1648, where they lived to old age; from whence he repeatedly visited his suffering brethren at Boston, and had an extensive correspondence both in Europe and America; and he copied several hundred of his own and others' letters into a book, which I am now favored with; containing a fund of intelligence, from 1641 to 1688. The writings and papers also of our elders, Holmes, Comer, Callender and others, have been useful in this design. Though, for want of room, I have been forced to leave a great many valuable articles out of this volume, and to give but a sketch of things in latter times. However I propose by divine leave to preserve and digest them in the best manner I can, for the use of those who may come after us; and should be glad to obtain accounts of the rise, progress and present state of all our churches for the same end.

In the following work, Plymouth Register intends an account of their church from its beginning, written by our County Register, and annexed to Mr. Robbins's Ordination Sermon, 1760.[1] The History of Providence means what was published of that nature in their Gazette in 1765.[2] Perhaps the rest of my authorities are sufficiently described. So great a part of this history is given in the words of others, that continued marks of quotation would have been tedious; therefore many passages only begin and end therewith.³ In the excellent letter you have in pages 311—313, I have marked the words which were necessarily supplied to complete the sense; but though I have as strictly kept to the true sense in all my quotations as in that, yet I have not thought it necessary to continue such marks in all. In the dates, where our fathers began the year with March, I have either plainly noted it, or else have begun the year with January, only have let the old style stand till it was altered here by law. Of the moneys, Mr. Prince says they were reckoned sterling till 1640. In 1652, when they first coined silver here, one pound of it was fifteen shillings sterling, and so it continued to 1690, when they began to make paper money, which gradually depreciated from six shillings to forty-five shillings for a Spanish milled dollar. In 1750 our currency was brought back to what it was a hundred years before, and that is our lawful money ever since. A dash [—] in a quotation signifies the omission of something there for brevity's sake;⁴ betwixt figures, it is to extend the reference from one number to the other.

Whoever considers the difficulty of compiling such a work with exactness, together with the confusion of the present times, and the author's distance from the press, will not be severe upon him for every imperfection that may be discovered therein; though he has named his principal vouchers on purpose to have his performance thoroughly examined, and every material mistake corrected. Sincerity and impartiality are allowed to be the most essential rules of history; how far they appear in this the reader will judge. Only the author must say, that he has acted under a full belief, that with what measure we mete, it shall be measured to us again; so that we cannot injure others in any case, without therein wronging our own souls. And to impress this great truth upon all minds, is the aim and earnest desire of their humble servant,

ISAAC BACKUS.

MIDDLEBOROUGH, July 9, 1777.

---

¹"An account of the church of Christ in Plymouth, the first church in New England, from its establishment unto the present day. By John Cotton, Esq., member of said church." This work was published in 1760. It is republished in the Massachusetts Historical Collections, Vol. IV, pp. 107—141.—ED.

²"This tract has been usually ascribed to the venerable Stephen Hopkins, who for eight years had been Governor of the colony, and served in that office one year after, but is better known as one of the signers of the Declaration of Independence." Introductory note to "An Account of Providence, R. I.," as republished in the Massachusetts Historical Collections, Second Series, Vol. IX.—ED.

³According to modern usage, this is the case with all the quotations in the present edition.—ED.

⁴In the present edition, such omissions are indicated by dots [....].—ED.

History of the Baptists in New England.

CHAPTER I.

THE SENTIMENTS AND CHARACTER OF THE FIRST PLANTERS OF THIS COUNTRY, WITH THEIR PROCEEDINGS DOWN TO THE YEAR 1634.

To obtain clear and just ideas of the affairs of the Baptists in New England, it seems necessary for us to look back to its first settlement, and carefully to examine what were the sentiments and character of the original planters. Those that began the first colony were called Separatists, because of their withdrawal from the national church of England; and different parties have accused them with rigidness therein; but ingenuous minds will not choose to be turned off with hard names, without knowing what is meant by them; therefore let us hear those fathers tell their own story. They separated from the national church near the beginning of the last century, and formed societies for worship by themselves; till, after suffering much from the ruling party in their native country, they left it, and sojourned about twelve years in Holland, and then removed to this land.

About the time of their fleeing into Holland, Mr. Richard Bernard, an Episcopal minister in Nottinghamshire, out of which many of those fathers removed, published a book against them, which he called "The Separatist's Schism," to which Mr. John Robinson, the pastor of the church which afterward began the settlement of New England, published an answer in 1610, entitled, "A Justification of Separation from the Church of England." As I am favored with this performance, containing four hundred and seventy-six pages in quarto, I shall from thence give the reader the author's own words upon the most material points of their controversy, and the rather, because the writings of that eminent father of our country are very little known at this day among us.

Mr. Bernard began his book with some things which he called "Christian Counsels of Peace," to which Mr. Robinson answers[1]:—

As God is the God of peace, so are not they God's children which desire it not; yea, even in the midst of their contentions. But as all vices use to clothe themselves with the habits of virtues, that under their [those] liveries they may get countenance, and find the more free passage in the world, so especially in the church, all tyranny and confusion do present themselves under this color, taking up the politic pretence of peace, as a weapon of more advantage, wherewith the stronger and greater party useth to beat the weaker. The papists press the protestants with the peace of the church, and, for the rent [which] they have made in it, condemn them beyond the heathenish soldiers, which forebore to divide Christ's garment; as deeply do the bishops charge the ministers refusing conformity and subscription,[2] and both of them us. But the godly wise must not be affrighted

---

[1] It is perhaps unfortunate, rhetorically, that these long and, to the general reader, somewhat tedious extracts from the work of Robinson are introduced at the commencement of the History. Such a reader may need to pass lightly over these first pages, suspending his judgment of the work till he reaches the commencement of the narrative.

These extracts have been carefully collated with the work from which they were taken, as found in Vol. II of the works of John Robinson, published by the Congregational Board, London, 1851. The differences found, where there was not an obvious error, are here indicated in brackets. Many words and phrases, not strictly necessary to the sense, were found to have been omitted, some of which are here supplied in brackets. The figures in brackets refer to the pages of the above-mentioned volume.—Ed.

[2] The main of those who afterward settled the Massachusetts colony were of this sort; they refused full conformity to the national church, and yet condemned an entire separation from it.

either from seeking or embracing the truth with such bugs as these are, but seeing "the wisdom which is from above, is first pure, then peaceable," he must make it a great part of his Christian wisdom to discern betwixt godly and gracious peace, and that which is either pretended for advantage, or mistaken by error, and so [to] labor to hold peace in purity. Let it then be manifested unto us, that the communion which the church of England hath with all the wicked in the land, without separation, is a pure communion; that their service book, devised and prescribed in so many words and letters, to be read over and over with all the appurtenances, is a pure worship; that their government by national, provincial and diocesan bishops, according to their canons, is a pure government, and then let us be blamed if we hold not peace with them in word and deed; otherwise, though they speak [spake] unto us never so oft, both by messengers and mouth of peace, and again of peace, as Jehoram did to Jehu, yet must we answer them in effect as Jehu did Jehoram, What peace, whilst the whoredoms of the mother of fornications [fornicators], the Jezebel of Rome, do remain in so great number amongst them? And I doubt not but Mr. Bernard, and a thousand more ministers in the land (were they secure of the magistrate's sword, and might they go on with [his] good license) would wholly shake off their canonical obedience to their ordinaries, and neglect their citations and censures, and refuse to sue in their courts, for all the peace of the church which they commend to us for so sacred a thing. Could they but obtain license from the magistrate to use the liberties [liberty] which they are persuaded Christ hath given them, they would soon shake off the prelates' yoke, and draw no longer under the same in spiritual communion with all the profane in the land, but would break those bonds of iniquity, as easily as Samson did the cords wherewith Delilah tied him, and give good reasons also from the word of God for their so doing. Pp. 13, 14. [12, 13.]

Whoever reads and well observes the history of the Massachusetts colony, I believe, will find that those remarks were neither enthusiastic nor censorious, but that they discover great knowledge, and a good judgment both in human and divine concernments. Mr. Robinson proceeds and says:—

These things I thought good to commend to the reader, that he may be the more cautious of this and the like colorable pretences, wishing him also well to remember, that peace in disobedience is that old theme of the false prophets, whereby they flattered the mighty, and deceived the simple. Jer. vi. 14, and viii. 11. ..... In the church of England we do acknowledge many excellent truths of doctrine, which we also teach without commixture of error, many Christian ordinances which we also practise, being purged from the pollution of antichrist; and, for the godly persons in it, (could we possibly separate them from the profane) we would gladly embrace them with both arms. But, being taught by the apostle, speaking but of one wicked person, and of one Jewish ordinance, that "a little leaven leaveneth the whole lump," 1 Cor. v. 6, Gal. v. 9, we cannot be ignorant how sour the English assemblies must needs be; neither may we justly be blamed though we dare not dip in their meal, lest we be soured by their leaven. Pp. 15, 16. [14, 15.]

To Mr. B., who counsels that we should "bear with lighter faults for a time, till fit occasion be offered to have them amended," he replies:—

1. No sin is light in itself, but being continued in and countenanced, destroyeth the sinner. Matt. v. 19. 2. It is the property of a profane and hardened heart evermore to extenuate and lessen sins. 3. Though the bearing and forbearing, not only of small but even of great sins also, must be for a time, yet it must be but for a time, and that is whilst reformation be orderly sought and procured. Lev. xix. 17. But what time hath wrought in the church of England, all men see growing daily, by the just judgment of God, from evil to worse, and being never aforetime so impatient either of reformation or other good as at this day. 4. A man must so bear evil, as he be no way accessory unto it, by forbearing any means appointed by Christ for the amending it. P. 16. [15.]

I see not upon what occasion the author should shuffle into this controversy, which is merely ecclesiastical, such considerations as he doth concerning the frame and alteration of civil states, except he would either insinuate against us, that we went about to alter the civil state of the kingdom; or, at least, that the alteration of the state ecclesiastical, must needs draw with it the alteration of the civil state; with which mote the prelates have a long time bleared the eyes of the magistrates; but how deceitfully, hath been sufficiently manifested, and offer made further to manifest the same by solemn disputation. And the truth is, that all states and policies which are of God, whether monarchical, aristocratical or democratical, or how mixed soever, are capable of Christ's government. Neither doth the nature of the state, but the corruption of the persons, hinder the same in one or other. . . . . . And where Mr. Bernard further adviseth, rather to offend many private persons than one lawful magistrate, I doubt not he gives no worse counsel than he himself follows, who (except I be much deceived in him) had rather offend half the private persons in the diocese, than one archbishop, though he be an unlawful magistrate. But let us remember our care be not to offend the Lord, and if with the offence of a private person, though never so base, be joined the offence of the Lord, better offend all, both lawful and unlawful magistrates, in the world, than such a little one. Matt. xviii, 6. Pp. 17, 18. [17, 18.]

Another piece of counsel given by Mr. B. is, "Use the present good which thou mayest enjoy, to the utmost; and an experienced good, before thou dost trouble thyself to seek for a supposed better good, untried, which thou enjoyest not." To this Mr. R. says:—

We may not stint or circumscribe either our knowledge, faith, or obedience, within straiter bounds than the whole revealed will of God, in the knowledge and obedience whereof we must daily increase and edify ourselves; much less must we suffer ourselves to be stripped of any liberty which Christ our Lord hath purchased for us, and given us to use for our good. Gal. v. i. And here, as I take it, comes in the case of many hundreds in the church of England, who what good they may enjoy (that is safely enjoy, or without any great bodily danger) that they use very fully. Where the ways of Christ lie open for them, by the authority of men, and where they may walk safely with good leave, there they walk very uprightly, and that a round pace; but when the commandments of Christ are, as it were, hedged up with thorns, by men's prohibitions, there they foully "step aside, and pitch their tents by the flocks of his fellows." Cant. i. 7. P. 23. [23, 24.]

Again Mr. B. says, "Never presume to reform others, before thou hast well ordered thyself." To which Mr. Robinson answers:—

True zeal, it is certain, ever begins at home, and gives more liberty unto other men than it dares assume unto itself; and there is nothing more true, and [or] necessary to be considered, than that every man ought to order himself in [and] his own steps first. That is good and the best, but not all; for if by God's commandment we ought to bring back our enemy's ox or ass that strayeth, how much more to bring into order our brother's soul and body, wandering in by-paths? P. 24. [25.]

Mr. Bernard went on to lay down a number of things, which he supposed would render it very unlikely that a separation from them could be right, before he came to the merits of the cause; as, 1. "The novelty thereof differing from all the best reformed churches in Christendom." To which Mr. Robinson replies:—

It is no novelty to hear men plead custom, when they want truth. So the heathen philosophers reproached Paul as a bringer of new doctrine. Acts xvii. 19. So do the papists discountenance the doctrine and profession of the church of England; yea, even at this day, very many of the people in the land call popery the old law, and the profession there made the new law. But for our parts, as we believe, by the word of God, that the things we teach are not new, but old truths renewed; so are we no less [fully] persuaded, that the church constitution, in which we are set, is cast in the apostolical and primitive mould, and not one day nor hour younger, in the nature and form of it, than the first church of the New Testament. P. 40. [42, 43.]

2. "For that it agreeeth so much with the ancient schismatics, condemned in former ages by holy and learned men." Answer:—

Can our way both be a novelty, and yet agree so well with ancient schismatics? Contraries cannot be both true, but may both be false, as these are. P. 42. [44, 45.]

Mr. Robinson tells us, that another article which Mr. B. alleged against them is, "That we have not the approbation of any of the reformed churches for our course." Answer:—

This is the same in substance with the first, and that which followeth in the next place the same with them both; and Mr. B. by [his] so ordinarily pressing us with human testimonies, shews himself to be very barren of divine authority. Nature teacheth every creature, in all danger, to fly first and oftenest to the chief instruments either of offence or defence, wherein it trusteth, as the bull to his horn, the boar to his tusk, and the bird unto her wing; right so this man shews wherein his strength lies, and wherein he trusts most, by [his] so frequent and usual shaking the horn, and whetting the tusk, of mortal man's authority against us. But for the reformed churches the truth is, they neither do imagine, nor will easily be brought to believe, that the frame of the church of England stands as it doth. The approbation which they give [of you] is in respect of such general truths of doctrine, as wherein we also, for the most part, acknowledge you; which notwithstanding you deny in a great measure in the particulars and practice. But touching the gathering and governing of the church, which are the main heads controverted betwixt you and us; they give you not so much as the left hand of fellowship, but do, on the contrary, turn their backs upon you. Pp. 46, 47[1]. [49, 50.] Thus much of the learned abroad. In the next place, Mr. Bernard draws us to the learned at home, from whose dislike of us he takes his fifth likelihood, which he thus frameth : "The condemnation of this way by our divines, both living and dead, against whom, either for godliness of life or truth of doctrine, otherwise than for being their opposites, they can take no exception."

To this, Mr. Robinson answers :—

No marvel. We may not admit of parties for judges. How is it possible we should be approved of them in the things wherein we witness against them? And if this argument be good and [or] likely, then is it likely that neither the reformists have the truth in the church of England, nor the prelates; for there are many of those both godly and learned, which in their differences do oppose, and that very vehemently, the one the other. Now, as for my own part, I do willingly acknowledge the learning and godliness of most of the persons named by Mr. B. and honor the memory of some of them ; so neither do I think them so learned, but they might err, nor so godly, but in their error they might reproach the truth they saw not. I do confess to the glory of God, and mine own shame, that a long time before I entered this way, I took some taste of the truth in it by some treatises published in justification of it, which [the Lord knoweth] were sweet as honey unto my mouth; and the principal thing which for the time quenched all further appetite in me, was the over-valuation which I made of the learning and holiness of these and the like persons, blushing in myself to have a thought of pressing one hair-breadth before them in this thing, behind whom I knew myself to come so many

---

[1] The ways of the church of England, wherein we forsake her, do directly and *ex diametro* cross and thwart the ways of the reformed churches, in these three main heads :—I. The reformed churches are gathered of a free people, joined together by voluntary profession, without compulsion of human laws. On the contrary, the church of England consists of a people forced together violently by the laws of men into their provincial, diocesan and parishional churches (as their houses stand) be they never so unwilling or unfit. 2. The reformed churches do renounce the ministry of the church of England, as she doth theirs; not admitting of any by virtue of it to charge of souls, as they speak, where, on the contrary, all the mass-priests made in Queen Mary's days, which would say their book-service in English, were continued ministers by the same ordination which they received from popish prelates. 3. The government by archbishops, lord bishops and their substitutes, in the church of England, is abhorred and disclaimed in the reformed churches as antichristian; as is, on the contrary, the Presbyterian government, in use there, by the church of England refused, as anabaptistical and seditious. P. 52. [55, 56.]

Here we may see how the very name of Anabaptist was used as a weapon to fight against reformation in Mr. Robinson's day, and the practice is still followed by many.

miles in all other things; yea and even of late times, when I had entered into a more serious consideration of these things, and, according to the measure of grace received, searched the Scriptures, whether they were so or no, and by searching found much light and truth, yet was the same so dimmed and overclouded with the contradictions of these men, and others of the like note, that had not the truth been in my heart as a burning fire shut up in my bones, Jer. xx. 9, I had never broken those bonds of flesh and blood, but had suffered the light of God to have been put out in my [mine own] unthankful heart, by other men's darkness.

Every man stands bound to give this reverence to the graces of God in other men, that in his differences with [from] them he be not suddenly nor easily persuaded, but that being jealous of his own heart, he undertake the examination of things, and so proceed with fear and trembling, and having tried all things, keep that which is good; 1 Thes. v. 21; so shall he neither wrong the graces of God in himself, nor in others. But on the other side, for a man so far to suffer his thoughts to be conjured into the circle of any [mortal] man's or men's judgment, as either to fear to try what is offered to the contrary, in the balance of the sanctuary, or finding it to bear weight, to fear to give sentence on the Lord's side, yea though it be against the mighty, this is to honor men above God, and to advance a throne above the throne of Christ, who is Lord and King forever. And to speak that in this case, which by doleful experience I myself have found, many of the most forward professors in the kingdom are well nigh as superstitiously addicted to the determinations of their guides and teachers, as the ignorant papists unto theirs; accounting it not only needless curiosity, but even intolerable arrogancy, to call in question the things received from them by tradition. But how much better were it for all men to lay aside these and the like prejudices, that so they might understand the things which concern their peace, and seeing with their own eyes, might live by their own faith.

And, for these famous men named by Mr. B., (with whose oppositions, as with Zedekiah's horns of iron, he would push us here and everywhere) as we hear their reproofs with patience, and acknowledge their worth [worths] without envy or detraction, so do we know they were but men, and through human frailty might be abused as well, or rather as ill, to support antichrist in a measure, as others before them have been, though godly and learned as they. It will not be denied but the fathers, as they are called, Ignatius, Irenæus, Tertullian, Cyprian, Ambrose, Jerome, Austin, and the rest, were both godly and learned, yet no man, if he have but even saluted them, can be ignorant what way, though unwittingly, they made for the advancement of antichrist which followed after them; and if they, notwithstanding their learning and godliness, thus ushered him into the world, why might not others, and that more likely, though learned and godly as the former, help to bear up his train? especially considering that as his rising was not, so neither could his fall be perfected at once. And, for us, what do we more or otherwise, for the most part, than walk in those ways into which divers of the persons by Mr. B. named have directed us by the word of God, in manifesting unto us by the light thereof what the ministry, government, worship, and fellowship of the gospel ought to be[1]? We then being taught, and believing that the word of God is a light and lantern, not only to our eyes, but to our feet and paths, as the psalmist speaketh, Psal. cxix. 105, cannot possibly conceive how we should justly be blamed by these men for observing the ordinances which themselves not only acknowledged, but contended for, as appointed by Christ, to be kept inviolable till his appearing, as some of them have expressly testified.

To conclude, let not the Christian reader cast our persons, and the persons of our opposites, whether these or others, in the balance together; but rather our cause and reasons, with their oppositions and the grounds of them, and so with [a] steady hand, and impartial eye, poise cause with cause, that so the truth of God may not be prejudiced by men's persons, nor held in respect of them. Pp. 48—53. [51—54.]

By these free and plain declarations the reader may be able to judge, whether the reproach of rigidness properly belongs to Mr. Robinson, or to his accusers and persecutors; yet because he would not stay in the church of England, when he was convinced of its being wrong so to do, Mr. Bernard accuses him and his brethren of either denying

---

[1] For proof of this, Mr. Robinson, in another place, cites a number of passages, written, he says, "by such men as I dare say Mr. B. reckons amongst the painful and conscionable ministers." Their words are these:—" The names and offices of archbishops, archdeacons, lord bishops, &c. are, together with their government, drawn out of the pope's shop, antichristian, [devilish] and contrary to the Scriptures. Parsons, vicars, parish priests, stipendiaries, &c. be birds of the same feather." 2d Admo. to the Parliament, [By Thos. Cartwright.] "There is no true visible church of Christ, but a particular congregation only." Christian Offer, prop. 4. "Every true visible church of Christ, or ordinary assembly of the faithful, hath, by Christ's ordinance, power in itself immediately under Christ to elect, to ordain, deprive and depose their ministers, and to execute all other ecclesiastical censures." Ibid., prop. 5. "The visible church of Christ, wheresoever it be, hath the power of binding and loosing annexed unto it, as our Saviour, Christ teacheth;" Matt. xviii. Discovery of Dr. Bancroft's Slanders. [Preface.] "Amongst us the holy mysteries of God are profaned, the Gentiles enter into the temple of God, the holy things are indifferently communicated with the clean and unclean." Plain Declaration. "Now," says Mr. Robinson, "let the [indifferent] reader judge whether these men in thus writing have not opened the door unto us, by which themselves enter not." Pp. 75, 76. [81, 82.]

their conversion there, or else of accounting it a false one. To which Mr. R. answers:—

For our personal conversion in the church of England, we deny it not, but do, and always have done, judge and profess it true there; and so was Luther's conversion true in the church of Rome, else could not his separation from Rome have been of faith, or accepted of God. P. 69. [75.]

And now for particular sentiments about church affairs. Mr. Robinson's opponent had said, "The word is the constitution of the church." To which he replies:—

His meaning is or should be, that the word is the ordinary [outward] means for collecting and constituting the church of God. I grant it. But how considered? Not the word in men's Bibles alone, for then all the heretics in the world were true churches [are true Christians]; nor yet the word preached simply, for Paul preached the word to the scoffing Athenians, and to the blasphemous Jews, yet I think he will not say that either the one or the other were churches truly constituted. How then? The word published, understood, believed and obeyed, outwardly at the least, as the spiritual sword or axe, hewing the stones in the rock, and the trees in the forest, and preparing them to be the Lord's spiritual house. And thus much the very places produced by Mr. B. [like Goliath's sword drawn out to cut off his own head,] do evidently declare.

Matt. xxviii. 19, which is the first place, shows that such as by preaching of the word were made disciples, for so much the word [$Μαθητεύσατε$] importeth, were to be gathered into the church and baptized. Mark xvi. 15, shows the same, especially if you add verse 16, inferring that men by preaching must believe, and so believe as they have the promise of salvation. 2 Cor. v. 19, and xi. 2, prove that the word of reconciliation and ministry of the gospel, believed and obeyed to the forgiveness of sins, and to the preparation and sanctification of the church of [to] Christ, is the means of gathering and building up the same. Acts ii. 14, 37, 38, 41, and xvi. 32—34, are of the same nature [with the former], and do prove that sundry of the Jews at Jerusalem, by Peter's preaching, and that the jailer's household at Philippi, by Paul's preaching, were brought to repentance, and faith in Christ, and so added to the church. But what will be the conclusion of all these premises? The proposition is this:—The true apostolic churches having a true constitution, were gathered and constituted of such men and women as by the preaching of the gospel were made disciples, had faith and repentance wrought in them, to the obtaining of the forgiveness of sins, and promise of life eternal, and to sanctification and obedience. Pp. 89, 90. [95, 96.]

Of baptism Mr. Robinson says :—

The proper ends and uses of baptism are to initiate the parties baptized into the church of Christ, and to consecrate them to his service, and so to serve for badges of Christianity, by which it is distinguished from all other professions. Matt. xxviii. 19, 1 Cor. xii. 13. P. 26. [28.] The sacrament of baptism is to be administered by Christ's appointment, and the apostles' example, only to such as are, externally, and so far as men can judge, taught and made disciples [Matt. xxviii. 19.]; do receive the word gladly; Acts ii. 41; believe and so profess; Acts viii. [12, 13, 37]; have received the Holy Ghost; Acts x. 47; and to their seed; Acts ii. 39, 1 Cor. vii. 14. P. 92. [99.] Baptism administered to any others is so far from investing them with any saintship in that estate, that [as] it makes guilty, both the giver and receiver, of sacrilege, and is the taking of God's name in vain. P. 110. [115.]

Of the Lord's Supper he says :—

The apostle teacheth, 1 Cor. x. 16, that the bread and wine in the supper are the communion of the body and blood of Christ, that is, effectual pledges of our conjunction and incorporation with Christ, and one with another; and in ver. 17, that all which eat of one bread or one loaf, are one mystical body. This place alone, if Mr. B. and his fellow ministers would seriously consider, and set themselves faithfully to observe, they would rather offer their own bodies to be torn in pieces by wild beasts, than the holy mysteries of Christ's body to be profaned as they are. P. 92. [98.]

Of the keys, Matt. xvi. 18, 19, he says :—

It is granted by all sides that Christ gave unto Peter the keys of the kingdom, that is, the power to remit and retain sins declaratively, as they speak; as also that in what respect this power was given to Peter, in the same respect it was, and is, given to such as succeed Peter; but the question is, in what respect or consideration this power spoken of was delegated to him? The papist affirms it was given to Peter as the prince of the apostles, and so to the bishops of Rome, as Peter's successors, and thus they stablish the pope's primacy. The prelates say Nay, but unto Peter an apostle, that is, a chief officer of the church, and so to us, as chief officers succeeding him. Others affirm it to belong to Peter here as a minister of the word and sacraments, and the like, and so consequently to all other ministers of the gospel equally, which succeed Peter in those and the like administrations. But we, for our parts do believe and profess that this promise is not made to Peter in any of these respects, nor to any office, order, estate, dignity or degree in the church or world, but to the confession of faith, which Peter made by way of answer to Christ's question, [who, demanding of the disciples whom, amongst the variety of opinions that went of him, they thought him to be, was answered by Peter in the name of the rest] "Thou art Christ, the Son of the living God." To this Christ replies, "Blessed art thou; thou art Peter, and upon this rock will I build my church; I will give unto thee the keys," &c. So that the building of the church is upon the rock of Peter's confession, that is, Christ whom he confessed. This faith is the foundation of the church; against this faith the gates of hell shall not prevail; this faith hath the keys of the kingdom of heaven; what this faith shall loose or bind on earth, is bound and loosed in heaven. Thus the Protestant divines, when they deal against the pope's supremacy, do generally expound this Scripture; [though Mr. B. directly makes the pope and his shavelings, Peter's successors in this place, as hereafter will appear.] Now it followeth, that whatsoever person hath received the same precious faith with Peter, as all the faithful have, 2 Pet. i. 1, that person hath a part in this gift of Christ. Whosoever doth confess, publish, manifest or make known Jesus to be the Christ, the Son of the living God, and Saviour of the world, that person opens heaven's gates, looseth sin, and partakes with Peter in the use of the keys; and hereupon it followeth necessarily, that one faithful man, yea, or woman either, may as truly and effectually loose and bind, both in heaven and earth, as all the ministers in the world. Pp. 149, 159. [157, 158.]

But here I know the lordly clergy, like the bulls of Bashan, will roar loud upon me, as speaking things intolerably derogatory to the dignity of priesthood; and it may be some others also, either through ignorance or superstition, will take offence at this speech, as confounding all things; but there is no such cause of exception. For howsoever the keys be one and the same in nature and efficacy, in what faithful man, or men's hands soever, as not depending either upon the number or excellency of any persons, but upon Christ alone; yet is it ever to be remembered, that the order and manner of using them is very different.

The [These] keys in doctrine may be turned as well upon them which are without the church, as upon them which are within, and their sins either loosed or bound, Matt. xxviii. 19; but in discipline not so, but only upon them which are within; 1 Cor. v. 12, 13. Again, the apostles by their office had these keys to use in all churches, yea, in all nations upon earth; ordinary elders for their particular flocks; Acts xiv. 23, and xx. 28. Lastly, there is a use of the keys publicly to be had, and a use privately; a use of them by one person severally, and a use of them by the whole church jointly, and together; a use of them ministerially, or in office, and a use of them out of office. But the power of the gospel, which is the keys, is still one and the same, notwithstanding the diverse manner of using it. P. 151. [158, 159.]

If the keys of the kingdom of heaven be appropriated unto the officers, then can there be no forgiveness of sins, nor salvation, without officers; for there is no entrance into heaven but by the door. Without the key the door cannot be opened. So then, belike, if either there be no officers in the church (as it may easily come to pass in some extreme plague or persecution, [howsoever in England a man may have a priest for the whistling,] and must needs be in the churches of Christ in our days, either in their first planting, or first calling out of Babylon; for antichrist's mass-priesthood is not essentially Christ's true ministry,) or if the officers take away the key of knowledge, as the scribes and pharisees did, and will neither enter themselves nor suffer them that would; then must the miserable multitude be content to be shut out and perish eternally, for ought is known to the contrary. To admonish the officers of their sin, [it] were "against common sense, as that the father should be subject to his children, the work domineer over the workman, the seedsman be ordered by the corn," and to excommunicate them and call new, were intolerable usurpation of the keys; "this power is given to the chief officers only;" Pp. 94, 95, and to separate from them is as intolerable. P. 88.[1] Miserable were the Lord's people, if these things were so; but the truth is, they are miserable guides who so teach.

They which may forgive sins and sinners, save souls, gain and turn men unto the Lord, to them are the keys of the kingdom given, by which they open the door unto such as they thus forgive, gain and save. But all these things, such as are not ministers may do, as these Scriptures, which I entreat the godly reader to consider, do most clearly manifest; Matt. xviii. 15; 2 Cor. ii. 5, 7;—10; Acts viii. 1, 4, with xi. 19—21; James v. 19, 20; 1 Pet. iii. 1; Jude 22, 23. Erroneous, therefore, and derogatory is it to the nature of the gospel, and free donation of Christ, thus to impropriate and engross the keys, which lie common to all Christians in their place and order. Pp. 152, 153. [160, 161.]

Concerning ordination Mr. Robinson observes :—

The officers of the church are the servants of the church; and their office a service of the Lord, and of his church. Matt. xx. 25, 26, 27. 2 Cor. iv. 5. Rom. xv. 31. Whereupon it followeth necessarily, that what power the offiers have, the body of the church hath first. P. 411. [435.] To these things I add, that what power any of the pope's clergy receive from him, the same he takes from them, and deprives them of, when they withdraw their obedience, or separate from that church. For our better proceeding, I will first consider what ordination is; and secondly how far

---

[1] These are quotations from Bernard,

the brethren may go by the Scriptures, and the necessary consequences drawn from them, in this and the like cases in the first planting of churches, or of reducing of them into order, in or after some general confusion. The prelates, and those which level by their line, highly advance ordination [and] far above the administration of the word, sacraments and prayer; making it, and the power of excommunication, the two incommunicable prerogatives of a bishop above an ordinary minister. But surely herein these chief ministers do not succeed the chief ministers, the apostles, except as darkness succeeds light, and antichrist's confusion Christ's order. When the apostles were sent out by Christ, there was no mention of ordination; their charge was, "Go teach all nations, and baptize them;" and, that the apostles accounted preaching their principal work, and after it baptism and prayer, the Scriptures manifest. Acts vi. 4; 1 Cor. i. 17. P. 412. [436, 437.]

Ordination doth depend upon the people's lawful election, as an effect upon the cause, by virtue of which it is justly administered, and may be thus described, or considered of us, as the admission of or putting into possession a person lawfully elected into a true office of ministry. .... The right unto their office they have by election, the possession by ordination, with the ceremony of imposition of hands. The apostle Peter, advertising the disciples or brethren that one (fitted as there noted) was in the room of Judas to be made a witness, with the eleven apostles, of the resurrection of Christ, when two were by them presented, did with the rest present them two and none other to the Lord, that he, by the immediate direction of the lot, might show whether of them two he had chosen. Acts i. In like manner the twelve being to institute the office of deaconry in the church at Jerusalem, called the multitude of the disciples together, and informed them what manner of persons they were to choose; which choice being made by the brethren accordingly, and they so chosen presented to the apostles, they forthwith ordained them, by virtue of the election [so] made by the brethren. To these add, that the apostles Paul and Barnabas (being thereunto called by the Holy Ghost) did pass from church to church, and from place to place, and in every church where they came did ordain them elders by the people's election, signified by their lifting up of hands, as the word[1] is, and as the use was in popular elections, throughout those countries. Act. xiii. 2, and xiv. 23. .... The judgment and plea (when they deal with us) of the most forward men in the land, in this case, I

---

[1] Χειροτονήσαντες. Mr. Robinson's argument from this word is not approved by the best criticism. "The interpretation *having appointed for them* [elders] *by their outstretched hands*, i. e., by taking their opinion or vote in that manner, is unwarranted; for it transfers the hands to the wrong persons."—Hackett; Commentary on Acts xiv: 23.—ED.

may omit; which is, that they renounce and disclaim their ordination by the prelates, and hold their ministry by the people's acceptation. Now if the acceptation of a mixed company, under the prelate's government (as is the best parish assembly in the kingdom) whereof the greatest part have by the revealed will of God no right to the covenant, ministry, or other holy things, be sufficient to make a minister, then much more the acceptation of the people with us, being all of them jointly, and every one of them severally, by the mercy of God, capable of the Lord's ordinances.[1] I acknowledge that where there are already lawful officers in a church, by and to which others are called, there the former, upon that election, are to ordain and appoint the latter. The officers, being the ministers of the church, are to execute the determinations [and judgments] of the church under the Lord. . . . . Ordination is properly the execution of election. Pp. 413—415. [437—440.]

The apostle Paul writes to the churches of Galatia to reject, as accursed, such ministers whomsoever as should preach otherwise than they had already received: and the same apostle writes to the church of [at] Colosse, to admonish Archippus to take heed to his ministry. So [did] John also, to the church of Ephesus, commendeth, [commending] it for examining, and so consequently for silencing, such as pretended themselves

---

[1] Mr. Robinson gives us a number of the Protestants' testimonies upon this point, of which take the following:—

"Gal. i. 8; 'If any man teach another gospel, let him be anathema.' Only the assembly where the true doctrine soundeth is the church: in it is the ministry of the gospel: in it are the keys of the kingdom of heaven. Wherefore in that very assembly [*in eo ipso cœtu*] there is the right of calling and ordaining the ministers of the gospel, because we must fly the enemies of the gospel, as anathema. And besides, if we should desire of them the ceremony of ordination, they would not give it, except we would bind ourselves to renounce the true doctrine; and other wicked bonds would they cast upon us. It is the confusion of order, to seek shepherds from the wolves. This hath ever been the right of the true church, to choose and call out of her own assembly fit ministers of the gospel."
Philip Melancthon.

"In the planting of churches anew, when men [want] are wanting, which should preach the gospel, a woman may perform that at the first; but so as when she hath taught any company, that some one man of the faithful be ordained, which may afterwards minister the sacraments, teach, and do the pastor's duty faithfully."
Peter Martyr.

"Tilenus being demanded of the Earl of Lavall, from whom Calvin had his calling answered, From the church of Geneva, and from Farrel, his predecessor; who also had his from the people of Geneva; who had right and authority to institute and depose ministers: which thing he also confirms by Cyprian, Epist. xiv." Pp. 421, 422. [446, 447.]

These were the sentiments of those who knew how they came out of Rome, and upon what grounds the Protestant churches were formed; but how differently are things represented by aspiring men at this day?

apostles, and were not: as also to the church of Thyatira, reproving it for suffering unsilenced the false prophetess Jezebel. Now as these things did first and principally concern the officers, who were in these and all other things of the same nature to go before and govern the people; so are [were] the people also in their places interested in the same business and charge. Neither could the officers' sin (if they should have been corrupt or negligent) discharge the people of their duty in the things which concerned them; but they were bound notwithstanding to see the commandments of the apostles, and of the Lord Jesus by them, executed accordingly. And if the people be in cases, and when their officers fail, thus solemnly to examine, admonish, silence, and suppress their teachers, being faulty and unsound; then are they also by proportion, where officers fail, to elect, appoint, set up and over themselves such fit persons as the Lord affordeth them, for their furtherance of faith and salvation. Pp. 417, 418. [442, 443.]

Against this doctrine many objections have been raised; the chief of which are about the people's instability, and their tendency to confusion. In answer to which, Mr. Robinson reminds his opponent, that though his ignorant people had readily changed their religion with their prince, even back to popery in Mary's days; yet, "The prelates and priests were as unstable as the rest, yea their ringleaders." Says he :—

For [ourselves, Mr. B., and that whereof we take] experience in this our popularity, as you term it, I tell you, that if ever I saw the beauty of Sion, and the glory of the Lord filling his tabernacle, it hath been in the manifestation of the divers graces of God in the church, in that heavenly harmony, and comely order, wherein by the grace of God we are set and walk; wherein, if your eyes had but seen the brethren's sober and modest carriage one towards another, their humble and willing submission unto their guides in the Lord, their tender compassion towards the weak, their fervent zeal against scandalous offenders, and their long-suffering towards all, you would, I am persuaded, change your mind, and be compelled to take up your parable, and bless where you purposed to curse. P. 212. [223.] For mine own part, knowing mine own infirmities, and that I am subject to sin, yea and to forwardness in sin, as much as the brethren are; if by mine office I should be deprived of the remedy which they enjoy, that blessed ordinance of the church's censures, I should think mine office accursed, and myself by it, as frustrating and disappointing me of that main end for which the servants of Christ ought to join themselves unto the church of Christ, furnished with his power for their reformation. . . . . As, on the contrary, God is my record, how, in the very writing of these things, my soul is filled with spiritual joy, that I am under this easy yoke of Christ, the censures of the church, and how much I am comforted in this [very] consideration, against my vile and corrupt nature, which, notwithstanding, I am persuaded the Lord will never so far suffer to rebel, as that it shall not be tamed and subdued by this strong hand of God, without which it might every day and hour so hazard my salvation. That doctrine which advanceth an inferior and meaner state [estate] in the church, above that which is superior and the chief, that is unsound, and indeed serving in a degree for the exaltation of that man of sin above all that is called God. But the doctrine of setting the elders without and above the judgments and censures of the church, doth advance an inferior above a superior. The point I thus manifest:—

The order of kings is the highest order or estate in the church. But the order of saints is the order of kings, and we are kings as we are saints, not as we are officers. . . . . As the Lord Jesus did prove against the scribes and pharisees, that the temple was greater than the gold, because it sanctified the gold, and that the altar was greater than the offering, because it sanctified the offering, so by proportion the condition of a saint, which sanctifieth the condition of an officer, is more excellent [and greater] than it is. To our saintship, and as we have faith, is promised the forgiveness of sins, the favor of God, and life eternal, but not to our office, or in respect of it. The estate of a saint is most happy and blessed, though the person never so much as come near an office; but on the contrary, an officer, if he be not also and first a saint, is a most wretched and accursed creature. Pp. 216, 217. [227, 228.]

The reader will not wonder that those who were for national churches, and unconverted ministers, discovered a strong prejudice against such writings as these; but how well do they agree with the apostles' doctrine. 1 Cor. xii. 31, and xiii. 1—3 ; Gal. i.

Of reformation, Mr. Robinson says to his opponent:—

You speak much of the reformation of your church after popery. There was indeed a great reformation of things in your church, but very little of the church, to speak truly and properly. The people are the church; and to make a reformed church, there must be first a reformed people; and so there should have been with you, by the preaching of repentance from dead works, and faith in Christ; that the people, as the Lord should have vouchsafed grace, being first fitted for, and made capable of, the sacraments, and other ordinances, might afterwards have communicated in the pure use of them; for want of which, instead of a pure use, there hath been, and is at this day, a most profane abuse of them, to the great dishonor of Christ and his gospel, and to the hardening of thousands in their impenitency. Others also, endeavoring yet a further reformation, have sued and do sue to kings, and queens, and parliaments, for the rooting out of the prelacy, and with it, of such other evil fruits as grow from that bitter root; and on the contrary, to have the ministry, government and discipline of Christ set over the parishes as they stand; the first fruit of which reformation, if it were obtained, would be the [further] profanation of the more of God's ordinances upon such, as to whom they appertained not; and so the further provocation of his [great] Majesty unto anger against all such as so practiced, or consented thereunto. Is it not strange that men, in the reforming of a church, should almost, or altogether, forget the church, which is the people, or that they should labor to crown Christ a King over a people, whose Prophet he hath not first been? or to set him to rule by his laws and officers, over the professed subjects of antichrist and the devil? [or] is it possible that ever they should submit to the discipline of Christ, which have not first been prepared, in some measure, by his holy doctrine, and taught with meekness to stoop unto his yoke? Pp. 300, 301. [316, 317.]

A main plea for such confusion, both then and now, was and is drawn from the parable of the tares. But, says Mr. Robinson:—

Since the Lord Jesus, who best knew his own meaning, calls the field the world, and makes the harvest, which is the end of the field, the end of the world, and not of the church, why should we admit of any other interpretation? Neither is it like [likely] that Christ would in the expounding of one parable speak another, as he should have done, if, in calling the field the world, he had meant the church. As God then in the beginning made man good, and placed him in the field of the world, there to grow, where by the envy of the serpent he was soon corrupted, so ever since hath the seed of the serpent, stirred up by their father the devil, snarled at the heel of the woman's seed, and like noisome tares vexed and pestered the good and holy seed; which though the children of God both see and feel to their pain, yet must they not therefore, forgetting what spirit they are of, presently call for fire from heaven, nor prevent the Lord's hand, but wait his leisure, either for the converting of these tares into wheat, which in many is daily seen,—and then how great pity had it been they should so untimely have been plucked up—or for their final perdition in the day of the Lord, when the church shall be no more offended by them. And that the Lord Jesus no way speaks of the toleration of profane persons in the church, doth appear by these reasons:—

1. Because he doth not contradict himself, by forbidding the use of the keys in one place, which in another he hath turned upon impenitent offenders. Matt. xviii. [15—17.] 2. In the excommunication of sinners apparently obstinate, with due circumspection, and in the spirit of wisdom, meekness, and long-suffering, with such other general Christian virtues, as with which all our special sacrifices ought to be seasoned, what danger can there be of any such disorder, as the plucking up of the wheat with the tares, which the husbandman feareth? 3. The Lord Jesus speaks of the utter ruinating and destruction of the tares,—the plucking them up by the roots;—but excommunication rightly administered, is not for the ruin and destruction of any, but for the salvation of the party thereby humbled. 1 Cor. v. 5. The Lord's field is sown only with good seed,—his church, saints [and] beloved of God, all and every one of them, though by the malice of Satan, and negligence of such as should keep this field, vineyard and house of God, adulterated seed, and abominable persons, may be foisted in, yea and suffered also. Pp. 119, 120. [125—127.] I deny not but, as it hath been said of old, there are many sheep without, and many wolves within; many of the visible church which are not of the invisible church, and many of the invisible church which never come into the visible church. But this, say I, is not according to the revealed will of God in his word; but by men's default and sin. It is their sin of ignorance, or infirmity, which, being of the invisible church, do not, if possibly they can, join themselves unto the visible church, there to partake in the visible ordinances. It is their sin of hypocrisy and presumption, which not being of the invisible church, do adjoin themselves to the visible church, there to profane the Lord's covenant and ordinances, to which they have no right. For how can they, being wicked and unholy, challenge the Lord to be their God, that is, all happiness and goodness unto them, which is one part of the covenant; or profess themselves to be his people, which is another part, when the devil and their lusts is their God? Pp. 313, 314. [330.]

OF THE DIFFERENCE BETWEEN CIVIL AND ECCLESIASTICAL GOVERNMENT.

1. Civil officers [are, and] are called in the word of God, princes, heads, captains, judges, magistrates, nobles, lords, kings, them in authority, principalities and powers, yea in their respect, gods; and according to their names so are their offices. But on the contrary, ecclesiastical officers are not capable of these, or the like titles, which can neither be given without flattery unto them, nor received by them without arrogancy. Neither is their office an office of lordship, sovereignty or authority, but of labor and service, and so they, the laborers and servants of the church, as of God. 2 Cor. iv. 5; 1 Tim. iii. 1.

2. Magistrates may publish and execute their own laws in their own

names. Ezra i. 1, &c.; Esther viii. 8; Matt. xx. 25. But ministers are only interpreters of the laws of God, and must look for no further respect at the hands of any to the things they speak, than as they manifest the same to be the commandments of the Lord. 1 Cor. xiv. 37.

3. Civil administrations, and their forms of government, may be and ofttimes are altered, for the avoiding of inconveniences, according to the circumstances of time, place and persons. Exod. xviii. 13, &c. But the church is a kingdom which cannot be shaken, Heb. xii. 28, wherein may be no innovation in office, or form of administration, from that which Christ hath left, for any inconveniency whatsoever.

4. Civil magistrates have authority by their offices to judge offenders, upon whom also they may execute bodily vengeance, using their people as their servants and ministers for the same purpose; but in the church the officers are the ministers of the people, whose service the people is to use for the administering of the judgments of the church, and of God first, against the obstinate, which is the utmost execution the church can perform. . . . . But here it will be demanded of me, if the elders be not set over the church for her guidance and government? Yes, certainly, as the physician is set over the body, for his skill and faithfulness, to minister unto it, to whom the patient, yea though his lord and [or] master, is to submit; the lawyer over his cause, to attend unto it; the steward over his family, even his wife and children, to make provision for them: yea, the watchman over the whole city, for the safe keeping thereof. Such, and none other, is the elder's or bishop's government. Pp. 135—137. [143—145.]

But, says Mr. Robinson :—

What sway authority hath in the church of England, appeareth in the laws of the land, which make the government of the church alterable at the magistrate's pleasure; and so the clergy, in their submission to King Henry VIII, do derive, as they pretend, their ecclesiastical jurisdiction from him, and so execute [exercise] it. Indeed many of the late bishops and their proctors, seeing how monstrous the ministration is of divine things, by a human authority and calling, and growing bold upon the present disposition of the magistrate, have disclaimed that former title, and do professedly hold their ecclesiastical power and jurisdiction *de jure divino*, and so consequently by God's word unalterable: of whom I would demand this one question:—What if the king should discharge and expel the present ecclesiastical government, and plant instead of it the presbytery or eldership, would they submit unto the government of the elders? Yea or No? If Yea, then were they traitors to the Lord Jesus, submitting to a government overthrowing his government, as doth the Presbyterian government that which is Episcopal: if No, then how could they free themselves from such imputations of disloyalty to princes, and disturbance of states, as wherewith they load us and others opposing them? But to the question itself. As the kingdom of Christ is not of this world, but spiritual, and he a spiritual King, John xviii. 36, so must the government of this spiritual kingdom under this spiritual King needs be spiritual, and all the laws of it. And as Christ Jesus hath, by the merits of his priesthood, redeemed as well the body as the soul, 1 Cor. vi. 20, so is he also by the sceptre of his kingdom to rule and reign over both, unto which Christian magistrates, as well as meaner persons, ought to submit themselves, and the more Christian they are, the more meekly to take the yoke of Christ upon them, and the greater authority they have, the more effectually to advance his sceptre over themselves and their people, by all good means. Neither can there be any reason given why the merits of saints may not as well be mingled with the merits of Christ, for the saving of the church, as the laws of men with his laws, for the ruling and guiding of it. He is as absolute and [as] entire a King as he is a Priest, and his people must be as careful to preserve the dignity of the one, as to enjoy the benefit of the other. P. 38. [39, 40.]

Of Ministers' Maintenance.

Mr. Bernard charged his opponents with error, in holding that ministers ought not to live of tithes, but of the people's voluntary contribution; and says, "This is against the wisdom of God, who allowed a settled maintenance under the law; and there is nothing against it in the gospel." But in reply Mr. Robinson says:—

As the Lord appointed under the law a settled maintenance by tithes and offerings, so did he a settled land of Canaan, which was holy, and a sacrament; so did he also appoint that the Levites to be maintained there, should have no part nor inheritance with the rest of the Israelites their brethren. And hath God's wisdom so appointed now? If it had, I fear many would not rest in it, so wise are they for their bellies. And where you add that there is nothing in the gospel against this ordinance in the law, the author to the Hebrews might have taught you, that the law is abolished by the gospel, in the sense we speak of; and the Old Testament by the New, in respect of ordinances, whereof this was one. If it be said that tithes were in use and given by Abraham to Melchizedec, priest of the most high God, before the law or Old Testament was given by Moses, I answer, that so was circumcision ministered and sacrifices offered before Moses; which notwithstanding were parts of the Old Testament, and assumed by Moses into the body of it, and so are abolished by the New. To conclude this point, since tithes and offerings were appurtenances unto the priesthood, and that the priesthood, both of Melchizedec and Levi, are abolished in Christ, as the shadow in the substance; and that the "Lord hath ordained that they which preach the gospel, should live of the gospel;" we willingly leave unto you both your priestly order and maintenance, contenting ourselves with the people's voluntary contribution, whether it be less or more, as the blessing of God upon our labor, the fruit of our ministry, and a declaration of their love and duty. Pp. 439, 440. [466, 467.]

In all these passages[1] I have recited Mr. Robinson's own expressions, without knowingly adding a single word. The spelling I have brought to the present times, but the language is entirely his; and it may be questioned whether any talked a purer one in that day or not, if there does in this.

About the time of his publishing this book, and for some years following, "many came to his church at Leyden from divers parts of England, so that they grew a great congregation;" "even so as to have three hundred communicants[2]." And as the Arminian controversy caused great troubles in Holland, and especially at Leyden, their two divinity professors being divided, Episcopius appearing for, and Polyander[3] against the Arminian tenets; Mr. Robinson, though he preached thrice a week, and went through much other labor, yet went constantly to hear them both, whereby he got well grounded in the controversy; so that when Episcopius, about the year 1613, set forth sundry Arminian theses at Leyden, which he would defend against all opposers, Polyander insisted upon Mr. Robinson's engaging against him, telling him, that "such was the ability and expertness of the adversary, that the truth is in danger to suffer, if he would not help them; is so importunate as at length he yields; and when the day comes, he so defends the truth, and foils the

---

[1] Changed from "In all these passages which begin and end with marks of quotation."—ED.

[2] Prince's Chronology, [125]; Plymouth Register.

[3] In the original edition this name stands as Polydore. Mr. Backus corrected the error in his Abridgment.—ED.

opposer, as he puts him to an apparent nonplus in this great and public audience. The same he does a second and a third time, upon the like occasions, which, as it causes many to give praise to God that the truth had so famous a victory, so it procures Mr. Robinson much respect and honor from those learned men and others[1]."

Several attempts were made to plant New England from worldly motives, but they all proved abortive. In 1607 a hundred men were sent over to Sagadahoc[2] with furniture to lay the foundation of a great state, and all lived through the winter but their president; yet the next year, " the whole colony breaks up and returns to England, and brands the country as over cold and not habitable by our nation, and the adventurers give over their design[3]." Other fruitless attempts were made for a while, and then were given over. " Sir Ferdinando Gorges and Captain Mason spent twenty thousand pounds each, in attempts for settlement, and each of them thought it advisable to give over their [his] designs, and sit down with the loss. Whether Britain would have had any colonies in America at this day, if religion had not been the grand inducement, is doubtful[4]."

The people whose religious sentiments are described above, after long consideration, many earnest requests to heaven for direction and help, and well consulting matters with English friends, at last determined to come over to this wilderness; and divine providence made them the honored instruments of laying the foundation of this now flourishing country. In December, 1617, Mr. Robinson and Elder Brewster wrote to the Council for Virginia, who then had the management of these affairs, wherein they say:—

---

[1] Prince's Chronology, pp. 36, 38. [130, 131.]
[2] In Maine, near the mouth of the Kennebec.—ED.
[3] Prince's Chronology, pp. 21—25. [116—119.]
[4] Massachusetts History, Vol. I, p. 3. [11, note.]

For your encouragement we will not forbear to mention these inducements. 1. We verily believe and trust the Lord is with us, to whom and whose service we have given ourselves in many trials; and that he will graciously prosper our endeavors according to the simplicity of our hearts. 2. We are well weaned from the delicate milk of our mother country, and inured to the difficulties of a strange land. 3. The people are, for the body of them, industrious and frugal, we think we may safely say, as any company of people in the world. 4. We are knit together as a body, in a most strict and sacred bond and covenant of the Lord; of the violation whereof we make great conscience, and by virtue whereof we hold ourselves straitly tied to all care of each other's good, and of the whole. 5. It is not with us as with other men; whom small things can discourage, or small discouragements cause to wish ourselves at home again[1].

Herein they were not mistaken, as will soon appear; for though contentions among the said Council, and other things, obstructed their proceeding till 1620, and they could not then obtain any royal promise of liberty of conscience in this country, only that "the king would connive at them, and not molest them if they carried it peaceably;" "yet, casting themselves on the care of Providence, they resolve to venture[2]." But as they could not obtain shipping and provision enough to carry half their company the first year, Mr. Robinson was obliged to tarry in Holland with the larger part, while Mr. William Brewster, their ruling elder, came over with the other. Most of their brethren came with them from Leyden to Delft-Haven, where they spent the night in friendly, entertaining and Christian converse. And July 22, the wind being fair, they go aboard, their friends attending them, when "Mr. Robinson falling down on his knees, and they all with him, he with watery cheeks commends them with most fervent prayer to God; and then with mutual embraces, and many tears, they take their leave, and with a prosperous gale come to Southampton," in England. July 27, 1620, Mr. Robinson wrote a letter, which was received

---

[1] Prince, pp. 51, 52. [143.]   [2] Prince, [148, 151.]—ED.

and read to the company at that place[1]; which I think worthy of a place here. The letter is as follows[2]:—

LOVING CHRISTIAN FRIENDS:—I do heartily and in the Lord salute you, as being those with whom I am present in my best affections, and most earnest longing after you, though I be constrained for a while to be bodily absent from you: I say constrained; God knowing how willingly, and much rather than otherwise, I would have borne my part with you in this first brunt, were I not by strong necessity held back for the present. Make account of me in the mean time as a man divided in myself, with great pain, and as (natural bonds set aside) having my better part with you; and, although I doubt not but in your godly wisdoms you both foresee and resolve upon that which concerneth your present state and condition, both severally and jointly, yet have I thought it but my duty to add some further spur of provocation unto them who run [well] already, if not because you need it, yet because I owe it in love and duty.

And first, as we are daily to renew our repentance with our God, especially for our sins known, and generally for our unknown trespasses; so doth the Lord call us in a singular manner, upon occasions of such difficulty and danger as lieth upon you, to both a narrow search and careful reformation [of your ways] in his sight, lest he, calling to remembrance our sins forgotten by us, or unrepented of, take advantage against us, and in judgment leave us [for the same] to be swallowed up in one danger or other; whereas, on the contrary, sin being taken away by earnest repentance, and the pardon thereof from the Lord sealed up to a man's conscience by his Spirit, great shall be his security and peace in all dangers, sweet his comforts in all distresses, with happy deliverance from all evil, whether in life or death. Now next after this heavenly peace with God and our own consciences, we are carefully to provide for peace with all men, what in us lieth, especially with our associates; and for that, watchfulness must be had, that we neither at all [in] ourselves do give, no, nor easily take offence being given by others. Wo be to the world for offences, for although it be necessary, considering the malice of Satan and man's corruption, that offences come, yet wo unto the man, or woman either, by whom the offence cometh, saith Christ. Matt. xviii. 7. And if offences in the unseasonable use of things, in themselves indifferent, be more to be feared than death itself, as the apostle teacheth; 1 Cor. ix. 15; how much more in things

---

[1] Prince, pp. 70, 71. [159, 160.]

[2] This letter, as given in the different editions of Morton's Memorial, and in Mourt's Relation and Neal's History of New England, is considerably varied. The words here added in brackets are from the edition of the Memorial published by the Congregational Board, Boston, 1855.—ED.

simply evil, in which neither the honor of God nor love of man is thought worthy to be regarded? Neither yet is it sufficient that we keep ourselves, by the grace of God, from giving offences, except withal we be armed against the taking of them, when they are given by others; for how imperfect and lame is the work of grace in that person, who wants charity to cover a multitude of offences? as the Scripture speaks. Neither are you to be exhorted to this grace only upon the common grounds of Christianity, which are, that persons ready to take offence, either want charity to cover offences, or [wisdom] duly to weigh human frailties; or, lastly, are gross though close hypocrites, as Christ our Lord teacheth; Matt. vii. 1—3; as indeed, in my own experience, few or none have been found which sooner give offence, than such as easily take it; neither have they ever proved sound and profitable members in societies, who have nourished this touchy humor. But besides these, there are divers motives provoking you above others to great care and conscience this way; as first, there are many of you strangers as to the persons, so to the infirmities one of another, and so stand in need of more watchfulness this way, lest when such things fall out in men and women as you expected not, you be inordinately affected with them, which doth require at your hands much wisdom and charity for the covering and preventing of incident offences that way. And lastly, your intended course of civil community will minister continual occasion of offence[1], and will be as fuel for that fire, except you diligently quench it with brotherly forbearance. And if taking offence causelessly or easily at men's doings be so carefully to be avoided; how much more heed is to be taken that we take not offence at God himself? Which yet we certainly do, so oft as we do murmur at his providence in our crosses, or bear impatiently such afflictions wherewith he is pleased to visit us. Store up therefore patience against the evil day; without which we take offence at the Lord himself in his [holy and] just works. A fourth thing there is carefully to be provided for, viz. that with your common employments, you join common affections, truly bent upon the general good, avoiding as a deadly plague of your both common and special comforts, all retiredness of mind for proper advantage; and all singularly affected every manner of way, let every man repress in himself, and the whole body in each person, as so many rebels against the common good, all private respects of men's selves, not sorting with the general convenience. And as men are careful not to have a new house shaken with any violence, before it be well settled, and the parts firmly knit; so be you, I beseech you my brethren, much more careful that the house of God, which you are and are to be, be not shaken with unnecessary novelties, or other oppositions, at the first settling thereof.

---

[1] For several years their affairs were managed in one common stock, but they afterward found the way of distinct property to be much better.

Lastly whereas you are to become a body politic, using amongst yourselves civil government, and are not furnished with persons of special eminency above the rest, to be chosen by you into office of government, let your wisdom and godliness appear, not only in choosing such persons as do entirely love, and will promote the common good; but also in yielding unto them all due honor and obedience in their lawful administrations, not beholding in them the ordinariness of their persons, but God's ordinance for your good; not being like the foolish multitude, who more honor the gay coat, than either the virtuous mind of the man, or the glorious ordinance of the Lord; but you know better things, and that the image of the Lord's power and authority, which the magistrate beareth, is honorable, in how mean persons soever; and this duty you may the more willingly, and ought the more conscionably to perform because you are, at least for the present, to have them for your ordinary governors, which yourselves shall make choice of for that work. Sundry other things of importance I could put you in mind of, and of those before mentioned, in more words; but I will not so far wrong your godly minds, as to think you heedless of these things, there being also divers amongst you so well able both to admonish themselves and others of what concerneth them. These few things therefore, and the same in few words, I do earnestly commend to your care and conscience, joining therein with my daily incessant prayers unto the Lord, that he who has made the heavens and the earth, and sea, and all rivers of waters, and whose providence is over all his works, especially over all his dear children for good, would so guide and guard you in your ways, as inwardly by his Spirit, so outwardly by the hand of his power, as that both you, and we also for and with you, may have after matter of praising his name all the days of your and our lives. Fare you well in him in whom you trust, and in whom I rest, an unfeigned well-wisher to your happy success in this hopeful voyage.

JOHN ROBINSON.[1]

This excellent letter properly describes the sentiments, temper and rules of conduct of the chief founders of New England; and may the same be duly regarded to their latest posterity!

By Dutch intrigues and others' ill conduct they were hindered long, and at last forced to come with only one ship instead of two; which sailed from Plymouth, in England, on September 6, and arrived in Cape Cod harbor, November 11, and at the place which they named Plymouth, in December, 1620.

[1] Morton, pp. 7—10. [15—19.]

And now compare this company with that of Sagadahoc. That company, who came upon worldly designs, had a hundred men; this religious society consisted of but one hundred and one souls, men, women and children; the one arrived at the place designed for settlement in August, the other not till winter had set in; the worldly company only buried their president, and all returned the next year to their native country again;[1] whereas this religious people, in about five months time, buried their governor and full half their number, and yet with fortitude and patience they kept their station; yea, though they were afterwards deserted and abused by some who had engaged to help them. We cannot now form an adequate idea of what those pious planters endured, to prepare the way for what we at this day enjoy. In the year 1623 they say, " By the time our corn is planted, our victuals are spent; not knowing at night where to have a bit in the morning, and have neither bread nor corn for three or four months together; yet bear our wants with cheerfulness, and rest on Providence."[2]

It pleased God further to try their faith, by sending a great drought and heat from the third week in May till the middle of July, which caused their corn to wither as if it were truly dead; and a ship that they had long expected did not arrive, but they thought they saw signs of its being wrecked on the coast. " The most courageous are now discouraged. Upon this the public authority set apart a sol-

---

[1] This paragraph seems hardly just to the company at Sagadahoc. Doubtless their object was gain, and they lacked the fortitude and patience which religious principle inspired in the colonists of Plymouth. But they were not without trials. The Indians proved hostile; the climate is naturally much more rigorous on the Kennebec than at Plymouth; and the winter of 1607-8 was everywhere remarkably severe; in mid-winter a fire broke out in the settlement and consumed their storehouse, with most of their provisions and part of their lodgings; in addition to the loss of their president, his brother, lord-chief-justice Popham, the chief patron of the enterprise, died in England, and Sir John Gilbert, brother of their second president, died, leaving him an estate, the care of which compelled his return. Bancroft, I. 268; Prince, 117, 119; Hutchinson, I. 10.—ED.

[2] Prince, p. 135. [216.]

emn day of humiliation and prayer, to seek the Lord in this distress, who was pleased to give speedy answer, to our own and the Indians' admiration; for though in the former part of the day it was very clear and hot, without a sign of rain, yet before the exercise is over the clouds gather, and next morning distill such soft and gentle showers as give cause of joy and praise to God." Their corn recovers, and soon after arrives the ship they expected, bringing over about sixty more of their friends, and a letter from others, wherein they say to those here, " Let it not be grievous to you, that you have been instruments to break the ice for others who come after with less difficulty. The honor shall be yours to the world's end. We bear you always in our breasts, and our hearty affection is towards you all, as are the hearts of hundreds more who never saw your faces, who doubtless pray for your safety as their own."[1] Their harvest was plentiful; and above twenty years after, Governor Bradford says, " Nor has there been any general want of food among us since to this day."[2]

Mr. Robinson and many of his people were detained in Holland, till, after about a week's illness, he died there on March 1, 1625, aged near fifty years. Governor Bradford says, " His and our enemies had been continually plotting how they might hinder his coming hither, but the Lord has appointed him a better place." Mr. Prince says, " His son Isaac came over to Plymouth colony, lived to above ninety years of age, a venerable man, whom I have often seen, and has left male posterity in the county of Barnstable."[3]

The cause why Mr. Robinson and the remaining part of his church were kept back so long, was their inability to transport themselves; and several merchants who had engaged in the affair deserted them, pursuing separate schemes of their own, and sent over one company of sixty stout

---

[1] Prince, pp. 137—140. [218—220.] [2] Prince, p. 141. [221.]
[3] Prince, pp, 159, 160. [238.]

men, who began a plantation at Weymouth; but soon reduced themselves to such straits that several perished, and the rest were forced to be beholden to the charity of Plymouth people, to keep them alive till they could get back whence they came. Another worldly scheme was begun at Braintree, which also proved abortive; while our Christian fathers at Plymouth were enabled to keep their station. Some of the adventurers wrote to them on December 18, 1624, and said, " We are still persuaded you are the people that must make a plantation in those remote places, when all others fail."[1] They were long destitute of a pastor, and yet constantly maintained divine worship among them; of which a noted author gives this account:—

> To satisfy the reader, how a Christian church, could, in any tolerable measure, carry on the public worship of God without suitable officers, as was the case of those people of Plymouth, we must know that those were a serious and religious people, that knew their own principles, knew and were resolved on the way of their worship, but in many years could not prevail with any to come over to them, and undertake the office of a pastor amongst them, at least none in whom they could with full satisfaction acquiesce, and therefore in the mean while they were peaceably and prudently managed by the wisdom of Mr. Brewster, a grave and serious person, ruling elder among them. . . . . Besides also several of his people were well gifted, and did spend part of the Lord's day in their wonted prophesying, to which they had been accustomed by Mr. Robinson. Those gifts while they lasted made the burthen of the other defect more easily borne.[2]

The names of those first planters were, John Carver, William Bradford, Edward Winslow, successive Governors;

---

[1] Prince p. 155. [233.]

[2] Hubbard. [p. 65.] Mr. Robinson says, " The disciples of Christ did not then first receive power to teach when they were possessed of their apostleship, but long before they were admitted into office, as did others also besides them, without office, as well as they. Matt. x. 5, 6. 7, Luke x. 1—3, 9, 10." Answer to Bernard, P. 148. [156.] " That we call prophesying, I affirm not to be so appropriated to the ministry, but that others having received a gift thereunto, may and ought to stir up the same, and to use it in the church, for edification, exhortation and comfort, though not yet called into the office of the ministry. Rom. xii. 6; 1 Cor. xiv. 3; 1 Pet. iv. 10, 11." Ibid, P. 235. [246. 247.]

William Brewster, elder; Captain Miles Standish,[1] John Alden, Samuel Fuller, Richard Warren, Stephen Hopkins, and others, each of whom have posterity remaining among us to this day. "I am not preserving from oblivion the names of heroes, whose chief merit is the overthrow of cities, provinces and empires; but the names of the founders of a flourishing town and colony, if not of the whole British empire in America."[2] Their deep poverty and the abundance of their joy, abounded unto the riches of their liberality, so as not only to enable them to relieve many in distress, but also to launch out so as to help over about thirty-five families more of their friends from Leyden, who were transported hither in 1629, at the charge of their brethren here, which was cheerfully borne by them, though it amounted to above five hundred and fifty pounds sterling, besides supporting them after their arrival for sixteen or eighteen months, till they had a harvest of their own, which cost near as much more. "Meanwhile," says Governor Bradford, "God gives us peace and health, with contented minds, and so succeeds our labors that we have corn sufficient, and some to spare, with other provisions. Nor had we ever any supply from England but what we first brought with us."[3] The first horned cattle that they ever had here were a bull and three heifers, which Governor Winslow brought over to Plymouth in March, 1624.

About that time, "the fame of the plantation at New Plymouth being spread in all the western parts of England, the Rev. Mr. White, a famous Puritan minister of Dor-

[1] The original edition here gives the name of Robert Cushman. Mr. Backus evidently discovered the mistake, as he omits the name in his Abridgment. Mr. Cushman came in the ship Fortune, in November, 1621, and returned in the same ship after a stay of "not above fourteen days." He was the agent of the colony until his death in 1626. Morton calls him "their ancient friend who was as their right hand with their friends the adventurers, and for divers years had done and agitated all their business with them, to their great advantage." Morton's Memorial, pp. 26, 50, 83—85; Prince, pp. 172, 220, 221, 238; Hubbard, 69.—ED.

[2] Massachusetts History, Vol II. pp. 462, 463. [412, note.]

[3] Prince, pp. 156, 201. [235, 264, 265.]

chester, excites several gentlemen there to make way for another settlement in New England."[1] This was the beginning of the Massachusetts colony. In the year 1624 a few persons gathered at Cape Ann, who removed the next year, and began the town of Salem, to whom others resorted from time to time, till in the summer of 1628, Mr. John Endicott came over to govern them, and in 1629, Mr. Francis Higginson and Mr. Samuel Skelton, two Nonconformist ministers came with many others, and formed and organized a church in that place. Upon which we may see Mr. Robinson's words verified; for these Puritans who had blamed him for an entire separation from the national church, yet were no sooner settled on this side the Atlantic, than they cast off the prelates' yoke in such a manner, that when John Brown and Samuel Brown, two of the "first patentees, men of estates, and men of parts," attempted to set up Episcopal worship at Salem, Governor Endicott convented them before him, where they "accused the ministers as departing from the orders of the church of England; that they were separatists, and would be Anabaptists, &c., but for themselves they would hold to the orders of the church of England." These speeches and practices were judged by the Governor and Council to be such as tended "to mutiny and faction, and the Governor told them that New England was no place for such as they, and therefore sent them back for England, at the return of the ships, the same year."[2]

By this and many other instances we may see, that the men who drew off from the national establishment, as soon as they were convinced that truth called them to it, were not so severe against dissenters from themselves, as they were who stayed till interest and civil power would favor the cause before they separated.

In the year 1630, Governor Winthrop with about fifteen

[1] Prince, p. 144. [224.]   [2] Morton's Memorial, pp. 84, 85. [100, 101.]

hundred people came over, and planted Charlestown, Boston, Dorchester, and Watertown, and soon formed churches in each town. Of these people Mr. Hubbard says :—

> Intending not to write an apology, but a history of their practice, nothing shall here be interposed by way of defence of their way, only to give a clear discovery of the truth, as to matter of fact, both what it was at first, and still continues to be. Those that came over soon after Mr. Endicott, namely Mr. Higginson and Mr. Skelton, Anno 1629, walked something in an untrodden path, therefore it is the less to be wondered at, if they went but in and out; in some things complying too much, in some things too little, with those of the separation; and it may be in some things not sufficiently attending to the order of the gospel, as themselves thought they understood afterwards. For in the beginning of things they only accepted of one another according to some general profession of the doctrine of the gospel, and the honest and good intentions they had one towards another, and so by some kind of covenant soon moulded themselves into a church in every plantation where they took up their abode[1]; until Mr. Cotton and Mr. Hooker came over, which was in the year 1633, who did clear up the order and method of church government, according as they apprehended was most consonant to the word of God. And such was the authority they, especially Mr. Cotton, had in the hearts of the people, that whatever he delivered in the pulpit was soon put into an order of court, if of a civil, or set up as a practice in the church, if of an ecclesiastical concernment. After that time, the administration of all ecclesiastical matters was tied up more strictly than before to the rules of that which is since owned for the Congregational way. The principal points wherein they differ from others may be reduced to these four heads :—

---

[1] The covenant of the first church in Boston was in these words :—
"In the name of our Lord Jesus Christ, and in obedience to his holy will and divine ordinance, we whose names are here underwritten, being by his most wise and good providence brought together into this part of America, in the Bay of Massachusetts, and desirous to unite ourselves into one congregation or church, under the Lord Jesus Christ our Head, in such sort as becometh all those whom he hath redeemed and sanctified to himself, do hereby solemnly and religiously (as in his most holy presence) promise and bind ourselves to walk in all our ways according to the rule of the gospel, and in all sincere conformity to his holy ordinances, and in mutual love and respect each to other, so near as God shall give us grace.
JOHN WINTHROP.
THOMAS DUDLEY.
ISAAC JOHNSON.
JOHN WILSON." &c.
Mr. Foxcraft's Century Sermon at Boston.

1. The subject matter of the visible church, saints by calling; such as have not only attained the knowledge of the principles of religion, and are free from gross and open scandal, but are willing, together with the profession of their repentance and faith in Christ, to declare their subjection to him in his ordinances, which they account ought to be done publicly before the Lord and his people, by an open profession of the doctrine of the gospel, and by a personal relation of their spiritual estate, expressive of the manner how they were brought to the knowledge of God by faith in Christ Jesus; and this is done either with their *viva voce*, or by a rehearsal thereof by the elders in public before the church assembly, they having beforehand received private satisfaction, the persons openly testifying their assent thereunto, provided they do not scandalize their profession by an unchristian conversation, in which case a profession is with them of small account.

2. In the constitutive form of a particular visible church; which they account ought to be a restipulation, or mutual covenanting to walk together in their Christian communion, according to the rules of the gospel; and this they say is best to be explicit, although they do not deny but an implicit covenant may suffice to the being of a true church.

3. In the quantity or extensiveness of a particular church; concerning which they hold that no church society, of gospel institution, ought to be of larger extent, or greater number, than may ordinarily meet together in one place, for the enjoyment of all the same numerical ordinances, and celebrating of all divine worship, nor ordinarily fewer than may conveniently carry on church work.

4. That there is no jurisdiction, to which such particular churches are or ought to be subject, be it placed in classis or synod, by way of authoritative censure, nor any church power, extrinsical to the said churches which they ought to have dependence upon any other sort of men for the exercise of.

"After this manner," says Mr. Hubbard, "have their ecclesiastical affairs been carried on ever since the year 1633;" that is, down to 1680, when he wrote his history.

Here let it be well observed and ever remembered, that these were the main points wherein they differed from others; and the reader is welcome to search through all their history from that day to this, and see if he can find that these principles, in themselves considered, ever produced any evil effects. But this people brought two other principles with them from their native country, in which they did not differ from others; which are, that natural birth, and the doings of men, can bring children into the covenant of grace; and, that it is right to enforce and support their own sentiments about religion with the magistrate's sword. And those, let them live in England, Scotland, Rome, or elsewhere, who reproach and condemn New England for the evils which these two principles have produced, while they hold the same things, ought to consider that in so doing they will be found inexcusable before our Great Judge.

The root of a compulsive uniformity was planted at a General Court in Boston, May 18, 1631, when it was "ordered and agreed, that for the time to come, no man shall be admitted to the freedom of this body politic, but such as are members of some of the churches within the limits of the same[1]." This test in after times had such influence, that he who "did not conform, was deprived of more civil privileges than a nonconformist is deprived of by the test in England. Both the one and the other must have occasioned much formality and hypocrisy. The mysteries of our holy religion have been prostituted to mere secular views and advantages[2]."

If in any instances this people carried their zeal to a greater severity than Episcopalians have often done, let it be remembered, that the latter hold a power in their church to decree rites and ceremonies, and so consequently a power to abate or alter the same as occasion suits; but the fathers of the Massachusetts held the Scriptures to be their unalterable rule, and having formed a plan which they thought was truly scriptural, Captain Johnson in 1651 said, "To them it seems unreasonable, and to savor too much of hypocrisy, that any people should pray unto the Lord for the speedy accomplishment of his word in the overthrow of antichrist, and in the meantime become a patron to sinful opinions and

---

[1] Prince's Annals, pp. 28, 29. [354.]
[2] Massachusetts History, Vol. I, p. 431. [380.]

damnable errors that oppose the truths of Christ, admit it be but in the bare permission of them[1]." Hence it appears, that it was this erroneous notion of using carnal weapons against what they looked upon as false opinions, that ought to bear the blame and reproach of those persecutions, and not their particular religious denomination, nor any of their zeal to promote religion by gospel means and methods.

That they were not aware how unscripturally they had confounded church and state together, appears from many facts. They were so much concerned to keep them distinct, that in 1632 the church of Boston wrote to the elders and brethren of the churches of Plymouth, Salem, &c. for their advice in three questions; 1. Whether one person might be a civil magistrate and a ruling elder at the same time? 2. If not, then which should he lay down? 3. Whether there might be divers pastors in the same church? The first was agreed by all negatively; the other two doubtful[2]." In consequence of which, Mr. Nowell resigned his office of ruling elder, to which he had been ordained in the church, to hold those of a magistrate and secretary in the state[3]. On the other hand, Mr. John Doan, having been formerly chosen to the office of deacon in the church of Plymouth, at his and the church's request, was freed from the office of Assistant in the commonwealth[4].

Again our late Governor says, " I suppose there had been no instance of a marriage lawfully celebrated by a layman in England, when they left it. I believe there was no instance of marriage by a clergyman after they arrived, during their charter; but it was always done by a magistrate, or by persons specially appointed for that purpose. It is difficult to assign a reason for so sudden a change[5]." I happened to observe a passage in Mr. Robinson which I suppose gives us

[1] Johnson's History, p. 206.
[2] Prince's Annals, p. 64. [398.]
[3] Hubbard, 186.—Ed.
[4] Prince's Annals, p. 92. [432.]
[5] Massachusetts History, Vol. I, p. 444. [392.]

the true reason of that great change. Mr. Bernard had charged the Separatists with an error, which he said they had given neither reason nor Scripture for, in holding that ministers may not celebrate marriage, nor bury the dead. To which Mr. Robinson answers:—

> In our third petition to the king, and the fourth branch of the sixth proposition, there are almost twenty several Scriptures, and nine distinct reasons grounded upon them, to prove, that the celebration of marriage, and burial of the dead, are not ecclesiastical actions, appertaining to the ministry, but civil, and so to be performed. . . . . The apostle testifieth that the Scriptures, being divinely inspired, do make perfect, and fully furnished, the man of God, or minister, to every good work of his calling. Now I suppose Mr. B. will not be so ill advised, as to go about to prove that the celebration of marriage, and burial of the dead, are duties prescribed by the Lord Jesus to be done in the pastor's office, or that the Scriptures lay this furniture upon the man of God for the proper works of his office. They are then other spiritual lords than the Lord Christ, that prescribe these duties to be done by their men, furnished by other Scriptures than the divine Scriptures, the bishop's Scriptures, their canons and constitutions; whereby they are furnished indeed with ring, service-book, and other priestly implements for the business[1].

This I suppose accounts for that change in our fathers' conduct then; though it is likely we are agreed in general now, that, as it was an error of popery to call marriage a sacrament, and to limit its administration to the clergy, so on the other hand that it was a mistake in those fathers to think that the civil state might not as well appoint ministers to celebrate marriages as any other persons.

These and many other things prove that those fathers were earnestly concerned to frame their constitution both in church and state by divine rule; and as all allow that nothing teaches like experience, surely they who are enabled well to improve the experience of past ages, must find it easier now to discover the mistakes of that day, than it was for them to do it then. Even in 1637, when a number of puritan ministers in England, and the famous Mr. Dod among them, wrote to

---

[1] Justification of Separation, p. 438. [465.]

the ministers here, that it was reported that they had embraced certain new opinions, such as "that a stinted form of prayer and set liturgy is unlawful; that the children of godly and approved Christians are not to be baptized, until their parents be set members of some particular congregation; that the parents themselves, though of approved piety, are not to be received to the Lord's Supper until they be admitted set members," &c., Mr. Hooker expressed his fears of troublesome work about answering of them[1], though they may appear easy to the present generation.

[1] Massachusetts History, Vol. I, p. 81. [80, 81.]

CHAPTER II.

MR. ROGER WILLIAMS'S SENTIMENTS, AND HIS BANISHMENT, WITH OTHER AFFAIRS, FROM 1634 TO 1644.

Mr. Hubbard tells us, that "February 5, 1631,[1] arrived Mr. William Peirse at Nantasket; with him came one Mr. Roger Williams,[2] of good account in England for a godly

[1] Hubbard, p. 202. Hubbard, according to the custom of his time, commences the year with March 25, and thus gives this date 1630. Winthrop (Vol. I, page 41) does the same. Backus, according to his plan, as stated in the preface to his first volume, has changed the date to conform to the present mode of reckoning. If Mr. Knowles had read and remembered this preface he would not have charged Backus with error in this date, or with neglect to observe the difference between the old and the new style. See Knowles's Memoir of Roger Williams, p. 45.—ED.

[2] Of the life of Roger Williams, previous to his arrival in America, the accounts are meagre and often untrustworthy and contradictory. It is a tradition that he he was born in Wales, in 1599. With this agrees his own statement in a letter written in July, 1679, quoted in Chapter III, in which he speaks of himself as being "near to four score years of age." He appears to have become early a subject of experimental religion. In 1673 he wrote, "From my childhood, now about three score years, the Father of lights and mercies touched my soul with a love to himself, to his only begotten, the true Lord Jesus, to his holy Scriptures." In his youth he was taken under the patronage of the famous lawyer and statesman, Sir Edward Coke. It is said that Coke's interest in him was aroused by seeing him in church taking notes of the discourse, and upon asking to look at the notes he was so much impressed with the ability of the boy that he at once obtained permission from his parents to superintend his education, (Knowles's Memoir of Roger Williams, p. 24.) In the library of Trinity College, Cambridge, there is still preserved a letter from Roger Williams to Mrs. Sadlier, daughter of Sir Edward Coke, to which she has appended the words, "This Roger Williams, when he was a youth, would, in a short-hand, take sermons and speeches in the Star Chamber, and present them to my dear father." His patron placed him in school at Sutton's Hospital, now the Charter House, from the records of which we learn that he entered there in 1621,

and zealous preacher. He had been some years employed in the ministry in England."[1] Accordingly I find Mr. Williams reminding Mr. Cotton of conversation he had with him and Mr. Hooker, while they were riding together, " to and

and obtained an exhibition in 1624. (Elton, Life of Roger Williams, p. 11.) From Sutton's Hospital there is little doubt that he was sent to the University of Cambridge, where Coke himself was graduated. A Williams, whose first name is not given, entered Pembroke College, Cambridge, in 1623, and a Roger Williams, probably the same person, was matriculated a pensioner there in 1625, and took the degree of Bachelor of Arts in 1627. His signature upon the college books in subscribing to the thirty-nine articles, a prerequisite of graduation, is said to bear unmistakable resemblance to that of the founder of Providence. (Arnold's History of Rhode Island, Vol. I, p. 49. Bancroft, Vol. I, p. 361. Guild's Biographical Introduction to the writings of Roger Williams, Publications of the Narragansett Club, Vol. I, pp. 5-8.) It is the tradition indeed, that Roger Williams was graduated at Oxford: and Elton, (p. 10,) would identify him with Rodericus Williams who entered Jesus College, April 30, 1624, aged eighteen. But this is inconsistent with Williams's own statement of his age, already quoted, and would make him only twenty-five when he landed on the shores of the new world,—evidently allowing him too little time to have passed through the experiences which had already fitted him for the part that awaited him here. Moreover, Wood, in his Athenae Oxonienses, in connection with another of the same name, mentions Roger Williams who wrote the key to the language of New England, with the words, " But of what university the said Williams was, if any, I know not."

After his graduation, Williams is said to have studied law under the direction of Coke, but if so, he must have soon abandoned this pursuit for the more congenial one of theology. He received Episcopal ordination, and is said to have assumed the charge of a parish. At this time the line of separation between conformists and nonconformists was rigidly drawn. Charles I succeeded to the throne in 1625, and at once disappointed the hopes of the puritans by showing himself even less liberal than James, his father. In 1628, he placed Laud in the See of London, and in effect, entrusted to him the whole government of the English church. It was Laud's ambition to secure universal conformity. Says Macaulay, " Under his direction, every corner of the realm was subjected to a constant and minute inspection. Every little congregation of separatists was tracked out and broken up. Even the devotions of private families could not escape the vigilance of his spies." The associations of Williams's previous life were such as would incline him towards the nonconformists. Sir Edward Coke was not unfavorable to them; they had large influence in the University of Cambridge, and Dr. Williams, bishop of Lincoln, under whom there are indications that Roger Williams held his living, was on the eve of suffering severest persecution for his leaning towards them. Moreover, Roger Williams's natural character, the Calvinism of his doctrinal views, and the fervor of his piety, all contributed to make him a puritan. He was not a man who could hide his views and principles. It was evident that persecution could not long fail to reach him, and to escape it, and to secure for himself " soul-freedom," he left his native country for the wilds of America. His subsequent history is sufficiently told in the pages that follow.—ED.

[1]It appears by his own account that he was then in the thirty-second year of his age.

[1634.]　　　ARRIVAL OF ROGER WILLIAMS.　　　41

from Sempringham."[1] From whence it appears that Mr. Williams was acquainted with those two famous men, in our mother country, and the subject of that conversation shows that he could not then conform to the national church so far as they did.

Mr. Hubbard says, " Immediately after his arrival he was called by the church of Salem to join with Mr. Skelton; but the Governor and Council being informed thereof, wrote to Mr. Endicott, to desire they would forbear any further proceeding therein, till the said council had conferred further about it. 1. Because he refused to join with the congregation [i. e. church] of Boston, because they would not make a public declaration of their repentance, for holding communion with the church of England while they lived there. 2. Because he declared it his opinion, that the civil magistrate might not punish any breach of the first table; whereupon they for the present forbode proceeding with him, which occasioned his being called to Plymouth;"[2] where, Governor Bradford says, " He was freely entertained, according to our poor ability, and exercised his gifts among us; and after some time was admitted a member of the church, and his teaching well approved; for the benefit whereof I still bless God, and am thankful to him even for his sharpest admonitions and reproofs, so far as they agreed with truth."[3]

As the two points which were so offensive to the rulers at Boston, were the foundation cause of their after proceedings against Mr. Williams, and closely affect the history of our country to this day, they demand our close attention. The Governor and Company of the Massachusetts colony held communion with the national church, and reflected upon their brethren who separated from her, while in their native island; and on their departure from it, they from ' on

---

[1] Hubbard, p. 203.—ED.　　　[2] Prince. p. 48. [377.]
[3] Reply to Cotton on the Bloody Tenet, p. 12.

board their chief ship wrote to those who were left behind, April 7, 1630, in these words[1]:—

REVEREND FATHERS AND BRETHREN :— .... Howsoever your charity may have met with some occasion of discouragement, through the misrepresentation of our intentions, ... yet we desire you would be pleased to take notice of the principles and body of our company, as those who esteem it our honor to call the church of England, from whence we rise, our dear mother, and cannot part from our native country, where she specially resideth, without much sadness of heart, and many tears in our eyes; ever acknowledging that such hope and part as we have obtained in the common salvation, we have received in her bosom, and sucked it from her breasts. We leave it not therefore, as loathing that milk wherewith we were nourished there, but blessing God for the parentage and education, as members of the same body, shall always rejoice in her good. ....

JOHN WINTHROP, Governor.
CHARLES FINES.
GEORGE PHILIPS.
RICHARD SALTONSTALL.
ISAAC JOHNSON.
THOMAS DUDLEY.
WILLIAM CODDINGTON. &c.[2]

Now as Episcopalians down to this day, try to improve this address, as an evidence that New England was first planted by members of their church (though the foregoing history shows that it was not so) we may safely conclude that the ruling party of the nation did not neglect the advantage hereby given to strengthen themselves then in their way, which was so corrupt, that when the archbishop of Canterbury a little after commenced a prosecution against Mr. Cotton, the Earl of Dorset interceded for him, till he found matters were got to such a pass that he sent Mr. Cotton word, " that if he had been guilty of drunkenness or uncleanness, or any such lesser fault, he could have obtained his pardon; but inasmuch as he had been guilty of noncon-

[1] The letter was printed in London a few days after. Neal's History of New England, Vol. I, p. 147.
[2] Massachusetts History, Vol. I, pp. 487—489. [431, 432.]

formity and puritanism, the crime was unpardonable; and therefore," said he, "you must fly for your safety[1]." Can we wonder that Mr. Williams, who came over the year after the aforesaid address was made, should not incline to join in fellowship with the authors of it, without some honest retraction? Yet he was not so rigid but that he did hold occasional communion at the Lord's table in the church of Plymouth, with Governor Winthrop, and his minister, Mr. Wilson, of Boston, October 28, 1632[2].

Mr. Williams preached at Plymouth between two and three years, and then discerning in a leading part of the church a disagreement with some of his sentiments, and being invited to Salem, he requested a dismission there; and though a number were unwilling for it, yet elder Brewster prevailed with the church to grant his request, fearing, he said, " that he would run the same course of rigid separation and anabaptistry, which Mr. John Smith at Amsterdam had done[3]. Such as did adhere to him were also dismissed, and removed with him, or not long after him to Salem[4]." The Court again

---

[1] Magnalia, B. 3, p. 19. [Vol. I. p. 241.]

[2] Prince's Annals, p. 70. [406.] —B.
See also, Winthrop, Vol. I, p. 91; Hubbard, p. 204.—ED.

[3] Mr. Smith's church separated from the church of England with Mr. Robinson's, and removed a little before him into Holland. After Mr. Smith's death a number of his church returned and promoted the Baptist cause in London. Crosby's History, Vol. I, p. 268.—B.

Mr. John Smith began his ministry in the church of England. Early in the reign of James I, he renounced the discipline and ceremonies of that church and escaped impending persecution by flight to Holland. Here he joined the church of Brownists or Separatists, and soon became a man of note among them. Continuing to measure his belief and practice by the rule of Scripture, he was next compelled to renounce infant baptism. He was excluded by the Brownists, but his views spread so rapidly that a Baptist church was soon founded of which he became the pastor, and the other English churches in Holland were largely leavened with Baptist sentiments. Churchmen pointed to him as a warning to all separatists and nonconformists, exemplifying the legitimate end of their heresies; and the separatists themselves wrote no less than six distinct treatises against him. He was accused of having baptized himself, a charge which has since been sufficiently disproved. See Crosby, Vol. I, pp. 90—99, 265—268; Neal's History of the Puritans, Vol. II, pp. 72, 73; Cutting's Historical Vindications, pp. 57—60.—ED.

[4] Morton, pp. 86, 87. [102.]

wrote to Salem against Mr. Williams, but could not prevent his being called to office there; and we are told that, " in one year's time he filled that place with principles of rigid separation, and tending to anabaptism[1]." For this they afterwards banished him; though as it was a confused piece of work for them thus to deal with him, so their historians have given the world a very confused account about it. Morton, Hubbard, Dr. Cotton Mather, and others, have set his banishment in 1634, yet all agree that he was not ordained till after Mr. Skelton's death, which was in August that year, and they tell us of a twelvemonth's labor with him and his church after his ordination, before his banishment; neither do they give us a better account of the true causes of that sentence, than they do of the date of it. I have taken much pains to collect as exact an account of this affair as possible, and have succeeded beyond my expectation.

The dates I find to be as follows:—Governor Winthrop and his Council first wrote to Salem against Mr. Williams, April 12, 1631[2], which occasioned his going to Plymouth. His first child was born there the first week in August, 1633[3], and Mr. Cotton, who arrived at Boston the fourth of September following, says he had removed into the Bay colony before his arrival[4]. Mr. Skelton died August 2, 1634[5], and we shall find proof enough that Mr. Williams was not banished till above a year afterward; so that instead of such hasty proceedings at Salem as his opponents would represent, he preached there more than a year before he was ordained, and as long after it.

As to the causes of his sentence, Mr. Morton has given us five articles, Mr. Hubbard six; Mr. Williams has reduced them to four, but Mr. Cotton is not willing to let them stand as he stated them, but tells us:—

[1] Morton, [103.] Hubbard, [204.]
[2] Prince, p. 26. [351.]
[3] Providence Records.
[4] Tenet washed, Part 2d, p. 4.
[5] Magnalia, B. 3, p. 76. [Vol. I, p. 331.]

Two things there were, which (to my best observation and remembrance) caused the sentence of his banishment; and two others fell in that hastened it.

1. His violent and tumultuous carriage against the patent.

By the patent it is, that we received allowance from the king to depart his kingdom, and to carry our goods with us, without offence to his officers, and without paying custom to himself. By the patent, certain select men, as magistrates and freemen, have power to make laws, and the magistrates to execute justice and judgment amongst the people, according to such laws. By the patent we have power to erect such a government of the church[1], as is most agreeable to the Word, to the estate of the people, and to the gaining of natives, in God's time, first to civility, and then to christianity.

This patent Mr. Williams publicly and vehemently preached against, as containing matter of falsehood, and injustice: falsehood, in making the king the first Christian prince who had discovered these parts; and injustice, in giving the country to his English subjects which belonged to the native Indians[2].

Let it be here noted, that we have no proof that Mr. Williams ever preached or objected against the whole patent, or charter, without distinction, much less against that part of it which constituted them a civil government. His own account of this matter informs us, that the sin of the patents which lay so heavy on his mind was, that therein "Christian kings (so called) are invested with a right, by virtue of their Christianity, to take and give away the lands and countries of other men." And he tells us that this evil so deeply afflicted his soul, that, "before his troubles and banishment, he drew up a letter, not without the approbation of some of the chief of New England, then tender also upon this point before God, directed unto the king himself, humbly acknowledging the evil of that part of the patent which respects the donation of lands, &c[3].

What grounds Mr. Williams and others had for this concern will plainly appear by what follows; for in the said patent from Charles the First, he recites that which was given by his father, King James the First, dated November 3, 1620, wherein he

---

[1]This clause is not truth.   [2]Tenet washed, p. 27.
[3]Reply to Cotton on the Bloody Tenet, pp. 276, 277.

Gave and granted unto the Council established at Plymouth, in the county of Devon, ... all that part of America lying and being in breadth from forty degrees of northerly latitude from the equinoctial line to forty-eight degrees of the said northerly latitude inclusively, and in length of and within all the breadth aforesaid throughout the main land from sea to sea, together also with all the firm lands, soils, grounds, havens, ports, rivers, waters, fishing, mines and minerals, ... jurisdictions, privileges, franchises, and pre-eminences, both within the said tract of land upon the main, and also within the islands and seas adjoining; provided always, that the said islands, or any of the premises by the said letters patent intended and meant to be granted, were not then actually possessed or inhabited by any other Christian prince or state. .... To have and to hold, possess and enjoy, all and singular the aforesaid continent lands, ... and every part and parcel thereof, unto the said Council, and their heirs and assigns forever. .... To be holden of our said most dear and royal father, his heirs and successors, as of his manor of East Greenwich in the county of Kent.

Then King Charles went on to name the Massachusetts Company, and to describe the limits of their colony through the main lands of America, and granted it to them in the same manner, "to be holden of us, our heirs and successors, as of our manor of East Greenwich[1]," &c.

Can any man claim a fuller property in any land in the world, than here was assumed over this vast tract of America? And though the men who had taken this patent banished Mr. Williams out of it, yet before we have done we may see this very principle which he abhorred turned back into their own bosoms, and made use of by a tyrannical party to give them a severe scourging, after their patent was vacated.

The other foundation cause of Mr. Williams's banishment Mr. Cotton gives in these words:—

2. The magistrates, and other members of the General Court, upon intelligence of some Episcopal and malignant practices against the country, made an order of Court to take trial of the fidelity of the people, not by imposing upon them, but by offering to them an oath of fidelity; that in case any should refuse to take it, they might not betrust them with place of public charge and command. This oath when it came abroad he vehe-

---

[1] Massachusetts History, Vol. 3, pp. 1—4.

mently withstood, and dissuaded sundry from it, partly because it was, as he said, Christ's prerogative to have his office established by oath; partly because an oath was part of God's worship, and God's worship was not to be put upon carnal persons, as he conceived many of the people to be. So the Court was forced to desist from that proceeding[1].

This case thus stated carries a sad face with it, but one acquainted with the history of the country would be ready to doubt whether it was truly stated or not; for every freeman had taken an oath of fidelity to the government before that time, and if there was no intent of imposing but only of offering this new oath, could they not find men enough for officers that would take it? Indeed when I come to find how the truth of this matter was, by the colony records, and to think that Mr. Cotton had them at his door when he wrote, I am the most shocked about him by this publication of his against Mr. Williams, of anything I ever met with concerning him. Upon the colony records, when the General Assembly met at Boston, May 14, 1634, I find these words:—

It was agreed and ordered, that the former oath of freemen shall be revoked, so far as it is dissonant from the oath of freemen here underwritten, and that those that received the former oath shall stand bound no further thereby to any intent or purpose than this new oath ties those that take the same.

The Oath of a Freeman.

I, A. B., being by God's providence an inhabitant and freeman within the jurisdiction of this commonweal, do freely acknowledge myself to be subject to the government thereof, and therefore do here swear, by the great and dreadful name of the ever living God, that I will be true and faithful to the same, and will accordingly yield assistance and support thereunto with my person and estate as in equity I am bound, and I will also truly endeavor to maintain and preserve all the liberties and privileges thereof, submitting myself to the wholesome laws and orders made and established by the same. And further, that I will not plot nor practise any evil against it, nor consent to any that shall so do, but will truly discover and reveal the same to lawful authority now here established, for the speedy preventing thereof. Moreover I do solemnly bind myself in the sight of

---

[1] Tenet washed, pp. 28, 29.

God, that when I shall be called to give my voice, touching any such matter of this state, wherein freemen are to deal, I will give my vote and suffrage, as I shall judge in mine own conscience may best conduce and tend to the public weal of the body, without respect of persons or favor of any man; so help me God in the Lord Jesus Christ.

This oath was framed and taken before they proceeded to election at the time above said. When the Assembly met again at Newtown, now Cambridge, March 4, 1635, they enacted as follows:—

It is ordered that every man of or above the age of sixteen years, who hath been or shall hereafter be resident within this jurisdiction, by the space of six months (as well servants as others) and not enfranchised, shall take the oath of residents, before the Governor, Deputy Governor, or two of the next Assistants, who shall have power to convent him for that purpose, and upon his refusal, to bind him over to the next Court of Assistants, and upon his refusal the second time, to be punished at the discretion of the Court.

It is ordered, that the freeman's oath shall be given to every man of or above the age of sixteen years, the clause for election of magistrates only excepted[1].

Now let the candid reader judge,

1. Who was the best friend to charter-rights? The Massachusetts Company were limited, in three different passages of their patent, not to make any laws contrary to the laws of England; yet one professed design of this new oath, was to guard against Episcopal practices, to effect which they left out the clause in their former oath, which bound them to submit to " all such laws, orders, sentences and decrees, as should be lawfully made and published by them;" and instead of it obliged men to swear to submit "to the wholesome laws and orders made and established" by the government of this commonwealth. And though Mr. Cotton asserts that they did not impose but only offer this new oath, yet the colony records are express, that every man who resided within their jurisdiction six months, ser-

[1] Massachusetts Records.

vants as well as others, must swear to obey all their wholesome laws and orders, or be punished at their discretion; yea, and also swear to reveal any plot that they should know of against such government, " to lawful authority now here established;"— that is, not to complain to any but themselves.

2. From whence came the power that presumed to absolve themselves and others from their oath, to keep to acts lawfully made, and to substitute the word *wholesome* in the room of it? Let the learned Cotton Mather answer the question. Says he,—

> The reforming churches, flying from Rome, carried some of them more, some of them less, all of them something, of Rome with them; especially in that spirit of imposition and persecution, which has too much cleaved unto them all[1].

That spirit of imposition and persecution ran so high in England at the time we are upon, that King Charles the First gave a commission, April 28, 1634, to Archbishop Laud, and ten courtiers more[2], some of them known paptists, as follows :—

> We do constitute you, our said Archbishop of Canterbury, &c., or any five or more of you, our counsellors; and to you or to any five or more of you, do commit and give power of protection and government, as well over the English colonies already planted, as over all such other colonies, which by any of our people of England hereafter shall be deduced into any other like parts whatsoever, and power to make laws, ordinances and constitutions, concerning either the state public of the said colonies, or utility of private persons and their lands, goods, debts and succession, within the precincts of the same, and for ordering and directing of them, in their demeanors towards foreign princes and their people, and likewise towards us and our subjects, as well within any foreign parts whatsoever beyond the seas, as during their voyages, or upon the seas to and

---

[1]His son Dr. Samuel Mather's Apology for the churches of New England, Appendix, p. 149.

[2]Lord Coventry, the Archbishop of York, the Earls of Portland, Manchester, Arundel, and Dorset, Lord Cottington, Sir Thomas Edmunds, and the Secretaries Cook and Windebank.

from the same; and for relief and support of the clergy, and the rule and cure of the souls of our people living in those parts, and for consigning of convenient maintenance unto them by tithes, oblations and other profits accruing, according to your good discretion, with the advice of two or three of our bishops, whom you shall think fit to call unto your consultations, touching the distribution of such maintenance unto the clergy, and all other matters ecclesiastical, and to inflict punishment on all offenders or violators of constitutions and ordinances, either by imprisonments or other restraints, or by loss of life or members, according as the quality of the offence shall require; with power also, our royal assent being first had and obtained, to remove all Governors and Presidents of the said colonies, upon just cause appearing, from their several places, and to appoint others in their stead: . . . . and power also to ordain temporal judges and civil magistrates to determine of civil causes, with such powers, in such a form, as to you or any five or more of you shall seem expedient; and also to ordain judges, magistrates and officers for and concerning courts ecclesiastical, with such power and such a form, as to you or any five or more of you, with the advice of the bishops suffragan to the Archbishop of Canterbury for the time being, shall be held meet. . . . . Giving, moreover, and granting to you, that if it shall appear, that any officer or Governor of the said colonies shall unjustly wrong one another, or shall not suppress all rebels to us, or such as shall not obey our commands, that then it shall be lawful, upon advice with ourself first had, for the causes aforesaid, or upon any other just reason, to remand and cause the offender to return into England, or into any other place, according as in your good *discretions* you shall think just and necessary. And we do furthermore give unto you, or any five or more of you, letters patent and other writings whatsoever, of us or of our royal predecessors granted, for or concerning the planting of any colonies, in any countries, provinces, islands or territories whatsoever beyond the seas; and if upon view thereof, the same shall appear to you, or any five or more of you, to have been surreptitiously and unduly obtained, or that any privileges or liberties therein granted be hurtful to us, our crown or prerogative royal, or to any foreign princes, to cause the same to be revoked, and to do all other things, which shall be necessary for the *wholesome* government' and protection of the said colonies, and our people therein abiding[1].

Thus the words "*discretion*" and "*wholesome*" were brought in to violate charters and all public faith, and to set up tyranny over the colonies. But Mr. Edward Winslow being

[1] Massachusetts History, Vol. I. pp. 502—506. [440—443.]

sent over agent for the country, by his indefatigable endeavors, and the influence of some great men, prevented the taking place of this arbitrary commission; upon which Laud turned his resentment against him, and got him imprisoned seventeen weeks in the Fleet prison, in London, for having sometimes taught publicly in the church of Plymouth, and for marrying people, which Laud called "assuming the Ministerial office[1]."

Had the Massachusetts fathers taken only lawful and prudent methods to guard against such Episcopal and malignant practices as these, they would have been justified, and applauded by posterity; but now we mourn to think that they brought so much of the same distemper into this country with them as they did.

The same Court that passed the act to oblige all to take the above oath, or be punished at their discretion, also passed the following, viz. :—

> This Court doth entreat of the brethren and elders of every church within this jurisdiction, that they will consult and advise of one uniform order of discipline in the churches, agreeable to the Scriptures, and then to consider how far the magistrates are bound to interpose for the preservation of that uniformity and peace of the churches[2].

Upon this Mr. Williams publicly preached against the oath they had framed, of submission to such a power; for which the Governor and Assistants called him before them, March 30, 1635, when "he was heard before all the ministers, and," according to Governor Winthrop's opinion, was "clearly refuted[3]." The two things which Mr. Cotton says hastened his banishment were, Mr. Williams's stirring up his church to write to other churches to which those rulers belonged, admonishing them of injustice about some land near Salem; and his separating from his own church when

[1] Plymouth Register, pp. 12.—14.   [2] Massachusetts Records.
[3] Winthrop's Journal. [Vol. I, p. 158.]

they turned against him in these things[1]. Concerning the first of these articles Governor Winthrop says,—

"Salem men preferred a petition at the General Court, May, 1635, for some land in Marblehead neck, which they did challenge as belonging to their town; but because they had chosen Mr. Williams their teacher while he stood under question of authority, and so offered contempt to the magistracy, &c. their petition was refused till, &c. Upon this the church of Salem wrote to other churches to admonish the magistrates of this as a heinous sin, and likewise the deputies, &c.[2]

By the colony records I find that the town of Marblehead was first granted by the Assembly which met May 6, 1635, when sundry parcels of land which Salem had improved were granted to them as soon as they should want them, only with order that Marblehead should pay Salem for what they had done upon the land; among the rest, "the land betwixt the clift and the forest river, near Marblehead" was so granted, but with this proviso, "that if in the meantime the inhabitants of Salem can satisfy the Court that they have true right unto it, that then it shall belong unto the inhabitants thereof."

The generality of those inhabitants turned the next fall, and joined with the rulers in banishing Mr. Williams, and when the General Assembly met again, March 3, 1636, I find these words, viz.: "It was proved this Court that Marble Neck belongs to Salem[3]." Now what can be more natural

---

[1] Tenet washed, pp. 29, 30.   [2] Winthrop's Journal. [Vol I. p. 164.]
[3] Massachusetts Records.

There are indications that Salem was not bribed into acquiescence with Williams's banishment as easily as these words might suggest. Neal writes, "Sentence of banishment being read against Mr. Williams, the whole town of Salem was in an uproar; for he was esteemed an honest, disinterested man and of popular talents in the pulpit; and such was the compassion of the people, occasioned by his followers raising a cry of persecution against him, that he would have carried off the greater part of the inhabitants of the town if the ministers of Boston had not interposed by sending an admonition to the church of Salem, with a confutation in writing of Mr. Williams's errors, showing their tendency to disturb the public peace both in church and State, though he always opposed what he called the Bloody Tenet, that is, every kind and degree of persecution for conscience sake; but by this means the greater part of the people were satisfied, or content at least to abandon their dear Mr. Williams, to whose opinions and doctrine they were but too much devoted." Neal's History of New England, Vol. I, pp. 159, 160. ED.

than to conclude from hence that the way for Salem to satisfy the Court that they had a true right to their land, was to submit their ecclesiastical as well as civil affairs to their direction?

At a General Court, July 8, 1635,—

Mr. Williams, of Salem, was summoned, and did appear. It was laid to his charge, that being under question before the magistracy and churches for divers dangerous opinions, viz.: 1. That the magistrate ought not to punish the breach of the first table, otherwise than in such case as did disturb the civil peace. 2. That he ought not to tender an oath to an unregenerate man. 3. That a man ought not to pray with such, though wife, children, &c. 4. That a man ought not to give thanks after sacrament, nor after meals [meat]; and that the other churches were about to write to the church of Salem to admonish him of these errors, understanding [notwithstanding] the church had called him to the office of a teacher. The said opinions were adjudged by all the magistracy and ministers (who were desired to be present) to be erroneous, and very dangerous, and the calling of him to office at that time was judged a great contempt of authority. So in fine there was given to him and the church of Salem to consider of these things till the next General Court, and then either to give satisfaction to the Court, or else to expect the sentence; it being professedly declared by the ministers (at the request of the Court to give their advice) that they who should obstinately maintain such opinions (whereby the church might come [run] into heresy, apostacy or tyranny, and yet the civil magistrate could not intermeddle) were to be removed, and that the other churches ought to request the magistrate so to do[1].

This is the most plain and ingenuous account of the real cause of Mr. Williams's banishment that I have ever met with, from any who were opposed to him and carries the more weight with it, as it was written by one of the greatest gentlemen in the country, in the time of it, and who was personally concerned in these transactions. And by the first and last of this account it is evident, that the grand difficulty they had with Mr. Williams was, his denying the civil magtrate's right to govern in ecclesiastical affairs.

This honorable writer informs us, that on August 15, 1635,

[1]Governor Winthrop's Journal, Vol. I, pp. [162. 163.]

Mr. Williams, pastor of Salem, being sick, and not able to speak, wrote to his church a protestation. that he could not communicate with the churches in the Bay, neither would he communicate with them, except they would refuse communion with the rest: but the whole church was grieved thereby.

September 1.—At this General Court, Mr. Endicott made a protestation, in justification of the letters formerly sent from Salem to the other churches against the magistracy and deputies, for which he was committed; but the same day he came and acknowledged his fault, and was discharged[1].

October.—At this General Court Mr. Williams, the teacher of Salem, was again convented, and all the ministers in the Bay being desired to be present, he was charged with his said two letters, that to the churches, complaining of the magistrates for injustice, &c. and the other to his own church. . . . . He justified both these letters, and maintained all his opinions; and being offered further conference or disputation, and another respite, he chose to dispute presently, so Mr. Hooker was appointed to dispute with him, but could not reduce him from any of his errors, so the next morning the court sentenced him to depart out of our jurisdiction, within six weeks, all the ministers approving the sentence; and his own church had him under question also for the same case, and he at his return home refused communion with his own church, who openly disclaimed his errors, and wrote an humble submission to the magistrates, acknowledging their fault in joining with Mr. Williams in that letter to the churches against them[2].

[1]Winthrop's Journal. [Vol. I, p. 166.] Mr. Endicott afterwards acted at the head of the most bloody persecutions in this country.—B.

The above sentence refers to the proceedings against Quakers, which culminated in the hanging of four persons of that sect in 1659. See Chap. v.—ED.

[2]Winthrop's Journal, [Vol. I, pp. 170, 171.] The next time the Court met they confirmed their land to them, as before observed. The province records agree with this account, only they do not set any date after the Court met in September, before Mr. Williams's sentence; but it might be October before it was passed.—B.

The exact date of Roger Williams's banishment is still undetermined. Knowles writes in his Memoir of Roger Williams, p. 73, note, "Winthrop places the banishment under date of October, but the Colonial Records, (I. 163,) state that it took place November 3, 1635." Elton, Life of Roger Williams, p. 32, gives the same date, doubtless taking it from Knowles. It were well if the matter could be thus easily settled; but the dates of the Colonial Records on this point are most uncertain. The Records give account of three sessions of the Court, dating them respectively September 1, November 3, and September 2. In the last of these, after a few items of business, there is the date September 3, in the margin; and after many other items, comes the sentence of Roger Williams. Mr. Knowles seems to have regarded the two last named sessions as belonging to the date November 3, either overlooking the dates September 2 and September 3, or rejecting them as spurious.

John Smith was banished at the same time with Mr. Williams, for his dangerous opinions, but we are not told what they were. It seems that the Court after this gave Mr. Williams liberty to stay till Spring, only enjoining it upon him not to go about to draw others to his opinions; but in January, 1636, the Governor and Assistants were informed, that he received and preached to companies in his house, "even of such points as he had been censured for." Upon which they agreed to send him into England by a ship then ready to depart. "The reason was, because he had drawn about twenty people to his opinions, who intended to erect a plantation about the Narragansett Bay, from whence infection would easily spread into these churches, the people being many of them much taken with the apprehension of his godliness." They sent for him to come to Boston, but he sent an excuse; upon which they sent a pinnace, with a commission to Captain Underhill, to apprehend him and carry him on board the ship then at Nantasket; but when they "came to his house, they found he had been gone three days[1]."

This I believe is the exact date of his departure, instead of being in 1634, as their historians have represented. Sixteen years after, Mr. Williams, referring to words of Mr. Cotton, says,—

"These passages occasion me to remember a serious question which many fearing God have made, to wit, whether the promise of God's Spirit blessing conferences, be so comfortably to be expected in New England

That there is an error is evident, but it cannot be remedied by rejecting entirely the dates last named, for that would assign to November 3 much more business than could possibly be transacted in one day. Probably no better explanation can be given than that of Backus. By that, we must regard the record dated November 3 as out of place, inscribed where it is by mistake; and must suppose that the business under date of September 3 really occupied the Court till October. Unless the Court was more diligent than similar bodies in later times, a full month's work is recorded there. Thus the Colonial Records will be made to harmonize with Winthrop's Journal which is almost invariably accurate, and the probable date of Williams's banishment remains as Backus gives it, October, 1635.—ED.

[1] Winthrop's Journal. [Vol. I, pp. 175, 176.]

because of those many public sins which most of God's people in New England lie under, and one especially, to wit, the framing a Gospel. or Christ to themselves without a cross, not professing nor practicing that in Old, which they professedly came over to enjoy with peace and liberty from any cross of Christ in New. I know those thoughts have deeply possessed not a few, considering also the sin of the patents, wherein Christian kings, so called, are invested with right, by virtue of their Christianity, to take and give away the lands and countries of other men; as also considering the unchristian oaths swallowed down, at their coming forth from Old England, especially in superstitious Laud his time and domineering[1]."

It is evident by the foregoing list of errors charged upon Mr. Williams, that the Massachusetts ministers and rulers meant to carry their uniformity so far, as to oblige ministers and Christians, throughout their jurisdiction, not only to ask a blessing at the Lord's table and at common meals, but also to return thanks afterward; and it is likely that this straining of that matter beyond Scriptural example, has had not a little influence upon many since to carry them to the other extreme. Be that as it may, what human heart can be unaffected with the thought that a people who had been sorely persecuted in their own country, so as to flee three thousand miles into a wilderness for religious liberty, yet should have that imposing temper cleaving so fast to them, as not to be willing to let a godly minister, who testified against it, stay even in any neighboring part of this wilderness, but it moved them to attempt to take him by force, to send him back into the land of their persecutors! To avoid this he fled to the heathen in the depth of winter, and obtained such favor in their sight, that Osamaquin (otherwise called Massasoit) chief sachem at Mount Hope, made him a grant of part of that which is since called Rehoboth; yet the place was so far then from answering to its present name, that a letter and messenger was sent from Plymouth to let him know there was not *room* for him in

---

[1] Reply to Cotton, p. 276. Note, it was not all oaths, but those only which he esteemed unchristian ones that he objected against.

that place, because within their patent. "This is a lamentation, and shall be for a lamentation."

Mr. Williams's own testimony, upon a particular occasion at Providence, twenty-five years after, I think deserves notice here. Says he:—

> I testify and declare in the holy presence of God, that when at my first coming into these parts I obtained the lands of Secunk of Osamaquin, the then chief sachem on that side, the Governor of Plymouth, Mr. Winslow, wrote to me, in the name of their government, their claim of Secunk to be in their jurisdiction, as also their advice to remove but over the river unto this side, where now by God's merciful providence we are, and then I should be out of their claim, and be as free as themselves, and loving neighbors together[1]. After I had obtained this place, now called Providence, of Canonicus and Myantinomy, the chief Nanhigganset sachems deceased, Osamaquin (the sachem aforesaid, also deceased) laid his claim to this place also. This forced me to repair to the Nanhigganset sachems aforesaid, who declared, that Osamaquin was their subject, and had solemnly, himself in person, with ten men, subjected himself and his lands unto them at the Nanhigganset, and now he seemed to revolt from his loyalty, under the shelter of the English at Plymouth[2]. This I declared from the Nanhigganset sachems to Osamaquin, who without any stick acknowledged to be true, that he had so subjected as the Nanhigganset sachems had affirmed; but withal he affirmed that he was not subdued by war, which himself and his father had maintained against the Nanhiggansets; but God, said he, subdued us by a plague, which swept away my people, and forced me to yield. This conviction and confession of his, together with gratuities to himself, brethren and followers, made him often profess, that he was pleased that I should here be his neighbor, and the rather because he and I had been great friends at Plymouth; and also because his and my friends at Plymouth advised him to be at peace and friendship with me; and he hoped that our children after us would be good friends together. And whereas there hath been often speech of Providence falling in Plymouth jurisdiction by virtue of Osamaquin's claim; I add unto the testimonies abovesaid, that the Governor, Mr.

[1] This by the way shows a great difference between the temper of Plymouth and Massachusetts rulers of which we shall yet see more. The chief sachems' names are very differently spelt in the different writings I have met with.

[2] This perfectly agrees with the account we have of Massasoit's or Osamaquin's league he made with Plymouth people the spring after their last coming, and of the Narragansett's threatenings on that account. Prince's Chronology, pp. 102, 116, [187, 188, 199, 200.]

Bradford, deceased, and other of their Magistrates, declared unto me, both by conference and writing, that they and their government were satisfied, and resolved never to molest Providence, nor to claim beyond Secunk, but to continue loving friends and neighbors (among the barbarians) together. This is the true sum and substance of many passages between our countrymen of Plymouth and Osamaquin, and me.

ROGER WILLIAMS.[1]

The above date of Mr. Williams's removal is confirmed by Mr. Winslow's being then Governor of Plymouth; for 1636 was the only year that he sustained that office between 1633 and 1644. And as it appeared by Plymouth records that he entered on his government the first of March that year, we may conclude that Mr. Williams fled to Secunk in the depth of winter, and removed with a few friends over the river in the spring[2]. Here let us admire the wisdom

---

[1]Copied from the original, in his own hand writing, dated "Providence, 13, 10, 1661, (so called)."

[2]It is said that he, with Thomas Angell, a hired servant, and some others, went over in a canoe, and were saluted by the Indians near the lower ferry, by the word *Whatcheere?* i. e. How do you do? which gave name to a field, which Mr. Williams sold many years after, and in the deed says he satisfied the owner for it, and planted it, at his first coming, with his own hands. They went round till they got to a pleasant spring above, where is now the great bridge, where they landed; and near to which both he and Angell lived to old age.—B.

The date of Roger Williams's removal from Seekonk to Providence can be reached only approximately. In a letter to Major Mason of Connecticut, written June 22, 1770, published in the Massachusetts Historical Collections, Vol. I. p. 275, he writes that he "begun to build and plant at Seekonk," and that his removal occasioned his "loss of a harvest that year." His letter to the Massachusetts colony announcing the murder of Oldham, which Governor Winthrop states (Vol. I, p. 190) was received July 26, seems to have been written from Providence. If so, his removal must have been before this date, and after the beginning of planting time. From these dates Knowles (Memoir, p. 104) conjectures that it took place about the middle of June. Elton, (Life of Roger Williams, p. 38,) and Gamwell, (Life of Roger Williams, p. 64,) place it in the latter part of June. The words "I *begun* to build and *plant* at Seekonk" might suggest a somewhat earlier date, as the season of planting does not extend beyond the last of May. There is perhaps another clue which will fix the time more definitely. In the letter to Major Mason already quoted, Williams writes that between his "friends of the Bay and Plymouth,' he was "sorely tossed for one fourteen weeks, not knowing what bread or bed did mean." His departure from Salem was in January; at what part of the month we do not know. Elton states (p. 33) that his citation before the General Court, the immediate cause of his flight, was January 11th, but here he evidently mistakes the words of Winthrop, "11 mo. January" which mean only January the eleventh

that governs the world. "As Joseph was sold by his envious brethren, with intent to get him out of their way, yet divine providence overruled this cruel action quite otherwise than they intended, and made it the means of their future preservation; so the harsh treatment and cruel exile of Mr. Williams seem designed by his brethren for the same evil end, but was, by the goodness of the same over-ruling hand, turned to the most beneficent purposes[1]."

Just at this juncture, the Pequods, a powerful Indian tribe, who lived upon the lands where are now the towns of Groton and Stonington, were forming plots against the English colonies, even the very year that those of Connecticut and Providence began, and when Boston was but six years old; and as a vessel was sent by the government from thence, under the command of John Oldham, to trade with the natives at Block Island, about fourteen Indians boarded the vessel, and murdered him; but as John Gallop happened to come upon them, in his return from Connecticut river, they leaped into the sea, where some were drowned, and others reached the shore. The first news of this sad event that they received was from Mr. Williams's pen, by two Indians who went with Oldham, and one from Canonicus, a Narragansett sachem, who arrived at Boston, July 26, 1636. Governor Vane wrote back to Mr. Williams, to let the Narragansetts know that they expected them to send home two boys who were with Oldham, and to take revenge upon the islanders. Four days after the boys came home with one of Miantinomy's men, with another letter from Mr. Williams, informing that said sachem had caused the sachem of Niantick to send to Block Island for them, and that he had near

---

month, according to the old style of reckoning. If we suppose Williams's escape to have taken place the latter part of January, counting fourteen weeks, we have near the middle of May, as the date of his settlement in Providence. This would be late enough for him to have "begun to plant at Seekonk," and, considering the bargains which he must make with the Indians and other delays in founding a new settlement, late enough to occasion his "loss of a harvest that year."—ED.

[1]History of Providence.

a hundred fathom of peag[1], and much other goods of Oldham's which should be reserved for them, and that three of the seven Indians who were drowned were sachems[2]. August 26 came a third letter from Mr. Williams. Governor Winthrop says :—

In these Indian troubles Mr. Williams was assiduous to influence the Narragansetts in favor of the English, and to keep them from joining with the Pequods[3].

Sept. Canonicus sent word of some English whom the Pequods had killed at Saybrook, and Mr. Williams wrote that the Pequods and Narragansetts were at truce, and that Miantonomoh told him that the Pequods had labored to persuade them that the English were minded to destroy all the Indians. Whereupon we sent for Miantonomoh to come to us.

Accordingly he and two of Canonicus's sons and another sachem, and near twenty of their men whom they call sannups, came to Boston October 21, where the Governor called together all the magistrates and ministers, and next day a firm league was signed between them. " But because they could not make them well understand the articles, they told them they would send a copy of them to Mr. Williams, who

---

[1] Wampum.—ED.

[2] Hubbard, [249, 250.] Hubbard also quotes from Winthrop's Journal, Vol. I, p. 190, the statement that ten or eleven Indians were drowned.—ED.

[3] Hubbard's Journal.—B.

" The warlike tribe [the Pequods] courted the alliance of its neighbors, the Narragansetts and the Mohegans, that a union and a general rising of the natives might sweep the hated intruders from the ancient hunting grounds of the Indian race. The design could be frustrated by none but Roger Williams; and the exile, who had been the first to communicate to the Governor of Massachusetts the news of the impending conspiracy, encountered the extremity of peril with magnanimous heroism. Having received letters from Vane and the Council of Massachusetts requesting his utmost and speediest endeavors to prevent the league, neither storms of wind nor high seas could detain the adventurous envoy. Shipping himself alone in a poor canoe, every moment at the hazard of his life, he hastened to the house of the sachem of the Narragansetts. The Pequod ambassadors, reeking with blood, were already there, and for three days and nights the business compelled him to lodge and mix with them, having cause every night to expect their knives at his throat. The Narragansetts were wavering; but Roger Williams succeeded in dissolving the formidable conspiracy. It was the most intrepid and most successful achievement in the whole Pequod war;—an action as perilous in its execution as it was fortunate in its issue." Bancroft, Vol. I, p. 398.—ED.

could best interpret the same to them. So after dinner they took leave[1]." What would the Massachusetts have now done, if Mr. Williams had been sent to England, as they had intended, the winter before!

Let us now review their religious state. In October, 1635, arrived Mr. Thomas Shepard and Hugh Peters, two ministers, who were much improved afterward; also Mr. afterward Sir Henry Vane, the latter of whom was admitted a member of Boston church November 1[2]. At the General Assembly held March 3, 1636, it was

> Ordered, that all persons are to take notice that this Court doth not, nor will hereafter, approve of any such companies of men, as shall henceforth join in any pretended way of church fellowship, without they shall first acquaint the magistrates and the elders of the greater part of the churches in this jurisdiction with their intentions, and have their approbation herein. And further it is ordered, that no person being a member of any church which shall hereafter be gathered without the approbation of the magistrates and the greater part of said churches, shall be admitted to the freedom of this commonwealth[3].

At the election at Boston, May 25, Mr. Vane was chosen Governor, and Mr. Winthrop Deputy Governor; and a standing Council was formed of three men. "The reason was, for that it was shewed from the word of God, &c., that the principal magistrates ought to be for life." Mr. Winthrop and Mr. Dudley were chosen for life, and Governor Vane to be their President[4]. The next year Mr. Endicott

---

[1] Winthrop, [Vol. I, pp. 196, 199]; Hubbard, [253.]
[2] Winthrop, [Vol. I, p. 170.]
[3] Massachusetts Records.
[4] Winthrop's Journal, [184.] Mr. Cotton wrote this year to Lord Say and Seal, and says, "God hath so framed the state of church government and ordinances, that they may be compatible to any commonwealth, though never so much disordered in its frame. But yet when a commonwealth hath liberty to mould its own frame, I conceive the Scripture hath given full direction for the right ordering of the same, and that in such sort as may best maintain the *euexia* [well being] of the church. Mr. Hooker doth often quote a saying out of Mr. Cartwright, that no man fashioneth his house to his hangings, but his hangings to his house. It is better that the commonwealth be fashioned to the setting forth of God's house, which is his church; than to accommodate the church frame to the civil state. . . . . Nor need

was chosen for life in Vane's room. This Council soon found work to do, one article of which here follows :—

To the Constable of Salem:

Whereas we are credibly informed that divers persons (both of men and women) within your town, do disorderly assemble themselves both on the Lord's days and at other times, contemptuously refusing to come to the solemn meetings of the church there (or being some of them justly cast out) do obstinately refuse to submit themselves, that they might be again received; but do make conventions, and seduce diverse persons of weak capacity, and have already withdrawn some of them from the church, and hereby have caused much (not only disturbance in the church, but also) disorders and damage in the civil state; .... these are therefore to require you forthwith to repair unto all such disorderly persons; and signify to them that said course is very offensive to the government here, and may no longer be suffered, and therefore command them from us, to refrain all such disordered assemblies, and pretended church meetings; and either to conform themselves to the laws and orders of this government, being established according to the rule of God's word; or else let them be assured that we shall by God's assistance take some such strict and speedy course for the reformation of these disorders, and preventing the evils which may otherways ensue, as our duty to God and charge over his people do call for from us. And when you have given them this admonition you shall diligently attend how it is observed, and certify us accordingly, as you will answer your neglect herein at your peril.

H. VANE, Gov.
JO. WINTHROP, Dept.
THO. DUDLEY[1].

From Boston this 30th of the 3d month, 1636.

They were somewhat too short in declaring the laws and orders of their government already established, for that work was yet to do; therefore this Court now passed the following act, viz. :—

The Governor, Deputy Governor, Thomas Dudley, John Haynes, Richard Bellingham, Esquires, Mr. Cotton, Mr. Peters, and Mr. Shepard, are

we fear, that this course will, in time, cast the commonwealth into distractions, and popular confusions. .... Purity preserved in the church, will preserve well ordered liberty in the people, and both of them establish well balanced authority in the magistrates." Massachusetts History, Vol. I, pp. 497, 500. [219, 220.] His great mistake herein will soon appear.

[1] Winthrop.

entreated to make a draught of laws agreeable to the word of God, which may be the fundamentals of this commonwealth, and to present the same to the next General Court; and it is ordered that in the mean time the magistrates and their associates shall proceed in the courts to hear and determine all causes according to the laws now established, and where there is no law, then as near the laws of God as they can[1].

Soon after this came on such disputes in the country about grace and works, that " it began to be as common there to distinguish between men being under a covenant of works, and a covenant of grace, as in other countries between protestants and paptists[2]." It divided the General Court,

---

[1] Massachusetts Records. From the beginning, their Governor and Assistants had been their executive court, till the March preceding, when they took in associates with the magistrates, and formed inferior courts in their several towns, to try causes not exceeding ten pounds; from whence appeals might be made to the Court of Assistants.

[2] Hubbard, [294]. Captain Johnson says, " That you may understand their way of broaching their abominable errors, it was in dividing those things the Lord hath united in his work of conversion continued, carrying on a soul to heaven, in these four particulars:

" 1. In dividing between the word and the word, under pretense of a legal gospel, persuading the people their ministers were legal preachers, teaching them little better than popery, and unfit for gospel churches; denying them to be any ministers of Christ, that preach any preparation work, by shewing men what the law requires. Here's nothing, says one of them, but preaching out of the law and the prophets. Truly, says another, I have not heard a pure gospel sermon from any of them.

"2. In separating Christ and his graces, in manifesting himself to be in the soul; and this they say makes much for the magnifying of free grace; and indeed they made it so free, that the soul that receives it shall never taste any of it by their consent, but remain still a dry branch as before. These legal Pharisees, says one of them, tell us of a thing they call inherent grace, and of a man being made a new creature; but I am sure the best of them go on in their legal duties and performances still, sorrowing for sin, hearing of sermons, observing duty morning and evening, and many such like matters. Tush man, says another, you shall hear more than this; I was discoursing with one of their scholastic preacher's disciples, a professed convert, and yet when he came to pray he begged for the forgiveness of his sins; I asked him why he used that vain repetition. since he did believe he was justified by Christ already? He made me an answer not worth repeating; but when I told him God could see no sin in his people, no more than I could see that which was covered close from my eyesight, he told me I spake little less than blasphemy. So ignorant are these men, and their learned guides also; who persuade them the more they have of the indwelling of the spirit of Christ, the better they shall be enabled to these legal duties. Nay, quoth the other, I can tell you more than all this; they make it an evidence of their good estate, even their sanctification, and yet these men would make people believe they are against popery.

and from thence it was carried into Boston church, where it caused sharp debates on Lord's day, December 31, between the two ministers, Cotton and Wilson, and between the Governor and Deputy Governor, who were members of it[1]. In this controversy Mr. Cotton found what it was to fall into the minority, for none of the ministers held fully with him but Mr. Wheelwright, who was not a settled minister, but was preaching to a branch of Boston church, at the place now called Braintree; where, at a general fast on January 19, 1637, he delivered a discourse that greatly increased the flame. Under his third use, we are told that he said, "The second sort of people that are to be condemned, are all such as do set themselves against the Lord Jesus Christ, such are the greatest enemies to the State as can be; if they can have their wills, you see what a lamentable state both church and commonwealth will be in; then we shall have need of mourning; the Lord cannot endure those

"3. The third dividing tenet, by which these persons prosecuted their errors, was between the word of God and the Spirit of God: And here these sectaries had many pretty knacks to delude withal, and especially to please the female sex, they told of rare revelations of things to come from the Spirit, as they say. . . . . Come along with me, says one of them, I will bring you to a woman that preaches better gospel than any of your black coats, that have been at the university*; a woman of another kind of spirit, who hath had many revelations of things to come; and for my part, saith he, I had rather hear such a one that speaks from the mere motion of the Spirit, without any study at all than any of your learned scholars, although they may be fuller of Scripture, and, admit they speak by the help of the Spirit, yet the other goes beyond them.

"4. To divide between Christ and his ordinances; and here they played their game to purpose, even casting down all ordinances as carnal, and that because they were polluted by the ordinance of man; as some of these sectaries have said to the ministers of Christ, you have cast off the cross in baptism, but you would do well to cast off baptism itself; as also for the sacrament of the Lord's Supper, for to make use of bread, or the juice of a silly grape, to represent the body and blood of Christ, they accounted it as bad as necromancy in ministers of Christ to perform it." Johnson's History, pp. 94—97.

[1]Winthrop, [Vol. I, 210.]—Hubbard [291.]

*In Johnson's History, both the original edition and the recent excellent reprint edited by Mr. Poole, this word is *ninneversity*. Backus seems to have taken as a mistake what was meant for a pun.—ED.

that are enemies to himself and kingdom and people, and unto the good of his church[1]."

At the General Court, March 9, Mr. Wheelwright was called to account for the words which tended to sedition in his sermon, but the matter was deferred from Court to Court till fall, when he was banished. Contention arose to a great height. Stephen Greensmith, for saying "that all the ministers, except A. B. C[2]. did teach a covenant of works, was censured to acknowledge his fault in every church, and fined forty pounds[3]."

At the General Court, May 17, 1637, after a hot dispute they proceeded to election, when Mr. Vane and his friends were left out[4]; and a law was made, "that no town or person shall receive any stranger resorting hither with intent to reside in this jurisdiction, nor shall allow any lot or habitation to any above three weeks, except such persons shall have allowance under some one of the Council, or of two other of the magistrates their hands, upon pain that every town that shall give or sell any lot or habitation to any such not so allowed shall forfeit one hundred pounds for every offence; and every person receiving any such for longer time than is here expressed, or than shall be allowed in some special case . . . . shall forfeit for every offence forty pounds, and for every month after such person shall there continue twenty pounds[5]."

Mr. Cotton was for a while so much dissatisfied with this law, that he had thoughts of removing out of that jurisdiction[6]. Governor Winthrop wrote a defence of it, in which

---

[1] Gorton's Glass for New England, pp. 19, 20. Gorton says, in this, Wheelwright "bore testimony to the light;" and the words above he says he transcribed out of Mr. Wheelwright's manuscript.

[2] "Mr. Cotton, Mr. Wheelwright, and he thought, Mr. Hooker." Hutchinson, Vol. I, p. 62.—ED.

[3] Winthrop, [Vol. I, p. 215.]

[4] He sailed for England the 3d of August following.

[5] Massachusetts Records.

[6] Massachusetts History, Vol. I, p. 63. [64.]

he does not deny but that a principal design of that law was to keep away persons of Mr. Wheelwright's opinions, and says:—

> If we find his opinions such as will cause divisions, and make people look at their magistrates, ministers, and brethren, as enemies to Christ, antichrists, &c., were it not sin and unfaithfulness in us, to receive more of their opinions, which we already find the evil fruit of? Nay, why do not those who now complain join with us in keeping out such, as well as formerly they did in expelling Mr. Williams for the like, though less dangerous? Where this change of their judgments should arise I leave to themselves to examine[1].

Ah! less dangerous, sure enough! for Mr. Williams was banished for holding that the magistrate's sword ought not to be brought in to decide religious controversies; but Wheelwright would have turned that sword against the rulers, ministers, and people, that he judged to be under a covenant of works, and so enemies to grace.

Mr. Wheelwright was brother-in-law to Mrs. Anne Hutchinson, who had been a principal instrument of the division in the country about grace and works. We are told that she brought these two errors out of England with her, viz.:—
" 1. That the person of the Holy Ghost dwells in a justified person. 2. That no sanctification can help to evidence our justification[2]." A synod of ministers and messengers from all parts of the country met at Newtown, the 30th of August, and spent three weeks in debates upon these controversies, and drew up and condemned fourscore errors. The General Court adjourned to attend on their debates, and after their result was signed by all the settled ministers except Mr. Cotton, who also appeared to incline towards the majority, they met, September 26, when it is recorded,—

> Mr. Wheelwright appearing, was dismissed until he should be sent for by the Court or Courts which shall succeed. This present Court is dissolved, until a new one be called, and to be kept at Newtown.[3]

[1]Massachusetts History, Vol. 3, p. 71.   [2]Winthrop's Journal, [Vol. I, p. 200.]
[3]Massachusetts Records.

Here opens something that I never heard of till I found it upon the colony records. It was customary to elect their deputies twice a year, namely, in the spring and fall; but to choose them twice in one fall was an unprecedented act, of which I believe no parallel can be found from the foundation of the country to this day. It seems that a major vote of those deputies, to execute the decrees of the late synod, could not be obtained, therefore the House was dissolved, and a new one convened on November 2, 1637;[1] to which a remonstrance against those former proceedings was presented, signed by above sixty men; of whom William Aspinwall, who drew it, and John Coggshall were members of the Assembly. For this they were now excluded, and an order was sent for Boston to choose two other deputies. Also, " John Oliver, justifying the seditious libel called a remonstrance or petition, was dismissed from being a deputy in this Court."[2] The Court then proceeded to pass the following sentences, viz. :—

Mr. John Wheelwright being formerly convicted of contempt and sedi-

[1] It was enacted July 14, 1634, that there should be "four General Courts held yearly," and that Deputies should be chosen " before every General Court." March 3, 1636, it was enacted that it should " be lawful for the Governor or Deputy Governor, or any two magistrates, upon special and urgent occasions, to appoint Courts," at other than the regular times. At the same time it was ordered that thereafter there should be " only two General Courts kept in a year," one in May and one in October. In the case under consideration, probably the Governor deemed the occasion sufficiently urgent to demand a special Court, and a new election was held according to the law above cited, which required that Deputies be chosen before every Court. See Massachusetts Records.—ED.

[2] Massachusetts Records; Winthrop. The remaining members of the Assembly were Governor Winthrop, Deputy Governor Dudley, John Endicott, John Humfrey, Richard Bellingham, Roger Harlakenden, Israel Stoughton, Simon Bradstreet, and Increase Nowell, Assistants, and thirty-one Deputies. The House that was dissolved in September had twenty-six Deputies, of whom but eleven were in this new House. Mr. Atherton Hough was one who was left out, though he was a magistrate two years before. John and Isaac Heath, John Johnson, Thomas Lynde, Nicholas Danforth, William Spencer, Samuel Appleton, Joseph Metcalf, John Upham and Thomas Gardner, were also of those they left out.*

These and such like proceedings caused the removal of Mr. William Blaxton about this time. He was a minister in the church of England, but came early to this

*According to the printed records of this former Court, it had twenty-seven Deputies. The name of John Heath is not among them. It is proper to remark, however, that the printed records are not infallible.—ED.

tion, and now justifying himself and his former practice, being the disturbance of the civil peace, he is by the Court disfranchised and banished, having fourteen days to settle his affairs.

Mr. John Coggshall being convented for disturbing the public peace, was disfranchised, and enjoined not to speak anything to disturb the public peace, upon pain of banishment.

Mr. William Aspinwall being convented for having his hand to a petition or remonstrance, being a seditious libel, and justifying the same, for which and for his insolent and turbulent carriage, he is disfranchised and banished, putting in sureties for his departure before the end of the first month next ensuing.

Mrs. Hutchinson, the wife of Mr. William Hutchinson, being convented for traducing the ministers and their ministry in this country, she declared voluntarily her revelations were the ground, and that she should be delivered, and the Court ruined with their posterity, and hereupon was banished; and the meanwhile was committed to Mr. Joseph Weld, until the Court shall dispose of her.

Captain Underhill, and two sergeants, were put from office and disfranchised, one of the sergeants being fined forty pounds the other twenty pounds. Four men more were disfranchised for having their hands to said petition, one of whom was William Dyer, afterward the first Secretary of Rhode Island colony. Ten men retracted their signing that remonstrance, and were forgiven. Then upon the 20th of November the court passed the following sentence:—

Whereas the opinions and revelations of Mr. Wheelwright and Mrs.

country. It appears by Johnson's History, p. 20, that he was here in 1628, but not agreeing with Mr. Endicott and others about church affairs, he betook himself to agriculture. He had planted himself upon the neck of land where Boston stands, which from him was called Blaxton's Point, when the Massachusetts company first arrived with their charter. At a Court in Boston, April 1, 1633, they made him a grant of fifty acres of land near his house there. Massachusetts Records. Yet now he said, "I came from England because I did not like the lord bishops; but I cannot join with you, because I would not be under the lord brethren." Magnalia, [Vol. I, p. 221.] He went and settled six miles north of Mr. Williams, near what is now called Whipple's Bridge, in Cumberland, where he lived to old age, and used at times to preach at Providence, and other places adjacent, and left behind him the character of a godly and pious man. His family is extinct. He planted an orchard near where he lived, which we are told is the first that ever bore fruit in Rhode Island colony; and one hundred and forty years after, many of the trees continued to be thrifty and fruitful.

Hutchinson have seduced and led into dangerous errors many of the people of New England, insomuch as there is just cause of suspicion that they, as others in Germany in former times, may upon some revelation make sudden irruption upon those that differ from them in judgment; for prevention whereof it is ordered that all those whose names are underwritten (upon warning given at their dwelling-houses) before the 30th day of this month of November, deliver in at Mr. Keayne's house, at Boston, all such guns, pistols, swords, powder, shot and match, as they shall be owners of, or have in their custody, upon pain of ten pounds for every default to be made thereof; which arms are to be kept by Mr. Keayne till this Court shall take further order therein. Also it is ordered, upon like penalty of ten pounds that no man who is to render his arms by this order, shall buy or borrow any guns, swords, pistols, powder, shot or match, until this Court shall take further order therein.

Seventy-six men are named as being disarmed by this sentence, only if any of them would acknowledge and not justify said petition before two magistrates, they should then be free from it.[1] Of these men fifty-eight belonged to Boston, five to Roxbury, two to Charlestown, six to Salem, two to Ipswich, and three to Newbury; of whom Richard Dummer, of Newbury, had been an Assistant, and Hutchinson, Underhill, Aspinwall, Coggshall and Oliver, of Boston, Robert Moulton, of Salem, and others, had been deputies.

Directly upon the foregoing act the Assembly added the following, viz. :—

The Court being sensible of great disorders growing in this commonwealth, through the contempts which have been of late put upon the civil authority, and intending to provide remedy for the same in time, doth order and decree, that whosoever shall hereafter openly or willingly defame any court of justice, or the sentence or proceedings of the same, or any of the magistrates or other judges of any such court, in respect of any act or sentence therein passed, and being thereof lawfully convicted in any General Court or Courts of Assistants, shall be punished for the same, by fine, imprisonment, or disfranchisement or banishment, as the quality and measure of the offence shall deserve ; . . . . provided always, that seeing

---

[1] Massachusetts Records. It appears that the Court had much difficulty afterward with Keayne about these arms.

the best judges may err through ignorance or misinformation .... it is not the intent of this Court to restrain the free use of the way of God, by petition, &c.

A complaint being made at the same time that some ministers were not well maintained, the Court sent out a request, "That the several churches will speedily enquire hereinto, and if need be to confer together about it, and send some to advise with this Court at the next session thereof, that some order may be taken according to the rule of the gospel."[1] The effects of these proceedings we shall soon see; though, by the way, it is proper to observe, that as Mr. Williams had been instrumental of procuring the Narragansetts' help against the Pequods, the several colonies sent out their forces against them, and Governor Winthrop says, May 24, "By letters from Mr. Williams we were notified, that Capt. Mason was gone to Saybrook with eighty English and one-hundred Indians,"[2] &c., so that he was constantly engaged for their good. The army was successful, the Pequods were subdued, and I find a proposal of a day of thanksgiving for the soldiers' return, at the General Court, August 1. But at the same time, they say, "Mr. John Greene, of New Providence, having spoken against the magistrates contemptuously, stands bound over in one hundred marks to appear at the next Quarter Court." At that Court he was fined twenty pounds, and committed till it was paid; though upon a submissive petition to the General Court, September 26, he was released.[3] He with others had resorted to Mr. Williams's plantation, to which there was a great addition the next spring. A new one was begun at Rhode Island; of which take the following account.

Mr. John Clarke, a learned physician, who I find was admitted a freeman at Boston, May 6, 1635,[4] as his brother

---

[1]Massachusetts Records.   [2]Winthrop's Journal, Vol. I. p. 223.—ED.
[3]Massachusetts Records.
[4]The John Clarke who was admitted a freeman at Boston, May 6, 1635, must have been a different person from the founder of Rhode Island plantation. The latter

Joseph had been the March before, seeing how things were turned at the Court, in November, 1637, made a proposal to his friends, for peace sake, and to enjoy the freedom of their consciences, to remove out of that jurisdiction. The motion was accepted, and he (being then a gentleman in his 29th year) was requested with some others to look out for a place. They did so; and by reason of the heat of the preceding summer, they first went northerly into that which is now the province of New Hampshire; but the coldness of the following winter made them incline to turn the other way. "So having sought the Lord for direction, they agreed that while their vessel was passing about Cape Cod they would cross over by land, having Long Island and Delaware Bay in their eye, for the place of their residence." At Providence Mr. Williams lovingly entertained them, and being consulted about their design, readily presented two places before them; Sowams, now called Barrington, and Aquetneck, now Rhode Island. They being determined to go out of the other jurisdictions, Mr. Williams, Mr. Clarke, and two others, went to Plymouth to enquire how the case stood, who, [those at Plymouth,] lovingly entertained them, and let them know that they claimed Sowams, but advised them to settle at Aquetneck, and promised that they should be looked upon as free, and to be treated and assisted as loving neighbors." Upon their return nineteen men incor-

---

writes in his "Narrative,"—"In the year '37 I left my native land, and in the ninth month of the same, I (through mercy) arrived at Boston. I was no sooner on shore but there appeared to me differences among them concerning the covenants, and, in point of evidencing a man's good estate, some pressed hard for a covenant of works and for sanctification to be the first and chief evidence; others pressed as hard for the covenant of grace that was established upon a better foundation, and for the evidence of the Spirit as that which is a more certain, constant and satisfactory witness." Mass. Historical Collections, fourth series, Vol. II. p. 22, The date thus given in the "Narrative" is verified by the fact that the difficulty on the question of covenants, which Clarke found in the colony as soon as he was on shore, does not seem to have arisen till 1636. See p. 63.—ED.

A biographical notice of John Clarke will be found in Chapter VII. —ED.

porated themselves into a body politic, and chose Mr. Coddington to be their judge or chief magistrate.[1]

Now to take things in their order, it is to be observed, that though Mr. Williams and a few of his friends had, with the consent of the Narragansett sachems, been settled at Providence near two years, yet the first deed of the place that is extant bears date the same day with that of Aquetneck; and is as follows:—

At Nanhiggansick the 24th of the first month, commonly called March, in the 2d year of our plantation, or planting at Mooshausick, or Providence: Memorandum, that we Caunannicus and Miantinomu, the two chief sachems of Nanhiggansick, having two years since sold unto Roger Williams the lands and meadows upon the two fresh rivers called Mooshausick and Wanaskatuckett,[2] do now by these presents establish and confirm the bounds of those lands, from the rivers and fields of Pawtuckett, the great hill of Neoterconkenitt on the northwest, and the town of Mashapauge on the west. As also, in consideration of the many kindnesses and services he hath continually done for us, both for our friends of Massachusetts, as also at Quininkticutt and Apaum, or Plymouth; we do freely give unto him all that land from those rivers reaching to Pautuxett River, as also the grass and meadows upon Pautuxett River; in witness whereof we have hereunto set our hands.

The mark of ‡ CAUNANNICUS,
The mark of ‖ MIANTINOMU.

In presence of
The mark of † SEATAGH,
The mark of * ASSOTEMEWETT.

1639, Memorandum, 3 month 9 day, this was all again confirmed by Miantinomu; he acknowledged this his act and hand; up the stream of Pautuckett and Pawtuxett without limits we might have for our use of cattle; witness hereof.

ROGER WILLIAMS,
BENEDICT ARNOLD.[3]

---

[1] Clarke's Narrative. [Mass. Historical Collections, fourth series, Vol. II. p. 25.]—Callender's Sermon. [R. I. Historical Collections, Vol. IV. pp. 83, 84.]

[2] The first of these rivers falls into the cove above Providence great bridge from the north, the other from the west.

[3] Literally transcribed from Providence Records. Pawtucket River riseth in or near Rutland, and runs through Leicester, Sutton, Grafton and Uxbridge, and entering Rhode Island colony, passes between Smithfield and Cumberland, and falls into Narragansett Bay, between Providence and Rehoboth. Pawtuxet River rises near the borders of Connecticut, and passing through Gloucester, Scituate and Cranston, falls into said bay, five miles south of Providence.

The deed of Rhode Island was also given the same March 24, 1638; and twenty years after Mr. Williams having occasion to give his testimony concerning it, says,—

I have acknowledged (and have and shall endeavor to maintain) the rights and properties of every inhabitant of Rhode Island in peace; yet since there is so much sound and noise of purchase and purchasers, I judge it not unseasonable to declare the rise and bottom of the planting of Rhode Island in the fountain of it. It was not price nor money that could have purchased Rhode Island. Rhode Island was obtained by love; by the love and favor which that honorable gentleman Sir Henry Vane and myself had with that great sachem Miantinomu, about the league which I procured between the Massachusetts English, &c., and the Narragansetts in the Pequod war. It is true I advised a gratuity to be presented to the sachem and the natives, and because Mr. Coddington and the rest of my loving countrymen were to inhabit the place, and to be at the charge of the gratuities, I drew up a writing in Mr. Coddington's name, and in the names of such of my loving countrymen as came up with him, and put it into as sure a form as I could at that time (amongst the Indians) for the benefit and assurance of the present and future inhabitants of the Island. This I mention, that as that truly noble Sir Henry Vane hath been so great an instrument in the hand of God for procuring of this Island from the barbarians, as also for procuring and confirming of the charter, so it may by all due thankful acknowledgment be remembered and recorded of us and ours which reap and enjoy the sweet fruits of so great benefits, and such unheard of liberties amongst us.[1]

Mr. Williams having obtained the aforesaid grant of Providence, conveyed the same to his friends by the following instrument:—

Providence, 8th of the 8th month, 1638 (so called.) Memorandum, that I, Roger Williams, having formerly purchased of Caunannicus and Miantinomu this our situation or plantation of New-Providence, viz., the two fresh rivers Wanasquatuckett and Mooshausick, and the ground and meadows thereupon; in consideration of thirty pounds received from the inhabitants of said place, do freely and fully pass, grant and make over equal right and power of enjoying and disposing of the same grounds and lands unto my loving friends and neighbors, Stukely Westcoat, William

---

[1] This I copied from the original manuscript, in Mr. Williams's own hand writing, dated "Providence, 25,6, 1658 (so called)." The affair of procuring the charter we shall hear more of anon.

Arnold, Thomas James, Robert Cole, John Greene, John Throckmorton, William Harris, William Carpenter, Thomas Olney, Francis Weston, Richard Waterman, Ezekiel Holliman, and such others as the major part of us shall admit into the same fellowship of vote with us. As also I do freely make and pass over equal right and power of enjoying and disposing of the lands and grounds reaching from the aforesaid rivers unto the great river Pautuxett, with the grass and meadows thereupon, which was so lately given and granted by the aforesaid sachems to me; witness my hand, ROGER WILLIAMS.[1]

Those who were thus received signed the following covenant, viz. :—

We whose names are here underwritten being desirous to inhabit in the town of Providence, do promise to submit ourselves in active or passive obedience to all such orders or agreements as shall be made for public good of the body in an orderly way, by the major consent of the present inhabitants, masters of families, incorporated together into a township, and such others whom they shall admit into the same, *only in civil things.*

By the records, compared with a more ample and full deed of Mr. Williams to the town, executed December 20, 1661, which is entered there, it appears that he generously gave the aforesaid twelve men their interest in the town freely, and the thirty pounds were paid by the next who were admitted, at the rate of thirty shillings a man, the names of whom were Chad Brown, William Field, Thomas Harris, William Wickenden, Robert Williams, Richard Scott, William Reynolds, John Field, John Warner, Thomas Angell, Benedict Arnold, Joshua Winsor, Thomas Hopkins, Francis Weeks, &c.[2] In the last mentioned deed,

---

[1] Providence Records. It seems the first deed of this tenure was lost, therefore this was drawn as exactly as could be remembered in 1666. Of the above men, Olney, Weston, Westcoat, Waterman and Holliman, did not depart the Massachusetts colony till April, 1638. Massachusetts Records. They, with Throckmorton, came from Salem. Massachusetts History, Vol. I, p. 421, [371], and records aforesaid. Weston had been a deputy in court.

[2] Of these I find Williams (brother to Mr. Roger) among the Massachusetts freemen, but no more of their names upon those records. Perhaps most of them might have newly arrived; for Governor Winthrop assures us that not less than three thousand arrived this year in twenty ships; and Mr. Hubbard tells us that those who inclined to Baptist principles went to Providence; others went to Newport. Seven of the first twelve, with Angell, I suppose began the settlement with Mr. Williams in 1636.

after referring to the former ones, and expressing that the sachems' deed was two years after his first purchase, he more fully explains the nature and motives of those transactions. Says he,—

Notwithstanding I had the frequent promise of Miantinomu, my kind friend, that it should not be land that I should want about those bounds mentioned, provided that I satisfied the Indians there inhabiting, I having made covenant of peaceable neighborhood with all the sachems and natives round about us, and having, in a sense of God's merciful providence unto me in my distress, called the place PROVIDENCE, I desired it might be for a shelter for persons distressed for conscience; I then considering the condition of divers of my distressed countrymen, I communicated my said purchase unto my loving friends, John Throckmorton and others, who then desired to take shelter here with me. .... And whereas by God's merciful assistance I was the procurer of the purchase, not by money nor payment, the natives being so shy and jealous that money could not do it, but by that language, acquaintance and favor with the natives, and other advantages which it pleased God to give me; and also bore the charges and venture of all the gratuities which I gave to the great sachems, and other sachems and natives round about us, and lay engaged for a loving and peaceable neighborhood with them, to my great charge and travel; it was therefore thought by some loving friends that I should receive some consideration and gratuity.

Thus, after mentioning the said thirty pounds, and saying, " This sum I received, in love to my friends, and with respect to a town and place of succor for the distressed as aforesaid, I do acknowledge the said sum and payment a full satisfaction;" he went on in full and strong terms to confirm those lands to said inhabitants; reserving no more to himself and his heirs than an equal share with the rest; his wife also signing the deed.

I trust the reader will excuse the length of this account, when he considers that these were the foundations of a now flourishing colony, which was laid upon such principles as no other civil government had ever been, as we know of, since antichrist's first appearance; " and ROGER WILLIAMS justly claims the honor of having been the first legislator in the world, in its latter ages, that fully and effectually provided for and established a free, full and absolute LIBERTY OF CONSCIENCE[1]."

[1] History of Providence. [Mass. Historical Collections, Second Series, Vol. IX, p. 190.] Massachusetts was so far from favoring this cause, that the General Court of March 12, 1638, passed this act, viz. : "Whereas a letter was sent unto this Court, subscribed by John Greene, dated from New Providence, and brought by one of that company, wherein the Court is charged with usurping the power of Christ over the churches and men's consciences, notwithstanding he had formerly acknowledged his fault in such speeches by him before used; it is now ordered, that the said John Greene shall not come into this jurisdiction, upon pain of imprisonment and further censure. And because it appears to this Court that some others of the same place are confident in the same corrupt judgment and practice, it is ordered, that if any other of the inhabitants of the said plantation of Providence shall come within this jurisdiction, they shall be apprehended, and brought before some of the magistrates, and if they will not disclaim the said corrupt opinion and censure, they shall be commanded presently to depart, and if such persons shall after be found within this jurisdiction they shall be imprisoned, and punished as the Court shall see cause."

Massachusetts Records.

Lamentable case indeed! that none of the inhabitants of that infant plantation, who were not able to send out shipping themselves, might go into the colony which was the only place where many of the necessaries as well as comforts of life were to be obtained by them; but they must either be exposed to dissemble, or to suffer imprisonment, if not worse; for how could they honestly declare that the Massachusetts did not usurp a power over men's consciences?—B.

We cannot forbear to add the oft-quoted tribute paid to Roger Williams by the historian Bancroft:—" He was the first person in modern Christendom to assert in its plenitude the doctrine of the liberty of conscience, the equality of opinions before the law; and in its defence he was the harbinger of Milton, the precurser and the superior of Jeremy Taylor. For Taylor limited his toleration to a few Christian sects; the philanthrophy of Williams compassed the earth. Taylor favored partial reform, commended lenity, argued for forbearance, and entered a special plea in behalf of each tolerable sect; Williams would permit persecution of no opinion, of no religion, leaving heresy unharmed by law, and orthodoxy unprotected by the terrors of penal statutes. . . . . We praise the man who first analyzed the air, or resolved water into its elements, or drew the lightning from the clouds, even though the discoveries may have been as much the fruits of time as of genius. A moral principle has a much wider and nearer influence on human happiness; nor can any discovery of truth be of more direct benefit to society, than that which establishes a perpetual religious peace, and spreads tranquillity through every community and every bosom. If Copernicus is held in perpetual reverence, because, on his death-bed, he published to the world that the sun is the centre of our system; if the name of Kepler is preserved in the annals of human excellence for his sagacity in detecting the laws of the planetary motion; if the genius of Newton has been almost adored for dissecting a ray of light, and weighing heavenly bodies in a balance,—let there be for the name of Roger Williams, at least some humble place among those who have advanced moral science and made themselves the benefactors of mankind." Vol. I, pp. 375—377.—ED.

None might have a voice in government in this new plantation, who would not allow this liberty. Hence about this time I find the following town act, viz.: "It was agreed that Joshua Verin, upon breach of covenant, or restraining liberty of conscience, shall be withheld from the liberty of voting till he shall declare the contrary." It appears from Mr. Hubbard, that the way in which he restrained that liberty was, in not letting his wife go to Mr. Williams's meeting so often as she was called for. Verin soon removed to Barbadoes, and left his interest in Providence in such a state as has caused much trouble since.

We will now turn to the affairs of the Rhode Island people, who, on March 7, 1638, signed the following instrument:—

We whose names are underwritten do swear solemnly, in the presence of Jehovah, to incorporate ourselves into a body politic, and as he shall help us, will submit our persons, lives and estates, unto our Lord Jesus Christ, the King of kings, and Lord of lords, and to all those most perfect and absolute laws of his, given us in his holy word of truth, to be guided and judged thereby.

Thomas Savage,	William Coddington,
William Dyre,	John Clarke,
William Freeborne,	William Hutchinson,
Philip Sherman,	John Coggshall,
John Walker,	William Aspinwall,
Richard Carder,	Samuel Wilbore,
William Baulstone,	John Porter,
Edward Hutchinson, Sen.,	Edward Hutchinson, Jun.,
Henry Bull,	John Sanford[1]."
Randal Holden,	

[1]Colony Records. Of these William Hutchinson died on the island; the other Hutchinsons, Aspinwall and Savage, went back, got reconciled. and were promoted in the Massachusetts colony afterward. Near all the others were considerably promoted afterward in Rhode Island colony, and have posterity still remaining there. All but two of the above nineteen men were disarmed by the sentence of November 20, 1637, viz.: Messrs. Coddington and Holden. Messrs. Coddington, Coggshall, Baulston, E. Hutchinson, Wilbore, Porter, Bull, Sherman, Freeborne and Carder, were all excluded or driven out of the Massachusetts colony by an act of their Assembly, on March 12, 1638, in these words, viz. :—

"Whereas you have desired and obtained license to remove yourselves and your

This was doubtless in their view a better plan than any of the others had laid, as they were to be governed by the perfect laws of Christ. But the question is, how a civil polity could be so governed, when he never erected any such state under the gospel? As much as they had been against the legal covenant, yet they now went back to the first order of government after Israel came into Canaan, and to imitate it chose Mr. Coddington their judge, and Messrs. Nicholas Easton, J. Coggshall, and William Brenton, elders to assist him. This form continued, till, on March 12, 1640, they altered it, and chose Mr. Coddington Governor, Mr. Brenton Deputy Governor, and Messrs. Easton, Coggshall, William Hutchinson, and John Porter, Assistants, Robert Jeffries Treasurer, and William Dyre Secretary, which form continued till they received a charter.

Before we proceed further upon their affairs, it may be

families out of this jurisdiction, and for that information hath been given to the Court, that your intent is only to withdraw yourselves for a season, that you may avoid the censure of the Court, for some things that may be objected against you; the Court doth therefore signify unto you that you may depart according to the license given you, so as your families be removed before the next General Court. But if your families be not so removed, then you are to appear at the next Court, to abide the further order of the Court herein." Mr. Nicholas Easton, of Newbury, who went to Newport, and Messrs. Francis Weston, Richard Waterman, Thomas Olney, and Stukely Westcoat, of Salem, who went to Providence, were also included in this sentence. Beside these there were William Lytherland, Robert Hardng, John Briggs, George Barden, John Odlin, Richard Wayte, and others that were disarmed at Boston, who removed into this colony, and have left a respectful remembrance therein.—B.

Massachusetts Records, as published, give the name of but one Edward Hutchinson among those disarmed.—ED.

On page 71, the number of these signers is given, according to the above list and that in the printed Colony Records of Rhode Island, as nineteen. In the first edition it was printed eighteen, but the table of *errata* at the close of volume first directed the change. In his Abridgment, Backus gives but eighteen names, omitting from this list that of Randal Holden. In this he agrees with Callender in his Century Sermon and Hopkins in his History of Providence. Arnold, in his History of Rhode Island, (Vol. I, p. 124,) explains the discrepancy. "Holden's name is separated from the others by a line. He is believed to be one not concerned in the purchase, as his name and that of Roger Williams are signed as witnesses to the deed. There were eighteen original proprietors and nineteen signers of the compact."—ED.

proper to observe, that the Assembly, who met at Boston, September 6, 1638, made the two following laws:—

1. Whereas it is found by sad experience, that divers persons, who have been justly cast out of some of the churches, do profanely contemn the same sacred and dreadful ordinance, by presenting themselves over-boldly in other assemblies, and speaking lightly of their censures, to the great offence and grief of God's people, and encouragement of evil-minded persons to contemn the said ordinance; it is therefore ordered, that whosoever shall stand excommunicated for the space of six months, without laboring what in him or her lieth to be restored, such person shall be presented to the Court of Assistants, and there proceeded with by fine, imprisonment, banishment, or further, for the good behavior, as their contempt and obstinacy upon full hearing shall deserve.

2. The Court taking into consideration the necessity of an equal contribution to all common charges in towns, and observing that the chief occasion of the defect herein arises hence, that many of those who are not freemen, nor members of any church, do take advantage thereby to withdraw their help, in such voluntary contributions as are in use; it is therefore hereby declared, that every inhabitant in any town is liable to contribute to all charges both in church and commonwealth whereof he doth or may receive benefit; and withal it is also ordered, that every such inhabitant who shall not voluntarily contribute proportionably to his ability with other freemen of the same town, to all common charges, as well for upholding the ordinances in the churches as otherwise, shall be compelled thereto by assessment and distress, to be levied by the constable or other officer of the town, as in other cases[1].

Here, my dear countrymen, let us make a little pause. Not long since, in the presence of a number of gentlemen, mention was made of the former persecutions in New England, upon which one of their legislators arose and said, "It is monstrous cruelty and injustice, thus to rake up the ashes of our good fathers, and to reproach their children therewith, when we never think of those transactions without grief and abhorrence!" If so, why are those deeds imitated by our present rulers? And why do the people love to have it so? Certainly the support of good order and government in the church is of greater importance than ministers' maintenance; and to vindicate the methods then taken to

[1] Massachusetts Records.

support the former of these, Mr. Cotton brought that plain text, " Thou shalt surely kill him, because he hath sought to thrust thee away from the Lord thy God ;" and, said he, " This reason is of moral, that is, of universal and perpetual equity."[1] But I never heard any man say so of that other text, " Thou shalt give it me now, and if not, I will take it by force," which is the most like the practice of many in this generation of anything that I could ever find in our Bible. Governor Winthrop informs us, that the next May after the above laws were passed, Mr. Cotton, in preaching from Heb. viii. 8, taught " that when magistrates are forced to proceed for the maintenance of ministers, &c., then the churches are in a declining state. Here he shewed that the ministers' maintenance should be by voluntary contribution." But the law to impower their executive court to punish excommunicates, for disregarding the churches' authority, was repealed the next fall, while that to maintain ministers by assessment and distress was continued in full force. Their practice upon it in Watertown moved Nathaniel Briscoe to write a book against it, the consequence of which was, that he was brought before the Quarter Court, at Boston, March 7, 1643, and fined ten pounds. " John Stowers, for reading of divers offensive passages (before company) out of a book, against the officers and church of Watertown, and for making disturbance there, was fined forty shillings." This severity brought Briscoe to a public acknowledgment, and then his fine was remitted to forty shillings, " and that to be taken."[2] The ministers thus left it to the secular arm to convince him, and said, " his arguments were not worth the answering; for he that shall deny the exerting of the civil power, to provide for the comfortable subsistence of them that preach the gospel, *fuste potius erudiendus, quam argumento,* as they say of them that are wont, *negare principia,* let him that is taught communicate to him that teacheth in

---

[1] Bloody Tenet washed, p. 67. [2] Massachusetts Records.

all good things,¹ that is, he that shall deny such an exertion of power, is rather to be taught by a cudgel than argument, as they say of them who are wont to deny first principles. But let us take heed that we are not imposed upon, by a confounding of two things together, which are as distinct in their nature as light and darkness, namely duty itself, and the right way of enforcing it. The duty of offering daily or continual thanksgivings to our great Creator, and of a liberal communication to Christ's ministers and members, are both called sacrifices to God, in Heb. xiii., and why do our rulers neglect to enforce the daily exercise of family worship, by the same sword as they do ministers' maintenance? Is not God's honor of greater concernment than men's livings! A college was founded this year in Newtown, and for that reason the place was called Cambridge; and the importance of receiving learning at that or like places, to qualify men for the ministry, has been much insisted upon ever since; and those who have not been educated at such places have commonly been called laymen. And among the many reflections that have been cast upon them, one is, that they often beg the question in argument. But who are guilty of this mean sort of conduct now? The question between us is not, whether it be the duty of those who are taught to communicate unto their teachers or not; but it is, whether that duty ought to be enforced by the sword, or only by instruction, persuasion and good example? And what have learned ministers ever done towards proving their side of the question better than begging?

The great events of this year have taken up considerable room, yet I must request a place for a few articles more, that will affect the following part of our history.²

¹Hubbard. [412.] Massachusetts History, Vol. I, p. 427. [377.]

²Mr. Hansard Knollys came over in the spring of this year, who was ordained by the Bishop of Peterborough, June 29, 1629; but he says, "About the year 1636 I was prosecuted in the High Commission Court, by virtue of a warrant, wherewith I was apprehended in Boston (in Lincolnshire) and kept a prisoner in the man's

On June 5, Uncas, the sachem of the Mohegan Indians, "having entertained some of the Pequods, came to the Governor at Boston with a present, and was much dejected because at first it was not accepted; but afterward, the

house who served the warrant upon me. But God helped me to convince him, and he was so greatly terrified in his conscience, that he set open his doors, and let me go away! but before I went, I tarried so long in London, waiting for a passage, that when I went abroad I had but just six brass farthings left, and no silver nor gold, only my wife had five pounds that I knew not of, which she gave me when we came there. By the way, my little child died with convulsion fits, our beer and water stank, our biscuit was molded and rotten, and our cheese also, so that we suffered much hardship, being twelve weeks in our passage; but God was gracious to us and led us safe through the great deeps: and ere we went on shore came one and enquired for me, and told me a friend that was gone from Boston to Rhode Island had left me his house to sojourn in, and to which we went, and two families more with us, who went suddenly to their friends and other relations in the country; and I being very poor, was necessitated to work daily with my hoe, for the space of almost three weeks. The magistrates were told by the ministers that I was an antinomian, and desired they would not suffer me to abide in their patent. But within the time limited by their law in that case, two strangers coming to Boston from Piscataqua, hearing of me by mere accident, got me to go with them to that plantation, and preach there, where I remained about four years, and then being sent for back to England, by my aged father, I returned with my wife and one child, about three years old, and she great with another. We came safe to London on the 24th of December, 1641, in which year the massacre in Ireland broke forth, and the next year wars broke forth in England, between King and Parliament." See Knollys's account of his own life. He embraced the Baptist principles, gathered a church of that persuasion in London, and used seldom to have less than a thousand auditors. He baptised Mr. Henry Jessey, an eminent minister in that city, and others; suffered much for religion, continued pastor of that church till he died in London, September 19, 1691, aged 93. Crosby, [Vol. I, pp. 226—232, 311, 334—344.] Though he was reproached as an antinomian, yet Dr. Mather says he had a "respectful character in the churches of this wilderness." Magnalia, B. 3, p. 7, [Vol. I. p. 221.] After his return to England, " he suffered deeply in the cause of nonconformity, being universally esteemed and beloved by all his brethren. Neal, Vol. 1, p. 216.—B.

To this account of Hansard Knollys it may be well to make a few additions. He was a graduate of the University of Cambridge. For two or three years after his admission to orders, he had charge of a parish in Humberstone, Lincoln. He then " began to scruple the lawfulness of several ceremonies and usages of the national church, as the surplice, the cross in baptism, the admitting wicked persons to the Lord's Supper," &c. He resigned his living, but for several years continued preaching in the established churches, refusing, however, to read the service. In 1636 he publicly joined the Dissenters. Persecuted in England he fled to America. Forbidden at once to remain in Massachusetts he went to Piscataqua, soon afterwards called Dover. Here he met with immediate opposition, but according to Winthrop, (Vol. I, p. 326,) "he gathered some of the best minded into a church

Governor and Council being satisfied about his innocency, they accepted it; whereupon he promised to submit to the orders of the English, both touching the Pequods he had received, and as concerning the differences between the

body and became their pastor." Backus says in a subsequent chapter, "Mr. Hansard Knollys was minister there from the spring of 1638 to the fall of 1641." The precise character of the church it is now impossible to determine. Benedict says, (General History of the Baptist Denomination, p. 497.) "The church at Dover to which Mr. Knollys officiated was probably on the mixed communion plan, as was very common in those days in incipient movements of this kind." The church was traduced from without and was rent with dissension within; and its pastor returned to England. He was imprisoned in London for preaching against infant baptism. In Suffolk, on one occasion he was stoned out of the pulpit, and on another, when he and the congregation who had gathered to hear him were shut out of the church and he preached to them in the church-yard, he was arrested and sent to London again as a prisoner. He afterwards established a meeting at Great St. Helen's, London, "where the people flocked to hear him, and he had commonly a thousand auditors."

Mr. Knollys was a Particular or Calvanistic Baptist, and one of the signers of the so-called Confession of 1646. He was a good scholar, especially in the ancient languages, and, besides his ministerial labors, was almost constantly engaged in teaching, and by this means, for the most part, gained his own support, He lived, says Crosby, "to a good old age, and went home as a shock of wheat that is gathered in its season," departing this life, " in a great transport of joy."

Winthrop calls Knollys, a "weak minister," and accuses him of slandering the government, and holding "familistical opinions." Vol. I, pp. 291, 306, 326. Winthrop's words were enough for the plagiarizing and narrow-minded Hubbard to repeat and build upon, till he represents the character of Knollys as anything but what it should be. P. 369. Savage in his edition of Winthrop, says that Knollys's history in this country was "little creditable to his morals." Vol. I, p. 292, note. There is abundant evidence, however, not only to vindicate the character of Knollys, but to prove him a man of extraordinary conscientiousness and piety. See Crosby, Vol. I, pp. 226—232, 334—344. Neal's History of the Puritans, Toulmin's edition, Vol. III, pp. 551—553.

The name of Henry Jessey, mentioned in the foregoing note of Backus, merits a more particular notice. He was born in Yorkshire in 1601. After studying six years at St. John's College, Cambridge, and being graduated Master of Arts, he received episcopal ordination in 1627, and six years later became rector of a church in his native county. The next year he was removed for nonconformity. He soon began preaching to a dissenting congregation in London, of which, in 1637, he assumed the pastoral charge. Perceiving that Baptist sentiments were making rapid progress in his congregation, Mr. Jessey was led to consider them, and after "a diligent and impartial examination of the Holy Scriptures and antiquity" "not without great deliberation, many prayers, and divers conferences with pious and learned men of different persuasions," was compelled to embrace them. He was baptized in 1644. The historian, Crosby, says, "It proved no small honor and advantage to the Baptists to have a man of such extraordinary piety and substantial.

Narragansetts and himself; and confirmed all with this compliment; laying his hand upon his heart he said " this heart is not mine, but yours; I will never believe any Indian against the English any more;" and so he continued ever after. Uncas was alive and well in the year 1630[1]

Mr. Cotton had entertained a favorable opinion of Mrs. Hutchinson, and when she was upon examination before the Court that banished her, he was asked what he thought of her revelation concerning her deliverance? He replied, "If she doth look for deliverance from the hand of God by his providence, and the revelation be in a word, or according to a word, I cannot deny it." Upon which Mr. Endicott said, " You give me satisfaction." " No, no," said Mr. Dudley, " he gives me none at all. . . . . You weary me, and do not satisfy me." Mr. Nowell said, " I think it is a devilish delusion." And Governor Winthrop said, " Of all the revelations that ever I heard of, I never heard the like ground laid as is for this. The enthusiasts and Anabaptists had never the like." Mr. Dudley added, " I never saw such revelations as these among Anabaptists, therefore am sorry that Mr. Cotton should stand to justify her;" and he and others of the Court would have brought him upon trial also, but the Governor prevented it[2].

---

learning among them." As these words indicate, Mr. Jessey was a man of extensive cultivation. The languages of the original Scriptures, and other ancient oriental dialects were his especial pursuit. He began a new translation of the Bible, in which he was assisted by some of the most eminent scholars of the age. For many years, Mr. Jessey escaped persecution, largely by reason of the respect which all were compelled to pay to his learning; but soon after the restoration he was imprisoned for heresy and died in confinement in 1663. See Crosby, Vol. I, pp. 307—320.—ED.

[1]Winthrop, [Vol. I, pp. 265, 266.] Hubbard, [255] Mr. Hubbard dates his coming in July, but I follow the Governor who acted in the affair. Uncas's headquarters were about eight miles above the mouth of New London river, on the west side of it. Though the Mohegans as well as other Indians, are greatly diminished, yet a considerable body of that tribe remain there to this day. In 1741 a remarkable work of God was wrought among them; a church of Christian Indians was afterwards gathered, and continues there, many of whom give great evidence of true piety. Mr. Samson Occum is of that tribe.

[2]Massachusetts History, Vol. II, pp. 514, 515. [443, 444.]—B.

It is perhaps too much to say, on the foundation of the report of the examination

After a year's consideration, at a public fast, December 13, 1638, Mr. Cotton

Did confess and bewail, as the churches' so his own security and credulity, whereupon so many and dangerous errors had gotten up, and spread in the churches, and went over all the particulars, and shewed how he came to be deceived; the errors being formed, in words, so near the truth he had preached, and the falsehood of the maintainers of them was such, as they usually would deny to him what they had delivered to others. He acknowledged that such as had been seducers of others (instancing in some of those of Rhode Island, though he named them not) had been justly banished; yet he said such as only had been misled, and others who had done any thing out of misguided conscience (not being grossly evil) should be borne withal, and first referred to the church, and if that could not heal them, they should rather be imprisoned or fined than banished, it being likely that no other church would receive them. . . . . If he were not convinced, yet he was persuaded to an amicable compliance with the other ministers, by a studious abstaining on his part from all expressions that were like to be offensive; for although it was thought he did still retain his own sense, and enjoy his own apprehension, in all or most of the things then controverted (as is manifest by some expressions of his in a treatise of the new covenant, since published by Mr. Thomas Allen, of Norwich)yet was there an healing of the breach that had been between him and the rest of the elders, and a putting a stop to the course of errors in the country for the future. . . . . By that means did that reverend and worthy minister of the gospel recover his former splendor throughout the country of New England[1].

in Hutchinson's History, that the Court would have brought Mr. Cotton upon trial but for the Governor. That which most nearly accords with this statement is the following:—

DEPUTY GOVERNOR. "I never saw such revelations as these among the Anabaptists, therefore am sorry that Mr. Cotton should stand to justify her."

Mr. PETERS. "I can say the same, and this runs to enthusiasm, and I think that is very disputable which our brother Cotton hath spoken."

Mr. COLLICUT. "It is a great burden to us that we differ from Mr. Cotton, and that he should justify these revelations. I would entreat him to answer concerning that about the destruction of England."

GOVERNOR. "Mr. Cotton is not called to answer to anything, but we are to deal with the party here standing before us." Ibid.—ED.

[1]Winthrop, [Vol. I, p. 280]—Hubbard, [297, 302.] Roger Harlakenden, one of the magistrates, died at Cambridge, November 17, this year. Winthrop, [Vol. I, p. 277.] Near the same time a church was gathered at Exeter, on Piscataqua river, and soon after Mr. Wheelwright, at his and their request, was dismissed with others to it, from the church of Boston, and became their minister. Hubbard. These facts help to discover the spirit of those times.

This year, upon an occurrence, Governor Winthrop wrote to Mr. Clarke at Aquetneck, and styled him, "A physician and a preacher to those of that island."

We are now come to an event which has made much noise in the world, I mean Mr. Williams's baptism. The reader may remember that he was charged with advancing principles at Plymouth that tended to anabaptism, and that he filled Salem therewith; and could he have found an agreeable administrator, it is not likely that he would have neglected the putting of this principle into practice so long as he did. At length, being in such a state of exile in a heathen land, it is probable he concluded that the case about baptism, which Mr. Robinson recites, was applicable to theirs, which is in these words:—

> Zanchy, upon the fifth to the Ephesians, treating of baptism, propounds a question of a Turk coming to the knowledge of Christ, and to faith, by reading the New Testament, and withal teaching his family, and converting it and others to Christ; and being in a country whence he cannot easily come to Christian churches, whether he may baptize them, whom he had converted to Christ, he himself being unbaptized? He answers, I doubt not of it but that he may, and withal provide, that he himself be baptized of one of the three converted by him. The reason he gives is, because he is a minister of the word extraordinarily stirred up of Christ. And so as such a minister may, with the consent of that small church, appoint one of the communicants, and provide that he be baptized by him.[1]

Mr. Williams took such a method, with only this difference, that one of the community was first appointed to baptize him, and then he baptized the rest; for Mr. Hubbard says, he "was baptized by one Holliman,[2] then Mr. Williams

---

[1] Robinson's answer to Bernard, p. 422. [447]

[2] This is the Ezekiel Holliman mentioned on page 74. We should not deem it needful to notice this, if an error in Cramp's Baptist History, pp. 461, 594, had not given the name, Thomas. As has been stated, (p. 74, note.) Holliman did not leave Massachusetts till 1638. In the Records of the General Court for that year are the words, "Ezekiel Holliman, appearing upon summons, because he did not frequent the public assemblies, and for seducing many, he was referred by the Court to the ministers for conviction." He seems to have been a leading man in Providence and afterwards in Warwick, and held various positions of trust.—ED.

rebaptized him, and some ten more." With this Governor Winthrop agrees, and sets the date of it in March, 1639. The Governor called Holliman a poor man, and Hubbard styles him a mean fellow; but after the year 1650, I find him more than once a deputy from the town of Warwick in their General Court. The above gentlemen represent that Mrs. Hutchinson's sister, the wife of one Scott, stirred Mr. Williams up to this action; though afterward Mr. Hubbard does not pretend to certainty as to that, and says it was difficult for one to give an exact account of their religious affairs in that colony, that did not live among them. It is certain that he and the Governor were both mistaken in calling "those of Providence all Anabaptists;" for it appears from under Mr. Williams's own hand, seventeen years after, that Arnold and Carpenter, two of the first twelve, were not such;[1] neither have I met with any proof that Gorton, Weston or Waterman, who went to Warwick, were ever of that denomination.[2]

[1] Massachusetts History, Vol. 3, p. 277. [310.]—B.
The document here referred to, is a letter from Roger Williams to the colony of Massachusetts Bay, complaining that, under the name of that colony, four persons in Pawtuxet were obstructing all law and order in the Providence Plantations. Massachusetts is especially appealed to in reference to two of the four. One, Stephen Arnold, was manifesting a better spirit, and "desired to be uniform" with those in Providence, "Zecharie Rhodes" says the letter, "being in the way of dipping, is (potentially) banished from you. Only William Arnold and William Carpenter, very far also in religion from you if you know all, they have some color," that is, some pretext of protection from Massachusetts. It is a fair inference that Arnold and Carpenter were not Baptists.—ED.

[2] This Baptist Church at Providence appears to be the second distinct society of that denomination in all the British empire. There had been many of them intermixed with other societies from their first coming out of popery, but the first distinct church in our nation was formed out of the Independent church in London, whereof Mr. Henry Jacob was pastor from 1616 to 1624, when he went to Virginia, and Mr. John Lothrop was chosen in his room. Prince's Chronology, [225.] But nine years after, "several persons in the society, finding that the congregation kept not to their first principles of separation, and being also convinced that baptism was not to be administered to infants, but such only as professed faith in Christ," desired and obtained liberty, and formed themselves into a distinct church, Sept. 12, 1633, having Mr. John Spilsbury for their minister. A second Baptist church was constituted in London this year, but I believe later in the year than ours at Providence. Crosby's History, Vol. 1, pp. 148, 149. Mr. Lothrop came over to Boston in

Before this time Mr. Peters had become minister of Salem, and he wrote to the church of Dorchester on July 1, this year, to acquaint them that their " great censure" was past upon Roger Williams and his wife, John Throgmorton and his wife, Thomas Olney and his wife, Stukely Westcoat and his wife, Mary Holliman, and the widow Reeves, and that all but two of these were rebaptized.[1]

Besides the above men, we are well informed that William Wickenden, Chad Brown, and Gregory Dexter, were of this Baptist church in Providence, and in 1765, Governor Hopkins, who is not a Baptist, said, " This first church of Baptists at Providence hath from its beginning kept itself in repute, and maintained its discipline to this day; hath always been, and still is, a numerous congregation, and in which I have with pleasure observed very lately sundry descendants from each of the above named founders, except Holliman."[2] It seems he removed away.

I am sensible that this testimony is very different from the accounts of many New England historians, who represent that the church soon broke up, because Mr. Williams did not walk long with it. His stop in that travel Governor

1634, was minister a while at Scituate, and then at Barnstable. Winthrop, [Vol. I, pp. 143, 144.] Prince, [225.]—B.

Crosby states that the church "commonly but most falsely called Anabaptists," which John Smith had founded in Holland, removed in 1614, with their pastor, Mr. Helwisse, to London, "where they continued their church state and assemblies for worship as publicly as the evil of the times would permit.." Vol. I, pp. 271, 272. Mr. Helwisse and his church were General Baptists, as is proved by their Confession of Faith; (Hansard Knollys Society, Confessions of Faith, &c., pp. 3—10,) though Crosby not having seen their Confession of Faith when he wrote his first volume, supposed them to be Particular Baptists. Crosby, Vol. I, pp. 270, 271. Taylor in his History of the English General Baptists, quoted by Guild, (Biographical Introduction to the writings of Roger Williams, Publications of the Narragansett Club, vol. I, p. 36, note,) "states that they formed distinct societies and had regular church officers twenty-five years prior" to the date of the founding of Mr. Spilsbury's church. That this was the first Particular Baptist church in the British empire may be true.—ED.

[1] Massachusetts History, Vol. I, p. 421. [371.]
[2] History of Providence. Olney and Dexter were much improved in their day in public offices in the colony.

Winthrop mentions in July following; and Richard Scott, who afterward turned to the Quakers, says,—

> I walked with him in the Baptists' way about three or four months, in which time he brake from the society, and declared at large the ground and reasons of it; that their baptism could not be right because it was not administered by an apostle. After that he set upon a way of seeking (with two or three of them that had dissented with him) by way of preaching and praying; and there he continued a year or two, till two of the three left him. That which took most with him was to get honor amongst men. After his society and he in a church way were parted, he then went to England, and there got a charter; and coming from Boston to Providence, at Seaconk, the neighbors of Providence met him with fourteen canoes, and carried him to Providence. And the man being hemmed in the middle of the canoes, was so elevated and transported out of himself, that I was condemned in myself, that amongst the rest I had been an instrument to set him up in his pride and folly. .... Though he professed liberty of consience, and was so zealous for it at the first coming home of the charter, that nothing in government must be acted till that was granted; yet he could be the forwardest in their government to prosecute against those that could not join with him in it; as witness his presenting of it to the Court at Newport.[1]

Thus Quakers, as well as pædobaptists, could cast out hard reflections against him; whether justly or not, the reader, when he has heard the whole story will judge. At present I would only remark, that this man had been Mr. Williams's neighbor thirty-eight years when he wrote this letter, and the spirit of it fully proves that he was not prejudiced at all in his or the Baptists' favor; yet the facts according to him were, that but two or three persons went off with Mr. Williams, leaving the rest in a church way still; neither does he say a word of Mr. Williams's expecting to be an apostle himself. Indeed as to that point, Mr. Hubbard goes no further than to say, "expecting (as was supposed) to become an apostle;" and Governor Winthrop has the same parenthesis; so that it was no more than a suppostion in that day; but a late historian has delivered

[1] Scott's letter in George Fox's answer to Williams, 1677, p. 247.

it off as fact, without the parenthesis; and Dr. Mather from his grandfather Cotton, says, they " broke forth into anabaptism, and then to antibaptism and familism, and now finally into no church at all.[1] Such naked untruths have one generation after another told about these people!

An evident cause of Mr. Williams's refraining from a farther proceeding in church ordinances, was an apprehension of the necessity of a visible succession of regular ordinations from the apostles, to empower men to it, which succession he could not find. Yet how fond are many ministers in our day of this successive notion? A minister's preaching upon it was vindicated in the Boston Evening Post of May 9, 1774, which informs us that the preacher said,—" God the Father sent forth the Son; he sent forth the apostles as the Father sent him; they sent forth others, with command to commit these things to faithful men. And the preacher said that Christ had never committed this power (to put into office) to any but such as were in office; and consequently no other had a power to put out of office." But I am not afraid boldly to assert, that I verily believe, according to this doctrine, that there is not a minister this day under heaven but what must stop from administering baptism, as Mr. Williams did, if he is as honest as he was. A minister in Connecticut a few years ago published a pamphlet to support the above opinion; wherein, to get over the difficulty that arises for want of any proof of such a lineal succession, he observed that none under the law were to be priests but the lawful posterity of Aaron, yet supposing a bastard son of that family should have posterity, in so long a succession that the knowledge of his illegitimacy was lost, he asserted that such priests might well be admitted into office with others. According to which doctrine, knowledge must be very detrimental to such priests, and ignorance must be the mother of such devotion. The min-

[1] Magnalia, B. 7, p. 9. [Vol. II, p. 433.]

ister who published said pamphlet is a trustee of Yale College; and likely he is better acquainted with philosophy and school divinity than he is with his Bible, or else he would have known that Ezra the priest, a scribe of the law of the God of heaven (in distinction from earthly gods) refused to admit or suffer men upon negatives; and such as sought but could not find "their register," were, "as polluted, put from the priesthood." Ezra ii. 62. And if we review the text[1] that is now so much harped upon, we shall find that the apostolic succession is in the line of "faithful men;" and no others are truly in it, though false brethren have sometimes crept in unawares.

Mr. John Spilsbury, pastor of the first Baptist church in London, says,—

> Because some think to shut up the ordinance of God in such a strait, that none can come by it but through the authority of the popedom of Rome; let the reader consider who baptized John the Baptist before he baptized others, and if no man did, then whether he did not baptize others, he himself being unbaptized. We are taught by this what to do on the like occasions. I fear men put more than is of right due to it, that so prefer it above the church, and all other ordinances; for they can assume and erect a church, take in and cast out members, elect and ordain officers, and administer the supper, and all anew, without looking after succession, any further than the Scriptures; but as for baptism, they must have that successively from the apostles, though it comes through the hands of Pope Joan. What is the cause of this, that men can do all from the Word but only baptism?[2]

The learned Mr. John Tombes also in that day produced the foregoing passage from Zanchy, for the same purpose that I have now done[3].

I would just add, that though the express rule to Israel was, that every male must needs be circumcised at eight days old, or be cut off from his people, yet this general rule was so far dispensed with in a particular case, that circumcision

---

[1] II Tim. ii. 2.—Ed.
[2] Crosby, Vol. I, pp. 103, 104.
[3] Crosby, Vol. I, pp. 104, 105.

was omitted forty years in the wilderness; and multitudes of them stood before God, and entered into or renewed their father Abraham's covenant in the plains of Moab, who yet were not circumcised till after they came over Jordan. Deut. xxix.; Joshua v. 4—7. But the Christian church had been through a worse wilderness than that of Arabia, between the apostolic age and that we are now treating of; therefore that ancient example seems to give light in the case before us.

Mr. Pelatiah Mason, who was born near Providence Ferry in 1669, told his sons (three of whom are now public preachers in Swanzey) that he heard from the fathers of that day, that in the trial they then had, they heard that the Queen of Hungary, or some in those parts, had a register of a regular succession from the apostles, and they had thoughts of sending Mr. Thomas Olney (who succeeded Mr. Williams as their pastor) into that country for it; but at length concluded that such a course was not expedient, but believing they were now got into the right way, determined to persevere therein.

Mr. Hubbard speaking of that colony says:—

> As to matters of religion, it was hard to give an exact account to the world of their proceedings therein, by any who have not been conversant with them from the beginning of their plantations; yet this was commonly said by all that ever had any occasion to be among them, that they always agreed in this principle, that no man or company of men ought to be molested by the civil power upon the account of religion, or for any opinion received or practiced in any matter of that nature; accounting it no small part of their happiness that they may therein be left to their own liberty; by which means the inhabitants are of many different persuasions. But what tendency that liberty had, by so long experience, towards the promoting of the power of godliness, and purity of religion, they are best able to judge that have had occasion to be most conversant amongst them[1].

By this and many other passages, that learned writer, as well as Governor Winthrop, discovered more candor of mind

---

[1] Hubbard, pp. 335, 336.—Ed.

toward Mr. Williams and Rhode Island colony, than almost any other of the Massachusetts writers have ever done, first or last. Mr. Hubbard says, that at Rhode Island "they gathered a church, but in a very disordered way; taking in some excommunicate persons, and others which were members of the church of Boston, but not dismissed; .... yet had they afterwards one Mr. Clarke for their minister, who had been bred to learning."

At the General Court at Boston, March 13, 1639, acts were passed as follows:—

John Smith for disturbing the public peace, by combining with others to hinder the orderly gathering of a church at Weymouth, and to set up another there, contrary to the orders here established, and the constant practice of all our churches, and for undue procuring the hands of many to a blank for that purpose, is fined twenty pounds and committed during the pleasure of the Court or the Council.

Richard Silvester, for going with Smith to get hands to a blank, was disfranchised and fined forty shillings.

Ambrose Morton, [Marten], for calling the church covenant a stinking carrion, and a human invention, and saying he wondered at God's patience, feared it would end in the sharp, and said the ministers did dethrone Christ and set up themselves; he was fined ten pounds and counselled to go to Mr. Mather to be instructed by him.[1] Thomas Mackpeace, because of his novel disposition, was informed we were weary of him unless he reformed.[2]

The fourth of the 2d month was thought fit for a day of humiliation, to seek the face of God, and reconciliation with him by our Lord Jesus Christ in all the churches. Novelties, oppression, atheism, excess, superfluity, idleness, contempt of authority, and troubles in other parts, to be remembered.

Mr. Robert Lenthal, upon his free acknowledgment under his hand, given into the Court, was appointed to appear at the next Court, and enjoined to acknowledge his fault and give satisfaction to the church at

[1] Mr. Richard Mather, of Dorchester.
[2] With this deserves to be quoted a record of the next Court, Dec. 1, 1640:—"Mr. Thomas Lechford, acknowledging that he had overshot himself and is sorry for it, promising to attend to his calling and not to meddle with controversies, was dismissed."—ED.

Weymouth, and to give a copy of that he gave into the Court to the church of Weymouth.[1]

John Smith and John Spur are bound in forty pounds to pay twenty pounds the first day of the next Court.[2]

Mr. Lenthal went to Rhode Island, was admitted a freeman there on August 6, 1640; and he kept school and preached there for a while, but before March, 1642, went back to England. The first settlement of the island began the same spring they purchased it; the second the spring after; the latter of which was named Newport, on May 16, 1639; the other was called Portsmouth, at a General Court, March 12, 1640.

At a General Court at Boston, October, 7, 1640, the following was enacted:—

It is ordered, that the letter lately sent to the Governor by Mr. Eaton, Mr. Hopkins, Mr. Haynes, Mr. Coddington, and Mr. Brenton, but coming also to the General Court,[3] shall be thus answered by the Governor, that the Court doth assent to all the propositions laid down in the aforesaid letter, but that the answer shall be directed to Mr. Eaton, Mr. Hopkins and Mr. Haynes only, excluding Mr. Coddington and Mr. Brenton, as men not to be capitulated withal by us, either for themselves or the people of the island where they inhabit, as their case standeth.[4]

---

[1]Mr. Lenthal was a minister whom the people of Weymouth had invited to visit them with the purpose of calling him to become their pastor. Winthrop, Vol. I, p 287.—ED.

[2]Massachusetts Records. Their crime was this, Mr. Lenthal held, "that only baptism was the door of entrance into the visible church; the common sort of people did eagerly embrace his opinion, and some labored to get such a church on foot, as all baptized ones might communicate in, without any further trial of them. For this end they procured many hands in Weymouth to a blank, intending to have Mr. Lenthal's advice to the form of the call. . . . . Mr. Lenthal, having before conferred with some of the magistrates and ministers, did openly and freely retract. . . . . So the Court forbore any further censure, though it was much urged by some." Hubbard, [275.] The next Court, Smith was fined five pounds more for contempt; but upon making his submission, and presenting his money, he got released by paying fifteen pounds. Massachusetts Records.—B.

This was not the last time that John Spur was called to suffer as a Baptist. In Chap. IV. we shall find him sentenced to pay a fine of forty shillings or to be whipped for the crime of shaking hands with Obadiah Holmes as the latter came from the whipping post.—ED.

[3]The published Records read, "but concerning also the General Court."—ED.

[4]Massachusetts Records. They at this Court granted to Mr. John Winthrop, junior, all their right to Fisher's Island, which still belongs to his posterity.

Eaton was of New Haven, the other of Connecticut, which had no more of a charter from England than Rhode Island had; therefore it was a difference about religious affairs that caused this partiality.

> Our neighbors of Plymouth had procured from hence[1] this year one Mr. Chauncy, a great scholar and a godly man, intending to call him to the office of a teacher; but before the fit time came, he discovered his judgment about baptism, that the children ought to be dipped, and not sprinkled. .... There arose much trouble about it. The magistrates and the elders there, and the most of the people, withstood the reviving [receiving] of that practice, not for itself so much as for fear of worse consequences; as the annihilating our baptism, &c. Whereupon the church there wrote to all the other churches, both here and at Connecticut, &c. for advice, and sent Mr. Chauncy's arguments. The churches took them into consideration, and wrote [their] several answers, wherein they shewed their dissent from him, and clearly confuted all his arguments; .... yet he could not give over his opinion; and the church of Plymouth, ... being much taken with his able parts, were very loth to part with him. He did maintain also that the Lord's Supper ought to be administered in the evening, and every Lord's day. And the church at Sandwich (where one Mr. Leveridge was minister) fell into the practice of it. But that being a matter of no great ill consequence, save some outward inconvenience, there was little stir about it. This Mr. Chauncy was after called to office in the church of Scituate[2].

At a Quarter Court at Boston, December 1, it is recorded:—

> The jury found Hugh Buet to be guilty of heresy, and that his person and errors are dangerous for infection of others. It is ordered that the said Hugh Buet should be gone out of our jurisdiction by the 24th present, upon pain of death, and not to return upon pain of being hanged.

This is the first instance that I find upon the Massachusetts records of banishment for heresy upon this penalty. Two years before they banished three persons at once, on pain of death, for adultery. The records give no account of what Buet's heresy was, but Governor Winthrop says, it was

---

[1] England.—ED.
[2] Winthrop's Journal, [Vol. I, pp. 330, 331.]

"for holding he was free from original sin, and from actual also, for half a year before, and for holding that true Christians are enabled to live without committing actual sin[1]."

The learned and pious Mr. Henry Dunstar came over this summer, and on August 27, was chosen President of Harvard College, which flourished under his care and influence fourteen years; till having openly renounced infant baptism, such a temper was manifested against him on that account, that he resigned that office[2]. About this time it appears by Mr. Hooker's letters, that many inclined toward the Baptist way, and he expressed his apprehensions that the number would increase[3]; which it seems moved him to "resolve that he would have an argument able to remove a mountain before he would recede from" infant baptism. This resolution Mr. Mitchell, thirteen years after, adopted from him, as a shield against Mr. Dunstar's arguments[4].

The estate of Mr. Humphry, one of their magistrates, being much impaired, he sold his plantation at Lynn to the Lady Moody, and returned to England[5]. She soon embraced the Baptist principles, and suffered therefor. And divers of those at Aquidneck[6] turned professed Anabaptists[7]. Mr. Hubbard says:—

[1] Winthrop's Journal, Vol. II, p. 19. Buet removed to Providence, and for many years was well known and honored there. He was one of the Commissioners for Providence, General Sergeant of Rhode Island and Providence Plantations, Solicitor General, and held other offices. Backus has further occasion to mention him, and spells his name as he himself spelled it, Bewit.—ED.

[2] Magnalia, B. 4, pp. 127, 128. [Vol. II, p. 10.]

[3] Massachusetts History, Vol. I, p. 227. [208.]

[4] Mitchell's Life, p. 70.—B.

Magnalia, B. 4, Vol. II, p. 79. After quoting with evident approval this resolution of Hooker and Mitchell, on the next page Mather speaks of those who were troubled by the "hydrophobie of anabaptism," and who could only reply to the arguments against them, "Say what you will, we will hold our mind." For those on the one side to refuse to be convinced by reasonable argument he seems to have regarded as wisdom, for those on the other, as madness.—ED.

[5] Massachusetts History, Vol. I, p. 15. [21.]—B.

See further notice of Lady Moody near the close of this chapter.—ED.

[6] On page —, this name is spelled Aquetneck. Other writers give it in still different forms.—ED.

[7] Winthrop, [Vol. II, p. 38.]

AFFAIRS AT RHODE ISLAND.

Nicholas Easton .... used to teach at Newport. .... He maintained, that man had no power nor will in himself, but as he was acted by God; and seeing that God filled all things, nothing could be or move but by him, and so must needs be the author of sin, and that a Christian is united to the essence of God. Being shewed what blasphemous consequences would follow therefrom, they seemed to abhor the consequences, but still defended the position. .... Mr. Coddington, Mr. Coggshall, and some others, joined with Nicholas Easton in those delusions; but their minister, Mr. Clarke, and Mr. Lenthal, and Mr. Harding, with some others, dissented and publicly opposed; whereby it grew to such a heat of contention that it made a schism amongst them.[1]

Mr. Coddington and Mr. Easton afterward joined the Quakers. Mr. Clarke and his friends formed the first Baptist church on Rhode Island.

In June this year the General Assembly of the Massachusetts sent to Plymouth to know why they might not take Seekonk into their jurisdiction. They tried for it about three years, till the commissioners of the United Colonies confirmed it to Plymouth.

At a Quarter Court at Boston, September 7, Mr. William Collins, a man of learning, who had married Mrs. Hutchinson's daughter, being "found a seducer," and Francis Hutchinson, for calling the church of Boston "a whore," &c., were both fined and banished upon pain of death.[2] About two years after, they were both killed by the Indians, with their mother Hutchinson, near New York. It is evident that the planters of Rhode Island did not at first see into the true nature and grounds of liberty of conscience, but their Assembly at Portsmouth, March 16, 1641, passed an act for that purpose, which on the 17th of September following was confirmed as a perpetual law. And at an Assembly in Newport, September 19, 1642, they appointed Messrs. Coddington, Brenton, Easton, Coggshall, Baulston, Porter, Dyer,

---

[1]Hubbard, p. 343.—B.

As usual, he borrows almost word for word from Winthrop. See Vol. II, pp. 40, 41. Nicholas Easton was five years Governor at Rhode Island.—ED.

[2]Massachusetts Records.

Clarke, Harding and Jeffries, a committee to improve the first and best opportunity that presented to send home for a charter, and to write to Sir Henry Vane to solicit his assistance and influence in the design. They accordingly sent over by Mr. Williams, and obtained their request; though in the mean time a most dreadful broil broke out, and prevailed to a terrible degree among them, of which take the following account:

Samuel Gorton, a man of learning from London, arrived at Boston in 1636, and doubtless had a considerable hand in the mystical disputes that then embroiled the Massachusetts colony. From thence he went to Plymouth, where he treated their pastor Mr. Smith in such a manner, as caused the authority to take him in hand, and require bonds of him for his good behavior. This occasioned his departure to Rhode Island, where such a difficulty arose, that by Mr. Coddington's order he was imprisoned and whipped. From thence he came to Providence, where he was kindly treated by Mr. Williams and others; and he and his friends sat down at Pawtuxet, now called Cranston. I find by the records that Mr. Gorton bought half of Robert Cole's interest there on January 10, 1641. And as the Court at Newport in March following disfranchised Richard Carder, Randal Holden, Sampson Shatton, and Robert Potter, they and John Wickes, who had followed Gorton[1] from Plymouth, came and formed

[1] In Winthrop's Journal, Vol. II, p. 58, note, Mr. Savage quotes from an anonymous correspondent as follows:—"It does not appear that he [Samuel Gorton] was ever a freeholder or freeman of Rhode Island, though 20th, 4th, 1638, he was admitted an inhabitant. In March, 1642, Randal Holden, Richard Carder, and others, were disfranchised the Island. These, Backus says, *followed* Gorton to Newport from Plymouth, though Carder and Holden were two of the original purchasers of the Island, and both signed the original deed of incorporation. Holden, with Roger Williams, witnessed the deed to Coddington, etc., dated 24th, 1st month, 1637. I mention these facts to show how easy it is to write carelessly about men whom we hate or despise." Mr. Savage's correspondent, though described as an "inquisitive antiquary," was most unfortunate in these investigations. A glance at the words of Backus will show that they do not necessarily state that Carder, Holden, &c., but only that John Wickes followed Gorton; and this is undoubtedly their meaning. The Rhode Island Records, in a list of those admitted as inhabitants at Newport in

a considerable party at Pawtuxet. Such a contention was raised between them and the former inhabitants, that " they came armed into the field, each against the other; but Mr. Williams pacified them for the present. This caused the weaker party to write a letter to the Massachusetts rulers, complaining of the wrong they suffered, desiring aid, or if not, counsel from them. They answered them, that they could not levy war without a General Court. For counsel they told them, that except they would submit to some jurisdiction (Plymouth, or theirs) they had no calling or warrant to interpose in their contentions, but if they would submit to any, then they had a call to protect them."[1] How different was the temper here discovered, from that of the pious Mr. Williams? He was ever ready wherever he came to exert all his influence to make peace so far as he could with a good conscience, but the Court at Boston seemed willing to play one party against another, till all would submit to their power. Gorton took a like method to defend himself against them; the consequence of which was terrible indeed; the true state thereof I shall give with all the exactness I can.

William Arnold, Robert Cole, William Carpenter, and Benedict Arnold of Pawtuxet, went to the General Assembly at Boston, September 3, 1642, and submitted themselves and their lands to that government. At the same time Mr. Leveret and Edward Hutchinson were sent to Miantinomu to demand satisfaction of him, and first to tell him "of credible information received, partly by relation of the Indians

---

1638, give the name of Samuel Gorton, with the date 20th, 3d, not 20th, 4th, as stated in the above quotation; and next after him the name of John Wickes, with the date 20th, 4th, so that, as Backus states, Wickes followed Gorton. It is well nigh certain, too, that our unknown writer is in error in stating that Holden was one of the original purchasers of Rhode Island. See p. 78, note, and Arnold's History of Rhode Island, Vol. I, p. 124. Backus, in this case at least, did not write carelessly about men whom he hated or despised; and the charge comes with ill grace from one who, in the very act of making it, crowds three errors into as many brief sentences.—ED.

[1] Winthrop, [Vol. II, p. 59]; Hubbard, [343, 344.]

themselves, that they have drawn in many other sachems to join with the Narragansetts, in making war upon the English." Benedict Arnold and Ahauton, the Indian, were to be their guides and interpreters.[1] Then, October 28, a warrant was sent from Boston to cite Gorton and his friends to come to their Court, to answer to the complaints of Arnold's company against them, signed by the Governor and three Assistants. To this an answer was returned on November 20, signed by Samuel Gorton, Randal Holden, Robert Potter, John Wickes, John Warner, Richard Waterman, William Woodale, John Greene, Francis Weston, Richard Carder, Nicholas Power, and Sampson Shatton. It contained a long mystical paraphrase upon their warrant and many provoking sentences against those rulers and their ministers, and a refusal to come to them. But in order to get out of their reach they removed and purchased Shawomet for a hundred and forty-four fathoms of wampum, and obtained a deed of it, signed by Miantinomu, Pumham, and others, on January 12, 1643. John Greene had received a deed of an island, neck of land and meadow, called Ocupassutuxet Cove, dated October 1, 1642, signed by Miantinomu and Socononco.[2]

The General Court at Boston, May 10, 1643, appointed Messrs. Atherton and Tomlyns, with William Arnold to speak with Messrs. Greene, Warner, and their company. On June 22, through Benedict Arnold's influence and assistance, Pumham, sachem of Shawomet, and Socanocho, sachem of Pawtuxet, signed at Boston a submission of their persons and lands to that government; and Arnold was allowed four pounds for his pains.[3] Governor Winthrop tells us that

[1] Hubbard, [447.] Massachusetts Records.

[2] Gorton's Defence, [59.] Callender [89, 90.] Colony Records. The hundred and forty-four fathoms of peag it is said was computed at forty pounds sixteen shillings sterling. Massachusetts History, Vol. I, p. 118, [113.]

[3] Massachusetts Records. The colonies of Massachusetts, Plymouth, Connecticut and New Haven, by their commissioners, signed articles of confederation together for mutual assistance and defence on May 19, 1643, from whence they were called the United Colonies.

they had two or three hundred men under them. The plea for this action was, that Gorton's company and Miantinomu had oppressed these sachems, and wronged them of their lands. Pumham said he was forced to sign the deed, but would take none of the pay. The Governor, with another magistrate, wrote to Shawomet people about it; and also to Miantinomu, and he came down and met said sachems at Boston, where they were forced to confess that they had sometimes sent him presents, and had aided him in his wars against the Pequods; yet they and Arnold would have it, that they were as free sachems as he was, because their people paid tribute to them. So the Court received them (as is before noted) under their protection. We are told that before this, Gorton and his company had sent a writing of four sheets " full of reproaches against the magistrates, ministers and churches, and stuffed likewise with absurd familistial stuff, and wherein they justified the purchase of the sachem's lands, and professed to maintain it to the death."[1]

Miantinomu had already seen Uncas, a warlike sachem to the west of him, putting himself and his people under the protection of the English; and he was accused of hiring a young Pequod to murder Uncas, but he brought the young man with him, who told the Court that Uncas cut his own arm with a flint, and then charged him to report that Miantinomu had hired him to murder him. But upon private examination, the Court were persuaded the young man was guilty, and advised Miantinomu to send him to Uncas; but instead of doing it, he cut off his head by the way, as he returned home."[2] What followed till his own death, we have recorded by Governor Winthrop, in a more distinct and clear light than has ever been published. I shall therefore give it to the reader in his own words :—

August. Onkus being provoked by Sequassion, a sachem of Connecticut (who would not be persuaded by the magistrates there to a reconcilia-

[1]Hubbard, [405.]   [2]Johnson, pp. 182—184.

tion) made war upon him, and slew divers of his men, and burnt up his wigwams; whereupon Miantinomu, being his kinsman, took offence against Onkus, and went with near one thousand men, and set upon Oukus before he could be provided for defence; for he had not then with him above three or four hundred men. But it pleased God to give Onkus the victory, after he had killed about thirty of the Narragansetts, and wounded many more; and among these, two of Canonicus's sons, and a brother of Miantinomu, who[1] fled, but having on a coat of mail[2] he was easily overtaken, which two of his captains perceiving, they laid hold of him and carried him to Onkus, hoping thereby to procure their own pardon. But so soon as they came to Onkus he slew them presently; and Miantinomu standing mute, he demanded of him, why he would not speak? "If you had taken me," (saith he) "I would have besought you for my life." The news of Miantinomu's captivity coming to Providence, Gorton and his company . . . . wrote a letter to Onkus, willing him to deliver their friend Miantinomu, and threatened him with the power of the English if he refused. Upon this Oukus carries Miantinomu to Hartford to take advice of the magistrates there; and, at Miantinomu's earnest entreaty, he left him with them, yet as a prisoner. They kept him under guard, but used him very courteously. So he continued till the commissioners of the United Colonies met at Boston,[3] who, taking into serious consideration what was safest and best to be done, were all of opinion that it would not be safe to set him at liberty; neither had we sufficient ground for us to put him to death. In this difficulty we called in five of the most judicious elders (it being in the time of the general assembly of the elders) and propounding the case to them, they all agreed that he ought to be put to death. Upon this concurrence we enjoined secresy upon ourselves and them, lest if it should come to the notice of the Narragansetts, they might attempt somewhat against Hartford for this reason, or might set upon the commissioners, &c., upon their return, to take some of them to redeem him (as Miantinomu himself had told Mr. Haynes had been in consultation amongst them) and agreed that upon the return of the commissioners to Hartford, they should send for Onkus, and tell him our determination, that Miantinomu should be delivered to him again, and he should put him to death so soon as he came within his own jurisdiction, and that the[4] English should go along with him to see the execution. And if any Indians should invade him for it, we would send men to defend him. If Onkus should refuse to do it, then Miantinomu should be sent in a pinnance to Boston, there to be kept until further consideration.

[1]Miantinomu.—ED.
[2]Johnson calls it a Corslet, and both he and Hubbard say he had it of Gorton.
[3]In September.
[4]Savage reads "two" in place of "the," and is probably correct.—ED.

"The reasons of this proceeding with him were these :—1. It was now clearly discovered to us that there was a general conspiracy among the Indians to cut off all the English, and that Miantinomu was the head and contriver of it. 2. He was of a turbulent and proud spirit, and would never be at rest. 3. Although he had promised us in the open Court to send the Pequod to Onkus, who had shot him in the arm, with intent to have killed him (which was by the procurement of Miantinomu, as did probably appear) yet in his way homeward he killed him. 4. He beat one of Pumham's men, and took away his wampum, and ,then bid him go and complain to the Massachusetts. According to this agreement the commissioners, at their return to Connecticut, sent for Onkus, and acquainted him herewith, who readily undertook the execution ; and taking Miantinomu along with him, in the way between Hartford and Windsor (where Onkus hath some men dwell) Onkus's brother following after Miantinomu, clave his head with an hatchet, some English being present. And that the Indians might know that the English did approve of it, they sent twelve or fourteen musqueteers home with Onkus to abide a time with him, for his defence, if need should be.[1]

Alas! when good men get into an evil path, where will it carry them? The next news we hear is as follows. September 12,[2] the General Court sent a warrant to require Gorton and his company to come to Boston, to answer the Indians' complaints against them. To which they sent a verbal answer, that they were out of that jurisdiction, and would own subjection to none but the government of Old England. Upon which the Court wrote the 19th, informing them that they intended to send commissioners to seek to right these things among them.[3] The commissioners were, Captain George Cook, Humphrey Atherton, and Edward Johnson, who were sent, " with forty able men to attend them, which had authority and order to bring Samuel Gorton and his company, if they should not give

[1]Winthrop, [Vol. II, pp. 130—134.]
[2]In the published Records the date of this warrant is given, September 7.—ED.
[3]Gorton's Defence, [p. 97.]—B.
This reference to Gorton's Defence and those that follow are to Staples's edition, Collections of the R. I. Historical Society, Vol. II. The exact words here referred to are these :—"This you may rest assured of; that if you will make good your own offer to us of doing us right, our people shall return and leave you in peace, otherwise we must right ourselves and our people by force of arms."—ED.

them satisfaction." A Sergeant Major-General was appointed in the colony, and the country put into a posture of war. "They of Aquidneck" were "granted to buy a barrel of powder, provided Lieutenant Morris give caution that it be employed for the defence of the island, by the advice of the Governor and Deputy." It was ordered "that the deputies should acquaint the elders, to desire them in special manner to commend this undertaking to God."

A large committee of magistrates and deputies was appointed in the recess of the General Court, " not knowing," say they, " what may fall out, concerning the expedition now on foot against Samuel Gorton, and the rest of that company.

It was ordered "that Pumham and Sochonoco should have each of them, lent them a fowling piece, and Benedict Arnold hath liberty to supply them with shot as he sees occasion."[1]

Hearing of their coming, Gorton's company sent a letter to meet them, dated September 28, to let them know, that if they came in a way of loving neighborhood, they were welcome; but if with a band of soldiers, they charged them not to set foot on their land at their peril.[2] The commissioners wrote a reply, signifying their great desire of having conversation with them, with hope of reclaiming them from

[1] Massachusetts Records.—B.
This enactment was passed at a later session of the Court, October 17.—ED.

[2] If you come to treat with us . . . . shaking a rod over our heads, in a band of soldiers, be you assured, we have passed our childhood and nonage in that point, and are under commission of the great God not to be children in understandings, neither in courage, but quit to ourselves as men. We straitly charge you therefore, hereby, that you set not a foot upon our lands in any hostile way, but upon your peril; and that if any blood be shed, upon your own heads shall it be. . . . . If you spread a table before us as friends, we sit not as mere invective, envious or malcontent, not touching a morsel nor looking for you to point us unto our dish; but we eat with you by virtue of the unfeigned law of relations, not only to satisfy our stomachs but to increase friendship and love, the end of feasting. So also, if you visit us as combatants or warriors, by the same law of relations, we as freely and cheerfully answer you unto death." Extract from the letter of the "owners and inhabitants in Shawomet," "to certain men styled Commissioners, sent from the Massachusetts." Gorton's Defence, p. 99.—ED.

their errors; but if that could not be done, that they should then "look upon them as men prepared for slaughter, and accordingly should address themselves with all convenient speed;"[1] which we may well suppose was very surprising to their wives and children, and it is said it scattered them and occasioned some their deaths.[2] Some of the people of Providence went with those commissioners and soldiers, and procured a parley with Shawomet men, who demanded the reason of this proceeding; to which the others answered, that they had done wrong to certain of their subjects, and also held blasphemous errors. Shawomet men offered to appeal to England, but that was refused; then they offered to leave the controversy to indifferent men in this country. This appeared so reasonable that a truce was agreed upon, till they could send to Boston to know the mind of the Court upon it. Accordingly, Chad Brown, Thomas Olney, William Field, and William Wickenden of Providence, wrote a letter to persuade the rulers of Massachusetts to comply with this proposal. But an answer was returned, dated October 3, refusing any such thing.[3] After this those men were seized and forcibly carried to Boston, where the General Court by adjournment met October 17, when the accusation following was exhibited, viz.:—

The charge of the prisoners, Samuel Gorton and his company.

Upon much examination and serious considerations of your writings, with your answers about them, we do charge you to be a blasphemous

---

[1] "It is our great desire that we might speak with them concerning the particulars which we were sent to them about; certainly persuading ourselves that we shall be able through the Lord's help, to convince some of them at least of the evil of their way and cause them to divert their course, that so doing they may preserve their lives and liberties, which otherwise must lead to the eternal ruin of them and theirs. .... But if there be no way of turning them, we then shall look upon them as men prepared for slaughter, and accordingly shall address ourselves with all convenient speed, not doubting of the Lord's presence with us, being clear in the way we are in." Extract from the letter of the Commissioners to John Peise, messenger from those at Shawomet. Gorton's Defence, p. 101.—ED.

[2] Two women are named as having died in consequence to the exposure incident to their flight; and others are said to have suffered severe physical injury. Gorton's Defence, p. 102.—ED.

[3] Gorton's Defence, [pp. 103—111.]

enemy of the true religion of our Lord Jesus Christ, and his holy ordinances, and also of all civil authority among the people of God, and particularly in this jurisdiction.

It is ordered that Samuel Gorton shall be confined to Charlestown, there to be set on work, and to wear such bolts or irons as may hinder his escape, and to continue during the pleasure of the Court; provided that if he shall break his said confinement, or shall in the mean time, either by speech or writing, publish, declare or maintain any of the blasphemous or abominable heresies wherewith he hath been charged by the General Court, contained in either of the two books sent unto us by him or Randal Holden; or shall reproach or reprove the churches of our Lord Jesus Christ in these United Colonies, or the civil government, or the public ordinances of God therein (unless it be by answer to some question propounded to him, or conference with any elder, or with any other licensed to speak with him privately under the hand of one of the Assistants) that immediately upon accusation of any such writing or speech, he shall, by such Assistant, to whom such accusation shall be brought, be committed to prison till the next Court of Assistants, then and there to be tried by a jury, whether he hath so spoken or written, and upon conviction thereof shall be condemned to death and executed. Dated 'the third of the ninth month, 1643.

A like sentence was passed, by which John Wickes was confined to Ipswich, Randal Holden to Salem, Robert Porter to Rowley, Richard Carder to Roxbury, Francis Weston to Dorchester, and John Warner to Boston; all on the same penalty with Gorton. William Woodale was confined to Watertown during the pleasure of the Court, and if he escaped to be punished as they see meet. Further:—

It is ordered, that all such cattle of Samuel Gorton, John Greene,[1] &c., as have been or shall be seized upon, for such satisfaction of charges as the country hath been put unto, by sending and fetching them in, and other charges about the trial in the Court, and expense in the prison or otherwise, shall be appraised and sold to the most advantage, and disposed of accordingly, and the overplus to be reserved, by the treasurer for their maintenance. .... If any of them will not do such work as they may, and as shall be appointed them, they are to be left to shift as they may.

[1] I can't find that Greene was carried now to Boston. Hubbard says Woodale was found to be an ignorant young man.—B.

Staples says that Greene " escaped entirely," running from the house when the commissioners came to apprehend him. Gorton's Defence, p. 137, note.—Ed.

Richard Waterman is dismissed for the present, so that what is taken of his, is to go toward payment of the charge, and the rest of his estate is bound in one hundred pounds that he shall appear at the General Court the third month, and not depart without license, and to submit to the order of the Court.

Nicholas Power appearing, and denying that he set his hand to the first book, was dismissed with an admonition.

For appraising the cattle brought from Providence, the prisoners have liberty to name two, Robert Turner and the soldiers two, and the Court one. The prisoners refusing, the Court, Robert Turner, and the soldiers, chose Mr. Colbron, John Jephson and William Parks.[1]

The whole of the aforesaid charges were adjudged to amount to an hundred and sixty pounds. They were detained through the winter under the above sentence; "but finding that they could not keep them from seducing others, nor yet bring them to any sight of their folly and wickedness, the General Court (March 7, 1644,) sent them away."[2] Ah, sent them away sure enough! it was with the words following, viz. :—

It is ordered that Samuel Gorton and the rest of that company, who now stand confined, shall be set at liberty, provided that if they or any of them shall, after fourteen days after such enlargement, come within any part of our jurisdiction, either in the Massachusetts, or in or near Providence, or any of the lands of Pumham and Soconocho, or elsewhere within our jurisdiction, then such person or persons shall be apprehended, wheresoever they may be taken, and shall suffer death by course of law; provided also, that during all their continuance in our bounds inhabiting for the said time of fourteen days, they shall be still bound to the rest of the articles of their former confinement, upon the penalty therein expressed.[3]

Such a way of treating our fellow servants as this, will doubtless appear very surprising to the present generation;

---

[1]Massachusetts Records. Nicholas Power and many of his posterity have been of good note among the Baptists in Providence. Hubbard says he was released "freely, for that he was in his master's house."

[2]Hubbard, [407].—B.

Hubbard is almost the last man in whose behalf one need enter a complaint of injustice, but a wrong impression seems to be conveyed by quoting from him only the above fragment. His sentence ends with the words, "——sent them away with this caution, that they should not come into any place where the said Court had jurisdiction, upon pain of death."—ED.

[3]Massachusetts Records.

and many will be ready to say, How was it possible for any, if they had been endowed with the least spark of Christianity, or even humanity, to treat their neighbors as those rulers did? Let Captain Johnson, who was one of the three commissioners that took them, answer the question; says he:—

That holy man of God, Mr. John Cotton. among many others, hath diligently searched for the Lord's mind herein, and hath declared some sudden blow to be given to this blood-thirsty monster [the man of sin] but the Lord Jesus Christ hath inseparably joined the time, means and manner of this work together; and therefore all men that expect the day (of his fall) must attend the means.[1]

And speaking of Gorton and his company, he says:—

To be sure there be them in New England that have Christ Jesus and his blessed ordinances in such esteem, that, the Lord assisting, they had rather lose their lives, then suffer them to be thus blasphemed, if they can help it; and whereas some have favored them, and endeavored to bring under blame such as have been zealous against their abominable doctrines, the good God be favorable unto them, and prevent them from coming under the like blame with Ahab; yet they remain in their old way, and there is somewhat to be considered in it to be sure, that in these days, when all look for the fall of antichrist, such detestable doctrines should be upheld, and persons suffered, that exceed the beast himself for blasphemy, and this to be done by those that would be counted reformers, and such as seek the utter subversion of antichrist.[2]

This plain account of the reasons and motives they acted upon, takes off the edge in some measure of Gorton's keen satire upon them, which he wrote from Warwick, Sept. 16, 1656, to the first Quakers that were imprisoned in Boston, saying,—

I marvel what manner of God your adversaries trust in, who is so fearful of being infected with error, or how they think they shall escape the wiles and power of the devil, when the arm of flesh fails them, whereby they seek to defend themselves for the present; sure they think their God will be grown to more power and care over them, in and after death, or else they will be loth to pass through it.

This remark is cutting indeed, if we leave out any con-

---

[1] Johnson's History, p. 230. [2] Ibid, p. 187.

sideration of duty in the case; but if that be brought in, then it is a presumption, and not faith, to expect protection and support from God in a way of disregard of the means of his appointment. Hence, the error of supposing that God has appointed the use of secular force in religious affairs, ought to bear all the blame and scandal of those cruel proceedings; and instead of venting our resentment against our dead fathers, let these things rouse the living to repentance and reformation. Those fathers could find warrant enough in the Old Testament for the use of force against idolaters and blasphemers; but the use of force to collect the priests' support was plainly censured in those times. With what face then can those who profess to be under the law of liberty, forcibly take a farthing from any to maintain professed ministers of him who has said, "Freely ye have received, freely give;" and who commanded his disciples to shake off, and therefore not to carry away, so much as the dust of a city or house that would not receive them!

It is likely that the reader may wish to know what Gorton's sentiments really were which were so offensive. To this I answer, that he evidently was a man of smart capacity, and of considerable learning, and when he pleased could express his ideas as plainly as any man; but he used such a mystical method in handling the Scriptures, and in speaking about religion, that people are not agreed to this day what his real sentiments were. It is so common for parties to misrepresent the opinions of their opponents, that little regard is paid by many to what those in Massachusetts have said against him. I will therefore give a taste of what he published to the world, not in a way of controversy, but of friendly correspondence with the aforesaid prisoners at Boston. He first wrote a letter to them of the date I have given; to which they returned an answer; then he made a reply, October 6, 1656, wherein he gives various remarks on the sentiments expressed in their letter, and says:—

In us a child is born, in us a son is given[1], but the government is upon his shoulder, and he is called Wonderful, Counsellor, The mighty God, The everlasting Father, The Prince of Peace. So that wherever this lowly and meek spirit is, there is also the spirit of the Lion of the tribe of Judah, and the Lord thereby shall roar out of Zion, and utter his voice from Jerusalem, and the heavens and the earth shall shake ; but the Lord is the hope of his people, and the strength of the children of Israel. True lowliness of spirit, and the loftiest mind that ever was, are never separated ; for these twain are made one so as never to be separated, no more than a child (in point of all human abilities) and the Ancient of Days shall ; for as we receive the kingdom of heaven as a little child, so we are never otherwise in the same respect, which we know, no wisdom human, serpentine, or upon principles proper to a creature, can ever yield unto or find out ; and therefore we are fools unto the world, being bereaved of all their principles, in regard of any exercise of them according to their proper intent in any of our designs. .... And therefore as brute beasts are unto them, so are they to us in the things of God.

Again he says :—

We conclude that the wisdom of God, though become foolishness unto the world, yet doth it contain sufficiency of power in argument to overtop any council, synod, synedrim or assembly, composed by human art or learning. .... For as it is in that way of the devil, to propose his temptations from the letter of the Scriptures, to subdue Christ thereby ; so is there sufficiency of spirit and wisdom, in the true interpretation thereof, to confound and bring them (in the party proposing them) to nought. A Christian is still saying, Let there be light, and it is so ; he shall ever divide the light from the darkness, and the waters that are above the firmament from the waters that are below the outspread firmament. In a word, he is for ever to form all things out of that ancient chaos of God and man being made one.

Once more he says :—

If I witness to the Son, word, light, life, law, or peace of God, I must witness unto the being of such a thing, that such a thing is, as also to the manner of its being, how it comes to be such a thing, together with its necessary and proper operations, which must inevitably accompany such a manner of being, with the comprehensions and extensions of such operations and motion, or else I am not that faithful and true witness, the beginning of the creation of God, or that head and masterpiece of his work.[2]

[1] Observe, the word of truth says, " *Unto us*," but this perverter of Scripture says, " *In us*."

[2] These letters are annexed to a book he published in 1636, pp. 272—294.

These extracts from his own writings, may give the reader some idea of his way of handling the Scriptures. Our Saviour vanquished the tempter by appealing to what was written, and shewing thereby that Satan perverted the text he pretended to quote; but the *lofty mind* of this writer soared so much above that method, as to say of the world of mankind, "As brute beasts are unto them, so are they to us in the things of God." Well therefore might Mr. Williams say, "I am no more of Master Gorton's religion than of Master Cotton's; and yet if Master Cotton complain of their obstinacy in their way, I cannot but impute it to his bloody tenet and practice, which ordinarily doth give strength, vigor, spirit and resolution to the most erroneous, when such unrighteous and most unchristian proceedings are exercised against them."[1] Besides their difference about gospel doctrines, they evidently differed in the following points of practice. 1. Mr. Williams used great plainness of speech, so that his meaning was obvious to common understandings; but Mr. Gorton's writings are not so. 2. Mr. Williams openly stood for what he believed to be the truth, in the face of the greatest danger; but when Mr. Gorton saw himself greatly exposed in Boston, he explained their mystical writings in such a manner, that Governor Winthrop said "he could agree with him in his answer, though not in their writings."[2] 3. Mr. Williams set a noble example of overcoming evil with good; but Mr. Gorton was sadly ensnared in rendering evil for evil, and railing for railing. Though after he had been to England, and obtained liberty to return to and enjoy the lands they had purchased, he and sundry of his suffering companions became very useful members of civil society. But as corruption is ever the most dangerous when covered with a religious mask, it is of great importance for us all to learn to distinguish between that and true religion. Paul said to the contending Corinthians, "Are ye

---

[1] Reply to Cotton, p. 123.   [2] Gorton's Defence, [132.]

not carnal and walk as men?" The same query may be made concerning those contentions betwixt Gorton and his opponents.

Those in Massachusetts professed a high regard to their charter, when they banished Mr. Williams; but that gave them no right to any land or government, further than three miles south of their bay, and of every part of Charles River. That line crosses the great post road near landlord Maxcy's, in Attleborough, from whence to Pawtuxet river is nineteen miles; and Shawomet is still further southward; yet we are plainly told that Arnold and his company were received "partly to draw in the rest, either under themselves or Plymouth.[1] And when Gorton and his friends were got out of Arnold's reach, two petty sachems were taken in to found a claim upon, though it was known that Miantinomu was so much above them, that he sold Providence and Pawtuxet over their heads, some years before, in which was contained the best title that Arnold's company had to their lands. What work then did they make, in first enticing subjects to revolt from their prince, and then in killing him because he was uneasy about it! Had they not been blinded with such a zeal as the disciples had, when they were for having fire to come down and consume the Samaritans, surely they would not have violated the rules of justice and equity as they did. They tried afterwards to vindicate their conduct by the claim of Plymouth to that land, and upon an act of the commissioners of the United Colonies concerning it.[2] But Plymouth patent extended no farther westward than Narragansett river, and the utmost limits of Pocanokit or Sawamset, that is Osamaquin or Massasoit's territories;[3] and we have before heard how they fell short of the lands in question. Further, the commissioners pleaded, that Miantinomu engaged by treaty, not to begin war with Uncas without first appealing to the English; yet had broken that

---

[1]Hubbard, [344.]   [2]Massachusetts History, Vol. I, p. 125, [117.]
[3]Prince's Chronology, p. 197. [269.]

agreement.[1] But a very credible writer of their own informs us, that Miantinomu first sent his complaint to Hartford against Uncas; and when they refused to meddle in Sequastion's quarrel, he would know whether they would be offended if he should make war upon Uncas? And that they left him to take his course,[2] so that their case in truth was, like that of other invaders of their neighbor's rights; they were in danger of being awfully requited, by a man so sensible and powerful as Miantinomu, if he was not taken out of the way. This evil is greatly to be lamented, and should ever stand as a solemn warning to us all, to beware of taking one step into any course of injustice, deceit or cruelty; for it will surely prove bitterness in the latter end.

Had Gorton been duly aware of this, he would not have armed Miantinomu against Uncas, for no better reason, that we know of, than because he, being a warlike prince, stood in the way of his forming an Indian party sufficient to withstand or overcome the Massachusetts; which proceeding, together with his irritating writings against their rulers and ministers, was the evident cause of things being carried to the dreadful extremity they were. Mr. Williams ever bore as plain and full testimony against their persecuting any man for matters of conscience, as Gorton could; and had a much greater influence over the Indians than he ever had; yet he was so far from trying to raise a heathen party against Christians, to correct them for injuries done to himself, that he exerted himself with great assiduity to prevent any thing of that nature; by which he undoubtedly was the greatest instrument of saving New England of any one man that lived in that day, and for which his memory is and will be blessed.

Among the reasoners of our world, some will not allow, that men are influenced in all their voluntary actions by previous causes and motives, while others incline so much to

---

[1] Massachusetts History, Vol. III, p. 140.   [2] Hubbard, [450.]

infidelity as to represent, that the very notion of religion, or of persons thinking that the Deity loves them better than others, tends to make them hate and treat those ill who, as they suppose, are not thus beloved. But as nothing teaches like experience, let the experience of those fathers be considered, and the light which facts give in the case be regarded, beyond all the suppositions or wrangles of disputants. Is it not evident, that those several contending parties were influenced in all their bad actions by the same principles of ambition, avarice, deceit, and resentment, that other men are? And is it not as evident, that those actions which were good and praiseworthy, flowed from a hearty belief of revealed religion, especially of free salvation by Christ Jesus? At present we will take a view of the head men of the three parties of Boston, Warwick and Providence.

Governor Winthrop was in such esteem in his native country, as to be made a justice of peace at the age of eighteen; had an estate of six or seven hundred pounds sterling per annum; yet sold it, and spent the main of it in promoting a religious settlement in this wilderness; where for all his vast labor and pains, in settling and managing the government, he for some years had no stated salary, and never had more than one hundred pounds a year; was several times very ungratefully treated by his own people; and what could carry him through all this with cheerfulness to the end, but the power of religion?[1]

[1] What his religious sentiments were, the reader may form some judgment by the following extracts. In the first part of his administration as Governor, he said, " In the infancy of plantations, justice should be administered with more lenity than in a settled state; because people are more apt then to transgress; partly out of ignorance of new laws and orders, partly out of oppression of business and other straits." But when some leading and learned men took offence at his conduct in this matter, and upon a conference, gave it as their opinion, that a stricter discipline was to be used in the beginning of a plantation, than after its being with more age established and confirmed, the Governor being readier to see his own errors than other men's, professed his purpose to endeavor their satisfaction with less lenity in his administrations." [Magnalia, B. 2, Vol. I, pp. 110, 111.] From this we may guess at the cause of the severities we have been treating of.

His expenses were great, and for two years he had no settled salary, yet the divine

Gorton, as we have seen, had a notion that the child was born in him and his followers, who had the government upon his shoulders, and he concurred with Wheelwright in treating those who opposed their religious sentiments as enemies to the state; which principle evidently moved him to

precept against taking bribes, had such influence upon his mind, that when he was the third time chosen Governor, May 8, 1632, he told the people publicly, "that he had received gratuities from divers towns, which he received with much comfort and content; he had also received many kindnesses from particular persons, which he could not refuse, lest he should be accounted uncourteous, &c., but he professed he received them with a trembling heart, in regard to God's rule, and the consciousness of his own infirmity, and therefore desired that hereafter they would not take it ill if he should refuse presents from particular persons, except the assistance of some special friends. To which no answer was made; but he is told after, that many good people were much grieved at it, for that he never had any allowance toward the charge of his place." [Prince's Chronology, pp. 394, 395.]

After he had acted in banishing Mr. Wheelwright and others, many of their friends in Boston church, whereof he was a member, were earnest with the elders to have the church call him forth as an offender, for passing that sentence, which he understanding, took occasion to make a public speech to them upon it, in which he said :— "As for myself, I did nothing in the causes of any of the brethren, but by advice of the elders of the church. Moreover, the oath which I have taken there is this clause, 'In all causes wherein you are to give your vote, you shall do as in your judgment and conscience you shall see to be just, and for the public good.' And I am satisfied it is most for the glory of God, and the public good, that there be such a sentence passed; yea, those brethren are so divided from the rest of the country in their opinions and practices that it cannot stand with the public peace for them to continue with us; Abraham saw that Hagar and Ishmael must be sent away." [Magnalia, B. 2, Vol. I, pp. 114, 115.]

Seven years after, upon a hot debate between the magistrates and deputies about who should have the negative vote, Governor Winthrop wrote his mind upon it, some passages whereof gave offence to some noted men, which he understanding, made the following speech at the next General Court, viz.: "As for the matter of my writing, I had the concurrence of my brethren; it is a point of judgment which is not at my own disposing. I have examined it over and over again, by such light as God has given me, from the rules of religion, reason and custom; and I see no cause to retract anything of it; wherefore I must enjoy my liberty in that, as you do yourselves. But for the manner, this, and all that was blameworthy in it, was wholly my own; and whatsoever I might allege for my own justification before men, I waive it, as now setting myself before another judgment-seat. However, what I wrote was upon great provocation, and to vindicate myself and others from great aspersion; yet that was no sufficient warrant for me to allow any distemper of spirit in myself; and I doubt I have been too prodigal of my brethren's reputation. I might have maintained my cause without casting any blemish upon others. When I made that my conclusion, 'And now let religion and sound reason give judgment in the case,' it looked as if I arrogated too much unto myself, and too little to others. And when I made that profession, 'that I would maintain what I wrote before all the world,' though such words might modestly be spoken, yet I perceive an unbe-

endeavor to raise what force he could against them, even from among the barbarians; and also to treat them with such a temper as he did from time to time. Even so late as the year 1676, the very title of the book he then published shows the spirit of it; which is exactly in these words, viz.:—

A glass for New England, in which they may see themselves and spirits, and, if not too late, repent and turn from their abominable ways and cursed contrivances. By S. G.

seeming pride of my own heart breathing in them. For these failings I ask pardon both of God and man. Ibid, [p. 115.]

Once more; when a great disturbance had been made in the colony by Dr. Child and others, in 1646, Governor Winthrop was called to an account for his actings against them, before a great assembly, but he was openly acquitted; upon which he said. "Though I am justified before men, yet it may be the Lord hath seen so much amiss in my administrations, as calls me to be humbled; and indeed for me to have been thus charged by men, is itself a matter of humiliation, whereof I desire to make a right use before the Lord. If Miriam's father spit in her face, she is to be ashamed. But give me leave before you go to say something that may rectify the opinions of many people, from whence the distempers have risen that have lately prevailed upon the body of this people. The questions that have troubled the country have been about the authority of the magistracy, and the liberty of the people. It is you who have called us unto this office; but being thus called, we have our authority from God; it is the ordinance of God, and it hath the image of God stamped upon it; and the contempt of it has been vindicated by God by terrible examples of his vengeance. I entreat you to consider, that when you choose magistrates, you take from among yourselves men subject unto like passions with yourselves. If you see our infirmities, reflect on your own, and you will not be so severe censurers of ours. We count him a good servant who breaks not his covenant. The covenant between us and you is the oath you have taken of us, which is to this purpose, 'that we shall govern you, and judge your causes, according to God's laws, and our own, according to our best skill.' As for our skill, you must run the hazard of that; and if there be an error, not in the will, but in the skill, it becomes you to bear it. Nor would I have you to mistake in the point of your own liberty. There is a liberty of corrupt nature, which is affected both by men and beasts, to do what they list; and this liberty is inconsistent with authority, impatient of all restraint; by this liberty, *sumus omnes deteriores*: It is the grand enemy of truth and peace, and all the ordinances of God are bent against it. But there is a civil, a moral, a federal liberty, which is the proper end and object of authority; it is a liberty for that only which is just and good; for this liberty you are to stand with the hazard of your very lives; and whatsoever crosses it, is not authority, but a distemper thereof. This liberty is maintained in a way of subjection to authority; and the authority set over you, will in all administrations for your good be quietly submitted unto, by all but such as have a disposition to shake off the yoke, and lose their true liberty, by their murmuring at the honor and power of authority." Ibid. [pp. 116, 117.]

O, had it not been for the mistaken notion of using secular force in religious affairs, how gloriously would this and other New England fathers have shined!

And as the Quakers were about that time accused by authority of setting up their posts by God's posts, he says:—

> I hope none will be so blind and ignorant as to set their posts or thresholds to the devil's post, and the professors of New England's posts, viz., their whipping-post or gallows-post; no nor yet join their threshold to their gaol-thresholds, nor their bridewell-threshold, over which and in which professors and talkers of God and Christ do and have hauled over lambs and followers of Christ, and in which they crop their ears, and out of which they bring them in their wills and madness, and banish, whip and hang them in their blind zeal. Pp. 17, 18.

And he annexes to said book a letter to Governor Bellingham, dated from Boston prison June 15, 1667, written by John Tyso, a Quaker, who speaks of it as a great error in Dr. Increase Mather to say, " there was nothing in him that he hoped to be saved by, and that there was none cleansed from all sin on this side the grave." P. 35. Gorton likewise speaking of Wheelwright's being first called before the General Court for his sermon, at their session in March, 1637, tells us that Mr. Cotton then said:—

> Brother Wheelwright's doctrine was according to God, in the point controverted, and wholly and altogether; and nothing did I hear alleged against the doctrine proved by the word of God. . . . . But, [says G.] that which is most to be lamented, is that those which once had a good testimony in their hearts and mouths for God, and his light and spiritual appearance; and they not being faithful and constant to that which is made manifest and committed to them, it has even happened to them according to the saying of the Lord God, by the mouth of his prophet, that "in the day in which a righteous man turns from his righteousness, and doth wickedly, all the righteousness that he hath done shall be forgotten, and in the sin which he hath sinned he shall surely die the death." Pp. 6, 7.

Now is it not evident, that the Massachusetts were moved by the same unreasonable principle of grasping at power and gain that belonged not to them, in their dealings with Gorton, as operates in other men, though it went under a cloak of religion? And is it not as evident that he was moved with self-conceit, and carnal wit and resentment, in his carriage towards them, notwithstanding all his talk of the child's being born in him, and of a creating power " for ever to form all things out of that ancient chaos of God and man being made one!" Neither of these things can hurt the truth and excellency of the Christian religion, any more than the self confidence, rashness and dissimulation of Peter did on the one hand, or the blasphemy of Hymeneus and Alexander on the other. Though some would have it, that Mr. Williams, after his banishment, left revealed religion, and took to the exercise of reason and humanity, in distinction from it, yet his own testimony is exceeding clear to the contrary. In his address to the Quakers thirty-seven years after his banishment he says:—

> The truth is, from my childhood, now above threescore years, the Father of lights and mercies touched my soul with a love to himself, to his only begotten, the true Lord Jesus to his holy Scriptures, &c. His infinite wisdom hath given me to see the city, court and country, the schools and universities of my native country, to converse with some Turks, Jews, papists, and all sorts of protestants, and by books to know the affairs and religions of all countries. My conclusion is, that, "Be of good cheer; thy sins are forgiven thee," Matt. ix., is one of the joyfulest sounds that ever came to poor sinful ears. How to obtain this sound from the mouth of the Mediator that spoke it, is the greatest dispute between the protestants and the bloody whore of Rome. This is also the great point between the true protestant and yourselves; as also, in order to this, about what man is now by nature, and what the true Lord Jesus is."[1]

And upon their use of those words spoken to the saints, "The manifestation of the spirit is given to *every man* to profit withal," and other like expressions, which they would apply to mankind in general, he says:—

> The Papists catch hold upon a letter, " *This is my body* ;" you as simply as do the Generalists catch hold upon the letter: "*All*," "*Every man*," &c., whereas the scope and connection in all writings, and in all matters in the world, is rationally to be minded. The sense and meaning is, in all speech

---

[1] Dedication of his book against the Quakers, 1673.—B.

In a subsequent notice of this book, Backus gives its proper title,—" George Fox digged out of his Burrowes,"— but with a censure of such personalities of language on the part of both Williams and his opponents. He uniformly quotes the work as Williams's " book against the Quakers."—ED.

and writing, the very speech and writing itself. The words *All*, and *Every one*, in our own and other tongues, are often used figuratively. It is so all the Scripture over, and thrice in one verse, Col. i, 28, where reason cannot imagine that Paul did literally and individually admonish every man, teach every man, and present every man that comes into the world perfect in Christ Jesus, which could not, cannot possibly be true, without another sense and exposition than the words literally hold out.[1]

And when they demanded the reason why he condemned them for not holding to the external use of baptism and the supper, while he did not live in the practice thereof himself, he answered:—

> It is one thing to be in arms against the King of kings, and the visible administration of his kingdom, and to turn off all to notions of an invisible kingdom, officers, and worship, as the Quakers, do, and another thing, among so many pretenders to be the true church, to be in doubt unto which to associate himself. After all my search and examinations, I said, I do profess to believe, that some come nearer to the first churches and institutions of Christ than others; as in many respects, so in that gallant, heavenly and fundamental principle, of the *true matter* of a Christian society, viz.: *actual believers, true disciples and converts*, and *living stones*, such as can give some account how the grace of God hath appeared to them, and wrought that heavenly change in them. I professed that if my soul could find rest in joining unto any of the churches professing Christ now extant, I would readily and gladly do it, yea, unto themselves whom I now opposed. But not finding rest, they knew there is a time of purity, and primitive sincerity; there is a time of transgression and apostacy, and there is a time of the coming out of the Babylonian and wilderness apostacy[2].

These extracts may assist the reader in forming a true judgment of the motives upon which those several noted men acted in those difficult times, which also may be useful now to teach us all, what to avoid and what to pursue; the importance of which I hope will sufficiently apologize for the length of this acconnt, and also make the reader willing to take an article or two more before we conclude this chapter.

The church at Plymouth was so unwilling to part with "a man of such eminence" as Mr. Chauncy, that they conceded

[1] Against the Quakers, pp. 8, 9.   [2] Against the Quakers, pp. 65, 66.

in case he would settle with them, that he should act according to his persuasion, which was that "baptism ought only to be by dipping or plunging the whole body under water," with such as desired it, either for themselves or infants, provided he could without offence suffer their other minister, Mr. Reyner, to practice in the other way, with those who desired it; "but he did not see light to comply."[1] From thence he was called to office in the church at Scituate. Mr. Winthrop says:—

> Mr. Chauncy of Scituate, persevered in his opinion of dipping in baptism, and practiced accordingly, first upon two of his own children, which being in very cold weather, one of them swooned away. Another, having a child about three years old, feared it would be frighted, (as others had been, and one caught hold of Mr. Chauncy, and had near pulled him into the water) she brought her child to Boston (with letters testimonial from Mr. Chauncy) and had it baptised here.[2]

This last action was in July, 1642; and not long after Mr. Winthrop writes:—

> The lady Moody, a wise and amiable[3] religious woman, being taken with the error of denying baptism to infants, was dealt withal by many of the elders and others, and admonished by the church at Salem, (whereof she was) but persisting still, and to avoid further trouble, she removed to the Dutch, against the advice of her friends. Many others infested with Anabaptism, &c., removed thither also. She was after excommunicated.[4]

Here as well as elsewhere appears the honesty and ingenuousness of this great man, in stating facts plainly, when they make directly against his own persuasion. Those who deny infant baptism have been reproached from age to age with the name of Anabaptists, under which have been couched such dreadful ideas, that even to this day we see the very name used as an argument in various controversies; so that if a

---

[1] Plymouth Register, pp. 5, 6.   [2] Winthrop, Vol. II, p. 72.—ED.

[3] Savage reads "anciently" instead of "amiable;" and adds in a note, "I fear we must infer from the text that her perversion to Anabaptism deprived her in the writer's opinion, of the 'anciently religious' character." Winthrop, Vol. II, p. 123. If this reading and inference be correct, it will detract somewhat from the praise awarded to Winthrop in the next paragraph.—ED.

[4] Winthrop, [Vol. II, pp. 123, 124.]

disputant can tell his opponent, he in that point agrees with the Anabaptists, it is thought that therein he must be in an error; but our honorable author gives, without a covering, the good characters and virtues of that father and that mother in our Israel, at the same time that he describes plainly what he disliked in them; leaving fair grounds for others to judge upon, without being biased with any old stories of German madness. By this it appears that the grand difficulty in the way of burying in baptism, is their admitting of subjects to it who have not the faith or the discretion which is necessary for such an action.

Though Mr. Williams had done such great services for his English neighbors, in the late wars, yet he was not permitted to pass through their coasts, but was forced to repair to the Dutch to get a passage to his native country. Yea, it must needs be so, because the blessings of a peacemaker were to come upon him, among the Dutch as well as English.[1]

[1] As a distinct account of this affair has not been published among us, I shall give it a place here. When the commissioners of the United Colonies met in September, 1643, they were informed of a Dutch ship that had arrived in Hudson's River, which brought four thousand pounds of powder, and seven hundred pieces, to trade with the natives; but the Dutch governor, having notice thereof, prudently confiscated them to the use of the company; thereby depriving their enemies of arms, whereby they might themselves have been destroyed, and furnishing themselves and friends with weapons for their safety; for at this time the Indians had fierce war with the Dutch, and if it had not been for the assistance for the English, they might have been all cut off. The occasion of the war was this:—An Indian being drunk, had slain an old Dutchman; the Dutch required the murderer, but he could not be had. The people called often upon the governor to take revenge, but he still put it off, because he thought it not just, or not safe. It fell out in that time, that the Maquas or Mohawks, either upon their own quarrel or (as the report was) being set on by the Dutch, came suddenly upon the Indians near the Dutch, and killed about thirty of them; the rest fled for shelter to the Dutch. One Marine, a Dutch captain, hearing of it, went to the governor and obtained a commission to kill as many as he could of them, and accordingly went with a company of armed men, and set upon them, when they feared no such thing from the Dutch, and killed seventy or eighty men, women and children. Upon this the Indians burnt divers of their farm houses, and their cattle in them, and slew all they could meet with, to the number of twenty or more, of men, women and children, and pursued hard upon the Dutch, even home to their fort Aurania (Albany) so that they were forced to call in the English to their aid, and entertained Captain Underhill in their service. Marine was so much

When Mr. Williams arrived in England, he found the country involved in the dreadful calamities and horrors of a war between the king and parliament; but the parliament having the command of the fleet, did by an ordinance of November 2, 1643, appoint commissioners to manage the affairs of the islands and other plantations; from whom, by the kind assistance of Sir Henry Vane, who was one of them, Mr. Williams obtained a charter, including the lands "bordering northward and northeast on the patent of the Massachusetts, east and southeast on Plymouth patent, south on the ocean, and on the west and northwest by the Indians called Narragansetts; the whole tract extending about twenty-five miles, unto the Pequod river and country;" "to be known by the name of THE INCORPORATION OF PROVIDENCE PLANTATIONS, IN THE NARRAGANSETT BAY, IN NEW ENGLAND." To the English inhabitants of the tract aforesaid, the charter gives "full power and authority to rule themselves, and such others as shall hereafter inhabit within any part of the said tract of land, by such form of civil government, as by vol-

enraged to see Underhill preferred before him, that his governor was forced at last to send him home in chains. About this time Captain Patrick, who went from Boston, was shot dead by a Dutchman, upon a Lord's day, at Stamford. Though the people were all for war before, yet now they were so much offended with the governor, that he entertained a guard of fifty English about his person. And the Indians annoyed them so by sudden assaults out of swamps, &c., that he was forced to keep a running army to oppose them upon all occasions. The Indians killed and drove all before them as far as Stamford; slew Mrs. Hutchinson and her family, all except one whom they captivated. They passed over to Long Island, and the natives there took part with them, and began to burn the Dutchmen's houses; assaulted the house of the lady Moody, who not long before moved away from Salem upon the account of Anabaptism; but she was defended by forty men that gathered to her house, which they assaulted divers times. But the Long Island Indians, by the mediation of Mr. Williams, (who was then there to take ship for England,) were pacified, and peace re-established between the Dutch and them. But still upon the main, they set upon the Dutch with an implacable fury, killing all they could come by, burning their houses, and destroying their cattle. without any resistance; so as the governor and such as escaped betook themselves to their fort at Manhatoes (New York) and there lived upon their cattle. But many of the Indians being destroyed by Captain Underhill and his followers, at last they began to be weary of the sport, and condescended to terms of peace." Winthrop, [Vol. II, pp. 135, 151.] Hubbard, [440—442.]

untary consent of all, or the greater part of them, they shall find most suitable to their estate and condition," provided " the civil government of the said plantations, be conformable to the laws of England, so far as the nature and constitution of the place will admit."

This charter was signed March 14, 1644, by Robert Warwick, Philip Pembroke, Say and Seal, Philip Wharton, Arthur Haslerig, Cornelius Holland, Henry Vane, Samuel Vassel, John Rolle, Miles Corbet, and William Spurstow.[1]

[1] See said charter in the History of Providence.

CHAPTER III.

FROM 1644 TO 1651, CONTAINING THE FIRST LAW THAT WAS MADE IN NEW ENGLAND AGAINST THE BAPTISTS, AND A VARIETY OF OTHER EVENTS.

The first Baptist church in Newport, we are told, was formed and set in order about the year 1644, under the ministry of Mr. John Clarke. It is the first church of any denomination on Rhode Island that has continued by succession, and the second in the colony.[1] Also in Massachusetts

[1] The first certain date in their church records is taken from a manuscript of Mr. Samuel Hubbard in 1648, which says the church was formed about the year 1644, and by what I have quoted from Winthrop and Hubbard, it appears as likely to be earlier as later than that time.—B.
    The entry in the records of the first Baptist church in Newport, here referred to, was made by John Comer as late as 1725, and is as follows :—" Having found a private record of Mr. Samuel Hubbard, who was a member of the church, by which I find that the church was in being so long back as October 12, 1648, (but how long before, justly, by any manuscript I can't find, but by private information it was constituted in the year 1644)—." Backus should therefore have given the above date on the authority of John Comer, and not of Samuel Hubbard. Comer repeated this testimony in a manuscript now in the library of the Backus Historical Society, in the words, "The church was first gathered by Mr. John Clarke about the year 1644." Callender wrote in 1738, " It is said that in 1644, Mr. John Clarke and some others formed a church on the scheme and principles of the Baptists." Century Sermon, Rhode Island Historical Collections, Vol. IV. p. 117. There is probably no evidence that Callender or any subsequent writer who has given the above date, had any authority for it beyond the tradition preserved by Comer. Backus represents that an earlier date is possible. Many regard the weight of evidence as in its favor. Some have placed it as far back as 1638, supposing that the church was founded by Clarke and his company upon their arrival on Rhode Island. See Minutes of the Warren Association, 1849, p. 14. Winthrop, indeed, mentions a church that had been gathered at Aquiday as early as 1639, but Lechford wrote in 1640, " There was a church where one Master Clark was elder; the place where the church was, is

we are told that "Anabaptists increased and spread in the country."[1] Upon which they framed and passed the following act at their General Court, November 13, 1644:—

> Forasmuch as experience hath plentifully and often proved, that since the first rising of the Anabaptists, about one hundred years since, they have been the incendiaries of the commonwealths, and the infectors of persons in main matters of religion, and the troublers of churches in all places where they have been, and that they who have held the baptizing of infants unlawful, have usually held other errors or heresies together therewith, though they have (as other heretics use to do) concealed the same till they spied out a fit advantage and opportunity to vent them, by way of question or scruple; and whereas divers of this kind have since our coming into New England appeared amongst ourselves, some whereof (as others before them) denied the ordinance of magistracy, and the lawfulness of making war, and others the lawfulness of magistrates, and their inspection into any breach of the first table; which opinions, if they should be connived at by us, are like to be increased amongst us, and so must necessarily bring guilt upon us, infection and trouble to the churches, and hazard to the whole commonwealth; it is ordered and agreed, that if any person or persons, within this jurisdiction, shall either openly condemn or oppose the baptizing of infants, or go about secretly to seduce others from the approbation or use thereof, or shall purposely depart the congregation at the ministration of the ordinance, or shall deny the ordinance of magistracy, or their lawful right and authority to make war, or to punish the outward breaches of the first table, and shall appear to the Court willfully and obstinately to continue therein after due time and means of conviction, every such person or persons shall be sentenced to banishment.[2]

called Newport; but that church, I hear, is now dissolved," Winthrop's Journal, Vol. I, p. 297; Plain Dealing, Trumbull's edition, p. 93, Some place the date of the present church in or about 1640, supposing that it succeeded the one which, according to Lechford, was dissolved. They reason from the improbability that the inhabitants of Rhode Island would remain four years without an organized church, and from the testimony of Winthrop in 1641, that "divers of them turned professed Anabaptists," and that there arose a contention and a schism among them. See Winthrop's Journal, Vol. II, pp. 38, 41. These indications are not without force, still, if a church was formed in 1640 or 1641, whether fully or partially Baptist, it may have had but a brief existence and have been succeeded by the present church in 1644. There seems to be as yet no wiser conclusion than that of Backus, when he gave 1644 as the only date which has any positive authority, and at the same time allowed the possibility of a date still earlier.—ED.

[1] Winthrop, [Vol. II, p. 174.]—ED.
[2] Massachusetts Records. Mr. Hubbard speaking of their making this law, says, "But with what success is hard to say; all men being naturally inclined to pity

Let it be here noted, that the evident design of this law was to guard against such as refused to countenance infant baptism, and the use of secular force in religious affairs; which the Baptists have ever done from that day to this; but the other articles inserted in this act they have not owned; and the Court then had no proof at hand, but were forced to have recourse to surmises, distant times, and foreign countries, for them. A like method of treating the Baptists, in Courts, from pulpits and from the press, has been handed down by tradition ever since. And can we believe that men so knowing and virtuous in other respects, as men on that side have been, would have introduced and continued in a way of treating their neighbors, which is so unjust and scandalous, if they could have found better arguments to support that cause upon? I have diligently searched all the books, records and papers I could come at upon all sides, and have found a great number of instances

them that suffer, how much soever they are incensed against offenders in general. Natural conscience and the reverence of a Deity, that is deeply engraven on the hearts of all, make men more apt to favor them that suffer for religion, true or false." [P. 373.] A judicious remark; yet in another instance we may see how party influence can blind great men. For this author in 1638 tells us of Arnold's opposing their censuring Verin at Providence, for refusing to let his wife go to Mr. Williams's meeting so often as she was called for, and represents that to censure Verin therefor, would be a breach of God's ordinance, about the "subjection of wives to their husbands." [P. 437.] But the same author informs us, that in 1644 one Painter, a poor man, was suddenly turned Anabaptist, "and having a child born, would not suffer his wife to carry it to be baptized. He was complained of for this to the Court, and enjoined by them to suffer his child to be baptized." And because he refused to obey them therein, and told them it was an antichristian ordinance, they tied him up and whipped him; which he bare without flinching, and declared he had divine help to support him; "upon which," says our author, "two or three honest men that were his neighbors affirmed that he was of very loose behavior at home," &c. [P. 342.] Be it so or not, we have no better account of Verin's character than of his, yet Verin must not be censured for withholding his wife from meeting; but if poor Painter would not give up the disposal of his children to his wife, at the Court's commandment, he must not only be censured, but also suffer corporal punishment; yea, and into the bargain, be publicly reproached for his private failings! Governor Winthrop tells us he belonged to Hingham, and says he was whipped "for reproaching the Lord's ordinance." [Vol. II, p. 175.] But did not they reproach infant sprinkling, by taking such methods to support it, much more than Painter did?

of Baptists suffering for the above points that we own; but not one instance of the conviction of any member of a Baptist church in this country, in any Court, of the errors or evils which are inserted in this law to justify their making of it, and to render our denomination odious.[1] Much has been said to exalt the characters of those good fathers; I have no desire of detracting from any of their virtues; but the better the men were, the worse must be the principle that could ensnare them in such bad actions.

The contrast betwixt their treatment of Mr. Wheelwright and Mr. Williams this year deserves notice. Upon a new running of the line, the Massachusetts had taken Exeter into their colony, which caused Mr. Wheelwright to remove to Wells, from whence he wrote to the Governor at Boston for a reconciliation, Dec. 7, 1643, and said, "It is the grief of my soul that I used such vehement censorious speeches. I repent me that I did so much adhere to persons of corrupt judgments, to the countenancing and encouraging of them in any of their errors, or evil practices, though I intended no such thing." The Court inclined to hear him of which the Governor sent him a written account, and received such a reply as would make one think of Bishop Burnet's remark. Said he, "There are none of us but what will acknowledge in general terms that our church is imperfect, though when we come to particulars, we are always in the right."[2] Yet

---

[1] There is not one instance in any government that supported Pœdobaptism by force. But Mr. Williams, when Governor of Providence colony in 1655, acted with the Court in punishing a man for opposing all government, who then was called a Baptist, but after turned to the Quakers.

[2] Said letter to the Governor is in these words:—

R. W.*

"I have received your letters, wherein you signify to me, that you have imparted my letter to the H. C.† and that it finds good acceptance, for which I rejoice with all thankfulness; as also for liberty of safe conduct granted by the Court, and, in case I desire, letters for that end. I should very willingly (upon letters obtained) express by word of mouth, openly in Court, that which I did by writing, might I without offence express my true intent and meaning more fully to this effect; that notwithstanding my failures (for which I crave pardon) yet I cannot with a good

*Right Worshipful.—Ed. †Honored Court.—Ed.

without waiting for his personal appearance, they at the General Court in Boston, May 29, 1644, passed the following act, viz. :—

It is ordered that Mr. Wheelwright (upon a particular, solemn, and serious acknowledgment and confession, by letters, of his evil carriages, and of the Court's justice upon him for them) hath his banishment taken off, and is received as a member of this Commonwealth.[1]

Mr. Williams returned with the charter he had procured, to Boston, the 17th of September following,[2] and brought the ensuing letter with him :—

To the Right Worshipful the Governor and Assistants and the rest of our worthy friends in the plantation of Massachusetts Bay, [in New England.][3]

OUR MUCH HONORED FRIENDS :—Taking notice some of us of long time of Mr. Roger Williams's [Williams his] good affections and conscience, and of his sufferings by our common enemy [enemies] and oppressors of God's people the prelates, as also of his great industry and travels [travail] in

conscience condemn myself for such capital crimes, dangerous revelations and gross errors, as have been charged upon me. The concurrence of which, as I take it, makes up the substance of all my sufferings. I do not see but in so mixed a cause, I am bound to use, may it be permitted, my just defence, so far as I apprehend myself to be innocent, and to make my confession where I am convinced of any delinquency, otherwise I shall seemingly and in appearance fall under guilt of many heinous offences, for which my conscience doth acquit me. If I seem to make suit to the Court for relaxation to be granted as an act of mercy upon my sole confession, I must offend my conscience; if by an act of justice, upon my apology and lawful defence, I fear here I shall offend your Worships. I leave all things to your wise and holy consideration, hoping you will pardon my simplicity and plainness, which I am forced upon by the power of an overruling conscience. I rest your Worship's in the Lord,

J. WHEELWRIGHT."

Wells, (I) I, 1643.

Winthrop, [Vol. II, p. 163.] Hubbard, [367.] Note, their way was to begin the year with March 25, so that according to our reckoning this was March 1, 1614.

[1] At the same time they passed a sentence, that "Richard Waterman, being found erroneous, heretical and obstinate, it was ordered that he should be detained prisoner till the Quarter Court in the seventh month, unless five of the magistrates find cause to send him away, which if they do, it is ordered, he shall not return within this jurisdiction upon pain of death."

Massachusetts Records.

[2] Winthrop, [Vol. II, p. 193.]

[3] This letter has been often quoted and considerably changed. The form here given is taken almost literally from Hutchinson. The words added in brackets will indicate its form as given by Winthrop. Vol. II, p. 193.—ED.

his printed Indian labors[1] in your parts (the like whereof we have not seen extant from any part of America) and in which respect it hath pleased both houses of parliament [freely] to grant unto him and friends with him a free and absolute charter of civil government for those parts of his abode, and withal sorrowfully resenting that amongst good men (our friends) driven to the ends of the world, exercised with the trials of a wilderness, and who mutually give good testimony each of the other [of other] (as we observe you do of him, and he abundantly of you[2]) there should be such a distance; we thought it fit upon divers considerations to profess our great desires of both your utmost endeavors of nearer closing and of ready expressing those good affections (which we perceive you bear each to other) in effectual [in the actual] performance of all friendly offices. The rather because of those bad neighbors you are likely [like] to find too near you in Virginia, and the unfriendly visits from the west of England and Ireland. That howsoever it may please the Most High to shake our foundations, yet the report of your peaceable and prosperous plantations may be some refreshings [refreshing] to your true and faithful friends.

Cor. Holland,   Robert Harley,
John Blackistow, John Gurdon,
Isaac Pennington, Northumberland,
Miles Corbet,   P. Wharton,
Oliver St. John, Thomas Barrington.
Gibert Pickering, William Masham."[3]

Hubbard says:—

Upon the receipt of this letter, the Governor and magistrates of the Massachusetts found, upon examination of their hearts, no reason to con-

---

[1] Mr. Williams's printed Indian labors referred to, which had considerable influence in procuring their charter, were three years before the famous Mr. Elliott began to preach to the Indians at Natic, or Mr. Thomas Mayhew at Martha's Vineyard. Magnalia, B. 3, p. 193. [Vol. I, p. 507.] Mayhew's Indian Converts, p. 5.

[2] Mr. Williams confirmed his profession of love to them by his practice, in constantly doing them all the good in his power, both in this country and at the British court, where also his great friend, Sir Henry Vane, this year showed a truly Christian spirit of forgiveness towards Massachusetts; for when upon a certain affair "a heavy complaint was made against the government, and they were threatened with the loss of their privileges, Sir Henry Vane stood their friend, and by his great interest with the Parliament, appeased their resentment, and laid the storm which was gathering and hung over them."

Massachusetts History, Vol. I, p. 66, [67.]

[3] Massachusetts History, Vol. I, pp. 39, 40, [42.] King Charles the First's party at that time had the command of the west of England, Ireland and Virginia, and fear of visits from them is what they refer to. That party was defeated the next year and the king taken prisoner.

demn themselves for any former proceedings against Mr. Williams; but for any offices of Christian love, and duties of humanity, they were very willing to maintain a mutual correspondence with him; but as to his dangerous principles of separation, unless he can be brought to lay them down, they see no reason why to concede to him, or any so persuaded, free liberty of ingress and egress, lest any of their people should be drawn away with his erroneous opinions.[1]

The reader may remember that Wheelwright in his sentence of banishment, was charged with contempt and sedition, which he never confessed; and that Governor Winthrop declared his opinions to be worse than Mr. Williams's;[2] yet now the one is received to favor and liberty again, while the other is denied it, though he had done the colony such great and essential services as the former never did. How can we account for this? The best answer I can give is, that Mr. Wheelwright held to infant baptism, and to the magistrates' power to govern in religious affairs, and now yielded to their exercise of it; but Mr. Williams denied both, for which he was excommunicated by the church, after the Court had sent him away. Wheelwright was also in such favor with Mr. Cotton, that he was dismissed from his church in fellowship, after the Court had banished him for sedition; and he now appeared very complaisant and submissive to men in power. But Williams was so "self-conceited, turbulent and uncharitable, as to give public advertisements and admonitions to all men, whether of meaner or more public note and place, of the corruptions of religion which himself observed, both in their judgments and practices; of which there needs no

---

[1] Hubbard, [348.]

[2] The Court's sentence against him was in these words:—"Whereas Mr. Roger Williams, one of the elders of the church of Salem, hath broached and divulged divers new and dangerous opinions, against the authority of magistrates, as also written [writ] letters of defamation both of the magistrates and churches here, and that before any conviction, and yet maintaineth the same without retraction: It is therefore ordered, that the said Mr. Williams shall depart out of this jurisdiction within six weeks now next ensuing, which if he neglect to perform, it shall be lawful for the Governor and two of the magistrates to send him to some place out of this jurisdiction, not to return any more without license from the Court."

Massachusetts Records, 1635.

other evidence, than what is obvious to the view of every indifferent reader, in his dealing with that famous and reverend divine, Mr. John Cotton, in his book called The Bloody Tenet."

These words Mr. Hubbard quotes from another, as the received opinion of that day. But who was this reverend divine, and how was he dealt with? Was not Mr. Williams as truly a minister of Christ as he? Does self-conceit move men to give plain warnings to great men, which have a tendency to expose self to heavy sufferings? And does it move persons to do every kind office they can from year to year, for those who will not hear reproof, but requite evil for good? This is a different sort of pride from what most men are acquainted with. However, that the reader may have a fair opportunity of judging for himself, I shall endeavor to plainly state the occasion and nature of this controversy between Cotton and Williams.

A prisoner in Newgate wrote some arguments against persecution, which were presented to Mr. Cotton, and he wrote an answer to them in a letter to one Mr. Hall, of Roxbury; who not being satisfied therewith, sent them to Mr. Williams at Providence, requesting him to write upon the subject.[1] And as Mr. Cotton closed his letter to Mr.

[1] "Mr. Cotton says in 1647, 'Mr. Williams sent me about a dozen years ago (as I remember) a letter, penned (as he wrote) by a prisoner in Newgate, touching persecution for conscience sake; and entreated my judgment of it for the satisfaction of his friend.' This 'letter' was a part,—the sixth, seventh, eighth and ninth chapters,—of a work printed in 1620, entitled, 'A most humble supplication of the King's Majesty's loyal subjects, ready to testify all civil obedience by the oath of allegiance, or otherwise, and that of conscience; who are persecuted, (only for differing in religion) contrary to divine and human testimonies: as followeth.' It is signed by 'your Majesty's loyal subjects unjustly called Anabaptists.' It is reprinted by Crosby, History of the English Baptists, II, Appendix, pp. 10—51, and in Tracts on Liberty of Conscience, &c., Hansard Knollys Society, pp. 189—231. According to Williams 'the author of these arguments being committed by some then in power, close prisoner to Newgate, for the witness of some truths of Jesus, and having not the use of pen and ink, wrote these arguments in milk, in sheets of paper, brought to him by the woman, his keeper, from a friend in London, as the stopples of his milk bottle.' Bloody Tenet, p. 18. Dr. Underhill conjectures that it must have been written by John Murton, or as Crosby calls him, Morton, who

Hall with saying, "I forbear adding reasons to justify the truth, because you may find that done to your hand, in a treatise sent to some of the brethren, late of Salem, who doubted as you do." Mr. Williams wrote to Mr. Sharp, elder of Salem church, for it, and obtained it.[1] He then wrote his sentiments upon the whole, under the title of " The Bloody Tenet of Persecution for Conscience Sake;" which I suppose he now brought with him from London, though I have not been able to obtain it.[2] Mr. Cotton wrote an answer to him, which he called " The Bloody Tenet washed, and made white in the Blood of the Lamb." It was printed in London in 1647. To this Mr. Williams pub-

was associated with Helwisse in Holland, and after his return, in England, and against whom John Robinson directed one of his controversial works. Tracts on Liberty of Conscience, &c., pp. 89, 187. Williams denies that this treatise was sent by him to Cotton, or that the reply was private, as Cotton alledged in complaint against its being printed in this work. He says, " To my knowledge there was no such letter or intercourse passed between Master Cotton and the discusser," but what I have heard is this,—One Master Hall, of Roxbury, presented the prisoner's arguments against persecution to Master Cotton, who gave this present controverted answer; with the which Master Hall not being satisfied, he sends them unto the discusser, who never saw the said Hall, nor those arguments in writing: (though he well remembers that he saw them in print some years since.) Bloody Tenet yet more Bloody, p. 4." S. L. Caldwell, Preface to the Bloudy Tenent, Narragansett Club. Vol. III, pp, iv., v.—ED.

[1]Williams's Reply to Cotton, pp. 290, 291.—B.

This treatise was entitled " A Model of Church and Civil Power." It probably was never printed, and its author is unknown. See Narragansett Club, Vol. III, Preface, pp. vi.—viii.—ED.

[2]The exact title of the first edition was " The Bloudy Tenet of Persecution, or the cause of Conscience, discussed, in a conference between Truth and Peace; who, in all tender Affection, present to the High Court of Parliament, (as the result of their Discourse) these, (amongst other passages) of highest consideration." In his Bloody Tenet yet more Bloody, p. 38, Williams says of this Work:—" When these discussions were prepared for public in London, his [the author's] time was eaten up upon attendance upon the service of the parliament and city, for the supply of the poor of the city with wood (during the stop of coal at Newcastle, and the mutinies of the poor for firing. God is a most holy witness that these meditations were fitted for public view in charge of rooms and corners, yea, sometimes (upon occasion of travel in the country, concerning that business of fuel) in variety of strange houses, sometimes in the fields, in the midst of travel; where he hath been forced to gather and scatter his loose thoughts and papers." Two editions of the work are said to have been published in London, in 1644. Backus is undoubtedly right in supposing that Roger Williams brought the book with him upon his return from England with the charter of " Providence Plantations." See Narragansett Club, Vol. III, Preface, pp. iii., iv.—ED.

lished a reply in 1652, entitled, "The Bloody Tenet yet more bloody, by Mr. Cotton's Endeavor to wash it white."[1] The last two of these performances are now before me, and from thence I shall give the reader their own words upon the most material points of their dispute.[2]

First. Mr. Cotton's Memory failed him so much as that he represented that what he wrote in answer to the prisoner's arguments, was in a private letter to Mr. Williams, and upon that said:—

I wrote my conscience, in the sight of God, and the truth of God, according to my conscience; why should he punish me with open penance, and expose me (as much as in him lieth) before the world to open shame, as a man of blood, for the liberty of my conscience? How will it stand with his own principles, to plead for liberty of conscience and yet to punish it? Besides let him remember, if I did offend him with such an error, it was but a private offence, and the rule of the gospel required he should first have convinced and admonished me privately of it, and so have proceeded upon my contumacy, at length to have told the church, before he had published it to the world. C.,[3] p. 2.

Mr. Williams in his reply mentions Mr. Cotton's mistake about the one to whom he wrote the letter, and that he supposed his answer to the prisoner's arguments had been as public as his profession and practice was upon that tenet, and then says:—

But grant it had been a private letter, and the discourse and the opinion private; yet why doth he charge the discusser with breach of rule, in not

[1] "The Bloody Tenent yet more Bloody, by Mr. Cotton's endeavor to wash it white in the Blood of the Lamb; of whose precious Blood, spilt in the Blood of his Servants, and of the Blood of millions spilt in former and later wars for Conscience sake, that most Bloody Tenent of persecution for cause of Conscience, upon a second trial, is found now more apparently and more notoriously guilty."—ED.

[2] The following quotations have been verified from the reprint of Williams's work, Narragansett Club. Vol. III, and a copy of Cotton's work in the library of the American Antiquarian Society, Worcester. Many words and phrases were found to have been omitted. As it was the object of Backus simply to give a brief abstract of the arguments of the two writers, in their own words, it has not been thought needful to notice the omissions except in the few instances in which it is required in order that the full sense of the passages may appear. There are a few unimportant instances of verbal change, probably by error of transcription, which are indicated in brackets.—ED,

[3] Note, C. and W. in this account stand respectively for Cotton's and Williams's books abovesaid; the figures for the pages therein.

using orderly ways of admonition, and telling the church, when Master Cotton in this book blames the discusser for disclaiming communion with their church, and they also (after he was driven by banishment from civil habitation amongst them) had sent forth a bull of excommunication against him in his absence! Such practice the Lord Jesus and his first apostles or messengers never taught. .... I never heard that disputing, discoursing and examining men's tenets or doctrines by the word of God, was, in proper English, persecution for conscience. Well had it been for New England, that no servant of God, nor witness of Christ, could justly take up complaint for other kinds of persecution. W., pp. 4, 5.

The main point of all Mr. Cotton's washings is a denial of the charge of persecuting any for cause of conscience, and he says:—

I expressly profess, 1. That no man is to be persecuted at all, much less for conscience sake. 2. I profess further, that none is to be punished for conscience sake, though erroneous, unless his errors be fundamental, or seditiously and turbulently promoted, and that after due conviction of conscience; that it may appear, he is not punished for his conscience, but for sinning against his conscience. .... If this tenet have any appearance of blood in it, it is because it is washed in the blood of the Lamb, and sealed with his blood. And then though it may seem bloody to men of corrupt minds and destitute of the truth (as Paul seemed to such to be a pestilent fellow) yet to faithful and upright souls, such things as are washed in the blood of the Lamb, are wont to come forth white. C., p. 3.

In reply to this, Mr. Williams says:—

Is not this the guise and profession of all that ever persecuted or hunted men for their religion and conscience? Are not all histories and experiences full of the pathetical speeches of persecutors to this purpose? You will say you are persecuted for your conscience, you plead conscience, thou art a heretic, the devil hath deceived thee, thy conscience is deluded, &c. .... Time hath and will discover that such a blackamore cannot be washed in the blood of Christ himself, without repentance.

He goes on to observe, that the setting up of state religions has been the grand source of persecution in every age. W., pp. 6, 7. Against which he brought our Lord's parable of the tares of the field. Upon which Mr. Cotton said:—

It is true, Christ expoundeth the field to be the world, but he meant not the [wide] world, but (by a usual trope) the church scattered throughout the world. C., p. 41.

Mr. Williams says:—

It is no wonder to find Master Cotton so entangled, both in his answers and replies touching this parable; for men of all sorts in former ages have been so entangled before him. To which purpose I will relate a notable passage recorded by that excellent witness of God, Master Fox, in his book of Acts and Monuments. It is this: In the story of Mr. George Wisehart, in the days of King Henry VIII, there preached at the arraignment of said Wisehart one John Winryme, sub-prior of the abbey of St. Andrews; he discoursed on the parable of the tares; he interpreted the tares to be heretics; and yet contrary to this very Scripture, (as Mr. Fox observeth, though elsewhere himself maintains [maintaining] it the duty of the civil magistrate to suppress heretics) I say the said Winryme concludeth that heretics ought not to be let alone until the harvest, but to be suppressed by the power of the civil magistrate. So that both the popish prior and the [that] truly Christian Fox were entangled in contradictions to their own writings about this heavenly Scripture. W., p. 46.

To support the notion of calling the church the world, Mr. Cotton quoted some texts wherein the redeemed are so called. C., p. 43. In reply, Mr. Williams says:—

Grant that it hath pleased the Lord in his infinite wisdom to cause the term world to be used in various significations; yet let any instance be given of any Scripture, wherein the Lord opposing the church and world, wheat and tares, doth not distinguish between the church redeemed out of the world, and the world itself, which is said to lie in wickedness, and to be such as for which Jesus would not pray. John xvii. W., p. 56.

He further argued that sowing of the seed in four sorts of ground by Christ's messengers, he called the kingdom of heaven, which four sorts cannot be supposed to be of the church. Mr. Cotton answers:—1. That Christ preached himself to those four sorts of hearers, yet he was the minister of circumcision, and seldom preached to any but members of the church of Israel. C., p. 44. Reply:—

When they grew incurable, and received not the admonitions of the Lord, by the Lord Jesus and his servants preaching unto them, the Lord cast them out of his sight, destroyed that national church, and established the Christian church. W., p. 57.

But Cotton says:—

It is an error to say, the church consisteth of no more sorts of hearers but one, the honest and good ground; for if the children of church members be in the church, and of the church, till they give occasion of rejection, then they growing up to years, become some of them like the highway side, others like the stony, others like the thorny, as well as others like the honest and good ground. C., p. 44.

Mr. Williams replies:—

Admit the Christian church were constituted of the natural seed and offspring, (which yet Mr. Cotton knows will never be granted to him, and I believe will never be proved by him,) yet he knows, that upon the discovery of any such portion of ground in the church, the church is bound to admonish, and upon impenitency after admonition, to cast them into the world, the proper place of such kinds of hearers and professors. W., p. 57, 58.

Mr. Cotton adds:—

Is it not a main branch of their covenant with God, that as God giveth himself to be a God to them, and to their seed, so they should give up themselves and their seed to be his people? Besides hath not God given pastors and teachers, as well for the gathering together of the saints, as for the edification of the body of Christ? And hath he not given the church, and the gospel preached in the church, to lie like leaven in three pecks of meal till all be leavened? C., p. 44.

Mr. Williams says:—

I answer, the proper work of pastors and teachers is to feed the sheep in the flock, and not the herds of wild beasts in the world. And although it is the duty of parents to bring up their children in the nurture and fear of the Lord; yet what if those children refuse to frequent the assemblies of the church, and what if those three sorts of [bad] ground or hearers will not come within the bounds of the pastors' and teachers' feeding? Hath not the Lord Jesus appointed other officers in Eph. iv. for the gathering of the saints, that is, sending out of the church of Christ apostles or messengers, to preach Christ to the three sorts of bad ground, to labor to turn them into good ground? But alas! to salve up this, the civil sword is commonly run for, to force all sorts of ground to come to church, instead of sending forth the heavenly sowers according to the ordinance of Christ. W., p. 58.

Another argument Mr. Cotton draws from the servants wondering to see the tares, which would not have been strange in the highway. C., p. 45. In reply to which Mr. Williams says:—

Let the highway, stony and thorny ground, be considered in their several qualities of profaneness, stoutness, stoniness and worldliness, and all the sons of men throughout the world naturally are such ; and it is no wonder, nor would the servants of Christ be so troubled, as to desire their plucking up out of the world. But again consider all these sorts of men as professing the name and anointing of Christ Jesus, in a false, counterfeit antichristian way, and then it may well be wondered whence such monstrous Christians or anointed ones arose ; and God's people may easily be tempted rather to desire their rooting out of the world, than the rooting out of any such sorts of ground or men, professing any other religion, Jewish, Mahometan or Pagan. A traitor is worse than a professed fox. W., pp. 58, 59.

Again, while Mr. Cotton pleaded for the exertions of the civil power against heretics and antichristians, he says:—

No ordinance or law of God, nor just law of man, commandeth the rooting out of hypocrites, either by civil or church censure, though the church be bound to endeavor as much as in them lieth to heal their hypocrisy. C., p. 47.

To this Mr. Williams answers:—

Hypocrisy discovered in the fruit of it, is not to be let alone in the church or state ; for neither the church of Christ nor civil state can long continue safe, if hypocrites or traitors (under what pretence soever) be permitted to break forth in them, without due punishment and rooting out; this hypocrisy being especially the great sin against which Christ so frequently and so vehemently inveighed, and against which he denounced the sorest plagues and judgments. W., p. 62.

He then proceeded to plead, that the civil state should punish only civil offences. Upon which Mr. Cotton asks :—

What if their worship and consciences incite them to civil offences? C., p. 50.

Mr. Williams says:—

I answer, the conscience of the civil magistrate must incite him to civil punishment ; as a Lord Mayor of London once answered that he was born to be a judge, to a thief that pleaded he was born to be a thief. If the conscience of the worshippers of the beast incite them to prejudice prince or state, although these consciences be not as the conscience of the thief, commonly convinced of the evil of his fact, but persuaded of the lawfulness of their actions; yet so far as the civil state is endamaged or endangered, I say the sword of God in the hand of civil authority is strong enough to defend itself, either by imprisoning or disarming, or other wholesome means, while yet their consciences ought to be permitted in what is merely point of worship, as prayer and other services and administrations. Against any civil mischief the civil state is strongly guarded. Against the spiritual mischief, the church or city of Christ is guarded with heavenly armories, wherein there hang a thousand bucklers, Cant. iv. 4, and most mighty weapons. 2 Cor. x. W., pp. 66, 67.

But as he still pleaded that the civil sword was never appointed by Christ for an antidote or remedy in spiritual evils and dangers, Mr. Cotton denies it, and says:—

It is evident the civil sword was appointed for remedy in this case; Deut. xiii.[1] and appointed it was by that Angel of God's presence, whom God promised to send with his people. Exod. xxxiii., 2, 3. And that Angel was Christ, whom they tempted in the wilderness. 1 Cor. x. 9. Therefore it cannot truly be said, that the Lord Jesus never appointed the civil sword for a remedy in such a case: For he did expressly appoint it in the Old Testament; nor did he ever abrogate it in the New. The reason of the law (which is the life of the law) is of eternal force and equity in all ages. "Thou shalt surely kill him because he hath sought to thrust thee away from the Lord, thy God." This reason is moral, that is, of universal and perpetual equity to put to death any apostate, seducing idolator, or heretic.[2] C., pp. 66, 67.

In reply Mr. Williams says:—

How grievous is this language of Master Cotton! Moses in the Old Testament was Christ's servant, yet being but a servant, dispensed his power by carnal rites and ceremonies, laws, rewards and punishments, in that holy nation, and that one land of Canaan. But when Jesus the Son and Lord himself was come, to bring the truth, life and substance, of all those shadows; to break down the partition-wall between Jew and Gentile, and establish the Christian worship and kingdom in all nations of the

[1] This incident is older than any "Lord Mayor of London," and has suffered transformations which have little improved it. Ζήνων δοῦλον ἐπὶ κλοπῇ ἐμαστίγου. Τοῦ δὲ ειπόντος, Εἵμαρτό μοι κλέψαι. Καὶ δαρῆναι, ἔφη. "Zeno was scourging a slave for theft. Upon his saying 'It was fated that I should steal,' 'And that you should be skinned,' said Zeno. Diogenes Laertius.—Ed.

[2] Does not this and such like sentences make the tenet to appear *yet more bloody*.

world, Master Cotton will never prove, from any of the books and institutions of the New Testament, that unto those spiritual remedies appointed by Christ against spiritual maladies, he added the help of the carnal sword. If it appear, as evidently it doth, that Jesus, the antitype of the kings of Israel, wears his sword in his mouth, being a sharp and two-edged sword, then the answer is as clear as the sun, that scatters the clouds and darkness of the night. Besides, Master Cotton need not fly to the pope's argument for children baptism, to wit, to say Christ never abrogated Deut. xiii. therefore, &c., for Mr. Cotton knows the profession of the Lord Jesus, John xviii. that his kingdom was not earthly, and therefore his sword cannot be earthly. Mr. Cotton knows that Jesus commanded a sword to be put up, when it was drawn in the cause of Christ, and added a dreadful threatening, that all that take the sword (that is the carnal sword in his cause) shall perish by it. W., pp. 95, 96.

The reader may remember, that Mr. Williams was often blamed for holding that the civil magistrate's work was confined to the precepts of the second table. His main argument therefor was, that Rom. xiii. speaks the most fully of that subject of any place in the New Testament, and there the discourse is confined to the duties included in love to our neighbor. Mr. Cotton grants his premises, but not his conclusion, and says:—

Though subjection to magistrates, and love to all men, be duties which concern the second table, yet the inference will not follow, that therefore magistrates have nothing to do to punish any violation, no, not the weightiest duties of the first table. It is a clear case, among the duties of the second table people may be exhorted to honor their ministers, and children may be exhorted to honor their parents; but will it hence follow, that therefore ministers have nothing to do with matters of religion in the church, or parents in the family?" C., p. 96.

Mr. Williams answers:—

If people are bound to yield obedience to civil things to civil officers of the state, Christians are much more bound to yield obedience to the spiritual officers of Christ's kingdom; but how weak is this argument to prove, that therefore civil officers of the state are constituted rulers, preservers and reformers of the Christian and spiritual state, which differs as much from the civil, as the heavens are out of the reach of the [this] earthly globe? W., pp. 147, 148.

Mr. Cotton often recurs, through his book, to his notion of not punishing men for any matter of conscience, but only for sinning against their own consciences after conviction. One great article of Mr. Williams's sentence of banishment was, his writing letters against the rulers and churches before any conviction. And Mr. Cotton says of ministers and churches, "None of us had any further influence, than by private and public conviction of himself, and of the demerit of his way." C., 2d part, p.12. And when one of the magistrates was going to the Court that banished Mr. Williams, and asked Mr. Cotton what he thought of it? his answer was, "I pity the man, and have interceded for him, whilst there was any hope of doing good; but now he having refused to hear both his own church and us, and having rejected us all, as no churches of Christ, before any conviction, we have now no more to say in his behalf, nor hope to prevail for him." C., Part 2, p. 39.[1]

This notion of not punishing any in matters of religion, till they had first convinced their consciences, runs through Mr. Cotton's whole book, as those who have it may see in the quotations below;[2] and he tries to support it by Tit. iii.

---

[1] The charge in Roger Williams's sentence, "Whereas Mr. Roger Williams, one of the elders of the church at Salem, hath broached and divulged divers, new and dangerous opinions against the authority of magistrates, as also writ letters of defamation both of the magistrates and churches here, and that before any conviction, &c.," (see p. 131,) seems to mean that he had given public expression by word and letter to his opinions against the magistrates and churches, without affording them the opportunity of discoursing with him and convicting him of his errors. Cotton, as above represented, holds that no one should be punished for religious error, except he advance or adhere to the error *after conviction*, that is, after the error has been plainly set before him so that, in candor, he must admit it, and to cling to it longer will be a sin of obstinacy rather than of ignorance. There does not seem to be quite the inconsistency of Williams's sentence with Cotton's words, or of Cotton's words with each other in different parts of his book, that Backus represents, though it is not strange that he mistakes the ambiguous expressions. Williams is charged with expressing his opinions before any conviction, but he was not sentenced till after conviction, in their sense of the word, that is, till after the magistrates and ministers had disputed with him, and, in their view, "clearly confuted" him, and yet he persisted in adhering to his views and making them public. See pp. 51, 54.
—ED.

[2] Pp. 3, 26, 189; Second Part, pp. 12, 17, 32, 37, 39.

11, which refers entirely to ecclesiastical, and not to civil government; and there not to every error, but only to gross heresy, which was to be judged of by those who were well acquainted with spiritual things. But said Mr. Williams:—

Every lawful magistrate, whether succeeding or elected, is not only the minister of God, but the minister or servant of the people also (what people or nation soever they be, all the world over) and that minister or magistrate goes beyond his commission, who intermeddles with that which cannot be given him in commission from the people, unless Master Cotton can prove that all the people and inhabitants of all the nations in the world have spiritual power, Christ's power, naturally, fundamentally and originally residing in them, to rule Christ's spouse, the church, and to give spiritual power to their officers to exercise their spiritual laws and commands;[1] otherwise it is but profaning the holy name of the Most High. It is but flattering of magistrates, it is but the accursed trusting to an arm of flesh, to persuade rulers of the earth that they are kings of the Israel or church of God, who were in their institutions and government immediately from God, the rulers of his holy church and people. W., p. 96. Not a few of his opposites will say, and that aloud, that he and they were or might have been convinced, whatever he or they themselves thought. The truth is, the carnal sword is commonly the judge of the conviction or obstinacy of all supposed heretics.[2] Hence the faithful witnesses of Christ, Cranmer, Ridley, Latimer, had not a word to say in the disputations at Oxford. Hence the

---

[1] Those who are called lords spiritual in England have no power, since the pope excommunicated them, but what they derive from the civil state.

[2] Dr. Owen wrote a piece upon toleration soon after Mr. Cotton's book was published in London, and upon this point he says, "He that holds the truth may be confuted, but a man cannot be convinced but by the truth. That a man should be said to be convinced of a truth, and yet that truth not shine in upon his understanding, to the expelling of the contrary error, to me is strange. To be convinced is to be overpowered by the evidence of that, which before a man knew not. I once knew a scholar invited to a dispute with another man, about something in controversy in religion; in his own, and in the judgment of all the bystanders, the opposing person was utterly confuted. And yet the scholar, within a few months, was taught of God, and clearly convinced, that it was an error which he had maintained, and the truth which he opposed; and then, and not till then, did he cease to wonder, that the other person was not convinced by his strong arguments, as before he had thought. To say a man is convinced, when either for want of skill and ability, or the like, he cannot maintain his opinion against all men, is a mere conceit. That they are obstinate and pertinacious is a cheap supposal, taken up without the price of a proof. As the conviction is imposed, not owned, so is this obstinacy; if we may be judges of other men's obstinacy, all will be plain; but if ever they get uppermost, they will be judges of ours." Collection of Owen's Sermons and Tracts, 1721, p. 312.

nonconformists were cried out as obstinate men, abundantly convinced by the writings of Whitgift and others; and so in the conference before King James at Hampton Court. W., p. 192.

Mr. Williams in discussing his opponent's arguments observed, that his opponent had taken many charges and exhortations which Christ gave to his ministers, and directed them to the civil magistrate. But Mr. Cotton says, " The falsehood of the discussor in this charge is palpable and notorious." C., p. 88. Yet fifty pages forward in the same discourse Mr. Cotton says :—

> The good that is brought to princes and subjects by the due punishment of apostate seducers, idolaters and blasphemers, is manifold. First, it putteth away evil from the people, and cutteth off a gangrene, which would spread to further ungodliness. Deut. xiii. 5 ; 2 Tim. ii. 16, 17, 18. Secondly, it driveth away wolves from worrying and scattering the sheep of Christ. False teachers be wolves. Matt. vii. 15 ; Act. xx. 29. C., p. 137, 138.

This is a clear proof that great men cannot go straight in a crooked path.

Mr. Williams had argued that Mr. Cotton's doctrine tended to the setting up of a Spanish inquisition in all parts of the world, and to frustrate the great design of our Saviour's coming. He denies it, and accuses Mr. Williams of rather promoting the principal end of the Spanish inquisition, "by proclaiming impunity to all their whorish and wolvish emissaries. Nor is it," says he, " a frustrating of the sweet end of Christ's coming, which was to save souls, but rather a direct advancing of it, to destroy, if need be, the bodies of those wolves, who seek to destroy the souls of those for whom Christ died. C., p. 93.

Mr. Williams replies :—

> I cannot without great horror observe, what is this but to give a woful occasion, at least to all civil powers in the world, to persecute Christ in his poor saints and servants? Yea, if Master Cotton and his friends of his conscience should be cast by God's providence (whose wheels turn about in the depth of his councils wonderfully) I say should they be cast under the reach of opposite swords, will they not produce Master Cotton's own

bloody tenet and doctrine to warrant them (according to their consciences) to deal with him as a wolf, an idolater, a heretic, and as dangerous an emissary and seducer as any whom Master Cotton so accuseth [accounteth]? Master Cotton hath no reason to charge the discusser with indulgence or partiality towards Romish and wolvish emissaries; his judgment and practice is known so far different, that for departing too far from them (as is pretended) he suffers the brands and bears the marks of one of Christ's poor persecuted heretics to this day.[1] All that he pleaded for, is an impartial liberty to their consciences in worshipping God, as well as [to the] consciences and worships of other their fellow-subjects." W., pp. 141, 142.

This book Mr. Williams dedicated to the rulers of New England, wherein, after several useful remarks, he says:—

There is one commodity for the sake of which most of God's children in New England have run mighty hazards; a commodity marvellously scarce in former times, in our native country. It is the *liberty of searching after God's most holy mind and pleasure.* Of this most precious and invaluable jewel if you suffer Satan to bereave you, and that it shall be a crime humbly and peaceably to question even laws and statutes, or whatever is even publicly taught and delivered, you will find yourselves after all your long run (like that little Frenchman who killed the Duke of Guise, and was taken next morning near the place from whence he had fled upon a swift horse all night); I say you will most certainly find yourselves but where you were, enslaved and captivated in the chains of those popish darknesses, viz.: Ignorance is the mother of devotion, and, We must believe as the church believes, &c. O remember that your gifts are rare, your professions of religion rare, your persecutions and hidings from the storms abroad rare and wonderful![2] So in proportion your transgressions and public sins cannot but be of a rare and extraordinary guilt. Amongst the crying sins of our own or other sinful nations, those two are ever among the loudest, viz.: Invented devotions to the God of heaven; 2dly, Violence and oppression on the sons of men, especially of his sons, for dissenting. That the impartial and dreadful hand of the most holy and jealous God, a consuming fire, tear and burn not up at last the roots of these plantations, but graciously discerning [discovering] the plants which are not his, he may graciously sanctify and cause to flourish what his right hand will own, this is the humble and unfeigned desire and cry at the throne of grace, of you so long despised outcast; ROGER WILLIAMS." W., dedication, pp. 26, 27.

[1] One of the two points upon which the Massachusetts began their contention with him was his refusing to countenance the fellowship they had with popish corruptions in the church of England.

[2] Persecution drove them into this land, where they were hid from the bloody storm of intestine wars in England.

Thus I have laid before the reader some of the most material points of that controversy in their own words, that he may see what those principles were which New England writers have often reproached, under the name of rigid separation and anabaptism; and also how the ruling party with all their boast of orthodoxy, could confound Jewish types with Christ's institutions, in order to keep up pædobaptism, and the use of secular force in religious affairs; and could separate from the common rights of humanity, good Christians, and some of their own best friends, only for testifying against such confusion.

Mr. Hubbard says:—

At a General Court, March,[1] 1645, two petitioners were preferred, one for suspending (if not abolishing) a law made against Anabaptists the former year; the other was for easing a law of like nature made in Mrs. Hutchinson's time, forbidding the entertaining of any strangers, without license of two magistrates: which was not easily obtained in those days. .... Some at this time were much afraid of the increase of anabaptism. .... This was the reason why the greater part prevailed for the strict observation of the aforesaid [foresaid] laws, although peradventure [on some accounts] a little moderation as to some cases might have done very well, if not [much] better. .... Many books coming out of England in the year 1645, some in defence of anabaptism and other errors, and for liberty of conscience, as a shelter for a general toleration of all opinions, &c., others in maintenance of Presbyterian [Presbyterial] government (agreed upon by the assembly of divines at Westminster) against the Congressional way which was practiced in New England; the ministers of the churches through all the United Colonies agreed upon a meeting at Cambridge, where they conferred their counsels, and examined the writings which some of them had prepared, in answer to the said books; which being agreed upon and perfected, were sent over into England to be printed,

---

[1]Hubbard evidently mistook this date. In the Massachusetts Records it is October 18. The enactment is as follows:—" Upon a petition of divers persons for consideration of the law about new comers not staying above three weeks without license; and the law against Anabaptists, the Court hath voted that the laws mentioned should not be altered at all nor explained." The attempt to secure the repeal of the latter law seems to have continued. Under date of May 6, 1646, is the record:—" The petition of divers of Dorchester, Roxbury, &c., to the number of seventy-eight, for the continuance of such orders without abrogation or weakening as are in force against Anabaptists and other erroneous persons, whereby to hinder the spreading or divulging of their errors, is granted.—Ed.

viz.: Mr. Hooker's Survey, in answer to Mr. Rutherford; Mr. Mather, Mr. Allen and Mr. Shepard, [Mr. Mather's, Mr. Allen's, and Mr. Shepard's discourses] about the same subject, &c.[1]

Our friends in London, hearing of the law made at Boston last year to banish Baptists, and the learned Mr. John Tombes having written an examination of Mr. Stephen Marshall's sermon upon infant baptism, dedicated to the Westminster Assembly, Mr. Tombes was moved to send a copy of his examination to the ministers of New England, and wrote an epistle with it to them, dated from the Temple in London, May 25, 1645; hoping thereby to put them upon a more exact study of that controversy, and to allay their vehemency against the Baptists.[2] But the Westminster Assem-

---

[1] Hubbard, [413—415.]
[2] Crosby's history, Vol. I, pp. 121, 122.—B.

John Tombes was born at Bewdly, Worcestershire, in 1603. At the age of fourteen he was admitted at Magdalen Hall, Oxford, and at the age of twenty-one was made Catechetical Lecturer there. Six years later he entered the ministry, and was settled at Lemster and afterwards at Bristol. Driven from these places successively by the civil war, in 1643 he went to London. For several years he had questioned the scriptural authority of infant baptism and held that there was only one passage, I Cor. vii, 14, on which it could be defended. He had recently been led to yield this passage also, as affording it no support. Upon coming to London where he had greater advantages for investigation, he determined to examine the subject in the light of church history, and as the result of the examination, he was as fully convinced that infant baptism was without support from antiquity as from Scripture. At a meeting of ministers in London, he proposed the question, "What Scripture is there for infant baptism?" and avowed his own renunciation of the rite. The Westminster Assembly was then in session, with the declared object of reforming religion in England and Scotland, and had appointed a committee on infant baptism. Mr. Tombes drew up in Latin his arguments against it, and sent them to the chairman of the committee, asking that they would answer his objections or reform the practice of the churches on the point in question. After a delay of months, he learned that they gave the matter no consideration save to pass a vote of censure on any who should dispute upon it.

Mr. Tombes became pastor of Fenchurch, London, agreeing with the church that he would not preach against infant baptism, and that they should admit no one to preach in their pulpit in its favor. Here he published two treatises against infant baptism, one of which was his Examen of Mr. Marshall's sermon, and, as the result, he was dismissed from his church. He next assumed charge of a parish in Bewdly, his native town. While here, he was immersed upon profession of faith, and gathered a church of those who were in agreement with him. He still continued to act as minister of the parish, and because of his acknowledged learning and ability, and of services which he had rendered to the government, he was held in repute, was entrusted with important offices in the national church and enjoyed the friendship of leading men in the country notwithstanding his religious views and practice. Several times he held public disputes upon baptism, once with Richard Baxter, when, says Anthony Wood, "all scholars there and present, who knew the way of disputing and managing arguments, did conclude that Tombes got the better of Baxter by far." Many of his most distinguished contemporaries testify to

bly were more ready to learn severity from this country, than these were to learn lenity from any; for the Independents on December 4, 1645, presented a request to that Presbyterian Assembly, "that they might not be forced to communicate as members in those parishes where they dwell; but many have liberty to have congregations of such persons who give good testimonies of their godliness, and yet out of tenderness of conscience cannot communicate in their parishes;" but the Assembly returned a flat denial, and said, "This opened a gap for all sects to challenge such a liberty as their due; and that this liberty was denied by the churches of New England, and we have as just ground to deny it as they."[1]

Sir Henry Vane also, when his interest in Parliament was very great, wrote to Governor Winthrop in the following terms:—

HONORED SIR:—I received yours by your son, and was unwilling to let him return without telling you as much. The exercise and troubles which God is pleased to lay upon these kingdoms, and the inhabitants in them, teaches us patience and forbearance one with another in some measure, though there be difference in our opinions, which makes me hope that, from the experience here, it may also be derived to yourselves; lest while the

---

his great learning and talent. A catalogue of his writings gives the titles of twenty-six works, fourteen of which are against infant baptism.

The manuscript copy of his Examen of Mr. Marshall's sermon which was sent to New England, is now in the library of the American Antiquarian Society, Worcester. With it is the following letter:—

"To all the elders of the churches of Christ in New England and to each in particular by name; to the pastor and teacher of the church of God at Boston, these present:

REVEREND BRETHREN:—Understanding that there is some disquiet in your churches about pædobaptism, and being moved by some that honor you much in the Lord, and desire your comfortable account at the day of Christ, that I would yield that a copy of my Examen of Master Marshall his sermon of infant baptism might be transcribed to be sent to you; I have consented thereto, and do commend it to your examination, in like manner, as you may perceive by the reading of it, I did to Master Marshall, not doubting but that you will, as in God's presence, and accountable to Christ Jesus, weigh the thing; remembering that your Lord Jesus Christ, John vii, 24, "Judge not according to appearance but judge righteous judgment." To the blessings of him who is your God and our God, your Judge and our Judge, I leave you and the flock of God over which the Holy Ghost hath made you overseers, and rest.

Your brother and fellow-servant,

JOHN TOMBES.

From my study at the Temple in London, May 25th, 1645."

See Crosby, Vol. I, pp. 120—122, 278—297; Hague's Historical Discourse, pp. 152—155.—ED.

[1] Crosby's history, Vol. I, pp. 185, 186.

Congregational way amongst you is in its freedom and is backed with power, it teach its oppugners here to extirpate it and root it out, from its own principles and practice. I shall need say no more, knowing your son can acquaint you particularly with our affairs. Sir, I am your affectionate friend, and servant in Christ,

H. VANE.[1]

June 10, 1645.

Had not the notion of securing religion to their posterity, by infant baptism and the magistrates' power, strongly prepossessed their minds, how could they have resisted all these motives to lenity as they did? That they were under a very strong bias may be seen in three pieces which were written this year against the Baptists. One of them was by Mr. Cotton, who was so much afraid of having both sides of the argument examined, that he gives us neither the names of the authors he wrote against nor the titles of their works; only he owns them to be such as did not " deny magistrates, or predestination, nor original sin; nor maintain free will in conversion, nor apostacy from grace; but only deny the lawful use of baptism of children, because it wanteth a word of commandment and example from the Scripture." And he says:—

> I am bound in Christian love to believe, that they who yield so far, do it out of conscience, as following herein the example of the apostle, who professed himself, and his followers, We can do nothing against the truth, but for the truth. But yet I believe withal, that it is not out of love to the truth that Satan yielded so much to the truth, but rather out of another ground, and for a worse end. He knoweth the times that how, by the good and strong hand of God, they are set upon purity and reformation. And now to plead against the baptism of children upon any of those Arminian and popish grounds, which be so grossly ungracious as those above named, Satan knoweth and seeeth they would be utterly rejected.[2] He chooseth therefore rather to play small game, as they say, than to lose all. He now pleadeth no other argument in these stirring times of reformation than may be urged from a main principle of purity and reformation, viz., That no duty of God's worship, nor any ordinance of religion, is to be ad-

---

[1]Massachusetts History, Vol. III, p. 137.
[2]Here is an acknowledgment, that the Baptists of that day did not hold the errors charged upon them in the aforesaid law.

ministered in the church, but such as hath *just warrant from the word of God*. And by urging this argument against the baptism of children, Satan transformeth himself into an angel of light; and the spirit of error and profaneness into a minister of truth and righteousness. And so he hopeth to prevail, either with those men who do believe the lawful and holy use of children's baptism to renounce that principle, and so to renounce also all reformation brought in by it; or else, if they stick to that principle, then to renounce the baptism of children; and so the reformation begun will neither spread far, nor continue long. For if godly parents do withdraw their children from the covenant, and from the seal of the covenant, they do make void (as much as in them lieth) the covenant both to themselves, and to their children; and then will the Lord cut off such souls from his people. Gen. xvii. 14. And so the reformation, begun with a blessing, will end in a curse, and in a cutting separation either of parents or of children, or both, from the Lord and his people.[1]

About the same time a minister at Lynn wrote a volume against various Baptist authors; but before he came to any of their arguments he said:—

Ever since that word of old, "I will put enmity betwixt thee and the woman, and betwixt thy seed and her seed," Satan hath had a special spite at the seed of the church. Witness that act of Cain, who was therein of that evil one, in killing his brother Abel. Whence also that project of Satan, all the ways that may be, to lay foundations of corrupting, and in time ruining the seed of the church by unequal marriages, &c. Gen. vi. 1, 2; Neh. xiii. 23, 24. Whence also that act of his, in stirring up his instruments to deride little Isaac. Whence also that satanical practice of seeking to cut them off by Pharoah, Exod. i. [15—17]; by Edomites, Psalm cxxxvii. 8, 9; by Babylonians, Jer. ix. [21]; Syrians, Dan. i. 1—8; Herod, Matt. ii. [16—18,] &c.; or, if they be not cut off in such sort, yet to stir up persons under pretence of religion, to devote them unto the very devil, Jer. vii. 31, &c.; Ezek. xvi. 20, &c.; or if they live, yet to persuade to their detainment under an Egyptian estate, and exclusion from any church care or privilege. .... Who seeeth not how Satan doth seek by such suggestions to undermine the succession of the true religion, and of true visible churches, which have used to be continued in and by the church seed? And what is Satan's fetch to bring this about, but the old trick, to create, (as I may say) scruples in the hearts of God's people, knowing well that it is a taking wile first to bemist through such legerdemain the eyes of the mind, and then to spoil them of truth. It took with our grandmother Eve, and was the inlet of all error and evil. "*Hath God*

---

[1] Cotton's Grounds and Ends of Children's Baptism, printed in 1647, pp. 3, 4.

said it?" was the old serpentine insinuation to blind and buzzle, and so corrupt first the judgment in point of warrant of this or that practice. . . . . How many precious professors, to outward view at least, did at first entertain some scruples about the external interest of church members' children in the covenant, and initiatory seal of it, which now peremptorily censure the same as antichristian and human inventions? Let my advice be grateful to thee thus far, Christian reader, to take heed of unnecessary discourses and disputes with satanical suggestions, under what promising and plausible pretences soever they come. . . . . It is not the first age or time, that satanical suggestions, " *Thus it is written,*" and " *Thus saith the Lord,*" hath been propounded.[1]

The question has often been asked in our day, what do you think of our good fathers who held to infant baptism? How did they get along? Here you have an answer in their own words; and the famous Dr. Thomas Goodwin ushered these performances into the world with a recommendatory preface to each of them; and the sentiments and temper of them have evidently been handed down by tradition ever since. But I appeal to the conscience of every reader, whether he can find three worse things on earth, in the management of controversy, than, first, to secretly take the point disputed for truth without any proof; then, secondly, blending that error with known truths, to make artful addresses to the affections and passions of the audience, to prejudice their minds, before they hear a word that the respondent has to say; and, thirdly, if the respondent refuses to yield to such management, then to call in the secular arm to complete the argument? And were not these the methods that were then taken to support pædobaptism? The protestants' way of defending their cause against the papists was, "If that ye will prove that your ceremonies proceed from faith, and do please God, ye must prove that God in express words hath commanded them, or else shall you never prove that they proceed from faith, nor yet that they please

---

[1] Mr. Thomas Cobbet's Vindication of the Covenant and Church Estate of Children of Church Members, printed in London, 1643, preface, pp. 7—9. Mr. Tombes says Mr. Cotton wrote to him, that the piece he sent them was delivered to Mr. Cobbet answer.

God."[1] But when this argument was urged against infant baptism, Cotton without any proof asserts that " Satan transformeth himself into an angel of light." And the whole of the above-recited addresses to men's and women's passions, is evidently founded upon the supposition, that infant baptism is as infallibly required by God, as abstaining from the forbidden fruit was, or Abraham's circumcising his children. Having taken the very point which is disputed for truth, without any evidence, they blended that with many known facts recorded in Scripture, and thereupon rank the opposers of that point with the old serpent the devil and Satan, and with his instruments Cain, Pharoah, Herod, and other murderers; yea, with such as sacrifice their children to devils! This history contains abundant evidence of their adding the magistrate's sword to all these hard words, which were used in their prefaces before they came to any of the Baptists' arguments. When Mr. Cotton came to them, the first of them is, that in Christ's commission to his ministers, he ordered them first to teach or make disciples, and then to baptize them; and he says two arguments offer themselves for his way from hence:—

" 1. Such as be disciples, they are to be baptized; but the children of the faithful, they are disciples; therefore children of the faithful, they are to be baptized." To support this assertion he turns to Isaiah liv. 13, " All thy children shall be taught of God;" and says he, " If they be taught of God, then are they his disciples; for that is the meaning of the word. Disciples are taught or learnt of God."[2] This is true, and our Lord quotes this text to shew how the father draws souls to himself, and says upon it, "Every man[3] therefore that hath heard, and hath learned of the Father, cometh unto me," John vi. 45. Can we desire

[1] Knox's History of the Reformation, p. 104.
[2] Cotton's Grounds and Ends, pp. 5, 6.
[3] Note. Christ shows that the word " children" in that text means posterity; men that are taught.

a more exact and certain definition of the word disciple than we have here? Let conscience speak before him who will judge us all. Do you who practice in this disputed way, believe when you bring your infants to be sprinkled, that they *have heard and learned of the Father*, so as to *come unto Christ*? And do you bring them because they *are taught of God*? If they are not, they are *not disciples* according to the known meaning of the word.

Mr. Cotton frames his second argument from Exod. xii. 48, where God required every proselyte to have all his males circumcised, before he could come to the passover; upon which Cotton says:—

> If then our Lord's Supper come in the room of the passover, and our baptism in the room of circumcision, like as he that hath not circumcised his males, was accounted as one uncircumcised himself, and so to be debarred from the passover, so he who hath not baptized his children, is accounted of God as not baptized himself, and so to be debarred from the Lord's Supper. If therefore you forbid baptism to children, you evacuate the baptism of their parents, and so make the commandment of God, and the commission to the apostles, and the baptism of believers, of none effect.[1]

These are the two main arguments for infant baptism to this day; and they both hang upon the little word *if*, which I think is a very small pin to rest the weight of whole provinces and kingdoms upon. *If* infants are disciples by virtue of their parents' profession, then they are to be baptized; and if our baptism comes in the place of the circumcision of Jewish proselytes, then we cannot lawfully admit bringing our infants thereto. But what if this supposition should prove to be as contrary to truth as darkness is to light, will men persist in that way still? Abraham had no warrant to circumcise any but such as were either born in his house or bought with his money. The first order that was given for bringing in others by households was in the day that Israel came out of Egypt. Now as we make no pretence of being Abraham's natural posterity, nor of being bought with Jew-

---

[1] Cotton's Grounds and Ends, p. 11.

ish money, the argument all turns upon a supposal that Gentile believers ought to bring their households with them to baptism, as the said proselytes did theirs to circumcision. But I know not how words can express the contrary more plainly than God himself has done in this case; for he says his new covenant is not according to that he made with Israel on said day. Heb. viii. 8—11. Upon this men often assert that the ordinances differ, while the subjects are the same. But the text assures us expressly, that the main difference is in the subjects; that the subjects of the new covenant *all know God from the least to the greatest.* When this is mentioned, they would then turn it to the difference betwixt the outward administration and inward efficacy of the covenant; but that cannot be here intended, because that distinction was as real in Abraham's time as it is now, as the apostle shows in Rom. iv. 11; which text is often brought for a proof that the covenant is the same now as with Abraham. It does prove that the internal efficacy of divine institutions was the same upon believers then as now; only their faith was fixed on a future Messiah, ours on one already come. The difference then betwixt the two covenants we are speaking of, is not internal, but external. By divine institution a whole family and a whole nation were then taken into covenant; now none are added to the church by the Lord but believers who shall be saved. Acts ii. 41, 47. Professors who had not this character were "false brethren unawares brought in." Gal. ii. 4. Their being in was owing to men's imperfection, and not to God's institution; yet because the Baptists refused to yield to a practice they viewed to be not only without, but directly against divine institution, they were abused in the manner above described. And Mr. Cobbet concludes his discourse with a few inferences, in which he says:—

See the danger and detestableness of anabaptistical tenets, giving God and Christ (in part) the lie, vailing the glory of his preventing grace of covenant; Num. xiv. 18; .... condemning the judgment and practice of former churches, Jews and Gentiles. .... Whence that profane trick of some to turn their back upon the churches [when they sprinkled infants] as if all their persons, and prayers, and fellowship, were unclean? whence the styling of it antichristian? &c. What is this but to blaspheme the name and tabernacle and saints of God? Rev. xiii. [6.]

Thus the Baptists were accused by those noted authors of profaneness and blasphemy, only for their manifesting by word and gesture their dissent from infant sprinkling.

Mr. Nathaniel Ward, of Ipswich, (the Indian name of which was Agawam,) who, with Mr. Cotton, had often been improved by the Court in composing their law-book, published a tract this year under a fanciful title, which contains the following addresses to the Anabaptists:—

1. To entreat them to consider, what a high pitch of boldness it is, for a man to cut a principal ordinance out of the kingdom of God; if it be but to make a dislocation, which so far disgoods the ordinance, I fear it altogether unhallows it. To transplace or transtime a stated institution of Jesus Christ, without his direction, I think is to destroy it.[1] 2. What a cruelty it is, to divest children of that only external privilege which their Heavenly Father has bequeathed them, to interest them visibly in himself, his Son, his Spirit, his covenant of peace, and the tender bosom of their careful mother the church. 3. What an inhumanity it is, to deprive parents of that comfort they may take from the baptism of their infants dying in their childhood. 4. How unseasonably [unseasonable] and unkindly it is, to interturbe the state and church with their Amalakitish onsets, when they are in their extreme pangs of travail with their lives? 5. To take a thorough view of those who have perambled this by-path; being sometimes in the crowds of foreign *wederdropers*, i. e. Anabaptists, and prying into their inward frames with the best eyes I had, I could but observe those disguised guises in the generality of them. 1. A flat formality of spirit, without salt or savor in the spiritualities of Christ; as if their religion had begun and ended with their opinion. 2. A shallow slighting of such as dissent from them, appearing too often in their faces, speeches and carriages. 3. A feeble yet peremptory obstinacy. Seldom are any of them reclaimed.[2]

[1] How easily may this reasoning be retorted? Christ's institution, and the apostles' administration of baptism, were expressly to such as believed, gladly received the word, and should be saved; and those who professed such a faith, went into the water, and were buried in baptism; and according to this writer's doctrine, how does it destroy the ordinance to change it into sprinkling of infants?

[2] Simple Cobbler of Agawam, pp. 16, 17; Hubbard, [155.]

By these extracts the reader may see the temper and language of Pædobaptists in that day, and how much of the same has there been in later times? of charging us with cruelty, because we hold that no acts of men can interest children in the grace of God, before they are taught and believe his truth; and because we dare not place our hopes of infants' salvation upon the doings of ministers and churches, instead of the sovereign mercy of God in Jesus Christ, unto whom we would commit them by believing prayer, and if they live, we would use all gospel methods for their conversion, and obedience to all his commands. How much also have we seen of their assuming God's prerogative, in judging the hearts of such as yield not to their arguments?

As all the foregoing means were ineffectual, some of the ministers presented a bill to the General Court this year, for the calling a synod to settle these and other ecclesiastical affairs. "The magistrates passed the bill, but some of the deputies questioned the power of the Court, to require their churches to send their messengers to such a convention, as not being satisfied that any such power was given by Christ to the civil magistrates over the churches in such cases." This caused a debate the conclusion of which was, "that the ensuing synod should be convened by way of motion only to the churches, and not in words of command."[1] The order of it began thus:—

BOSTON, 15th 3d Month, 1646.

The right form of church government and discipline being agreed, part of the kingdom of Christ upon earth, therefore the establishing and settling thereof by the joint and public agreement and consent of churches, and by the sanction of civil authority, must needs greatly conduce to the honor and glory of our Lord Jesus Christ, and to the settling and safety of church and commonwealth, where such a duty is diligently attended and performed. Upon which they sent out their motion for said synod.

[1] Hubbard, [533, 534.]

To enforce this they say :—[1]

For [Through] want of the thing here spoken of, some differences of opinion and practice of one church from another do already appear amongst us; and others (if not timely prevented) are like speedily to ensue, and this not only in lesser things, but even in points of no small consequence and very material; to instance in no more but those about baptism, and the persons to be received thereto, in which one particular the apprehensions of many persons in the country are known not a little to differ; for whereas in most churches the ministers do baptize [only such children whose nearest parents, one or both of them, are settled members in full communion with one or other of these churches, there be some one who do baptize][2] the children if the grandfather or grandmother be set [such] members, though the immediate parents be not, and others, though for avoiding of difference of neighbor churches they do not [as] yet actually so practice, yet they do much incline thereto [as thinking more liberty and latitude in this point ought to be yielded than hath hitherto been done]. And many persons living in this country who have been members of the congregations in England, but are not found fit to be received at the Lord's table here, there be notwithstanding considerable persons in these churches who do think that children of these also, upon some conditions and terms, may and ought to be baptized. Likewise on the other side, there be some among us who do think that whatever be the state the parents, baptism ought not to be dispensed to any infants whatsoever; which various apprehensions being seconded with practices according thereto, as in part they already are, and are like to be more, must needs, if not timely remedied, beget such differences as will be displeasing to the Lord, and offensive to others, and dangerous to ourselves.

These were their reasons for calling the synod. The work assigned to them was to "discuss, dispute, and clear up by the word of God, such questions of church government, and discipline, in the things aforementioned, or any other as they shall think needful and meet, and to continue so doing, till they or the major part of them shall have

[1] The records mention two reasons besides those here given, for calling this synod:—that it is a time of peace, and therefore convenient for settling religious questions; and that divers friends in England have urged this good work.— ED.

[2] Backus evidently here committed an error which is one of the most frequent errors of transcription. The word "baptize" occurs twice near together, and he, misled by the recurrence, omitted the intervening words, and thus, as is shown by the words supplied, his statement in this clause is just the opposite of that of the document which he is copying.—ED.

agreed [and consented] upon one form of government and discipline, for the main and substantial parts thereof, as that which they judge agreeable to the holy Scriptures;" which when it was finished was to be presented to the General Court, " to the end that the same being found agreeable to the word of God, it may receive from the said General Court such approbation as is meet, that the Lord being thus acknowledged by church and state, to be our Judge, our Lawgiver, and [our] King, he may be graciously pleased still to save us, as hitherto he hath done.[1]

Here we may plainly see wherein their great mistake lay. They confounded the judgment that they formed upon the Scripture with the rule itself. Also the majority assumed the power of judging for the whole, and of punishing dissenters from their judgments, as breakers of God's law; a delusion that the world is not clear of to this day, though light and truth have gained much since that time.

We are told that opposition was made in some of the churches against sending to that synod, notwithstanding the moderate expressions in the Court's ordered for it. Mr. Hubbard says:—

> The principal men who raised the objections were some who lately came from England, where such a vast liberty was pleaded for, by all that rabble of men that went under the name of Independents, whether Anabaptists, Antinomians, Familists and Seekers, far beyond the moderate limits pleaded for by [the] Congregational divines in the assembly at Westminster, such as Dr. Goodwin, Mr. Nye, Mr. Burroughs, &c., who yet [it may be intending to double the Cape of Good Hope, then in view, as was thought,] tacked about further than they need to have done. A great part of the Parliament also, then in being inclined much that way, and had by their commissioners sent word to all the English plantations in the West Indies, and Summer Islands, that all men should enjoy their liberty of conscience; and had by their letters also intimated the same to those of New England. Some few of the church at [of] Boston adhered to these principles which made them stickle so much against the calling of the synod at that time; against which they raised a threefold objection. 1. That by a

[1] This request was also sent to the churches of Plymouth and Connecticut colonies. Massachusetts Records.

liberty already established among the laws of New England, the elders or ministers of the churches have [allowance or] liberty to assemble upon all occasions, without the compliance of the civil authority. 2. It was observed that this motion came originally from some of the [elders or] ministers, and not from the Court. 3. In the order was expressed, that what the major part of the assembly should agree upon should be presented to the Court for their confirmation.

To the first it was answered, that [the] said liberty was granted only for help in case of extremity, if in time to come either the civil authority should grow opposite to the churches, or neglect the care of them, and not with any intent to practice the same while the civil rulers were nursing fathers to the church.[1] To the second it was answered, it was not for the churches to enquire what or who gave the occasion; but if they thought fit to desire the churches to afford them help of council in any matter[s] which concerned religion and conscience it was the churches' duty to yield it to them; for as [so] far as it concerns their command or request, it is an ordinance of man, which all are to submit unto for the Lord's sake, without troubling themselves about the occasion or success. .... For the third, where the order speaks of the major part,

---

[1] Mr. Williams in discussing Mr. Cotton's arguments observed, that the higher powers in Rom. xiii. were strangers to God and true religion, from whence he argued, that for Paul to command subjection to such in spiritual causes would have been to put out the eye of faith, reason and sense, at once. [Bloody Tenet, p. 77.] To which Mr. Cotton answers, "The cases of religion wherein we allow civil magistrates to be judges, are so fundamental and palpable, that no magistrate studious of religion in the fear of God, but if he have any spiritual discerning, he cannot but judge of such gross corruptions as unsufferable in religion.... But [as] for such magistrates as are merely natural and pagan, though Christians be bound to subject themselves to them with patience; yet such magistrates ought to forbear the exercise of their power, either in protecting or punishing matters of religion, till they have learned so much knowledge of the truth, as may enable them to discern of things that differ." Tenet washed, pp. 101, 102. In reply to which Mr. Williams says, "O the miserable allowance which Master Cotton hath brought the kings and governors of the world unto! We allow them to judge in such fundamental, &c." ....The magistrates must wait at their gates for their poor allowance. They shall judge, and they shall not judge; they shall judge that which is gross and palable [and] enough to hold the people in slavery, and to force them to sacrifice to the priest's belly; but the more sublime and nicer mysteries they must not judge or touch but attend upon the tables of the priest's infallibility." Williams's Reply, p. 152. "If Christ Jesus have left such power with the civil rulers of the world, [kingdoms and counties, of or] for the establishing, governing, and reforming his church, what is become of his care and love, wisdom and faithfulness, since in all ages since he left the earth, for the general [beyond all exception] he hath left her destitute of such qualified princes and governors, and in the course of his providence furnished her with such, whom he knew would be [and all men find] as fit as wolves to protect and feed his sheep and people!" Ibid. p. 202.

it speaks in its own language, ... but it never intended thereby to restrain [or direct] the synod in the manner of their proceeding : nor to hinder them but that they might first acquaint the churches with their conclusions, and have their assent to them, before they did present them to the Court. . . . .

This matter was two Lord's days in agitation with the church in Boston, before they could be brought to any comfortable conclusion ; but on a lecture day intervening, Mr. Norton, teacher of the church at Ipswich, was procured to supply the place at Boston, where was a great audience ; and the subject then handled was, [suitable to the occasion, viz. :] Moses and Aaron kissing each other in the mount of God. . . . . On the next Lord's day, after much debate in Boston church, it was agreed by the vote of the major part, that the elders and three of the brethren should be sent [as messengers] to the synod.[1]

This account from one of their noted ministers, may give us considerable light about the actings of that day. He informs us that the synod did not meet till near winter, when after a session of fourteen days, they adjourned to June 8,[2] 1647 ; and that summer proving sickly,[3] they were forced to adjourn again. But on August 16, 1648, they met, and completed the Cambridge platform ; the last article of which says :—

"If any church, one or more, shall grow schismatical, rending itself from the communion of other churches, or shall walk incorrigibly or obstinately in any corrupt way of their own, contrary to the rule of the word ; in such case the magistrate [Josh. 22,] is to put forth his coercive power, as the matter shall require.[4]

This principle the Baptists and others felt the cruel effects of for many years after. A clause was also inserted at the end of their tenth chapter, that no church act can be consummated without the consent of both elders and brethren ; which implicitly gives ministers a power to negative the churches' acts, and which many in later times have contended for, though that would give them such a lordly power over the church, as chief judges in the state are not allowed to

---

[1] Hubbard, [534—536.]

[2] In the original edition this date is given erroneously, June 18.—ED.

[3] The celebrated Mr. Hooker, minister of Hartford, died July 7, 1647. Hubbard, 536, 537.—ED.

[4] Magnalia, B. 5, Vol. II, p. 203.—ED.

have in the executive courts of our nation. As to baptism, though the order for calling the synod asserted that most ministers do baptize the grandchildren of church members,[1] yet that assertion was so far from truth, that those who "labored much to have this principle declared and asserted in the platform," could not effect it because of " many worthy men."[2] Mr. Hooker had published his testimony, wherein he asserted " that children as children have no right to [not right unto] baptism, so that it belongs not to any predecessors either nearer or farther off removed from the next parents to give right of this privilege to their children."[3] Mr. Thomas Shepard, pastor of the church where this synod met, had also publicly asked what members every particular visible church ought to consist of? and answered, that " Christ being the head of every particular church, and it his body, hence none are to be members of the church but such as are members of Christ by faith." And though he observes that hypocrites do sometimes creep in, yet he says, "If they could have been known to be such, they ought to be kept out; and when they are known they are orderly to be cast out."[4] And there was still more regard paid to this first principle of the New England churches, than could consist with the admission of persons to bring their children to baptism, who were " not found fit " for the other ordinance.

It may be proper now to take a further view of the affairs of Mr. Gorton and his company. Upon their being released and banished, as I have related, they went to Rhode Island, and from thence over to Narragansett, where, on April 19, 1644, they procured a deed from the sachems, whereby they resigned themselves, people, lands, rights, inheritances, and possessions, over unto the protection and government of King Charles; and appointed Samuel Gorton, and others their

---

[1] See p 156, note 2.—ED.   [2] Magnalia, B. IV, p. 176.
[3] Survey of Church Discipline, part 3, pp. 12, 13.
[4] First Principles of the Oracles of God, pp. 25, 26. [Works of Thomas Shepard, Doctrinal Tract and Book Society, Boston, 1853, Vol. I, p. 350.]

agents, to carry the same to him. This was signed by Passicus, Canaunicus and Maxan, and witnessed by two Indians and three English. The loss of their great sachem Miantinomu lay very heavy upon their spirits. Hubbard says, he "was a very goodly personage, of tall stature, subtile and cunning in his contrivements."[1] In May came a letter to the rulers at Boston, signed by Canaunicus, though written by some of Gorton's company, to this effect, that they purposed to make war upon Uncas, in revenge of the death of Miantinomu and others of their people, and marvelled that the English should be against it; and that they had put themselves under the government and protection of the king of England, and so were become their fellow subjects, and therefore if any difference should fall between them, it ought to be referred to him; professing withal their willingness to continue all friendly correspondence with them. The General Court received another letter from Gorton and his company, to the like effect. "June 23, news came that the Narragansetts had killed six of Uncas's men and five women, and had sent two hands and a foot to Pumham, to engage him to join with them, but he chose to keep to Massachusetts."[2] Contentions increased so much the next year that an extraordinary meeting of the Commissioners of the United Colonies was called at Boston, on July 28, 1645, when they sent three messengers to the Narragansetts, who on their return brought a letter from Mr. Williams to the Commissioners, assuring them that " war would presently break forth, and that the Narragansett sachems had lately concluded a neutrality with Providence, and the towns on Aquedneck Island." Upon which they determined to raise an army of three hundred men, in the following proportion, viz.:—One hundred and ninety out of the Massachusetts, forty out of Plymouth, forty out of Connecticut, and thirty out of New Haven colonies. Forty were raised immediately, and sent away under the

[1]Hubbard, 446.—ED.
[2]Winthrop, [Vol. II, pp. 166, 167, 169]; Hubbard, [452, 453.]

command of Lieutenant Humphrey Atherton, to protect Uncas, till Captain Mason should meet him there with the western forces, who were then to proceed to meet the remainder of the forces from the eastward, in Narragansett, under the command of Edward Gibbons, Major General. After which Governor Winthrop informed the Commissioners, "that since Miantinomu's death the Narragansett sachems by messengers sent him a present, expressing their desire to keep peace with the English, but desiring to make war with Uncas for their sachem's death." The present was about the value of fifteen pounds in wampum, but he refused to receive it upon those terms. The Commissioners concluded to take the present into their hands, and thereupon sent Captain Harding and Mr. Wilbore to those sachems, who were to take Benedict Arnold with them, and inform them that their present was returned and not accepted, unless they would be at peace with Uncas as well as the English; but if said sachems would come with them to Boston, they should have liberty safely to come and return without molestation, to treat of peace, though deputies in their stead would not now do. The messengers returning brought back the present, and informed the Commissioners that they found not Benedict Arnold at Providence, and heard that he durst not adventure himself again amongst the Narragansett Indians without a sufficient guard. They also understood that Mr. Williams, sent for by the Narragansett sachems, was going thither, wherefore they acquainted him with their message, shewed him their instructions, and made use of him as an interpreter." He prevailed with Passicas and others to go to Boston, and moved the messengers to write and acquaint Captain Mason of the prospect there was of peace; which last article the Commissioners censured them for, as going beyond their instructions. The English demanded two thousand fathoms of wampum to pay the costs of this expedition, and for other damages; which the Indians were compelled to yield to, and to give hostages till it was paid; and so articles of peace were drawn up and signed between them. The Commissioners afterward drew up a formal declaration, to justify their proceedings in said war.[1]

The Indians were far from being easy under these things; and in August, 1648, about a thousand Indians from various parts were collected in Connecticut, with three hundred guns among them; and it was reported that they were hired by the Narragansetts to fight with Uncas. The magistrates of Hartford sent three horsemen to enquire what they designed, and to let them know that if they made war with him the English must defend him, upon which they dispersed. When the commissioners met at Plymouth the next month, they ordered four men to be sent to the Narragansetts, "with instructions how to treat with them, both concerning their hiring other Indians to war upon Uncas, and also about the tribute of wampum that was behind. Captain Atherton and Captain Prichard undertook the service, and going to Mr. Williams, they procured that the sachems should be sent for; but they, hearing that many horsemen were come to take them, shifted for themselves; Passicus fled to Rhode Island; but soon after they were, by Mr. Williams's means, delivered of their fears, and came to the messengers as they were desired, and denied their hiring the Mohawks to war against Uncas, though they owned that they had sent them a present.[2]

Gorton, Holden, and Greene, went to England to carry the Narragansett's surrender of themselves and lands, as well as their own complaints, to the king; but found him not able to help either himself or them. However, they published their case and a narrative of their sufferings, in 1645, under the title of "Simplicity's Defence against seven-headed Policy." They also applied themselves to the Commissioners whom the Parliament had appointed over the

[1] Records of the United Colonies. Massachusetts History, Vol. III, pp. 138—145.
[2] Canaunicus died a very old man, on June 4, 1648. Hubbard, [464.]

affairs of the plantations, and at length obtained from them the following letter to the authority in the Massachusetts colony, viz. :—

We being especially intrusted, by both houses of parliament with ordering the affairs and government of the English plantations in America, have some months since received a complaint from Mr. Gorton and Mr. Holden, in the name of themselves and divers other English, who have transported themselves into New England, and now are or lately were inhabitants of a tract of land called the Narragansett Bay; (a copy of which complaint the enclosed petition and narrative will represent unto your knowledge) we could not proceed [forthwith proceed] to a full hearing and determining [determination] of the matter, it not appearing unto us that you were acquainted with the particular charge, or that you had furnished any persons [person] with power to make defence in your behalf; nor could we conveniently respite some kind of resolution, without a great prejudice to the petitioners, who could have lain under much incouveniency if we had detained them from their families, till all the formalities and circumstances of proceeding (necessary at this distance) had regularly prepared the cause for a hearing. We shall therefore let you know in the first place, that our present resolution is not grounded upon an admittance of the truth of what is charged; we knowing well how much God hath honored your government, and believing that your spirit and affairs are acted by principles of justice, prudence and [of] zeal to God; and therefore cannot easily receive any evil impressions concerning your proceedings. In the next place you may take notice that we found the petitioners' aim and desire, in the result of it, was not so much a reparation of what was passed, as a settling their habitations for the future, under that government, by a charter of civil incorporation, which was heretofore granted them by ourselves. We find withal that the tract of land called the Narragansett Bay, concerning which the question is [has] arisen, was divers years since inhabited by those of Providence, Portsmouth and Newport, who are interested in the complaint; and that the same is wholly without the bounds of the Massachusetts patent granted by his Majesty. We have considered that they be English, that the forcing of them to find out new places of residence will be very chargeable, difficult and uncertain, and therefore, upon the whole matter, do pray and require you to permit and suffer the petitioners, and all the late inhabitants of Narragansett Bay, with their families, and such as shall hereafter join with them, freely and quietly to live and plant upon the Shawomet, and such other part [parts] of the said tract of land, within the bounds mentioned in our said charter, on which they have formerly planted and lived, without extending your jurisdiction to any part thereof, or otherwise disquieting them in their consciences or civil peace, or interrupting them in their professions, until such time as we shall have received your answer to their claim in point of title, and you shall thereupon have received our further order therein. And in case any others, since the petitioners' address to England, have taken possession of any part of the lands heretofore enjoyed by the petitioners, or any [of] their associates, you are to cause them that are newly possessed as aforesaid to be removed, that this order may be fully performed. And, till our further order, neither the petitioners are to enlarge their plantations, nor are any others to be suffered to intrude upon any part of the Narragansett Bay; and if they shall be found hereafter to abuse this favor, by any act tending to disturb your rights, we shall express a due sense thereof, so as to testify our care of your honorable [honored] protection and encouragement. In order to the effecting of this resolution we do also require, that you suffer the said Mr. Gorton, Mr. Holden, Mr. Greene, and their company, with their goods and necessaries, to pass through any part of that territory which is under your jurisdiction, toward the said tract of land, without molestation, they demeaning themselves civilly, any former sentence of expulsion [or] otherwise notwithstanding. We shall only add, that to these orders of ours we shall expect a conformity [conforming to], not only from [for] yourselves, but from all other governments and plantations in New England whom it [which they] may concern. And so commending you to God's gracious protection, we rest your loving friends.

From the Governor in Chief, loving Admiral, and Commissioners for foreign plantations, sitting at Westminster, 15 May, 1646.[1]

To our loving friends the Governor, Deputy Governor and Assistants of the Massachusetts plantations, in New England.

WARWICK, Governor and Admiral,
NORTHUMBERLAND,   JOHN HOLLAND,
NOTTINGHAM,   H. VANE,"[2] &c.

With this order and resolution Mr. Gorton and his friends returned to Boston, where they were in motion to apprehend them, till upon shewing the State's order they were permitted to return to Shawomet, which, in honor to their friend the Admiral, they called Warwick. Sundry of them lived there to old age, and were considerably improved in the government of the colony.

[1] In the printed Rhode Island Colony Records, this clause stands as follows:— "[Office of the] Chiefe Lo Adm'll and Comm'rs for foreign plantations, sitting at Westminster, 15 day of May, 1646.—ED.
[2] Providence Records.

As there was no particular form of government, nor appointment of officers in their charter, it took a length of time to settle upon a method that was agreeable to the majority of the inhabitants. Their first General Assembly met at Portsmouth on May 19, 1647, when Mr. John Coggshall was chosen President, Mr. Roger Williams Assistant for Providence, Mr. John Sanford for Portsmouth, Mr. William Coddington for Newport, and Mr. Randal Holden for Warwick. Mr. William Dyre was chosen Recorder. They agreed upon a body of laws, chiefly taken from the laws of England, with the addition of a few suited to their particular circumstances. They also ordered as follows:—

Forasmuch as Mr. Roger Williams had taken great pains, and expended much time, in [the] obtaining [of] the charter for this province, of our noble Lords and Governors, be it enacted and established, that in regard to his so great trouble, [travail] charges and good endeavors, we do freely give and grant unto the said Mr. Roger Williams an [one] hundred pounds, to be levied out of the three towns, viz.: fifty pounds out of Newport, thirty pounds out of Portsmouth, [and] twenty pounds out of Providence; which rate is to be levied and paid in by the last of November.

The form of Government which they came into was thus to elect a President and four Assistants, annually, who had executive power, were judges in the courts of law, and kept the peace. An Assembly of sx Commissioners, or Representatives from each town, made laws and ordered their general affairs; but their laws must be sent to every town, to be deliberately considered in their town meetings, from whence the clerk was to send an account of their votes to the General Recorder,[1] and if the majority of the towns approved the law, it was confirmed, if not, it was disannulled. The Assembly chose yearly a General Recorder and General Sergeant, which are only other names for a secretary and sheriff. In each town six persons were yearly chosen, who were called the Town-council, who had the powers of

---

[1] In May, 1660, they enacted that the return of their votes to the Recorder must be made in three months.

a court of probate, of granting licenses to inn keepers and retailers, and the care of the poor.

Persons of almost all sentiments and tempers had resorted to this new colony, and various contentions and parties had appeared, which were not easily composed and reconciled; but toward the obtaining of such a desirable end, the following covenant was drawn and signed at Providence, viz. :—

Considering the [that] great mercy afforded unto us, in this liberty thus to meet together, being denied to many of our countrymen in most parts, especially in our poor native country, now deploring their distressed condition in most sad and bloody calamities; that ingratitude and disacknowledgments for favors received, are just causes for the deprivation of them, together with [our] home divisions and home conspiracies, the ruination of families, towns and countries; [town and country]moreover, the many plots and present endeavors at home and abroad, not only to disturb our peace and liberties, but utterly to root up both root and branch of this our being; that government held [holds] forth through love, union and order, although by few in number and mean in condition, yet (by experience) hath withstood and overcome mighty opposers; and above all, the several [and] unexpected deliverances of this poor plantation, by that mighty Providence who is still able to deliver us, through love, union and order, therefore being sensible of these great and weighty premises, and now met together to consult about our peace and liberty, [liberties] whereby our families and posterity [posterities] may still enjoy these favors; and that we may publicly declare upon all the free discharge of all our consciences and duties, whereby it may appear upon record that we are not willfully opposite, nor careless and senseless, and thereby the means of our own and others ruin and destruction; and especially in testimony of our fidelity and cordial affection unto one another here present, that so there may be a current placable [peaceable] proceeding, we do faithfully and unanimously, by this our subscription, promise unto each other to keep unto these ensuing particulars:—
First, that the foundation in love may appear among us, what causes of difference have heretofore been given either by word [s] or misbehavior, in public or private, concerning particular or general affairs, by any of us here present, not to mention or repeat them in the assembly, but that love shall cover the multitude of them in the grave of oblivion. Secondly, that union may proceed from love, we do promise to keep constant unto those several engagements made by us, both unto our town and colony, and that to the uttermost of our powers and abilities to maintain our lawful rights and privileges, and to uphold the government of this plantation. Also that love may appear in union, we desire to abandon all causeless fears and jeal-

ousies of one another, self-seeking [s] and striving [s] one against another, only aiming at the general and particular peace and union of this town and colony. Lastly, for our more orderly proceeding in this Assembly, whereby love, [peace] and union may appear in order, if in our consultations differences in judgment shall arise, then moderately in order, through argumentation, to agitate the same; considering the cause how far it may be hurtful, or conducing unto our union, peace and liberty, [liberties] and accordingly act, not after the will or person of any, but unto the justice and [or] righteousness of the cause. Again, if [in case] such cause [s] shall be presented wherein such difficulties shall appear, that evident arguments cannot be given for present satisfaction, but that either town or colony or both shall suffer, then to take into our consideration a speech of a beloved friend, " Better to suffer an inconvenience than a mischief," better to suspend with a loss which may be inconvenient, than to be totally disunited and bereaved of all rights and liberties, which will be a mischief indeed. Moreover that offences and distractions may be prevented, that so the current of business [disturbances] may peaceably proceed in this Assembly, we do faithfully promise to carry ourselves, in words and behavior, so moderately and orderly as the cause shall permit, and if [in case or] any of us shall fly out in provoking, scurrilous [or] exorbitant speeches, and [or] unsuitable behavior, that he or they so doing shall be publicly declared, branded and noted upon record to be a covenant violator, and disturber of the union, peace, and liberrty [liberties] of this plantation. We do here subscribe without partiality. Dated December, 1647.

ROBERT WILLIAMS,   ROGER WILLIAMS,
JOHN SMITH,   HUGH BEWIT,
WILLIAM WICKENDEN,   JOHN FIELD,[1]
THOMAS HOPKINS,   WILLIAM HAWKINS.

This preferring of the public good to private interest or inclination, Mr. Williams discovered as much of, through his life, as perhaps any man has done in latter ages; but alas! he had to do with many who were not of this disposition.

In their General Assembly at Providence, May 16, 1648, Mr. Coddington was elected President, and Jeremiah Clarke, Roger Williams, William Baulston, and John Smith, Assistants; Philip Sherman, Recorder, and Alexander Partridge,

---

[1] The original edition reads "John Tripp," instead of John Field. The error has been corrected from the Rhode Island Colonial Records. The person here referred to is undoubtedly the John Field mentioned on page 74.—ED.

General Sergeant; but Mr. Coddington absented himself, Mr. Dyre, the late recorder, having exhibited divers bills of complaint against him, and he did " not attend this Court for the clearing of the accusations charged upon him;" upon which the Assembly passed an act that in such a case the Assistant of the town where the President lived should supply his place"[1]

Mr. Coddington wrote to Governor Winthrop the 25th of the same month:—

> Mr. Baulstone, and some others of this island, are in disgrace with the people in Providence, Warwick, and Gorton's adherents on the island, for that we will not interpose or meddle at all in their quarrels with the Massachusetts, and the rest of the colonies; and do much fear that Gorton will be a thorn in their [and our] sides, if the Lord prevent not.[2]

And when the Commissioners of the United Colonies met in September this year, he and Captain Partridge went to them and said:—

> Our request and motion is in the behalf our island, that we the islanders of Rhode Island may be received into a combination with all the United Colonies of New England, into a firm and perpetual league of friendship and amity, for [of] offence and defence, mutual advice and succor, upon all just occasions, for our mutual safety and welfare, and for preserving of peace amongst ourselves, and preventing as much as may be, all occasions of war or [and] differences, and to this our motion we have the consent of the major part of our island.
> WILLIAM CODDINGTON,
> ALEXANDER PARTRIDGE.[3]

Thus, under a pretence of promoting peace, they would have separated the island from the rest of that little colony. However the Commissioners were not willing to own them as a distinct colony, but would have the island to be included in Plymouth patent, and if the majority of its inhabitants would acknowledge themselves to be under that jurisdiction,

---

[1] All the articles from Mr. Gorton's return till now are taken from the colony and Providence town records, compared with Mr. Callender and others.
[2] Hutchinson's Collection, p. 225.—ED.
[3] Ibid, p. 226.—ED.

and their principles have now had a very extensive spread in those parts. Thus Mrs. Scammon's bread, cast upon the water, seems to have been found after many days; the books that she freely dispersed being picked up, and made useful to many. Neither did the writings of learned ministers against the Baptists, weaken their cause, but strengthen it, as what follows will shew.

Mr. Moses Mather, of Stamford, in his first piece upon the covenant, published in 1769, owns ingenuously, that the covenant of circumcision, in Gen. xvii. was not, strictly speaking, the covenant of grace, but a divine institution whereby that nation was taken into visible covenant with God; and that the ordinances of that church were appointed as means for the regeneration as well as comfort and strengthening of its members. And he labors hard to prove that the covenant is the same with the Christian church; and that the Lord's Supper is " a converting ordinance." And to those who hold that persons ought to profess saving faith, in order to come to full communion, he says, " This scheme makes infant baptism a mere nullity, or thing of naught. To me this conclusion appears just and unavoidable."[1] Mr. Ebenezer Farris, of Stamford, was roused hereby to such an examination of the subject, as not only brought him to embrace believers' baptism, but also to publish a defence of that doctrine at New York. And he and others called Elder Gano from thence to baptize them in 1770; and in 1773 a Baptist church was constituted at Stamford, and another at Greenwich, ten miles nearer to New York. At the same time, the increase of the Baptists in Boston (above sixty members being added to the First Baptist church there) caused a great uneasiness among other ministers, and Dr. Chauncy published five sermons in 1772, to persuade people that it was their indispensable duty to come up to full communion in their churches. And after laboring hard to

[1] Discourse, pp. 17, 54, 57.

swords, is cruel and merciless; to trouble the state and lords of England, is most unreasonable, most chargeable; to trouble our neighbors of other colonies, seems neither safe nor honorable. Methinks, dear friends, the colony now looks with the torn face of two parties, and that the greater number of Portsmouth, with other loving friends adhering to them, appear as one grieved party; the other three towns, or greater part of them, appear to be another. Let each party choose and nominate three; Portsmouth and friends adhering three, the other party three, one out of each town. Let authority be given to them to examine every public difference, grievance and obstruction of justice, peace and common safety. Let them, by one final sentence of all or the greater part of them, end all, and set the whole into an unanimous posture and order, and let them set a censure upon any that shall oppose their sentence. One log, without your gentle help, I cannot stir. It is this. How shall the minds of the towns be known? How shall the persons chosen be called? time and place appointed in any expedition? For myself I can thankfully embrace the help of Mr. Coddington or Mr. Clarke, joined or apart, but how many are there who will attend (as our distempers are) to neither! It is, gentlemen, in the power of the body to require the help of any of her members, and both king and parliament plead, that in extraordinary cases they have been forced to extraordinary ways for common safety. Let me be friendly construed, if (for expedition,) I am bold to be too forward in this service, and to say, that if within twenty days of the date hereof, you please to send to my house, at Providence, the name of him whom you please to nominate, at your desire I will acquaint all the persons chosen with place and time, unto which in your name I shall desire their meeting within ten days, or thereabouts, after the receipt of your letter. I am your mournful and unworthy ROGER WILLIAMS.[1]

This address had such effect, that Mr. Williams was received to act as President of the colony, till their election at Warwick, May 22, 1649, when Mr. John Smith was chosen President, and Thomas Olney, John Sanford, John Clarke, and Samuel Gorton, Assistants; Philip Sherman, Recorder; Richard Knight, Sergeant, and John Clarke, Treasurer. Mr. Williams was chosen " to take a view of the records delivered into the Court by Mr. William Dyre." And they made a law that if a President should be elected, and should refuse to serve, he should be fined ten pounds; and if an Assistant refused, five pounds. Also it was " ordered that a

[1] Providence Records.

messenger be sent to Pumham and the other sachems, to require them to come to this Court; and that letters be sent to Benedict Arnold and his father, and the rest of Pawtuxet, about their subjecting to this colony." Mr. Dyre again presented his complaints against Mr. Coddington, but they were deferred.

At the Assembly at Newport, May 23, 1650, a fresh order was sent to the towns, to collect and pay what they owed to Mr. Williams for the charter, within twenty days. William Arnold and William Carpenter, instead of submitting to the government of their own colony, went again and entered complaints against some of their neighbors to the Massachusetts rulers, and they sent a citation to them to come and answer the same in their courts, dated from Boston, June 20, 1650, signed by Edward Rawson, secretary.[1] Such obstructors of good government were they who have made a great noise in the world about the disorders of Rhode Island colony! In 1651, Mr. Coddington caused a terrible difficulty among them, as will be seen in its place, though another affair must be attended to first.

[1] Providence Records.

CHAPTER IV.

AN ACCOUNT OF MR. CLARKE AND MR. HOLMES, AND OF THEIR SUFFERINGS AT BOSTON IN 1651.

It has already been seen that Mr. John Clarke was a principal instrument in procuring Rhode Island for a people who were persecuted elsewhere, and that he was the first religious minister on the island, and serviceable also in their civil government; yet all this did not prevent his being most abusively treated this year in Boston, with two other members of his church.

The best account of Mr. Obadiah Holmes that I have seen, is in a manuscript which he left to his children, that a gentleman of his posterity has favored me with, an extract of which I will give in his own words. Says he:—

First, I must remember my honored parents, who were faithful in their generation, and of good report among men, and brought up their children tenderly and honorably. Three sons they brought up at the university in Oxford; but the most of their care was to inform and instruct them in the fear of the Lord; and to that end gave them much good counsel, carrying them often before the Lord by earnest prayer; but I, the most rebellious of all, did neither hearken to counsel nor any instruction, for from a child I minded nothing but folly and vanity, and as years did grow on, and wisdom should have taken place, then the wisdom I had was wise to do evil, but to do well had no knowledge. .... As days and strength increased, even so did my transgressions, so that I became hardened in sin, not only to be drawn into it by others, but was as forward to draw others into evil as my fellows, ... being come to that height of wickedness that I did think it best when I could do the most wickedness, and began to think that it was but a foolish thing to talk of God, that should bring man to judgment; .... continuing in such a course for four or five years, and then began to bethink what counsel my dear parents had given me, many a time with tears and prayers; my rebellion to my honored parents then looked me in open face, and my dear mother being sick, it struck to me my disobedient acts, which forced me to confess the same to her. After this I began to go to hear the Word preached, but every word was against me, and left me without hope of mercy; and sometimes passing over a field called the Twenty Acres, stood still and said, Oh! that I might lie in hell but so many years as here are grass! It would have an end. .... That word was ever before me, "The wicked shall be turned to hell;" "Where the worm dieth not," &c. And yet at this time Satan tells me, It is best to put such thoughts out of mind, and take pleasure while thou art here, and return to thy former merry companions. and friends; which I did for a time; but the worm in the conscience did still gnaw. I went to hear the most noted men I could, but found it still against me; yet often heard them say, I must repent and be humbled, and must pray, and then should find mercy; but must confess sins and forsake them; which brought me to a resolution, in the most public way or company I could find, ever so to do; and had done it through ignorance, had not a friend advised me to the contrary, and that upon good grounds. But he also put me upon prayer and hearing. I then fell to prayer and duties, but found no rest or quiet in my soul; for then Satan let fly at me, and told me, it was too late to return, for there was no hope for me. I answered him, and did instance several of my wicked companions God had shown mercy unto a little before. He answered, Remember thou scorned, mocked and derided them; yea saying the devil was in them, they were all mad, and become fools; and withal he told me I had read and heard that there was a sin that never could be forgiven, the which sin I had committed. With this assault he fooled me a long time, even my life was a burden to me. Oh! the knives, ropes, trees, coal pits, can witness the many escapes of them, as one in a most undone, desperate condition, as one appointed to eternal destruction. The perplexity of mind brought me to great weakness in body, and yet for ease and comfort I turned over every stone, hearkened to all my acquaintance and friends, as to leave off my old ways, and all my old companions, which I had done before; but all this while I never considered sin according to the true nature of it, as being loathsome to the Lord, but as it brought judgment upon me; yet was I fearful to sin, and began to love to read the Scriptures, and frequent prayer and other duties, and took delight among professors that were of the strictest sort, easily seeing the gross evil and danger of the formal ministers and professors, and so that conformity was only superstition and a name. Yet for all that I had no rest in my soul, though I was in a manner as strict as any. As I was enlarged in sorrow for sin, deep in humiliation, enlarged in prayer, or filled with tears, my comfort came in and increased; but as I failed in them, so my sorrows renewed; and when I looked over my best performances found them full of sin. Oh! then the fears, doubts and questioning of my own estate! I judged it was all done in hypocrisy, which sin my soul did then abhor. In this sad and doubtful state I continued very long, yea many years. And although I could speak comfortably to others, yet had often much disquiet within my soul; my comforts were according to my enlargements. Not long after this there was in me a great love to the Lord; but alas! I was deceived by my own heart, and the ministers who told me there must be such and such a love to him, as to keep to him [me] in duty, and to part with all for him, but they left me short of understanding him as I should, and my selfish heart was willing to love him or part with all for him, yea my dear honored father, brethren and friends, house and lands, and my own native country, for time, and to avoid those popish relics of the bishops, and that filthy rabble, and to separate from them, and all those that mention them: and was fully known in my own country, and adventured the danger of the seas to come to New England, where I tried all things in several churches, and for a time thought I had made a good choice or change; but in truth it little differed from former times, and my spirit was like a wave tossed up and down, as not yet come to dig so deep as I should, or to consider the only ground of a well grounded hope, which God at last brought me to consider, which is, His own love to poor lost man, which first was in his own secret council and purpose before man was, and revealed to man in his time; and that there is no preparative necessary to obtain Christ, nor any thing to deserve that love, or to merit the same. And nothing could stay or satisfy my soul till I came to consider why, when and upon whom he laid sin and transgression, namely, on the Lord, and on him alone. And looking at me when a rebel, an enemy, yea dead in sin and trespasses, yea in my blood, he then said, Live, through the blood of Christ be cleansed, and in him be loved, for his own love to poor man, and that the election may obtain it, for he knows who are his; but good will is manifested before they have done either good or evil, so that neither good foreseen shall prevail, nor evil original or actual shall hinder, but that free grace may have its free course; but manifested when he giveth faith to believe the promise of the Father in giving a full discharge to the soul, by taking full satisfaction from his only Son, who became sin for us, who knew no sin, that we might be made the righteousness of God through him; and so remission and free pardon is granted forth, that whosoever believes in him shall not perish, but have everlasting life; and all those that so come to him he will no ways cast away. And when God had given me to see in any measure this love of his, then and not till then could I give over working for life, and to live in working. But at last he caused me to say, that *from* life I must work, and then all my former turnings and re-turnings must come to nought, yea all my righteousness as filthy rags, and to account all as dung, so I might obtain Christ, or rather that I might be accepted by him; and so removed me from the covenant of works to the covenant of grace, even that new covenant of life alone by himself, who paid so dear a price, as to lay down his own blood to wash, cleanse and purify the soul, and to redeem both soul and body to serve the Lord; and that is now the life I live by faith in the Son of God; and this faith causes works of faith, or rather fruits that flow from that root, so that now love hath constrained me to yield myself to live to him, as to a King to rule me by his holy laws and commandments, and as to an only Prophet to teach and instruct me, both to know and to do his holy will, and as my only Chief Priest to offer a sacrifice for me, which he did even for all, whereby my poor imperfect prayers and all other services became accepted of the Father; and this love, shed abroad in my heart, wrought in me a restless desire to know his will, that I might shew forth the praises and glory of him, that had called me by his grace.

As the sentiments of the ancient Baptists in this country have been grossly misrepresented, and as Mr. Holmes was no small sufferer in that cause, I thought it expedient to let the reader thus far hear him speak for himself, and tell his own experience and ideas about the nature of true religion. When he first came to this land he joined with the church in Salem, with whom he walked six or seven years; and then about the year 1645 was dismissed to the Congregational church in Seaconck (Rehoboth) newly settled there, under the ministry of Mr. Samuel Newman. He continued in that relation about four years, till an unrighteous act, as he judged, of the minister and part of the church, for which they would not give satisfaction, caused Mr. Holmes and several more to withdraw, and set up a meeting by themselves. And being convinced that the Baptists' way was right, a number of them were baptized, I suppose by the aforesaid Mr. Clarke, for they joined to his church. After this Mr. Newman pronounced a sentence of ex-communication against Mr. Holmes, upon which he and two more were presented to the General Court at Plymouth, June 4, 1650, where they met with four petitions against them, one from their own town with thirty-five hands to it, one from the church at Taunton, one from all the ministers but two in Plymouth colony, and a fourth from the Court at Boston, under their secretary's hand, urging Plymouth rulers to suppress them speedily.[1]

Here we may observe the great difference between our Plymouth fathers, and the Massachusetts. With all these stimulants to severity, the Court of Plymouth only charged them to desist from their practice, which others had taken such offence at, and one of them yielding thereto, the others, viz., Obadiah Holmes and Joseph Tory, were bound over to the next October Court, but were not so much as bound to their good behavior, nor any other sureties required, only they were bound " one for another in the sum of ten pounds apiece," for their appearance at said Court.

At a General Court holden at New Plymouth the second of October, 1650, before William Bradford, gentleman, Governor, Thomas Prince, William Collyare, Captain Miles Standish, Timothy Hetherly, William Thomas, John Alden, gentlemen, Assistants, [and a House of Deputies.]

PRESENTMENT BY THE GRAND INQUEST.

OCTOBER 2d, 1650.

Wee whose names are heer underwritten, being the grand inquest, doe present to this Court John Hazell, Mr. Edward Smith and his wife, Obadiah Holmes, Joseph Tory and his wife, and the wife of James Mann, William Deuell and his wife, of the towne of Rehoboth, for the continuing of a meeting uppon the Lord's-day from house to house, contrary to the order of this Court, enacted June 12, 1650.

THOMAS ROBINSON,
HENRY TOMSON, [&c., to the number of 14.[2]]

This is an exact copy of their presentment, but no sentence appears upon record against them. How different is

---

[1] Clarke's Narratives, pp. 18, 25, [46, 53, 54.] Plymouth Records.—B.

The figures in brackets appended to the references to Clarke's Narrative on this page and those that follow, refer to Massachusetts Historical Society, fourth series, Vol. II, where the Narrative is published.—ED.

[2] Plymouth Records.—B.

In the published Records the second of these names is Henry Sampson.—ED.

this from the actings of Boston Court the next year![1] For on July 19, 1651, Messrs. Clarke, Holmes and Crandal, "being the representatives of the church in Newport, upon the request of William Witter, of Lynn, arrived there, he being a brother in the church, who, by reason of his advanced age, could not undertake so great a journey as to visit the church."[2] He lived about two miles out of town, and the next being the Lord's day they concluded to spend it in religious worship at his house. Mr. Clarke says:—

> Finding by sad experience, that the hour of temptation spoken of was coming upon all the world (in a more eminent way) to try them that are upon the earth, I fell upon the consideration of that [word of] promise, made to those that keep the word of his patience, which present thoughts, while in conscience toward God, and good will unto his saints, I was imparting to my companions in the house where I lodged, and to four or five strangers that came in unexpected after I had begun, opening and proving what is meant by the hour of temptation, what by the word of his patience, and their keeping it, and how he that hath the key of David (being the promiser) will keep those that keep the word of his patience from the hour of temptation; while, I say, I was yet speaking, there comes into the house where we were two constables, who, with their clamorous tongues, made an interruption in my discourse, and more uncivilly disturbed us than the pursuivants of the old English bishops were wont to do, telling us that they were come with authority from the magistrate to apprehend us. I then desired to see the authority by which they thus proceeded, whereupon they plucked forth their warrant, and one of them with a trembling hand (as conscious he might have been better employed) read it to us; the substance whereof was as followeth:—
>
> "By virtue hereof, you are required to go to the house of William Witter, and so to search from house to house, for certain erroneous persons, being strangers, and them to apprehend, and in safe custody to keep, and to-morrow morning by eight o'clock [of the clock] to bring before me,
>
> ROBERT BRIDGES."

---

[1] Mr. Hazel wrote to his cousin Hubbard, of Newport, June 23, 1651, that they were then threatened with a fine of ten shillings a day for every person who set up any other meeting, and that their absence from the town meeting the day before should prove costly. Samuel Hubbard's Manuscript. Mr. Hazel died soon after, near Boston. The rest of them moved to Newport, where I find that Edward Smith, Joseph Torry, James Man and William Deuell, were admitted freemen, May 17, 1653. Smith was afterward a magistrate, and Torry many years Secretary of the colony, as well as a teacher in Mr. Clarke's church, in which Mr. Holmes also ministered for many years.

[2] Newport church papers.

When he had read the warrant, I told them, Friends, there shall not be, I trust, the least appearance of a resisting of that authority by which you come unto us; yet I tell you, that by virtue hereof you are not so strictly tied, but if you please you may suffer us to make an end of what we have begun, so may you be witnesses either to or against the faith and order which we hold. To which they answered they could not; then said we, Notwithstanding the warrant, or anything therein contained, you may..... They apprehended us, and carried us away to the ale-house or ordinary, where at [after] dinner one of them said unto us, Gentlemen, if you be free I will carry you to the meeting; to whom it was replied, Friend, had we been free thereunto we had prevented all this, nevertheless we are in thy hand; and if thou wilt carry us to the meeting, thither will we go; to which he answered, Then will I carry you to the meeting; to this we replied, If thou forcest us unto your assembly, then shall we be constrained to declare ourselves, that we cannot hold communion with them. The constable answered, that is nothing to me; I have not power to command you to speak when you come there, or to be silent. To this I again replied, [Friend, know a little further;] since we have heard the word of salvation by Jesus Christ, we have been taught, as those that first trusted in Christ, to be obedient unto him both by word and deed; wherefore if we be forced to your meeting, we shall declare our dissent from you both by word and gesture. After all this, when he had consulted with the man of the house, he told us he would carry us to the meeting; so to their meeting we were brought, while they were at their prayers, and uncovered; and at my first stepping over the threshold I unveiled myself, civily saluted them, and turned into the seat I was appointed to, put on my hat again, and sat down, open my book, and fell to reading. [Hereupon] Mr. Bridges being troubled, commanded the constable to pluck off our hats, which he did, and where he laid mine there I let it lie, until their prayers, singing, and preaching was over; after this I stood up, and uttered myself in these words following:—I desire as a stranger [if I may] to propose a few things to this congregation, hoping in the proposal thereof I shall commend myself to your consciences, to be guided by that wisdom that is from above, which being pure, is also peaceable, gentle, and easy to be entreated; and therewith [I] made a stop, expecting if the Prince of peace had been among them, I should have had a suitable answer of peace from them.....[1]Their

---

[1]Supplying the words here omitted, the Narrative reads as follows:—"But no other voice I heard but of their pastor, as he's called, and their magistrate. Their pastor answered by way of query whether I was a member of a church. Before I could give an answer, Mr. Bridges spoke, saying, 'If the congregation please to give you leave, well; if not, I shall require you silence, for,' said he, 'we will have no objections, &c.'" These last words, then, were spoken by the magistrate, and not, as represented above, by the pastor.—ED.

pastor answered, We will have no objections against what is delivered. To which I answered, I am not about at present to make objections against what is delivered, but as by my gesture at my coming into your assembly, I declared my dissent from you, so lest that should prove offensive unto some whom I would not offend, I would now by word of mouth declare the grounds, which are these :—First, from the consideration we are strangers each to other, and so strangers to each other's inward standing with respect to God, and so cannot conjoin and act in faith, and what is not of faith is sin. And in the second place, I could not judge that you are gathered together, and walk according to the visible order of our Lord; which when I had declared, Mr. Bridges told me, I had done, and spoke that for which I must answer, and so commanded [me] silence. When their meeting was done, the officers carried us again to the ordinary, where being watched over that night, as thieves and robbers, we were the next morning carried before Mr. Bridges, who made our mittimus, and sent us to the prison at Boston.[1] The words of the mittimus are these :—

" To the Keeper of the Prison at Boston :

By virtue hereof, you are required to take into your custody from the constable of Lynn, or his deputy, the bodies of John Clarke, Obadiah Holmes and John Crandal, and them to keep until the next County Court to be held at Boston, that they may then and there answer to such complaints as may be alleged against them; for being taken by a [the] constable at a private meeting at Lynn, upon the Lord's day, exercising among themselves, to whom divers of the town repaired, and joined with them, and that in the time of the public exercise of the worship of God; as also for offensively disturbing the peace of the congregation, at their coming into the public meeting in the time of prayer in the afternoon, and for saying and manifesting that the church in [of] Lynn was not constituted according to the order of our Lord, and for such other things as shall be alleged against them, concerning their seducing and drawing [aside of] others after their erroneous judgments and practices, and for suspicion of having their hands in [the] re-baptizing of one or more among us, as also for neglecting or refusing to put [give] in sufficient security for their appearance at the said Court. Hereof fail not at your peril.

22, 5, 51.   ROBERT BRIDGES."[2]

On July 31, Mr. Clarke was brought before the Court, and fined twenty pounds, or to be well whipped. The crimes he was charged with, beside what is above mentioned, were,

---

[1] It appears that somehow they were permitted to meet again on Monday, and were sent to prison on Tuesday.

[2] Clarke's Narrative, pp. 1—4. [27—31.]

that he met again the next day after his contempt, as they call it, of their public worship, " at the house of Witter, and in contempt of authority, being then in the custody of the law, did there administer the sacrament of the Lord's supper to one excommunicated person, to another under admonition, and to a third that was an inhabitant of Lynn, and not in fellowship with any church, and yet upon answer in open Court did affirm, that he never re-baptized any," &c.[1] Says Mr. Clarke :—

None were able to turn to the law of God or man by which we were condemned. At length the Governor stepped up, and told us we had denied infants' baptism, and being somewhat transported, told me, I had deserved death, and said he would not have such trash brought into their jurisdiction. Moreover he said, " You go up and down, and secretly insinuate into those that are weak, but you cannot maintain it before our ministers. You may try and dispute with them."

To this I had much to reply, but he commanded the gaoler to take us away. So the next morning having so fair an opportunity, I made a motion to the Court in these words following :—

To the honorable [honored] Court assembled at Boston :

Whereas it pleased this honored Court yesterday to condemn the faith and order which I hold and practice ; and after you had passed your sentence upon me for it, were pleased to express, I could not maintain the same against your ministers, and thereupon publicly proffered me a dispute with them ; be pleased by these few lines to understand, I readily accept it, and therefore desire you would appoint the time when, and the person with whom, in that public place where I was condemned, I might with freedom, and without molestation of the civil power, dispute that point publicly, where I doubt not by the strength of Christ to make it good out of his last Will and Testament, unto which nothing is to be added, nor from which nothing is to be diminished. Thus desiring the Father of lights to shine forth, and by his power to expel the darkness, I remain your well-wisher, JOHN CLARKE.

From the prison, this 1, 6, 51.

This motion, if granted, I desire might be subscribed by their Secretary's hand, as an act of the same Court by which we were condemned."[2]

[1]Neal's History of New England, Vol. I, p. 30. [2]Clarke's Narrative, p. 7, [33, 34.]

This was presented, and after much ado, one of the magistrates informed Mr. Clarke, that a disputation was granted to be the next week; but on Monday their ministers came together and made no small stir about the matter, and near the close of the day the magistrates sent for Mr. Clarke into their chamber, and queried with him about the matter, and demanded of him whether he would dispute upon the things contained in his sentence, and maintain his practice; "for" said they, " the Court sentenced you not for your judgment and conscience, but for matter of fact and practice." To which, says Mr. Clarke, I replied:—

You say the Court condemned me for matter of fact and practice. Be it so. I say that matter of fact and practice was but the manifestation of my judgment and conscience. And I make account, that man is void of judgment and conscience, with respect unto God, that hath not a fact and practice suitable thereunto.... If the faith and order which I profess do stand by the word of God, then the faith and order which you profess must needs fall to the ground; and if the way you walk in remain, then the way that I walk in must vanish away. They cannot both stand together. To this they seemed to assent; therefore I told them, that if they please to grant the motion under the Secretary's hand, I would draw up the faith and order which I hold, as the sum of that I did deliver in open Court, in [into] three or four conclusions, which conclusions I will stand by and defend, until he whom you shall appoint shall by the word of God remove me from them. In case he shall remove me from them, then the disputation is at end; but if not, then I desire like liberty by the word of God to oppose the faith and order which he and you profess, thereby to try whether I may be an instrument in the hand of God to remove you from the same. They told me the motion was very fair, and the way like unto a disputant, ...saying, Because the matter is weighty, and we desire that what can, may be spoken, when the disputation shall be, therefore would we take a longer time. .... So I returned with my keeper to prison again, drew up the conclusions, which I was resolved through the strength of Christ to stand in defence of, and through the importunity of one of the magistrates, the next morning very early I shewed them to him, having a promise I should have my motion for a dispute granted, under the Secretary's hand. The conclusions were as followeth:—

The testimony of John Clarke, a prisoner of Jesus Christ at Boston, in behalf of my Lord, and of his people, is as followeth:—

1. I testify that Jesus of Nazareth, whom God raised from the dead, is

made both Lord and Christ; this Jesus I say is the Christ, in English, the Anointed One; hath a name above every name; he is the Anointed Priest, none to or with him in point of atonement; the Anointed Prophet, none to him in point of instruction; the Anointed King, who is gone unto his Father, for his glorious kingdom, and shall ere long return again; and that this Jesus Christ is also the Lord; none to or with him by way of commanding and ordering, with respect to the worship of God, the household of faith, which being purchased with his blood as Priest, instructed and nourished by his spirit as Prophet, do wait in his appointments as the Lord, in hope of that glorious kingdom which shall ere long appear.[1]

2. I testify that baptism, or dipping in water, is one of the commandments of this Lord Jesus Christ, and that a visible believer or disciple of Christ Jesus (that is one that manifesteth repentance towards God, and faith in Jesus Christ) is the only person that is to be baptized, or dipped with that visible baptism, or dipping of Jesus Christ in water, and also that visible person that is to walk in that visible order of his house, and so to wait for his coming the second time, in the form of a Lord and King, with his glorious kingdom according to promise, and for his sending down in the time of his absence the Holy Ghost, or Holy Spirit of promise, and all this according to the last Will and Testament of that living Lord, whose will is not to be added to or taken from.[2]

[1]To confirm this article Mr. Clarke says, "If the nature of the commanding and ordering power, that suits both with the worship, and with the worshippers, which the Father of Spirits seeks for, be [also] considered, which is not a law of a carnal commandment, seconded with carnal weapons, or an arm of flesh; but a spiritual law, as the apostle calls it, Rom. viii., 'a law of the spirit of life from Christ Jesus,' spoken unto, or rather written in the heart of a Christian by the Spirit of Christ, by reason whereof he obeys from the heart readily, willingly and cheerfully, that form of doctrine which is engraven and laid up therein; Heb. viii. 10, II Cor. iii. 3, Rom. vi. 17; If this I say be considered, that the worship is spiritual, such as must begin in, spring up and rise from, the heart and spirit, and so be directed to the Father of Spirits, and so the commanding power that suits herewith must speak to the heart and spirit of the man, then there is no Lord in this matter to Christ Jesus, who speaks to the heart and spirit, and his words are as commands from the head to the members, which convey [together] spirit and life to obey them, by reason of which his commands are not grievous, for where the Spirit of the Lord is there is liberty; &c. II Cor. iii. 17, 18." pp. 48, 49, [81.]

[2]To confirm the first part of this article Mr. Clarke says, "Although there be frequent mention made of that appointment of Christ in his last Will and Testament, yet it is never expressed by the word that may be rendered *rantism*, or sprinkling, but by the word that is rendered *baptism*, or dipping;" to which he adds many proofs, pp. 50—52, [82.] The other part, which concerns the subjects of baptism, he confirms by the apostles' commission, and by their practice, and notes in particular, that on the day of Pentecost they baptized none but such as were *called, gladly received his word, were added and continued in the apostles' doctrine and fellowship, &c.* p. 54, [87.]

3. I testify or witness, that every such believer in Christ Jesus, that waiteth for his appearing, may in point of liberty, yea ought in point of duty, to improve that talent his Lord hath given unto him, and in the congregation may either ask for information to himself; or if he can, may speak by way of prophecy for the edification, exhortation and comfort of the whole; and out of the congregation at all times, upon all occasions, and in all places, as far as the jurisdiction of his Lord extends, may, yea ought to walk as a child of light, justifying wisdom with his ways, and reproving folly, with the unfruitful works thereof, provided all this be shown out of a good conversation, as James speaks, with meekness of wisdom.

4. I testify that no such believer or servant of Christ Jesus hath [any] liberty, much less authority, from his Lord, to smite his fellow servant, nor yet with outward force, or arm of flesh to constrain, or restrain his conscience, no nor yet his outward man for conscience sake, or worship of his God, where injury is not offered to the person, name or estate of others, every man being such as shall appear before the judgment-seat of Christ, and must give an account of himself to God, and therefore ought to be fully persuaded in his own mind for what he undertakes, because he that doubteth is damned if he eat, and so also if he act, because he doth not eat or act in faith, and what is not of faith is sin.[1]

When Mr. Clarke had thus freely given them his testimony, instead of openly and fairly meeting him as they had talked of, to vindicate their proceedings, the next news that he hears from them is this :—

To the Keeper of the Prison :

By virtue hereof you are to release and set at liberty the body of Mr. John Clarke, and this shall be your discharge for so doing. Given under my hand the 11th of the 6th month, 1651.

WILLIAM HIBBINS.[2]

Great expectations had been raised in the country of hearing these points disputed, and Mr. Clarke knowing well how they would try to turn all the blame upon him, immediately drew up the following address :—

Whereas through the indulgence of tender hearted friends, without my consent, and contrary to my judgment, the sentence and condemnation of

---

[1] Narrative, pp. 9, 10, [34—37.]

[2] Narrative, p. 10, [37.] Four years after, Hibbins's wife was hanged for a witch.

the Court at Boston (as is reported) have been fully satisfied on my behalf, and thereupon a warrant hath been procured, by which I am secluded the place of my imprisonment, by reason whereof I see no other call for present but to my habitation, and to those near relations which God hath given me there; yet lest the cause should hereby suffer, which I profess is Christ's, I would hereby signify, that if yet it shall please the honored magistrates, or General Court of this colony, to grant my former request under their Secretary's hand, I shall cheerfully embrace it, and upon your motion shall, through the help of God, come from the island to attend it. And hereunto I have subscribed my name.

11th, 6, 51. JOHN CLARKE.

This was the next morning sent to the magistrates, who were met at the Commencement at Cambridge, upon which it was noised abroad that the motion was granted, and that Mr. Cotton was to be the man; "a man," says Mr. Clarke, " best of all approved of by myself for that same purpose, he being the inventor and supporter of that way in these parts wherein they walk." But a little before their lecture the next Thursday, he received the following paper :—

MR. JOHN CLARKE:

We conceive you have misrepresented the Governor's speech, in saying you were challenged to dispute with some of our elders, whereas it was plainly expressed, that if you would confer with any of them, they were able to satisfy you, neither were you able to maintain your practice to them by the word of God, all which we [was] intended for your information and conviction privately; neither were you enjoined to what you were then [then were] counselled unto; nevertheless if you are forward to dispute, and that you will move it yourself to the Court, or magistrates about Boston, we shall take order to appoint one who will be ready to answer your motion, you keeping close to the questions to be propounded by yourself; and a moderator shall be appointed also to attend upon that service; and whereas you desire you might be free in your dispute, keeping close to the points to be disputed on, without incurring damage by the civil justice, observing what hath been before written, it is granted; the day may be agreed, if you yield the premises.

JOHN ENDICOTT, Governor,
THOMAS DUDLEY, Dep. Governor,
RICHARD BELLINGHAM,
WILLIAM HIBBINS,
INCREASE NOWEL."

11th[1] of the 6th, 1651.

[1] It seems that this should be the 12th.

Says Mr. Clarke:—

My answer followeth superscribed,

To the honored Governor of the Massachusetts, and the rest of that honorable Society, these present:

WORTHY SENATORS:—I received a writing, subscribed with five of your hands, by way of answer to a twice repeated motion of mine before you, which was grounded as I conceive sufficiently upon the Governor's words, in open Court, which writing of yours doth no way answer my expectation, nor yet that motion which I made; and whereas, (waiving that grounded motion) you are pleased to intimate, that if I were forward to dispute, and would move it myself to the Court, or magistrates about Boston, you would appoint one to answer my motion, &c., be pleased to understand, that although I am not backward to maintain the faith and order of my Lord, the King of saints, for which I have been sentenced yet am I not in such a way so forward to dispute, or move therein, lest inconvenience should thereby arise; I shall rather once more repeat my former motion, which if it shall please the honored General Court to accept, and under their Secretary's hand shall grant a free dispute, without molestation or interruption, I shall be [so] well satisfied therewith; that what is past I shall forget, and upon your motion shall attend it; thus desiring the Father of mercies not to lay that evil to your charge, I remain your well wisher, JOHN CLARKE.[1]

From Prison this 14, 6, 51.

I have transcribed the whole of these letters with great care, to give the reader a fair opportunity to judge for himself, whether those rulers and ministers were not afraid of the light, though they pretended the contrary. For they knew that they had then laws in force to punish any man who should dispute against infant baptism, as well as other of their ways, and what they now sent was no act of Court, but only a writing from some of their rulers met at Commencement. Mr. Clarke says, it was in Mr. Cotton's handwriting. They would thus fain have stopped Mr. Clarke's mouth, or else have drawn him again under the lash of their laws. This he says gave ground for others to conclude, "that the utmost they can say for themselves, and to stop the mouth of him that is contrary minded, lies in

---

[1] Narrative, pp. 11—13. [40.]

the sword and power of the magistrate, which, although it be a good ordinance of God in this present evil world to restrain the oppressor, and to let the oppressed go free, and so approved and owned by Christ and all true Christians, in case of wrong and wicked lewdness, ... yet was it never appointed by Christ (to whom all power, not only in earth, but also in heaven, is committed, and by whom all earthly powers are to be judged; I say it was never appointed by Christ) to inform and rectify the minds and consciences of men in the worship of God, in that great mystery of godliness, and in those mystical matters concerning the kingdom of Christ, that being a matter that only belongs to the Holy Spirit of promise, and to the sword of that Spirit, which is the word (not of man, but) of God, to effect, much less to conform their outward man contrary to their minds and consciences in the worship of God; and therefore that sword and power ought to take heed how they meddle herein, lest they attempt to take the place and enter upon the throne and kingdom of Christ."[1]

Mr. Crandal, who was fined five pounds, only for being with the others, was released upon promise of appearing at their next Court (though they did not let him know when it was, till it was over, and they exacted the fine of the keeper) and he with Mr. Clarke returned home. Mr. Holmes was kept in prison till their Court met in the beginning of September, and then, after their public lecture in Boston, the sentence of Court was executed upon him; a particular account of which we have written with his own hand, as follows:—

Unto the well beloved brethren, John Spilsbury, William Kiffen, and the rest that in London stand fast in the faith, and continue to walk steadfastly in that order of the gospel which was once delivered unto the saints by Jesus Christ; Obadiah Holmes, an unworthy witness that Jesus is the Lord, and of late a prisoner for Jesus' sake at Boston, sendeth greeting:

DEARLY BELOVED AND LONGED AFTER:—My heart's desire is to hear from you, and to hear that you grow in grace, and in the knowledge of our

[1] Narrative, pp. 13, 14. [41.]

Lord and Saviour Jesus Christ, and that your love to him, and one unto another, as he hath given commandment, aboundeth, would be the very joy and great rejoicing of my soul and spirit. Had I not been prevented by my beloved brethren of Providence, who have wrote unto you, wherein you have my mind at large; and also by our beloved brother Clarke, of Rhode Island, who may, if God permit, see you, and speak with you mouth to mouth, I had here declared myself in that matter, but now I forbear; and because I have an experimental knowledge in myself, that in members of the same body, while it stands in union with the head, there is a sympathizing spirit, which passeth through, and also remaineth in each particular, so that one member can neither mourn nor rejoice, but all the members are ready to mourn and rejoice with it; I shall the rather impart unto you some dealings which I have had therein from the sons of men, and the gracious supports which I have had from the Son of God, my Lord and yours, that so like members you might rejoice with me, and might be encouraged, by the same experiment of his tender mercies, to fear none of those things which you shall suffer for Jesus' sake. It pleased the Father of lights, after a long continuance of mine in death and darkness, to cause life and immortality to be brought to light in my soul, and also to cause me to see that this life was by the death of his Son, in that hour and power of darkness procured, which wrought in my heart a restless desire to know what the Lord, who had so dearly bought me, would have me to do, and finding that it was his last will (to which none is to add, and from which none is to detract,) that they which had faith in his death for life, should yield up themselves to hold forth a lively consimilitude or likeness unto his death, burial and resurrection, by that ordinance of baptism, I readily yielded thereto, being by love constrained to follow the [that] Lamb (that takes away the sins of the world) whithersoever he goes. I had no sooner separated from their assemblies, and from communion with them in their worship of God, and thus visibly put on Christ, being resolved alone to attend upon him, and to submit to his will, but immediately the adversary cast out a flood against us, and stirred up the spirits of men to present myself and two more to Plymouth Court, where we met with four petitions against our whole company to take some speedy course to suppress us; one from our own plantation, with thirty-five hands to it; one from the church, as they call it, at Taunton; one from all the ministers in our colony, except two, if I mistake not, and one from the Court at Boston, in the Massachusetts, under their Secretary's hand; whereupon the Court straitly charged us to desist, and neither to ordain officers, nor to baptize, nor to break bread together, nor yet to meet upon the first day of the week; and having received these strait charges, one of the three discovers the sandy foundation upon which he stood, who, when the flood came and the wind blew, fell, yet it pleased the Father of mercies (to whom be the praise) to give us strength to stand, and to tell them it was better to obey God [rather] than man; and such was the grace of our God to us-ward, that though we were had from Court to Court, yet were we firmly resolved to keep close to the rule, and to obey the voice of our Lord, come what will come.

Not long after these troubles I came upon occasion of business into the colony of Massachusetts, with two other brethren, as brother Clarke being one of the two can inform you, where we three were apprehended, carried to [the prison at] Boston, and so to the Court, and were all sentenced. What they laid to my charge, you may here read in my sentence,[1] upon the pronouncing of which, as I went from the bar, I expressed myself in these words:—I bless God, I am counted worthy to suffer for the name of Jesus. Whereupon John Wilson (their pastor, as they call him) struck me before the judgment-seat, and cursed me, saying, The curse of God or Jesus go with thee.[2] So we were carried to the prison, where not long after I was deprived of my two loving friends, at whose departure the adversary stepped in, took hold of [on] my spirit, and troubled me for the space of an hour, and then the Lord came in, and sweetly relieved me,

---

[1] The sentence of Obadiah Holmes, of Seaconk, the 31st of the 5th month, 1651.

Forasmuch as you Obadiah Holmes, being come into this jurisdiction about the 21 of the 5 month, did meet at one William Witter's house, at Lynn, and did here privately (and at other times, being an excommunicate person, did take upon you to preach and baptize) upon the Lord's day, or other days, and being taken then by the constable, and coming afterward to the assembly at Lynn, did, in disrespect to the ordinance of God and his worship, keep on your hat, the pastor being in prayer, insomuch that you would not give reverence in vailing your hat, till it was forced off your head, to the disturbance of the congregation, and professing against the institution of the church, as not being according to the gospel of Jesus Christ; and that you the said Obadiah Holmes did upon the day following meet again at the said William Witter's, in contempt to authority, you being then in the custody of the law, and did there receive the sacrament, being excommunicate, and that you did baptize such as were baptized before, and thereby did necessarily deny the baptism that was before administered to be baptism, the churches no churches, and also other ordinances, and ministers, as if all were a nullity; and also did deny the lawfulness of baptizing of infants; and all this tends to the dishonor of God, the despising the ordinances of God among us, the peace of the churches, and seducing the subjects of this Commonwealth from the truth of the gospel of Jesus Christ, and perverting the strait ways of the Lord, the Court doth fine you thirty pounds, to be paid, or sufficient sureties that the said sum shall be paid by the first day of the next Court of Assistants, or else to be well whipped, and that you shall remain in prison till it be paid, or security given in for it. By the Court,

INCREASE NOWEL.

[Clarke's Narrative, p. 44.]

[2] "Mr. Wilson is represented by his cotemporaries as one of the most humble, pious and benevolent men of the age." Massachusetts History, Vol. I, p. 258. [237.] But when that darling point, infant sprinkling, was in danger, see how it makes the most benevolent act like cruel persecutors!

causing to look to himself; so was I stayed, and refreshed in the thoughts of my God. And although during the time of my imprisonment the tempter was busy, yet it pleased God so to stand at my right hand, that the motions were but sudden, and so vanished away. And although there were that would have paid the money if I would accept it, yet I durst not accept of deliverance in such a way, and therefore my answer to them was, that although I would acknowledge their love to a cup of cold water, yet could I not thank them for their money, if they should pay it. So the Court drew near, and the night before I should suffer according to my sentence, it pleased God I rested and slept quietly. In the morning my friends come [came] to visit me, desiring me to take the refreshment of wine, and other comforts; but my resolution was not to drink wine, nor strong drink that day until my punishment was over, and the reason was, lest in case I had more strength, courage and boldness than ordinarily could be expected, the world should either say, He is drunk with new wine, or else that the comfort and strength of the creature hath carried him through. My course was this:—I desired brother John Hazel to bear my friends company, and I betook myself to my chamber, where I might communicate with my God, commit myself to him, and beg strength from him. I had no sooner sequestered myself, and come into my chamber, but Satan lets fly at me, saying, Remember thyself, thy birth, breeding, and friends, thy wife, children, name and credit; but as this was sudden, so there came in sweetly from the Lord as sudden an answer, 'Tis for my Lord; I must not deny him before the sons of men (for that were [is] to set men above him) but rather lose all, yea wife, children, and mine own life also. To this the tempter replies, Oh! but that is the question, is it for him? and for him alone? is it not rather for thy own, or some other's sake? thou hast so professed and practiced, and now art loth to deny it; is not pride and self in the bottom? Surely this temptation was strong, and thereupon I made diligent search after the matter, as formerly I had done, and after a while there was even as it had been a voice from heaven in my very soul, bearing witness with my conscience, that it was not for any man's case or sake in this world, that so I had professed and practiced, but for my Lord's case and sake, and for him alone; whereupon my spirit was much refreshed; as also in the consideration of these three Scriptures, which speak on this wise:— "Who shall lay any thing to the charge of God's elect?" "Although I walk through the valley and shadow of death I will fear no evil, thy rod and thy staff they shall comfort me;" and "He that continueth to the end, the same shall be saved."

But then came in the consideration of the weakness of the flesh to bear the strokes of a whip, though the spirit was willing, and thereupon [hereupon] I was caused to pray earnestly unto the Lord, that he would be pleased to give me a spirit of courage and boldness, a tongue to speak for him, and strength of body to suffer for his sake, and not to shrink or yield to the strokes, or shed tears, lest the adversaries of the truth should thereupon blaspheme and be hardened, and the weak and feeble-hearted discouraged; and for this I sought [besought] the Lord earnestly. At length he satisfied my spirit to give up, as my soul so my body to him, and quietly to leave the whole disposing of the matter to him; and so I addressed myself in as comely a manner as I could, having such a Lord and Master to serve in this business. And when I heard the voice of my keeper come for me, even cheerfulness did come upon me, and taking my Testament in my hand, I went along with him to the place of execution, and after common salutation here stood. There stood by also one of the magistrates, by name Increase Nowel, who for a while kept silent, and spoke not a word, and so did I, expecting the governor's presence, but he came not. But after a while Mr. Nowel bade the executioner do his office. Then I desired to speak a few words, but Mr. Nowel answered, It is not now a time to speak. Whereupon I took leave, and said, Men, brethren, fathers and countrymen, I beseech you give me leave to speak a few words, and the rather because here are many spectators to see me punished, and I am to seal with my blood, if God give strength, that which I hold and practice in reference to the word of God, and the testimony of Jesus. That which I have to say in brief is this, Although I confess I am no disputant, yet seeing I am to seal what I hold with my blood, I am ready to defend it by the Word, and to dispute that point with any that shall come forth to withstand it. Mr. Nowel answered me, now was no time to dispute. Then said I, Then I desire to give an account of the faith and order I hold; and this I desired three times, but in comes Mr. Flint, and saith to the executioner, Fellow, do thine office, for this fellow would but make a long speech to delude the people.[1] So I being resolved to speak, told the people; That which I am to suffer for is the Word of God, and testimony of Jesus Christ. No, saith Mr. Nowel, it is for your error, and going about to seduce the people. To which I replied, Not for error, for in all the time of my imprisonment wherein I was left alone (my brethren being gone) which of all your ministers in all that time came to convince me of an error; and when upon the governor's words a motion was made for a public dispute, and upon fair terms so often renewed, and desired by hundreds, what was the reason it was not granted. Mr. Nowel told me, it was his fault that went away, and would not dispute, but this the writings will clear at large. Still Mr. Flint calls to the man to do his office; so before and in the time of his pulling off my clothes I continued speaking, telling them, that I had so learned, that for all Boston I would not give my body into their hands thus to be bruised upon another account, yet upon this I

---

[1] Thomas Flint was chosen one of their magistrates in 1642.

would not give the hundredth part of a *wampum peaque*[1] to free it out of their hands, and that I made as much conscience of unbottoning one button, as I did of paying the thirty pounds in reference thereunto. I told them moreover, The Lord having manifested his love towards me, in giving me repentance towards God and faith in Jesus Christ, and so to be baptized in water by a messenger of Jesus into the name of the Father, Son and Holy Spirit, wherein I have fellowship with him in his death, burial and resurrection, I am now come to be baptized in afflictions by your hands, that so I may have further fellowship with my Lord, and am not ashamed of his sufferings, for by his stripes am I healed.

And as the man began to lay the strokes upon my back, I said to the people, Though my flesh should fail, and my spirit should fail, yet my God would not fail. So it pleased the Lord to come in, and so to fill my heart and tongue as a vessel full, and with an audible voice I broke forth praying unto the Lord not to lay this sin to their charge; and telling the people, that now I found he did not fail me, and therefore now I should trust him forever who failed me not; for in truth, as the strokes fell upon me, I had such a spiritual manifestation of God's presence as the like thereof I never had nor felt, nor can with fleshly tongue express; and the outward pain was so removed from me, that indeed I am not able to declare it to you, it was so easy to me, that I could well bear it, yea and in a manner felt it not although it was grievous as the spectators said, the man striking with all his strength (yea spitting in [on] his hand three times as many affirmed) with a three-corded whip, giving me therewith thirty strokes. When he had loosed me from the post, having joyfulness in my heart, and cheerfulness in my countenance, as the spectators observed, I told the magistrates, You have struck me as with roses; and said moreover, Although the Lord hath made it easy to me, yet I pray God it may not be laid to your charge.

"After this many came to me rejoicing to see the power of the Lord manifested in weak flesh; but sinful flesh takes occasion hereby to bring others in trouble, informs the magistrates hereof, and so two more are apprehended as for contempt of authority. Their names were John Hazel and John Spur, who came indeed and did shake me by the hand, but did use no words of contempt or reproach unto any. No man can prove that the first spoke any thing, and for the second, he only said thus: Blessed be the Lord; yet these two for taking me by the hand, and thus saying after I had received my punishment, were sentenced to pay forty shillings, or to be whipped. Both were resolved against paying their fine; nevertheless after one or two days imprisonment, one paid John Spur's fine and he was released; and after six or seven days imprisonment of brother Hazel, even

---

[1] A *wampum peaque* is the sixth part of a penny with us.

the day when he should have suffered, another paid his, and so he escaped; and the next day went to visit a friend about six miles from Boston, where the same day he fell sick, and within ten days [he] ended his life. When I was come to the prison, it pleased God to stir up the heart of an old acquaintance of mine, who, with much tenderness, like the good Samaritan, poured oil into my wounds, and plastered my sores;[1] but there was present information given what was done, and inquiry made who was the surgeon, [chirurgeon] and it was commonly reported he should be sent for, but what was done I yet know not. Now thus it hath pleased the Father of mercies so to dispose of the matter, that my bonds and imprisonments, have been no hindrance to the Gospel; for before my return, some submitted to the Lord, and were baptized, and divers were put upon the way of inquiry. And now being advised to make my escape by night, because it was reported that there were warrants forth for me, I departed; and the next day after, while I was on my journey, the constable came to search at the house where I lodged, so I escaped their hands, and was by the good hand of my heavenly Father brought home again to my near relations, my wife and eight children. The brethren of our town, and Providence, having taken pains to meet me four miles in the woods where we rejoiced together in the Lord. Thus have I given you as briefly as I can, a true relation of things; wherefore, my brethren, rejoice with me in the Lord, and give all glory to him, for he is worthy, to whom be praise forevermore; to whom I commit you, and put up my earnest prayers for you, that by my late experience who have trusted in God, and have not been deceived, you may trust in him perfectly. Wherefore, my dearly beloved brethren, trust in the Lord, and you shall not be ashamed nor confounded; so I also rest.

Yours in the bond of charity,

OBADIAH HOLMES.[2]

Thus I have given the reader his own testimony, without adding or diminishing a single word, that all who understand may judge; for the Scriptures assure us, that " the ear trieth words, as the mouth tasteth meat." You have heard from Mr. Holmes, that two men were put to trouble for the respect they showed to him after his sufferings. Mr. Clarke

---

[1] In a manuscript of Governor Joseph Jencks, written near fifty years ago, he says:— "Mr. Holmes was whipped thirty stripes, and in such an unmerciful manner, that in many days, if not some weeks, he could take no rest but as he lay upon his knees and elbows, not being able to suffer any part of his body to touch the bed whereon he lay. But Mr. Clarke being a scholar bred, a friend of his, paid his fine.

[2] Clarke's Narrative, pp. 16—23, [45—52.]

says, it was reported that warrants were sent forth to the number of thirteen, but that "some through fear were fain to hide themselves, and being strangers, to hasten away, or to change their habit." John Spur, one of their church members, who was taken, gives us the following testimony. Says he:—

Mr. Cotton in his sermon immediately before the Court gave their sentence against Mr. Clarke, Obadiah Holmes, and John Crandal, affirmed, that denying infant baptism would overthrow all, and this was a capital offence; and therefore they were soul-murderers. When therefore the Governor, Mr. John Endicott, came into the Court to pass sentence against them, he said thus, You deserve to die, but this we agreed upon, that Mr. Clarke shall pay twenty pounds fine, and Obadiah Holmes thirty pounds fine, and John Crandal five pounds, and to remain in prison until their fines be either paid or security given for them, or else they are all of them to be well whipped. When Obadiah Holmes was brought forth to receive his sentence, he desired of the magistrates, that he might hold forth the ground of his practice; but they refused to let him speak, and commanded the whipper to do his office; then the whipper began to pull off his clothes, upon which Obadiah Holmes said, Lord lay not this sin unto their charge; and so the whipper began to lay on with his whip; upon which Obadiah Holmes said, O Lord, I beseech thee to manifest thy power in the weakness of thy creature. He neither moving nor stirring at all for their [the] strokes, breaks out in these expressions, Blessed and praised be the Lord, and thus he carried it to the end, and went away rejoicingly. I John Spur being present, it did take such an impression in my spirit to trust in God, and to walk according to the light that God had communicated to me, and not to fear what man could do unto me, that I went to the man (being inwardly affected with what I saw and heard) and with a joyful countenance took him by the hand when he was from the post and said, Praised be the Lord; and so I went along with him to the prison; and presently that day there was information given to the Court what I had said and done; and also a warrant[1] [was] granted out that day to arrest both myself and John Hazel, which was executed on the morrow morning upon us, and so we were brought to the Court and examined. The Governor asked me concerning Obadiah Holmes, according as he was informed

---

[1] To the keeper or his deputy:

By virtue hereof you are to take into your custody and safe keeping, the body of John Spur for a heinous offence by him committed; hereof fail not [not to fail.] Dated the 5th of the 7th month, 1651. Take also into your safe keeping John Hazel. By the Court,

INCREASE NOWEL.

by old Mr. Cole and Thomas Buttolph, of my taking of him by the hand, and smiling, and I did then freely declare what I did, and what I said, which was this :—Obadiah Holmes, said I, I do look upon as a godly man ; and do affirm that he carried himself as did become a Christian, under so sad an affliction ; and his affliction did so affect my soul, that I went to him being from the post, and said, Blessed be the Lord. . . . . But said the Governor, What do you apprehend concerning the cause for which he suffered ? My answer was, That I am not able to judge of it. Then said the Governor, we will deal with you as we have dealt with him. I said unto him again, I am in the hands of God. Then Mr. Symonds, a magistrate, said, "You shall know that you are in the hands of men." The Governor then said, Keeper, take him ; and so I was presently carried away to prison.

The next day about one of the clock, I was sent for again into the Court. The Governor (being then about to go out of the Court when I came in) delivered his [this] speech to me ; said he, You must pay forty shillings or be whipped. I said then to those of the Court that remained, That if any man suffer as a Christian, let him glorify God in this behalf. Then I desired to know what law I had broken, and what evil I had done.? but they produced no law, only they produced what the two witnesses had sworn against me.[1] My speech thereto was this :—My practice and carriage is allowed by the word of God, for it is written in Rom. 12. Be like affectioned one towards another ; rejoice with them that rejoice ; and it is contrary to my judgment and conscience to pay a penny. Then said Mr. Bendal, I will pay it for him, and there presented himself. I answered then and said, I thanked him for his love, but did believe it was no acceptable service for any man to pay a penny for me in this case ; yet notwithstanding, the Court accepted of his proffer, and bid me begone. Then came John Hazel to be examined. JOHN SPUR.[2]

[1] "J. Cole being in the market place, when Obadiah Holmes came from the whipping-post, John Spur came and met him presently, laughing in his face, saying, 'Blessed be God for thee brother,' and so did go with him, laughing upon him up towards the prison, which was very grievous to me to see him harden the man in his sin, and shewing much contempt of authority by that carriage, as if he had been unjustly punished, and had suffered as a righteous man under a tyrannical government. Deposed before the Court, the 5th of the 7th month. INCREASE NOWEL."

"I, Thomas Buttolph, did see John Spur come to Obadiah Holmes, so soon as he came from the whipping-post, laughing in his face, and going along with him towards the prison to my great grief to see him harden him in his sin, and to shew such contempt of authority. Deposed the 5th of the 7th month, 1651, before the Court. INCREASE NOWEL."
[Narrative, p. 58.]

[2] Narrative, pp. 26—28. [56—58.]
I find that John Hazel was admitted a freeman at Boston, March 9, 1637, and John Spur, May 22, 1639. Massachusetts Records.

Mr. Hazel was one of Mr. Holmes's brethren of Rehoboth, who, though above threescore years old, and infirm in body, had traveled near fifty miles, partly indeed on other business, but chiefly to visit his beloved brother in prison; and how he was treated there, he has given us an account, written and subscribed with his own hand as follows:—

A relation of my being brought before the magistrates the 6th of the 7th month, 1651.

I, going from place to place, to buy and take up commodities for my use, was attached or arrested by the marshal, by virtue of a warrant from the Court, to appear in the Court, and there to answer for a high misdemeanor committed by me; and coming into the Court (which was then privately kept in the chamber) they asked me divers questions, among[st] which this was one, Whether I did think that Obadiah Holmes did well or not, in coming among them to baptize, and administer the sacrament? laying this to my charge, that I was one with him, and of the same judgment, and, Whether I did think he did well or no, in his so carrying himself? To which I answered, I had here nothing to do with that which another man did, but I was here to answer for what I myself had committed against their law. Then said they, You have offended our law, and have contemned authority, for you took him by the hand, and did countenance him in his sin, so soon as he was gone from the post. To which I said, If I have broken any law of the place, by what I then did, I am willing to submit unto punishment. Yea, said the Governor you took him by the hand, did you not? and spake to him; what said you? did you not say so and so? Blessed be God, &c. To which I said, I shall refer myself unto the testimonies that may or can be brought against me. Well, said the Governor, we shall find testimony enough against you. Take him to you, keeper, and we will call you forth in public, for what [that] we do with you we will proceed in public with you. And so I went to prison. This was the sum and substance of the first time I was called before them. The next day being the last day of the week, and the last day of their Court, I was in expectation all the forenoon to be called forth, but was not. So after dinner, when (as appeareth) the Court was risen, and some of the magistrates departed, I was sent for again into the chamber, where was the Governor with three others, *scil*, Mr. Bellingham, Mr. Hibbins, and Mr. Increase Nowel. As soon as I was come into the room, the Governor read my sentence, which was, that I must pay forty shillings, or be well whipped; and so immediately he departed, and when he was gone (for could not have time before) I answered, that I desired the privilege of an English subject, which was to be tried by the country, to wit, a jury, and to be made to appear (if they can) to be a transgressor by a law. To which they said, I had contemned authority, and they had a law to punish such, and said they, You did show your contempt of authority in that you did take such a person by the hand, as soon as he was from the post. To which I answered, I could not do that which I did in contempt to authority, seeing he had satisfied the law to the full, and was departed from the place of suffering; and in the next place, what I did, I did unto him as my friend; and further I said, If I had taken him by the hand so soon as he was loosed from the post, and had led him out of the town, I should not have broken any law either of God or man. To this they said, that there was a law in all Courts of justice, both in Old England and other countries, to punish contempt of authority, and so had they such a law among themselves. To which I said, that in Old England and other places, they had such a law I denied not, but that law also was both enacted and published, but what law have I broken in taking my friend by the hand, when he was free, and had satisfied the law? To this they replied, that he had not satisfied the keeper. To this I answered, that he had talked with the keeper, and there was some agreement between them, and so in that sense also not under the law, but free. Then said they, if you would have showed kindness unto your friend, you might have forborne in that place, and done it more privately. To which I answered, I knew not but that place was as free as another, he having satisfied the law. The testimony that was given by Mr. Cole, was this, "I saw John Hazel take Obadiah Holmes by the hand, but what he said I cannot tell." This is the substance of all the proceedings until the last day at night, and then they said I should be whipped; but said some of their officers, The whipper cannot be found. Then they commanded that they should be ready by the second day morning, and then I did expect to be called forth; but neither that day, nor the third, nor fourth, was I called, but am as I understand reserved unto the fifth day, to be more public in the view of the world. And when the fifth day came, as I had many before, so also then, that would have paid the fine, if I would give my consent which I denied to do, and so set myself by the power of Christ to suffer what should be inflicted upon me; but when noon came I was told I should not suffer whipping; yet not having a discharge I did not look to be freed until the keeper told me I might go about my business. Then I demanded a discharge, (meaning under the magistrates' hands) so he bade me go; he would discharge me.

The strokes I was enjoined by the Court to have, were ten with a three-corded whip; the very same number I understand, that the worst malefactors that were there punished had; of which some were guilty of common whoredom, another of forcing a little child, and one Indian for coining of money. Thus far have you a relation according to my best remembrance from the first to the last of all the passages concerning this matter; by me John Hazel, written with mine own hand in Boston prison, the 13th day of the seventh month, 1651.

A postscript. Since I wrote, I understand there is report that I was willing to pay my fine, and that the magistrates would not accept of it without I were willing. Gentle reader, be pleased to understand that this is false, for it was without my consent or approbation; and further understand, that the fine was taken by them, upon the proffer of Mr. Bendal for John Spur. It was willingly accepted by the magistrates, and approved of, although John Spur did to their faces contradict it, and oppose it; therefore, good reader, believe not such reports.

By me, JOHN HAZEL."[1]

Thus far we have attended to those sufferers' own testimony, the last of whom wrote the postscript of his relation on his death-bed; and how much the abusive treatment he met with was the cause of his death, God only knows. Let us now hear what others had to say about them. Mr. Clarke went to England in November, 1651, and the next year printed the narrative from whence we have taken these accounts; upon which Sir Richard Saltonstall, one of the Massachusetts' first magistrates, then in our mother country, wrote to Messrs. Cotton and Wilson, of Boston, in this manner:—

REVEREND AND DEAR FRIENDS, WHOM I UNFEIGNEDLY LOVE AND RESPECT :—

It doth not a little grieve my spirit to hear what sad things are reported daily of your tyranny and persecutions in New England, as that you fine, whip and imprison men for their consciences. First, you compel such to come into your assemblies as you know will not join with you in your worship, and when they show their dislike thereof or witness against it, then you stir up your magistrates to punish them for such (as you conceive) their public affronts. Truly, friends, this your practice of compelling any in matters of worship to do that whereof they are not fully persuaded, is to make them sin, for so the apostle (Rom. 14 and 23) tells us, and many are made hypocrites thereby, conforming in their outward man for fear of punishment. We pray for you and wish you prosperity every way, hoped the Lord would have given you so much light and love there, that you

---

[1] Narrative, pp. 29—32, [59—62.] Here note, that Mr. Neal mistakes in representing that it was the General Court that fined these men, for it was only the Court of Assistants.

might have been eyes to God's people here, and not to practice those courses in a wilderness, which you went so far to prevent. These rigid ways have laid you very low in the hearts of the saints. I do assure you I have heard them pray in the public assemblies that the Lord would give you meek and humble spirits, not to strive so much for uniformity as to keep the unity of the spirit in the bond of peace.[1]

Mr. Cotton's answer:—

HONORED AND DEAR SIR:—My brother Wilson and self do both of us acknowledge your love, as otherwise formerly, so now in the late lines we received from you, that you grieve in spirit to hear daily complaints against us..... Be pleased to understand we look at such complaints as altogether injurious in respect of ourselves, who had no hand or tongue at all to promote either the coming of the persons you aim at into our assemblies, or their punishment for their carriage there. Righteous judgment will not take up reports, much less reproaches against the innocent. The cry of the sins of Sodom was great and loud, and reached up to heaven; yet the righteous God (giving us an example what to do in the like case) he would first go down to see whether their crime were altogether according to the cry, before he would proceed to judgment. And when he did find the truth of the cry, he did not wrap up all alike promiscuously in the judgment, but spared such as he found innocent.[2] We are amongst those whom (if you knew us better) you would account, [as the matron of Abel spake of herself,] peaceable in Israel. Yet neither are we so vast in our indulgence or toleration, as to think the men you speak of, suffered an unjust censure. For one of them, (Obadiah Holmes) being an excommunicate person himself, out of a church in Plymouth patent, came into this jurisdiction, and took upon him to baptize, which I think himself will not say he was compelled here to perform.[3] And he was not ignorant that the rebaptizing of an elder person, and that by a private person out of office and under excommunication, are all of them manifest contestations against the order

---

[1] Massachusetts History, Vol. III, pp. 401, 402.

[2] Alas! how often do men act contrary to the good rules they prescribe for others! How often was Mr. Cotton guilty of censuring others, without a fair and full hearing! He does it to Mr. Holmes before he has got to the end of this letter. And where there are some things wrong, yet how little care has been used by his party to distinguish the innocent from the guilty, among the Baptists! So far from such a care, that from his day to ours, it has been a common trade of that party to ransack Germany, in order to reproach the English Baptists with errors and bad actions, which we never had any more concern with, than our accusers have with the whoredom of pope Joan!

[3] What an evasion is this! Sir Richard spake of compelling persons into their worship, and Cotton here turns it as if he meant a compelling persons out of one government into another to worship in their own way.

and government of our churches, established (we know) by God's law, and he knoweth) by the laws of the country. As for his whipping, it was more voluntarily chosen by him than inflicted on him. His censure by the Court was to have paid (as I know) thirty pounds, or else be whipped; his fine was offered to be paid by friends for him freely, but he chose rather to be whipped; in which case, if his suffering of stripes was any worship of God at all, surely it could be accounted no better than will-worship.[1] The other (Mr. Clarke) was wiser in that point and his offence was less, so was his fine less, and himself (as I hear) was contented to have it paid for him, whereupon he was released.[2] The imprisonment of either of them was no detriment. I believe they fared neither of them better at home, and I am sure Holmes had not been so well clad of many years before.

But be pleased to consider this point a little further. You think to compel men in matter of worship is to make them [men] sin. If the worship be lawful in itself, the magistrate compelling him to come to it, compelleth him not to sin, but the sin is in his will that needs to be compelled to a Christian duty. If it do make men hypocrites, yet better be hypocrites than profane persons. Hypocrites give God part of his due, the outward man, but the profane person giveth God neither outward nor inward man. You know not, if you think we came into this wilderness to practice those courses here which we fled from in England. We believe there is a vast difference between men's inventions and God's institutions; we fled from men's inventions, to which we else should have been compelled; we compel none to men's inventions. If our ways (rigid ways as you call them) have laid us low in the hearts of God's people, yea, and of the saints (as you style them) we do not believe it is any part of their saintship. Nevertheless, I tell you the truth, we have tolerated in our church some Anabaptists, some Antinomians and some Seekers, and do so still at this day. We are far from arrogating infallibility of judgment to ourselves or affecting uniformity; uniformity God never required, infallibility he never granted us.[3]

Here I would remark :—

1. That they were not infallible, can easily be believed, by all who see what great absurdities and self-contradictions they were driven to, in trying to support that way. Mr.

[1] "Although the paying of a fine seems to be but a small thing in comparison of a man's parting with his religion, yet the paying of a fine is the acknowledgment of a transgression; and for a man to acknowledge that he has transgressed when his conscience tells him he has not, is but little, if any thing at all, short of parting with his religion; and 'tis likely that this might be the consideration of those sufferers." Governor Jencks.

[2] If the reader will look back to page 185, he may see how contrary this is to truth.

[3] Mass. History, Vol. III, pp. 403—406.

Cotton here asserts that they were far from arrogating infallibility to themselves, and yet in the same letter had said, our churches are established, " *We know* by God's law," and that in the points Mr. Holmes contested. And the use of force in religious matters naturally carries men into this absurdity; for it would sound very odd in any men, to compel others to their way by the magistrate's sword, and yet own at the same time that they did not know but they were compelling them into errors. When I first came into the parish where I now dwell, as they were without a minister, their committee requested me to preach to them for some time, which I did. But in the year following, they got a major vote to hire another sort of preaching, and taxed me with our society thereto. This caused our society to present an address to that party, dated November 21, 1748, wherein they say, " Pray consider, would you like it if we were a few more in number than you, to be forced to help us build a meeting-house, and maintain our minister? We doubt it much." To this the other party, by the help of a neighboring minister, returned a long answer, the turning point of which was in these words, viz.:—

> What we demand of you is equal and right; what you demand of us is evil and sinful; and hence we have the golden rule upon our side, while you are receding and departing from it; for if we were in an error, and out of the right way, as we see and *know* that you are in several respects, and you see and *know* it of us, as *we do* of you, we think the golden rule would oblige you to tell us of our error, and not let us alone to go on peaceably in it, that is without using proper means to recover and reclaim us; whether by the laws of God, or the good and wholesome laws of the land, as we now treat you.

Now, only allow it to be right to join the laws of the land with the laws of God, in supporting what the majority calls the right way of worship, and then how can any one fairly withstand this reasoning? For we are required not to suffer sin upon our neighbor; and if secular force be a means that Christians ought to use, to bring their neighbors from error to attend and support the truth, how can Mr. Cotton's party be condemned for seizing and punishing Mr. Clarke and his brethren for worshipping in a private house, when they had an Orthodox meeting in the town, established by public authority? And how can the major party in any parish be blamed for imprisoning men for their minister's rates (as my neighbors did me) though they never heard him, or received the least benefit from him? If any think these two are not parallel cases, I ask what is the difference? Mr. Clarke and Holmes might have gone to the established worship, if they *would;* and Mr. Holmes might have had his fine paid it seems if he *would*, and so all his devotion under the whip is declared to be "no better than will worship." According to Mr. Cotton's own words, men might then be Anabaptists, Antinomians, and what not, if they would but come to hear the right ministers, and join with the right churches; and is not the greatest complaint they have at this day against the Baptists, because they refuse to commune with Pedobaptist churches? They professed to grant liberty of conscience then, as well as now. Captain Johnson who wrote in the time we are upon, says of erroneous persons:—

> They report in all places where they come, that New England government doth persecute the people and churches of Christ; which, to speak truth, they have hitherto been so far from, that they have endeavored to expel all such beasts of prey (who will not be reclaimed) that here might be none left to hurt or destroy in all God's holy mountain. .... Neither do they exercise civil power to bring all men under their obedience, to a uniformity in every point of religion, but to keep them in the unity of the spirit, and the bond of peace; nor yet have they ever mixed their civil powers with the authority peculiarly given by Christ to his churches and officers of them, but from time to time have labored to uphold their privileges, and only communion one with another.[1]

It is readily granted that the sentiments of Mr. Williams and Mr. Clarke, about religious liberty, have had a great spread since that day, so that men of a contrary mind can-

[1] Johnson's History, p. 107.

not carry their oppressive schemes so far now as they did then; yet as to such as still hold that they have a right to use secular force to support worship, I think the chief difference between them and their fathers in 1651, lies in these two points: Then they gave the church the whole power of electing and settling ministers; now the world is empowered to control the church in her choice; then they obliged men to hear, as well as support their good ministers; now men may hear whom they please, if they will but let the parish minister have their money; but if that is refused, men are as liable to imprisonment or confiscation of goods now as then; and whether the compelling of a man to pay for that which is no benefit to him, be not an action more void of the very appearance of justice, than the compelling of men to hear what the compellers esteemed good preaching was, is freely referred to every reader's conscience; as it also is, whether the real error in both cases does not lie in blending divine and human laws together, rather than in any mistake about applying of them then, more than now.

2. We have abundant reason to think that Mr. Clarke's narrative of their sentiments and sufferings, is a true and just one; for he published it in 1652, and it greatly concerned the Massachusetts colony to confute the same if they could, and they did not want for men of ability and inclination to vindicate themselves in that respect, if they had found matter to work upon. But Captain Johnson who published his history of that colony in 1654, is silent about this remarkable affair. Mr. John Leverett, their agent at the British Court, wrote to Governor Endicott about it; but he in a letter of June 29, 1657, says, "I cannot for the present answer your expectation touching Rhode Island, and Clarke and Holmes."[1] Mr. Morton printed his New England Memorial in 1669, in which he endeavors to vindicate the country against many other complaints, but leaves this narrative

[1] Massachusetts History, Vol. III, p. 309.

untouched. Mr. Hubbard wrote a large history of the country in 1680, yet touches not this affair unless in an obscure hint which confutes nothing. Dr. Cotton Mather published his folio history of New England in 1702, but passes over these sufferings in silence; yea, and so does Governor Hutchinson, though his history is the most impartial upon religious disputes of any that has been written in this country, yet he says, " The first persecution I find upon record of any of the people called Anabaptists was in the year 1665."[1] In his third volume, which is a collection of ancient papers, are a few references to these sufferers, which I have now made use of, but instead of confuting, they confirm Mr. Clarke's Narrative. Mr. Neal who wrote in London, 1720, has from that narrative given a brief account of their sufferings, and has done them the most honor of any Pedobaptist author I ever saw; though he has made several mistakes about them.[2]

---

[1] Massachusetts History, Vol. I, p. 226. [208.]

[2] As in Vol. I, p. 298, he says, " Mr. Newman admonished Holmes of his offence; but finding him obstinate, and not willing to give an account of his conduct to the church, he excommunicated him;" for which he gives no other proof than Mr. Clarke's Narrative, and that informs us, p. 24, [53, 54,] that the first occasion of Mr. Holmes's separation was, "That seven of the brethren should pass an act of admonition upon a brother, without the consent of the rest, we (says Mr. Holmes) being twenty-three in number, who might all in one hour's space, if in health, have come together; so when I heard of it I went to Mr. Newman, and told him of the evil which he and the other six had done; he told me they were the church representative, and if four of them had done it, it had been a church act. When this comes to the congregation, with much ado, he got five more to himself, and then they were twelve and we eleven; then they owned themselves to be the church, and began to deal with me for saying, they had abused the church, and had took from them their power; whereupon I told them I should renounce them, till either they saw their sin, or I further light." After which a number more drew off and set up a meeting by themselves, and there was public notice of the day when they were to be baptized, and many witnesses of the transaction, yet says he, "Not one man or woman of Mr. Newman's company ever come to deal with me for evil either in judgment or practice till a long time after." Now is it just to charge Mr. Holmes with obstinacy, only for his refusing to submit to the other party after this? Again Mr. Neal, p. 302, charges Mr. Clarke, with standing upon a *punctilio* against *very fair concessions* of the Massachusetts rulers, only because he refused to dispute without an exemption from the lash of their law.

3. By all that appears, those Baptist fathers were sound in the faith and much acquainted with experimental and practical religion. All that was proved against them may be summed up in their noble testimony, that there is "none to or with Christ the Lord, by way of commanding and ordering with respect to the worship of God; that baptism or dipping in water is one of his commandments, and that a visible believer or disciple of Christ is the only person that is to be baptized; that every such believer, may in point of liberty, yea, ought in point of duty to improve that talent his Lord hath given him with meekness of wisdom; and that no such believer hath any liberty, much less authority from his Lord, to smite his fellow-servant, nor yet with outward force to restrain his conscience, nor outward man for conscience sake, where injury is not offered to the person, name or estate of others." This is the sum of all the principles for which they suffered such cruel things, though their opposites have constantly accused them of others. The assembly of Massachusetts begin their law against the Baptists in 1644, with saying, that "since the first arising of the Anabaptists about one hundred years since, they have been the incendiaries of the commonwealths, and the infectors of persons in main matters of religion, and the troublers of churches in all places where they have been;" and great pains have been taken by teachers and writers from that day to this, to connect these odious ideas with the very name of Anabaptists. But let the reader judge whether it be possible for ministers of any denomination, to visit and worship with any of their brethren, more peaceably than these ministers did with their brother at Lynn; and whether he can find one of their martyrs who showed less of a disposition for denying the lawful authority of magistrates, or more of a Christian temper in sufferings, under their unlawful usurpations, than these Baptists did. And whether they were heterodox or not in main matters of religion, may be partly

gathered from the foregoing account, and still further by the confession of their faith inserted below.[1]

I shall close this chapter with an address of Mr. Roger Williams to Governor Endicott, concerning these affairs.

[1] Mr. Clarke left a confession of his faith in writing, from whence an extract was inserted in the records of his church, the main of which here follows :—

"The decree of God is that whereby God hath from eternity set down with himself whatsoever shall come to pass in time. Eph. i. 2. All things with their causes, effects, circumstances and manner of being, are decreed by God. Acts, ii. 23. 'Him, being delivered by the determinate counsel and foreknowledge of God,' &c. Acts, iv. 28. This decree is most wise; Rom. xi. 33; most just; Rom. ix. 13. 14; eternal; Eph. i. 4, 5; II Thes. ii. 13; necessary; Psa. xxxiii. 2, Prov. xix. 21; unchangeable; Heb. vi. 17; most free; Rom. ix. 13; and the cause of all good; Jam. i. 17; but not of any sin; I John, i. 5. The special decree of God concerning angels and men is called predestination. Rom. viii. 30. Of the former, viz., angels, little is spoken in the Holy Scripture; of the latter more is revealed, not unprofitable to be known. It may be defined, the wise, free, just, eternal and unchangeable sentence or decree of God, determining to create and govern man for his special glory, viz., the praise of his glorious mercy and justice; Rom. ix. 17, 18, and xi. 36. Election is the decree of God, of his free love, grace and mercy, choosing some men to faith, holiness and eternal life, for the praise of his glorious mercy; I Thes. i. 4, II Thes. ii. 13, Rom. viii. 29, 30. The cause which moved the Lord to elect them who are chosen, was none other but his mere good will and pleasure, Luke xii, 32. The end is the manifestation of the riches of his grace and mercy, Rom. ix. 23, Eph. i. 6. The sending of Christ, faith, holiness, and eternal life, are the effects of his love, by which he manifesteth the infinite riches of his grace. In the same order God doth execute this decree in time, he did decree it in his eternal counsel. I Thes. v. 9; II Thes. ii. 13. Sin is the effect of man's free will, and condemnation is an effect of justice inflicted upon man for sin and disobedience. .... A man in this life may be sure of this election, II Pet. i, 10, I Thes. i, 4; yea of his eternal happiness, ... but not of his eternal reprobation; for he that is now profane, may be called hereafter." Thus far Mr. Clarke.

Mr. Holmes says:—"Having had two or three requests from my friends and brethren, in special my brother Robert, to give some information of my present state and standing with reference to the Lord and my own soul, [I] shall as briefly as I can, give account thereof. .... But before I come to speak to the point in hand, I cannot forget the rock out of which I was hewn, and the cistern out of which I was digged; who was by nature a child of wrath as well as others, and by actual transgression added sin to sin, as my conscience and others did know. But God had mercy for me in store when I neither deserved it nor desired it, for he knows who are his; and the elect shall obtain it, forever blessed be his holy name, to whom be glory forever. Amen. Now in this faith or belief I stand, not doubting but it is the faith of God's elect.

1. "I believe there is one Essence or Being, even one God, who made heaven and earth, the waters, and all things therein contained, who governs all things by the word of his power, and hath appointed life and death to men, and bounded their habitations, whose providence extendeth to the least creature and actions. 2. I believe this God is Father to our Lord Jesus Christ; in a special understanding may be dis-

The governor having occasion (as they often had,) to write to Mr. Williams about the "peace of the English and Indians," and having at the entrance of his letter said, "Were I as free in my spirit as formerly I have been to

tinguished as Father, Son and Holy Spirit, and yet but one in Essence. 3. I believe that as God made the world, so by his word made he man in his own image without sin, and gave him a most excellent place and being, giving him commandment what he should do, and what he should forbear; but through the malice of Satan working with his wife was deceived; for she did eat, and gave her husband and he did eat, which was the first cause of the curse to him, and reached to all his posterity, by which came death natural, and death eternal. 4. I believe in this interim of time the Lord manifested his great love in that word, 'The seed of the woman shall break the head of the serpent,' but enmity was between the two seeds. 5. I believe that at that and after time the Lord was worshipped by sacrifices, though darkly held forth to us. 6. I believe after that God in his own time chose a people to himself, and gave them his laws and statutes in a special manner, though he had always his chosen ones in every generation. 7. I believe with this people he made a choice covenant to be their God, and they to be his people; which covenant they brake though he was a Father to them, and was grieved for them, and yet did not only give them his laws, but sent his prophets early and late, but they would not hear; and in fullness of time sent his only Son; but as they had abused his prophets, so they killed his only Son. 8. I believe God in his Son made a new covenant, a sure and everlasting covenant, not like that he made with Israel, of which Moses, that faithful servant, was mediator, but a covenant of grace and peace through his only Son, that whosoever believed in him should not perish, but have everlasting life. 9. I believe that all those that are in this covenant of grace, shall never fall away nor perish, but shall have life in the Prince of Life, the Lord Jesus Christ. 10. I believe no man can come to the Son but they that are drawn by the Father to the Son, and they that come, he in no wise will cast away. 11. I believe he came to call sinners to repentance, for the whole need him not, but they that are sick. 12. I believe that by the shedding of his precious blood is my redemption, and not mine only, but all that are or shall be saved. 13. I believe that as he was God so was he man, for he did not take the nature of angels, but the nature of Abraham. 14. I believe God hath laid the iniquity of all his elect and called ones, upon him. 15. I believe the Father is fully satisfied, and the debt is truly paid to the utmost farthing, and the poor sinner is quit, and set free from all sin past, present and to come. 16. I believe the Holy Scriptures which testify of Christ in dark shadows and types, and all that was written of Christ in the Prophets and Psalms; and that he was born of a virgin at Bethlehem, and come to his own and they received him not. 17. I believe he was put to death and hanged upon a tree, called the cross, and was buried, and the third day rose again according to the Scriptures, and appeared to many. 18. I believe he ascended to his Father and sitteth at his right hand, having made request for his. 19. I believe that the Father's commandment and his declaration of him is to be observed, when the Father uttered that voice saying, 'This is my beloved Son in whom I am well pleased; hear ye him.' 20. I believe there is no salvation but by him alone; no other name under heaven by which man can be saved. 21. I believe he is sent unto the world, and to be published to all men; but some, yea, many reject the counsel of God against themselves. 22. I believe

write unto you, you should have received another manner of salutation than now, with a good conscience I can express; however God knoweth who are his, and what he is pleased to hide from sinful man in this life, shall in that great day be

none have power to choose salvation, or to believe in Christ for life; it is only the gift of God. 23. I believe although God can bring men to Christ, and cause them to believe in him for life, yet he hath appointed an ordinary way to effect that great work of faith, which is by means of sending a ministry into the world, to publish repentance to the sinner, and salvation, and that by Jesus Christ; and they that are faithful shall save their own souls and some that hear them. 24. I believe that they that are sent of God are not to deliver a mission of their own brain, but as it is in the Scripture of truth, for holy men wrote as they were inspired by the Holy Spirit. 25. I believe the precious gifts of the Spirit's teaching were procured by Christ's ascension and given to men for begetting of souls to the truth, and for establishment and consolation of those that are turned to the Lord; for none shall pluck them out of his Father's hand. 26. I believe no man is to rush into the ministry without a special call from God, even as gospel ministers had of old, which was the call of the Holy Spirit, with some talent or talents to declare the counsel of God to poor sinners, declaring the grace of God through Jesus Christ, even to those that are yet in the power of Satan; yea, to bring glad tidings by and from the Lord Jesus Christ. 27. I believe this ministry is to go forth, and he that hath received grace with a talent or talents, as he hath received freely of the Lord, so he is freely to give, looking for nothing again but the promise of the Lord. 28. I believe none is to go forth but by commission, and carefully to observe the same according as Christ gave it forth without adding or diminishing; first to preach Christ, that is to make disciples, and then to baptize them, but not to baptize them before they believe; and then to teach them what Christ commanded them. For as the Father had his order in the former dispensation, so hath the Son. In former times the Lord spake in divers ways and manners, but now hath he spoken by his Son. 29. I believe that as God prepared a begetting ministry, even so doth he also prepare a feeding ministry in the church, where a called people out of the world, by the word and Spirit of the Lord, assembling of themselves together in a holy brotherhood, continuing in the apostles' doctrine, fellowship, breaking bread and prayer. 30. I believe such a church ought to wait for the Holy Spirit of promise, on whom it may fall, and to choose out among themselves either pastor, teacher, or elders ·to rule, or deacons to serve the table, that others may give themselves to the word and prayer, and to keep them close to the Lord, and their fellowship clear and distinct, not to have fellowship with the unfruitful works of darkness, but rather to reprove them. 31. I believe the church of Christ, or this company gathered, are bound to wait on the Lord for the Spirit to help them, and have liberty, and are under duty, that they may prophesy one by one. 32. I believe that the true baptism of the gospel, is a visible believer with his own consent to be baptized in common water, by dying, or as it were drowning, to hold forth death, burial and resurrection, by a messenger of Jesus, into the name of the Father, Son, and Holy Spirit. 33. I believe the promise of the Father, concerning the return of Israel and Judah, and the coming of the Lord to raise up the dead in Christ, and to change them that are alive, that they may reign with him a thousand years, according to the Scripture. 34. I believe the resurrection of the wicked to receive their just judgment, Go ye cursed to the devil and his

manifested to all." Mr. Williams referring to the sufferings of Mr. Clarke and Mr. Holmes, says:—

Sir, at the reading of this line, the speech of that wise woman of Tekoa unto David came fresh unto my thoughts: Speaks not the King this thing as one that is guilty? for will my honored and beloved friend not know me for fear of being disowned by his conscience? Shall the goodness and integrity of his conscience to God cause him to forget me? Doth he quiet his mind with this (God knoweth who are his; God hides from sinful man; God will reveal before all?) Oh how comes it then that I have heard so often [and] heard so lately, and heard so much, thàt he that speaks so tenderly for his own, hath yet so little respect, mercy or pity to the like conscientious persuasions of other men? are all the thousands of millions of millions of consciences at home and abroad, fuel only for a prison, for a whip, for a stake, for a gallows? are no consciences to breathe the air, but such as suit and sample his? may not the Most High be pleased to hide from his as well as from the eyes of his fellow-servants, fellow-mankind, fellow-English? .... Who can shut when he will open? and who can open, when he that hath the key of David will shut? ....

Objection. But what makes this to heretics, blasphemers, seducers, to them that sin against their conscience (as Mr. Cotton saith) after conviction? .... First, I answer, he was a tyrant that put an innocent man into a bear's skin, and so caused him as a wild beast to be baited to death.

angels forever. 35. I believe, as eternal judgment to the wicked, so I believe the glorious declaration of the Lord saying, Come ye blessed of my Father, enter into the joy of your Lord, which joy, eye hath not seen, ear hath not heard, neither can it enter into the heart of man to conceive the glory that God hath prepared for them that love and wait for his appearance; wherefore come Lord Jesus, come quickly!

For this faith and profession I stand, and have sealed the same with my blood in Boston, in New England, and hope through the strength of my Lord I shall be enabled to witness the same to death, although I am a poor unworthy creature, and have nothing to plead or fly unto but to grace, grace; and have nothing to rest on but only the mercy, the free mercy of God in and through Jesus Christ my Lord and Saviour; to whom be honor, glory and praise forever and ever, Amen. Thus have I given you an humble and true account of my standing, and of my dear wife's standing in our faith and order, that you may consider the same, comparing what is written by the Holy Scriptures, which are our rule towards God and man; committing this and you to the wisdom and counsel of God. Yours in all love to serve continually having you in our prayers; fare ye well.

"This for Mr. John Angher, and my brother Robert Holmes, and my brother-in-law, and sisters, with Mary Nonly, and to them that love and fear the Lord. For Robert Holmes in the parish of Manchester, Lancashire." Obadiah Holmes's Manuscript, 1675.

Secondly, This is the common cry of haunters [hunters] or persecutors, heretics, blasphemers, &c., and why, but for crossing the persecutors' consciences (it may be but their superstitions) whether Turkish, Popish, Protestant, &c. This is the outcry of the pope and prelates, and of the Scotch Presbyterians, who would fire all the world, to be avenged on the sectarian heretics, the blasphemous heretics, the seducing heretics, &c., had it not pleased the God of heaven who bounds the insolent rage of the furious ocean to raise up a second Cromwell to stay the fury of the oppressor, whether English, Scottish, Popish, Presbyterian, Independent, &c. . . . .

Let it not be offensive in your eyes, that I single out a point, a cause of my banishment, wherein I greatly fear one or two sad evils have [which hath] befallen your soul and conscience. The point is that of the civil magistrate's dealing in matters of conscience and religion, as also of persecuting [and hunting] any for any matter merely spiritual and religious. The two evils intimated are these: first, I fear you cannot after so much light, and so much profession to the contrary (not only to myself [and so] often in private,[1] but) before [so] many witnesses; I say, I fear you cannot say and act so much, against so many several consciences, former and latter, but with great checks, great threatenings and inward throes [great blows and throes] of conscience. Secondly, If you shall thank God, that it is not so with you, but that you do what conscience bids you in God's presence, upon God's warrant, I must then be humbly faithful to tell you, that I fear your underprizing of holy light, hath put out the candle, and the eye of conscience in these particulars, and that delusions, strong delusions, and that from God, (by Satan's subtilty) hath seized upon your very soul's belief, because you prized not, loved not the persecuted Son of God in his despised truths and servants. . . . . I desire to say it tremblingly and mournfully, I know not which way he will please to raise his glory, only I know my duty, my conscience and my love, all which enforce me to knock, to call, to cry at the gate of heaven, and at yours, and to present you with this loving, though loud and faithful noise, and sound of a few grounds of deeper examination of both our souls and consciences, uprightly and impartially at the holy and dreadful tribunal of him that is appointed the Judge of all the living and the dead.

Be pleased then (Honored Sir) to remember that the thing which we call conscience is of such a nature, especially in Englishmen, as once a pope of Rome, at the suffering of an Englishman in Rome himself observed that although it be groundless, false and deluded, yet it is not by any arguments of torments easily removed. I speak not of the stream of the multitude of all nations, which have their ebbings and flowings in religion (as

[1] Governor Endicott was once a member of Salem church, under Mr. Williams's ministry.

the longest sword and strongest arm of flesh carries it[1] (but I speak of conscience, a persuasion fixed in the mind and heart of a man, which enforceth him to judge (as Paul said of himself a persecutor) and to do so and so with respect to God, his worship, &c. This conscience is found in all mankind more or less. .... To this purpose let me freely without offence remember you (as I did Mr. Clarke, newly come up from his sufferings amongst you) I say, remember you of the story I did him of William Hartly in queen Elizabeth, her days, who receiving the sentence of hanging, ... spake confidently (as afterward he suffered) "What tell you me of hanging? if I had ten thousand millions of lives, I would spend them all for the faith of Rome!" Sir, I am far from glancing the least countenance on the consciences of papists .... all that I observe is, that boldness and confidence. zeal and resolution, as it is commendable in a kind when it seriously respects a Deity, so also the greatest confidence hath sometimes need of the greatest search and examination. .... Wise men use to enquire what motives, what occasions, what snares, what temptations were there which moved, allured, &c. .... Surely sir, the baits, the temptations, the snares laid to catch you were not few, nor common. .... It is no small offer, the choice and applause and rule over so many towns, so many holy, so many wise, in such a holy way as you believe you are in. .... I cannot but fear and lament, that some of these and others have been too strong and potent with [for] you. .... Sir, I must be humbly bold to say, it is [that 'tis] impossible for any man or men to maintain their Christ by the sword, and to worship a true Christ! to fight against all consciences opposite to theirs, and not to fight against God in some of them, and to hunt after the precious life of the true Lord Jesus Christ. Oh remember whither your principles and consciencies, must in time and opportunity force you! .... Yourself and others have said it by your principles, such whom you count heretics, blasphemers, seducers, ought to be put to death. You cannot be faithful to your principles and consciences, if you satisfy them with but imprisoning, fining, whipping and banishing the heretics, and by saying that banishing is a kind of death, as some chief with you formerly said in my case.[2] I end with an humble cry to the Father of

---

[1] The following words are remarkable, viz.: "It is made by learned and judicious writers, one of the undoubted rights of sovereignty to determine what religion shall be publicly professed and exercised within their dominions. Why else do we in New England that profess the doctrines of Calvin, yet practice the discipline of them called Independent, or Congregational churches, but because the authority of the country is persuaded, that is most agreeable to the mind of God." Mr. Hubbard's Election Sermon at Boston, May 3, 1676, p. 35.

[2] Cotton, on the contrary, declared that in this country, "where a man may make his choice of a variety of more pleasant and profitable seats than he leaveth behind

mercies, that you may take David's counsel, and silently commune with your own heart upon your bed, reflect upon your own spirit, and believe him that said [it] to his over-zealous disciples, "You know not what spirit you are of;" that no sleep may seize [upon] your eyes, nor slumber upon your eye-lids, until your serious thoughts have [seriously] calmly, and unchangeably, through help from Christ, fixed, first on a moderation towards the spirit and consciences of all mankind, merely differing from, or opposing yours with only religious and spiritual opposition; .... secondly, a deep and cordial resolution to search, to listen, to pray, to fast, and more fearfully, more tremblingly to enquire what the holy pleasure, and the holy mysteries of the Most Holy are; in whom I humbly desire to be, your poor fellow servant, unfeignedly, respective, and faithful.

ROGER WILLIAMS.[1]

How happy had it been for New England, and for Governor Endicott in particular, if they had then regarded this faithful admonition of their old friend! but disregarding it, Mr. Williams's words a few years after were fully verified, when, under Governor Endicott's administration, the blood of the Quakers was shed, which has left an indelible stain upon their characters, and "sullied the glory of their former sufferings from the bishops; for now it appeared that the New England Puritans were no better friends to liberty of conscience than their adversaries, and that the question between them was not, whether one party of Christians should have power to oppress another, but who should have that power?"[2]

him," "banishment is not counted so much a confinement as an enlargement." Reply, &c., pp. 8, 9.—ED.

[1] Appendix of his Reply to Cotton, 1652, pp. 303—313. Mr. Cotton died the twenty-third of December, that year.

[2] Neal's History of New England, Vol. I, p. 320.

CHAPTER V.

A VARIETY OF EVENTS, FROM 1651 TO 1664.

A review of 1651, presents before us such a dark cloud and threatening gloom, upon the cause of believers' baptism, and true liberty of conscience, as must affect every heart that is not extremely obdurate. The friends of that cause had been so cruelly treated in Europe, that a number of them fled into America, where a persecuting temper followed them and expelled them out of Massachusetts colony; but God gave them favor in the eyes of the heathen, from whom they obtained a grant of lands, upon which to begin the first civil government that ever allowed equal liberty of conscience, since our Saviour died for us. With great hazard and expense Mr. Williams had procured a charter for that purpose, which they had enjoyed about seven years, when alas! Mr. Coddington, who had the deeds and records of the island in his own hands, went to England, and procured from the Council of State, a commission, dated April 3, 1651, signed by J. Bradshaw, constituting him Governor of the islands, to rule them with a council of six men, nominated by the people and approved by himself; which split this little colony into two parts, and Mr. Clarke and his brethren were to submit to a Governor that they had no hand in choosing, and their estates lay at his mercy. This melancholy news arrived just about the time that he and his brethren had been so cruelly handled in the Massachusetts, only for visiting and worshiping with an aged brother there. At the same time a party both of English and savages were supported in the heart of Mr. Williams's part of the colony, in opposition to all the good orders that he endeavored to establish among them. What could they now do? where could they go for relief? banished from their mother kingdom, and from neighboring colonies, who were exerting all their power to divide and conquer them! Indeed a man of the greatest worldly note among them, seemed as if he was like to do it effectually.[1]

[1] Near the same time the Court at Boston imposed a large fine upon the church in Malden, for calling a man to be their minister, without the approbation of the rulers and other ministers; and as they had before a law against gathering churches without their consent, their assembly now made another wherein they enacted, "that no minister should be called unto office in any of the churches, without the approbation of some of the magistrates, as well as the neighboring churches; on which ground in the year 1653, the Court would not allow the north church in Boston to call Mr. Powell, a well gifted though illiterate person to the stated office of a public teacher or minister; wherefore the people contented themselves with his being called to the place of a ruling elder. .... And whereas the plantations of New England had never as yet been acquainted, with the way of paying tithes for the support of the ministry, it was now left to the power of the county courts throughout the whole jurisdiction, to make sufficient provision for the maintenance of the ministry in the respective towns of the colony." [Hubbard, p. 551.]—B.

The Massachusetts Records give the following account of the above-mentioned dealings with the church in Malden. Under date of May 22, 1651, is the record:— "Whereas Mr. Marmaduke Matthews hath formerly and lately given offence to the magistrates, elders and many brethren, in some unsafe if not unsound expressions in his public teachings, and as it hath been manifested to this Court, and has not yet given satisfaction to those magistrates and elders that were appointed to receive satisfaction from him, since which time there hath in his public ministry been delivered other unsafe and offensive expressions by him, whereby both magistrates, ministers and churches were occasioned to write to the church of Malden to advise them not to proceed to the ordination of Mr. Matthews, which offences taken against him were also made known, yet, contrary to all advice and the rule of God's word, as also the peace of the churches, the church of Malden hath proceeded to the ordination of Mr. Matthews; this Court therefore, taking into consideration the premises and the dangerous consequences and effects that may follow such proceedings, &c." After this preamble, the act proceeds to appoint a committee of nine deputies to examine the affair, with permission to "call in the help or advice of any of the reverend elders whom they shall think meet." "The offence of the church" is then "referred to the next Court," but Mr. Matthews, for "suffering himself to be ordained contrary to the rules of God's word," is required to "give satisfaction at this session of this Court, by an humble acknowledgment of his sin for his so proceeding; which, if he refuse to do, to pay the sum of ten pounds within one month." Mr. Mathews "gave no satisfaction before the Court," and a warrant was issued to

Captain Johnson at that time said, "Familists, Seekers, Antinomians, and Anabaptists, [they] are so ill armed, that they think it best sleeping in a whole skin, fearing that if the day of battle once go on they shall fall among anti-

"levy the fine on his goods." The reverend gentleman seems not to have been encumbered with a heavy weight of worldly means, for, at the next session of the Court his fine was respited "till other goods appear besides books." He made an acknowledgment to the next General Court, and asked the remission of his fine, which was at first refused but afterwards granted.

October 14, 1651, the Court "appointed the church of Malden speedily to consider the errors Mr. Matthews stands charged with in Court," and if they refused, the Secretary was directed to give notice to the churches of Cambridge, Charlestown, Lynn and Reading, "to send their messengers in way of counsel and advice unto the church of Malden," "to debate the doctrines there delivered by Mr. Matthews." At the same session it is recorded, "The Court having perused an answer of the church of Malden touching those things wherein they have given offence, are not satisfied therewith, and do therefore judge that the members of the church of Malden shall be fined for their offences the sum of fifty pounds." This fine was levied on the estates of three members of the church, and they were empowered to apportion it upon the rest of the church except "such as consented not to Mr. Matthews's ordination." Ten pounds of the fine were afterwards remitted. May 23, 1655, certain of the church presented an acknowledgment and a petition for the repayment of the remainder of the fine, but were answered, "The Court doth not think meet to grant the petitioners' request herein."

The case of the "north church in Boston" appears from the records of the Court to have been as follows:—The church seems to have referred the question of Mr. Powell's ordination to the General Court for advice, representing themselves satisfied of his "abilities and fitness," notwithstanding his limited education; whereupon, October 19, 1652, the Court expressed themselves willing that Mr. Powell should "exercise in public" with the new church in Boston, "till it please God to provide better for them," but they advised against their proceeding to establish him as teaching elder. They gave as reasons, that Boston is "a place of such public resort," and the humor of the times to discourage learning. Four days later is the record, "The General Court having received credible information that the new church in Boston have chosen Mr. Powell to be their minister, and that he hath accepted their choice, they think it meet, in respect of the trust the country hath committed to them, lovingly to advise both the church and Mr. Powell to desist from any further proceeding." The church petitioned the next Court for liberty to call and ordain Mr. Powell, but the Court replied that they could not but judge Mr. Powell unfit for the office of pastor or teacher, nor could they consent thereto, because they could not be satisfied that Mr. Powell had such abilities, learning and qualifications as are requisite and necessary for an able ministry of the gospel. They added, "The Court conceives the church may call Mr. Powell to the office of ruling elder, and then they may enjoy all the ordinances of Christ amongst them save the sacrament, which they are supplied with in Boston; and their waiting till the Lord shall send unto them an able minister of the gospel, they hope, will not be in vain." The next year the church repeated its petition, and was curtly answered by being referred to the records of the previous Court.—ED.

christ's armies; [and] therefore they cry out like cowards, If you will let me alone, I will let you alone; but assuredly the Lord Christ hath said, ' He that is not with us, is against us;' there is no room in his army for *toleratorists*."[1] Had this been true, how could Mr. Williams and Mr. Clarke have persevered like heroes, in the cause of equity and liberty as they did? For being requested by their injured neighbors, they again crossed the boisterous ocean, and appeared as advocates for them at the British court; and also published to the world their pleas for equal liberty of conscience; and where can any writers be found of so early date, who defended that important right of mankind, so well as they did? Mr. Locke's excellent letters upon that subject were written near forty years afterward.

A little look back will give a more clear and just view of the important concerns of Mr. Williams's agency at this time. When the Commissioners of the United Colonies met at Plymouth, September 7, 1648, Mr. Coddington and Captain Partridge tried for a confederacy with them, but were denied it, unless they would come in as part of Plymouth colony. Mr. Henry Bull then complained to them, that some Narragansett Indians had beat him, and done him other injuries; and Mr. John Smith, Assistant for Warwick, sent a writing by Messrs Holden and Warner, in the behalf of the whole town, " wherein they complain, among other things, of divers injuries, insolences and affronts offered them by the Indians that are about them, and near inhabitants to them, as, namely, killing their cattle, about a hundred hogs, abusing their servants when they take them alone, [and] sometimes making violent entrance into their houses, and striking the masters thereof, stealing and purloining their goods; and hereupon do earnestly desire to know the minds of the Commissioners herein, and to receive advice from them." Upon which the Commissioners gave them a writing to the

[1] Johnson, p. 231.

sachems and others to warn them " to prevent and abstain from all such miscarriages for the future, and if any of them receive any injury from the English, upon complaint in due place and order, satisfaction shall be endeavored them according to justice, as the like will be expected from them." When the Commissioners met at Boston, July 23, 1649, Warwick wrote again to them; but they refused to do any thing for their defence, till they could find under what colony their plantation fell; and it was then disputed whether it belonged to the Massachusetts, or Plymouth; and they advised the latter to take it. When the Commissioners met again at Hartford, September 5th, 1650, they received a letter from Mr. Easton, President, in the name of the council of that colony, in which he declared, that " Rhode Island and Warwick were combined and bound mutually to support one another." Upon this the Commissioners mention a former article of advice which they had received from the honorable committee of parliament, " that in this and like cases the bounds of patents should be first set out by a jury, of uninterested persons, and that all inhabiting within the limits so set forth, should fall under the government established by patent." But instead of following this direction, after mentioning that the inhabitants of Warwick claimed an interest in Mr. Williams's patent, and refused to be brought under the Massachusetts government, they advised the authority of Plymouth " forthwith to resume [reässume] the right they formerly had by patent to the place." And that if the inhabitants refused to submit to them, then the advice of said committee should be taken, and if the same was not complied with, " that real damages duly proved, be levied by legal force, though with as much moderation and tenderness as the case will permit."[1] This was the treatment that was shown to Warwick; and hearing of what Mr. Coddington had done, they joined with Providence in send-

[1] Records of the United Colonies.

ing Mr. Williams to England. William Arnold hired a messenger secretly to carry a letter to Boston, to apprize their rulers of it,[1] but they were notified of it in a better way; for at a meeting of the Commissioners of the United Colonies at New Haven, September 4, 1651, they received the following letter, viz.:—

> May it please this honored committee to take knowledge, that we, the inhabitants of Shawomet alias Warwick, having undergone divers oppresions and wrongs, amounting to great damage since we first possessed this place; being forced thereby to seek to that honorable state of Old England for relief, which did inevitably draw great charge upon us, to the further impairing of our estates; and finding favor for redress, were willing to waive for that time (in regard to the great troubles and employment that then lay on that State) all other lesser wrongs [other losses and wrongs] we then underwent, so that we might be replaced [replanted] in and upon this [that] our purchased possession, and enjoy it peaceably for time to come, without disturbance or molestation by those from whom we had formerly suffered. But since our gracious grant from the honorable parliament, in replacing [replanting] of us in this place, we have been and daily are pressed with intolerable grievances, to the eating up of our labors, and wasting of our estates, making our lives, together with our wives and children, bitter and uncomfortable; insomuch, that groaning under our burthens, we are constrained to make our address[es] to the honorable parliament and state, once again, to make our just complaint against our causeless molesters, who by themselves and their agents, are the only cause of this our reüttering of our distressed condition. May it please therefore this honored Assembly, to take notice of this our solemn intelligence (given unto you as the most public authorized society appertaining unto, and instituted in the United Colonies, whom our complaints do concern) that we are now preparing ourselves with all convenient speed for Old England, to make our grievances known again to the state, which fall upon us by reason that the order of parliament [of England] concerning us hath not been observed, nor the enjoyment of our granted privileges permitted to us, that we are as it were bought and sold from one patent and jurisdiction to another; in that we have been prohibited and charged to acquit this place since the order of parliament given out and known to the contrary; in that we have had warrants sent us, to summon us to the Massachusetts Court, and officers employed amongst us for that purpose; in that these barbarous Indians about us, with evil minded English mixed among us, under pretence of some former personal subjection to the government of

---

[1] Massachusetts History, Vol. III, pp. 237—239.

the Massachusetts countenancing of them, cease not to kill our cattle, offer violence to our families, vilify authority of parliament vouchsafed to us, justifying their practices with many menaces and threatenings, as being under the protection of the Massachusetts; in that we [are and] have been restrained this seven or eight years past of common commerce in the country, and that only for matters of conscience; in that our estates formerly taken from us remain yet unrestored, with these additions thereunto. These and the like are the grounds of our complaints, with our serious desires that you would be pleased to take notice of them, as our solemn intelligence given hereof, that as yourselves shall think meet, you may give further seasonable intelligence to your several colonies whom it may concern, so that their agent or agents may have seasonable instructions to make answer, and we hereby shall acquit ourselves, that we offer not to proceed in these our complaints, without giving due and seasonable notice thereof. By me,

JOHN GREENE, Jun., Clerk.

In behalf of the town of Warwick.

Warwick, the first of September, 1651.

This brought matters to a close trial among them and the Commissioners, for those of Massachusetts (who were Mr. Simon Bradstreet, and Mr. William Hathorne, Esq'rs.) made a long declaration, how Plymouth gave up their right in that land to them in 1643; which was approved by all the Commissioners, who advised them to proceed against Gorton and his company, and had silently assented to what they had done from time to time since; and that when in 1649 they were advised to return those lands back to Plymouth, their Court sent two deputies to the Assembly at Plymouth, with orders to offer, to "resign and submit the said [aforesaid] lands, and persons residing thereon to the government of Plymouth; they only promising to do equal justice both to English and Indians there, according to our engagements; but the government of Plymouth chose rather to ratify the aforesaid resignment of their Commissioners;" after which they had "out of their own treasury allowed a large gratuity [quantity] of corn to the Indians under their government there, to keep them alive, the cattle of Gorton's company having destroyed most of theirs, rather than force to compel them, till all other means and ways of prudence for issuing these and the like differences were used." They closed with asking what aid the other jurisdictions would afford them, for the righting their injured and oppressed people, and bringing delinquents to condign punishment. The Connecticut and New Haven Commissioners answered, by owning that they had their advice in 1643, to proceed against Gorton's company, and that when Plymouth Commissioners yielded up their right to the Massachusetts, the others, being neither concerned, nor understanding where the right lay, saw no cause to dissent, &c. The Commissioners for Plymouth (who were Mr. John Brown, and Mr. Timothy Hatherley (declared that what was done by the Commissioners for their colony in 1643, in resigning said lands to the Massachusetts, was not at all in their power, neither could the Massachusetts receive any such resignation without injuring the third and sixth articles of their confederation; and that what right the authority of the Massachusetts had to send for Samuel Gorton and company, " inhabiting so far out of their jurisdiction they understand not." As to what the Governor of Plymouth and some others did in 1650, about ratifying that former resignation of Warwick to the Massachusetts, they said they had " protested against it in the Court of Plymouth, as being directly contrary to the order of the honorable committee of the parliament of England, and contrary to the articles of confederations with the rest of the colonies. " And whereas we are informed, that the Court of the Massachusetts have lately sent out several [summons or] warrants to several persons inhabiting [Shawomet, alias] Warwick and Pawtuxet, and have made seizure upon some of their estates, we do hereby protest against such proceedings if any there be."[1] Those in Massachusetts were so unwilling to have these things laid before the parliament, that they put Mr. Williams

[1] Records of the United Colonies.

to great distress only for attempting to take his passage through their colony.

The town of Newport signed an engagement and request to Mr Clarke in these words:—

We whose names are here underwritten,[1] being resolved to make our address unto the parliament of England, in point of our lands and liberties, do earnestly desire those six men that were last chosen the council of the town of Newport, and such as they shall consult with, to improve their best abilities for the managing thereof. We also do earnestly request Mr. John Clarke to do his utmost endeavors in soliciting our cause in England; and we do hereby engage ourselves to the utmost of our estates to assist them, being resolved in the mean time peaceably to yield all due subjection unto the present power set over us. Witness our hands the 15th of October, in the year of our Lord, God, 1651.

He sailed for England the next month.

Mr. Coddington having gotten the command of the islands, Providence and Warwick, each chose six deputies, who met at Providence, November 4, and unanimously concluded to stand embodied and incorporated as before, by virtue of their charter; and as president Easton had given place to Mr. Coddington, they chose another in his room, and made several laws, one of which was to prohibit any from purchasing lands of the Indians, without the Assembly's approbation, on penalty of forfeiting the same to the colony. When those two agents arrived in England, they united in a petition to the council of state, who on April 8th, 1652, referred the same to the Committee for Foreign Affairs. The Court of election at Warwick, May 18, made a law to forbid

---

[1] This was signed by John Easton, James Barker, John Cranston, Robert Carr, John Sheldon, Samuel Hubbard, John Allen, Henry Bull, Edward Thurston, Nathaniel West, William Dyre, William Lytherland, Richard Knight, Thomas Clarke, Thomas Dungan, &c., to the number of sixty-five, who with the six counsellors were almost all the free inhabitants of Newport, as Mr. Clarke said afterward to their General Assembly. Forty-one of the inhabitants of Portsmouth signed a like request. Copied from the original papers now before me.

Many of the above men were afterwards noted rulers in that colony; and Mr. Dungan was a member of Mr. Clarke's church, till about the year 1684; when he went to Pennsylvania, and became the first Baptist minister in that colony, where he left a numerous posterity. Edwards's History of the Baptists in that colony, p. 10.

the Dutch who were not inhabitants among them, from trading with the Indians in this colony, upon penalty of forfeiting both goods and vessel to the colony if they did; and the president was ordered to give the Governor of Manhatoes notice of it. When their Assembly met again in the fall at Providence, they wrote the following letter to Mr. Williams, viz.:—

HONORED SIR:—We may not neglect any opportunity to salute you in your absence, and have not a little cause to bless God, who hath pleased to select you to such a purpose, as we doubt not but will conduce to the peace and safety of us all, as to make you once more an instrument to impart and disclose our cause unto those noble and grave senators our honorable protectors, in whose eyes God hath given you honor [favor] (as we understand) beyond our hopes, and moved the hearts of the wise to stir on your behalf. We give you hearty thanks for your care and diligence, to watch all opportunities to promote our peace, for we perceive your prudent and comprehensive mind stirreth every stone to present it unto to the builders, to make firm the fabric unto us about which you are employed, laboring to unweave such irregular devices wrought by others amongst us, as have formerly clothed us with so sad events, as the subjection of some amongst us, both English and Indian to other jurisdictions; as also to prevent such near approach of our neighbors upon our borders on the Narragansett side, which might much annoy us, with your endeavors to furnish us with such ammunition as to look a foreign enemy in the face, being that the cruel begin to stir in these western parts, and to unite in one again, such as of late have had seeming separation in some respects; to encourage and strengthen our weak and enfeebled body to perform its work in these foreign parts, to the honor of such as take care, have been, and are so tender of our good, though we be unworthy to be had in remembrance by persons of so noble places, indued with parts of so excellent and honorable and abundantly beneficial use.

Sir, give us leave to intimate thus much, that we humbly conceive (so far as we are able to understand) that if it be the pleasure of our protectors to renew our charter for the re-establishing of our government, that it might tend much to the weighing of men's minds, and subjecting of persons who have been refractory, to yield themselves over as unto a settled government, if it might be the pleasure of that honorable state, to invest, appoint and empower yourself to come over as Governor of this colony for the space of one year, and so the government to be honorably put upon this place, which might seem to add much weight forever hereafter in the constant and successive derivation of the same. We only present it to your deliberate thoughts and consideration, with our hearty desires that your time of stay there for the effectual perfecting and finishing of your so weighty affairs may not seem tedious, nor be any discouragement unto you; and rather than you shall suffer for loss of time here, or expense there, we are resolved to stretch forth our hands at your return beyond our strength for your supply. Your loving bed-fellow is in health, and presents her endeared affection; so are all your family. Mr. Sayles also his, with the rest of your friends throughout the colony, who wish and desire earnestly to see your face.

Sir, we are yours, leaving you unto the Lord, we heartily take leave.

From the General Assembly of this colony of Providence Plantations, assembled in the town of Providence the 28th of October, 1652.[1]

JOHN GREENE, General Recorder.

On the 2d of October, the Council of State gave an order and wrote letters to vacate Mr. Coddington's commission, and to confirm their former charter; which were sent over by William Dyre. And about the 16th of February, 1653, he brought a letter to Providence, signed by Messrs. Sanford, Baulston, Porter and William Jefferies, requesting the two towns on the main to appoint a time to meet those on the Island, to hear and act upon the State's letters. Providence met upon the affair, and inquired why those letters were not brought to them, seeing they had continued to act upon the charter, after the Island was parted from them? Dyre told them that the two agents had united in their petition, and that as it appeared to him that the Island was the major part of the colony, therefore they had the greatest interest in the letters, and he had left them there. President Smith, William Field, and some others, joined with Dyre, and strove to persuade them to "account themselves a disordered, confused rout, as he acknowledged the islanders were, and to account all officers' orders of court, laws and cases depending, as null, and to come to a popular meeting to lay a new foundation of government for the colony." This they could not consent to, but each town chose six commissioners who met at Pawtuxet on February 25th, and sent four messen-

[1] Providence Records.

gers to the Island for those letters or a copy of them; and that if the state's orders were for them all to unite again, then to agree upon a meeting for that purpose. Dyre seeing no other way to carry his own scheme, assumed the power to himself to call the whole colony together by the following instrument :—

> Loving friends and neighbors, these are to signify unto you, that it hath pleased the right honorable, the Council of State, authorized by the supreme authority of the commonwealth of England to betrust myself with letters and orders concerning this colony, and the welfare thereof; be pleased therefore to understand, that upon Tuesday come seven night, at Portsmouth on Rhode Island, at Mr. Baulston's house, I shall be there (God willing) ready to attend the communication of the trust committed to my charge, unto all such free inhabitants as shall there make their personal appearance. Given under my hand this present 6th day of the week, being the 18th of February, 1652.
>
> WILLIAM DYRE.[1]

A copy of this he sent to each town, and many of the freemen met on the said March first, but instead of throwing all up, they ordered, "that all officers who were in place when Mr. Coddington's commission obstructed, should stand in their places, to act according to their former commissions, upon the Island; and the rest in the colony according as they had been annually chosen, until a new election according to former order." The Commissioners met again at Pawtuxet on March 9th, to receive the answer of their messengers from the Island, who reported what was done, but that they could not obtain so much as a copy of those letters from England. Upon which they sent again therefor, and also a proposal of joining with the towns on the Island in the next election, if they would agree to it in their

---

[1]This document, together with many others relating to the early history of Rhode Island, was copied for Backus by David Howell, then Professor in Rhode Island College, afterwards Judge in the United States' Court. The manuscript is among the Backus papers in the library of the Backus Historical Society. Appended to the above document are the words, "This the town of Providence in their letter to R. W. [Roger Williams], Agent in England, call *Dyre's Mandamus.* His conduct herein gave great offence to Providence and Warwick."—ED.

former method, and give them ten days' notice. By some means such notice was not given, therefore the two towns on the main met at Providence, May 17th, 1653, and elected their officers. An assembly met at the same time on the Island, and chose Mr. Sanford their President, and some freemen coming from the main, they chose an Assistant for each town in the colony; and they sent Mr. James Barker, and Mr. Richard Knight to Mr. Coddington, to demand the statute book, and book of records. And as it was then a time of war betwixt England and Holland, and mention was made of it in the letters which confirmed their charter, Dyre thought to make his advantage thereby, and procured commissions for himself, Captain Underhill, and Edward Hull to act against the Dutch in America; and some cannon with twenty men were sent to the English[1] on the east end of Long Island, to enable them to act against the Dutch who lay to the westward of them. This alarmed Providence colony, who met again in June, and a third time at Warwick, on August 13th, when they answered a letter from the Massachusetts, and remonstrated against being drawn into a war with the Dutch;[2] and wrote to Mr. Williams an account of Dyre's conduct, and of their being urged to give up their former actings as null; but say they, "being still in the same order you left us, and observing two great evils that such a course would bring upon us; first, the hazard of involving in all the disorders and bloodshed which have been committed on Rhode Island since their separation from us; secondly, the invading and frustrating of justice in divers weighty causes then orderly depending in our courts, in some of which causes Mr. Smith, President, William Field, &c., were deeply concerned;" therefore they could not yield to such a notion.[3]

[1] "They shall have two great guns and what *murtherers* are with us, on promise of returning them." R. I. Colonial Records.—ED.

[2] The remonstrance was made in June; the letter to Massachusetts was written in August. R. I. Colonial Records.—ED.

[3] Callender, [p. 99.] Colony Records. To give a clear idea of their difficulties I would insert the following things:—

Before we proceed further upon their affairs, some transactions in the Massachusetts call for our attention. Their ministers have often tried to persuade people, that ignorance of the original languages in which our Bible was written, is

"The 24th of the first month called March, in the year (so commonly called) 1637-8, Memorandum, that we Canonicus and Miantinomo, the two chief sachems of the Narragansetts, by virtue of our general command of this Bay, as also the particular subjecting of the dead sachems of Aquedneck and Kitackamuckqut, themselves and lands unto us, have sold to [unto] Mr. Coddington and his friends united unto him, the great island of Aquedneck, laying [from]hence eastward in this Bay, as also the marsh or grass upon Quinunnuqut, and the rest of the islands in this bay (excepting Chibachuwesa [Prudence] formerly sold to [unto] Mr. Winthrop, the now Governor of the Massachusetts, and Mr. Williams of Providence) also the grass upon the rivers and bounds [coves] about Kitackamuckqut, and from thence [these] to Paupusquatch, for the full payment of forty fathoms of white beads, to be equally divided between us; in witness whereof we have here subscribed. Item, that by giving, by Miantonomo's hands, ten coats and twenty hoes to the present inhabitants, they shall remove themselves from off the Island before next winter.

        In presence of,   Witness our hands,
The mark X of YOTUESH,   The mark † of CANONICUS,
ROGER WILLIAMS,   The mark ‡ of MIANTINOMO."
RANDAL HOLDEN,
The mark ‡ of ASSOTEMUIT,
The mark ‖ of MISHAMMOH,
    CANONICUS his son.

"Memorandum, that I, Osamaquin freely consent that Mr. William Coddington, and his friends united unto him, shall make use of any grass or trees on the main land on Pawakasick side, and I do promise loving [and just] carriage of myself and all my men to the said Mr. Coddington, and English, his friends united to him, having received of Mr. Coddington five fathoms of wampum, as gratuity for [from] himself and the rest.

    Witness, { ROGER WILLIAMS,   The mark X of OSAMAQUIN.
            { RANDAL HOLDEN.
Dated the sixth day of the fifth month, 1638.

These deeds, with a number of receipts from the Indians, are upon the colony records which Mr. Coddington had in his power when he obtained a commission to be their Governor without the people's consent, and when they contended hotly with him, it seems that he fled to Boston, where they sent after him, and prevailed with him to sign an engagement on April 14th, 1652, in the presence of Robert Knight and George Manning, to deliver up said deeds and records to such men as the majority of the purchasers and freemen should appoint to receive them, and to claim no more to himself than an equal share with the other purchasers. And the above record shows that he had those deeds in his hands till May. 1653. The main instance of bloodshed above referred to, was of a principal inhabitant of Newport, who was charged with a capital crime before a town meeting, and was condemned by them, and carried forth and shot to death in their presence. History of Providence. [Mass. Hist. Coll., Second series, Vol. IX, p. 184.]

the cause why any embrace Baptist principles. How well this agrees with their fear of a fair dispute with the learned Mr. Clarke the reader will judge, and what follows may afford further light.

Captain Johnson, speaking of the first president of Harvard College, says, that he was "fitted from the Lord for the work, and, by those that have skill that way, reported to be an able proficient both in the Hebrew, Greek and Latin languages, an orthodox preacher of the truths of Christ, and very powerful through his blessing to move the affections."[1] Mr. Hubbard speaking of Mr. Dunstar's being made president in 1640, says, " Under whom, that which was before but at best *schola illustra*, grew to the stature and perfection of a College, and flourished in the profession of all liberal sciences for many years." And Mr. Prince, upon the New England Psalm Book, says, " For a further improvement it was committed to the Rev. Mr. Henry Dunstar, president of Harvard College ; one of the greatest masters of the oriental languages, that hath been known in these ends of the earth."[2]

[1] Johnson, p. 168.
[2] Prince's preface to his own version of the psalms.—B.

"Among the early friends of the college none deserves more distinct notice than Henry Dunstar. He united in himself the character of both patron and President; for, poor as he was, he contributed, at a time of its utmost need, one hundred acres of land towards its support, besides rendering to it for a succession of years a series of official services well directed, unwearied and altogether inestimable. Under his administration the first code of laws was formed, rules of admission, and the principles on which degrees should be granted, were established. .... The charter of 1642, was probably, and that of 1650 was avowedly obtained on his petition. By solicitations among his personal friends, and by personal sacrifices he built the President's house. He was instant in season and out of season with the General Court for the relief of the College in its extreme wants. ....

" Dunstar's usefulness however was deemed to be at an end and his services no longer desirable, in consequence of his falling in 1653, as Cotton Mather expresses it, 'into the briars of anti-pædobaptism,' and of his having borne 'public testimony in the church at Cambridge against the administration of baptism to any infant whatever.' .... Indicted by the grand jury for disturbing the ordinance of infant baptism in the Cambridge church, sentenced to a public admonition on lecture day, and laid under bonds for good behavior, Dunstar's martyrdom was consummated by being compelled in October, 1654, to resign his office of President. .... He found the seminary a school, it rose under his auspices to the dignity of a college. No man ever questioned his talents, learning, exemplary fidelity, and usefulness.' Quincy's History of Harvard University, Vol. I, pp. 15—18.—ED.

This eminent man was brought so far this year that, " he not only forbore to present an infant of his own unto baptism, but also thought himself under some obligation to bear his testimony in some sermons, against the administration of baptism to any infant whatsoever." His brethren were so vehement and violent against him therefor, as to desire him to cease preaching there, and procured his removal both from his office and from his living in the town;[1] and Mr. Jonathan Mitchell, their minister at Cambridge, wrote December 24th, 1653:—

> That day after I came from him, I had a strange experience; I found hurrying and pressing suggestions against pædobaptism, and injected scruples and thoughts whether the other way might not be right, and infant baptism an invention of men, and whether I might with good conscience baptize children, and the like. And these thoughts were darted in with some impression, and left a strange confusion and sickliness upon my spirit. Yet methought, it was not hard to discern that they were from the *evil one*. First, because they were rather injected, hurrying suggestions, than any deliberate thoughts, or bringing any light with them. Secondly, because they were unseasonable; interrupting me in my study for the sabbath, and putting my spirit into [a] confusion, so I had much ado, to do ought in my sermon. It was not now a time to study that matter; but when in the former part of the week, I had given myself to that study, the more I studied it, the more clear and rational light I saw for pædobaptism, but now these suggestions hurried me into scruples. .... It was a check to my former self-confidence, and it made me fearful to go needlessly to Mr. D., for methought I found a venom and poison, in his insinuations and discourses against pædobaptism. .... I resolved also on Mr. Hooker's principle, that I would have an argument, able to remove a mountain, before I would recede from, or appear against a truth or practice received among the faithful.[2]

Query. How did he know but that his hurry and darkness was caused by the opposition of his heart, and the injections of the devil against the truth? Can anything be more unreasonable than his conclusion drawn from the time of his

---

[1] Governor Dudley died July 31, 1653, with these lines in his pocket, viz.:—
" Let men of God in courts and churches watch
O'er such as do a *toleration* hatch."

[2] Mitchell's Life, pp. 67—70. [Magnalia, Vol. II, p. 79.]

scruples? The fact was just this; in his own study he thought he saw a light for infant baptism, but when he came to converse with a gentleman who knew more than he did, it raised scruples in his mind about that practice. But where was the modesty of a youth not thirty years old, when he accused one of the most venerable fathers of that age, of having venom and poison in his discourses, only because his own self-confidence was shocked thereby? Sure I am that if any Baptist minister had told such a story, and that it made him fearful of going near a learned gentleman, whose arguments had brought him to scruple whether he had not been educated in a wrong way, but that he was resolved to have an argument able to work miracles before he would leave it, the other party would then have had such grounds, to charge the Baptist with wilfulness and obstinacy as they never yet had.

Rigidness is a word that both Episcopalians and Presbyterians have often cast upon our Plymouth fathers. Yet the Massachusetts now discovered so much more of that temper than they, that Mr. Dunstar, on October 24, 1654, resigned his office among them, and removed and spent his remaining days at Scituate, in Plymouth colony. And it seems remarkable that Mr. Charles Chauncy who, though he allowed believers to bring their infants, yet held that baptism was dipping, was, on the 27th of November following, made president of Harvard College in Mr. Dunstar's room.[1] Mr. Chauncy was born in Hartfordshire, in 1589; was educated in the university of Cambridge; "was incomparably well skilled in all the learned languages, especially in the oriental, and eminently in the Hebrew; in obtaining whereof his conversation with a Jew for the space of a year, was no little advantage.[2] He was successful in the ministry at Ware, in England, till, being persecuted, and having suffered much from Laud's party, he came to Ply-

---

[1] Magnalia, Book IV, p. 128. [Vol. II, p. 10.] [2] Ibid, Vol. I, p. 419.—ED.

mouth in 1638; in which place he preached about two years, and then, as has been noted, he removed and settled at Scituate, where, upon his taking the charge of that flock, he preached from that text, "Wisdom hath sent forth her maidens!" and reflecting in his discourse upon some compliances with the High Commission Court that he had been guilty of in his own country, he, with tears said, "Alas, Christians, I am no maiden! my soul hath been defiled with false worship! how wondrous is the free grace of the Lord Jesus Christ, that I should still be employed among the maidens of wisdom!" Upon an invitation from his old people at Ware, he now came to Boston, with a design of returning to them, when the overseers of the college, "by their vehement importunity prevailed with him to accept the government of that society."[1] Here we will leave him, till we shall have further occasion to mention his testimony against degeneracy in our land.

Mr. Williams had many enemies and difficulties to encounter in pleading for the rights of his colony, but was wonderfully supported and carried through them all; of which some account is given in the following letter:—

From Sir Henry Vane's at Belleau, Lincolnshire.

April 1st, '53 (so called.)

MY DEAR AND LOVING FRIENDS AND NEIGHBORS OF PROVIDENCE AND WARWICK:—Our noble friend Sir Henry Vane, having the navy of England mostly depending on his care, and going down to the navy at Portsmouth, I was invited by them both to accompany his lady to Lincolnshire, where I shall yet stay as I fear until the ship is gone; I must therefore pray your pardon that by the post I send this to London. I hope it may have pleased the most high Lord of sea and land to bring Capt. Ch-rst-n's ship and dear Mr. Dyre unto you, and with him the council's letters, which answer the petition Sir Henry Vane and myself drew up, and the council by Sir Henry's mediation granted us, for the confirmation of the charter, until the determination of the controversy. This determination you may please to understand is hindered by two main obstructions. The first is the mighty war with the Dutch, which makes England and Holland and the nations [to] tremble. This hath made the parliament set Sir Henry

[1]Magnalia, Book IV, pp. 134—136. [Vol. I, pp. 120—122.]

Vane and two or three more as commissioners to manage the war, which they have done with much engaging the name of God with them, who hath appeared in helping [of] sixty of ours against almost three hundred of their men-of-war, and perchance to the sinking and taking about one hundred of theirs, and but one of ours which was sunk by our own men. Our second obstruction is the opposition of our adversaries, Sir Arthur Haselrig and Colonel Fenwicke, who hath married his daughter, Mr. Winslow[1] and Mr. Hopkins, both in great place; and all the friends they can make in the parliament and council, and all the priests both Presbyterian and Independent; so that we stand as two armies ready to engage, observing the motions and postures each of other, and yet shy each of other. Under God the sheet anchor of our ship is Sir Henry, who will do as the eye of God leads him, and he faithfully promised me that he would observe the motion of our New England business, while I stayed some ten weeks with his lady in Lincolnshire. Besides here is [are] great thoughts and preparation for a new parliament; some of our friends are apt to think another parliament will more favor us and our cause than this has done. You may please to put my condition into your souls' cases; remember, I am a father and an husband; I have longed earnestly to return with the last ship, and with these, yet I have not been willing to withdraw my shoulders from the burthen lest it pinch others, and may fall heavy upon all; except you are pleased to give to me a discharge. If you conceive it necessary for me still to attend this service, pray you consider if it be not convenient that my poor wife be encouraged to come over to me, and to wait together on the good pleasure of God for the end of this matter. You know my many weights hanging on me, how my own place stands, and how many reasons I have to cause me to make haste, yet I would not lose their estates, peace and liberty [liberties] by leaving hastily. I wrote to my dear wife, my great desire of her coming while I stay; yet left it to the freedom of her spirit, because of the many dangers. Truly at present the seas are dangerous, but not comparably so much nor likely to be, because of the late great defeat of the Dutch, and their present sending to us offers of peace. My dear friends although it pleased God himself, by many favors to encourage me, yet please you to remember, that no man can stay here as I do, leav- in a present employment there, without much self-denial, which I beseech God for more, and for you also, that no private respects or gains or quarrels may cause you to neglect the public and common safety, peace and liberties. I beseech the blessed God to keep fresh in your thoughts what he hath done for Providence Plantations. My dear respects to yourselves, wives and children; I beseech the eternal God to be seen amongst you. So prays your most faithful and affectionate friend and servant,

ROGER WILLIAMS.

P. S. My love to all my Indian friends.

[1] Winslow died in the West Indies in 1655.

As men of all tempers and sentiments had resorted to that colony, and there had been from various quarters such interruptions of a regular administration of government as have been mentioned, it is not to be wondered at if many disorders appeared among them, of which enemies to their liberties did not fail to make all the advantage they could. Mr. Williams attended upon the difficult and important affairs of his agency another year, and then leaving the cause there with Mr. Clarke and other friends, he came over to take care of things here. He brought with him the following epistle, viz. :—

LOVING AND CHRISTIAN FRIENDS :—I could not refuse this bearer, Mr. Roger Williams, my kind friend and ancient acquaintance, to be accompanied with these few lines from myself to you, upon his return to Providence colony; though perhaps my private and retired condition, which the Lord of his mercy hath brought me into, might have argued strongly enough for my silence; but indeed something I hold myself bound to say to you, out of the Christian love I bear you, and for his sake whose name is called upon by you and engaged on your behalf. How is it that there are such divisions amongst you? Such headiness, tumults, disorders, injustice? the noise whereof echoes into the ears of all, as well friends as enemies, by every return of ships from those parts. Is not the fear and awe of God amongst you to restrain? Is not the love of Christ in you to fill you with yearning bowels one towards another, and constrain you not to live to yourselves but to him that died for you, yea, and is risen again? Are there no wise men amongst you? No public self-denying spirits, that at least upon grounds of common safety, equity and prudence can find out some way or means of union and reconciliation for you amongst yourselves, before you become a prey to common enemies? Especially since this state, by the last letter from the Council of State, gave you your freedom, as supposing a better use would have been made of it than there hath been. Surely when kind and simple remedies are applied and are ineffectual, it speaks loud and broadly, the high and dangerous distempers of such a body, as if the wounds were incurable. But I hope better things from you, though I thus speak, and should be apt to think, that by commissioners agreed on and appointed on all parts, and on behalf of all interests, in a general meeting, such a union and common satisfaction might arise, as through God's blessing might put a stop to your growing breaches and distractions, silence your enemies, encourage your friends, honor the name of God which of late hath been much blasphemed by reason of you; and in particular refresh and revive the sad heart of him who mourns over your present evils, as being your affectionate friend, to serve you in the Lord.

H. VANE.[1]

Belleau, the 8th of February, 1653—4.

With this Mr. Williams returned to Providence ; but at first met with such treatment as caused him to address the town in the following manner :—

WELL BELOVED FRIENDS AND NEIGHBORS :—I am like a man in a great fog. I know not well how to steer. I fear to run upon the rocks at home, having had trials abroad. I fear to run quite backward (as men in a mist do) and undo all that I have been a [this late] long time undoing myself to do, viz. : to keep up the name of a people, a free people, not enslaved to the bondages and iron yokes of the great (both soul and body) oppressions the English and barbarians about us ; nor to the divisions and disorders within ourselves. Since I set the first step of any English foot into these wild parts, and have maintained a chargeable and hazardous correspondence with the barbarians, and spent almost five years time with the state of England, to keep off the rage of the English against us, what have I reaped of the root of being the stepping stone to so many families and towns about us, but grief, and sorrow, and bitterness ! I have been charged with folly for that freedom and liberty which I have always stood for ; I say liberty and equality both in land and government. I have been blamed for parting with Mooshawsick, and afterward Pawtuxet (which were mine own, as truly as man's coat upon his back) without reserving to myself a foot of land or an inch of voice in any matter, more than to my servants or strangers. It hath been told me that I labored for a licentious and contentious people ; that I have foolishly parted with town and colony advantages, by which I might have preserved both town and colony in as good order, as any [town or colony] in the country about us. This and ten times more I have been censured for, and at this present am called a traitor by [the] one party, against the state of England, for not maintaining the charter and the colony ; and it is said that I am as good as banished by yourselves, and that both sides wished that I might never have landed, that the fire of contention might have had no stop in burning. Indeed the words have been so sharp between myself and some lately, that at last I was forced to say, They might well silence all complaints if I once began to complain, who was unfortunately fetched and drawn from my employment, and sent to so vast distance from my family to do your work of a high and costly nature, for so many days, and weeks, and months together, and there left to starve, or steal, or beg, or borrow. But

[1]Copied from the original letter.

blessed be God who gave me favor to borrow one while, and to work another, and thereby to pay your debts there, and to come over with your credit and honor, as an agent from you, who had in your name grappled with the agents and friends of all your enemies round about you. I am told that your opposites thought on me, and provided (as I may say) a sponge to wipe off your scores and debts in England, but that it was obstructed by yourselves, who rather meditated on means and new agents to be sent over to cross what Mr. Clarke and I had obtained. But gentlemen, blessed be God who faileth not, and blessed be his name for his wonderful providences, by which alone this town and colony, and that grand cause of truth and [and truth of] freedom of conscience hath been upheld to this day. And blessed be his name who hath again quenched so much of our fires hitherto, and hath brought your names and his own name thus far out of the dirt of scorn, reproach, &c. I find among[st] yourselves and your opposites that of Solomon true, that the contentions of brethren, some that lately were so, are the bars of a castle, and not easily broken, and I have heard some of both sides zealously talking of undoing themselves by a trial in England. Truly, friends, I cannot but fear you lost a fair wind lately, when this town was sent to for its deputies, and you were not pleased to give an overture unto the rest of the inhabitants about it; yea, and when yourselves thought that I invited you to some conference tending to reconciliation, before the town should act in so fundamental a business, you were pleased to forestall that, so that being full of grief, shame and astonishment [amazement]; yea, and fear that all that is now done (especially in our town of Providence) is but provoking the spirits of men to fury of desperation. I pray your leave to pray you to remember (that which I lately told your opposites) *Only by pride cometh contention.* If there be humility on the one side, yet there is pride on the other, and .... certainly the eternal God will engage against the proud; I therefore pray you to examine, as I have done them, your proceedings in this first particular. Secondly, love covereth a multitude of sins. Surely your charges and complaints each against other have not hid nor covered anything, as we used to cover the nakedness of those we love. If you will now profess not to have disfranchised humanity [humility] and love, but that (as [once] David in another case) you will sacrifice to the common peace, and common safety, and common credit, that which may be said to cost you something, I pray your loving leave to tell you that if I were in your souls' case, I would send unto your opposites such a line as this :—" Neighbors, at the constant request, and upon the constant mediation which our neighbor Roger Williams, since his arrival, hath used to us, both for pacification and accommodation of our sad differences, and also upon the late endeavors in all the other towns for an union, we are persuaded to remove our obstruction, viz., that paper of contention between us, and to deliver it into the hands of our aforesaid neighbor, and to obliterate that order which that paper did occasion. This removed, you may be pleased [please] to meet with, and debate freely, and vote in all matters with us as if such grievances had not been amongst us. Secondly, If yet ought remain grievous which we ourselves by free debate and conference cannot compose, we offer to be judged and censured by four men, which out of any part of the colony you shall choose two, and we the other.

Gentlemen, I only add, that I crave your loving pardon to your bold but true friend, ROGER WILLIAMS.

This address had the desired effect; and when the town came together, and Mr. Williams had a full hearing of the case, he, in the name of the town, drew an answer to Sir Henry Vane's letter, on August 27th, 1654, which now remains on record in his own hand writing as follows:—

SIR:—Although we are aggrieved at your late retirement from the helm of public affairs, yet we rejoice to reap the sweet fruits of your rest in your pious and loving lines, most seasonably sent unto us. Thus the sun [Thus sir, your sun] when he retires his brightness from the world, yet from under the very clouds we perceive his presence, and enjoy some light and heat and sweet refreshings. Sir, your letters were directed to all and every particular town of this Providence colony. Surely Sir, among the many providences of the most High, toward this town of Providence, and this Providence colony, we cannot but see apparently his gracious hand, providing your honorable self for so noble and true a friend to an outcast and despised people. From the first beginning of this Providence colony, (occasioned by the banishment of some in this place [these parts] from the Massachusetts) we say ever since, to this very day, we have reaped the sweet fruits of your constant loving-kindness and favor toward us. Oh Sir! whence then is it that you have bent your bow, and shot your sharp and bitter arrows now against us? Whence is it that you charge us with divisions, disorders, &c.? Sir, we humbly pray your gentle acceptance of our two-fold answer.

First, we have been greatly disturbed and distracted [distressed] by the ambition and covetousness of some amongst ourselves. Sir, we were in complete order until Mr. Coddington (wanting that public self-denying spirit which you commend to us in your letter) procured, by most untrue information, a monopoly of part of the colony, viz.: Rhode Island to himself, and so occasioned our general disturbance and distractions. Secondly, Mr. Dyre, with no less want of a public spirit, being ruined by party contentions with Mr. Coddington, and being betrusted to bring from England the letters of the Council of State for our re-unitings, he hopes for a recruit to himself by other men's goods; and (contrary to the State's intentions and expressions) plungeth himself and some others, in most unnecessary and unrighteous plundering, both of Dutch and French, and English also, [all] to our great grief, who protested against such abuse of our power from England; and the end of it is [even] to the shame and reproach of himself, and the very English name, [itself] as all these parts do witness."

Sir, our second answer is, (that we may not lay all the load upon other men's backs) that possibly a sweet cup hath rendered many of us wanton and too active; for we have long drunk of the cup of as great liberties as any people that we can hear of under the whole heaven. We have not only been long free (together with all New England) from the iron yoke of wolfish bishops, and their popish ceremonies (against whose cruel oppressions God raised up your noble spirit in parliament)[1] but we have sitten quiet and dry, from the streams of blood spilt by that war in our native country. We have not felt the new chains of the presbyterian tyrants, nor in this colony, have we been consumed with the over-zealous fire of the (so called) godly Christian magistrates. Sir, we have not known what an excise means; we have almost forgot what tythes are, yea, or taxes either, to church or commonwealth. We could name other special privileges, ingredients of our sweet cup, which your great wisdom knows to be very powerful (except more than ordinary watchfulness) to render the best of men wanton and forgetful. But blessed be your love, and your loving heart and hand, awakening any of our sleepy spirits by your sweet alarm; and blessed be your noble family, root and branch, and all your pious and prudent engagements and retirements. We hope you shall no more complain of the saddening of your loving heart, by the men of Providence town or Providence colony, but that [Sir,] when we are gone and rotten, our posterity and children after us shall read in our town records, your pious and favorable letters and loving-kindness to us, and this our answer, and real endeavor after peace and righteousness; and to be found Sir, your most obliged and most humble servants, the town of Providence, in Providence colony in New England.

GREGORY DEXTER, Town Clerk.

They chose commissioners who met with those from the other towns on August 31; when they agreed that the affairs that had been transacted by authority in each town should remain till further orders; and that for the future their government should be managed according to their

---

[1] When those cruel oppressors had regained their power in 1662, so as to eject two thousand Protestant teachers out of their places, they wreaked their vengeance on this noble man, so as to have him publicly beheaded; but he died in an heroic manner.

charter; and that an assembly of six commissioners from each town, should transact the business of making laws, and trying their general affairs; and they ordered, "that Mr. Ezekiel Holiman, and Mr. John Greene, jun'r, are to view the general laws of the colony, and to represent [present] them to the next Court of Commissioners;" and they appointed a general election at Warwick, on Sept. 12.[1] At that election Mr. Williams was chosen president of the colony; and the assembly ordered, " that Mr. Roger Williams, and Mr. Gregory Dexter [are desired to] draw forth and send letters of humble thanksgiving, to his Highness the Lord Protector, and Sir Henry Vane, Mr. Holland, and Mr. John Clarke, in the name of the colony, and Mr. Williams is desired to subscribe them by virtue of his office." Thus far things appeared encouraging; but as tyranny and licentiousness are equally enemies, both to government and liberty, Mr. Williams often had both of them to contend with. Soon after this settlement a person sent a paper to the town of Providence, That it was blood-guiltness, and against the rule of the gospel, to execute judgment upon transgressors, against the private or public weal. But said Mr. Williams:—

> That ever I should speak or write a tittle that tends to such an infinite liberty of conscience is a mistake, and which I have ever disclaimed and abhorred. To prevent such mistakes, I at present shall only propose this case. There goes many a ship to sea, with many [a] hundred souls in one ship, whose weal and woe is common; and is a true picture of a commonwealth, or an human combination, or society. It hath fallen out some-

---

[1] Providence Records. The names of the commissioners who composed and signed this amicable settlement were, Thomas Harris, Gregory Dexter, John Sayles, William Wickenden, John Brown and Henry Brown, for Providence; William Baulston, John Roome, Thomas Cornell, John Briggs and William Hall, for Portsmouth; Benedict Arnold, Richard Tew, John Coggshall, John Easton, William Lytherland and Thomas Gould, for Newport; John Greene, senior, Randal Holden, Ezekiel Holiman, John Greene, junior, John Townsend and Richard Townsend, for Warwick. Arnold left his father's party at Pawtuxet, and was received a freeman at Newport, in May, 1653; after which he was greatly promoted in the colony.—B.

The published R. I. Colonial Records give the name John Taylor, instead of John Sayles. Backus is undoubtedly correct, as it is known from other sources that

times that both Papists and Protestants, Jews and Turks, may be embarked into one ship. Upon which supposal, I [do] affirm that all the liberty of conscience, that ever I pleaded for, turns upon these two hinges, that none of the Papists, Protestants, Jews or Turks, be forced to come to the ship's prayers or worship; nor [secondly] compelled from their own particular prayers or worship, if they practice any. I further add, that I never denied that notwithstanding this liberty, the commander of this ship ought to command the ship's course; yea, and also command that justice, peace and sobriety to be kept and practiced, both among the seamen and all the passengers. If any of the seamen refuse to perform their service, or passengers to pay their freight; if any refuse to help in person or purse towards the common charges or defence; if any refuse to obey the common laws and orders of the ship, concerning their common peace or preservation; if any shall mutiny and rise up against their commanders and officers; if any should [shall] preach or write that there ought to be no commanders nor officers, because all are equal in Christ, therefore no masters nor officers, no laws nor orders, no corrections nor punishments; I say, I never denied but in such cases, whatever is pretended, the commander or commanders may judge, resist, compel and punish such transgressors, according to their deserts and merits. This, if seriously and honestly minded, may if it so please the Father of lights, let in some light to such as willingly shut not their eyes. I remain studious of your [our] common peace and liberty.

ROGER WILLIAMS.[1]

This clear description of the difference between civil and ecclesiastical affairs, and of the difference betwixt good government on the one hand, and tyranny or licentiousness on the other, confirmed by a correspondent practice through fifty years of incessant labors, is more than a sufficient balance to all the slanders that various parties have cast upon this ancient witness and advocate for the rights and liberties of men, against the superstitions and enthusiasms of his day. Having settled things as well as he could among his own people, he, as president of his colony, addressed the general

there was a John Sayles in Providence at about this time, and there seems to be no account of a John Taylor. After the name of William Baulston, should be inserted that of Richard Barden. It is given in the Colonial Records, and Backus by omitting it represents Portsmouth as having only five commissioners though he has said above that each town was to have six. The name which stands in the first edition as Richard Jew, we have changed to Richard Tew as it stands here and in many other places on the Records.—ED.

[1] History of Providence. [Mass. Hist. Coll., Second series, Vol. II. pp. 191, 192.]

assembly at Boston, in the following words, directed to their governor :—

Providence, 15, 9 month, '55 (so called.)

MUCH HONORED SIRS :—It is my humble and earnest petition unto God and you, that you may be so pleased to exercise command over your own spirits that you may not mind myself nor the English of these parts (unworthy with myself of your eye) but only that face of equity (English and Christian) which I humbly hope may appear in these representations following :—

First, May it please you to remember, that concerning the town of Warwick, [in this colony] there lies a suit of two thousand pounds damages against you before his Highness and the Lords of the [his] Council. I doubt not, if you so please, but that (as Mr. Winslow and myself had well nigh ordered it) some gentlemen from yourselves and some from Warwick deputed, may friendly and easily determine that affair between you.[1]

Secondly, The Indians which pretend your names at Warwick and Pawtuxet (yet live as barbarously if not more than any in the whole colony) please you to know their insolences upon ourselves and cattle (unto twenty pounds damages per annum) are insufferable by English spirits ; and please you to give credence that to all these they pretend your name, and affirm that they dare not (for offending you) agree with us, nor come to rules of righteous neighborhood, only they know you favor us not, and therefore send us for redress unto you.

Thirdly, Concerning four families at Pawtuxet, may it please you to remember the two controversies they have long (under your name) maintained with us, to the constant obstructing of all order and authority amongst

---

[1] Thus it appears that their invading their neighbors' rights at Warwick, caused troubles for them in England above ten years after, which Mr. Winslow, their agent, and Mr. Williams, could not quite settle ; and they not complying with his reasonable proposal now, Gorton entered a complaint against them before king Charles's Commissioners in 1665, in which, besides all their other sufferings, they alleged that the Massachusetts took away and sold eighty head of their cattle. Massachusetts History, Vol. I, p. 103.

The controversy not being then settled, drew consequences after it enough to make our ears to tingle ; an account of which I perceive was presented to king Charles the Second, in 1679, by Randal Holden and others, as agents from Warwick, wherein they, after describing their suffering at Boston, say, " and all this because that we (being without their jurisdiction) would not relinquish and forsake the sound doctrine and Christian principles taught us in our minority in the church of England." Upon which they go on to relate how that party disposition against them, after exasperating the Narragansetts in Philip's war, left Warwick defenceless to the fury of the savages ; and that the English themselves did them other great injuries afterward. How should these things warn all to leave off contention before it is meddled with?

us. .... To obey his Highness' authority in this charter, they say they dare not for your sakes, though they live not by your laws, nor bear your common charges, nor ours, but evade both under color of your authority. .... Be pleased to consider how unsuitable it is for yourselves [if these families at Pawtuxet plead truth] to be the obstructors of all orderly proceedings amongst us; for I humbly appeal to your own wisdoms and experience, how unlikely it is for a people to be compelled to order and common charges, when others in their bosoms are by such (seeming) partiality exempted from both.

He then observes that there were in reality only W. Arnold and W. Carpenter, " very far in religion from you, if you knew all," who continued this obstruction; and all their plea for it was a fear of offending the Massachusetts. And says he :—

I perceive your commerce with the people of this colony is as great as with any in the country, and our dangers (being a frontier people to the barbarians)[1] are greater than those of other colonies, and the ill consequences to yourselves would be not few nor small, and to the whole land, were we first massacred or mastered by them. I pray your equal and favorable reflection upon that your law, which prohibits us to buy of you all means of our necessary defence, of our lives and families; yea, in this [most] bloody and massacring time. We are informed that tickets have rarely been denied to any English of the country; yea, the barbarians, though notorious in lies, if they profess subjection, they are furnished;[2] only ourselves, by former and latter denial, seem to be devoted to be the Indian shambles and massacres. The barbarians all the land over are filled with artillery and ammunition from the Dutch, openly and horridly, and from the English all over the country, by stealth, I know they abound so wonderfully, that their activity and insolence is grown so high, that they daily consult and hope and threaten to render us slaves, as they long since [and now most terribly] have made the Dutch. For myself, as through God's goodness, I have refused the gain of thousands by such a murderous trade, and think no law yet extant among yourselves or us, secure enough against such villainy; so am I loth to see so many hundreds, if not some thousands, in this colony destroyed like fools and beasts without resistance. I grieve that so much blood should cry against yourselves; yea, and I grieve that at this instant by these ships, this cry and the premises should now trouble his Highness and his council. For the seasonable

---

[1] When Mr. Williams first began among the Narragansetts, he said they had five thousand fighting men. Callendar, p. 70. [124.]
[2] See page 104.

preventing of which is this humble address presented to your wisdom, by him who desires to be your unfeigned and faithful servant,

ROGER WILLIAMS,
Of Providence Plantations, President."

He then requested them to record an order which the Lords of the Council gave him upon his last return from England, for his free taking of ship or landing at their ports, lest, says he, "forgetfulness hereafter again put me upon such distresses as, God knows, I suffered, when I last passed through your colony to our native country."[1]

The above were not all the trying things that he met with this year. No, Mr. William Harris, to whom he generously gave a share in Providence lands, and who had professed himself a Baptist, "sent his writings to the main and to the Island, against all earthly powers, parliaments, laws, charters, magistrates, prisons, punishments, rates, yea, against all kings and princes, under the notion that the people should shortly cry out, *No lords, no masters;* and in open court protested, before the whole colony assembled, that he would maintain his writings with his blood!" This was done at the election at Newport, May 22d, 1655. Upon which the Assembly appointed Messrs. Olney, Baulston and Roome to deal with him;[2] and Mr. Williams soon after received the following letter from the Lord Protector, viz.:—

GENTLEMEN:—Your agent here hath represented unto us some particulars concerning your government, which you judge necessary to be settled

---

[1] Massachusetts History, Vol. III. pp. 275—278. [R. I. Colonial Records.] This year the church of Charlestown began their dealings with Mr. Gould, which issued in his gathering the first Baptist church in Boston.

[2] In the published R. I. Colonial Records of the Court which sat at Newport, May 25, 1655, the election of which was held May 22, is the following:—"It is ordered, ... that, whereas, it hath been debated in this Court of some rising or taking up of arms to the opposing of authority by Mr. Thomas Olnie, Mr. Baulston and Mr. Roome are desired to treat with him and to declare to him the mind of this Court and the proceedings of the Colony concerning him." If this is the record to which Backus refers in the above statement,—and there appears to be no other to which he could refer,—it has been materially misread, either by him or by the copyist who prepared it for the press. It was nearly a year later, May 20, 1657, that Roger Williams impeached Harris for high treason The articles of impeachment com-

by us here, but by reason of the other great and weighty affairs of this commonwealth, we have been necessitated to defer the consideration of them to [a] further opportunity; in the mean time we are [were] willing to let you know that you were [are] to proceed in your government according to the tenor of your charter, formerly granted on that behalf, taking care of the peace and safety of those plantations, that neither through [any] intestine commotions or foreign invasions, there do arise any detriment or dishonor to their [this] commonwealth or yourselves, as far as you by your care and diligence can prevent. And as for the things that are before us, they shall, as soon as the other occasions will permit, receive a just and sufficient [fitting] determination. And so we bid you farewell and rest,

Your very loving friend,   OLIVER, P.

March 29th, 1655.

To our trusty and well-beloved, the President, Assistants, and inhabitants of Rhode Island, together with the rest of the Providence Plantations in the Narragansett Bay, in New England.

Hereupon the Assembly met again, June 28th, and enacted as follows:—

Whereas, we have been rent and torn with divisions, and his Highness hath sent unto us an express command, under his hand and seal, to provide against intestine commotions, by which his Highness noteth, that not only ourselves are dishonored and endangered, but also dishonor and detriment redounds to the commonwealth of England; it is ordered, that if any person or persons be found, by the examination and judgment of the General Court of Commissioners, to be a ringleader or ringleaders of factions or divisions among us, he or they shall be sent over at his or their own charges, as prisoners, to receive his or their trial or sentence at the pleasure of his Highness and the Lords of his Council.

These means had such effect, that at their Assembly at Warwick, in March following, I find it thus recorded:—

I, William Coddington, do freely submit to the authority of his Highness in the colony as it is now united, and that with all my heart.

Whereas, there have been differences depending between William Coddington, Esq.; and Mr. William Dyre, both of Newport, we declare joy-

menced as follows:—"Whereas, William Harris, of Providence, published to all the towns in the colony dangerous writings containing his notorious defiance to the authority of his Highness the Lord Protector, &c., and the high Court of Parliament of England, as also his notorious attempts to draw all the English subjects of this colony into a traitorous renouncing of their allegiance and subjection, and whereas the said William Harris now openly in the face of the Court, declareth himself resolved to maintain the said writings with his blood," &c. Arnold's History of Rhode Island, Vol. I, p. 263.—ED.

fully for ourselves and heirs by this present record that a full agreement and conclusion is made between us, by our worthy friends, Mr. Baulston, Mr. Gorton, Mr. John Smith of Warwick, Mr. John Greene, jun. of Warwick, and Mr. John Easton; and in witness whereof we subscribe our hands, and desire this to be recorded, this present 14th of March, 1655, –56.

In the presence of
ROGER WILLIAMS, President,
JOHN ROOME,
BENEDICT ARNOLD,
JOHN GREENE, jun.[1]

WILLIAM CODDINGTON.
WILLIAM DYRE.

Harris now turned, and cried up government and magistrates as much as he had cried them down before.[2] Being desirous to make thorough work of it, Mr. Williams wrote again to the Massachusetts governor, and was encouraged by him to come to their Assembly at Boston, which he did, with an address, dated May 12th, wherein he says:—

HONORED SIRS:—Our first request was and is, for your favorable consideration of the long and lamentable condition of the town of Warwick, which hath been thus. They are so dangerously and so vexatiously intermingled with the barbarians, that I have long admired the wonderful power of God in restraining and preventing very great fires, of mutual slaughters, breaking forth between them. Your wisdoms know the inhuman insultations of these wild creatures, and you may be pleased also to imagine, that they have not been sparing of your name as the patron of all their wickedness against our English, men, women and children, and cattle, to the yearly damage of sixty, eighty and a hundred pounds. The remedy, under God is only your pleasure that Pumham shall come to an agreement with the town or colony, and that some convenient way and time be set for their removal. And that your wisdoms may see just grounds for such your willingness, be pleased to be informed of a reality of a solemn covenant between this town of Warwick and Pumham, unto which, notwithstanding [that] he pleads his being drawn to it by the awe of his superior sachems, yet I humbly offer that what was done was according to the law and tenor of the natives (I take it) in all New England and America, viz., that the inferior sachems and subjects shall plant and remove at the pleasure of the highest and supreme sachems, and I humbly conceive that it pleaseth the Most High and only wise to make use of such a bond of authority over

---

[1] This latter document is not in the published R. I. Colonial Records, it being regarded, perhaps, as the record of a merely private matter.—ED.

[2] Rhode Island Colony Records. Williams against the Quakers, pp. 11—20.

them, without which they could not long subsist in human societies, in this wild condition wherein they are. Please you not to be insensible of the slippery and dangerous condition of this their intermingled cohabitation. I am humbly confident that all the English towns and plantations in all New England put together, suffer not such molestation from the natives as this one town and people. . . . . Be pleased to review this copy from the Lord Admiral[1] that this English town of Warwick should proceed, and [also] that if any of yours were there planted, they should by your authority be removed. And [we humbly conceive that] if the English, whose removes are difficult and chargeable, how much more these wild ones, who remove with little more trouble and damage than the wild beasts of the wilderness? . . . . This small neck, whereon they keep and mingle fields with the English, is a very den of wickedness, where they not only practice the horrid barbarisms of all kinds of whoredoms, idolatries and conjurations, but living without all exercise of actual authority, and getting store of liquors (to our grief) there is a confluence and rendezvous of all the wildest and most licentious natives and practices of the whole country.

He then proceeded to inculcate his other former requests, which now had their effect.[2]

The journal of governor Winthrop shows, that before they received Pumham and his fellows under their protection, the Court made them promise to keep the Sabbath, and to observe other religious rules;[3] but this account manifests the pernicious evil of invading others' rights under the mask of religion. They were awfully requited therefor. Beside the manifold troubles that it cost the Massachusetts before, in Philip's war; they not only " lost more of their substance as well as inhabitants than both Plymouth and Connecticut colonies together,"[4] but Pumham and his family had so great a hand therein, that the dispatching of a grandson of his is mentioned among the heroic exploits of Captain Denison, nine months after that war began. Pumham himself was "accounted the most warlike and best soldier of all the Narragansett sachems," and he was so bloody and barbarous through the war that when he was killed a few days before

[1] See page 165.
[2] Massachusetts History, Vol. III, pp. 278—283.
[3] Winthrop's Journal, pp. 121, 122.—Ed.
[4] Massachusetts History, Vol. III, p. 493.

Philip, within about fifteen or twenty miles of Boston, he, after he could not stand, " catching hold of an Englishman, that by accident came near him, had done him a mischief, if he had not been presently rescued."[1]

No sooner had Mr. Williams obtained such a settlement of old controversies in the country, than new ones arose in the following manner. George Fox, a very zealous teacher, had raised a new sect in England, who, from his, and his companions' quaking and trembling when they were brought before Gervase Bennett, a justice in Derby, in 1650, were called QUAKERS; though Fox says, it was because, " we bid him and his company tremble at the word of God."[2] In July (this year) a number of his followers arrived at Boston, but were soon imprisoned. Mr. Gorton wrote to them as I have related,[3] to which they gave an answer Sept. 28th, wherein they say :—

Friend, in that measure which we have received, which is eternal, we see thee, and behold thee, and have oneness with thee, in that which is meek and low, and is not of this world;....and in that meek and low spirit we salute thee, and own that of God in thee, which is waiting for, and expecting the rising of that which is under the earth.....The ransomed of the Lord shall come to Zion with joy and gladness, being redeemed from kindreds, nations, tongues and people, by the blood of Jesus, which is spirit and life to all those that obey the light, which from the life doth come, for the life is the light of men, and whosoever believes in the light which they are enlightened with, shall not abide in darkness, which light we have obeyed in coming into these parts. The Lord is come and coming to level the mountains, and to rend the rocks of wisdom and knowledge, and to exalt that which is low and foolish to the wisdom of the world ; and blessed shall thou, and all those be, who meet him in this his work. From the servants and messengers of the Lord whom he hath sent and brought by the arm of his power into these parts of the world, for which we suffer bonds and close imprisonment.....Known in the world by these names,

| CHRISTOPHER HOLDEN, | WILLIAM BREND, |
| JOHN COPELAND, | THOMAS THURSTON. |

[1] Hubbard's History of that war, pp. 68—100.
[2] Williams's dispute with them, p. 27. Fox's answer, p. 26.—B.
[3] Page 165. See Appendix A at the close of this volume.—ED.

To this Gorton wrote a reply recited in page 110, and thereby as well as by what is in pages 116, 117, we may learn that he held with them about inward power, perfection in this life, and falling from grace received; but when he came to be acquainted with them, he did not concur with them about *Thee* and *Thou*, and the names of months and days, nor in the more important articles of refusing the oath of allegiance to civil government and a defensive war. After his return from England, his character as a member of civil society, and as a ruler, stands unimpeached in their records. And as Fox in his book in folio had said, "The Scriptures are the words of God, but Christ is the word of God in whom they end; and it is not blasphemy [as an author said it was] to say the soul is part of God, for it comes out of him, and rejoiceth in him;" which John Stubs tried to defend against Mr. Williams, from those words, God breathed into man the breath of life; Gorton, desiring liberty to speak, said, "If it be affirmed that God can be divided, and that man was a part of God, the Godhead was destroyed, and the soul of man. .... It is in the margin, the breath of *lives*, which Stubs acknowledged."[1]

On September 2, 1656, the Assembly at Boston wrote to the Commissioners of the United Colonies, and said:—

> Having heard some time since, that our neighbor colony of Plymouth, our beloved brethren, in a great part seem to be wanting to themselves, in a due acknowledgment and encouragement to the ministry of the gospel, so as many pious ministers (how justly we know not) have deserted their stations, callings, and relations; our desire is, that some such course may be taken, as that a pious orthodox ministry may be re-stated among them, that so the flood of errors, and principles of anarchy, [which will not long be kept out where Satan and his instruments are so prevalent as to prevail to the crying down of ministry and ministers] may be prevented. Here have [hath] arrived amongst us several persons, professing themselves Quakers, fit instruments to propagate the kingdom of Satan; for the securing of ourselves and our neighbors from such pests, we have imprisoned them till they be despatched away to the place from whence they came.

[1] Williams, 1672, pp. 144, 145.

.... We hope that some general rules may be commended to each General Court, to prevent the coming [in] amongst us, from foreign places such notorious heretics as Quakers, Ranters, &c.

The Commissioners replied as follows :—

The Commissioners having considered the premises, cannot but acknowledge the godly care and zeal of the gentlemen of the Massachusetts to uphold and maintain those professed ends of coming into these parts, and of combination of the United Colonies, which, if not attended in the particulars aforesaid, will be rendered wholly frustrate, our profession miserably scandalized, ourselves become a reproach in the eyes of those that cannot without admiration behold our sudden defection from our first principles.

From this they went on to inculcate what Massachusetts Assembly had proposed.[1]

Though the Massachusetts rulers knew not whether those ministers had deserted their stations justly or not, yet they had approved of the settlement of Mr. John Mayo in Boston, Mr. Edward Bulkley at Concord, Mr. John Reyner at Dover (who preached in Boston, the winter after he left Plymouth,) Mr. Richard Blinman at Cape Ann, &c., all of whom were ministers in Plymouth colony, when the colonies confederated together in 1643. We learn also that Mr. John Norton arrived at Plymouth in 1635, where he preached the following winter, and Mr. Smith their pastor resigned his place to him, " and the church used him with all respect, and large offers, yet he left them, ... alleging that his spirit could not unite with them.[2] He went and settled at Ipswich, but after Mr. Cotton's death removed and took his place in Boston, where he with his colleague had not a little hand in spiriting up others to the above described measures. Another vigorous hand in the same work was Mr. Cobbet, who arrived at Boston in 1637, wrote against the Baptists in 1645, was minister at Lynn, when they suffered there in 1651, but upon the death of Mr. Nathaniel Rogers, took his place at Ipswich, where the town, on Feb. 25th, this year, voted to give him a hundred pounds to buy

[1] Massachusetts History, Vol. III, pp. 283—285.
[2] Winthrop, [Vol. I, p. 175.] Hubbard, [274.]

or build him a house, and taxed all the inhabitants to pay it. This being a new thing with them, several persons would not comply with the scheme; therefore distress was made upon them in 1657. Samuel Symonds, Esq., descended from an ancient and honorable family in Essex in England, was then one of the Massachusetts magistrates, and at last died their Deputy Governor. Before him George Giddings prosecuted Edward Brown, for seizing his pewter for said tax. The justice gave the plaintiff damage and costs, for which judgment he rendered these reasons:—

> I understand this to be about a fundamental law; such a law as that God and nature has [have] given to a people; so that it is in the trust of their governors in highest place and others to preserve, but not in their power to take away from them. Of this sort are these, viz.: 1. Election of the supreme governors. 2. That every subject shall and may enjoy what he hath a civil right unto, so as it cannot be taken from him, by way of gift or loan, to the use or to be made the right or property of another man, without his own free consent. 3. That such laws, (though called liberties) yet more properly may be called rights, and in this sense this may be added, as a third fundamental law, viz.:—That no custom or precedent ought to prevail in any moral case, that may appear to be sinful in respect of the breach of any law of piety against the first table, or of righteousness against the second. .... I shall add .... that it is against a fundamental law in nature, to be compelled to pay that which others do give; for then no man hath any certainty, or right to what he hath; if it be in the power of others by pretence of authority or without, to give it away (when in their prudence they conceive it to be for the benefit of the owner) without his own consent. .... The parliament may tax, and that justly, the whole country to give a [gift or] reward to one man for some service, for they are betrusted so to do. The reason is, it is levied upon the whole country, with their consent, and for the immediate benefit of the whole. But if they should do it between persons (though they should do it [so do] by power, and the person wronged hath no remedy in this world) yet it should be accounted tyranny. Is it not to take from Peter and give unto [it to] Paul?

Then after mentioning the law for ministers' salaries,[1] he says:—

> Yet the law was framed so as such churches as chose to go in a volun-

[1] See page 79

tary way of weekly contribution, might so continue, as some churches in the country do to this day.

After an appeal to the County Court, the question, with the reasons each party had for and against it, was put to the General Court, whether the town vote for giving the said hundred pounds, bound the inhabitants, so that any of them who were unwilling, might be compelled to pay it, or not? On October 20th, 1657, the deputies resolved it in the negative, which was non-concurred by the Council; and influence enough was made the next day to bring a majority of the House round to the compelling side.[1]

Neither could they be content with using compulsion themselves, but the Commissioners of the United Colonies, wrote to that of Providence, September 25, 1656, to try to draw them into their measures towards the Quakers. To this the Assembly at Portsmouth, gave an answer, on March 13, 1657, wherein they say:—

> Whereas freedom of different consciences to be protected from inforcements, was the principal ground of our charter, both with respect to our humble suit for it, as also to the true intent of the honorable and renowned parliament of England, in granting of the same to us, which freedom we still prize, as the greatest happiness that men can possess in this world, therefore we shall for the preservation of our civil peace and order, the more especially [seriously] take notice that those people, and any others that are here, or shall come among us, be impartially required, and to our utmost, constrained to perform all civil duties requisite. .... And in case they refuse it, we resolve to [take and] make use of the first opportunity to inform our agent, residing in England, &c.

They close with thankful acknowledgments of the Com-

---

[1] Massachusetts History, Vol. III, pp. 287—308. So in October, 1658, the majority of the House were against the law, to banish Quakers on pain of death; but the Council, with the help of some ministers, at last prevailed to carry it, by the majority of only one vote; which, when deacon Wozel [or Wiswal] understood, he wept, and though illness caused his absence, yet had notice been given him, he said, "If he had not been able to go, he would have crept upon his hands and knees, rather than it should have been." Thus those oppressions were carried on by a few men, against the sense of the best part of the community. Endicott, Bellingham, Bradstreet and Denison, with the ministers they sat under, were as guilty in this respect as any. Bishop's New England Judged, [Grove's Abridgment, pp. 101, 102.] Massachusetts History, Vol. I, p. 198, [182.]

missioners' care they had expressed for the peace and welfare of the whole country, and saying :—

> We rest yours, most affectionately, desirous of your honorable [honors and] welfare.
> JOHN SANFORD, Clerk of Assembly.

This did not content those Commissioners; but they wrote again the next fall, to which Governor Arnold and his Court returned an answer, October 13th, which has been published.[1] And the contention growing more terrible the year after, the Assembly at Warwick, November 5th, 1658, appointed Mr. Olney, Mr. Gorton and Mr. Crandal, who had

---

[1] Massachusetts History, Vol. I, pp. 526, 527. [453, 454.]—B.
The letter was as follows :—

"MUCH HONORED GENTLEMEN :—Please you to understand that there hath come to our view a letter subscribed by the honored gentlemen, Commissioners of the United Colonies, the contents whereof are a request concerning certain people called Quakers, come among us lately, &c.

"Our desires are, in all things possible, to pursue after and keep fair and loving correspondence and intercourse with all the colonies and with all our countrymen in New England, and to that purpose we have endeavored (and shall still endeavor) to answer the desires and requests from all parts of the country, coming unto us, in all just and equal returns; to which end, the colony have made suitable provision to preserve a just and equal intercourse between the colonies and us, by giving justice to any that demand it among us, and by returning such as make escapes from you, or from the other colonies, being such as fly from the hands of justice, for matters of crime done or committed amongst you, &c. And as concerning these Quakers, (so called,) which are now among us, we have no law among us whereby to punish any for only declaring by words, &c., their minds and understandings concerning the ways and things of God as to salvation and an eternal condition. And moreover we find that in those places where these people aforesaid, in this colony, are most of all suffered to declare themselves freely, and are only opposed by arguments in discourse, there they least of all desire to come, and we are informed that they begin to loath this place, for that they are not opposed by the civil authority, but with all patience and meekness are suffered to say over their pretended revelations and admonitions, nor are they like or able to gain many here to their way; and surely we find that they delight to be persecuted by civil powers, and when they are so, they are like to gain more adherents by the conceit of their patient sufferings than by consent to their pernicious sayings. And yet we conceive that their doctrines tend to very absolute cutting down and overturning relations and civil government among men, if generally received. But as to the damage that may in likelihood accrue to the neighbor colonies by their being entertained, we conceive it will not prove so dangerous, (as else it might) in regard of the course taken by you to send them away out of the country as they come among you. But, however, at present we judge it requisite, and do intend to commend the consideration of their extravagant outgoings unto the General Assembly of our colony in March

suffered from them at Boston, with Mr. Trip, to draw a letter to their agent in England,[1] which is as follows :—

WORTHY SIR, AND TRUSTY FRIEND, MR. CLARKE :—We have found, not only your ability and diligence, but also your love and care to be such concerning the welfare and prosperity of this colony, since you have been entrusted with the more public affairs thereof, surpassing the [that] no small benefit which [formerly] we had of your presence here at home, that we in all straits and incumbrances, are emboldened to repair unto you, for further and continued care, counsel and help, finding that your solid and Christian demeanor hath gotten no small interest in the hearts of our superiors, those noble and worthy senators, with whom you had to do in our behalf, as it hath constantly appeared in our [your] addresses made unto them, [which] we have by good and comfortable proofs found, having plentiful experience thereof. The last year we had laden you with much employment, which we were then put upon by reason of some too refractory among ourselves, wherein we appealed unto you for advice, for the more public manifestation of it, with respect to our superiors ; but our intelligence [it seems] fell short in that great loss of the ship, which we concluded [is conceived] here to be cast away. We have now a new occasion given us by an old spirit, with respect to the colonies round about us, who [which] seem to be offended with us because of a sort of people, called by the name of Quakers, who are come amongst us, who [and] have raised up divers who at present seem to be of their spirit, whereat the colonies about us seem to be offended with us, being the said people have their liberty with [amongst] us, are entertained in our houses, or any of our assemblies ; and for the present we have found no just cause to charge them with the breach of the civil peace ; only they are constantly going forth amongst them about us, and vex and trouble them about [in point of] their religion and spiritual state, though they return with many a foul scar in their bodies

next, where we hope there will be such order taken, as may, in all honest and conscientious manner, prevent the bad effects of their doctrines and endeavors ; and so, in all courteous and loving respects, and with desire of all honest and fair commerce with you, and the rest of our honored and beloved countrymen, we rest,
Yours in all loving respects to serve you,
BENEDICT ARNOLD, President.
WILLIAM BAULSTON,
RANDALL HOWLDEN,
ARTHUR FENNER,
WILLIAM FIELD.
From Providence, at the Court of Trials held for the Colony, October 13, 1657.
To the much honored, the General Court, sitting at Boston, for the Colony of Massachusetts."—ED.

[1]They were " chosen and authorized to draw up a letter to be sent to Mr. John Clarke, in England, to be presented to his Highness and Council." Rhode Island Records.—ED.

for the same.¹ And the offence our neighbors take against us, is because we take not some course against the said people, either to expel them from amongst us, or take such courses against them as themselves do, who are in fear lest their religion should be corrupted by them. Concerning which displeasure that they seem to take, it was expressed to us in a solemn letter, written by the Commissioners of the United Colonies at their sitting, as though they would either bring us in to act according to their scantling, or else take some course to do us a greater displeasure. A copy of which letter we have herewith sent unto you, wherein you may perceive how they express themselves; as also we have herewith sent our present answer unto them, to give you what light we may in the matter. There is one clause in the [their] letter which plainly implies a threat, though courtly [covertly] expressed as their manner is; which we gather to be this, that [as] themselves (as we construe [conceive] it) have been much awed in point of [their] continued subjection to the state of England, lest in case they should decline, England might prohibit all trade with them, both in point of exportation and importation of any commodities, which were an host sufficiently prevalent to subdue New England, not being able to subsist; even so they seem [secretly] to threaten us, by cutting us off from all commerce and trade with them, and thereby to disable us of any comfortable subsistance, being that the concourse of shipping, and all other sorts [so of all kinds] of commodities are universally conversant among themselves; as also knowing that ourselves are not in a capacity to send out shipping of ourselves, which in great measure is occasioned by their oppressing of us, as yourself well knows; as in many other respects so in this for one, that we cannot have anything from them, for the supply of our necessities, but in effect they make the price, both of our commodities and their own. Also, because we have no English coin, but only that which passeth among these barbarians, and such commodities as are raised by the labor of our hands, as corn, cattle, tobacco, &c., to make payment in, which they will have at their own rates, or else not deal with us; whereby, though they gain extraordinarily by us, yet, for the safeguard of their [own] religion, they may seem to neglect themselves in that respect; for *what will not men do for their God?* Sir, this is our earnest and pressing request unto you in this matter, that as you may perceive by our answer unto the United Colonies [that] we fly as our refuge in all civil respects to his Highness and Honorable Council, as not being subject to any other in matters of our civil state, so may it please you to have an eye and ear open in case our adversaries should speak [seek] to undermine us in our privileges granted unto us, and plead our cause in such sort, as that we

---

¹Many were whipped, some were branded, and Holder, Copeland and Rouse, three single young men, had each his right ear cut off in the prison at Boston, the 16th of September this year. Grove's Abridgment of Bishop, pp. 64, 91, 92.

may not be compelled to exercise any civil power over men's consciences, so long as human orders in point of civility are not corrupted and violated, which our neighbors about us do frequently practice, whereof many of us have absolute [large] experience, and [do] judge it to be no less than a point of ABSOLUTE CRUELTY.

JOHN SANFORD, Clerk of Assembly.[1]

The Commissioners of the colonies who met at Boston, September 2, 1658, and continued their meeting to September 23, closed their acts with saying:—

Whereas there is an accursed and pernicious sect of heretics, lately risen up in the world, who are commonly called Quakers, who take upon them to be immediately sent of God, and infallibly assisted, who do speak and write blasphemous things, despising government, and the order of God in church and commonwealth; speaking evil of dignities, reproaching and reviling magistrates, and the ministers of the gospel, seeking to turn the people from the faith, and to gain proselytes to their pernicious ways; and whereas the several jurisdictions have made divers laws to prohibit their coming amongst them; (but they refusing to obey them, and still making disturbance) it is therefore propounded, and seriously commended to the several General Courts, ... to make a law, that all Quakers formerly convicted and punished as such, shall (if they return again) be imprisoned, and forthwith banished or expelled out of the said jurisdiction, under pain of death.

All the eight Commissioners signed this advice, only the Governor of Connecticut said, "Looking at the last as a query and not an act, I subscribe, John Winthrop."[2] Such

---

[1] As Oliver Cromwell died Sept. 3, 1658, and his son Richard was chosen Protector in his stead, their Assembly of May 17, 1659, sent an address to the latter, wherein they say, "May it please your Highness to know, that this poor colony of Providence Plantations, mostly consists of a birth and breeding of the providence of the Most High, we being an outcast people, formerly from our mother nation in the bishops' days, and since from the New English over-zealous colonies; our whole frame being like unto the present frame and constitution of our dearest mother England; bearing with the several judgments and consciences each of other in all the towns of our colony [the] which our neighbor colonies do not, which is the only cause of their great offence against us..... Sir, we dare not interrupt your high affairs with the particulars of our wilderness condition, only [we] beg your eye of favor to be cast upon our faithful agent, Mr. John Clarke, and unto what humble addresses he shall at any time present your Highness with in our behalf." Colony Records.

[2] Records of the United Colonies. The other Commissioners were Endicott and Bradstreet, of Massachusetts; Prince and Winslow, of Plymouth; Taliot, of Connecticut; and Newman and Leet, of New Haven.

a law was made at Boston the next month, but the like was not done in any of the other colonies. At Plymouth they had prevailed for two years past, with the majority of the Court, to imprison, fine and whip the Quakers, and to send some of them out of the colony; and the manner of their proceedings was as follows:—

Mr. John Brown, who had long been one of their magistrates, and often a commissioner for his colony, took a voyage to England. Captain James Cudworth of Scituate, was a magistrate these two years; and near the beginning of this year he entertained Copeland and Brend, two of the Quakers, at his house a night or two, and says:—

I thought it better so to do, than with the blind world, to censure, condemn and rail at them, when they neither saw their persons, nor knew any of their principles; but the Quakers and myself cannot close in divers things; and so I signified to the Court, I was no Quaker, but must bear my testimony against sundry things that they held, as I had occasion and opportunity. But withal I told them, that as I was no Quaker, so I would be no persecutor. This spirit worked in those two years that I was of the magistracy; during which time, I was on sundry occasions forced to declare my dissent, in sundry actings of that nature; which, although I did with all moderation of expression, together with respect unto the rest, yet it wrought great disaffection and prejudice against me.

A person took pains to go to Marshfield to procure a warrant to apprehend the Quakers he had entertained, which Mr. Hatherly understanding, said, "Mr. Envy hath procured this;" and in lieu of it, gave them a pass under his hand, with which they travelled to Plymouth; but were there seized and whipped by order of three other magistrates. And says Captain Cudworth:—

Truly the whipping of them with that cruelty as some have been, and their patience under it hath sometimes been the occasion of gaining more adherence to them, than if they had suffered them openly to have preached a sermon..... The Massachusetts after they have whipped them, and cut their ears, they have now gone the farthest step they can; they banish them upon pain of death, if ever they come there again. We expect we must do the like; we must dance after their pipe; now Plymouth saddle is on the *Bay* horse, we shall follow them on the career. .... All these carnal and antichristian ways being not of God's appointment, effect nothing as to hindering of them in their way or course. It is only the word and spirit of the Lord, that is able to convince gainsayers. They are the mighty weapons of the Christian warfare, by which great and mighty things are done and accomplished..... Our civil powers are so exercised in things appertaining to the kingdom of Christ, in matters of religion and conscience, that we can have no time to effect any thing that tends to the promotion of the civil weal, or prosperity of the place ; but now we must have a state religion, such as the powers of the world will allow, and no other ; a state ministry, and a state way of maintenance ; and we must worship and serve the Lord Jesus, as the world shall appoint us. We must all go to the public place of meeting, in the parish where we dwell, or be presented. I am informed of three or fourscore last Court, presented for not coming to public meetings ; and let me tell you how they brought this about. You may remember a law once made, called Thomas Hinckley's law, That if any neglected the worship of God, in the place where he lives, and set up a worship contrary to God, and the allowance of this government, to the public profanation of God's holy day and ordinance, [he] shall pay ten shillings. This law would not reach what then was aimed at ; because he must do so and so ; that is, all things therein expressed, or else break not the law. In March last, a Court of Deputies was called, and some acts touching Quakers were made ; and then they contrived to make this law serviceable to them ; and that was by putting out the word "And," and putting in the word " Or," which is a disjunctive, and makes every branch become a law. So now, if any neglect, or will not come to the public meetings, ten shillings for every defect..... And these men altering this law last March, yet left it dated, June 6th, 1651,[1] and so it stands as the act of a General Court ; they to be the authors of it seven years before it was in being ; and so yourselves have your part and share in it, if the records lie not. But what may be the reason that they should not by another law, made and dated by that Court, as well effect what was intended, as by altering a word, and so the whole sense of the law ; and leave this their act, by the date of it, charged on another Court's account? Surely the chief instruments in the business, being privy to an act of parliament for liberty, should too openly have acted repugnant to a law of England ; but if they can do the thing, and leave it on a Court, as making it six years

---

[1] These things Capt. Cudworth wrote to Mr. Brown, then in England, who let Bishop publish them, pages 168--176. Morton says that Mr. Dunstar, "was useful and helping in defending the truth against the Quakers; and that he fell asleep in the Lord, in 1659." [186.] After Mr. Brown returned from England, he and Cudworth were called to account for this letter, but were not punished. Cudworth was restored to the magistracy in 1674, and died their Deputy Governor, in 1681. Plymouth Records.

before the act of parliament, there can be no danger in this.....If we can but keep the people ignorant of their liberties and privileges, then we have liberty to act in our own wills what we please.....Through mercy we have yet among us worthy Mr. Dunstar, whom the Lord hath made boldly to bear testimony against the spirit of persecution.[1]

For the above things those two magistrates Hatherly and Cudworth were left out of all their offices, in June, this year. At the same time it is meet that posterity should know how those Quakers behaved under their sufferings. Humphrey Norton, one of their teachers and authors, was sent out of Plymouth colony in 1657, for being an extravagant person;[2] which charge, says Bishop, could not be proved. On election day, June 1st, 1658, he and John Rouse came again to Plymouth, and were taken up and whipped, Norton twenty-three lashes, and Rouse fifteen, which, Bishop says, "they received for no other thing but for coming into that colony in the will of God."[3] The records inform us, that when they were brought before the Assembly, June 3d, Norton " said unto the Governor sundry times, *Thou liest!* and said unto him, *Thomas, thou art a malicious man*, &c. For these things, and for refusing the oath of allegiance to any civil government, they were then whipped, and for officers' fees were imprisoned till the tenth, when they were released, and went to Rhode Island, where, on the 16th, Norton wrote a letter to Mr. Alden, one of their magistrates, and another to the Governor, with an answer to Christopher Winter's deposition against them, all which the Court ordered to be recorded." The beginning and end of that to the Governor, I took from thence with my own hand, which is in the words and letters following :—

Thomas Prince, thow who hast bent thy hart to worke wickedness, and with thy tongue hast thow set forth deceite ; thou imaginest mischief upon thy

---

[1] See page 178, note.

[2] In the Massachusetts Records his offense is somewhat differently stated. " October 6, 1657. At this Court, Humphrey Norton, one of those commonly called Quakers, being summoned, appeared and was examined and found guilty of divers horrid errors, and was sentenced speedily to depart the government and was forthwith expelled the government by the under marshal."—ED.

[3] New England Judged, [Grove's Abridgement,] pp. 163—179.

bed, and hatcheth thy hatred in thy cecrett chamber; the strength of darknes is over thee, and a malliciouse mouth hast thow opened against God and his anointed, and with thy tongue and lipps hast thow uttered perverse things; thow hast slaundered the innocent by railing, lying and false accusations, and with thy barborouse hart hast thow caused theire bloud to bee shed. Thow hast through all these things broke and transgresed the laws and waies of God, and equitie is not before thy eyes. The curse causles cannot come upon thee, nor the vengance of God unjustly cannot fetch thee up; thow makest thyself merry with thy cecrett mallice. .... The day of thy wailing will bee like unto that of a woman that murthers the fruite of her wombe; the anguish and paine that will enter upon thy reignes will be like knawing worms lodging betwixt thy hart and liver: When these things come upon thee, and thy backe bowed downe with pain, in that day and houre thow shalt know to thy griefe, that prophetts of the Lord God wee are, and the God of vengance is our God.

HUMPHREY NORTON.

I have sent thee heer inclosed a reply to C. Winter's deposition, alsoe I have sent already a true relation of parte of thy proceedings towards London, with a coppy of the fines laid on, and levied of the people of God, with a coppy of thy late laws.

Superscribed, For the governor of Plymouth pattent, this with care and speed.

After this prophecy Mr. Prince continued Governor of that colony near fourteen years, and then died in peace, (for ought we know). His son was a justice of peace in his day, and his grandson was a learned and pious minister at Boston, whose writings have furnished many valuable materials for our history. It ought also to be known, that in *rending the rocks of wisdom and knowledge*, and *exalting that which is low*, the Quakers meant to have civil as well as ecclesiastical government managed by the above described power. For in those times George Fox published a large book in folio, in the 170th page of which he said :—

The magistrate of Christ, the help government for him, he is in the light and power of Christ; and he is to subject all under the power of Christ, into his light, else he is not a faithful magistrate: and his laws here are agreeable, and answerable according to that of God in every man; when men act contrary to it, they do evil; so he is a terror to evil-doers, discerneth the precious and the just from the vile; and this is a praise to them that do well.

When Mr. Williams mentioned this passage, as one proof, that their spirit tended to arbitrary government, and fiery persecution, they said upon it :—

Is there one word of persecution here? Or can Roger Williams think himself a Christian, and look upon it to be persecution, for Christ's magistrates, by Christ's light and power, to subject all under the power of Christ, and to bring all into this light of Christ? Or can he think such an one an unfaithful magistrate? Or are those laws, and the execution of them, persecution, that are agreeable and answerable to that of God in every man? These are George Fox's words. Such magistrates, such laws, such power, and light, and subjection, is G. F. for, and no other.[1]

This opens the plain cause why they militated so hard against other magistrates and government, as in the lamentable instances following.

Our Lord directed his disciples to depart from any house or city, that they should travel into, when they refused to receive them; and when the Gadarenes besought him to depart out of their coasts, he did so; and we have no account of his forcing himself upon them again. The Quakers took another course. Three of them who were banished, on pain of death, returned again to Boston, and were condemned to die; and William Robinson gave in a paper to the Court, which contains the following reason for his conduct therein, viz. :—

On the eighth day of the eighth month, 1659, in the after part of the day, in traveling betwixt Newport in Rhode Island, and Daniel Gould's house, with my dear brother Christopher Holder, the word of the Lord came expressly to me, which did fill me immediately with life and power, and heavenly love by which he constrained me, and commanded me to pass to the town of Boston, my life to lay down in his will, for the accomplishing of his service, that he had there to perform at the day appointed. To which heavenly voice I presently yielded obedience, not questioning the Lord how he would bring the thing to pass. .... For the Lord had said unto me, My soul shall rest in everlasting peace, and my life shall enter into rest, *for being obedient* to the God of my life.

Marmaduke Stevenson, gave in another paper, informing the Court, how he heard a *voice* as he was plowing in York-

[1] Williams, p. 207. Fox's Answer, pp. 229, 230.

shire, saying, *I have ordained thee a prophet unto the nations;* and after he came to Rhode Island, he says :—

> The word of the Lord came unto me saying, Go to Boston, with thy brother William Robinson. .... This is given forth to be upon record, that all people may know, who hear it, that we came not in our own will, but in the will of God.[1]

This was their way of following what they called the light, and the clearest account of what they meant thereby, that I have seen, is contained in the following sentences directed to Mr. Williams, viz. :—

> Thou wrongest the Quakers in saying, they confess their light to be conscience. In this thou pervertest their words, and thou wouldest have it so; for George Fox's words are, The light which you call conscience, which is the light of Christ, as you may see all along in his book. .... Thou hast read our books with an evil eye, or else thou mightest see how often we mention, that Christ hath bought us with a price, which is his blood; and how that all died in Adam, and how that Christ died for all, that they that live, might live to him; and that all might believe in him, who died for them; and if they do not, they are condemned with the light, which they should believe in. .... Christ lighteth every man that cometh into the world,[2] with life in him, the word and faith. He is the light of the world, and saith, Believe in the light, that ye may become children of light, and he that believeth is saved, and he that doth not is condemned. And the condemnation is the light that is come into the world; which light is saving to them that believe in it, and condemning to them that do not believe in it, but hate it, whose deeds be evil. John 3.[3]

In all this there is a manifest confounding of grace and works, law and gospel, which the inspired writers took great pains to keep distinct. And since Christ himself says, "God sent, not his Son into the world to condemn the world; but that the world through him might be saved," "Think not that I will accuse you to the Father; there is one that accuseth you, even Moses, in whom ye trust;" John 3. 17, and 5. 45; was not the zeal of these men like that we read of Rom. 10. 2—4? Did they not trust in the law instead

---

[1] Bishop, [Grove's Abridgment,] pp. 127—133.
[2] Williams says, he believes Fox, in his book in folio, repeats these words, near or quite a thousand times. P. 186.
[3] Fox against Williams, Second Part, pp. 4, 6, 10.

of the gospel? As to the person of the Saviour, Mr. Williams says:—

Fox in all his book cannot endure to hear of the word *Human*, as being a new name, and never heard of in Scripture. I said in public, many words truly and properly English, are commendably used that are not in Scripture, in English. The word human comes from the Latin *humanus*, signifying pertaining, or belonging to man. So a human soul or body is such as all mankind have. Hence I told them that the word *anthropinos peirasmos*, I. Cor. 10, might have been turned *human*, but is truly turned, no temptation but such as is *common to man*. G. Fox knows, that if Christ Jesus be granted to have had such a soul and body as is human, or common to man, down falls their monstrous idol of a Christ, called light within.

To this Fox answers:—

For thee and the priests to give such names to Christ, our Lord and Saviour, which the Scriptures do not give, and yet say the Scriptures are the rule, that is abominable. And there is no such word in I. Cor. 10, that calleth Christ's body and soul *human;* and whether is Christ's body celestial or terrestial, or which glory doth he bear? I. Cor. 15, 14. G. F. doth grant, and all the Quakers, that Christ was made *like unto us*, sin excepted, and had *a body and soul*, or else how could he suffer? and is risen, the *same that descended is ascended*, as the apostle saith.[1]

And I have seen other of their writings which hold expressly, that Christ brought the same body from heaven, that he carried thither again. But they reckoned it "*abominable*" for Mr. Williams to use a word concerning our Saviour's humanity, that is not in our translation, while he at the same time approved of the reading as it is; yet when Hebrews i. 3, was brought in those times to prove the *personality* of the Trinity, the Quakers said, "That is falsely translated, for in the Greek it is not *person* but *substance*."[2] And said Mr. Samuel Hubbard, "They turn the Holy Scriptures into allegories, all unless some which they wrest to their own destruction, as the apostle Peter saith?"

They expressly held to a power of direction within them, superior to the Scriptures, which carried them into actions that light from thence, or from reason could not justify;

---

[1] Williams, p. 51; Fox, p. 43.   [2] Bishop, [Grove's Abridgment,] p. 360.

and their only way was to appeal to an inward motion or voice. As for instance, George Bishop speaks of Deborah Wilson, as a "modest woman, of retired life, and sober conversation; and that bearing a great burthen for the hardness and cruelty of the people, she went through the town of Salem naked, as a sign, which she having in part performed, was laid hold of, and bound over to appear at the next Court of Salem, where the wicked rulers sentenced her to be whipped."[1] Lydia Wardwel, a married woman of Hampton, went in the same manner into the meeting-house in Newbury, in time of public worship; for which she met with the like treatment.[2] Mr. Williams referred the Quakers to these instances which their own author had published; and told them they never could persuade souls not bewitched, that the Holy Spirit would move them to do so; to which they answer thus:—

> We do believe thee, in that dark, persecuting, bloody spirit, that thou and the New England priests are bewitched in, you cannot believe that you are naked from God and his clothing, and blind; and therefore hath the Lord in his power moved some of his sons and daughters to go naked; yea, and they did tell them in Oliver's days, and the long parliaments, that God would strip them of their church profession, and of their power, as naked as they were. And so they were true prophets and prophetesses to the nation, as many sober men have confessed since; though thou and the old persecuting priests in New England remain in your blindness and nakedness. .... As thou didst in the dispute, so now, thou makest a great ado with our men and women going naked. We told them then, we owned no such practice in any, unless they were called unto it by the Lord. .... He beginneth again to upbraid us with our men's and women's going naked, as if it were a thing commonly allowed among us in their wills, without the motion of God.[3]

As an impartial historian I thought it duty thus to state these plain facts and sentiments on both sides; for upon Dr. Mather's saying, that some good men formerly took that wrong way of reclaiming heretics by persecution, the Quakers spent seventeen pages in the most striking recital of what they suffered in those times that their art would admit of, in

---

[1] Bishop, [Grove's Abridgment] p. 383.—ED. [2] Ibid, p. 367.—ED. [3] Fox, pp. 9, 28, 32.

order to prove, that no good man could be an actor therein. To fix this prejudice more lastingly in the minds of all, they turned it into verse, saying :—

> These that in conscience cannot wrong a worm,
> Are fin'd and whip'd, because they can't conform ;
> And time hath been, which ne'er shall be forgot,
> God's servants have been hanged, none knows for what,
> Except for serving of their blessed Lord,
> For quaking and for trembling at his word.
> Let these black days, like the fifth of November,
> Be writ in red, for ages to remember.[1]

And they are remembered in such a manner to this day, that a person can hardly plead for equal liberty of conscience in Massachusetts without having the disorders of Rhode Island colony brought up against it ; nor for the good doctrine, and family orders of those fathers, among some in the latter colony, without having hot irons and halters thrown in his teeth ? Not only so, but we have lately seen artful men trying to prevent our union in the cause of our civil liberties by these means. But from the above facts the reader may judge, whether an invasion of each other's rights, under the name of religion, was not the real cause of those dreadful broils ; which a true acknowledgment thereof, both as to property and conscience, would have prevented ; whether the grand error on both sides, was not the assuming a power to govern religion, instead of being governed by it.

On October 20th, Robinson, Stevenson and Mary Dyre, received the sentence of death.[2] It was executed upon the

---

[1] Magnalia, Book 7, p. 22. [Vol. II, pp. 453, 454.] Whiting's Answer, pp. 11—29.

[2] In justice to the rulers on whom rests the responsibility of this persecution, its whole history should be related.

September 14, 1659, William Robinson, Marmaduke Stevenson, Nicholas Davis, and Mary Dyer, were banished on pain of death. "Nicholas Davis and Mary Dyer," says Bishop, addressing the rulers of Massachusetts colony, "found freedom to depart your jurisdiction, the one to Plymouth patent, the other to Rhode Island ; but the other two, were constrained in the love and power of the Lord, not to depart but to stay in your jurisdiction and to try your bloody law unto death." Remaining in Massachusetts, they were apprehended, whipped and again set free on pain of

two men, the 27th. The woman was brought with them to the gallows, but at the intercession of her son of Newport and others, she was then reprieved, and sent away.[1] Returning again the next spring, she was hanged, June 1st, 1660.[2] Twelve days after, the Court of Plymouth repealed one or more of the sharpest laws they had made against that people.[3] Charles the Second had been restored to the crown

death. October 8, Mary Dyer came to Boston to visit a Quaker imprisoned there. October 15, " W. Robinson and M. Stevenson," says Bishop, "came to Boston, and with them Alice Cowland, who came *to bring linen to wrap the dead bodies of them who were to suffer.*" Several other Quakers also attended them. "These all came together," continues Bishop, "in the moving and power of the Lord, as one, *to look your bloody laws in the face,* and to accompany those who were to suffer by them. Upon the trial of Robinson, Stevenson and Mrs. Dyer, the Governor said " that he desired not their death;" and again, " We have made many laws, and endeavored by several ways to keep ye from us, and neither whipping nor imprisonment nor cutting off ears, nor banishment upon pain of death will keep ye from us." This conduct of the Quakers in provoking their own punishment is certainly no excuse for the cruelty of the General Court of Massachusetts, but it is utterly inconsistent with the example of Christ and his apostles, and, as has been observed, p. 258, with Christ's direction. Far different was the conduct of Clarke, Crandall and Holmes in coming into Massachusetts, not to rush into danger, breaking no law, and, though bold in the face of suffering, at the first honorable opportunity retiring to a place of safety. See p. 193. Bishop's New England judged, Grove's Abridgment, pp. 114, 125. Massachusetts Records.—ED.

[1]This language might be misunderstood as stating that she was brought to the gallows to be executed, and there was reprieved. The record of the Court is as follows:—Whereas Mary Dyer is condemned by the General Court to be executed for her offences, on the petition of William Dyer, her son, it is ordered that the said Mary Dyer shall have liberty for forty-eight hours after this day to depart out of this jurisdiction; after which time, being found therein she is forthwith to be executed; and in the meantime that she be kept close prisoner till her son or some other be ready to carry her away within the aforesaid time. And it is further ordered that she shall be carried to the place of execution and there to stand upon the gallows with a rope about her neck till the rest be executed.—ED.

[2]Mary Dyer, like Robinson and Stevenson, came back deliberately, to challenge her own death. " Being asked what she had to say why sentence should not be executed, she gave no other answer but that she denied our law, came to bear witness against it, and could not choose but come and do as formerly." Bishop's New England judged, Grove's Abridgment, pp. 156, 157.—ED.

[3]In 1657 it was enacted " that no Quaker or person commonly so called, shall be entertained by any person or persons within this government, under penalty of five pounds for every such default, or be whipped;" also, "that if any Ranter or Quaker, or person commonly so called, shall come into any town within this government, and by any person or persons be known, or be suspected to be such, the person knowing or suspecting him shall forthwith acquaint the constable or his deputy of them, on pain of presentment;" and also that no meeting of Quakers or Ranters "shall be assembled or kept by any person in any place within this government, under the

of England, on May 29th, of which Plymouth could have had no knowledge then. After the news of it arrived, Governor Endicott and his Court wrote to him, December 10th, when they said:—

> Our liberty to walk in the faith of the gospel, with all good conscience, was the cause of our transporting ourselves, with our wives, little ones, and our substance, from that pleasant land over the Atlantic ocean, into this [the] vast wilderness, choosing rather the pure Scripture worship with a good conscience, in this remote wilderness, among the heathen, than the pleasures of England with submission to the [impositions of the] then so disposed and so far prevailing hierarchy, which we could not do without an evil conscience. .... Concerning the Quakers, open and capital blasphemers, open seducers from the glorious Trinity, our Lord Jesus Christ, the the blessed gospel, and from the Holy Scriptures as the rule of life, open enemies to the government itself as established in the hands of any but men of their own principles, [we were at last constrained, for our own safety, to pass a sentence of banishment against them upon pain of death.] .... The magistrate at last, in conscience, both to God and man, judged himself called for the defence of all, to keep the passage with the point of the sword held towards them; this could do no harm to him that would be warned thereby; their wittingly rushing themselves thereupon was their

penalty of forty shillings a time for every speaker and ten shillings a time for every hearer that are heads of families, and forty shillings a time for the owner of the place that permits them so to meet together." The same year it was enacted, "that in case any shall bring in any Quaker or other notorious heretic, by land or water, into any part of the government, [he] shall forthwith, from order from any one magistrate, return them to the place from whence they came, or clear the government of them, on the penalty of paying a fine of twenty shillings for every week that they shall stay in the government after warning."

These enactments were repealed, June 13, 1660; but, alas, they were repealed only to be reënacted on the spot, with slight modifications, or to give place to new laws quite as oppressive. The first law above mentioned, was passed again with the change of scarce a word. The second law, requiring any who might know or suspect the presence of a Quaker to give immediate notice thereof, was reënacted with a very little modification. The law prohibiting the holding of meetings by Quakers or Ranters was changed by the addition of a clause that all persons "under the government of others, as wives, children or servants," who might be present at such meetings, should be carried by the constable of the town "either into the stocks or cage," to continue there two hours, if in winter, or four, if in summer; and towns were required to provide cages for their confinement.

All these reënactments were made near the commencement of the session of the General Court which sat "at New Plymouth, June 10, 1660," probably the very day of the repeals. It was also enacted at this time that if any should furnish horses to Quakers, for travel in the colony or escape from it, such horses should be forfeited to the government. Laws of Plymouth Colony.—ED.

own act, we with [all] humility conceive, a crime bringing their blood upon their own head.¹

In like manner they proceeded and hanged William Leddra, March 14th, 1661; but their friends in England procured an express from White-Hall, of Sept. 9th, which was brought over by Samuel Shattock, of Salem, requiring these rulers to forbear such things for the future, and to send such Quakers as appeared to them so obnoxious, to be tried in England. Soon after the receipt of this, Mr. Norton and Mr. Bradstreet, were sent over as agents, by whom Governor Endicott and his Court wrote to the Earl of Manchester, " to beseech his Majesty to tender them in respect of those pestilent heretics the Quakers, who have lately obtained his Majesty's letter, requiring us to forbear their punishments; in observance whereof we have suspended execution of our laws against them respecting death or corporal punishments; but this indulgence they [do] abuse to insolency and seduction of our people, and unless his majesty strengthen our hands in the application of some suitable remedy to suppress these and others, ill affected to our tranquility, this hopeful plantation is likely in all probability to be destroyed." They had before said, that allowing such to have liberty here, would be "so contrary to our consciences to permit, and no less oppression of us than the destroying both us and ours by the sword."² How justly then did Mr. Williams call the use of force in such affairs, " *The bloody tenet !*"³

We will now return to the affairs of baptism. Mr. Hubbard upon the year 1656, says :—

Baptism unto this time had been administered unto those children only, whose immediate parents were admitted into full communion in the churches where they lived; but now the country came to be increased, and sundry families were found, that had children born in them, whose immediate parents had never attempted to join to any of the churches to which they belonged, and yet were very much unsatisfied that they could not ob-

¹Hubbard, [559.] Massachusetts History, Vol. III, pp. 326, 327.
²Massachusetts History, Vol. III, pp. 331—360.
³Upon what has been said in reference to Quakers, see Appendix A, at the close of this volume.—ED.

tain baptism for their children; the cause occasioned many debates between the ministers of the country.[1]

Connecticut took the lead therein, and sent a draught of questions about it to the rulers of the Massachusetts, requesting that the ablest ministers of both colonies might be called together, to answer the same. Such an assembly was therefore called by authority at Boston, June 4th, 1657, and sat till the 19th. Their answers to twenty-one questions were afterwards printed in London, under the title of "A disputation concerning church members, and their children." Therein they concluded, that the children of professing parents, " are by means of their parents' covenanting, in covenant also, and *members of the church*, by divine institution."

1. Because they are in that covenant for substance which was made with Abraham. Gen. 17, 7, compared with Deut. 29, 12, &c. 2. Because such children are, by Christ, affirmed to have a place and portion in the kingdom of heaven. 3. Else no children could be baptized, baptism being a church ordinance, and a seal of the covenant of grace.

And also they concluded :—

It is the duty of infants, who confederate in their parents, when grown up to years of discretion, though not yet fit for the Lord's Supper, to own the covenant they made with their parents, by entering thereinto in their own persons; and it is the duty of the church to call upon them for the performance thereof; and if, being called upon, they shall refuse the performance of this great duty, or otherwise continue scandalous, they are liable to be censured for the same by the church. And in case they understand the grounds of religion, are not scandalous, and solemnly own the covenant in their own persons, wherein they give up both themselves and their children unto the Lord, and desire baptism for them, we (with due reverence to any godly learned that may dissent) see not sufficient cause to deny baptism unto their children.

As this disputation had its first rise in Connecticut, so was there much difference and contention raised at Hartford, ... between Mr. Samuel Stone, their teacher, and the rest of the church, occasioned at the first on some such account; insomuch that sundry members of that church, having rent themselves off, removed to another place higher up the river, where they settled, and gathered a distinct church in that way of *schism* as the rest of the churches accounted.[2]

This unhappy difference overspread the whole colony of Connecticut, with such a monstrous enchantment upon the

[1]Hubbard, p. 562.—ED.   [2]Hubbard, [pp. 464—570.]

minds of Christian brethren that in all the towns round about, the people generally made themselves parties to one side or the other of the quarrel. A world of sin was doubtless committed, even by pious men on this occasion. It came at last to an open breach, which could not be healed, or made up among themselves, which put them upon a necessity of calling a convention of the messengers of sundry churches in Massachusetts, who met at Boston, in 1659, and made a reconciliation between them. The practice of church-care, about the children of our churches, met with such opposition as could not be encountered with any thing less than a synod of elders and messengers from all the churches of the Massachusetts colony. Accordingly the General Court, having the necessity of the matter laid before them at their second session in the year 1661, issued out their desire and order for the convening of such a synod at Boston in the spring. After long labor the majority of them approved of the above proposition, and obtained the concurrence of the General Court thereto, on October 8th, 1662.[1] Mr. Mitchel who was the chief draughtsman, of that result, said, " We make account that if we keep baptism within the non-excommunicable, and the Lord's Supper within the compass of those that have (unto charity) somewhat of the power of godliness, or grace in exercise, we shall be near about the right *middle-way* of church reformation."[2] And it has been called the " *Half-way* Covenant" ever since ; though this *halving* of matters in religion has done more mischief in this land as well as elsewhere, than tongue can express.

Mr. Eleazer Mather, the first minister of Northampton, wrote on July 4, this year, to Mr. Devenport, and said concerning this synod, " There was scarce any of the congregational principles, but what were layen at by some or other of the assembly; as relations of the work of grace, power of voting of the fraternity in admission," &c.[3] President

[1] Hubbard, 570. Magnalia, B, 3. pp. 117, 118, [Vol. I, p. 194,] and B. 5, pp. 63, 64. [Vol. II, p. 239.]
[2] His life, pp. 76, 80. [Magnalia Book 4, Vol. II, p. 83.]
[3] Massachusetts History, Vol. I, p. 224, [206.]

Chauncey published his testimony against this new scheme; and so did Mr. Devenport; to the last of which Mr. Increase Mather wrote a preface, containing a distinct apology for those who dissented from it. Mr. John Allen, of Dedham, answered Mr. Chauncey, and Mr. Richard Mather the other, while Mr. Mitchel was employed to answer his son's preface. Young Mr. Mather in that preface says, "The synod acknowledged, that there ought be to true saving faith in the parent, or else the child ought not to be baptized. We intreated and urged again and again, that this, which themselves acknowledged was a principle of truth, might be set down for a conclusion, and then we should all agree. But those reverend persons would not consent to this." No; and Mr. Mitchel was so far from doing it in his answer, that he tells of distinguishing between faith in its hopeful beginning, and faith in special exercise; initial faith and exercised faith, and says, "All reformed churches, unanimously grant the child's right unto baptism, by its being born within the visible church. Besides, what have infants more than mere membership to give them right unto baptism! We know of no stronger argument for infant baptism than this, that church members are to be baptized."[1] To which I would say, that the Jewish church indeed was first constituted of the household of Abraham, and all his offspring were born in the church, of whom the son of the bond woman was the first that was circumcised; but the Christian church is constituted of the household of God, the children of the free woman, in distinction from those who were born after the flesh, though from Abraham's body. Ephesians 2. Gal. 4.

Mr. Mitchell, by his reasonings drew Mr. Increase Mather over to that side; after which he acted many cruel things against the Baptists for near twenty years, till the same measures were meeted to him again, so as very sensibly to convince him of his error therein. Mr. Hubbard says,

[2] Magnalia, Book 5, page 77—79. [Vol. II, p. 262.]

"Some think Mr. Devenport's book hath overthrown the propositions of the synod, according to their own principles."[1] Mr. Devenport was a while in Holland, before he came here, where he testified against their promiscuous baptism; and he said:—

When a reformation of the church has been brought about in any part of the world, it has rarely been afterwards carried on any one step further than the first reformers did succeed in their first endeavors. He observed, that as easily might the ark have been removed from the mountains of Ararat, where it first grounded, as a people get any ground in reformation, after and beyond the first remove of the reformers. And this observation quickened him to embark in a design of reformation, wherein he might have opportunity to drive things in the first essay, as near to the precept and pattern of Scripture as they could be driven.[2]

We shall presently see other ministers promoting a separation from him for these attempts.

On the 8th of May, this year, the Assembly at Boston wrote to that of Rhode Island, and said:—

Our affection to peace and a fair correspondence, [with you] puts us upon a condescension far beneath our own reason, and the justice of our cause, once more to transmit [emit] this our last letter to you, concerning the unjust molestation and intrusion of some of your inhabitants, upon the undoubted rights of this jurisdiction, and the inhabitants thereof, in their grants and possessions in the Pequot and Narragansett country, upon pretence of authority from your Court, and purchase from [the] Indians, but producing no deed, record, order or commission for warranting the same; wherein, as we conceive, they act directly against reason, righteousness, precedent, grants from England, clear conquest, purchase and possession. It is not unknown to yourselves what means have been used from time to time, both by the Commissioners of the United Colonies, and by the Governor and magistrates, General Court and Council of this jurisdiction, by their several letters, to desire you to cause your people to desist [from] such proceedings, and extend [exert] your authority for suppressing injustice; but to this day [we] have received no satisfactory or particular answer in the premises; which has given [gives] us grounds to suppose, [suspect] that at least you indulge them in their proceedings. You may hereby have [take] notice, that two of your people, namely, Tobias Sanders, and Robert Bardick, [Burditt] being long since taken on the place, and secured by us

---

[1]Hubbard, p. 590.—Ed.   [2]Magnalia, Book 3, p. 53. [Vol. I, p. 295.]

to answer their trespass, we have now called them before the Court, and find nothing from them to justify their proceedings; therefore the Court hath fined them forty pounds for their [your]¹ offence, and towards satisfaction for the charges expended in carrying them before authority; and that they stand committed [to prison] till the [your] fine be satisfied, and security given to the Secretary to the value of one hundred pounds for their [your] peaceable demeanor toward all the inhabitants of this jurisdiction for the future. .... And we hereby signify unto you, that unless you command off your inhabitants that yet continue their possession at Sotherton and Pateskomscut, before the last of June next, you may expect we shall not continue to neglect the relief and protection of our people there [thus] molested; and shall account it our duty to secure all such persons and estates of yours as shall be found within our jurisdiction, until [all] just damages be satisfied. But this we heartily and earnestly desire may be avoided, by your prudent care and justice, and that peace and good agreement [government] may for the future be preserved between us.²

This reminds me of Mr. Locke's saying, "That dominion is founded in grace, is an assertion by which those who maintain it do plainly lay claim to the possession of all things; for they are not so wanting to themselves as not to believe, or at least as not to profess themselves to be the truly pious and faithful."³ Because Mr. Williams testified against that power when he first came to Boston, the Court wrote to Salem against him; whereupon he did not stay to contend with them, but peaceably withdrew to Plymouth, where his teaching was well approved as long as Mr. Bradford was Governor. But when Mr. Winslow came into that office, who with Massachusetts was against a full toleration in religious matters,⁴ Mr. Williams peaceably retired to Salem, and took the charge of that flock; but for the church's receiving him without the rulers' leave, they took away some of their possessions, till they would give up Mr. Williams; and, for his faithful admonitions to them on that account, they

---

¹The original document probably had in several instances the old abbreviation, "yr," which sometimes stood for *their*, and sometimes for *your*. Backus understood it in the former sense, and the copyist of the Rhode Island Records in the latter. Backus's interpretation seems far preferable to the other.—ED.

²Rhode Island Records.   ³On Toleration, p. 61.
⁴Massachusetts History, Vol. III, p. 154.

expelled him out of their jurisdiction. But who can tell how far that extends? When he came first into this country all the Indians from Boston and Plymouth bays to Paucatuck River were tributaries to the chief sachems of Narragansett; and from thence to Hudson's River, and over all Long Island, Sassicus had extended his power, even over twenty-six sachems.[1] The Pequots being thus powerful, made war upon the Narragansetts, who, in April, 1632, had a number of their tributaries out of Plymouth and Massachusetts colonies to assist them against him; yet Sassicus prevailed, and extended[2] his territories ten miles east of Paucatuck River. About the same time Natuwannute, a sachem of the country about where Hartford now stands, with a number of his men, "were driven out from thence by the potency of the Pequots," and came to our fathers at Plymouth, and requested them to go up and trade there, though "their end was to be restored to their country again." This motion was complied with, and a trading house was set up among them.[3] This was such an eyesore to the Pequots, that in 1634 they murdered Captain Stone and seven men with him, plundered his goods and sunk his vessel, because they were going up Connecticut river to trade there. Two years after they murdered Captain Oldham as I have related.[4] Upon the notice which Mr. Williams gave them of this sad event, Mr. Endicott with an armed force was sent in August 25, 1636, to try to bring the Pequots to terms; but Johnson says it proved a bootless voyage, only his leaving some men with Underhill, at Saybrook fort, prevented its being taken. Upon his return Sassicus applied to the Narragansetts for a reconciliation, that they all might join to expel these new comers; representing, "that if they should help, or suffer the English to subdue the Pequots, they would thereby make

[1]Connecticut Assembly's answer to the king's letter, 1773, written by Governor Trumbull.
[2]Prince's Annals, pp. 58, 59. [391, 392.]
[3]Massachusetts History, Vol. II, pp. 469, 470. [416.]
[4]Page 59.—ED.

way for their own future ruin; and that they need not come to open battle with the English; for only to fire their houses; kill their cattle, lay in ambush and shoot them as they went about their business, they would quickly be forced to leave the country, and the Indians not be exposed to any great hazard."[1]

Had two such politic and potent princes as Sassicus and Miantinomo were, united in this scheme, when Boston was but six years old, Providence and Hartford but a few months, and New Haven not begun, what would have become of all their claims they were now contending for? And it is most evident that Mr. Williams was the very instrument of preventing the junction of those two great Indian powers, and so of saving the vast interest we now have in this country. But how was he requited for it? Why, after Warwick men had obtained as fair a title to that town, as the Massachusetts ever had to Boston, yet because they were not orthodox they were fetched away by force of arms; and the captive sachem was murdered for fear he should revenge such doings. And when the orthodox party afterward proclaimed war upon his successors, because they were for revenging his death, and Mr. Williams, to prevent the further effusion of blood, had prevailed with them to go down and settle the matter at Boston, how were they treated?[2] They were not only compelled to sign an engagement to pay all damages and costs, and to quit any claim to the Pequot country, but also to say, "The Narragansett and Nyantick sagamores and deputy, hereby agree and covenant, to and with the Commissioners of the United Colonies, that henceforward, they will neither give, grant, sell, or in any manner alienate any part of their country, nor any parcel of land therein, either to any [of the] English or others, without consent or allowance of the said Commissioners."[3] Two years after,[4] upon

---

[1] Major Mason's history of the Pequot war and others. [Massachusetts Historical Collections, second series, Vol. VIII, p. 123.]
[2] Pp. 161—163.
[3] This agreement was made August 27, 1645.—ED.   [4] July 30, 1647.—ED.

their calling for their pay, Passicus sent them word, that "when he made this covenant, he did it in fear of the army, and though the English kept their covenant with him there, and let him go from them, yet the army was to go to Narragansett immediately and kill him there; therefore said the Commissioners, *Set your hands to such and such things, or else the army shall go forth to the Narragansetts.*" In answer to which the Commissioners say, "After covenants have been solemnly made, and hostages given, and a small part of the wampum paid, and all the rest due, now to pretend fears is a vain and offensive excuse."[1] This shows that they themselves did not neglect the rule they prescribed to their General in that expedition, viz. :—

> You are to use your best endeavors to gain the enemies' canoes, or utterly to destroy them, and herein you may make good use of the Indians, our confederates, as you may do upon other occasions, having due regard to the honor of God, who is both our sword and shield, and to the distance which is to be observed betwixt Christians and barbarians, as well in war as in other negotiations.[2]

Sixteen months before that covenant was made, Passicus and other heads of their tribes, had by an ample deed resigned over and submitted all those lands to the supreme authority in England, and Mr. Williams had procured a charter thereof from thence, extending unto the Pequot River and country.[3] The Massachusetts Records, upon granting Fisher's Island to Mr. Winthrop, say it lies against the mouth of Pequot River. What right of jurisdiction then had those colonies east of that river? and what right had Passicus to engage any of those lands to them, which he had submitted to another authority so long before? By re-

---

[1] Records of the United Colonies.
[2] Massachusetts History, Vol. III, p. 151.—B.

The words above quoted are from a document issued by the Commissioners of the United Colonies entitled, "Instructions for Sergeant-Major Gibbones, Commander-in-chief of our military forces, and for such as are joined with him in a council of war."—ED.

[3] Pp. 122, 161.

peated endeavors the Commissioners had got all the wampum that was promised in said covenant but three hundred and eight fathoms, before they met at Hartford, on September 5, 1650; and then Captain Atherton was sent, with twenty armed men, to demand the remainder, with orders to seize their goods if the Indians refused to pay it; and if resistance should be made so as any life was lost, that a special meeting of the Commissioners should then be called to make war upon them for it. He accordingly went, and placed his men round Passicus's tent, and going into it, seized the sachem by the hair of his head, and threatened to shoot him, if any resistance was made. This terrified them so much, that the wampum was presently paid. On July 25, 1651, at the desire of the Narragansett sachems, Mr. Williams wrote to the Governor at Boston, an account of sundry complaints they had against Uncas; which letter was laid before the Commissioners when they met at New Haven, the 4th of September following; but though Uncas was present, yet they acted nothing upon it, because the Narragansetts had not sent any of their men to support the charge. At the same time a tribute of three hundred and twelve fathoms of wampum was paid by Uncas, Ninecrost and others, on account of the Pequots they had among them; and upon laying of it down they demanded:—

Why this tribute was required, how long it should continue, and whether the children to be born hereafter were to pay it? All which being considered, the Commissioners by Thomas Stanton, answered, that the tribute by agreement hath been due yearly from the Pequots since *anno* 1638, for sundry murders without provocation committed by them upon several of the English at several times, as they found opportunity; refusing either to deliver up the murderers or to do justice upon them; [and] so drawing on a war upon themselves, to the great charge and inconvenience of the English; which war, through the good hand of our God, issued first in a conquest over that treacherous and bloody people, and after by agreement, (to spare as much as might be even such guilty blood,) in a small tribute, to be paid in different proportions, by, and for their males, according to their different ages yearly; but hath not hitherto been satisfied, though demanded. Wherefore, ... though twelve years' tribute were due before the year 1650, [this last year] and though the agreement was for a yearly tribute to be paid by them and theirs, so long as they continue in this part of the country; yet the Commissioners, something to ease their spirits [in reference to this just burthen,] and to engage them to an inoffensive and peaceable carriage, ... declared that the payment of this tribute shall be limited to ten years, [of which] this last year to be reckoned the first; after which, [time] unless they draw trouble unto themselves, they shall be free.[1]

Such an uneasiness among the Narragansetts was discovered two years after, that another army was raised and sent against them, which compelled them into another treaty, which not being otherwise fulfilled, the sachems were brought, on October 13, 1660, to mortgage all their lands, to Major Atherton, and about twenty associates with him, for six hundred fathoms of wampum, said then to be due to the Commissioners of the United Colonies. I find also by the records, that Massachusetts and Connecticut could never agree how to divide the Pequot lands betwixt them, till the Commissioners from Plymouth and New Haven had the case referred to them; and they on September 16, 1658, settled the line betwixt them, which was to be Mistick River (which runs in betwixt Stonington and Groton) up to the pond, by Lanthorn Hill, and thence from the middle of that pond to run a north course; Massachusetts to have both property and jurisdiction from thence to Wecapaug Brook, which was the easterly bounds of Sassicus's conquest. Pataquamscut purchase was made partly in 1657, and partly in 1658, by some inhabitants of Rhode Island, and John Hull of Boston, (who got a great estate by coining their silver money.) This purchase was about thirteen miles in length, and seven in breadth, in the heart of the Narragansett country.[2]

---

[1] Records of the United Colonies.

[2] In 1668, these purchasers gave three hundred acres of their best land, for an orthodox person, to preach God's word to the inhabitants; which has cost much contention in the law. Dowglass, Vol. II. p. 104.

In 1752, Dr. Macsparran said, " I have been engaged in a law suit about Glebe land twenty-eight years, and the Independent teacher has at last obtained a decree

When their Assembly met at Newport, May 21, 1661, they appointed a committee upon the letters they had then received from the Massachusetts, " who seriously considered and debated circumstances, concerning the matter in difference, betwixt the gentlemen, and some friends with them, that are active in sharing the Narragansett lands in the colony, without the consent of the colony ; and we [do] find by their letter, that those gentlemen, Major Atherton and associates, are not so well informed of the intent of the colony as might be requisite." They concluded to write and give them better information, and to offer to leave the case to referees to settle it ; but say :—

In case a fair issue cannot be had, as is desired, then, in a speedy and convenient time and season, to forbid the said gentlemen, or any of their company, in his Majesty's name, from further proceeding in the said purchase, as to possessing or sharing of any of the said lands, and to prosecute [against] them, or any of them, in case they still proceed without consent of the colony, as concluding that such their proceedings are contrary to the crown and dignity of his Majesty, and to the peace and well-being of his Majesty's subjects in this colony.

The 27th of August following, an Assembly met at Portsmouth, of which Mr. Williams was a member, when they sent a commission and letters to Mr. Clarke, to solicit for a new charter.[1] April 27th, 1662, the town of Providence gave Mr. Clarke a full purchase right of land therein as a free gift. The next month came the foregoing letter[2] from Boston to their Assembly, with account of their dealings

in council in his favor; so that I am forced to sit down by the loss of at least six hundred pounds sterling." America Dissected, p. 42.

I am told that Dr. Stennett, a Baptist minister in London, had a great hand in procuring this decree for Mr. Joseph Torry.

[1] This commission was drawn up and adopted by the previous Assembly which met in Warwick, October 16, 1660, and was " drawn out," that is, copied in due form, and sealed at the session in Portsmouth. Mr. Williams was not a member of the former Assembly. The commission simply appointed Mr. Clarke the "undoubted agent and attorney" of the colony, but did not direct him " to solicit a new charter." Probably this duty was assigned him in the letters, which seem to have had their origin in the later session of the Assembly. R. I. Colonial Records.—ED.

[2] See page 269.—ED.

with men whom they called trespassers, of whom Mr. Burdick was then a member of Mr. Clarke's church. He married Mr. Samuel Hubbard's daughter, and has a large posterity remaining in and about Westerly to this day. Mr. Sanford, and Mr. Greene, were now sent to Boston to make another trial for an amicable settlement of this controversy. It is to be noted, that neither of those colonies, which had made such a noise about their rights, had ever received any charter, either from king or parliament, of any lands to the west of Providence colony, till Connecticut, by the help of Mr. Winthrop, obtained one dated April 23, 1662, which took New Haven into the same colony. When the Commissioners met at Boston the 4th of September, they wrote to Rhode Island rulers in their former strain, and informed them of a warrant they had seen, signed by Joseph Torry, their Secretary, in the name of the General Court, " warning Captain Gookin and others to desist and forbear any further or future possession of any [of the] lands at or about Paucatuck as they shall answer the contrary at their peril; yet withal expressing your submission to his Majesty's determination. Wherefore (say the Commissioners) being earnestly[jointly] desirous to prevent any further disturbance of the peace of the colonies, though we have no doubt of the present right and interests of the Massachusetts to those lands we are willing to improve the argument which [that] yourselves have owned, and therefore thought meet to certify you, that we have read and perused a charter of incorporation, under the broad seal of England, sent over in the last ship, granted to some gentlemen of Connecticut, wherein the land at Paucatuck and Narragansett are contained, which we hope will prevail with you to require and cause your people to withdraw themselves, and desist from further disturbance."

The words in said charter which they built this upon, bounded that colony east, " by the Narragansett River, commonly called Narragansett Bay, where the said river, falleth into the sea." Now it is to be remembered, that Plymouth patent was bounded westward by Narragansett River and Bay, and these colonists pretended that Warwick was included therein, which could not be, unless Paucatuck was the river meant; and if it was, where is their right now to go east of it by Connecticut charter? The truth is, names are arbitrary, and those worthy governors, Bradford and Winslow, took Patucket to be the river intended in their patent.[1] And there was now less room left for this dispute; for on July 8, 1663, his Majesty granted Rhode Island charter, which describes their west boundaries to be the middle channel of Paucatuck River up to its head, and thence a north course to the south line of Massachusetts; which river says he, " having been yielded after much debate, for the fixed and certain bounds between these our said colonies, by the agents thereof; who have also agreed, that the said Paucatuck River shall be also called, alias, Narragansett River; and to prevent future disputes that otherwise might arise thereby forever hereafter, shall be construed, deemed and taken to be the Narragansett River, in our late grant to Connecticut colony, mentioned as the eastwardly bounds of that colony." This colony of Rhode Island and Providence Plantations, was to extend three English miles east and north-east of the most eastern and north-eastern parts of the Narragansett Bay, unto the mouth of Providence River, and thence by the eastwardly bank of it up to Patucket Falls, being the most westwardly line of Plymouth colony; and thence due north to the Massachusetts line, by which it is bounded on the north, and by the ocean on the south, including Block Island, and the other islands within their bay. As the Indians had formerly sent over a submission of themselves and land, to the king's father, they had now sent another to him; whereupon he says in this charter:—

> It shall not be lawful to, or for the rest of the colonies, to invade or molest the native Indians, or any other inhabitants inhabiting within the

[1] See pp. 57, 58.

bounds and limits hereafter mentioned; they having subjected themselves unto us, and being by us taken into our special protection, without the knowledge and consent of the governor and company of our colony of Rhode Island and Providence Plantations.

This charter appointed that a Governor, Deputy Governor, and ten Assistants should be elected annually on the first Wednesday in May, who, with deputies or representatives from each town, were to make laws, not contrary to the laws of England, make grants of land, constitute courts of justice, and appoint their officers both civil and military. Mr. Clarke sent over this charter, and Captain Gregory Dexter[1] fetched it from Boston; upon which a large assembly of the freemen in all the colony met at Newport, November 24th, and ordered Captain Dexter [Baxter] to take forth the charter and read it before all the people, and hold it up with the broad seal to their view, and then to have it safely deposited with Governor Arnold.[2] And they voted to pay all Mr. Clarke's disbursements in going to England, in their service there, and upon his intended return; as also one hundred pounds sterling as a free gratuity to him, besides those expenses; yea, and to give Captain Dexter [Baxter] twenty-five pounds sterling for his service and faithfulness in bringing the charter from Boston. Mr. Clarke's letters were read, upon which letters of thanks were ordered to be sent to the king, and to Lord Clarendon, for these great favors they had received by their means. The next day (after the

---

[1] This name should be "George Baxter." Bancroft says, Vol. II, p. 63, note, "Backus, almost always very accurate, here mistakes the name." He was doubtless led into the error by the fact that Gregory Dexter is a name well known in Rhode Island annals. Mistakes in deciphering old records are among the most excusable of mistakes; and the Records of Providence seem, from the wide difference between different copyists, to be especially obscure.—ED.

[2] "Voted; That the box in which the King's gracious letters were enclosed be opened, and the letters, with the broad seal thereto affixed, be taken forth and read by Captain George Baxter, in the audience and view of all the people; which was accordingly done, and the said letters, with his Majesty's royal stamp and the broad seal, with much becoming gravity, held up on high, and presented to the perfect view of the people, and then returned into the box and locked up by the Governor in order to the safe keeping of it." R. I. Colonial Records.—ED.

Governor, Deputy Governor, and six Assistants had taken their engagements) they called the sachems of the Narragansetts and Niantics before them, and let them know what the king had done for them; upon which they said, " they return his Majesty great thanks for his gracious relief, in releasing their lands from those forced purchases and mortgages by some of the other colonies." But another thing which is by no means to be omitted is, that the king says, in their petition for the charter they declared:—

> That it is much on their hearts, if they may be permitted, to hold forth a lively experiment, that a most flourishing civil state may stand and best be maintained, and that among our English subjects, with A FULL LIBERTY OF RELIGIOUS CONCERNMENTS, and that true piety rightly grounded upon gospel principles, will give the best and greatest security to sovereignty, and will lay in the hearts of men the strongest obligation to true loyalty.[1]

This petition was therefore fully granted; and above a hundred years after, a worthy gentleman well says:—

> This great experiment hath been made, [and hath fully answered the expectations of the beneficent, royal mind, that proposed it,] and it hath fully appeared, that a flourishing civil state, and the most unstained loyalty, may stand without the help of any religious party tests to support them; and the Christian religion is as little indebted to human laws for its support, as it is to human inventions, for the purity of its morals, and the sublimity of its doctrines.[2]

For seven years past there had been many contentions about lands, and strivings to strain Indian purchases, beyond their just limits, in Providence, Newport, and other parts of the colony, which Mr. Williams had a great hand in composing and settling; the particulars of which would be very instructive, had we room for them. And his HOPE in

---

[1] It is perhaps not strange that this familiar and noble sentence has been, by implication at least, ascribed to Roger Williams. See Morgan Edwards's History of the Baptists of Rhode Island; Benedict's History of the Baptists, Vol. II, pp. 489, 490. It was the product of a spirit kindred to that of Williams, it being part of John Clarke's second address or petition to the King. R. I. Colonial Records; Arnold's History of Rhode Island, Vol. I, p. 280.—ED.

[2] History of Providence. [Massachusetts Historical Collections, Second Series, Vol. IX, p. 196.]

1647, that government, held forth through love, union and order, though by few in number, and mean in condition, yet would withstand and overcome mighty opposers,[1] was wonderfully granted and confirmed; the memory of which, in the figure of an ANCHOR with this word for its motto, in their colony seal, has been continued from that time to this.[2] Mr. Clarke returned June 7, 1664, after he had served his colony at the British Court twelve years. In October following the Assembly appointed him, Mr. Williams and others, to inspect their laws, to see if any of them were contrary to their charter, and to make a table of them.[3] A committee was also appointed to consider of their eastern and western boundaries, and to write to the other colonies concerning them. Connecticut still contended for power and jurisdiction in Narragansett and offered to leave the case to the colonies of Massachusetts and Plymouth; which Rhode Island would not do.[4] The king's Commissioners who were now sent over, heard the complaints of the sachems and others, and entered upon the Narragansett country in the king's name, and called it the king's province. But on the

---

[1] Page 168.

[2] In 1647, the General Assembly ordered, "The seal of the Province shall be an ANCHOR; in 1664, they ordered that the seal be changed by inscribing above the anchor the word HOPE.—ED.

[3] Two years later Mr. Clarke was again assigned a similar duty. "It is ordered that Mr. John Clarke is deputed and authorized to compare all the laws of the colony into a good method and form, leaving out what may be superfluous, and adding what may appear unto him necessary, as well for the regulation of Courts as otherwise." R. I. Colonial Records.—ED.

[4] John Leverett, afterwards Governor of Massachusetts, wrote to Sir Thomas Temple of London, as follows:—"Connecticut have offered to refer the matter [of the boundary line] to the two colonies of Massachusetts and Plymouth; to which motion, divers of Rhode Island will come, but others refuse, upon what ground is not understood, these colonies not being interested in the quarrel or reason of it; [though some of the inhabitants may be in the land, or claim an interest therein, but the government do not,] so that that course might have been neighborly, to have tried for an issue that way before there had been giving a trouble to his Majesty in so small a matter as it is supposed that will be when heard." Massachusetts History, Vol. III, [Hutchinson's Collection of Original Papers,] p. 382. Any one who knows the attitude in which the colony of Plymouth, and especially that of Massachusetts stood toward Rhode Island, will readily understand upon what grounds some in Rhode Island should refuse this proposal.—ED.

I think I could do anything of myself to forward the work of regeneration; and here I got clear of one false hope, and began to build upon another; now I put great dependence in my non-dependence, and so went on with my reformation, thinking all the good I did that it was God who wrought it in me, and the evil came from the devil and my own corrupt nature; and this hope gave me great joy in my good performances, but great grief, guilt and repentance, for the commission of any known sin, or the omission of any known duty; and so I went on for ten or twelve years, and after that I grew more engaged after the treasures of the world, and then my delight in religion died away. .... At length I began to think I was blind, and ignorant both of my own miserable estate, and of the remedy God had provided. I prayed that God would enlighten my understanding; but still I grew more blind, ignorant and wicked, as I thought, but kept it to myself, till at last I got hedged up so that I could neither read nor pray, which lasted but a short time. This was a Sabbath morning, September 30, 1781. .... Now I began to see the base views I formerly had of the Lord Jesus Christ, and of the plan of salvation; for when I had a discovery of actual sins, and the danger I was exposed to thereby, I would repent and reform, and think what a glorious Saviour Christ was, and that some time or other he would save me from hell, and take me to glory, with a desire to be happy, but no desire to be holy. But, glory be to God, he now gave me another view of salvation; now I saw his law to be holy, and loved it, though I and all my conduct was condemned by it. Now I saw that God's justice did not strike against me as his creature, but as a sinner, and that Christ died not only to save from punishment, but from sin itself. I saw that Christ's office was not only to make men happy, but to make them holy, and the plan now looked beautiful to me; I had no desire to have the least tittle of it altered, but all my cry was to be conformed to it. .... On October 3, the load of guilt and condemnation was instantly removed, and my soul was filled with joy and peace. Then it was asked me, could I desire anything more? And at first I saw no want, till I found a want of love and gratitude in me to return thanks to God for this great deliverance, which I began to cry and plead for; and those words were spoken to me, Greater love hath no man than this, that a man lay down his life for his friend; which came with such light, life, love and power, that I knew it to be the voice of my blessed Jesus, who by his Holy Spirit set that glorious seal to my soul that God is true; and now, by his grace, I could speak forth redeeming love and free grace without dread or fear. At this time there was no work or moving of religion among us, or round about us.

But he was constrained to go and visit his neighbors from house to house, and to lay open to them the vast concerns of

tioned; and which, by a blessing upon their labors, increased by the close of the next year to fifty-five members. In 1651, forty more joined to it; forty-seven in 1652, and by the end of 1660, two hundred and sixty-three persons had joined to that church, whose names all now stand in a neat book of records which they kept; which contain a distinct account of the means and methods they took to promote vital and practical religion among the several branches of their society; as also letters of correspondence to and from their brethren in various parts of England and Ireland.

But here another scene opens.

The Presbyterians had been as much against equal religious liberty as the Episcopalians, and manifested as great bitterness against those who broke their power in the long parliament. These two parties joined in restoring the second Charles to the throne, who came in with plausible promises of indulgence to tender consciences; and great pains were taken to accommodate matters between them, without any good effect. The Episcopalians having got the power into their hands, determined to crush all that opposed it. Among the rest they wreaked their vengeance on Sir Henry Vane, whom they beheaded in August, 1662. "His indiscretion and insolence (says a great author) as well on his trial as his execution, have been extremely aggravated; but it is easy to see, it was only to save the king's honor, who having positively promised a pardon to all except the king's judges, could not avoid granting a pardon to Vane, without violating his promise."[1] And when Vane's friends persuaded him to make some submission in order to save his life, he said, "If the king does not think himself more concerned for his honor and word than I do for my life, I am very willing they should take it. Nay, I declare that I value my life less in a good cause, than the king can do his promise." A Presbyterian author who writes very bitterly against him,

---

[1] Rapin, Vol. II, p. 631. [The History of England, as well Ecclesiastical as Civil, by Mr. De Rapin Thoyras, London, 1731, Vol. XIII, p. 305.]

yet owns that, " the two things in which he had most success, and spake most plainly, were his earnest plea for universal liberty of conscience, and against the magistrates' intermeddling with religion, and his teaching his followers to revile the ministry, calling them ordinarily, *black coats, priests*, and other names which savored of reproach." And he says, " No man could die with greater appearance of a gallant resolution, and fearlessness, than he did, though before supposed a timorous man; insomuch that the manner of his death procured him more applause than all the actions of his life."[1] On the twenty-fourth of that month, called St. Bartholomew's day, an act of parliament was passed, which ejected all teachers, both of churches and schools, out of their places, who would not declare their assent or consent to all the forms and ceremonies of the church of England. About two thousand were turned out by it. The method the church party took to procure this act, was secretly to foment disturbances and tumults in different parts of England, and then to persuade the parliament that the Presbyterians did it, and that no peace could be had with them till dissenters were all turned out of place. Among those so ejected was our Mr. Miles.[2] Upon which he and some of his friends came over to our country, and brought their church records with them. And at Mr. Butterworth's house, in Rehoboth, in 1663, John Miles, elder, James Brown, Nicholas Tanner, Joseph Carpenter, John Butterworth, Eldad Kingsley, and Benjamin Alby, joined in a solemn covenant together.

This church was then in Plymouth colony, concerning whom Dr. Mather says, " there being many good men among those—I do not know that they have been persecuted with any harder means, than those of kind conferences to reclaim them."[3] I suppose it was so for some years, and that because

[1]Calamy's Abridgment. Vol. I, pp. 99, 101.
[2]Calamy's Abridgment, Vol. I, pp. 178—181, and Vol. II, pp. 731.
[3]Magnalia, Book I, p. 14. [Vol. I, p. 58.]

Mr. Newman, who persecuted Mr. Holmes died this year; but four years after I find it thus recorded, viz.:—

At the Court holden [held] at Plymouth the 2d of July, 1667, before Thomas Prince, Governor, John Alden, Josiah [Josias] Winslow, Thomas Southworth, William Bradford, Thomas Hinckley, Nathaniel Bacon, and John Freeman, assistants....Mr. Miles, and Mr. Brown, for their breach of order, in setting up of a public meeting without the knowledge and approbation of the Court to the disturbance of the peace of the place, are fined each of them five pounds, and Mr. Tanner the sum of one pound [twenty shillings] and we judge that their continuance at Rehoboth, being very prejudicial to the peace of that church and that town, may not be allowed; and do therefore order all persons concerned therein, wholly to desist from the said meeting in that place or township, within this month. Yet in case they shall remove their meeting unto some other place, where they may not prejudice any other church, and shall give us any reasonable satisfaction respecting their principles, we know not but they may be permitted by this government so to do.

And it was no longer than the 30th of October following, before the Court made them an ample grant of Wannamoiset which they called Swanzey. It then included what is now Warren and Barrington, and the district of Shawomet, as well as the present town of Swanzey.[1] There they made a regular settlement,[2] which has continued to this day. The

[1] Plymouth Records. Note. This town was named on March first, 1667-8. When by mistake the first grant is dated, in Swanzey Town Records; but the above I took from the Court Records at Plymouth.

[2] The grant of this town was made to "Capt. Thomas Willet, Mr. Paine, senior, Mr. Brown, John Allen, and John Butterworth." Of these, says John Comer, "the first two were Pædobaptists, the others Baptists." Captain Willet "made the following proposals unto those that were with him. 1. That no erroneous persons be admitted into the township either as an inhabitant or sojourner. 2. That no man of an evil behavior or contentious person, &c., be admitted. 3. That none may be admitted that may become a charge to the place.

"The church of Christ here gathered and assembling did therefore make the following address unto the said Captain Willet and his associates, the trustees, as aforesaid:—

SIRS: We being with you engaged (according to our capacities) in the carrying on a township according to the grant given us by the Honorable Court, and desiring to lay such a foundation thereof as may effectually tend to God's glory, our future peace and comfort, and the real benefit of such as shall hereafter join with us herein; as also to prevent all future jealousies and causes of dissatisfaction, or disturbances in so good a work, do, in relation to the three proposals made by our

families also of Luther, Cole, Bowen, Wheaton, Martin, Barnes, Thurber, Bosworth, Mason, Child, and others, which are numerous in those parts, sprang from the early planters of that town and church. Their first meeting-house was built a little west of Kelly's ferry, against Warren, but Mr. Miles settled the west side of the great bridge which still bears his name.

much honored Captain Willet, humbly present to your serious consideration (before we further proceed therein) that the said proposals may be consented to and subscribed by every townsman under the following explication:—

"That the first proposal relating to the non-admisson of erroneous persons may be only understood under the following explications, viz.: of such as hold damnable heresies, inconsistent with the faith of the gospel; as, to deny the Trinity, or any person therein; the deity or sinless humanity of Christ, or the union of both natures in him, or his full satisfaction to the divine justice of all his elect, by his active and passive obedience, or his resurrection, ascension into heaven, intercession, or his second coming personally to judgment; or else to deny the truth or divine authority of the Scriptures, or the resurrection of the dead, or to maintain any merit of works, consubstantiation, transubstantiation, giving divine adoration to any creature, or any other anti-christian doctrine directly opposing the priestly prophetical or kingly offices of Christ, or any part thereof; (2) or such as hold such opinions as are inconsistent with the well-being of the place, as to deny the magistrate's power to punish evil doers as well as to encourage those that do well, or to deny the first day of the week to be observed by divine institution as the Lord's day or Christian Sabbath, or to deny the giving of honor to whom honor is due, or to oppose those civil respects that are usually performed according to the laudable customs of our nation each to other, as bowing the knee or body, &c., or else to deny the office, use or authority of the ministry or a comfortable maintenance to be due to them from such as partake of their teachings, or to speak reproachfully of any of the churches of Christ in the country, or of any such other churches as are of the same common faith with us or them.

"We desire that it be also understood and declared that this is not understood of any holding any opinion different from others in any disputable point, yet in controversy among the godly learned, the belief thereof not being essentially necessary to salvation; such as pædobaptism, anti-pædobaptism, church discipline or the like; but that the minister or ministers of the said town may take their liberty to baptize infants or grown persons as the Lord shall persuade their consciences, and so also the inhabitants take their liberty to bring their children to baptism or to forbear."

This is followed by the "explication" of the other two proposals, and the document is signed by John Myles, pastor, and John Butterworth. Comer's Manuscript Diary. It is evident that this ancient Baptist church was not, at first, clear in the view that civil government has no right of interference with religious belief; and that it took upon itself the dangerous task of deciding between Christian doctrines as more or less essential.—ED.

CHAPTER VI.

AN ACCOUNT OF THE CONSTITUTION OF THE FIRST BAPTIST CHURCH IN BOSTON, IN 1665, AND OF THEIR SUFFERINGS DOWN TO 1675.

Mr. Hubbard says :—

As some were studying how baptism might be enlarged and extended to the seed of the faithful in their several generations, there were others as studious to deprive all unadult children thereof, and to restrain the privilege only to adult believers.[1]

And Dr. Mather, after confessing that very odious and unjust things had been published against Anabaptists ever since Luther's time, says :—

Infant baptism hath been scrupled by multitudes in our day, who have been in other points most worthy Christians, and as holy, watchful, fruitful and heavenly people as perhaps any in the world. Some few of these people have been among the planters of New England from the beginning, and have been welcome to the communion of our churches, reserving their particular opinion unto themselves. .... At last some of our churches used, it may be, a little too much cogency towards the brethren, who would weakly turn their backs when infants were brought forth to be baptized.[2]

Twenty years before, Mr. Cobbet had called their so doing a "profane trick." What their dealings were, which are here covered under the obscure term cogency, will presently

---

[1] Hubbard, p. 590.—ED.
[2] Magnalia, Book VII, p. 27, [Vol. II, p. 459.] Seth Sweetser, who came over to Charlestown in 1638, from Tring, in Hardfordshire, was one of those early Baptists. I find by the records that he was received a freeman that year. His son Benjamin was long a useful member of the Baptist church in Boston, and he has left a numerous posterity, one of whom has been schoolmaster and town clerk in Charlestown for sundry years past.

be seen. It was such that a number drew off and met by themselves in Charlestown, till, on May 28th, 1665, Thomas Gould, Thomas Osburne, Edward Drinker, and John George, were baptized, and joined with Richard Goodall, William Turner, Robert Lambert, Mary Goodall, and Mary Newel, " in a solemn covenant, in the name of the Lord Jesus Christ, to walk in fellowship and communion together, in the practice of all the holy appointments of Christ, which he had, or should further make known to them." Goodall came recommended from Mr. Kiffin's church in London; Turner and Lambert from Mr. Stead's church in Dartmouth, having been regular walkers in the Baptist order before they came to this country. Gould and Osburne separated from the church in Charlestown; Drinker and George had lived many years in this country, but had not joined to any of their churches.[1]

The king's Commissioners being here, caused the Court not to lay hold of these people so soon as otherwise they might have done. But in August a note was entered in Roxbury church records, and published in an Almanac, which has been communicated to me in these words:—

> The Anabaptists gathered themselves into a church, prophesied one by one, and some one among them administered the Lord's Supper after he was regularly excommunicated by the church at Charlestown; they also set up a lecture at Drinker's house once a fortnight.

As great noise was made about their receiving excommunicate members and officers, it is proper to give that matter a distinct consideration here. Dr. Mather says:—

> Our Anabaptists formed a church .... not only with a manifest violation of the laws in the Commonwealth, relating to the orderly manner of gathering a church, but also with a manifold provocation unto the rest of our churches, by admitting into their own society such as our churches had excommunicated for moral scandals, yea, and employing such persons to be administrators of the two sacraments among them.[2]

[1] Their Church Records. Russell's Narrative, pp. 1, 2.
[2] Magnalia, Book VII, p. 27, [Vol. II, p. 459.]

They would thus represent as though that church had many such members and officers; whereas, in fifteen years, among fourscore Baptist members, they have named but four excommunicated persons, and but one of them an officer, viz.. Thomas Gould, who, with Thomas Osburne, was of the first members; and as the impartial reader would be willing to hear both sides upon it, I will give him their story in their own words.

Mr. Samuel Willard of Boston, who wrote against this church, says of Thomas Gould:—

Though he was first called to an account about withholding his child from baptism, yet that was not the reason of his being admonished, nor because he could not be convinced of error; nor yet did the church proceed to admonition, till such time as he (not only spake contemptuously and irreligiously of the emptiness and nullity of that ordinance, but also) used unbecoming gestures in the time of administration, of which (being asked the reason) he (before the congregation) acknowledged they were to cast disrespect upon it; nor then neither till after much patience. 2. At his first admonition he was not sententially suspended, but only desired, for preventing of the offence of some, to abstain from coming to the other sacrament. 3. Upon this Thomas Gould took up a trade of absenting himself from the meetings of the church to worship God on the Sabbath, which made a new offence. 4. The church in much tenderness waited upon him, and proceeded not to excommunication, but tried with admonition upon admonition, and that by the space of seven or eight years; nor was he excommunicated, till (having left his own) he joined to another society, without the church's leave, or once asking it; and now also being twice sent for by the church, he disclaimed their authority over him. 5. Thomas Gould did not leave the church at Charlestown on the account of the Anabaptists' new church (as is pretended) but had many years before renounced his submission to that church. 6. He did (while under admonition) neglect public worship, and gather a private meeting on the Sabbath to his house. 7. He did wickedly slight the admonition of the church, declaring that they had by it, discharged him of all relation to them.

For Thomas Osburne; the church's proceedings with him were with the like patience as to Thomas Gould; only it is to be observed, that his first offence was this; whereas it is one thing which church members engage to upon admission, to walk with the church in constant attendance upon public worship, he (without notifying any offence) did withdraw and separate, frequenting those schismatic meetings at Gould's on the Sabbath;

this was the offence, nor did he when first dealt with pretend any dislike of infant baptism, but that the church gave no liberty to private brethren to prophesy, that they limited the ministry to learned men, and that he did not find his own spirit free to come; though afterwards he spake both of that, and of their severity to the Quakers, though that church meddled not with them, but to preach against their errors. In this practice he contumaciously persisted many years, denying himself to be subject to that church, or bound to assemble with them, slighting many admonitions; and afterwards (with Thomas Gould) went off to, and became a worthy pillar of an Anabaptist church.[1]

This is the Pædobaptist's story; Mr. Gould has given us his in the words following:—

It having been a long time a scruple to me about infant baptism, God was pleased at last to make it clear to me by the rule of the gospel, that children were not capable nor fit subjects for such an ordinance, because Christ gave this commission to his apostles, first to preach to make them disciples, and then to baptize them, which infants were not capable of; so that I durst not bring forth my child to be partaker of it; so looking that my child had no right to it, which was in the year 1655, when the Lord was pleased to give me a child; I staid some space of time and said nothing to see what the church would do with me. On a third day of the week when there was a meeting at my house, to keep a day of thanksgiving to God for his mercy shown to my wife, at that time one coming to the meeting, brought a note from the elders of the church to this effect, that they desired me to come down on the morrow to the elder's house, and to send word again what time of that day I would come, and they would stay at home for me; and if I could not come that day to send them word. I, looking on the writing with many friends with me, I told them I had promised to go another way on the morrow. Master Dunstan[2] being present desired me to send them word, that I could not come on the morrow, but that I would come any other time that they would appoint me; and so I sent word back by the same messenger. The fifth day, meeting with elder Green, I told him how it was; he told me it was well, and that they would appoint another day when he had spoken with the pastor, and then they would send me word. This lay about two months, before I heard any more from them. On a First-day, in the afternoon, one told me I must stop, for the church would speak with me. They called me out, and Mas-

---

[1] Willard's answer to Russell, pp. 13, 14. Note, Richard Russell, one of their magistrates, was a member of Charlestown church; and did not he act against the Quakers?

[2] I suppose, Mr. Henry Dunstar.

ter Sims told the church, that this brother did withhold his child from baptism, and that they had sent unto him to come down on such a day to speak with them, and if he could not come on that day to set a day when he would come, and they be at home, but he refusing to come would appoint no time, when we writ to him to take his own time and send us word.

I replied that there was no such word in the letter, for me to appoint the day; but what time that day I should come. Mr. Sims stood up and told me, *I did lie*, for they sent to me to appoint the day. I replied again that there was no such thing in the letter. He replied again, that they did not set down a time, and not a day, therefore he told me it was a lie, and that they would leave my judgment and deal with me for a lie; and told the church that he and the elder agreed to write, that if I could not come that day, to appoint the time when I could come, and that he read it, after the elder writ it, and the elder affirmed it was so; but I still replied, there was no such thing in the letter, and thought that I could produce the letter. They bid me let them see the letter, or they would proceed against me for a lie. Brother Thomas Wilder, sitting before me, stood up and told them, that it was so in the letter as I said, for he read it when it came to me. But they answered, it was not so, and bid him produce the letter, or they would proceed with me. He said, I think I can produce the letter, and forthwith took it out of his pocket, which I wondered at; and I desired him to give it to Mr. Russell to read, and so he did, and he read it very faithfully, and it was just as I had said, that I must send them word what time of that day I would come down; so that their mouths were stopped, and Master Sims put it off, and said he was mistaken, for he thought he had read it otherwise; but the elder said, This is nothing, let us proceed with him for his judgment. Now let any man judge what a fair beginning this was, and if you wait a while you may see as fair an ending. They called me forth to know why I would not bring my child to baptism. But before I speak to that, observe the providence of God in the carriage of this letter. Brother Wilder was with us when their letter came to my house, and after Mr. Dunstan [Dunstar] had read it, he gave it to brother Wilder and he put it into his pocket, and it lay there eight or nine weeks, till, that day I was called forth, going a good space from his house, finding it too cold to go in the clothes he had on, [he] returned again and put on another pair of breeches which were warmer, and when he had so done, put his hand into his pocket to see if he had any paper to write with, and there found that letter, and put it in again and went to meeting, yet not knowing what would be done that day concerning me. God had so appointed it, to stop their fierce proceedings against me for a lie, which they sought to take me in. Then asking me why I did not bring my child to baptism, my answer was, I did not see any rule of Christ for it, for that ordinance belongs to such as can make profession of their faith, as the Scripture doth plainly hold forth. .... They answered me, That was meant of grown persons, and not of children; but that which was most alleged by them was, that children were capable of circumcision in the time of the law, and therefore as capable in the time of the gospel of baptism; and asked me why children were not to be baptized in the time of the gospel, as well as children were circumcised in the time of the law? My answer was, God gave a strict command in the law for circumcision of children; but we have no command in the gospel, nor example, for the baptizing of children. Many other things were spoken, then a meeting was appointed by the church the next week at Mr. Russell's.

Being met at Mr. Russell's house, Mr. Sims took a writing out of his pocket wherein he had drawn up many arguments for infants' baptism, and told the church that I must answer those arguments, which I suppose he had drawn from some author; and told me I must keep to those arguments. My answer was, I thought the church had met together to answer my scruples, and to satisfy my conscience by a rule of God, and not for me to answer his writing. He said he had drawn it up for the help of his memory, and desired we might go on. Then I requested three things of them. 1st. That they should not make me offender for a word. 2d. They should not drive me faster than I was able to go. 3d. That if any present should see cause to clear up any thing that is spoken by me, they might have their liberty without offence; because here are many of you that have their liberty to speak against me if you see cause. But it was denied, and Mr. Sims was pleased to reply, that he was able to deal with me himself and that I know it. So we spent four or five hours speaking to many things to and again; but so hot, both sides, that we quickly forgot and went from the arguments that were written. At last one of the company stood up and said, I will give you one plain place of Scripture where children were baptized. I told him that would put an end to the controversy. That place in the second of the Acts, 39th, 40th verses. After he had read the Scripture, Mr. Sims told me that promise belonged to infants, for the Scripture saith, *The promise is to you and your children, and to all that are afar off;* and he said no more, to which I replied, *Even so many as the Lord our God shall call.* Mr. Sims replied, that I spoke blasphemously in adding to the Scriptures. I said, pray do not condemn me, for if I am deceived, my eyes deceive me. He replied again, I added to the Scripture, which was blasphemy. I, looking into my Bible, read the words again, and said it was so. He replied the same words the third time before the church. Mr. Russell stood up and told him it was so as I had read it. Ay, it may be so in your Bible, saith Mr. Sims. Mr. Russell answered, Yea in yours too if you will look into it. Then he said he was mistaken, for he thought on another place; so after many other words we broke up for that time.

At another meeting the church required me to bring out my child to baptism. I told them I durst not do it, for I did not see any rule for it in the word of God. They brought many places of Scripture in the Old and New Testaments, as circumcision and the promise to Abraham, and that children were holy, and they were disciples. But I told them that all these places made nothing for infants' baptism. Then stood up W. D. in the church and said, "*Put him in the Court! Put him in the Court!*" But Mr. Sims answered, I pray forbear such words; but it proved so, for presently after, they put me in the Court, and put me in seven or eight Courts, whilst they looked upon me to be a member of their church. The elder pressed the church to lay me under admonition, which the church was backward to do. Afterwards I went out at the sprinkling of children, which was a great trouble to some honest hearts, and they told me of it. But I told them I could not stay, for I look upon it as no ordinance of Christ. They told me that now I had made known my judgment I might stay, for they know I did not join with them. So I stayed and sat down in my seat when they were at prayer and administering that service to infants. Then they dealt with me for my unreverent carriage. ... One stood up and accused me, that I stopped my ears; but I denied it.

At another meeting they asked me if I would suffer the church to fetch my child and baptize it? I answered, If they would fetch my child and do it as their own act they might do it; but when they should bring my child, I would make known to the congregation that I had no hand in it; then some in the church were against doing of it. A brother stood up and said, Brother Gould, you were once for children's baptism, why are you fallen from it? I answered, It is true, and I suppose you were once for crossing in baptism, why are you fallen from that? The man was silent. But Mr. Sims stood up in a great heat, and desired the church to take notice of it, that I compared the ordinance of Christ to the cross in baptism! This was one of the great offences they dealt with me for. After this the Deputy Governor[1] meeting me in Boston, called me to him and said, Goodman Gould, I desire you that you would let the church baptize your child. I told him that if the church would do it upon their own account they should do it, but I durst not bring out my child. So he called to Mrs. Norton of Charlestown, and prayed her to fetch Goodman Gould's child and baptize it. So she spake to them, but not rightly, informing them, she gave them to understand that I would bring out my child. They called me out again and asked me if I would bring forth my child? I told them No, I durst not do it, for I see no rule for it. One of the brethren stood up and said, If I would not let my child partake of one ordinance, it was meet I should not partake of the other; so many of the church concluded to lay me under admonition; but before they did it Mr. Sims told me, it

[1] Mr. Bellingham, who was chief Governor when Mr. Gould was banished in 1668.

was more according to rule for me to withdraw from the ordinance, than for them to put me by; bringing that place of Scripture, If thou bring thy gift to the altar, and there rememberest that thy brother hath ought against thee, leave there thy offering and be reconciled first to thy brother. But I told them, I did not know that my brother had any thing justly against me; for they had not shewn me any rule of Christ that I had broken, therefore I durst not withdraw from that ordinance that I had found so much of God in; but if they would put me by, I hoped God would feed my soul another way. So they proceeded to admonition. Elder Green[1] said, Brother Gould, you are to take notice that you are admonished for three things; the first is, that you refused to bring your child to be baptized; the second is, for your contentious words, and unreverent carriage in the time of that ordinance; the third is, for a late lie you told; and therefore you are to take notice, that you are not to partake any more of the ordinance of Christ with us, till you give satisfaction for these things. But when that late lie was told I know not, except it was when the letter was found in brother Wilder's pocket. This admonition was between seven and eight years before they cast me out. After this I went to Cambridge meeting, which was as near to my house as the other; upon that they put me into the Court, that I did not come to hear; but many satisfied the Court that I did come constantly to Cambridge; so they cleared me. Then the church called me to account and dealt with me for schism, that I rent from the church. I told them, I did not rend from them, for they put me away. Master Sims was very earnest for another admonition for schism, which most of the church were against; but it seems he set it down for an admonition on a bit of paper. This continued for a long time before they called me out again. In the meantime, I had some friends who came to me out of old England, who were Baptists, and desired to meet at my house of a First-day, which I granted. Of these was myself, my wife and Thomas Osburne, that were of their church. Afterward they called me forth and asked why I kept the meeting in private on the Lord's day, and did not come to the public? My answer was, I know not what reason the church had to call me forth. They asked me if I was not a member of that church? I told them they had not acted toward me as a member, who had put me by the ordinances of Christ seven years ago; .... they had denied me the privileges of a member. They asked whether I looked upon admonition as an appointment of Christ? I told them, Yes, but not to lie under it above seven years, and to be put by the ordinances of Christ in the church; for the rule of Christ is first to deal with men in the first and in the second place, and then in the third place before the church; but the first time that ever they dealt with me, they called me before the whole

---

[1] Mr. Green, as I take it, was ruling elder; Mr. Zachariah Sims, was teaching elder.

church. Many meetings we had about this thing, whether I was a member or not, but could come to no conclusion; for I still affirmed that their actings rendered me no member. Then Mr. Sims told the church that I was ripe for excommunication, and [he] was very earnest for it; but the church would not consent. Then I desired that we might send to other churches for their help to hear the thing betwixt us; but Master Sims made me this answer: We are a church of Christ ourselves, and you shall know that we have power to deal with you ourselves. Then said Mr. Russell, We have not gone the right way to gain this our brother, for we have dealt too harshly with him. But still Master Sims pressed the church to excommunicate me. Mr. Russell said, There were greater errors in the church in the apostles' time, and yet they did not so deal with them. Mr. Sims asked him what they were? He said, How say some of you that there is no resurrection of the dead? Mr. Sims was troubled and said, I wonder you will bring this place of Scripture to encourage him in his error? Mr. Sims was earnest for another admonition. Then stood up Solomon Phips and said, You may clap one admonition on him upon another, but to what end, for he was admonished about seven years ago! Mr. Sims said, Brother! do you make such a light matter of admonition, to say, Clap them one upon another? Doth not the apostle say, After the first and second admonition reject an heretic? therefore there might be a second admonition. It was answered, it was a hard matter to prove a man an heretic, for every error doth not make a man a heretic. Mr. Sims said, It was not seven years ago, nor above three, since I was admonished, and that was for schism. A brother replied and said, it was seven years since I was admonished. On that there was some difference in the church what I was admonished for. Mr. Sims then pulled a bit of paper out of his pocket and said, This is that he was admonished for, and that was but three years since. Brother Phips asked him when that paper was writ, for he never heard of that admonition before? He answered, he set it down for his own memory; then he read it, that it was for schism, and rending from the church. I told him I did not rend from the church, but the church put me away from them, and that was four years before this. Then there was much agitation when the admonition was given, and what it was for? And this was all the church records that could be found, which was about seven years after the admonition was given; so after many words we broke up, which was the last time we met together. Now let any man judge of the church records that were drawn up against me, and read at the dispute in Boston, which contained three or four sheets of paper; read by Mr. Shepard,[1] and drawn up by him, a little while before the dispute, who was not an eye nor ear witness to the church's actings not above half the time.

[1] Son to Mr. Thomas Shepard, formerly of Cambridge.

Now after this, considering with myself what the Lord would have me to do; not likely to join with any of the churches of New England any more, and so to be without the ordinances of Christ; in the mean time God sent out of Old England some who were Baptists; we, consulting together what to do, sought the Lord to direct us, and taking counsel of other friends who dwelt among us, who were able and godly, they gave us counsel to congregate ourselves together; and so we did, being nine of us, to walk in the order of the gospel according to the rule of Christ, yet knowing that it was a breach of the law of this country; that we had not the approbation of magistrates and ministers, for that we suffered the penalty of that law, when we were called before them. After we had been called into one or two courts, the church understanding that we were gathered into church order, they sent three messengers from the church to me, telling me the church required me to come before them the next Lord's day. I replied, The church had nothing to do with me, for they had put me from them eight years before. They replied, that they had nothing to do with that, but were sent by the church to tell me it was the mind of the church to speak with me. I told them I was joined to another church, and that church was not willing I should come to them, they having nothing to do with me, therefore I would not come without the church's consent. Then they departed. The next week they sent three messengers more, who came to my house and told me that the church had sent them to require me to come to the church the next Lord's day after. I told them that the church had nothing to do to require me to come, who had put me from them eight years, and the church I now walked with would not let me come. They told me again that if I did not come, the church would proceed against me the next Lord's day. I told them that I could not come for we were to break bread the next Lord's day. They told me they would return my answer to the church. One of them asked if I would come the next Lord's day after? But another presently said, We have no such order from the church; so they departed. The last day of that week three loving friends coming to me of their own account, one of them was pleased to say to me, Brother Gould, though you look upon it as unjust for them to cast you out, yet there be many that are godly among them, that will act with them through ignorance, which will be a sin of them, and you are persuaded, I believe, that it is your duty to prevent any one from any sinful act; for they will cast you out for not hearing the church; now your coming will stop them from acting against you, and so keep many from that sin. Upon these words I was clearly convinced that it was my duty to go, and replied, Although I could not come the next day, yet I promised them that if I was alive and well, I would come the next Lord's day if the Lord permit. He replied, What if the church I was joined to was not willing? I told him I did not question that any one would be against it upon this ground. After I had propounded it to the church, not one was against it. I entreated these friends to make it known to the elders that I would come to them the next Lord's day after; yet, though they knew of it, they proceeded against me that day, and delivered me up to Satan for not hearing the church.

This narrative I met with among Mr. Callender's papers, and I have good reason to think it genuine, and that the manuscript now in my hands was written above a hundred years ago; which I have copied that the public may be better able to judge of what those excommunications were. It appears by Mr. Willard that the first charge they had against Mr. Osburne, was his going to meeting with that schismatical Gould; therefore, as the reader judges of the one, so likely he will of the other. Only it ought to be noted, that neither of them were excommunicated persons, when they formed that Baptist church, but had that sentence pronounced upon them afterwards, for refusing to return to those who had treated them so ill. And before that act, viz., on August 20, 1665, Richard Russell, Esq., issued a warrant to the constable of Charlestown, the original whereof is now before me, requiring him in his Majesty's name, to labor to discover where these people were assembled, and to require them to attend the established worship, which if they refused, he was to return their names and places of abode to the next magistrate. In consequence whereof they were brought before the Court of Assistants in September; to whom they exhibited a confession of their faith, which is copied into their records. The only article of which that I find objected against is in these words, viz.: "Christ's commission to his disciples is to teach and baptize, and those who gladly receive the word and are baptized, are saints by calling, and fit matter for a visible church." This was complained of as excluding all from a visible saintship but baptized persons, which we shall hereafter see they had no thought of. But their grand crime lay in not obeying the ruling party in their religious affairs.

The Court of Assistants charged them to desist from what they called their schismatical practice; and because they would not, the General Court that met October 11, convented Gould, Turner, Osburne, Drinker and George before them, to whom these Baptists exhibited the same confession as they had to the Court of Assistants, which was closed with saying, "If any take this to be heresy, then do we, with the apostle, confess, that after the way which they call heresy, we worship God the Father of our Lord Jesus Christ, believing all things that are written in the law and the prophets and apostles." This the Court called a "contemning the authority and laws here established, for the maintenance of godliness and honesty, as well as continuing in the profanation of God's holy ordinances;" and said:—

> This Court taking the premises into their serious consideration, do judge meet to declare, that the said Gould and company, are no orderly church assembly, and that they stand justly convicted of high presumption against the Lord and his holy appointments, as also the peace of this government, against which this Court doth account themselves bound to God, [to] his truth and his churches here planted, to bear their testimony, and do therefore sentence the said Thomas Gould, William Turner, Thomas Osburne, Edward Drinker and John George, such of them as are freemen, to be disfranchised, and all of them, upon conviction before any one magistrate or Court, of their further proceedings herein, to be committed to prison until the General Court shall take further order with them. Zechariah Rhodes being in Court when they were proceeding against Thomas Gould and company, and saying in Court, "The Court has not to do in [with] matters of religion;" he was committed likewise. Being sent for he acknowledged his fault, declaring he was sorry he had given them offence. The Court judged meet to discharge him, the Governor giving him an admonition for his said offence.[1]

Can any man believe that these were measures to promote either godliness or honesty, in Rhodes, or in any one else? rather did not the Court take Jehovah's name in vain in this

---

[1] Massachusetts Records. Rhodes was a Baptist, but had been of Arnold's party at Pawtuxet. Massachusetts History, Vol. III, p. 277.—B.

The Massachusetts Records as published give only the surnames of the offenders and arrange them in the following order, viz.: Gould, Osburne, Drinker, Turner and George.—ED.

act? The forementioned excuse, made by Dr. Mather, for this severity, viz., their joining in church fellowship without the approbation of other ministers and their rulers,[1] says Mr. Neal, " condemns all the dissenting congregations that have been gathered in England, since the act of uniformity in the year 1662. . . . . Let the reader judge, who had most reason to complain ; the New England churches, who would neither suffer the Baptists to live quietly in their communion nor separate peaceably from it ; or these unhappy persons who were treated so unkindly for following the light of their consciences."[2] Yet because they still followed that light, they were presented to the County Court at Cambridge, April 17, 1666, " for absenting themselves from the public worship." And when they asserted that they did steadily attend such worship,[3] the foregoing act of the Assembly was produced to prove that it was not in a lawful way ; and Gould, Osburne and George, were each of them fined four pounds therefor, and ordered to bind themselves in a bond of twenty pounds apiece, for their appearance at the next Court of Assistants ; and refusing so to do were committed to prison.[4] When the Court of Assistants came, they gave sentence that they should pay their fines and Court charges ; and when the Assembly sat on September 11, they ordered,

---

[1] See page 288.—ED.

[2] Neal's History of New England, Vol. I, pp. 304, 305.

[3] "Thomas Osburne answered that the reason of his non-attendance was that the Lord hath discovered unto him from his word and spirit of truth that the society wherewith he is now in communion is more agreeable to the word of God, asserted that they were a church and attended the worship of God together, and do judge themselves bound so to do, the ground whereof he said he gave in to the General Court. Thomas Gould answered that as for coming to public worship, they did meet in public worship according to the rule of Christ, the grounds whereof they had given to the Court of Assistants, asserted that they were a public meeting according to the order of Christ Jesus, gathered together. John George answered that he did attend the public meetings on the Lord's days where he was a member, asserted that they were a church according to the order of Christ in the gospel, and with them he walked and held communion in the public worship of God on the Lord's days. Massachusetts History, Vol. III, [Hutchinson's Collection of Original Papers,] p. 400.—ED.

[4] Massachusetts History, Vol. III, pp. 400, 401.

that if they would pay the same, they should be set at liberty; but added that, " the order of Court of October, 1665, referring to the said schismatical assembly, shall be, and hereby is declared to stand in full force."[1] Thus they went on from time to time, till the Court of Assistants at Boston, March 3, who adjourned to May 1, 1668, passed the following act, a copy of which I find among their church papers, exactly in these words, viz. :—

Thomas Gould, plaintiff, on appeal from the judgment of the last County Court at Charlestown. After the Court's judgment, reasons of appeal and evidences in the case produced were read, committed to the jury, and remain on files with the records of this Court. The jury brought in their verdict; they found for the plaintiff, reversion of the former judgment. The Court not accepting this verdict, commended it to the jury's further consideration, and sent them out again. And at the adjournment, on the further consideration, they brought in a special verdict, i. e., If the intent of this law, that the appellent is accused of the breach of, be that the presentment of the Grand Jury, without their certain knowledge, or other evidence, or the person so complained of is legally convicted of the breach of the law, thereby he not making it appear he had done his duty, then they confirmed the judgment of the former Court at Charlestown, but if otherwise they acquit the appellant. The Court, on a due consideration of this special verdict, do confirm the judgment of the County Court at Charlestown. This judgment was declared, and on the plaintiff's refusal to pay the fine imposed, [he] was committed to prison.

On the 7th of this March, they also said :—

The Governor and Council, accounting themselves bound by the law of God, and of this Commonwealth, to protect the churches of Christ here planted, from the intrusion thereby made upon their peace in the ways of godliness, yet being willing by all Christian candor to endeavor the reducing of the said persons from the error of their way, and their return to the Lord and the communion of his people from whence they are fallen, do judge meet to grant unto Thomas Gould, John Farnum, Thomas Osburne and company, yet further an opportunity of a full and free debate, of their grounds for their practice ; and for that end this court doth nominate and request the Rev. Mr. John Allen, Mr. Thomas Cobbet, Mr. John Higginson, Mr. Samuel Danforth, Mr. Jonathan Mitchel, and Mr. Thomas Shepard, to assemble with the Governor and magistrates, upon the 14th day of

[1] Massachusetts Records.

the next month, in the meeting-house at Boston, at nine in the morning; before whom, or so many of them, with any other the Reverend elders or ministers, as shall then assemble, the above-said persons and their company shall have liberty, freely and fully, in open assembly, to present their grounds as above-said, in an orderly debate of this following question :— Whether it be justifiable by the word of God, for these persons and their company to depart from the communion of these churches, and to set up an assembly here in the way of Anabaptism, and whether such a practice is to be allowed by the government of this jurisdiction? To Thomas Gould :—You are hereby required in his Majesty's name, according to the order of the Council above-written, to give notice thereof to John Farnum, senior, Thomas Osburne, and the company, and you and they are alike required to give your attendance, at the time and place above-mentioned, for the end therein expressed.

EDWARD RAWSON, Secretary.[1]

Mr. Clarke's church in Newport, hearing of this appointment, sent to the assistance of their brethren, Mr. William Hiscox, Mr. Joseph Tory, and Mr. Samuel Hubbard, who arrived at Boston, three days before the dispute. The author of Mr. Mitchel's life says :—

When the churches were troubled by a strong attempt upon them from the spirit of anabaptism, there was a public disputation appointed at Boston, two days together, for the clearing of the faith in that article; this worthy man was he, who did most service in this disputation; whereof the effect was, that although the erring brethren, as is usual in such cases, made this their last answer to the arguments, which had cast them into much confusion, *Say what you will, we will hold our minds!* yet others were happily established in the right ways of the Lord.

How well this corresponds with the preceding pages, the reader may judge. For therein we are informed, that Mr. Mitchel was fearful of going to a learned gentleman who had renounced infant baptism; and that he resolved that *he would have an argument able to remove a mountain*, before he would recede from that principle.[2] And a look back to our page 185, will show what fear the ruling party had, of disputing upon their way with another learned Bap-

---

[1] Copied from the warrant now before me in Mr. Rawson's hand writing.
[2] His Life, pp. 69, 70, 72. [Magnalia, Vol. II, pp. 79, 80.] The dispute was held both the 14th and 15th of April.

tist; but the whole power of the country now adventured to enter the lists with a few honest mechanics.

When the Assembly met at Boston in May following, they proceeded to the next argument and said :—

Whereas, the Council assembled in March last, did, for their further conviction, appoint a meeting of divers elders, and required the said persons to attend the said meeting, which was held [here] in Boston with a great concourse of people, ... this court, being sensible of their duty to God and the country, and being desirous that their proceedings in this great cause might be clear and regular, do order that the said Gould and company be required to appear before this Court, on the seventh instant, at eight in the morning, that the Court may understand from themselves, whether upon the means used, or other considerations, they have altered their former declared resolution, and are willing to desist from their former offensive practice, that accordingly a meet [and] effectual remedy may be applied to so dangerous a malady..... At the time they, Thomas Gould, William Turner and John Farnum, being summoned, made their appearance, and after the Court had heard what they had to say for themselves, proceeded. Whereas, Thomas Gould, William Turner, and John Farnum, senior, obstinate and turbulent Anabaptists, have some time since combined themselves with others in a pretended church estate, without the knowledge and [or] approbation of the authority here established to the great grief and offence of the godly orthodox ;.... the said persons did in open Court, assert their former practice to have been according to the mind of God, and that nothing that they had heard convinced them to the contrary ; which practice, being also otherwise circumstanced with making infant baptism a nullity, and thereby making us all to be unbaptized persons, and so consequently no regular churches, ministry, or ordinances ; as also renouncing all our churches, as being so bad and corrupt that they are not fit to be held communion with ; denying to submit to the government of Christ in the church, and entertaining of those who are under church censure, thereby making the discipline of Christ [in his churches] to be of none effect, and manifestly tending to the disturbance and destruction of these churches,—opening the [a] door for all sorts of abominations to come in among us, to the disturbance not only of [our] ecclesiastical enjoyments, but also contempt of our civil order, and the authority here established, ... which [our] duty to God and the country doth oblige us to prevent, by using the most compassionate effectual means to attain the same ; all of which considering, together with the danger of disseminating their errors, and encouraging presumptuous irregularities by their example, should they continue in this jurisdiction ; this Court do judge it necessary that they be removed to some other part of this country, or elsewhere, and accordingly doth order, that the said Thomas Gould, William Turner, and John Farnum, senior, do before the 20th of July next, remove themselves out of this jurisdiction, and that if after the said 20th of July [the said Thomas Gould, William Turner, and John Farnum, senior, or] either of them be found in any part of this jurisdiction, without license, [first] had [and obtained] from this Court or the Council, he or they shall be forthwith apprehended and committed to prison by warrant from any magistrate, and there remain without bail or mainprise, until he or they shall give sufficient security to the Governor or any magistrate, immediately to depart the jurisdiction, and not to return as above said. And all constables and other officers, are required to be faithful and diligent in the execution of this sentence. And it is further ordered, that the keepers of all prisons whereto the said Thomas Gould, William Turner and John Farnum, senior, or any of them shall be committed, shall not permit any resort of companies of more than two at one time to any of the said persons. And our experience of their high, obstinate and presumptuous carriage, doth engage us to prohibit them any further meeting together, on the Lord's day, or [upon any] other days, upon pretence of their church estate, or for the administration or exercise of any pretended ecclesiastical functions, or dispensation of the seals or preaching; wherein if they shall be taken offending, they shall be imprisoned until the tenth of July next, and then left at their liberty within ten days to depart the jurisdiction upon penalty as aforesaid. And, whereas, Thomas Gould is committed to prison in the county of Middlesex, by the last Court of Assistants, for non-payment of a fine imposed, this Court [having passed a censure on him and others] judgeth it meet, after the sentence of this Court is published this day after the lecture to them, that the said Gould shall be [declared to be] discharged from imprisonment in Middlesex as to his fine, that so he may have time to prepare to [and] submit to the judgment of this Court.[1]

This looked like a powerful way of arguing; but the Baptists were not convinced by it, either of its being duty to return into fellowship with those who managed the argument, or to quit their stations and enjoyments at their command. I find by the colony records, that John Farnum was admitted a freeman of that colony May 13, 1640; Thomas Gould, June 2, 1741; in which year John George bound himself to Governor Winthrop, I suppose, to pay for his

[1] Massachusetts Records.

passage over to this country. And I have a copy before me of a warrant for the commitment of Turner and Farnum to Boston jail, dated July 30, this year, signed by Governor Bellingham, Eleazer Lusher and Edward Tyng. When the Assembly met again in the fall, a petition was presented to them, whereof a copy found among their church papers, is before me, in these words :—

Whereas by the censure of this honorable Court, Thomas Gould, William Turner and John Farnum, now lie in prison deprived of their liberty, taken off from their callings, separated from their wives and children, disabled to govern or to provide for their families, to their great damage and hastening ruin, how innocent soever; beside the hazard of their own lives, being aged and weakly men, and needing that succor a prison will not afford; the sense of this, their personal and family most deplorable and afflicted condition, hath sadly affected the hearts of many sober and serious Christians, and such as neither approve of their judgment or practice; especially considering that the men are reputed godly, and of a blameless conversation; and the things for which they seem to suffer seem not to be moral, unquestioned, scandalous evils, but matters of religion and conscience; not in things fundamental, plain and clear, but circumstantial, more dark and doubtful, wherein the saints are wont to differ, and to forbear one another in love, that they be not exposed to sin, or to suffer for conscience sake. We therefore most humbly beseech this honored Court, in their Christian mercy and bowels of compassion, to pity and relieve these poor prisoners; whose sufferings (also being doubtful to many, and some of great worth among ourselves, and grievous to sundry of God's people at home and abroad,) may crave a further consideration, whereby perceiving this Court not likely to effect the end desired, but rather to grieve the hearts of God's people; now your wisdoms may be pleased to think of some better expedient, and seriously consider whether an indulgence, justifiable by the word of God, pleaded for and practiced by Congregational churches, may not, in this day of suffering to the people of God, be more effectual, safe and inoffensive than other ways, which are always grievous, and seldom find success. We in all humility hope, hereby occasions of difference being removed, that love and communion among all saints, which our dying Lord so weightily charged and earnestly prayed for, will more easily be preserved and practiced, to the glory of God, honor of the gospel, peace and welfare of all the churches, which this honored Court being the happy instruments of effecting, will oblige your poor petitioners, as in duty bound, to pray for your happiness both in this life and in that to come, and that your authority may be long continued as an unparalleled blessing to this Commonwealth.

We are informed that Captain Edward Hutchinson, Captain Oliver, and many others, signed this petition; but the Court were so far from granting it, that the chief promoters of it were fined, and others compelled to an acknowledgment of their fault in reflecting upon the Court herein. We are also told, that the Honorable Francis Willoughby, who was their Deputy Governor from 1665, till he died on April 4, 1671, " was a great opposer of these persecutions against the Baptists."[1] Leverett and Symonds, his successors in that office, appear also to have been on that side of the question. The ruling party printed their sentence against those Baptists, an answer to which I find among their church papers, which is closed with these words :—

This my husband would entreat of you, to take counsel of Master Bennet, and if he and you judge it meet, to send it to England, and the printed sentence with it. It is desired that no man see it but Goodman Sweetser, and that Josiah write it fair and plain.

I conclude the person here speaking is Elder Gould's wife ; and the most material points of her answer are as follows :—

First, They call them *obstinate and turbulent Anabaptists*. 1. I desire to know wherein their obstinacy doth appear? They desired the Court to show them, from the rule of Christ, of any point that they were out of the way of God ; and if the Lord was pleased to show them wherein they were out, they would freely lay it down ; but they shewed them no other rule than their own law ; and sentenced them to be fined and imprisoned; and this was all the rule they could give, which did not convince them. 2. They say they were *turbulent*. I desire them to prove wherein they were turbulent, when they did not disturb neither churches nor courts, neither by word nor by action, but desired to live quietly and peaceably among them, and they cannot tell of any one thing that they disturbed them in, but desired they might enjoy that liberty that Christ hath purchased for them. They know not that they spoke any word that gave offence to the Court, unless it was those few words, when Master Bradstreet pronounced that sentence against them, and charged them no more to meet together, whether on the Lord's day or on the week days, in their conventicles ; those words were returned by them, We ought to obey God rather than man ; we cannot but do the things we have heard and learned. 3. As for *Ana-*

[1] Massachusetts History, Vol. II, pp. 227, 269, [236, 246.]

baptists, they do not own that name, except they will be pleased to explain what they mean by it; for they own them to be of the baptized. Again, they say, *they combined together in a pretended church estate.* They need not have said so, unless they could have proved they set up their church contrary to a rule of Christ. Beside, they gave them in a writing wherein they gave a brief account of their faith, where they declared what they owned to be a church of Christ, and the order of it according to the rule of the Scripture, which neither the Court nor the elders ever answered to this day. They say it was *without the knowledge or approbation of the authority here established as the law required.* Answer:—1. If the apostles had not set up churches in their time, without the approbation of the authority and their priests, there had been few or no churches in their time. 2. Christ is Lord and King of his church, and he will set up his government therein, and hath given them rules from himself, how to set it up and to carry it along according to his appointment, and not to ask leave of the powers of the world to set up his church; for Christ's jurisdiction is the greatest jurisdiction in the world. 3. They had asked leave, had they found a command of Christ for it, but finding no rule of Christ they did not do it.

Again, they say some of themselves were *excommunicated persons.* First, it is true what they say, yet that some was but two that were cast out, and that after they were gathered into this pretended church, as they call it, a good space of time. But consider for what it was, and how it was?

Here the foregoing account of Messrs. Gould and Osburne is confirmed. And of the day they were cast out she says:—

The word was carried to the elder, that if they were alive and well they would come the next day, yet they were so hot upon it that they would not stay, but Master Sims when he was laying out the sins of these men, before he had propounded it to the church, to know their mind, the church having no liberty to speak, he wound it up in his discourse, and delivered them up to Satan, to the amazement of the people, that ever such an ordinance of Christ should be so abused, that many of the people went out; and these were the excommunicated persons. They say, *After long forbearance to use the utmost means to convince and reduce them, entreated the assistance of divers elders.* Answer:—1. It is true there were seven elders appointed to discourse with them, and there were a few plowmen and tailors to come before them; but how they were served with a warrant to appear before these elders in his Majesty's name! 2. When they were met, there was a long speech made by one of them, of what vile persons they were, and how they acted against the churches and government here, and stood condemned by the Court. The others desiring liberty to speak, they would not suffer them, but told them they stood there as delinquents, and ought not to have liberty to speak. Then they desired they might choose a moderator as well as they; they denied them. Two days were spent to little purpose..... In the close, Master Jonathan Mitchel pronounced that dreadful sentence against them in Deut. xvii. 8 to the end of the 12th, and this was the way they took to convince them, and you may see what a good effect it had. .... There was nothing spoken from the rule of Christ, neither from the Court nor the elders, but such sentences as these, fining, and whipping, and prisoning, and banishing, and Master Mitchel's sentence, and all these are not the weapons of Christ, but carnal weapons that never did convince any soul of the error of his ways.

Whereas, they say, *Which practice making infant baptism a nullity*, &c.; I answer, It is good for every one to be sure that they are upon good ground whatsoever the practice of others may seem to condemn. .... They say, *Tending to the disturbance and destruction of these churches.* For Answer, 1. If eight or nine poor Anabaptists, as they call them, should be the destruction of their churches, then let any seeing man judge what their churches are built upon; then we may think they are built upon a sandy foundation; for the church of Christ is built upon himself, and the gates of hell shall not prevail against it. 2. If they be the churches of Christ, and think they shall be overthrown by them, it is from the weakness of their faith, looking more to an arm of flesh and powers of the world to uphold them, than to Christ and his faithful promise. 3. If they fear they will be the destruction of their churches, now [that] all the power of the country is for them and [they] have an arm of flesh to help them, what will they do when all the powers of the country are against them, as are against the other, as you say yourselves of them, that when they were in examination before the Court, they professed themselves resolved to adhere to the same practice; and now suffer willingly for it. But for the men, what they are, I shall say nothing, for the sixty-five hands to the petition that was put into the General Court, does [do] plainly declare to their best discerning, that they have been honest and godly, and lived quietly and peaceably among them a good length of time. Again they say, *By using the most compassionate and effectual means to attain the same.* Answer:—1. The Lord keep every gracious soul from such compassionate means for the truth of the gospel! 2. For what compassionate means were used with them, let men fearing God judge; for one of them was called from prison when this sentence of banishment was read against them; and if any man desires to inform himself wherein their compassion appears, let him read their printed sentence against them, which was executed upon them; for, not moving themselves, they sent the constable, and fetched them away to prison on a public lecture day at Boston, when the said Thomas Gould,

William Turner and John Farnum, had been all there, and newly come home to their houses, and they remain in prison to this day.

How any that feared God, could be ensnared and held in such a way of treating their fellow-servants may doubtless appear unaccountable to many; but a careful search will help us to discover the nature of this mystery. The establishment of a Christian commonwealth, was the grand object that had been before those leaders for forty years, and it continued so to their last hours. Mr. Wilson, the first minister of Boston, had been famed for a gift of prophecy, or foretelling future events; and as his dissolution appeared near, a large number of ministers came round him on May 16, 1667, and desired him to declare unto them, what he conceived to be the sins among them that caused the displeasure of God against the country. He told them he had long feared the following sins as chief among others, which greatly provoked God, viz.:—

1. Separation. 2. Anabaptism. 3. Corahism. [The latter he did explain thus:] when people rise up as Corah, against their ministers or elders, as if they took too much upon them, when indeed they do but rule for Christ, and according to Christ; yet (said he) it is nothing for a brother to stand up and oppose, without Scripture or reason, the doctrine and word of the elder, saying I am not satisfied, &c., and hence, if he do not like the administration, be it baptism or the like, he will [then] turn his back upon God and his ordinances, and go away. And [saith he] for our neglect of baptizing the children of the church, those that some call grandchildren, I think God is provoked by it. 4. Another sin I take to be the making light of, [and] not subjecting to the authority of synods without which, the churches cannot long subsist. And so for the magistrates being Gallio-like, either not caring for these things, or else not using their power and authority for the maintenance of the truth, [and] gospel and ordinances of our Lord and Saviour Jesus Christ, and for bearing thorough witness against the contrary. Should the Lord leave them hereunto how miserable a people should we be!

And at night he blessed them upon their parting, with great affection, and with tears, "and all the ministers wept with him, and took their leave of him, even as children of their father, who having blessed them was about to die."

He died the 7th of August following.[1] These things affected their minds in such a manner, that upon his church's obtaining Mr. Devenport from New Haven to succeed him, who had printed his testimony against the result of the late synod about the Half-way Covenant, a minor part of the church drew off from the rest, and in May, 1669, other ministers assisted in forming them into a new church, in open separation from the first church in Boston, which schism continued about fourteen years, till an Episcopal invader of their rights drove them together again.[2] Hence see what a schismatical doctrine that is, of infant church membership, and of using secular force in religious affairs. What divisions and contentions did it produce both in Connecticut and

[1] Morton, pp. 195, 196. [211, 212.]
[2] Magnalia, B. 5., pp. 82, 83. [Vol. II, pp. 266, 267.] " There was a great difference betwixt the old church and the members of the new church, about baptism, and their members joining in full communion with either church. This was so high that there was imprisoning of parties, and great disturbances; but now hearing of my proposals for ministers to be sent over, they are joined together, about a fortnight ago, and pray to God to confound the devices of all who disturb their peace and liberties." Randolph's letter to the Bishop of London, May 9, 1682. Massachusetts History, Vol. III, pp, 531, 532. That new church is since called The Old South.—B.

The passage in the Magnalia above referred to, is as follows :—"That famous and faithful society of Christians, the first church in Boston, had, after much agitation, so far begun to attend the discipline directed in the doctrine of the synod that they proceeded ecclesiastically to censure the adult children of several communicants for scandals, whereinto they had fallen. But that church, for a supply of their vacancy upon the death of their former more synodical ministers, applying themselves unto Mr. John Devenport, the greatest of the antisynodists, all the interests of the synod came to be laid aside, therein, on that occasion. Hereupon thirty members of that eminent church offered several reasons of their dssent from their call of that worthy person. . . . . The difference produced so much division that the major part of the church, by far, proceeded to their election of that great man; this lesser part nevertheless carefully and exactly following the advice of councils fetched from other churches in the neighborhood, set up another church in the town of Boston, which hath since been one of the most considerable in the country. Very uncomfortable were the *paroxisms* which were the consequents of this ferment. *Longa est injuria, longa ambages*....Indeed, for a considerable while, though the good men on both sides really loved, respected and honored one another, yet, through some unhappy misunderstandings in particular persons, the communicants of these two particular churches in Boston, like the two distinguished rivers, not mixing, though running between the same banks, held not communion with one another at the table of the Lord."—ED.

Massachusetts? Is it not evident that they proceeded from a confounding of the Jewish and Christian churches together? for a right to membership and to office, in the former, proceeded in a natural, in the latter, in a spiritual line. The gainsaying of Korah was after an infallible authority had fixed the priesthood in the line of Aaron and his seed, who were types of Christ and his saints, but officers in distinction from the rest of the lively stones whereof his house is built, are never called priests in the New Testament; yea, we have seen ministers resenting others calling of them by that name, and yet they in the above instance and down to this day, have applied the case of Korah to those who refuse practically to own them as such. And they have often told us of David's error, in carrying the ark upon a new cart, instead of the priests' shoulders; but that error is theirs, not ours; and had they been as ready to imitate David in reformation as they were in transgression what happy times might we have seen before now? The oracles of God were then carried in the ark, but now his church is the pillar and ground of the truth. I Timothy 3. 15; I Peter 2. 5. Upon Uzza's being struck dead, David was turned to search the divine rules, which taught him to rest the cause of truth upon living shoulders, instead of an earthly machine drawn by beastly force. I Chron. 15. 2. But when the rulers of the Massachusetts were moved by their ministers to exert such force against the Baptists, though they saw the chief procurers of that sentence struck dead before the time came for its execution, and many more of them about that time, yet their posterity have approved their sayings even to this day.[1] I am well sensible that the

---

[1] Mr. Henry Flint of Braintree, and Mr. Samuel Shepard of Rowley, died about the time of their dispute with the Baptists in Boston. Mr. Mitchel, who was most active in procuring the sentence against them, died July 9, aged 43, and Mr. John Eliot, junior, October 13, 1668, aged 35, both of Cambridge. Mr. John Reyner of Dover, and Mr. Richard Mather of Dorchester, both died in April, and Eleazer Mather of Northampton, on July 24, 1669, aged 32. Mr. Sims, who had treated the Baptists so ill, and Mr. John Allen of Dedham, one of the disputants against them, both died within two years after, as well as many others.

divine judgments are a great deep, and that love or hatred is not to be known merely by such outward events; yet they ought to put us all upon searching and trying our ways (as David did) by the revealed will of God; which duty was excellently inculcated upon them at that time in a letter to Captain Oliver of Boston, in the words following:—

MY DEAR BROTHER: The ardent affection and great honors that I have for New England transport me, and I hope your churches shall ever be to me as the gates of heaven. I have ever been warmed with the apprehension of the grace of God towards me in carrying me thither. I have always thought that of the Congregational churches of New England in our days. But now it is otherwise, with joy as to ourselves and grief as to you be it spoken. Now the greater my love is to New England the more am I grieved at their failings. It is frequently said here, that they are swerved aside towards presbytery; if so, the Lord restore them all. But another sad thing that much affects us is, to hear that you even in New England persecute your brethren; men sound in the faith; of holy life [and] agreeing in worship and discipline with you; only differing in the point of baptism. Dear brother, we here do love and honor them, hold familiarity with them, and take sweet council together; they lie in the bosom of Christ and therefore they ought to be laid in our bosoms. In a word, we freely admit them into churches; few of our churches but many of our members are Anabaptists; I mean baptized again. This is love, in England; this is moderation; this is a right New Testament spirit. But do you now (as is abovesaid) bear with, yea, more than bear with, the Presbyterians? yea, and that the worst sort of them, viz., those who are the corruptest, rigedest; whose principles tend to corrupt the churches; [so] turning the world into the church, and the church into the world; and which doth no less than bring a people under mere slavery. It is an iron yoke which neither we nor our Congregational brethren in Scotland were ever able to bear. I have heard them utter these words in the pulpit, that it is no wrong to make the Independents sell all they have, and depart the land; and many more things I might mention of that kind; but this I hint only, to shew what cause there is to withstand that wicked tyranny which was once set up in poor miserable Scotland, which I verily believe was a great wrong and injury to the reformation. The generality of them here, even to this day will not freely consent to our enjoyment of our liberty; though, through mercy, the best and most reformed of them do otherwise. How much more therefore would it concern dear New England to turn the edge against [those] who, if not prevented, will certainly corrupt and enslave, not only their own, but also your churches? Whereas Anabaptists are neither spirited nor principled to injure nor hurt your government nor your liberties; but rather these be a means to preserve your churches from apostacy, and provoke them to their primitive purity, as they were in the first planting, in and admission of members to receive none into your churches but visible saints, and in restoring the entire jurisdiction of every congregation complete and undisturbed. We are hearty and full for our Presbyterian brethren's enjoying equal liberty with ourselves; oh that they had the same spirit towards us! but oh how it grieves and affects us that New England should persecute! will you not give what you take? is liberty of conscience your due? and is it not as due unto others that are sound in the faith? Read the preface to the declaration of the faith and order, owned and practiced in the Congregational churches in England, pp. 6, 7. Amongst many other Scriptures, that in the 14th of Romans much confirms me in liberty of conscience thus stated: To him that esteems any thing unclean, to him it is unclean; verse 13. Therefore though we approve of the baptism of the immediate children of church members, and [of] their admission into the church when they evidence a real work of grace; yet to [those] that in conscience believe the said baptism to be unclean, it is unclean. Both that and mere ruling elders, though we approve of them, yet our grounds are mere interpretations of, and not any express Scripture. I cannot say so clearly of any thing else in our religion, neither as to faith or practice. Now must we force our interpretation, upon others, Pope-like? In verse 5 of that chapter the Spirit of God saith, Let every one be fully persuaded in his own mind; therefore this being the express will of God, who shall make a contrary law, and say, Persuaded or not persuaded, you shall do as we say, and as we do! and verse 23, What is not of faith is sin; therefore there must be a word for what we do, and we must see and believe it, or else we sin if we do it. And Deut. 12, and last, as we must not add, nor may we diminish; what is commanded we must do. Also 28th of Matthew. And what principles is persecution grounded upon? Domination and infallibility. This we teach is the truth. But are we infallible, and have we the government? God made none, no not the apostles who could not err, to be lords over [of our] faith; therefore what monstrous pride is this? At this rate any persuasion getting uppermost may command, and persecute them that obey them not; all non-conformists must be ill-used. Oh wicked and monstrous principle! Whatever you can plead for yourselves against those that persecute you, those whom you persecute may plead for themselves against you. Whatever you can say against those poor men, your enemies say against you. And what! is that horrid principle crept into precious New England, who have felt what persecution is, and have always pleaded for liberty of conscience; Have not those run equal hazards with you for the enjoyment of their liberties; and how do you cast a reproach upon us, that are Congregational in England,

and furnish our adversaries with weapons against us? We blush and are filled with shame and confusion of face, when we hear of these things. Dear brother, we pray that God would open your eyes and persuade the hearts of your magistrates, that they may no more smite their fellow servants, nor thus greatly injure us their brethren; and that they may not thus dishonor the name of God, and cause his people to be reproached, nor the holy way of God (the Congregational way) to be evil spoken of. My dear brother! pardon my plainness and freedom, for the zeal of God's house constrains me. What cause have we to bless God who gives us to find favor in the eyes of his Majesty, and to pray God to continue him, and to requite it graciously to him in spiritual blessings. Well, strive I beseech you with God by prayers, and use all lawful ways and means, even to your greatest hazard, that those poor men may be set free. For be assured, this liberty of conscience, as we state it, is the cause of God; and hereby you may be a means to divert the judgments of God from falling upon dear New England, for our Father in faithfulness will afflict us if we repent not. Doth not the very gospel say, What measure we mete to others shall be measured to us? God is not unrighteous. What is more provoking to him than the persecuting of his saints? Touch not mine anointed, and do my prophets no harm! Did he not reprove kings for their sake? those who have the unction the apostle John speaks of, and the spirit and gift of prophecies. With what marvellous strength did holy Mr. Burroughs urge that place against persecution? Persecution is bad in wicked men, but it is most abominable in good men, who have suffered and pleaded for liberty of conscience themselves. Discountenance men that certainly err, but persecute them not. I mean gross errors. Well, we are travelling to our place of rest; with joy we look for new heavens and new earth. We shall ere long be in the fullness of bliss, holy, harmless in the bosom of Christ. Let us pray the earth may be filled with the knowledge of the Lord, that they may not hurt nor destroy in all his holy mountain. The Lord grant we may by the next hear better things of the government of New England. My most hearty love to [you and] your brother, and to all our brethren. My respects and my service to my dear cousin Leverett, and to Mr. Francis Willoughby. The Lord make them instrumental for his glory, in helping to reform things among you. I shall be glad to hear from you. I remember our good old sweet communion together. My dear brother, once again pardon me, for I am affected! I speak for God, to whose grace I commit you all in New England; humbly craving your prayers for us here, and remain,

      Your [most] affectionate brother,
              ROBERT MASCALL.

Finsbury, near Morefield, the 25th of March, 1669.[1]

---

[1] Samuel Hubbard's collection.

Never did I see the true nature of these controversies better stated by any on that side. Our opponents have no better grounds for accusing us of denying Scripture consequences, than because we refuse to yield to their interpretations, which appear to us unsound. Neither are we any more rigid than themselves; though because they hold to two or three ways of baptizing, while we believe our Lord has instituted but one baptism, they accuse us with it, if we cannot act with them as baptized persons, who appear to us not to be such. The plain question is, Whether each one shall be allowed to act the full persuasion of his own mind, according to God's law, or whether the ruling party in the State shall make the law void by their traditions? The learned and much esteemed Dr. Goodwin, Dr. Owen, Mr. Nye, Mr. Caryl, and nine other noted dissenting ministers in London wrote to the Massachusetts Governor, upon these things at the same time, and said:—

We shall not here undertake [in the least] to make any apology for the persons, opinions and practices of those who are censured among you. You know our judgment and practice to be contrary unto theirs, even as yours; wherein (God assisting) we shall continue to the end. Neither shall we return any answer to the reason of the reverend elders, for the justification of your proceedings, as not being willing to engage in the management of any the least difference with persons whom we so much love and honor in the Lord. But the sum of all which at present we shall offer to you is, that though the Court might apprehend, that they had grounds, in general, warranting their procedure (in such cases) in the way wherein they have proceeded; yet that they have any rule of command rendering their so proceeding indispensably necessary, under all circumstances of fines [times?] and places, we are altogether unsatisfied; and we need not represent unto you how the case stands with ourselves, and all your brethren and companions in the services of these latter days in these nations. We are sure you would be unwilling to put an advantage into the hands of some, who feel pretences, and occasions against our liberty, and to reinforce the former rigor. Now we cannot deny but this hath already in some measure been done, in that it hath been vogued, that persons of your [our] way, principles and spirit, cannot bear with dissenters from them. And as this greatly reflects on us, so some of us have observed how already it has turned unto your own disadvantage. We leave it to your wisdom to determine, whether under all these circumstances, and sundry others of the like nature that might be added, it be not advisable at present to put an end unto the sufferings and confinements of the persons censured, and to restore them to their former liberty.[1] You have the advantage of truth and order; you have the gifts and learning of an able ministry to manage and defend them; you have the care and vigilancy of a very worthy magistracy to countenance and protect them, and to preserve the peace; and above all, you have a blessed Lord and Master, who hath the keys of David, who openeth and no man shutteth, living forever to take care of his own concernments among his saints; and assuredly you need not be disquieted, though some few persons (through their own infirmity and weakness, or through their ignorance, darkness and prejudices) should to their disadvantage turn out of the way, in some lesser matters, into by-paths of their own. We only make it our hearty request to you, that you would trust God with his truths and ways so far, as to suspend all vigorous proceedings in corporal restraints or punishments, on persons that dissent from you, and practice the principles of their dissent without danger or disturbance to the civil peace of the place.

Dated March 25, 1669.

We may reasonably conclude that this address did not reach Boston till May or June; and Dr. Mather says, "I cannot say that this excellent letter had immediately all the effect it should have had."[2] So that though he allows that some of those Baptists were "truly godly men,"[3] yet it is likely that they were imprisoned a year or more, only for not banishing themselves for their religion. After their release, Elder Gould went and lived upon an island in the harbor; where they held their meeting for some years. But this could not make the ruling party easy, as the following

---

[1] "At a Court of Assistants held at Boston, March 2, 1669, the Governor and Magistrates being assembled in Council, and motion being made by Thomas Gould, in behalf of himself and William Turner, now in durance by the sentence of the General Court; the keepers of the prisons, under whose custody they now are, are ordered to permit them liberty for three days, to visit their families, as also to apply themselves to any that are able and orthodox, for their further convincement of their many irregularities in those practices for which they were sentenced; the said keeper staking the engagements of the said Gould and Turner, or other sufficient caution, for their return again to prison at the end of the said three days.

By the council, EDWARD RAWSON, Secretary."

[2] Magnalia, B. 7, pp. 27, 28. [Vol. II, pp. 460, 461.]
[3] Ibid. [Vol. II, p. 459.]

letter to Mr. Clarke and his church at Newport plainly shews :—

BELOVED BRETHREN AND SISTERS :—I most heartily salute you all in our dear Lord, who is our alone Savior in all our troubles, that we his poor members are exercised with for his name's sake. And blessed be God our Father, that has given us such a High Priest, that was touched with the feeling of our infirmities, which is no small comfort to the souls of his poor suffering ones; the which, through grace, the Lord hath been pleased to make us in some [small] measure partakers of. And at this present our dear brother William Turner, a prisoner for the Lord's cause in Boston, has some good experience of, both of that which Paul desired, to be comfortable to our Lord in his sufferings, and also of the promises of our Lord, in the giving forth [of] the comfort of his Spirit, to uphold us all, for that he is sensible of the sufferings of his poor members, and is ready to give forth supplies as are most suitable to such a condition as he calls his to. Friends, I suppose you have heard that both he and brother Gould were to be taken up; but only brother Turner is yet taken and has been about a month in prison. Warrants are in two marshals' hands for brother Gould also, but he is not yet taken, because he lives on Noddle's Island, and they only wait to take him at town [but he comes not over.] The cause why they are put in prison is the old sentence of the General Court in '68, because they would not remove themselves. There were six magistrates' hands to the warrant to take them up, viz., Mr. Bradstreet, Major Denison, Thomas Danforth, Captain Gookin, Major Willard and Mr. Pinchon. But all the deputies of the Court voted their liberty, except one or two at most, but the magistrates carry against all; and because some others of the magistrates were absent, and some that were there were Gallio-like, as one Mr. R. B. G.[1] But blessed be the Lord who takes notice of what is done to his poor servants, though men little regard. The town and country is very much troubled at our troubles; and especially the old church in Boston, and their elders, both Mr. Oxonbridge and Mr. Allen have labored abundantly, I think as if it had been for their best

---

[1] I suppose, Richard Bellingham, Governor. Thus a few men at the head of the government, by the clergy's help, carried on their oppressions against the minds of those worthy rulers, Willoughby, Symonds and Leverett, a whole House of Deputies, and the best part of the whole community. "That magistrates should thus suffer these incendiaries, and disturbers of the public peace, might justly be wondered at, if it did not appear that they have been invited by them unto a participation of the spoil, and have therefore thought fit to make use of their covetousness and pride, as a means whereby to increase their own power. For who does not see that these good men are indeed more ministers of the government, than ministers of the gospel. Locke on Toleration, pp. 71, 72.

friends in the world.¹ Many more gentlemen and solid Christians are for our brother's deliverance; but it cannot be had; a very great trouble [is it] to the town; and they had gotten six magistrates' hands for his deliverance, but could not get the Governor's hand to it.....Some say one end is, that they may prevent others coming out of England; therefore they would discourage them by dealing with us; a sad thing if so, when God would have Moab be a refuge for his banished ones, and that Christians will not. But God will be a refuge for his, which is our comfort. We keep our meeting at Noddle's Island, every First-day, and the Lord is adding some souls to us still, and is enlightening some others; the priests are much enraged. The Lord has given us another elder, one John Russell, senior, a gracious, wise and holy man that lives at Woburn, where we have five brethren near that can meet with him; and they meet together First-days when they cannot come to us, and I hear there are some more there looking that way with them. Thus, dear friends, I have given you an account of our troubles, that you may be directed in your prayers to our God for us; as also of the goodness of God to us, and the proceedings of his good work in our hands, both to our, and I doubt not, to your joy and comfort. That God may be glorified in all, is our earnest desire and prayer to God, in all his dispensations to us. Brother Turner's family is very weakly and himself to. I fear he will not trouble them long; only this is our comfort, we hear if he dies in prison, they say they will bury him. And thus, my dear friends, I desire we may be remembered in your prayers to our Heavenly Father, who can do abundantly above what we can ask or think; to whom I commend you all, and rest, your friend and brother,

EDWARD DRINKER.

November 30, 1670.

This occasioned the following epistle to them, viz. :—

Unto the church of Jesus Christ, meeting on Noddle's Island in New England. Grace, mercy and peace be mightily showered down upon you all, with such daily supplies to every one of you, according to your various conditions, strengthening the weak, and making you to press forward with life and courageous hearts, being valiant for the Lord and his holy truths, holding out to the end in what ye have received; not to look back, but pressing forward to know more of his holy will, like children desiring the sincere milk of the word, to grow up therein. Samuel Hubbard, a very poor and unworthy one, yet by great grace found in my sinful estate, among the sinners in a sinful world, in a sinful age, and by free grace called by a di-

---

¹Mr. Devenport died March 15, 1670, aged 72; and Mr. John Oxonbridge, who left England, after the cruel Bartholomew Act in 1662, was settled in his stead, collegue with Mr. James Allen, who came from thence about the same time.

vine call or power, being not able to resist it, but by grace shewed that it was his will to call sinners that were weary and heavy laden to come unto him, making a gracious promise, that they should find rest to their souls; Matt. 11; and by his grace hath made me willing, in my very weak measure, to be going on in what he hath shewed me; though I find a law in my members, contrary to God's holy law, which is written in my heart, leading me captive both in thoughts, words and deeds, which is a great burden, and makes me go heavily. But blessed be God, my rock, who hath shewed me that it is not by my works, but by faith in our precious Redeemer, I am accepted with the Father. Not thereby taken off from endeavoring to keep all his holy commandments and ordinances, but with righteous Zacharias and Elizabeth, desirous to be found blameless, when our Lord and King Jesus shall come, and by him enabled with joy to say, This is my Lord, I have waited for him; when you with others shall meet and sing the song of Moses and the Lamb, Hallelujah to God most High, &c. Dear and precious hearts, my love is such towards you, for what of God is in you, and what great grace hath appeared towards you, in bearing you up to stand in this hour of temptation, that your feet are not moved, and your arms are made strong by the mighty God of Jacob; yea, not only so, but hath crowned your endeavors with a blessing of increase of such precious helps, as I hear you have, in which I rejoice, desiring greatly of the Lord, that he would be still with you to the end of your race. Dear friends, it was upon my heart to have given you a visit, whereby I might have been refreshed by your mutual love, as I have been to see your precious order in the gospel; but it has pleased our heavenly Father to visit me and my dear wife, by a sore stroke in taking away our only son Samuel;[1] all we had; a man grown (whose we are also); but God of his grace hath borne us up, blessed be his name! by which I have been very much disappointed as in coming to you, so in many other things, and am learning in every condition to be content; a hard lesson to learn I find. Dear brethren and sisters, what am I, poor worm, to inform you! but to stir up your pure minds that you would be holding fast what you have received, that you may not lose your rewards, for this is a declining day. But know, the reward is laid up in most sure hands, for those who hold out to the end. I beseech you, pray with all manner of prayers, and for me, poor one, that I may have such fresh supplies of grace, that I may stand fast in what I have received of God, and not deny his name, knowing of whom I have received it. Pray for me that I may have more of the spirit

---

[1] He was in his 21st year, a very promising youth. Mr. Hubbard's daughter Ruth, married to Robert Burdick, and Bethia, married to Joseph Clarke, jun'r, have left a large posterity at Westerly; and Rachel, married to Andrew Langworthy, left a large family in Newport; and he hoped that all his children, and some of his grandchildren were savingly converted.

of adoption, to cry in faith, Abba, Father; more of faith in those precious promises made to his in the Holy Scriptures, and more strength to run the ways of his holy commandments with more delight and largeness of heart without partiality. Oh! my dear friends, pray for Sion! they that love her shall prosper. Oh! my brethren and sisters! pardon my boldness, and accept in love my weak endeavors, and let me have from you a few lines, which would be as a dew upon my poor weak heart, which needs information, instruction and comfort. Thus, desiring your prosperity in your inward man, and outward man also, knowing that if ye seek first the kingdom of God, we have our Lord's word for it, that all other things shall be added; committing you to the Almighty to bless you with spiritual blessings, with such daily fresh supplies as you stand in need of, whereby ye may abound for his name's praise, the good of sinners, strengthening of saints, comforting one another, drawing in love in all your ways, which is as precious ointment, giving forth such a precious savor as that all Christ's virgins may love and rejoice in you, and bless God on your behalf. The God of all grace be with you all. Amen. My wife desires to have her affectionate and entire love to you all remembered. Your poor weak brother in the best relation, SAMUEL HUBBARD.

Newport, this 4th day of the 9th Month, 1671.

Dear brother and sister, my kind love and respect with my wife's, be remembered to you with all the rest of our dear friends, hoping you welfare. These few lines are to let you understand, that your loving Christian letter you sent me I received, for which I give you hearty thanks. I delivered your letter according to your desire, and it was read in the church, wherein we understand the Lord has been pleased to take away your son, that was dear unto you. God sometimes tries his people in that which is most near and dear to them, even in their Isaacs. Jacob must part with his Benjamin, and say, All these things are against me; yet the Lord turned it about for good; and he has promised that all shall work for good unto those that love and fear him; and what he deprives us of in the creature, he is able to make up abundantly in himself. The good Lord grant that it may be so with you! Brother Turner has been near to death, but through mercy is revived, and so has our pastor, Gould. The Lord make us truly thankful, and give us hearts to improve them, and those liberties we yet enjoy that we know not how soon may be taken from us. The persecuting spirit begins to stir again. Elder Russell and his son, and brother Foster, are presented to the Court that is to be this month. We desire your prayers for us, that the Lord would keep us, that we may not dishonor that worthy name we have made profession of, and that the Lord would still stand by us, and be seen amongst us, as he has been in a wonderful manner in preserving of us until this day. We should be glad to hear how it is with you, and desire if it be the will of God, that love and peace may be continued betwixt you and the other society; although you may differ in some things, yet there may be endeavors to keep the unity of the spirit in the bond of peace, and as far as we have attained, to walk by the same rule. I shall not trouble you any further, but commit you to the guidance and protection of the Almighty, and remain your unworthy brother in the best relation, BENJAMIN SWEETSER.

Charlestown, the first, 10th month, '71.

The next news from them is as follows :—

I perceive you have heard as if our brother Russell had died in prison. Through grace he is yet in the land of the living, and out of prison bonds; but is in a doubtful way as to recovery of his outward health; but we ought to be quiet in the good will and pleasure of our God, who is only wise. I remain your loving brother, WILLIAM HAMLIT.

Boston, 14, of the 4th month, 1672.

We will now look a little back, and see how their oppressors got along. The breach in Boston church affected many; and the Governor appeared against the new party, and in July, 1669, called his Council together, fearing, he said, " a sudden tumult, some persons attempting to set up an edifice for public worship, which was apprehended by authority to be detrimental to the public peace." But the majority of the Council were not for hindering their proceeding. On May 11, 1670, Mr. Danforth of Roxbury, who was one of those that had been called to the Baptist dispute two years before, said to the Assembly in his election sermon :—

Is not the temper, complexion and countenance of the churches strangely altered? Doth not a careless, remiss, flat, dry, cold, dead frame of spirit grow upon us secretly, strongly, prodigiously? They that have ordinances are as though they had none; they that hear the word as though they heard it not; and they that pray as though they prayed not; and they that received sacraments as though they received them not; and they that are exercised in holy things, use them by the by, as matters of custom and ceremony. .... Pride, contention, worldliness, covetousness, luxury, drunkenness and uncleanness break in like a flood upon us; and good men grow cold in their love to God and one another.[1]

[1] Prince's Christian History, Vol. I, p. 97.—B.

This sermon is entitled "A brief recognition of New England's errand into the wilderness." Text, "What went ye out into the wilderness to see?" The quotations above given are from pages 12, 13.—ED.

Upon this the House of Deputies appointed a committee, to inquire into the prevailing evils that had procured the divine displeasure against the land; and they reported these among other causes, viz. :—

Declension from the primitive foundation work, innovation in doctrine and worship, opinion and practice; an invasion of the rights, liberties and privileges of churches, a usurpation of a lordly and prelatical power over God's heritage, subversion of gospel order, &c.

They then go on to speak of the late transaction of the elders, in constituting the third church in Boston, as " irregular, illegal and disorderly." But the effect was such, that among fifty deputies in their next Assembly, there were but twenty of those who were in this; and then fifteen ministers presented an address to the new-modeled house, wherein they mention their former connection with rulers, like Moses and Aaron, and then call the setting up of said church in Boston, " That weighty and worthy transaction." They prevailed with this house to correct and declare against what the preceding house had done to the contrary.[1] Such was the ministerial influence of that day. On May 15, 1672, the Assembly ordered their law-book to be revised and reprinted; and therein they say :—

Although no human power be lord over the faith and consciences of men, yet because such as bring in damnable heresies, tending to the subversion of the Christian faith, and destruction of the souls of men, ought duly to be restrained from such notorious impieties; it is therefore ordered and declared by the Court, that if any Christian within this jurisdiction, shall go about to subvert and destroy the Christian faith and religion, by broaching and maintaining any damnable heresies; as denying the immortality of the soul, or resurrection of the body, or any sin to be repented of in the regenerate, or any evil done by the outward man to be accounted sin, or denying that Christ gave himself a ransom for our sins, or shall affirm that we are not justified by his death and righteousness, but by the perfection of our own works, or shall deny the morality of the fourth commandment, or shall openly condemn or oppose the baptizing of infants, or shall purposely depart the congregation at the administration of that ordi-

[1] Massachusetts History, Vol. I, pp. 272—274. [249—251.]

nance, or shall deny the ordinance of magistracy, or their lawful authority to make war, or to punish the outward breaches of the first table, or shall endeavor to seduce others to any of the errors and heresies above mentioned; every such person continuing obstinate therein, after due means of conviction, shall be sentenced to banishment.[1]

The reader may here observe what advances they had made since the year 1644.[2] The two articles which the Baptists own, are now fenced with a much more formidable catalogue of heresies and errors, than were then inserted in their law against them. Though they still fall far behind their mother, the church of England; for the last man that she burnt for religion was a Baptist, and in the warrant for his burning, the King says:—

Whereas the reverend father in God, Kichard, bishop of Coventry and Litchfield, having judicially proceeded in the examination, hearing and determining of a cause of heresie against Edward Wightman, of the parish of Burton upon Trent, in the diocese of Coventry and Litchfield, concerning the wicked heresies of the Ebionites, Cerenthians, Valentinians, Arrians, Macedonians, of Simon Magus, of Manes, Manichees, of Photinus, and Anabaptists, and of other heretical, execrable and unheard of opinions, by the instinct of Satan, by him excogitated and holden, &c.

They went on to name sixteen articles, many of them so foolish and inconsistent, that, as the historian observes, he must be an idiot or a madman to hold them all. Three of them are in these words, viz.:—

13. That the baptizing of infants is an abominable custom. 14. That there ought not, in the church, the use of the Lord's supper to be celebrated in the elements of bread and wine, and the use of baptism to be celebrated in the element of water, as they are now practiced in the church of England; but the use of baptism is to be administered in water, only to converts of sufficient age and understanding, converted from infidelity to the faith. 16. That Christianity is not wholly professed and preached in the church of England but only in part.

For these things Mr. Wightman was burnt at Litchfield,[3]

---

[1] Massachusetts Law-book, printed 1672. pp. 58, 59.   [2] See page 126.

[3] Descendants of this martyr to Baptist principles are said to have come early to the country, where several of them have been well known pastors of Baptist churches. Benedict's History of the Baptists, Vol. I, pp. 196, 501, 521. Semi-centennial Discourse of the New London Baptist Association; Minutes, 1867, p. 40.—Ed.

April 11, 1611, by a warrant from that king, who in the preface to our Bible is compared to the rising sun,[1] and whose tyranny drove our fathers into New England.

The above clearly shows that the church of England far exceeded her daughters in this land, both in the number of hard names they imposed upon the Baptists, and also in their degree of cruelty towards them; though a lamentable imitation of those evils appears in this history. And to enforce the fore-cited law among the rest, the Massachusetts placed the following motto in the title page of their law book:—" Whosoever resisteth the power, resisteth the ordinance of God, and they that resist receive to themselves damnation." But whether the assuming and exerting of such power in religious affairs, be not the way to damnation, rather than the resistance of it, deserves the serious consideration of all. Some years ago, when the Presbyterians had the upper hand in England,[2] Mr. Samuel Oates, a noted and successful Baptist minister, was imprisoned, put in irons, and tried for his life as a murderer, at Chelmsford assize, only because Ann Martin, a young woman that he had baptized, happened to die a few weeks after. But when his case came to be tried, her mother and others declared upon oath, " that she was in better health for several days after her baptism than she had been for some years before; and was seen to walk abroad very comfortably," so that he was acquitted.[3]

And now when the Episcopalians had gotten the power again into their own hands, Mr. Neal truly observes, that the enemies to the Baptists tried to ruin them, " by as unparalleled a piece of villainy as ever was heard of."

A pamphlet was published in London, in 1673, entitled, "Mr. Baxter baptized in blood; or a sad history of the unparalleled cruelty of the Anabaptists in New England; faithfully relating the cruel, barbarous and bloody

[1] Crosby's History, Vol. I, pp. 108, and Appendix, pp. 1—3.
[2] See pp. 146, 147.
[3] Crosby's history, Vol. I, pp. 237, 238.

murder of Mr. Josiah Baxter, an orthodox minister, who was killed by the Anabaptists, and his skin most cruelly flead off from his body. Published by his mournful brother, Benjamin Baxter, living in Fenchurch street, London." This pamphlet was licensed by Dr. Parker, the archbishop's chaplain, and cried about streets by the hawkers.[1] The author represents his brother as worsting the Anabaptists in a public disputation at Boston; for which, by way of revenge, they sent four ruffians in vizors to his house a little way out of town, who, after they had bound his wife and three children, first whipped, and then flead [flayed] him alive. The author concludes, "I have published this narrative *in perpetuam rei memoriam*, that the world may see the spirit and temper of those men, and that it may stand as an eternal memorial of their hatred to all orthodox ministers."

But when search was made by authority, they could find no account of such a minister as Josiah Baxter in New England, nor of his brother Benjamin in London. The whole story was a naked and malicious forgery,[2] and verified the words of Lactantius, in the next century after Constantine first introduced the custom of supporting such ministers by force as the court called orthodox. Said he, "Among those who seek power and gain from their religion, there will never be wanting an inclination to forge and lie for it."[3]

As a contrast to the above, I will give a further taste of the spirit of those men who have often been accused of hatred to orthodox ministers. In the beginning of 1665, Mr. Stephen Mumford, a Seventh Day Baptist, arrived from London at Newport, and Mr. Hiscox, Mr. Hubbard, and other members of Mr. Clarke's church, soon embraced the keeping of that day; but in 1671, two or three men who had so done, turned back to the observance of the first day, which Mr. Hubbard and others called apostacy, though many accounted it a reformation; and in June that year Mr. Holmes preached smartly against the others' sentiments;

---

[1] Yea, it went off so current that a second edition was got into the press in a few weeks. Parker was thought to be its author. [Crosby, Vol. II, pp. 291, 292.]

[2] Neal's History of New England, Vol. I, pp. 374, 375.—B.

For a complete exposition of this forgery, see Crosby, Vol. II, pp. 278—294. —ED.

[3] Middleton's Letter from Rome, p. 97.

and the contention increased, till in December it caused an open separation;[1] upon hearing of which, our suffering fathers in the Massachusetts wrote the following letter :—

To brother William Hiscox, and the rest of our beloved brethren and sisters, that observe the Seventh day Sabbath with him, the church of Christ in or near Boston sends greeting.

BRETHREN, BELOVED OF THE LORD :—We having had a view of the proceedings between yourselves and the church, cannot but be grieved to see how busy the adversary hath been, and how easily he hath prevailed upon the corruptions of our nature, to make breaches and divisions among those whom [who], we dare not but judge, are united unto one Head, even Christ Jesus. And although we dare not judge your consciences in the observation of a day or days to the Lord, yet, brethren, your judging them that have so done, and we hope have not unadvisedly changed their minds, to be apostates, seems to our understandings to savor too much a censorious spirit. And we, as brethren, made partakers of the same grace of God through the influence of his Holy Spirit, not being enlightened in the observation of the Seventh day as a sabbath to the Lord, shall humbly beseech you all, to put on bowels of mercy, and not to be so strait in your spirits towards others ; but consider, the only wise God giveth to each soul what measure of light and knowledge he pleaseth ; and it is he must give wisdom to improve that measure of knowledge so given, or else we shall make a bad improvement thereof. Now, brethren, we dare not justify your action, nor the manner of the actions that have been between you and the church ; but should have been glad, if it had been the good pleasure of the Lord, that you could have borne each with other in the matter of difference, and so have left it for the Lord to reveal more light and knowledge to those that are yet in the dark. But may we not say, we are all in the dark, and see and know but in part? and the little part that any one knoweth, he is ready

---

[1] "The covenant drawn up by the Seventh Day church when they were first gathered, after they withdrew from the church under the pastoral care of Mr. John Clarke.

"After serious consideration and seeking God's face among ourselves for the Lord to direct us in a right way for us and our children, so as might be for God's glory and our souls' good, we, viz., William Hiscox, Samuel Hubbard, Steven Mumford, Roger Baxter, Tacy Hubbard, Rachel Langworthy, —— Mumford, entered into covenant with the Lord and with one another, and gave up ourselves to God and one to another, to walk together in all God's holy commandments and holy ordinances according to what the Lord had discovered to us or should discover to be his mind for us to be obedient unto; with sense upon our hearts of great need to be watchful over one another, did promise so to do, and in edifying and building up one another in our most holy faith; this 7th day of December, 1671." Manuscript of John Comer; Backus Historical Society's Library.—ED.

to conceive is the will of God, and so would have all to see with his eyes, and understand with his understanding; and cannot patiently wait on the Lord till he shall make discoveries of it to his brethren; so that our quick, narrow and impatient spirits are the cause of so many breaches and divisions amongst the citizens of Sion at this day. By all which we humbly desire the Lord may make you and us, and all the Lord's people, to see the corruption of our natures that is yet unsubdued, that so we may all with sincerity of soul, wait on him according to that measure of light and knowledge that each of us have [has] received from him. And now brethren, our desire is, if it may be the good pleasure of God, that this breach may be healed between you and the church. Our prayers shall be to the Lord for you, that each one of you may be truly sensible, wherein you have so far departed from the law of brotherly love, as to be an occasion of grief one to another, and to the Israel of God, and have given an occasion to the enemies to speak reproachfully of the ways of God; not doubting but you will be willing to look back over all those actions past in these differences, and if you find anything contrary to the mind and will of God, be willing to own it both to God and his people. We shall leave you to his care and guiding, who is able to comfort you in all your tribulations, and to establish, strengthen and settle you; to whom we leave you, and remain your poor unworthy brethren, who should rejoice in your prosperity, both in spirituals and temporals. By the appointment of the church assembled.

THOMAS GOULD,
WILLIAM TURNER,
JOHN WILLIAMS.

Noddle's Island, September 1, 1672.

This sweet letter, Mr. Hubbard has preserved, and it caused no alienation of mind, but there remained a great nearness between them as long as they lived. I find him in a letter the next year to his brother Hamlit saying, " I desire the welfare of the whole Sion, and the brethren with you; brother Foster, brother Farlow, elder Russell and his son; yea, to all the church, with thanks for their love to me and my wife." Mr. Hamlit wrote on June 19, 1673, that the Baptists were still persecuted for their withdrawing from the public meetings, and said, " Brother Trumbel and brother Osburne were fined last Court at Charlestown, twenty shillings apiece; they have appealed to the Court of Assistants." But Mr. Bellingham dying, and Mr. Leverett being chosen Governor, and Mr. Symonds, Deputy Governor, things took another turn, so that Mr. Hamlit wrote to his brother Hubbard, on January 9, 1674, and said, " Brother Drinker hath been very sick near unto death, but the Lord hath restored him to health again. The church of the baptized do peaceably enjoy their liberty. Brother Russell, the elder and the younger, have good remembrance of you." And while those governors lived, that church enjoyed the greatest liberty that ever they did under their first charter. After Governor Leverett's death, I find Mr. Russell and his church, in an appointment of a day of thanksgiving, expressing their sense of " the Lord's goodness in preserving our peace and liberty beyond all expectation; God having removed him, who was a friend to us in the authority, by reason of which our opposites have the greater advantage against us, who have not been wanting to do their endeavor to suppress us." We shall soon find how that advantage was improved. We are informed by their records, that the next members that were added, after the first constitution of the church, were Isaac Hull, John Farnum, Jacob Barney, John Russell, Jr., John Johnson, George Farlow, Benjamin Sweetser, all before Ellis Callender, who was received November 9, 1669. Mr. Hull was called also to be an elder in the church in the time of their sufferings. The next on the list are Joshua Turner, Thomas Foster, John Russell, Sr., (afterwards their pastor,) William Hamlit, James Landon, Thomas Skinner, John Williams, Philip Squire, Mary Gould, Susanna Jackson, Mary Greenleaf, &c. Elder Gould died October 27, 1675, having been a man, "in some good measure fitted and qualified (says Elder Russell) for such a work ; and proved an eminent instrument in the hand of the Lord, for the carrying on this good work of God in its low and weak beginnings." And including the other first constitutors with him, he says :—

Their trouble and temptations followed, one upon the neck of another, like the waves of the sea ; but these precious servants of the Lord, having in some good measure counted the cost beforehand, were not moved from

per. Psalm i. 1—3 ; xlvi. 4. And Jesus said, If any man thirst, let him come unto me and drink. He that believeth on me, as the Scripture hath said, out of his belly shall flow *rivers* of living water. John vii. 37, 38. But how often have men put human learning in the place of saving faith in the Son of God!

The first university in America is in Cambridge, where an early example of oppression appeared after the war. A Baptist church was constituted in that town in 1781, and they had a pastor ordained in 1783 ; yet they were all taxed for the support of Congregational ministers, and three men were imprisoned therefor in 1784. Therefore they sued the assessors who taxed them, and their case was carried through their inferior and superior courts in 1785, and was turned against the Baptists, which cost them more than a hundred dollars. The constitution of our government restrained our rulers from making any certificate law, as they did in Connecticut, whereby dissenters from the ruling party might be exempted from taxes to their worship; and if any persons might draw off from them without acknowledging that they had power to bind and loose in such affairs, the use of force to support religious ministers would come to an end. Therefore a great lawyer informed those oppressed people, that if they would give in certificates to the ruling sect, that they belonged to said Baptist society, and would have their money go to the minister thereof, he might sue the money out of the hands of those who took it. This advice he founded upon the words in our constitution which say :—

All moneys paid by the subject to the support of public worship, and of the public teachers aforesaid, shall, if *he* require it, be uniformly applied to the support of the public teacher or teachers of his own religious sect or denomination, provided there be any on whose instructions he attends; otherwise it may be paid towards the support of the teacher or teachers of the parish or precinct in which said moneys are raised.

This article was drawn by another great lawyer ; and men of that profession are interested in supporting religious

CHAPTER VII.

An account of Philip's war, of the further sufferings of the Baptists, and other events down to 1690.

The foregoing history may give the reader some idea, of the nature and causes of the contentions that long labored in the country, between the natives and the English. Mr. Samuel Hubbard in the close of Philip's war, wrote to a minister in England, and said:—

God has been long waiting with patience, by several signs and warnings, these forty years, as I can witness [to]; but we in our turnings have not so turned to the Lord as ought to be, and his displeasure is broke forth in the country by the natives, who were forced thereto, as some of them said (and in very deed I judge truly.)[1]

I find by their records, that the Commissioners of the United Colonies, in September, 1662, appointed Captain George Denison, Thomas Stanton, and James Averell, to manage their affairs at Paucatuck, to govern the Indians, and collect the tax imposed upon them on account of the Pequots; and then they say:—

They are also hereby authorized to act and do, or cause to be done, what, in their discretion, may best conduce, to reduce them to civility and the knowledge of God, as well by causing due punishment to be inflicted on disorderly persons according to their demerits, as by encouraging such as shall be sent to instruct them by order of the Commissioners, and by causing them to attend thereunto.

[1] Letter to Edward Stennett, 29th day 9th month, 1676. Samuel Hubbard's Manuscript.—Ed.

And nothing has been more common with their party ever since, than to represent the inhabitants of Rhode Island as an irreligious people; but I trust the foregoing facts show that they were not all so, to which I shall add, that Mr. Samuel Hubbard's daughter Ruth was converted and joined Mr. Clarke's church in 1652, when she was not thirteen years old, and on August 4, 1666, she wrote from Westerly thus:—

MOST LOVING AND DEAR FATHER AND MOTHER: My duty with my husband and children presented unto you, with all my dear friends..... My longing desire is to hear from you, how your hearts are borne up above these troubles which are come upon us, and are coming, as we fear; for we have the rumors of wars, and that almost every day. Even now we have heard from your island by some Indians who declared unto us, that the French have done some mischief upon the coast, and we have heard that twelve hundred Frenchmen have joined with the Mohawks, to clear the land both of English and Indians. But I trust in the Lord, if such a thing be intended, that he will not suffer such a thing to be. My desire and prayer to God is, that he will be pleased to fulfill his promise to us, that is, that as in the world we shall have troubles, so in him we shall have peace. The Lord of comfort, comfort your and our hearts, and give us peace in believing and joy in the Holy Ghost. Oh that the Lord would be pleased to fill our hearts with his good Spirit, that we may be carried above all these things! and that we may remember his saying, When ye see these things come to pass, lift up your heads, knowing that your redemption draws nigh. Then if these things be the certain sign of our Lord's return, let us mind his command, that is, Pray always that ye may be counted worthy to escape all these things, and to stand before the Son of Man. Let us have boldness to come unto him in the new and living way, which he hath prepared for us. Through grace I find the Lord doth bear up the spirits of his in this place, in some comfortable measure, to be looking above these things. The Lord increase it more and more unto the day of his appearing, which I hope is [near] at hand. Dear father and mother, the Lord hath been pleased to give us here many sweet and comfortable days of refreshing, which is great cause of thankfulness, and my desire is, that we may highly prize it, and you with us give the Lord the praise for this benefit. I pray remember my love to all my dear friends with you in fellowship. Sister Sanders desires to be remembered to you all; so doth sister Clarke. Your loving daughter to my power,

RUTH BURDICK.

Philip was son to Osamaquin and succeeded him as the chief sachem on the east side of Narragansett Bay. He had this name given him by Plymouth Court in 1660. Such rumors spread of his preparing for war, as brought Governor Prince, and two of his Assistants to Taunton, April 13, 1671, to meet three gentlemen from the Massachusetts, to examine into the matter. Philip kept at a distance, and sent to them to come to him at Three Mile River.[1] The Governor sent again for him to come to them, but he refused, till old Mr. Roger Williams and Mr. Brown, I suppose of Swanzey, offered to remain there as hostages; by which means he was brought forward and prevailed with to deliver up about seventy guns he had got, and to promise future fidelity, which suspended the war for four years.[2] And then it was brought on in the following manner. John Sasaman, an Indian that the English had given considerable instruction to, both as to human learning and religious affairs, being with Philip at Namasket, discovered that he was preparing for war, and informed the English of it; for which he was murdered upon a pond at Assawamset, both of which places are in Middleborough. Three Indians were apprehended for that murder, and were executed at Plymouth.

Mr. John Tracy of Norwich had married Mrs. Mary Winslow from Marshfield five years before, and returning from a visit there at this time, happened to fall in among a party of Indians in arms, waiting to hear whether their friends would be executed or not. They brought him to Philip, whom he satisfied that he was only a traveler and upon no ill design, so that he sent him away in peace.[3] But

---

[1] This river runs from Norton through the west part of Taunton, and falls into the Great River betwixt that town and Dighton.

[2] Massachusetts History, Vol. I, pp. 278, 279. [254, 255.]

[3] Callender's Century Sermon, p. 73. [127.] Mr. Tracy was my mother's grandfather.—B.

The only further information which we have of the person here mentioned is in a brief allusion to him in Mr. Backus's Gospel Comfort, a sermon on the death of his mother, in which he says, "Her father, Mr. John Tracy, was a man eminent for vital and practical religion, who died on March 27, 1726, with such comfortable

hearing soon after that those Indians were executed, they broke out on June 24, 1675, and killed nine men in different parts of Swanzey, and fired upon one in Rehoboth; which alarmed the country, and in four days an army was collected there, and made Mr. Miles's house their head-quarters. Philip soon left his station at Mount Hope, now Bristol, and retired to a great swamp east of the Great River. The Massachusetts part of the army went into the Narragansett country, and brought those Indians to promise not to join in the war, and then returned, and, with the other forces, attacked Philip at the swamp on July 18, but had little success therein. Soon after which, Philip and many of his men repassed the river, and crossing Seconk plain, made their way up to the Nepmuck Indians in Worcester county, who had begun the war on July 14.

These alarms caused Mr. Joseph Tory and Mr. Hubbard to send a boat which brought their friends from Westerly to Newport this month, and they continued on the island till the war was over. Soon after Philip had joined the Nepmucks, they violently assaulted a small English plantation at Brookfield, and as Captain Hutchinson with a company went to relieve them on August 2, they from an ambush gave him a mortal wound. But Major Willard came two days after with forty-eight men, and slew many of the enemy, and delivered his friends. Upon which the enemy steered further westward, and on September 1, burnt most of the houses in Deerfield, and killed eight men the next day at Northfield; and Captain Beers going with thirty-six men to fetch off the inhabitants there, had a terrible fight with the enemy, wherein he and above half of his men fell. September 18, sundry teams went to bring off a large quantity of grain from Deerfield, and Captain Lothrop went with about eighty men to guard them; but not seeing any of the

views of another world, that he charged his friends to give him up, and not hold him any longer with their prayers. He was very strict in the religious education of his family, which this daughter of his was ever thankful for as long as she lived."—ED.

enemy, they on their return, got to picking grapes by Muddy Brook, when the enemy got a dreadful advantage of them. I have seen the stone over the place where they tell me about seventy of them were buried in one grave. Presently after, an assault was made upon Springfield, where the minister's house and library was burnt, with thirty-one houses beside. But a large body of Indians making an onset upon Hadley, October 19, and having killed one man, were so bravely repulsed by the English, that in their flight some of them were drowned in Connecticut River, and others who escaped, retired into Narragansett. In that country on a small tract of upland within a great swamp, seven miles west from the south ferry that goes over from Newport, the Indians built and stored the strongest fort they ever had in this country. Therefore the colonies gathered an army of a thousand men, under the command of Governor Winslow, and after a fierce conflict, took and destroyed it, on December 19. They supposed that a thousand of the enemy were cut off; but it cost on our side the lives of six captains, and one hundred and seventy, some said two hundred and ten men, killed or wounded. They marched sixteen or eighteen miles from Major Smith's to that fight, and returned through a terrible snow-storm the same night.[1]

[1] I have met with the original of a testimony concerning that family, and that affair, which I will give a copy of here. It is as follows:—

Narragansett, 21 July, 1679, (*ut vulgo.*)

I, ROGER WILLIAMS, of Providence, in the Narragansett Bay, in New England, being (by God's mercy) the first beginner of the mother town of Providence, and of the Colony of Rhode Island and Providence Plantations, being now near to fourscore years of age, yet (by God's mercy) of sound understanding and memory, do humbly and faithfully declare, that Mr. Richard Smith, Sr., who for his conscience to God, left fair possessions in Gloucestershire, and adventured, with his relations and estate, to New England, and was a most acceptable inhabitant, and a prime leading man in Taunton, in Plymouth colony; for his conscience' sake, many differences arising, he left Taunton and came to the Narragansett country, where (by God's mercy and the favor of the Narragansett sachems) he broke the ice at his great charge and hazard, and put up in the thickest of the barbarians, the first English house amongst them. 2. I humbly testify that about forty years from this date, he kept possession, coming and going himself, children and servants and he had a quiet possession of his housing, lands and meadows; and there in his own house, with

Great stores of corn were destroyed in that fort, which reduced the Indians to terrible distress. But a thaw in January enabled them to get some sustenance out of the earth, upon which they burnt the deserted houses in Mendon, and on February 10, 1676, made an onset upon Lancaster, burnt their habitations, and killed or captivated forty persons, one of whom was Mrs. Rowlandson, wife of the minister, who was then gone to Boston to procure help against the enemy. The narrative she gave of her captivity has lately been reprinted.[1] Like mischiefs were done at Groton, Marlborough, Sudbury and Chelmsford; and on February 21, the enemy wheeled round and came down upon Medfield, (twenty miles from Boston,) and burnt half their houses, and slew eighteen men, notwithstanding two or three hundred soldiers that they then had in town. February 25, they did considerable damage in Weymouth, still nearer to Boston; and the like at Groton and Sudbury on March 10. The 12th, they cut off two families in Clarke's garrison at Plymouth; and the

---

much serenity of soul and comfort, he yielded up his spirit to God, (the Father of Spirits,) in peace. 3. I do humbly and faithfully testify as abovesaid, that since his departure, his honored son, Captain Richard Smith, hath kept possession (with much acceptance with English and pagans) of his father's housing, lands, and meadows, with great improvement, also by his great cost and industry. And in the late bloody pagan war, I knowingly testify and declare. that it pleased the Most High to make use of himself in person, his housing, goods, corn, provisions and cattle, for a garrison and supply for the whole army of New England, under the command of the ever-to-be-honored General Winslow, for the service of his Majesty's honor and country of New England. 4. I do also humbly declare, that the said Captain Richard Smith, Jr., ought by all the rules of equity, justice and gratitude (to his honored father and himself) to be fairly treated with, considered, recruited, honored, and by his Majesty's authority, confirmed and established in a peaceful possession of his father's and his own possessions in this pagan wilderness, and Narragansett country. The premises I humbly testify, as now leaving this country and this world. ROGER WILLIAMS.

It appears by Governor Winthrop's journal that Taunton was first planted in 1637, [Vol. I, pp. 252, 253,] so that Mr. Smith came there soon after. We are told that the mansion house of the Updike family, in North Kingstown stands where he began among the Narragansetts.

[1] "A narrative of the captivity, sufferings and removes of Mrs. Mary Rowlandson, who was taken prisoner by the Indians, with several others, and treated in the most barbarous and cruel manner by the savages, with many other remarkable events during her travels. 1773."—ED.

next day burnt almost all Groton, in Middlesex, to the ground.

Here I must open something that has been surprisingly concealed from this country. It has been the constant practice of all parties who are fond of an ecclesiastical establishment by human laws, to accuse the Baptists of disobedience to government, especially in the point of a defensive war. This the reader may see inserted in a law of the Massachusetts, but three years before this war began. Mr. Callender was then a member of the Baptist church in Boston, and was continued a great blessing to them for more than fifty years. The copy of Mr. Russell's Narrative that I am favored with, came out of his family, and in it is a manuscript note in the margin, against Mr. Russell's account of Mr. Turner, which says :—

> In the beginning of the war, William Turner gathered a company of volunteers, but was denied a commission and discouraged, because the chief of the company were Anabaptists. Afterwards when the war grew more general and destructive, and the country in very great distress, having divers towns burnt, and many men slain, then he was desired to accept a commission. He complained it was too late, his men on whom he could confide being scattered; however, was moved to accept.

They made him Captain, and his brother Drinker, Lieutenant, of a company that marched up with others in the beginning of this month, to relieve the western towns, under Major Savage as chief commander; and by them the Indians were repulsed and driven off from Northampton on March 14. The 17th, they burnt all but one of the houses in Warwick, most of the inhabitants being gone to Rhode Island. On Lord's day, March 26, Captain Pierce being at Rehoboth, with fifty English soldiers, and twenty friendly Indians, heard of a body of the enemy up Patucket River, and wrote to Captain Andrew Edmunds, of Providence, to meet him there with his company to attack them. He sent the letter by a person who was going over to Providence meeting, but who did not deliver it till their worship was done at noon. As soon as Captain Edmunds had read the letter, he gave the bearer a sharp reprimand, for not delivering it before, and expressed his fear of the consequence as it proved; for Captain Pierce engaging the enemy alone, who were also more numerous than he expected, he was surrounded and cut off, with all but thirteen of his men, only one of whom was of the English; and it is said he escaped by a friendly Indian's turning and running after him with a weapon, as if he was an enemy, which others seeing did not pursue him. They tell us that another of those friends escaped in this manner: being pursued by an enemy, he took shelter behind a rock, where, as each waited for an opportunity to shoot the other, our friend gently raising his hat above the rock upon a stick, the enemy discharged his gun at it, on which the other shot him down and escaped. It is reported that Captain Pierce and his men slew one hundred of the enemy in the conflict. The people both of Marlborough and Springfield suffered considerably the same day. March 28, forty houses were burnt in Rehoboth, and twenty-nine the next day at Providence, the people retiring into garrisons.

In the Clerk's office in that town is a paper, in which Mr. Williams said :—

> I pray the town, in the sense of the late bloody practices of the natives, to give leave to so many as can agree with William Field, to bestow some charge upon fortifying his house, for security to women and children; also to give me leave, and so many as shall agree, to put up some defence on the hill, between the mill and the highway, for the like safety of the women and children in that part of the town.

To this eleven principal inhabitants subscribed, the highest whereof was two pounds six shillings, except Mr. Williams, who subscribed ten pounds. Tradition says, that when the Indians appeared on the high lands north of their great cove, Mr. Williams took his staff and walked over towards them, hoping likely to pacify them as he had often done; but when some of their aged men saw him, they came out and met him, and told him that though those who had long known him would not hurt him, yet their young men were so enraged that it was not safe for him to venture among them; upon which he returned to the garrison. The house where their records were kept was plundered, and they thrown into the mill-pond, but were recovered, though by that means some passages are not legible, and likely many articles were lost.

In April, Captain George Denison of Stonington, with a number of English and Mohegan Indians, performed two great exploits. They penetrated into the Narragansett country, and slew forty-four of the enemy at one time, and sixty-six at another, without the loss of a man. In the mean time the Massachusetts met with a dreadful blow. Captain Wadsworth and Lieutenant Bruttlebank, with above thirty men, were cut off as they were going to relieve Sudbury on April 18. Bridgewater, which was planted in 1652, was now assaulted by a great body of the enemy on May 8, when twelve deserted houses were burnt, but there was never one of their people killed in that war; neither can we learn that any English person who was born in that town, was ever slain by the sword for eighty years after.[1] Major Savage and most of his men returning, he left Captain Turner to command in that quarter. Hereupon the enemy, thinking themselves more out of danger, resorted, seven or eight hundred of them, to the great falls above Deerfield, on the fishing design. Two captive lads made their escape, and gave information of their secure state, whereupon Captain Turner and young Captain Holioke of Springfield, collected what force they could on a sudden, being not much more than a hundred and fifty men, and went up silently in the night, tied their horses at some distance, and a little before daybreak, May 18, 1676, came unawares upon the enemy, " fired amain into their very wigwams, killing many upon

[1] It is remarkable that the inhabitants of the said Bridgewater never yet lost one person by the sword of the enemy, though the town is situate within Plymouth colony; yet have they helped to destroy many of the enemy. Hubbard's Narrative of the Indian wars; Stockbridge, 1803, p. 171.—ED.

the place, and frighting others with the sudden alarm of their guns, made them run into the river, where the swiftness of the stream carrying them down a steep fall, they perished in the waters; some getting into canoes, sank or overset by the shooting of our men; others, creeping for shelter, under the banks of the great river, were espied by our men and killed by their swords. . . . . 'Some of their prisoners afterwards owned that they lost above three hundred, some whereof were principal men, sachems, and some of their best fighting men that were left. . . . . Nor did they seem ever to have recovered themselves after this defeat, but their ruin immediately followed upon it." When our people first fired upon them they cried out, *Mohawks!* but in the morning discovering their mistake, they rallied their scattered men, and Captain Turner being unwell, and so "not able for want of bodily strength (no ways defective for want of skill or courage) to assist or direct in making a retreat; some of the enemy fell upon the guards that kept the horses, others pursued them in the rear, so as our men sustained pretty much damage as they retired, missing after their return thirty-eight of their men." One of these was Captain Turner, who was afterwards found and buried.[1] Dr. Stephen Williams says, "There were many remarkables in this affair (as related by Jonathan Wells, Esq., who was present) which are not taken notice of by Mr. Hubbard, or Dr. Mather."[2] Mr. Hubbard's account was examined and approved by three gentlemen of the Council, and so was published by authority. All the rest of the Baptists who were in that action, but their Captain, were preserved and returned. And as they again met with cruel treatment four years after, both from rulers and ministers, and the old charge of denying magistracy was revived, they said in answer thereto:—

1. It is directly against our principles, and contrary to what we asserted in a confession of our faith, that we gave into the Court, as also to that Con-

---

[1] Hubbard's History of that war, pp. 88, 94. [205—211.]
[2] Appendix to his father's and Deerfield's captivity, p. 66.

fession of our faith lately set forth by our brethren in old England, which Confession we own in every particular.[1] 2. Our continual prayer to God for them, according to I. Tim. ii. 1, 2, will witness against this charge. 3. Our constant subjection and obedience to their laws, both actively, as far as we can with a good conscience, and where we could not actively, there have we been passively obedient; in suffering what they inflicted on us, without seeking any revenge in the least. 4. In paying all due demands whatsoever; not being desirous to withhold from Cæsar at any time, any of his dues. In a word, both our persons and estates are always ready at command to be serviceable in the defence of the country; yea, and have been voluntarily offered on the high places of the field, in the time of the country's greatest extremity. .... Among whom was William Turner, whom they pleased to make Captain of that company, who had been one of the greatest sufferers among us, for the profession of religion. He was a very worthy man for soldiery; and Edward Drinker, who had been another sufferer, whom they pleased to make Lieutenant; and by the presence of the Lord with them, they were made instruments of the preservation of one town from the rage of the heathen, who violently broke into it, but they being there beat them out. And after that, by Captain Turner, who was then commander-in-chief, as an instrument in the hand of the Lord, was the greatest blow struck to the Indians of any they had received; for after this they were broken and scattered, so that they were overcome and subdued with ease. Here it is to be observed that those who had suffered so much from the country, and scandalized as enemies to the country, and their privileges, freely offering themselves in their service, have been (through the Lord's presence with them) some of the principal instruments

[1] The Confession published in London, in 1677, and revised in 1689.—B.

"God, the supreme Lord and King of all the world hath ordained civil magistrates to be under him over his people for his own glory and the public good, and to this end hath armed them with the power of the sword for defence and encouragement of them that do good, and for the punishment of evil doers. It is lawful for Christians to accept and execute the office of a magistrate when called thereunto; in the management whereof, as they ought especially to maintain justice and peace, according to the wholesome laws of each kingdom and commonwealth, so, for that end, they may lawfully now, under the New Testament, wage war upon just and necessary causes. Civil magistrates being set up by God, for the ends aforesaid, subjection in all lawful things commanded by them, ought to be yielded by us in the Lord, not only for wrath but for conscience sake; and we ought to make supplications and prayers for kings and all that are in authority, that under them we may live a quiet and peaceable life in all godliness and honesty." Confession of 1677, Chap. XXXIV. This Confession is published in Crosby, Vol. III, Appendix II; Confessions of Faith, &c., Hansard Knolly's Society, pp. 179—246; Cutting's Historical Vindications, pp. 131--188. It was highly esteemed among the early Baptists of this country. The Philadelphia Association made brief additions to it and adopted it in 1742.—ED.

to subdue the barbarous heathen, and to deliver the country from its greatest distress; which may stand as a witness of our fidelity to the government to the world's end. We have been vilified and greatly reproached, and are at this day, it being without any just reason laid to us, that we are one chief cause of all the judgments of God on the land. We do not excuse ourselves, as not having a share or part in many of the sins that have provoked the Lord against poor New England; neither have we been freed from having part with others in the general calamities that God hath brought on this poor place. Yet it is observable how graciously the Lord hath dealt with us; that in the time of great mortality by the small-pox, when so many hundreds died, though many of us were visited with that visitation, yet not one of our society was removed by it; but it was not for any thing in us, that the Lord spared us, but for his name's sake, that the mouth of our adversaries might be silent.[1]

In answer to this, Mr. Willard said:—

The German Anabaptists were enemies to civil government; we hope these (though they have shown too much contempt of authority) are not so far gone. But for his so gloriously emblazoning their service in the late wars, it is neither to the purpose, nor of much moment. That they did join against the common enemy is true. Swanzey (a place chiefly consisting of Anabaptists, and where they had a church) was the place where the enemy made the first onset. .... Besides, any man would fight, rather than have his throat cut; it was not for religion, nor civil government, but for lives and estates. .... Nor did the Indians receive the greatest blow at that time; nor is it the Anabaptists' true, but vain, glory, to set such an encomium upon their own deeds. .... We have dismissed the charge, now comes a strong argument of their orthodoxy, a witness from Heaven, viz., their happy preservation in the time of the small pox. Let it be remembered, that one of their persuasion died of it at Woburn, (where John Russell lived, and should have observed it) and many of their children. But be it so; their society is small, and scattered from Dan to Beersheba. And who knows, but God might spare them in judgment, to harden them? These are too high things for us; only when God comes to chasten his people, those that are not chastened, may ask whether they are not bastards?

He had before said:—

As the honored magistrates here are Christians, so have they judged it their duty to maintain the ways of Christ, and strengthen them by civil laws, which hath not only been the practice of reformers of old, but the constant judgment of the church of Christ ever since the apostles. .... On this principle our worthy rulers have made laws against many sects and

[1] Russell's Narrative, pp. 11, 12.

intruders, and among the rest the Anabaptists. That in quelling the Anabaptists they do not oppose the truth, but suppress error, they are fully persuaded; and although they never pretended to a lordship over men's consciences, yet they account the outward man is subject to them; and if they must tarry till all men are agreed about what is truth, before we oppose error, we shall stay till there is no need of it.[1]

According to this, we are not to imagine that those ministers ever intended to lord it over Thomas Gould's conscience, when they censured him for not standing up, and looking on when they sprinkled infants in the sacred name. He might have thought what he pleased of it inwardly, if he would but have honored them before the people;[2] and though for refusing so to do, they excluded him from the ordinance of the Supper for seven years, and then for taking another method to enjoy it, they moved the rulers to disfranchise, fine, imprison and banish him, yet all this was for error in his outward man, not in his conscience! neither must it be supposed, that vain glory had any influence in the emblazoning of things on their side; for all these things were done by orthodox ministers, and Christian rulers. But let the Anabaptists offer themselves ever so willingly, and at a time when the main of the enemy were remote from their churches, both of Boston and Swanzey; and let them do ever so great public service, yet it must not be thought that they were moved either by religion or loyalty. No, all proceeded either from love to the world, or else fear of having their throats cut by the Indians in Boston, if they had not gone a hundred miles into the country to meet them! This is spoken, not in contempt to any man's person, but to expose and detect that self-flattery which so often deceives mankind. The above is all the mention I ever saw, in any publication from that party, that shews the chief commander in the fall fight to have been a Baptist. Most of their histories of that war mention his name, but not a word of his being the man who had before suffered in the Baptists' cause. And lest it should detect the slanders they still were casting upon our denomi-

---

[1] *Ne sutor*, &c., pp. 23, 24.   [2] 1 Sam. xv. 30.

tion, they, having gained his son to their party, entirely concealed this fact from his numerous posterity. For though his grandson, Captain William Turner of Swanzey, embraced our principles, which he continued in after he removed to Newport, where he died in 1759, bequeathing, among other legacies in his will, his lands in Fall Town, adjoining to the place where his grandfather was slain; yet in June, 1774, I was conversing with one of his daughters, together with her son, William Turner Miller, Esq., both members of the Baptist church in Warren, and they told me, they had often heard of their ancestor's exploits and death in Philip's war, but never a word before of his being a Baptist, or of his sufferings in that cause. Neither have any of their historians ever ventured to publish a particular account of the Baptist sufferings, as they have of the Quakers. For which I can give no better reason than, because they could find encroachments upon their rights in the latter to found a plea upon, which they could not in the former. And the author of the Magnalia plainly expressed his unwillingness that the records thereof should be kept anywhere.[1]

Captain Benjamin Church of Duxbury near Plymouth, who had made some beginning at Sokonet, now Little Compton, east of Rhode Island, the year before the war, carried his family on that Island after it began, as a place in his opinion of greater safety than Duxbury or Plymouth; and he was an active and successful commander through the war. As he knew that Philip had forced the Sokonet Indians into the war, contrary to the minds of the leading part of them, he, against his friends' advice, went over in a canoe, and adventured himself among them in June this year, and gained them over to our side, by whose help he took great numbers of the enemy from day to day, who had now lost all their courage. At length returning to visit his wife, whose anxious mind fainted to see him again well, he was immediately informed by Major Sanford and Captain Gold-

---

[1] Magnalia, Vol. I, p. 58; Vol. II, p. 552.—ED.

ing, that one of Philip's men had fled from him (then at the foot of Mount Hope) and was come over to the Island. Hereupon they all put spurs to their horses, and having heard the Indian's account, crossed the ferry in the night with a few men, and after Captain Church had stationed his ambush, of the Rhode Island gentlemen, beat up Philip's head-quarters, upon which he set out to flee through a little swamp, but after an Englishman had snapped his gun at him without effect, Alderman, an Indian, fired a bullet through his heart, on August 12, 1676, a little before the break of day; after which the war was soon brought to a close.

This summary of that bloody war I have carefully collected from a great variety of histories and accounts. And upon the whole, it was said, that in this war were slain, twelve captains and about six hundred men; that about one thousand two hundred houses were burnt, eight thousand head of cattle, and many thousand bushels of grain destroyed; and also three thousand Indians. The loss to the English colonies was computed at one hundred and fifty thousand pounds sterling, and Captain Tom, with another chief of the Christian Indians at Natick, were taken and hanged at Boston, for being active instruments of those mischiefs.[1] Many others were faithful. Of those twelve captains, Gallop, Seily and Marshall, (who were slain at the Narragansett fort,) were of Connecticut; Hutchinson, Beers, Lothrop, Devenport, Gardner, Johnson, Wadsworth and Turner, were of the Massachusetts, and Pierce was of Scituate, in Plymouth colony. From Pierce, one Baptist elder of that name, and many members of the Baptist churches of Swanzey, Rehoboth and other places have sprung.

On November 29, this year, Mr. Samuel Hubbard wrote to Mr. Edward Stennett, in England;[2] and after what is re-

---

[1] Massachusetts History, Vol. III, pp. 492, 493.
[2] Mr. Stennett's son and grandson, named Joseph, and great-grandson, named Samuel, have been noted Baptist ministers in London; the two latter, Doctors of Divinity.

cited in the beginning of this chapter, he further said of the Indians :—

They have done much harm in our bordering towns, as Warwick, destroyed by fires; only most of the people are here, and their goods, and some of their cattle; and the like at Pawtuxet and Providence, though not altogether destroyed, for a garrison remaineth there to this day. And for the other side over against us on the main, which once was ours, and is, I judge, by charter, many are killed by the Indians, the rest came to us with what they could bring. Connecticut army, Plymouth and Bay armies being there, wasted very much; when they left it, the Indians burnt near all that was left. In Plymouth the wars began, and [they] are sore wasted [lost most men of all]; the Bay lost very many men. Connecticut did most service, and I have not heard of one town destroyed or fired in that colony. In the beginning of these troubles of the wars, Lieutenant Joseph Tory, elder of Mr. Clarke's church, having but one daughter living at Squamicot, [Westerly] and his wife being there, he said unto me, Come, let us send a boat to Squamicot; my all is there and part of yours. We sent a boat so as his wife, his daughter, and son-in-law, and all their children, and my two daughters and their children (one had eight, the other three, with an apprentice boy) all came, and brother John Crandal and his family, with as many others as could possibly come. My son Clarke came afterwards before winter, and my other daughter's husband came in the spring, and they all have been at my house to this day. .... Now, dear brother, although we are not destroyed by the Indians, God hath visited this land by taking away many by death, and in this place [very much, yea to this day, yea] of all sorts. Of the old church, first Mr. Joseph Tory, then my dear brother John Crandal, then Mr. John Clarke, then William Weeden, a deacon, then John Salmon; a sad stroke in very deed; young men and maids; to this day, I never knew or heard the like in New England. Last week four or five were buried in this town. .... Brother Turner went to war, and God prospered him for a time, but he is now killed by the Indians; the rest are well and enjoy their liberty. Mr. Miles, that was at Swanzey, is now with them. Brother William Gibson, who came from old England with brother Mumford, is now gone to New London to visit our brethren there.

Mr. Mumford had been over to London, and he with Mr. Gibson returned to Boston, in October 16, 1675. Mr. Gibson afterward succeeded Elder Hiscox in the pastoral office at Newport.

The above account of the preservation of Connecticut, as well as the other articles expressed, are just, as far as I can learn. The Mohegan Indians, under Uncas, did the English great service in that war. I have seen scarce any account of any other damages in Swanzey and Rehoboth, beside what have been recited, except the Indians' killing Captain Willet's son near the garrison in Swanzey this year. Middleborough and Dartmouth were but just begun before the war, and when it came on, the English and part of the Indians therein, removed to Plymouth and other places of greater safety; and the large body of natives near to and upon Cape Cod, continued in amity with the English, as those on the islands south of it also did. Of the latter I have met with the following entertaining account.

Thomas Mayhew, Esq., obtained a grant of Martha's Vineyard, with the islands adjacent, and began a settlement at Edgartown, on the east part of the Vineyard, in 1642, where he was their chief ruler, and his son their minister. In 1646, the son began to preach to the Indians with success; to promote which cause his father told them, "that by order from the crown of England, he was to govern the English who should inhabit those islands; that his royal master was in power far above any of the Indian monarchs; but that as he was great and powerful, so he was a lover of justice; and that therefore he would in no measure invade their jurisdictions, but on the contrary assist them if need required; that religion and government were distinct things, and their sachems might retain their just authority, though their subjects were Christians." And he practiced according to his profession; for "he would not suffer any to injure them either in their goods, lands or persons. They always found a father and protector in him; and he was so far from introducing any form of government among them against their wills, that he first convinced them of the advantage of it, and even brought them to desire him to introduce and settle it." This wise conduct and the gospel means that were used with them, produced such happy effects, that a Christian church was formed and organized among them five years before this war. And now in the time of it, the government furnished those Christian Indians with arms and ammunition and employed them to defend the islands against the enemy. "And so faithful were they, that they not only resolutely rejected the strong [and repeated] solicitations of the natives on the neighboring main, but, in observance of the general orders given them, when any landed to solicit them, though some were nearly related by marriage, and others by blood, yet the island Indians would immediately bring them before the Governor to attend his pleasure." By the divine blessing on these means, though the Indians there were twenty to one of the English, yet through this extensive and bloody war, " these islands enjoyed a perfect calm of peace; and the people wrought and dwelt secure and quiet.[1]

[1] Prince's Appendix to Mayhew's Indian converts, pp. 293—297. In that performance I find that Mr. Peter Foulger was early employed as a "school-master among those Indians, and when young Mr. Mayhew went to England, in 1667, Mr. Prince says, they had not only several Indian teachers on the island, but also 'an able, godly Englishman named Peter Foulger, employed in teaching the youth in reading, writing and the principles of religion by catechizing; being well learned likewise in the Scripture, and capable of helping them in religious matters." p. 291. I find by Mr. Samuel Hubbard, that Mr. Foulger became a Baptist, and joined Mr. Clarke's church about the time of this war; as Thomas West, an Englishman, and some Indians from thence, did to Mr. Hiscox's church in 1680. And Mr. Foulger promoted the Baptist principles among the Indians. Though one of them named Japheth, who had been his scholar, and now was got to be a noted teacher, reminded him that he had formerly warned them against false teachers that would come, and said he, "Now Sir, I find your prediction true, for you yourself are become one of these teachers, you cautioned us against; I am therefore fully resolved to take your good counsel, and not believe you, but will continue steadfast in the truths wherein you formerly instructed me." Mayhew, pp. 49, 50. However he found others not to be so resolute, for by the time that their Governor, Mayhew, died in 1680, the Baptist principles had prevailed considerably among them; and by the year 1694, they had one Baptist church on the Vineyard among the Christian Indians, and another on Nantucket. Magnalia, B. 6, p. 56. [Vol. II, p. 375.] The first Indian pastor over those Baptists on the Vineyard, that I have seen any account of, was Stephen Tackamason. He first joined a church of the other denomination, in or about 1690. Mr. Mayhew informs us, that he was re-baptized some years after, and became a membe and a teacher of that church, but says, "However, he appeared to be so serious a man, that I cannot but judge, that he acted according to the dictates of his conscience in what he did, and not out of any base or sordid ends." He died in Chilmark, in 1708; and our author says, "I had frequent conversation with him while he was in health, and sometimes . . . . in the time of that long sickness whereof he died; and never from first to last saw anything by him, that made me any ways suspect the integrity of his

Ninegret and his Nyantick subjects, who dwelt from Point Judith up to Westerly, on the shore south of the Narragansetts, did not join in that war; and a considerable number of their descendants now live there in Charlestown; and in 1741 a great reformation took place among them; a Baptist

heart, but did ever think him to be a godly and discreet man. The last time I went to see him, he professed his good opinion of those people and churches, from whom he differed in his apprehensions about the subjects and mode of baptism, and blamed some of his brethren for being too uncharitable and censorious towards them; and he on other subjects, discoursed like a good Christian. . . . . He seemed not to be at all terrified at the approaches of death towards him, of which he was very sensible, but appeared to enjoy that peace in his soul, which passeth understanding." Pp. 42—44. These are the words of Mr. Experience Mayhew, in his "Indian Converts," published in 1727. His worthy son, who succeeds him in the ministry among the Indians on the Island, treated one of my brethren in the ministry very friendly, when he was over and preached among those Baptists, near three years ago. I had requested my friend to collect some account of those Baptists, and he applied to Mr. Mayhew for that purpose; who promised he would get the best intelligence he could concerning them, from an aged aunt of his, who retained her mental powers remarkably, and from others. He sent the same in the following letter:—

"REVEREND SIR:—In compliance with your request I have got the best information I could, with respect to the origin of Anti-pædobaptists at Martha's Vineyard. My aged aunt informs me, that the first Baptist minister among the Indians on the island, that she knew or heard of, was one Isaac Decamy, who came from the mainland with his family, and preached and administered the ordinances of baptism and the Lord's Supper, a number of years. She is uncertain what year he came, but according to the best of her memory the said Decamy died near sixty years agone. She saith further, that he was a man of a sober life and conversation. The next Indian minister of this denomination, by the best intelligence I can get, was Jonas Horswet, who preached and administered the ordinances to a small society of Baptists at Gay Head. The next was Ephriam Abraham, originally of Chappaquidick, at the east end of the island, who had the charge of the society at Gay Head, as also of one, which about this time was formed at said Chappaquidick. The next ordained minister was Samuel Kakenehew, whom I had a personal acquaintance with; he lived at Chappaquidick, was esteemed by such as knew him, to be a man of sense, and of a regular and Christian life and conversation. There were several other preachers among them, but not ordained; except Silas Paul, who is now living, and is an ordained pastor of the Baptist church at Gay Head, and who also takes upon him the care of the small society of that denomination at Chappaquidick; preaching occasionally, and administering the ordinances to them. He is the only Indian minister of this denomination now upon this island.

This is the best information that can be obtained by your friend and fellow-laborer in the work of the ministry,
ZECHARIAH MAYHEW."

Chilmark, 27 August, 1774.

This was directed to Elder Hunt, who says, the said Paul informed him that he was then thirty-four years old, was baptized in 1758, ordained in 1763; that the church at Gay Head had thirteen members, and the other, sixteen.

348   HISTORY OF THE BAPTISTS IN NEW ENGLAND.

church was formed there some years after, over whom James Simons was ordained; and since that, Samuel Niles, both of their own nation; and a considerable number of them have given lasting evidence of their being pious Christians.

It may be proper to take some particular notice here of Mr. Clarke, who left as spotless a character as any man I know of, that ever acted in any public station in this country.[1] The Massachusetts writers have been so watchful and

[1] He was born October 8, 1609; married Elizabeth, daughter of John Harges, Esq., of Bedfordshire. In a power of attorney signed by them, May 12, 1656, he styles himself, John Clarke, physician, of London. It was for the recovery of a legacy of twenty pounds per annum during her life, that was given her by her father out of the manor of Wreslingworth, Bedfordshire. Where he had his education I know not; but the following clause in his will may give some idea of his learning, viz.: 'Item, unto my loving friend Richard Bailey, I give and bequeath, my Concordance and Lexicon to it belonging, written by myself, being the fruit of several years' study; my Hebrew Bibles, Buxtorff's and Passor's Lexicon, Cotton's Concordance, and all the rest of my books." His first wife died at Newport without any issue, and February 1, 1671, he married Mrs. Jane Fletcher, by whom, February 14, 1672, he had a daughter born; but the mother died the 19th of April following, and the daughter May 18, 1673. His third wife was the widow Sarah Davis, who survived him. He gave some legacies, both to her and to the children she had by her former husband, Mr. Bailey, who came from London with him in 1664.—B.

"It is not certainly known," says Elton, "where Mr. Clarke was born, but tradition makes him a native of Bedfordshire." Appendix to Callender's Century Sermon, Rhode Island Historical Collections, Vol. IV, p. 210. A different tradition, together with other valuable notes in connection with his history, is presented in the following extract from a letter from a descendant of the family:—" In the old family Bible, which was Thomas Clarke's, the father of John Clarke, is this notice, viz.: 'The 2 of the 10 month, 1674, Thomas Clarke, son of Thomas Clarke, of Wastrup, [Westthorpe, in Suffolk,] departed this life in Newport on Rod Island, in the house of his brother [John].' I have inserted in brackets the name of the place which I think is meant. I have many reasons for believing that the family were from Suffolk. The wife of Thomas Clarke, senior, was Rose Herrige, of an ancient Suffolk family. There is in the Bible a family record in the hand-writing of Thomas Clarke, commencing, 'John Clarke, my grandfather, was buried the 3d of March, A. D. 1559,' and ending with the birth and baptism of his own children, which were, ' Margret, born the 1st of February, 1600; [the dates of course are old style] Carewe, born the 3d of February, 1602; Thomas, baptized the 31st of March, 1605; Meric, baptized the 17th of July, 1607; John, born October 8th, 1609; William, baptized the 11th of February, 1610; Joseph, baptized the 16th of December, born 9th, 1618.'"

The services of John Clarke can scarcely be over-estimated. In the principles which he caused to be incorporated in the plantation of Rhode Island at its beginning, and which he diligently watched over and preserved, in the constant public employments in which he was engaged for the united plantations of the island and

careful, to publish whatever they could find, which might seem to countenance the severities, they used towards dissenters from their way, that I expected to find something of that nature against Mr. Clarke; but have happily been disappointed. Though he was disarmed by them in 1637,[1] and imprisoned and fined at Boston, in 1651, and he exposed their injustice and cruelty, to him and his brethren, in print the next year, and continued in England, to oppose and defeat all their attempts at the Court there against his colony, till he obtained their present charter; yet among all their authors or records, that I have searched, I have not met with a single reflection cast upon him by any one; which I think is very extraordinary. There was doubtless enough said against him, for his principles of believer's baptism and liberty of conscience, to secure him from the wo of being spoken well of by all men; yet, like Daniel, it seems as if

the main, and especially in his work as agent for the colony in England, in securing the liberal charter under which Rhode Island as a colony and afterwards as a State was governed and prospered for nearly two centuries, he took his rank second to none, certainly, but Roger Williams, among Rhode Island's benefactors. His work has probably never been appreciated as it deserves, his fame having been unduly overshadowed by that of his contemporary, the founder of Providence.

Whether he accepted the peculiar sentiments of the Baptists among those of that faith in England, or alone in the wilds of America, we do not know; but his views on these and other points of Christian doctrine, are so clear and scriptural that they might stand as the confession of faith of Baptists today, after more than two centuries of experience and investigation.

The testimony which Backus proceeds to give to the purity of his character and to his good name, even among his enemies, has been fully corroborated by later writers. Says Allen, in his Biographical Dictionary, "His life was so pure that he was never accused of any vice which has left a blot on his memory." Bancroft says of him, "Never did a young commonwealth possess a more faithful friend," and calls him "the modest and virtuous Clarke, the persevering and disinterested envoy, who, during a twelve years' mission had sustained himself by his own exertions and a mortgage on his estate; whose whole life was a continued exercise of benevolence, and who, at his death, bequeathed all his possessions for the relief of the needy and the education of the young. Others," he adds, "have sought office to advance their fortunes; he, like Roger Williams, parted with his little means for the public good. He had powerful enemies in Massachusetts, and left a name without a spot." History of the United States, Vol. II, pp. 61, 64, 65.—ED.

[1] A "Mr. Clarke" was among those disarmed, but whether the John Clarke of this history, may be questioned. See p. 70, note.—ED.

his enemies could find no fault in him in matter of the kingdom, but only concerning the law of his God.

Few men ever merited the title of a patriot more than he did; for he was a principal procurer of Rhode Island, for sufferers and exiles. And when their rights and liberties were grossly invaded, he crossed the boisterous ocean, and exerted all his influence, in twelve years' watchful and diligent labors for his colony, at the British Court, till he obtained a new charter for them, of great and distinguishing privileges; for the accomplishment of which, he mortgaged his own estate in Newport, willing to venture his all, in so good a cause, though he was not insensible of the covetousness and ingratitude of some great pretenders to liberty in that colony; whose influence had caused a great deal of trouble and expense to Mr. Williams, without any suitable recompence.[1] The inventions of men are scarce ever more

---

[1] Six years after Mr. Williams obtained their first charter, viz.: On March 22, 1650, he presented a paper to the deputies and inhabitants of Providence, which contained four requests for others, and a fifth for himself, wherein he says:—" I cannot be so unthankful to you, and so insensible of my own family's comfort, as not to take notice of your continued and constant love and care, in your many public and solemn orders for the payment of that money due unto me about the charter. It is true, I have never demanded it; yea, I have been truly desirous, that it might have been laid out for some further public benefit in each town; but observing your loving resolution to the contrary, I have at last resolved to write unto you (as I have also lately done to Portsmouth and Newport) about the better ordering of it to my advantage. I have here, through God's providence, conveniency of improving some goats; my request is therefore, that, if it may be without much trouble, you would please to order the payment of it in cattle of that kind. I have been solicited, and have promised my help about iron works, when the matter is ripe; earnestly desirous every way to further the good of the town of Providence, to which I am so much engaged, and to yourselves the loving inhabitants thereof, to whom I desire to be your truly loving and ever faithful

ROGER WILLIAMS."

Yet he never received all his pay for that first charter. And though the first Assembly that met after they received the second, voted Mr. Clarke the reward that has been mentioned, yet they were very backward about fulfilling their promise. Their General Assemblies from year to year, wrote to stir up the towns thereto; but at the Assembly of April 2, 1672, an account was exhibited, examined, approved and attested by Governor Arnold and three Assistants, which is now extant under their own hands, wherein it appears, that when Mr. Clarke obtained said charter, he had received but two hundred and twenty-one pounds, three shillings, though the char-

fruitful, than in finding out ways to get money, and excuses to keep it; but how few have parted with it for public good, so freely as Mr. Williams and Mr. Clarke did!

After Mr. Clarke's return, he was improved in various public offices; was elected Deputy Governor three years successively, in two of which he accepted the office; but all the concern of the State did not prevail with him, as it has done with many, to neglect the affairs of religion. His church records and other writings prove, the continuance of his pastoral relation to the first church in Newport, and his care and labors to uphold gospel worship, and discipline therein. And the instrument by which he settled his last concerns in this world, shows what his faith and hopes were, as to that which is to come; for therein he says:—

Whereas, I, John Clarke of Newport, in the colony of Rhode Island and Providence Plantations in New England, physician, am at this present, through the abundant goodness and mercy of my God, though weak in my body, yet sound in my memory and understanding, and being sensible of the inconveniencies that may ensue in case I should not set my house in order before this spirit of mine be called by the Lord to remove out of this tabernacle, do therefore make and declare this my last will and testament, in manner following; willing and readily resigning up my soul unto my merciful Redeemer, through faith in whose death I firmly hope and believe to escape from that second hurting death, and through his resurrection and life, to be glorified with him in life eternal. And my spirit being returned out of this frail body, in which it hath conversed for about sixty-six[1] years my will is, that it be decently interred, without any vain ostentation, between my loving wives Elizabeth and Jane, already deceased, in hopeful expectation, that the same Redeemer who hath laid down a price both for my soul

ter with his time and pains cost six hundred and fifty-one pounds, seventeen shillings, ten pence; one hundred pounds of which was then due to him, and was ordered to be paid in provision pay, two pounds for one; but he never received any of it in his life time. By his papers I find that he mortgaged his estate in Newport, to Captain Richard Deane, of London, the same month that he procured the charter, and that it was not taken up till September 5, 1699, when the last payment of one hundred and fifteen pounds was made to Captain Deane's heirs.

[1]The article on John Clarke in Allen's Biographical Dictionary, places his death at the age of fifty-six. It also states that Mr. Clarke paid the fine which was assessed upon him in Boston in 1651. See pp. 225, 237, 248. These things are mentioned because this article is often referred to, and, except these errors, is correct and valuable.—Ed.

and body, will raise it up at the last day a spiritual one, that they may together be singing hallelujah unto him to all eternity.[1]

Oh! what miserable things are all earthly pleasures or glories, when compared with such a life, and such a death! "Mark the perfect man, and behold the upright; for the end of that man is peace."

It has often been observed, that when one heavy affliction comes upon a person or people, others soon follow; which

[1] Copied from the original will, dated April 20, 1676. He quitted our world the same day. As he left no child, he gave many legacies to his relations and friends, both in that colony and in the Massachusetts. His brother Joseph Clarke was early a member of the church in Newport with him, and was often magistrate of the colony; whose son Joseph was also a member of that church, and then of the church in Westerly, where his posterity are numerous and respectable to this day. Elder Clarke, gave a particular lot of land in Newport, to his brother's son John, whose posterity have also been respectable among the Baptists ever since, one of whom is Mr. Edward Clarke, now a gospel preacher near Providence. Then, after giving a small lot in town to his church, and giving his wife the use of his house and farm, containing more than a hundred and fifty acres, of upland and marshes, together with ten acres in a part of Newport, called the Neck, during her life, he gave said farm and Neck to his friends, William Weeden, Philip Smith and Richard Bailey and to their assigns, "qualified and chosen in manner following forever; that is to say, that when it shall happen that either of them three decease, the two surviving shall make choice of an understanding person, fearing the Lord, to succeed in the place of him so deceased; and in case the two surviving differ in their choice of the person to succeed in the room of him so deceased, that then the choice shall be decided by lot; which person so chosen shall be the assignees of the said persons above-mentioned, and shall have equal power to act with them in all matters relating to the disposal of the profit or rent of the said land and farm, from time to time; and so all persons chosen as above said to make good the said number of three, shall be deemed and taken to be the assigns of the said William Weeden, Philip Smith and Richard Bailey, and none other; which said persons and their assigns, from time to time, chosen and succeeding as above said, shall be seized of the said farm and land called The Neck, to the use and uses following forever; that is to say, faithfully and truly to distribute and dispose of the rent and profit of my said farm and land, for the relief of the poor, or bringing up children unto learning, from time to time, forever, according to such instructions as I shall give unto them, bearing even date with these presents." Which instructions are in these words viz., "That in the disposal of that which the Lord hath bestowed on me, and I have now betrusted you with, you and your successors, shall have special regard and care, to provide for those that fear the Lord; and in all things, and at all times, so to discharge the trust which I have reposed in you, as may be most for the glory of the Most High, and the good and benefit of those for whom it is by me expressly designed. JOHN CLARKE."

His estate was appraised at one thousand and eighty pounds, twelve shillings, by James Barker, Thomas Ward, and Philip Edes, who made oath to the inventory May

observation was remarkably verified this year. For beside those already named, Mr. Mark Luker, an ancient member, and a ruling Elder of Mr. Clarke's church, died the December after him, leaving the character of a very worthy walker.

About the beginning of 1677, came out Mr. Williams's account of his dispute with the Quakers, upon which Mr. Coddington wrote over to his friend Fox, and said :—

Here is a lying, scandalous book of Roger Williams, of Providence, printed at Cambridge, in New England. .... I have known him about fifty years; a mere weathercock; constant only in inconstancy; poor man! that doth not know what should become of his soul, if this night it should be taken from him. He was for the priests, and took up their principles to fight against the truth, and to gratify them and bad magistrats, that licked up his vomit, and wrote the said scurrilous book; and so hath transgressed for a piece of bread. And so are all joined with the red dragon to pour out their flood against the man-child. Into their secrets let not my soul come; my honor be not thou united. Dear G. F., I may yet more prove what I have said. One while he is a Separatist at New Plymouth, joining with them till they are weary of him (as from Morton's Memorial, in print, doth appear;) another time you may have him placed a teacher or a member of the church at Salem. O, then a great deal of devotion is pleaded in women wearing of vails in their assemblies, as if the power of godliness was in it; and to have the cross out of the colors; and then to be against the king's patent and authority, and writeth a large book in quarto against it. And another time he is hired for money, and gets a patent from the Long Parliament, so that it is not long but he is off and on it again. One time for men's wearing caps, and not hats for covering their faces; and again, hats and no caps; one time for water baptism, men and women must be plunged into the water; and then throw it all down again;

17, 1666. Said farm and Neck they appraised at five hundred and thirty pounds, and its late annual income has been two hundred and twenty dollars; as the honorable Josias Lyndon, Esq., one of the assigns, informs me; who says, the first assigns being Mr. Clarke's intimate friends, were informed by him, that his intent was to provide for religious as well as civil instruction, though he did not insert the word *ministry*, lest the national clergy should lay claim to it. Therefore part of said profits have been improved to maintain religious teaching in that church ever since. Complaint was made in 1721, that one of these assigns was unfaithful in his trust, which caused the Assembly to take the case in hand; who at length made a law to empower the Town Council in each town to enquire how all charitable donations therein were managed, and by a jury of twelve men, upon oath, to assess damages upon delinquents; to whom therefore the assigns above-said have annually been accountable ever since.

so that Cotton (who in his day did know the power of God to salvation) said of him, that he was a harberdasher of small questions against the power. So they ought to have feared God and the king, that is to punish evil doers ; and therefore not to meddle to their hurt, with him that is given to change.

He goes on to say he was credibly informed that Governor Leverett said he would give twenty pounds, and Governor Winslow five pounds, rather than that book should not be printed. Scott's letter, which is mentioned in page 89, was also written on this occasion, wherein, after accusing Mr. Williams of acting contrary to his own principle of liberty of conscience, he says :—

> Witness his presenting of it to the Court at Newport; and when this would not take effect, afterwards when the Commissioners were two of them at Providence, being in the house of Thomas Olney, senior, Roger Williams propounded this question to them :—We have a people here among us, who will not act in our government with us ; what course shall we take with them? George Cartwright, one of the Commissioners, asked him what manner of persons they were? Do they live quietly and peaceably amongst you? This they could not deny. Then he made this answer, If they can govern themselves, they have no need of your government; at which they were silent. This was told again by a woman of the house where the speech was spoken, to another woman, whom the complaint, with the rest, was made against, who related it to me ; but they are both dead, and cannot bear witness with me, to what was spoken there.[1]

These letters being sent over with the book to Fox, he, with John Burnyeat, published them, with an answer to Williams, in 1678, which they entitled, A New England Firebrand Quenched. Fox's former book in folio, Williams says, was written against about six score authors and papers, to which Edward Burroughs wrote a preface ; and some things that they said in the dispute, turned his thoughts so, as from those names he called his work, George Fox digged out of his Burroughs. Such titles were more common in that day than ours, but I have nothing to say to justify them, nor a great deal of the language that was used on both sides. What I am concerned with is fact and not language. As Mr. Wil-

[1] Fox, Part Second, pp. 245, 248.

liams had occasion to vindicate many things in the writings of Mr. Richard Baxter, Dr. John Owen, and others that Fox had written against, whom Williams calls pious and learned men; he prefixed a particular address to them, in which he says :—

As to matters in difference between yourselves and me, I have willingly omitted them, as knowing that many able and honest seamen in their observations of the sun, (one picture of Christ Jesus) differ sometimes in their reckonings, though uprightly aiming at, and bound for one port and harbor. I humbly beg of you, 1. That you will more and more earnestly, candidly and Christianly study the things that differ without reflecting upon credit, maintenance, liberty, and life itself, remembering who it was that said, He that loves his life shall lose it. 2. More and more study the prophesies and the signs of the times. You know when it was that five bishops, twenty-two ministers, and almost three hundred other precious believers in the true Lord Jesus, were sacrificed in the flames, for his ever blessed sake, against that monstrous man of sin and bloody whore of Rome. These Foxians' fancy is but a feather to those high Pico's and Tenariffs, the Pope and Mahomet, whom some of you may live to see flung into the lake that burns with fire and brimstone.

To this they answer and say :—

Here you may see, though there is, and hath been, great difference betwixt R. W., R. B. and J. O.,[1] yet all these have written against God's people, that are in the truth. .... But it is well if they come to repentance for what they have done, for imprisoning and persecuting us, when they had both the sword and the bag. And so R. W. and the rest of the New England priests, have been one with them in the spirit of envy and malice against the people of God, like the wily foxes, whose blood lieth at all your doors. .... All may see what a devilish and unchristian mind is in this R. W. whose desires are to R. B. and J. O., that they may see Mahomet, and the Turk, and the whore of Rome, and us, (that he joins with them) flung into the lake of fire.[2]

And in answer to his attempt to prove that pride about spiritual matters was the root and branch of their religion they say :—

Roger, this is their condition, and the New England priests' and professors'. Oh! that your eyes were open that you might see it! and so what thou measurest to others, it will be measured to thee again, pressed down

[1] Roger Williams, Richard Baxter and John Owen.—ED.
[2] Fox, pp. 11, 12.

and running over; and the god of the world will fail thee in thy proofs, and hath failed thee; as he did thy[1] mother Eve, and thy father Adam. For this is the mouth of the pit, that thou speakest of, and Lucifer's boast in thee against the children of the Lord, that are daily in jeopardy of their lives, and some of them have lost their lives amongst you in New England, in obedience to the command of Christ their Saviour. And we know they hated Christ our Lord and Master without a cause, and so you do us. But R. W. may say, he doth not persecute with his hands; but let him read page 200 of his book, wherein he declares himself, that a due and moderate restraint he would have inflicted upon us, yea, through pretending conscience; and he would not have this called persecution. But would R. W. be so served himself? No, but now he lives in a peaceable government, where he cannot exercise his cruelty, and he hath not the sword in his hand, but is in a restless spirit, who grudgeth at the liberty of others, and cannot be content with his own.

Again, they mention his plea for liberty against the bloody tenet, in 1652, and say:—

But R. W. is fallen from that plea, who now desireth the magistrates to persecute us, &c., and it must not be called persecution neither, as in page 200, and many things we could bring out of his former books, which would render him very uncertain; but we shall forbear at the present, and leave him to the Lord, for his books declare, themselves, what he said then, and what he saith now. But the reader may see how R. W. hath invented and forged many words against us, the people of God, in scorn called Quakers, which we never spoke nor wrote.[2]

They refer to that page, from one end to the other of their book, to prove him a persecutor; and when the Magnalia came out in 1702, John Whiting wrote an answer the next year, wherein he said of the author, "He compares Roger Williams to a wind-mill, that by his rapid motion was like to set the whole country on fire, ... yet commends him, though such a wind-mill, for his opposition against the Quakers; .... but that haberdasher of small questions against the power of godliness, as their great Cotton called him, was answered by George Fox and John Burnyeat, in another book entitled, A New England Firebrand Quenched."[3] Joseph

[1] Why not *my*?
[2] Fox, pp. 10, 11, Part Second, p. 212. In pp. 241, and 242 they repeat their reference to that page, in like manner.
[3] Whiting against Mather, pp. 55, 56.

Grove published his Abridgment of Bishop, with notes, the same year. And against where Bishop had mentioned Mr. Norton, Grove says, " This is that priest Norton, whom Cotton Mather, in his late History of New England, so much commends, and with his brother in iniquity, John Wilson, ranks with John Cotton, a man of a better spirit in his day."[1]

Thus both parties could extol Mr. Cotton, while they vented their resentment against Mr. Williams at a high rate; and by these means, and by some connection with the Coddington family, Mr. Callender, in his Century Sermon, scrupled to own him for a Baptist,[2] and in the dedication of it, set Mr. Coddington up as the main founder and supporter of that colony. Though by his papers, I find he was afterwards convinced of his error herein. And let us now examine the evidences referred to, to prove those dreadful charges against Mr. Williams.

1. Morton does not represent that the people were weary of him at Plymouth, but that they were backward to grant his request of a dismission to Salem, though their elder pre-

[1] Bishop, p. 124.—B.
The above sentence misplaces the names Norton and Wilson. It should read as follows :—"And against where Bishop had mentioned Mr. Wilson, Grove says, ' This is that priest Wilson, whom Cotton Mather, in his late History of New England, so much commends, and, with his brother in iniquity, John Norton,'" &c.—ED.

[2] Callender says, "Mr. Roger Williams is said, in a few years after his settling at Providence, to have embraced the opinions of the people called (by way of reproach) Anabaptists, in respect to the subject and mode of baptism; and to have formed a church there, in that way, with the help of one Mr. Ezekiel Holliman." To this he adds a note, as follows :—" Since this was transcribed for the press, I find some reasons to suspect that Mr. Williams did not form a church of the Anabaptists, and that he never joined with the Baptist church there. Only, that he allowed them to be nearest the Scripture rule, and true primitive practice, as to the mode and subject of baptism; but that he himself waited for new apostles, &c. The most ancient inhabitants now alive, some of them above eighty years old, who personally knew Mr. Williams, and were well acquainted with many of the original settlers, never heard that Mr. Williams formed a Baptist church there, but always understood that Mr. Browne, Mr. Wickenden or Wiginton, Mr. Dexter, Mr. Olney, Mr. Tillinghast, &c., were the first founders of the church." Upon these words, Elton quotes from Morgan Edwards, " I have one of the Century Sermons of Mr. Callender, with a *dele* upon this note, in his own hand-writing." Century Sermon, Rhode Island Historical Collection, Vol. IV, pp. 109, 110; Materials for a History of the Baptists, Rhode Island Historical Collections, Vol. VI, p. 303.—ED.

vailed with them to do it;[1] and Governor Bradford blessed God for the good effects of his ministry many years after he was banished.[2] 2. Like those he calls New England priests, Coddington tries to draw women's veils, and men's hats and caps over people's eyes, to prevent a just view of those affairs. Mr. Hubbard speaks of those veils, as the first article in his account of the causes of Mr. Williams's banishment, though he is so honest as to let us know, that it was Mr. Skelton who introduced the custom at Salem, which Mr. Williams only concurred with; and Governor Hutchinson shows, that Mr. Cotton had spoken in favor of that mode of dress in England; but now he went to Salem, and preached the people out of conceit of it. And among all Mr. Williams's numerous writings, I have not met with any thing about it; no, nor about his hat or cap, though in the Massachusetts Records, I find that the year before they banished him, when Coddington was both a magistrate and their Treasurer, they made a law against *superfluous and expensive fashions*, wherein they prohibited the making or wearing of *beaver hats* upon penalty of forfeiting of them if they did. 3. As to the cross in the military colors, which Hutchinson also names as a sufficient ground for the authority to take hold of Mr. Williams, it is certain from Winthrop, Hubbard, and the Colony Records, that the Assembly took hold of Endicott, and not Williams, for that act, and put him out of all office for one year therefor; and the Magnalia assures us, that the scruple about that popish sign prevailed in their colony after Mr. Williams was gone out of

---

[1] "He desired his dismission to the church of Salem; which, though some were unwilling to, yet, through the prudent counsel of Mr. Brewster, the ruling elder there, fearing that his continuance amongst them might cause divisions, and there being many abler men in the Bay, they would better deal with him than themselves could, and foreseeing what he prophesied he feared concerning Mr. Williams, which afterwards came to pass, that he would run the same course of rigid separation and anabaptistry which Mr. John Smith, the Se-Baptist at Amsterdam had done, the church of Plymouth consented to his dismission." Morton's Memorial, p. 102.—Ed.

[2] See page 41.

it.¹ 4. Upon the affairs of the patent, Coddington artfully slips in the word "*authority*," willing, with his friend Cotton, to have Williams appear as a rebel against the king. We learn from Governor Winthrop, that Mr. Williams first wrote upon that subject at Plymouth, and after he came to Salem, the Court called for a copy of it, which he granted them, and then, near the close of 1633, they had him before them; but he gave them such satisfaction about it, that they dismissed him; yet they afterward brought in and reëxamined that matter, as one cause of his banishment.² 5. By the foregoing history, the reader may see with what grace the Quakers could accuse Mr. Williams of being mercenary or hired for money, in procuring their first charter. And I find that when he was setting off upon his second agency, to get Mr. Coddington's commission revoked, he, on September 3, 1651, sold his trading house and interest in Narragansett, for fifty pounds, to Mr. Richard Smith.³ His great crime therefore, was his advancing such questions as he did, against the power; which, in plain terms, was a power to frame to themselves a gospel and a Christ without the cross; a power to suspend obedience to what they looked upon to be truth in England, and to compel others to their judgments, when they had got out of the prelates' reach; yea, a power to confirm and support such corruptions by oaths, both there and here.⁴

Mr. Williams says:—

Cases have befallen myself in the chancery in England, &c., of the loss of great sums, which I chose to bear, through the Lord's help, rather than yield to the formality (then and still in use) in God's worship, though I offered to swear in weighty cases, by the name of God, as in the presence of God, and to attest or call God to witness; and the judges told me they would rest in my testimony and way of swearing, but they could not dispense with me without an act of parliament.⁵

¹Book 7, p. 11. [Vol. II, pp. 433--435.]—B.
The Magnalia also states that Mr. Williams was "but obliquely and remotely concerned" with this matter. Ibid, p. 433.—ED.
²Williams's reply to Cotton, p. 277.   ³Newport Records.
⁴See page 56.   ⁵Against the Quakers, Appendix, pp. 59, 60.

And in the face of all their reproaches, I am bold in it, that I know not of one Pædobaptist or Quaker, that came to this country in that age, who acted so consistently and steadily upon right principles about government and liberty, as Mr. Williams did; neither do I think that they had, or have, any cause to glory over him as to religion. Though Mr. Cotton represented it as a mere pretence for him to tell of church government, when he did not join fully with any church that was then extant, yet he replies and says:—

> The institution of any [state] government and order is one thing, and the administration and execution, which may be interrupted and eclipsed, is another. [Indeed] Jeremiah could not rightly have been judged a pretender, when he mourned for and lamented the desolations of the temple, priests, elders, altar and sacrifices; and neither he nor Daniel, nor any of God's [prophets or] servants, could, during the desolation and captivity, acknowledge either temple [or] altar, or sacrifice aright, extant upon the face of the earth..... Although the discusser be not satisfied in the period of the times, and the manner of Christ's [his] glorious appearing, yet his soul uprightly desires to see and adore, and to be thankful to Master Cotton, yea to the least of the disciples of Christ, for any coal or spark of true light, among so many false and pretended candles and candlesticks.[1]

Now as no man was permitted by Ezra, to officiate as a priest at God's altar, but those who could find their register of a lawful descent from Aaron, and the church had been through a more terrible captivity in mystical Babylon, between the apostolic age and that we are upon, than the Jews had in Chaldea; how could a man, so honest as Mr. Williams was, receive any man to administer the ordinance of the Supper to him, who could not produce a register of his succession from the apostles?[2] I know of no other consistent way, to get over this difficulty but this; that as the lawful seed of Aaron were to govern in the Jewish church, so are the spiritual seed of Christ to govern in his church, into which none ought to be admitted, without gospel evidence of their being such; and it seems that Mr. Williams had not attained to a clear settlement in this point. But in

[1] Reply to Cotton, pp. 106, 107.   [2] See page 91.

my opinion his greatest mistake, when he first came to this country was, his blending the duties of natural and revealed religion too much together. The light of nature teaches the importance of seeking to God for what we need, and of praising him for what we receive; which duties ought to be inculcated upon all men, as much as love to God or our neighbors; while the revealed institutions of baptism and the supper, are tokens of fellowship with Christ, and therefore cannot be our duty to perform before we are united to him. Psalms, 107; Acts 17. 27; Rom. 1. 20, 21, and 6. 3—5; I Cor. 10. 16. But for a while, Mr. Williams seemed to limit these two kinds of duties alike to the regenerate. It is also well known, that the divine rule is perfect, but that the best of men in this state are imperfect, and how far we are to exercise forbearance, and how far not, has not been an easy question to the most enlightened saints; yet Mr. Williams's grand crime in the view of both of these parties, was because he would not yield to their power in this matter. The passage the Quakers so often appealed to, as an evidence of his being a bloody persecutor, is as follows:—

An author had said, "The Quakers' spirit doth teach them to honor no man." Upon which Fox said:—

"That is a *lie*; for it teacheth them to have all men in esteem and to honor all men in the Lord; yet they are convinced by the law as transgressors if they respect men's persons as you do.

In reply to which Mr. Williams says:—

All men may see how truly they honor all in the Lord, and what Lord they mean, when his first word to his opposite is that most provoking term, *That is a lie*. It is true that Christ Jesus and his servants, used sharp reproofs, similitudes, &c., but thus suddenly, at the first dash, to give fire, *Thou liest, That is a lie*, &c., shows neither religion nor civility, but a barbarous spirit, for they that know the barbarians, know how common that word is in all their mouths..... The most Holy and only Wise knows how proudly and simply and barbarously they have run into uncivil and inhuman behavior towards all their superiors, the eldest and highest, how they have declared by principle and practice, that there are no men to be respected in the world but themselves, as being Gods and Christs. It is true our English Bibles and grammar (as Fox in his great learning often objects) makes *Thou* to a single person; and *Thou* in Holy Scripture is used in a grave and respective way unto superiors, unto kings and parents, and God himself. But, 1. the Hebrew and Greek signify no more *Thou* than *You*, and so may be truly turned. 2. Every nation, every shire, every calling, have their particular properties or idioms of speech, which are improper and ridiculous with others. Hence these simple reformers are extremely ridiculous in giving *Thou* and *Thee* to every body, which our nation commonly gives to familiars only; and they are insufferably proud and contemptuous unto all their superiors in using *Thou* to every body, which our English idiom or propriety of speech, useth in a way of familiarity, or anger, scorn and contempt. I have therefore publicly declared myself, that a due and moderate restraint, and punishing of these incivilities, (though pretending conscience) is so far from persecution, (properly so called) that it is a duty and command of God unto all mankind, first in families, and thence into all human societies.[1]

This is all the passage in his whole book that speaks in favor of punishing Quakers; and compared with the instance of Norton's incivilities to Governor Prince[2] and others, and observing that the emphasis lies upon their manner of using those words, the reader will judge, whether a moderate punishing of the same, is any ways inconsistent with Mr. Williams's plea for liberty, against Mr. Cotton. As to his practice, we learn expressly that the instance Scott refers to at Newport, was that of Harris, at the election, in 1655.[3] And though he and Mr. Coddington submitted to Mr. Williams's government the next year, (a few months before the Quakers arrived) yet, after that, they and others became so

---

[1] Williams, pp. 199, 200.—B.

In some parts of England, the pronoun of the second person, singular, is employed, as is the case in the German language, only in addressing those with whom the speaker is most intimate and familiar; and to use it in addressing others, and especially superiors, would be, not merely eccentric but highly disrespectful. There seems to have been something of this idiom in the New England colonies.

The explanation which Backus proceeds to give of the above-cited words of Williams, is undoubtedly correct, that it was not the mere use of *Thee* and *Thou*, by Quakers, which he thought proper to restrain, but such language to Magistrates as they had been often known to employ, plainly intended to express irreverence and disrespect.—ED.

[2] See page 256.—ED.   [3] See page 241.—ED.

spiritual as to refuse to act therein. This, it seems, caused Mr. Williams to ask Mr. Cartwright what they should do with them, which, in their view, was another proof of his persecuting disposition. In 1665 their Assembly framed an engagement to the government, which they hoped those men would have taken, and so have come in to act with them again; but in March, 1666, they pleaded that they could not in conscience do it, and prevailed with the Assembly to make a law, to allow those who pleaded that they could not in conscience take either that engagement or the oath of allegiance in England, to make their submission to the government, either before the Court or before two magistrates, in their own words, instead of any that others could frame for them. And no sooner was this point gained, than, at the election in May ensuing, they got in a Quaker Deputy Governor, and three magistrates; two of the latter being Coddington and Harris;[1] Harris was in the same office in 1667, when, on July 2, he procured an extraordinary meeting of the Assembly, to try Mr. Fenner, (another magistrate,) for a rout which Harris had charged him with making in Providence, on June 3. But the Assembly acquitted Fenner, and fined Harris fifty pounds, and put him out of office, choosing Stephen Arnold in his stead. The next fall he was fined ten shillings for breach of peace, and bound to his good behavior. Yet he had influence enough in May, 1668, to get again into the magistracy, and in the fall to have his fifty pounds remitted. He was likewise in the same office in 1669; and as Connecticut then revived their claim to the Narragansett country, he eagerly turned to assist them, hoping, doubtless, to share largely therein, if they prevailed.

It seems that the agents who procured their charters, agreed that some persons living near Mr. Smith's trading house in Narragansett, should have liberty to choose which

---

[1] Mr. Backus afterwards became convinced that Harris was not a Quaker. See Appendix A., at the close of this volume.—ED.

government they would be under; therefore from thence, and from the words of Connecticut charter, they set out afresh to grasp all that country to themselves. And for that end they would come over from Stonington and knock Westerly people down, and carry them off to jail, and persisted long in those encroachments, against the remonstrances of the authority of Rhode Island colony; one of which they sent by Mr. John Crandal to Hartford, in May, 1671. The Assembly at the same time made choice of Mr. Clarke as their agent, to go again to England upon the affair; though, after repeated applications to Connecticut Court, such a prospect appeared of having the matter settled by treaty, that they revoked that appointment the next year. But Harris, finding that the king's words in their charter had most explicitly fixed Paucatuck River as the bounds betwixt the two colonies, openly attacked the validity of the charter, because therein the king had granted full religious liberty, notwithstanding the penal laws in England. Upon which Harris declared, "that the king cannot dispense with the penal laws on the consciences of his subjects, papists or protestants, at home or abroad." Their rulers then were Benedict Arnold, Governor; John Clarke, Deputy Governor; John Cranston, John Coggshall, James Barker, William Carpenter, Thomas Harris, Roger Williams, William Baulston, John Albro, John Green, Benjamin Smith, Assistants; John Sanford, Recorder; James Rogers, General Sergeant; and Joseph Tory, Attorney General. They committed Harris to prison for denying the king's authority and prerogative. When the Assembly met at Newport, April 2, 1672, he presented a petition to them by the hand of a Quaker, but, because " not directed in those words which his Majesty, in his gracious charter, hath pleased to give the title unto the corporation, [viz., His Majesty's Colony of Rhode Island and Providence Plantations, &c.,"] the Assembly voted not to take cognizance of it.[1] At their election the next month, they chose the first

[1] Colony Records.

Quaker Governor[1] they ever had in that colony; and Mr. Williams says, "The Quakers prevailing, Harris, by their means gets loose."[2] These facts I have carefully collected from their colony records, compared with Mr. Williams's account; to which they return no better answer than to say, "It is like he doth belie W. H. as he hath done us; and, for thy story and anger against William Harris, he is of age and able enough to speak for himself."[3]

Fox and other noted teachers of theirs were now come over, and gained many proselytes; upon which Mr. Williams went to a general meeting they had at Newport, and began to present to them some considerations concerning the true Christ and the false, the true spirit and the false, but says, "I was cut off in the midst, by the sudden prayer of one, and singing of another," &c., which is afterward explained thus, viz.:—

> I was stopped by the sudden praying of the Governor's wife, who also told me of her asking her husband at home, (meaning Christ, which I touched upon). I rose and said, if a man had so alleged, I would have answered him; but I would not countenance the violation of God's order so much in making a reply to a woman in public. Hereupon J. Nichols stood up and said, In Christ Jesus neither male nor female. I was replying to him and to J. Burnyeat's speech concerning their spirit, but was stopped by Burnyeat's sudden falling into prayer, and dismissing the assembly. I resolved, with God's help, to be patient and civil, and so ceased, not seeing a willingness in them for me to proceed; which experience made me not trouble G. Fox and the assembly at Providence, but rather to make a fair and solemn offer of a dispute about these matters."[4]

To this they answer and say:—

> o here thou mayest see, it was thy spirit that was cut by the spirit of God, that led them to pray and sing in order, and this thou callest Confusion; and thus thou judgest of things thou knowest not, with thy doting spirit. For the true Christ we know, who is our Shepherd; and the false spirit of Christ is easily savored in thee, which was cut off by the spirit of prayer, and the spirit of singing, from the true spirit of Christ.[5]

---

[1] John Cranston.—Ed. [2] Williams, pp. 14, 206, 207.
[3] Fox, pp. 21, 229.   [4] Williams, pp. 2, 12.   [5] Fox, p. 17.

Thus each party call their own way Order; but the order and decency which the inspired apostle enjoined upon the church of Cornith, concerned the behavior of their women, as distinguished from men; their women who had husbands, in the plural number, who had each a distinct part to act in divine worship, which they ought to know and attend unto. As all saints are one in Christ, there is but one Husband and one bride; and viewing things in this distinct light, tends both to purity and peace; but the confounding of literal women with mystical husbands, has often produced the grapes of Sodom and clusters of Gomorrah. And among the many instances of the Quakers assuming a power to govern the Scriptures, instead of being governed by them, take the following.

The Baptist churches in Wales, gathered by our Mr. Miles and others, published a confession of their faith, wherein they adopted the words of David in Psalm, 51 : 5 ; to which Fox in page 214 of his former book said, " David doth not say, *You* were conceived in sin, but *I*. John was sanctified from the womb; and the Scriptures speak of children that are clean. And so you do not speak as elders and messengers of true churches, or men dividing the word aright, but you are one against another, though you are all against them you call Quakers that be in the truth." " In which passage," says Mr. Williams, " he discovers a strong presumption that he never felt what the woful estate of all mankind by nature is."[1] To which they reply and say, " Paul saith, I am crucified with Christ (mark *I am*) and Christ liveth in me; and the life that I live in the flesh, is by the faith of the son of God, &c.; is not the faith victory? and thou fallest a railing, and speaking of our conditions, which thou art ignorant of, and thy own, and hast abused both the Scriptures and us."[2]

In July, 1672, Mr. Williams drew up fourteen propositions, and inclosed them in a letter to Deputy Governor

---

[1] Williams, Appendix, pp. 66. 67. [2] Fox, Second part, p. 136.

Cranston, whom he styles, "My kind friend," for him to deliver them to Fox or his friends; in which Mr. Williams proposed a fair dispute upon those points with any of them, seven propositions to be handled at Newport, and the others at Providence, on the days they should appoint. By some means the matter was delayed till Fox had sailed for England; after which John Stubs, John Burnyeat and William Edmundson, engaged in the affair, and with them, Williams held the dispute at Newport, on the 9th, 10th and 12th of August, and at Providence the 17th. When they began at Newport, he publicly declared his motives to be these:—

1. The vindicating his most Holy Name, which my soul saw trodden in the dirt by Satan clothed in Samuel's mantle, and the bright garment of an angel of light, which once he was, but pride deceived him. 2. I had in my eye the vindicating this colony for receiving such persons whom others would not. We suffer for their sakes, and are accounted their abettors, that therefore, together with the improvement of our liberties which the God of Heaven, and our king's majesty have graciously given us, I might give a public testimony against their opinions in such a way and exercise, I judged it incumbent upon my spirit and conscience to do (in some regards) more than most in the colony. I may also truly say, 3. That I had it in my eye, that this exercise might occasion some soul-consideration in many.[1]

As they dwelt so much upon the word *Light*, and upon its coming into the world with all mankind, he asked them in public:—

Whether it comes into them at the conception, or at the birth, or when else? whether it was in all mankind before the coming and death of Christ, or to those since his coming, or both? whether it be in the understanding, will, memory, affections, in any of them severally, or lodged in all of them jointly?[2]

In answer to this they say:—

As to his unlearned questions, whether the light cometh into mankind at the conception, or at the birth, or when else? we leave him to what is written John 1: 9. Christ is the true light, that lighteth every man that cometh into the world. So it is evident, all are lighted that come into the world; and the believers witnessed it to shine in their hearts, and Abraham saw his light, or day; and in it David saw more light, which was

[1] Williams, pp. 25, 26.   [2] Williams, p. 35.

before Christ came in the flesh; John saith, in the Word which was in the beginning, was life, and the life was the light of men.[1]

Mr. Williams says:—

The hinge and pinch of the difference lies in the opposition which the Quakers make against the manhood of Christ Jesus to be yet extant..... Who questions but Christ Jesus, as the sun in the heavens, influenceth all parts of the world in several respects, and nothing is hid from his heat? He is felt in the bruised reed and smoking flax; in the poor in spirit; in the hungry and thirsty after righteousness; sometimes in the hope of glory to come, yea, in present joy unutterable and glorious; sometimes the Lamb's wife is visibly asleep though her heart wakes; sometimes she is alarmed by his knocking and is sluggishly unwilling to open to him; sometimes she rises and opens but he is gone, and she feels for him by day and night, and cannot find him.

Again he says:—

The Papists, Arminians and Quakers are one; 1. As to the power of nature and free will in heavenly and spiritual matters; 2. As to the losing of true saving grace; 3. As to election and predestination in time, upon obedience, and rejection, and reprobation upon rebellion and disobedience.. .... 4. The Quakers are brethren with the Socinians, in making Christ a type and figure, a pattern and example how Christians ought to walk; not that the blood which he shed upon the cross at Jerusalem, was a sufficient price and satisfaction unto God for the sins of the whole world.[2]

To which they say:—

This is like the rest of thy false charges and comparisons; and what dost thou talk of election and predestination, &c., when thou callest the light of Christ an idol? for these are mysteries to thee, who art not come to take heed unto the light that shineth in a dark place.[3] [See II Cor. 10. 12.]

His last proposition was, that their spirit tended to arbitrary government and fiery persecution; upon which he says:—

By an arbitrary government, I do not intend a ruling by force, for there could be no government in the world without the sword, but arbitrary, I said, came from *arbitrium*, which signifies will or pleasure; and so my argument is, that, persons immediately speaking from God, it is impertinent and profane to clog and cumber them with laws, for the voice of God, the law of laws, proceeds out of their mouth, than which there could be none

---

[1] Fox, p. 32.   [2] Williams, p. 137; Appendix, p. 56.   [3] Fox, p. 154.

more just, wise or holy. . . . . I told them I must crave their patience while I must profess my fears, lest the spirit by which they were guided, might run them upon their own and others' temporal destruction. I told them I thought they had no such thing in their eye at present; but if power of the sword came into their hands, it was easy to imagine, that whom the spirit (infallible) decreed to death, peasant or prince, if it were possible, he must be executed.[1]

To this they say :—

Where there is no force there is no fear of slavery, and such an arbitrary government no body was ever afraid of. . . . . But Roger, dost thou not accuse the people called Quakers of holding, that they are acted by the Spirit of God, and not by their own spirits? If so, it is the *arbitrium* or will and pleasure of their God, and not their own wills and spirits that they are acted by; and what harm is this to just government? or how doth this set up men's will and power? O, thy blindness! thy darkness! and thy confusion!²[2]

He then referred them to the passage before recited about the magistrate's subjecting all into his light; and closed that head with observing, that Christ says, Out of the abundance of the heart the mouth speaketh; and asks if any professors of the Christian name except Papists, were ever so sharp and cutting with their tongue, as they, even to knowing and conscientious persons? From whence he questions, what might be expected if whips, swords and halters were permitted to fall into their hands? To which they say :—

The tongues of God's people have in all ages been as a fire and a sword to the wicked. . . . . It may be as rationally questioned of the people of God in this age, as in former ages; and God will reckon with thee, thou ungodly, unjust man, that insinuatest these wicked things against a suffering, as well as harmless people! This spirit thou art led by, in writing against us, would burn us, as it led thy forefathers to burn the martyrs in Smithfield; for ye are all of Cain's race, and are found in his steps, and shall have Cain's reward if you repent not.[3]

This was their way of *quenching a firebrand.*

The Quakers prevailed so far, that in 1675, Mr. Coddington was Governor, and Mr. John Easton[4] Deputy Gov-

---

[1]Williams, p. 204. [2]Fox, p. 226. [3]Fox, p. 231.
[4]John Easton was the son of Nicholas Easton, mentioned on pp. 78, 97.—ED.

ernor; when, finding that their spiritual power would not secure them against the Indians, they gave out military commissions under their hands and seals to arm both vessels and garrisons against them.[1] Harris was again chosen an Assistant in the years '73, '74 and '76, in the last of which Mr. S. Hubbard said in a letter to Boston, " The Quakers are still uppermost in government among us; I mean in outward rule, though we have put out the chief, Mr. John Easton, from being Deputy, and now Major John Cranston is Deputy Governor." Mr. Williams's book came out soon after, and at their next election, May 2, 1676, the Quakers were left out of office; and on June 28, Mr. Coddington wrote the fore-cited letter to his friend Fox; which facts may enable us to account for the spirit of it. Mr. Williams was again chosen a magistrate, but excused himself from that service; yet he wrote thus to Providence, viz. :—

I pray the town that the place of meeting be certain, and some course settled for payments, that the Clerk and Sergeant be satisfied according to moderation; that the town business may go on cheerfully; that the busi-

[1]Callender, p. 80, [135.] Colony Records.—B.

"It is true the Governor and the Deputy Governor, that year, were both of the people called Quakers, but there are military commissions still in being under their hands and seals, to Mr. B. Arnold, Jun., and others, to go in *an armed sloop to visit the garrisons in Providence.*" Callender, R. I. Hist. Coll., Vol. IV, p. 134.

"To John Cranston, by this present Assembly appointed and chosen Major of this his Majesty's Colony of Rhode Island and Providence Plantations, for the well ordering and managing the military officers in this Colony, and for the defence of the king's subjects herein.

"You are therefore, in his Majesty's name, hereby fully and absolutely required, as Major of all, and singular, the land forces to this Colony belonging, to undertake the conduct, leading and training up of the said forces, and for the preservation of the king's subjects in this Colony, to take care that the said military be put in a suitable and absolute way of defence. You are also, by virtue hereof, to have the absolute command of all the captains and inferior officers with their respective companies within this Colony, to martial, array at your command, and to repair to such place or places as may be most for the king's interest and the safety of the inhabitants here;....and, upon assault of any enemy, with them, or either of them, to use your utmost endeavor to *kill, expulse, expel, take and destroy* all and every the enemies of this his Majesty's Colony, that shall in hostile manner be found acting against the public peace of this Colony and the inhabitants herein.....
WILLIAM CODDINGTON, Governor.
April 11th, 1676."
R. I. Colonial Records.—ED.

ness of the rate (paid by so many already) be finished; that the old custom of order be kept in our meetings, and those unruly be reproved, or upon obstinacy, cast out from sober and freemen's company; that our ancient use of arbitration be brought into esteem again; that (it being constantly reported that Connecticut is upon the gaining his Majesty's consent to enslave us to their parish worship) we consider what we ought to do.

A special Court of Commissioners met at Providence, October 3, 1676, procured by Harris; who by a jury gave his party five verdicts for land, the first of which was against Gregory Dexter, Arthur Fenner, and the town of Providence, wherein they gave, "two pounds in money, damage and cost of Court; and also that the said defendants run the line equally between Pawtuxet River and Wenasquatucket River, till they met with a thwart line from the head of Wenasquatucket River, directly running to Pawtuxet River." The next two verdicts gave that party thirty pounds damages in each, with lands further southward; of which the town of Warwick, by the hands of Mr. Holden and Mr. Greene, gave an account two years after to the king, wherein they mention the former ill treatment they had met with at Boston, and represent that the late war was wholly caused by the arbitrary conduct of the neighboring colonies. After the Narragansett fight in December, 1675, they say:—

> The neighboring colonies withdrew their forces from us, leaving our unguarded towns to the destroyer, whereby the town of Warwick was wholly burnt, great part of our goods and cattle lost and consumed, but the lives of most of us reserved as a prey, supported with hope that yet in time of peace, we might be enabled to rebuild and provide for our distressed families and succeeding generations..... But William Harris of Pautuxet, came over in 1674, and claimed land in Narragansett by Indian purchase, and the king appointed the case to be heard by Commissioners, chosen out of the several colonies of New England. We attended time and place according to summons, but the major part of the Commissioners, elected out of our professed and mortal enemies, out-voted those of Rhode Island, granting and awarding to him the lands bought and improved by your petitioners, also giving him great damages, notwithstanding the testimony of one Mr. Williams, the first Indian purchaser of those lands, and other material witnesses in our behalf, whereby above five thousand acres of land and meadows belonging to the poor town of Warwick, and parts adjacent are

taken away, and we prohibited to rebuild, or attempt anything for the support of our dependences.

They then went on to pray for relief.[1]

The people of Connecticut in the mean time had continued their encroachments upon the west part of that colony, till a letter was obtained from the king, dated July 9, 1679, confirming Rhode Island charter; upon which the Assembly wrote to warn them off their lands, and to charge their own people not to obey them. But at the same time Harris had procured an order from the king to the authority of the colony, to levy the aforesaid executions. In consequence whereof, I have seen warrants issued to John Smith of Newport, appointing him Marshal to levy three of them, signed November 24, 1679, by John Cranston, Governor, Caleb Carr, Joseph Clarke, Arthur Fenner and John Sanford, Assistants. But this not satisfying Harris, he soon set off again for England with new complaints. Mr. Samuel Hubbard wrote to his children at Westerly, the 7th of February, following, informing them of a rumor he heard of turning their Governor out of his place, and of putting a Quaker into it, and of setting Narragansett, which they called the king's province, off by itself; and said he, "William Harris is gone for Old England, displeased at our Court's act, and will not accept, though offered, it is said, to be Connecticut agent's attorney. God can have Ahithophel's counsel to fall and to hang himself." Poor man! he was taken and carried into Turkish slavery, from whence he never returned. Thus ended the controversy with him, whose first title to any of those lands was a free gift from Mr. Williams.

Two considerations have moved me to be much larger and more particular upon these unhappy affairs, than I had any thoughts of at first. One is, that harangues have often been made from pulpits, and in courts of justice, from that time to ours, upon the great disorders of Rhode Island colony, to prove that an established religion by human laws is

[1] See page 239.

exceeding necessary in every government. I thought it duty, therefore, to give the public a fair and full state of those facts, to enable them to judge righteously concerning such addresses. The other is, that I might plainly detect and expose the pernicious nature of imagining that dominion is founded in grace, or that religion endows the subjects of it with a right to act as lawgivers and judges over others. In the Assembly that banished Mrs. Hutchinson, in 1637, Mr. Coddington said, " I do not see any clear witness against her; and you know it is a rule of the Court, that no man may be a judge and accuser too."[1] But where was that rule when he, in his letter to Fox, acted the part of an accuser, witness and judge against Mr. Williams, even as to the inward state of his soul! With all their talk about light, Mr. Cotton formerly[2] and the Quakers now, accused Mr. Williams of counteracting his own principles about liberty of conscience, only for examining and bringing to light the nature of their principles and behavior; and the word of truth tells us what light that is. Matthew 6. 23; John 3. 19, 21. The Quakers have had a fame among many for honesty and liberty, and far be it from me to detract in the least from what has truly been among them of that nature; and I readily grant that not only in those respects, but also in their moderation in dress, and solemnity in worship, (though not singularity) and hospitality to strangers, they have merited high commendation, and more so for their zeal against the slave trade. Yet what a bondage is it to be under such a power as their first leaders assumed! What pope ever spake more haughtily than to say, " He lives in a peaceable government but is in a restless spirit, grudgeth at the liberty of others, and cannot be content with his own," only because he sought in a peaceably way to discharge his conscience, by bearing a plain testimony against what appeared to him to be very corrupt and dangerous? And what sentence was

---

[1] Massachusetts History, Vol. II, p. 516, [444, 445.]
[2] See page 134.

ever more unjust than that which is delivered in their martyr-book? Grove tells us the first part of it was published in 1661, the other in 1667, by that zealous servant of the Lord, George Bishop. He lived in the city of Bristol, and he entitled his work, "New England judged, not by man's, but the Spirit of the Lord." After his account of the whipping of Humphrey Norton and Deborah Wilson, among the rest, he reads off his sentence thus:—

> Whether they will hear or forbear, they shall know that his prophets have been amongst them.....So, see where you are, and in what case, ye blood thirsty enemies of God; ye men of Boston, of Plymouth patent, and New Haven; ye rulers of Sodom, and inhabitants of Gomorrah, who are hardened against the hour of your visitation; whose day is over; who delight in blood, in the blood of the saints of the Most High God, to whom blood will be given, for ye are worthy; the Lord will come upon ye, you that put his day afar off, and say, He delays his coming; I say, He will come upon you, in a day that ye think not of, and in an hour of which ye are not aware; and will cut you asunder, and appoint you your portion with hypocrites and sinners; and ye shall be cast into the lake that burneth with fire and brimstone, there to be tormented with the devil and his angels, which is the second death.

In 1703, in the margin against this sentence, Grove said, "This was fulfilled in the Indian wars, wherein many of them were cut to pieces."[1]

Now, if in Fox's view Mr. Williams discovered a devilish spirit, in telling the ministers he wrote to, that perhaps some of them might live to see the Pope and Mahomet cast into that lake,[2] what a spirit did this great writer of theirs discover? What God did he worship, if this sentence came immediately from him? The evident reason of their favorable opinion of Mr. Cotton above his colleague, was his countenancing the power by which Mrs. Hutchinson declared that she should be delivered, and the Court ruined with their posterity."[3] A gentleman of that Assembly said she told him in London, that she had never any great thing done

---
[1] Bishop Grove's Abridgment, pp. 206, 207.
[2] See page 355.—Ed.   [3] See page 84.

about her, but it was revealed to her beforehand; to which she, before the Court, replied, "I say the same thing again."¹ And how was that revelation fulfilled? Why Bishop says, "Some of your patents endeavored to get Rhode Island under some of your governments, which occasioned some to remove under the Dutch, where Anne Hutchinson, and her son Francis, and W. Collins her son-in-law, with others, were murdered by the Indians; the guilt and weight of whose blood lies upon you, as done by you; who were people of an honest life, and good behavior, only differing from you."² The first legislator and captain that was slain in Philip's war was her son Edward, who, as Bishop tells us, entered his protest at Boston, in 1658, against their making a law to banish Quakers on pain of death. I cannot learn that any man who had ever been an Assistant in either colony was then slain by the Indians, except Mr. John Wickes, of Warwick, who had been a sufferer with Gorton. He was killed at a very advanced age.³ Put all these things together and shall we not say with Solomon, That which is crooked cannot be made straight?

Mr. Williams's zeal appeared to be directed, not against the person of any man, but only against men's errors. In the Preface to his Reply to Mr. Cotton, he says:—

Since it pleased God to lay a command upon [on] my conscience, to come in as his poor witness in this great cause, I rejoiced that it pleased him to appoint so able and excellent [and consciable] an instrument to bolt out the truth to the bran; though [so] I can humbly say in God's holy presence, it is my constant heaviness and soul's grief [as] to differ from any fearing God; [so] much more, [ten thousand times] from Mr. Cotton, whom I have desired, and still desire, highly to esteem and dearly to respect, for so great a portion of mercy and grace vouchsafed unto him, and so many truths of Christ [Jesus] maintained by him. [And] therefore (notwithstanding some of no common judgment and respect to him, have said, he wrote his washings of the bloody tenet in blood against Christ [Jesus] and gall against me, yet) if upon so slippery and narrow a

¹Massachusetts History, Vol. II, p. 510. [441.]
²Bishop, pp. 225, 226. See page 97.
³Callender, p. 93. [148.]

passage, I have slipped into any term or expression unbeseeming his person, or the [matter, the] cause of the Most High in hand [considered,] I humbly crave pardon of God, and Mr. Cotton also.

Although he could not say the like of the chief teachers among the Quakers, yet he said, " Many truly humble souls may be captivated among them. .... And many of the Quakers I love and honor." And he said, "He that shall ponder the fathers' polygamy, the best kings of Judah suffering the high places, David's slaying Uriah, Asa's imprisoning the prophet, Peter's rash using the sword, the disciples' calling for fire from heaven, shall see cause to reprove the Quakers for their rash damning of others from whom they have suffered."[1] But when they came to answer him, they were so far from regarding this admonition, that where he spake of the matter of the Christian churches, viz.: true converts,[2] and said in the margin, " This was, and I hope is, the principle of the New English churches;" they spent three pages full of capitals about their sufferings, to prove that it could not be so, and at last said: " So it is clear, you that have destroyed men's lives, are not of God, but the devil."[3] This was the temper of their teachers; but of others, the two Easton's, father and son, Walter Clarke, and Henry Bull, were all worthy Governors of that denomination, and I find Mr. Samuel Hubbard expressing a considerable esteem also for Mr. Coddington, after his death, in a letter to a friend. Neither have I found one reflection upon his person in all Mr. Williams's writings, unless a plain recital of facts may be so called.

A new sect came out from among the Baptists about this time, who have caused not a little trouble to themselves and others, of whom I have collected the following brief account, chiefly from the letters preserved by Mr. Samuel Hubbard. In the close of the year 1674, the family of Mr. James Rogers, of New London, called Mr. Crandal over from Wes-

---

[1] Williams, pp. 3, 25, 71, 178.   [2] See page 119.   [3] Fox, p. 63, 66.

terly, who preached among them, and baptized his sons John and James, and an Indian named Japheth. This alarmed the other denomination; and Mr. Bradstreet, minister at New London, said he hoped the next Court would take a course with them. They sent to Newport, and Elder Hiscox, Mr. Hubbard and his son Clarke, were sent to visit them in March, 1675, when Jonathan Rogers was also baptized, and all four of them were received as members of their church, by prayer and laying on of hands. Hereupon John Rogers's father-in-law took his wife and children from him; and, upon her complaints against him, he was carried before their Deputy Governor, and committed to Hartford jail, from whence he wrote to Mr. Hubbard April 6, 1675. How long he continued there I do not find, only, he visited the church at Newport the next September. In September 18, 1676, those four members went with a boat, and brought Elder Hiscox and Mr. Hubbard to New London again, when old Mr. Rogers, his wife and daughter, were all baptized and received into that church; whereupon they were called before the magistrate, but were soon released; though, from that time, they began to imprison the Rogerses for working on the first day of the week. And when Mr. Hiscox and Mr. Hubbard visited them again, and held worship with them two miles out of town on their Sabbath, November 23, 1677, and Joseph Rogers's wife had next morning given them a satisfying account of her experiences, John must needs have them go up to town to baptize her there. Mr. Hubbard opposed it, but John carried the day; and while Mr. Hiscox was preaching at town, the constable came and took him, and they all went before the magistrate; where also was the minister, Mr. Bradstreet, who had much to say, about the good way that their fathers had set up. Upon which Mr. Hubbard, obtaining leave to speak, said, "You are a young man, but I am an old planter of about forty years, a beginner of Connecticut, and have been persecuted for my conscience from this colony, and I can assure you, that the old beginners were not for persecution, but we had liberty at first." After further discourse, the magistrate said, Could you not do it elsewhere? "A good answer," says Mr. Hubbard; and so they were released and went to Samuel Rogers's house, where his brother John put himself forward, prayed, and then went out to the water and baptized his sister; upon which Mr. Hiscox was seized again, as supposing he had done it, but John came before the magistrate, and was forward to make known his act therein; so the others were released and returned home.

Jonathan Rogers had married Naomi Burdick, granddaughter to Mr. Hubbard; and on March 2, 1678, Elder Hiscox baptized her at Westerly, together with James Babcock, George Lamphere, and two others; and on the 5th of May following, Joseph Clarke wrote from thence to his father Hubbard, that John and James Rogers with their father were in prison; having previously excommunicated Jonathan, chiefly because he did not retain their judgment of the unlawfulness of using medicines, nor accuse himself before authority, for working on the first day of the week. Hereupon the church at Newport sent messengers to New London about this matter, who reported on their return, that " a practice was started up, (out of conscience) that because the world, yea, most professors, pray in their families mornings and nights, and before meats and after, in a customary way, therefore to forbear prayer in their families or at meats publicly, except some are led forth upon some special occasion; saying they find no command in the word of God for it." About this time, Elder Hiscox's church received letters from Dr. Chamberlain, whereof one was directed to their church, he being of the same faith and order with them, the other was directed as follows:—

Peter Chamberlain, senior, Doctor of both universities, and first and eldest physician in ordinary to his Majesty's person, according to the world, but according to grace, a servant of the word of God; to the excellent and noble Governor of New England; grace, mercy, peace and truth, from

God our Father, and from our Lord Jesus Christ; praying for you, that you may abound in heavenly graces and temporal comforts. I have always had a love to the intended purity, and unspotted doctrine of New England; for Mr. Cotton was of the same college and university, of Emanuel in Cambridge, as I was, and so was Mr. Hooker and others with whom we were all contemporary; and I never knew them but of a holy life and conversation. I also knew Colonel Humfrey, Sir Richard Saltonstall and Mr. Peters, who were of note among you, and Sir Henry Vane, who all had some share in the foundation of your government. But certainly the first intentions were never to debar the truths of Scripture and liberty of conscience guided thereby; but to suppress sin and idolatry, and prevent all the adulteries of Rome, to whom all things are lawful, especially lies in hypocrisy, to promote their most damnable doctrines, covetous superstitions, and blasphemous supremacy. It is great wisdom to suppress sin, but not oppress the liberty of a good conscience; and whilst men grant liberty of conscience, not to admit liberty of sin. All magistrates have not attained to this wisdom, else England had been long since freed from popery and perjury. Whatsoever is against the ten commandments is sin. Rom. 3. 10; I John, 3. 4. And he that sinneth in one point is guilty of all, because he that spake one word of them spake all, and he added no more. Jam. 2. 10, 11; Exo. 20. 1. While Moses and Solomon caution men, so much against adding to, or taking from; Deut. 4. 2; Prov. 30. 5, 6; and so doth the beloved apostle; Rev. 22. 18, 19; what shall we say of those that take away of those ten words, or those that make them void, and teach men so? Nay, they dare give the lie to Jehovah, and make Jesus Christ not only a breaker of the law, but the very author of sin in others, also causing them to break them. Hath not the little horn played his part lustily in this, and worn out the saints of the Most High, so that they become little-horn men also? If you are pleased to inquire about these things, and to require any instances or informations, be pleased by your letters to command it from your humble servant in the Lord Jesus Christ,

PETER CHAMBERLAIN.

Most worthy Governor. September 1, 1677.

Copies hereof were sent to those whom it was directed to; and the church sent a letter therewith to Connecticut, from whence this answer was returned:—

HARTFORD, 8, 8, 78.

FRIENDS OF NEWPORT ON RHODE ISLAND; WILLIAM HISCOX, &c.:— Yours of 9, 4, 78, was received the 7th instant, with one enclosed from another, Peter Chamberlain, senior. The advice in both is readily complied withal and thankfully accepted. To be minded of any parts of the

Scriptures of truth is gratefully received, and were it not for a seducing devil, and a deceitful heart, they would be a rule of life unto all that have senses exercised therein, and make due application thereof. What yourselves or that worthy gentleman intend, or who or what he refers to, is not so easy to guess at. We have of late had to deal with Rogers and his of New London, towards whom the authority have shown all condescension imaginable to us; that if they would forbear to offend our consciences, we should indulge them in their persuasion, and give them no offence in the seventh day, in worshipping God by themselves. We may doubt (if they were governors in our stead) they would tell us, that their consciences would not suffer them to give us so much liberty; but that they must bear witness to the truth, and beat down idolatry, as the old kings did in Scripture; they judging so of our Lord's day worshipping. It may be that your counsel may be more taking with them, to make them forbear, than ours; which is all at present, with respects,

From your friend and servant in Christ,

WILLIAM LEETE.

The church repeatedly sent and labored with them, but to little effect. Mr. Gibson went and lived and preached a while among them at New London; but Mr. Hubbard wrote to their aged brother Thorton, (who had removed from Newport to Providence,) on November 8, 1679, informing him of his late visit to that people, when he found that "old Mr. Rogers, had the wheel of a loaded cart go over his leg a little below his knee, bruising it much, and had been so six weeks, but now could move it; their judgment is not to use any means." And, said he, "pray remember my respects to Mr. Roger Williams; I should be glad to hear of him and his wife;" a great respect to whom was shown in all their letters as long as he lived. On June 7, 1685, Mr. Hubbard wrote to Mr. Henry Reeve of Jamaica, and informed him that messengers were then gone from their church to New London, "to declare against two or more of them that were of us, who are declined to Quakerism, I might say more; of whom be thou aware, for by their principles, they will travel by land and sea to make disciples, yea, sorry ones too. Their names are John and James Rogers, and one Donham."

From this beginning proceeded a sect which has continued to this day, who from their chief leader have been called Rogerenes. In their dialect and many other things, they have been like the first Quakers in this country; though they have retained the external use of baptism and the supper, and have been singular in refusing the use of means and medicines for their bodies. Their greatest zeal has been discovered in going from meeting to meeting, and from town to town, as far as Norwich and Lebanon, (the one fourteen, the other twenty-four miles,) to testify against hireling teachers, and against keeping the first day of the week as a sabbath, which they call the idol-sabbath. And when the authorities have taken them up and fined them therefor, and have sometimes whipped them for refusing to pay it, they have soon published accounts of all such persecutions, which has been the very means of keeping their sect alive. When the small-pox was very terrible in Boston, in 1721, and great fear of it was discovered in the country, John Rogers, their founder, was confident he could go in where it was and not catch it; and to prove his faith, went a hundred miles to Boston, but caught the distemper, came home and died with it, and scattered it in his family; yet his successors still kept on in their way. So late as 1763, some of them repeatedly came and clapped shingles and pieces of boards together around the meeting-house in Norwich town, as well as delivered messages to the worshippers, against their keeping of the Lord's day. But as the rulers had learned so much wisdom as only to remove them away from disturbing others, without inflicting either fine or corporal punishment upon them, they have ceased from such things since in a great measure, and as they never were a large society, there is hope of a true reformation among them.[1] Besides these,

---

[1] Morgan Edwards gives the following account of this singular sect:—

"The most forward of the brothers was John; for he took upon him to form the family, and others that he baptized, into a church, and to make a creed, and to settle rules of discipline. The first act of discipline was the excommunication of his

there have been some Sabbatarian Baptists in that place from the beginning to the present time, though not a distinct church.

We must now return to our Baptist fathers at Boston. The liberty they had enjoyed, with a blessing upon the ministry of Mr. Miles and others, had caused such an increase of members, that, in February, 1677, they agreed to divide

brother Jonathan, for using medicine and refusing to do things which would bring on him the lash of the civil magistrate. And this John Rogers was not only the founder of the sect, and the person from whom they were called Rogerenes, but the hero of the cause, in suffering and writing and defying; I say defying, for he had not been long at the head of the cause, before he printed and published the following proclamation: 'I, John Rogers, a servant of Jesus Christ, doth here make an open declaration of war against the great red dragon, and against the beast to which he gives power; and against the false church which rides upon the beast; and against the false prophets who are established by the dragon and the beast; and against the image of the beast: and also a proclamation of derision against the sword of the devil's spirit, which is prisons, stocks, whips, fines and revilings, all of which is to defend the doctrines of devils.'

"His theory relative to baptism and the Lord's supper, is scriptural, for the Rogerenes baptize by immersing professed penitents and believers; the Lord's supper they administer in the evening, with its ancient appendages. Some other articles of Rogers's creed are orthodox. The particulars of it are, 1st, All days are alike since the death of Christ. 2d. No medicines are to be used, nor doctors nor surgeons employed. 3d. No grace at meals. 4th. All prayers to be mental, and not vocal, except when the spirit of prayer compels to the use of the voice. 5th. All unscriptural parts of religious worship are idols. 6th. All good Christians should exert themselves against idols, &c. Among these idols they placed the first day of the week, infant baptism, &c. The First-day sabbath they called the New England idol. The methods they took to demolish this idol were, they would be at work near meeting-houses and in the ways to meeting-houses, and take work into meeting-houses, the women knitting and the men whittling and making splits for baskets, and every now and then contradicting the preachers. This was seeking persecution, and they had plenty of it, insomuch that the New Englanders left some of them neither liberty, nor property, nor a whole skin.

"John Rogers was an author. He published a commentary on the Revelation. He that hath patience to read it, let him read it. He also published 'A Midnight Cry;' a 'Narrative of Sufferings,' &c." Materials for a History of the Baptists in New Jersey, pp. 147, 148.

Benedict says that after the death of John Rogers, Joseph Bolles published a second edition of his book, entitled, "A Midnight Cry from the temple of God to the ten virgins slumbering and sleeping. Awake! awake! arise! and gird your loins and trim your lamps, for behold the Bridegroom cometh, go ye therefore out to meet him!"

Even as late as 1813, according to Benedict, there was a "small company of the Rogerenes in Groton, Ct., near New London." History of the Baptists, Vol. II, pp. 425, 426.—ED.

into two churches; but in January, 1678, they revoked that act, and concluded to build them a meeting-house, in Boston, and to defer the affair of dividing, till they could obtain the settlement of an able, sufficient ministry there. They first nominated Mr. Russell for that end, and then talked of his going to Swanzey in Mr. Miles's room; but in conclusion, Mr. Miles returned to his old flock, and Mr. Russell was ordained their pastor in Boston, July 28, 1679, and removed there. Before this time Governor Leverett had deceased, and Mr. Bradstreet had been chosen in his stead; in consequence of which this church wrote to their brethren at Newport the 25th of January this year, that several of their brethren and sisters had been called to Court, censured, fined twenty shillings a piece and to pay Court charges, and others only admonished and to pay Court charges, which had not then been paid, and the constables were backward to make distress upon them if they could shift it off. February 9, the church met, and purchased their meeting house with the land it was built upon, of Philip Squire and Ellis Callender, for sixty pounds; and they met in it for worship the 15th. They had built with so much caution as not openly to call it by that name till it was done. They had been often censured and reproached for meeting in private houses, but now say, "Since we have for our convenience obtained a public house on purpose for that use, we are become more offensive than before."[1] The leaders of the society were convented before the General Court of May 10,[2] who, not finding any old law to suit their term then made a new one, in these words:—

It is ordered by the Court and the authority thereof, that no persons whatever, without the consent of the freemen of the town where they live, first orderly had, and obtained, at a public meeting assembled for that end, and license of the County Court, or in defect of such consent, a license by

[1] Russell, p. 10.—B.
[2] In the published Massachusetts Records, the date of this transaction is May 28. —Ed.

the special order of the General Court, shall erect or make use of any house as above said; and in case any person or persons shall be convicted of transgressing this law, every such house or houses wherein such persons shall so meet more than three times, with the land whereon such house or houses stand, and all private ways leading thereto, shall be forfeited to the use of the county, and disposed of by the County Treasurer, by sale or demolishing, as the Court that gives judgment in the case shall order.[1]

How different is this from the above language of Governor Leete! But instead of seeking for persecution as Rogers did, this peaceable people refrained from meeting in their own house for the present, waiting to see what God would do for them. And he who has the hearts of kings in his hand, moved their king to write to the Massachusetts rulers on July 24, requiring that liberty of conscience should be allowed to all Protestants, so as they might not be discountenanced from sharing in the government, much less that no such good subjects of his, for not agreeing in the congregational way, should by law, " be subjected to fines or forfeitures, or other incapacities for the same; which is a severity to be the more wondered at, whereas liberty of conscience was made a [one] principal motive for your first transportation into those parts."[2] Deplorable indeed was their case at this time. Their all was in great danger, for doing so much of that which they thought Heaven frowned upon them for not doing more of; and it was evidently the two errors I have mentioned on page 35, which brought them into this dilemna. Mr. William Hubbard, whom I have so often quoted, who was a minister at Ipswich, preached at their election in Boston, May 3, 1676; and as the permission of Quaker meetings had been declared by many ministers, to be one great cause of God's judgments upon them, which had stirred up the Court to severity against that people, he plainly gave his mind to the contrary; and that pride and worldly mindedness were the greatest evils then among them; yet lest Governor Leverett

[1]Massachusetts Records. [2]Massachusetts History, Vol. III, p. 520.

and his Court should be too favorable to the Baptists, he, in his dedication of that sermon to them, page 6, said, "If he were not much mistaken who said it is morally impossible to rivet the Christian religion into the body of a nation without infant baptism, by proportion it will as necessarily follow, that the neglect or disuse thereof, will as directly tend to root it out." And Dr. Increase Mather, who yielded to Mr. Mitchel's reasonings about the Half-way Covenant, and took the lead among the Massachusetts ministers after his death, in that capacity now moved the Assembly to convene what they called The Reforming Synod. First they kept a general fast in their churches, and then the Synod met at Boston, September 10, 1679, to answer these two questions: 1st. What are the evils that have provoked the Lord to bring his judgments on New England? 2d. What is to be done that so these evils may be reformed?

They had not gone far in their answer before they said:—

Men have set up their thresholds by God's thresholds, and their post by his post. Quakers are false worshippers; and such Anabaptists as have risen up among us, in opposition to the churches of the Lord Jesus, receiving into their society those that have been for scandal delivered unto Satan; yea, and improving those as administrators of holy things, who have been (as doth appear) justly under [church] censure, do no better than set up altar against the Lord's altar. Wherefore it must needs be provoking to God, if these things be not duly and fully testified against, by every one in their several capacities.

Their result was approved of by the General Court on October 15, which commended it to all their churches, "enjoining and requiring all persons in their respective capacities to a careful and diligent reformation of all those provoking evils mentioned therein, according to the true intent thereof, that so the anger and displeasure of God, many ways manifested, might be averted [from this poor people;] and his favor and blessing obtained."[1]

[1] Magnalia, B, 5, pp. 87, 89, [Vol. II, pp. 274, 275]; I. Mather's Life, p. 84. Mr. Stoddard informs us, that in this Synod "they had a dispute about persons giving, a relation of the work of God's Spirit upon their hearts, in order to coming to com-

This dreadful charge, coming out from the whole power of the colony against one small society, put them upon a critical review of their past conduct; and they found that among about eighty members that they had received, there were but two that had been censured in those other churches (since Mr. Gould and Mr. Osburne, of whom we have before spoken) one of whom was Mr. Thomas Foster, of Billerica, who, for turning and going away when infants were sprinkled, and for going at last and joining with the Baptists, and refusing, after they had presented him to Court, to return to the other church, was censured and excommunicated by

munion. .... The result was, that they blotted out that clause, ... and put in the room of it, the making a profession of their faith and repentance; and so I voted with the rest, and am of the same judgment still." That is, a profession of a saving change should not be required before they come to communion. Stoddard's Appeal, p. 94. Was this reformation, or was it apostasy?—B.

Evidently the moving spirit in this Reforming Synod, was Increase Mather. His son, Cotton Mather, in his account of his father's life, entitled, "Parentator, Remarkables of Dr. Increase Mather," pp. 84, 85, gives the following account of the Synod:—

"Upon motion of Mr. Mather, in conjunction with others excited by him first, the General Court called upon the churches to send their delegates for a Synod in Boston, to consider What are the evils? &c. The churches having first kept a general fast, that a gracious direction might be obtained of God in what was now to be done, the Synod met at Boston, September 10, 1679. The Synod also kept a day of prayer with fasting, in which Mr. Mather was chose for one of the preachers and the venerable old Mr. Cobbett was chose for the other. Several days were then spent in free discourses on the two questions, and at last a result, with a preface, were agreed unto, which were of Mr. Mather's drawing up. On the day when a Committee of the ministers presented it unto the General Court, Mr. Mather preached a very potent sermon on the danger of not being reformed by these things; and the General Court thereupon commended it unto the serious consideration of all the churches and people of the jurisdiction."

The Mr. Stoddard, mentioned in the above note, is Solomon Stoddard, who had succeeded Eleazer Mather as pastor of the church in Northampton, where he was afterwards succeeded by his grandson, Jonathan Edwards. The full title of his work above cited, is, "Appeal to the Learned; being a vindication of the right of visible saints to the Lord's Supper, though they be destitute of a saving work of God's Spirit in their hearts; against the exceptions of Mr. Increase Mather." Mr. Stoddard states in this work, page 94, that the dispute in the Synod, on the question whether persons, in order to be received to full communion, should be required to give a relation of the work of God's Spirit in their hearts, was chiefly between Mr. Mather on the affirmative, and himself on the negative. A further account of the sentiments of Solomon Stoddard on these points, and of their results, will be given in subsequent pages.—Ed.

them. The other was Mr. Farnum, who was the only one the Baptists had received, after others had cast him out; which was from the North Church in Boston, where Mr. Mayo and Dr. Mather were ministers. The Baptists now sent and obtained copies of the proceedings of that church against him, whereby it appeared, that they were in the height of their dealings with him, the same month that the Assembly disfranchised Gould and Osburne for constituting that Baptist church, viz., in October, 1665; and that Farnum got his temper up, and in sundry instances spake and acted very unadvisedly; for which the Baptists now required him to offer satisfaction to that church, before they would commune with him again. This he soon after did. Mr. Willard owns that he offered a confession therefor both orally and in writing; but because he refused to return into their communion they judged it not to be sincere. The Baptists say that some who had been baptized among them had afterward been refused communion by the other churches, when they had desired it. To which Mr. Willard says, "They know that our churches have received some that were scrupulous about infant baptism, who were willing to carry inoffensively; that we have refused such as were re-baptized among those excommunicated Anabaptists, is true hypothetically, viz., except they would acknowledge and repent of that act; because we judge it scandalous."[1] Upon which I would only remark, that God says, He that doubteth is damned if he eat; but the Massachusetts were willing to admit persons to eat with scruples, but excommunicated such as put their full persuasion about baptism into practice, and judged those not to be sincere, who would not repent of that act! A letter at this time to their Governor deserves notice, which is as follows:—

HONORED SIR:—I have often heard of your name by Colonel Eyers, whose first wife's name was Bradstreet; and the character I have of you, if you were her son, relates you a wise and understanding man. But your

[1] Russell, p. 10; Willard, p. 22.

report gives you as though some Lauderdale's counsel had possessed you, which set all Scotland in an uproar. God is wiser than man, more just and righteous; his counsel must stand. Beware of smiting your brethren, lest the ecclesiastical power of England invade you. A parliament is near at hand, when just grievances will be previously [grievously?] resented; I hope there shall be none during your government. Samson plucked a house on his head, and fell in it. If I can serve you in any honorable way, command your humble servant,

PETER CHAMBERLAIN,
His Majesty's physician in ordinary to his Royal Person.
September 2, 1679.

Mr. Samuel Hubbard sometime after sent a letter, with a copy of this, to Governor Leete, to check their imprisoning the Rogerses at New London. Notice being received by the Baptists in Boston, of the king's letter in their favor, they met again in their house; but had not so done above four times before the Court met, and issued a warrant to the constable of Boston, requiring him, "in his Majesty's name, forthwith to summon Philip Squire, Thomas Skinner, and Mr. Drinker, to make their appearance before the Court of Assistants now sitting, having liberty to bring with them three or four more of their friends, to give an account of their breach of the law in erecting a meeting-house; and that they appear at three of the clock this instant 5th March, 1680." They appeared accordingly, and the Court required a positive answer to the question, whether they would engage, either for the whole society, or for themselves in particular, to desist from meeting in said house till the next General Court? They said they were not prepared to answer it, and desired time to consult their brethren. This was then denied them, but upon renewing the request next morning, they were allowed so much time as from Saturday till Monday. The church met on Monday, and presented the following address, viz.:—

To the honorable the Governor and magistrates now assembled at Boston, at the Court of Assistants, the 8th of March, 1680, the petition and declaration of the society of the people commonly known or distinguished by the name of Baptists, residing in and about Boston, humbly showeth,

In primum, that whereas the only wise God, having by his providence led us into that order and way of the gospel of gathering into church fellowship, we do hereby confess, that what we did was not out of opposition to, or contempt of, the churches of Christ in New England, but in a holy imitation, merely for the better enjoyment of the liberty of our consciences, the great motive to this removal at first into this wilderness. 2. That the building a convenient place for our public church assembly, was not thought of affronting authority, there being no law in the country against any such practise at the erecting of this house, and we did therefore think, as the apostle saith, where there is no law, there is no transgression. The dictates of nature, or common prudence belonging to mankind, and the example or practice of the country throughout, lead to the seeking of this convenience. 3. There being a law made in May last against meeting in the place built, we submitted to the same, until we fully understood by letters from several in London, that it was his Majesty's pleasure and command (the common *supersedus* to all corporation laws in the English nation, that have not the royal assent[1]) that we should enjoy liberty of our meetings in the manner as other of his Protestant subjects; and the General Court at their last meeting not having voted a non-occurrence. 4. As therefore the two tribes and half did humbly and meekly vindicate themselves, upon the erecting of their altar, when challenged for it by Eleazer and the messengers of the ten tribes, so do we hereby confess in like manner, that we have not designed by this act any contempt of authority, nor any departing from the living God, or churches of his worship; the Lord God of gods he knows it; Joshua xxii, 22; though it be our lot, with the apostles, in the way that some call heresy so to worship the God of our fathers. Your petitioners, therefore, having no design against the peace of this place, but being still as ready as ever to hazard our lives for the defence of the people of God here, do humbly request that this our profession and declaration may find acceptance with this honorable Court, as that of the two tribes did with Eleazer; and that we may still, through your allowance and protection, enjoy the liberty of God's worship, in such places as God hath afforded us, which will greatly oblige your petitioners, as in duty bound, humbly to pray.

Signed by us in the name and with the consent of the church.

ISAAC HULL,
JOHN RUSSELL,
EDWARD DRINKER,
THOMAS SKINNER."

---

[1] Their charter was originally designed for a corporation in England, to be executed only by a deputation in this country, as the King observes in the letter referred to. Massachusetts History, Vol. III, p. 519.

But instead of having any ears to hear this loyal and Christian address, their marshal was sent, and finding their gate locked, forced his way through Mr. Squire's ground, and nailed up their meeting-house doors, putting a paper thereon which said :—

All persons are to take notice, that by order of the Court the doors of this house are shut up, and that they are inhibited to hold any meeting therein, or to open the doors thereof, without license from authority, till the General Court take further order, as they will answer the contrary at their peril.

Dated in Boston, 8th March, 1680.

By order of the Council,

EDWARD RAWSON, Secretary.

The Baptists required a copy of the marshal's warrant, but he refused it; they then went to the Secretary for one, who plainly told them, " he was not to let them have any." They met the next Lord's day in their yard, and in the week ensuing prepared a shed therein for the purpose; but when they came together the second Lord's day, they found the doors open; and considering, say they, " that the Court had not done it legally, and that we were denied a copy of the constable's order and marshal's warrant, we concluded to go into our house, it being our own, having a civil right to it." And they met therein till the Assembly sat, before whom they were convented on May 11; when they gave in these pleas :—

1. The house was our own. 2. It was built before the law was made, therefore no transgression. 3. The express will and pleasure of the king, that we should enjoy our liberty. After some debate of the matter (in which we met with some hard and reviling speeches from some of them) we were dismissed for that time. Next morning we put up a humble petition, (being blamed by some in the Court that we had not done it before) that there might be a suspension of any proceedings against us.

These accounts I have taken from their church records and papers. On the colony records, under May 19, I find it thus written, viz. :—

After the Court had heard their answer and plea, perused their petition and what else was produced, the parties were [the persons being] called in, the Court's sentence in the name of the Court was published to them; that the Court, in answer to their petition, judged it meet and ordered, that the petitioners be admonished by the present honored Governor for their offence, and so granted them their petition, so far as to forgive them their offence past, but still prohibited them as a society of themselves, or joined with others, to meet in that public place they have built, or any [other] public house except such as are allowed by lawful authority; and accordingly the Governor in open Court gave them their admonition.

Dr. Mather had published a piece the preceding March, entitled, The Divine Right of Infant Baptism, containing some injurious reflections upon this people; which, with others, were briefly answered in Mr. Russell's Narrative, dated from Boston the 20th of this month, with the consent of the whole church, and sent to London, where Messrs. William Kiffen, Daniel Dyke, William Collins, Hansard Knollys, John Harris and Nehemiah Cox, noted Baptist ministers, wrote a preface to it, in which they say:—

As for our brethren of the Congregational way in old England, both their principles and practice do equally plead for our liberties as for their own; and it seems strange that such of the same way in New England, yea, even such (a generation not yet extinct, or the very next successors of them) who with liberal estates chose rather to depart from their native soil into a wilderness, than be under the imposition and lash of those, who upon religious pretences took delight to smite their fellow servants, should exercise towards others the like severity that themselves with so great hazard and hardship sought to avoid; especially considering that it is against their brethren, who avowedly profess and appeal to the same rule with themselves for their guidance in, and decision of, all matters relating to the worship of God, and the ordering of their whole conversation. . . . . For one Protestant congregation to persecute another, where there is no pretence to infallibility in the decision of all controversies, seems much more unreasonable than the cruelties of the church of Rome towards them that depart from their superstitions: and if prejudices were removed and opportunities of power not abused, but the golden rule of our Saviour were duly attended unto and rightly applied in the present case, certainly more moderation, yea, even compassion would be exercised towards these our Christian friends by such as now give them trouble.

They close with observing That Dr. Stillingstreet had already declared in his Mischief of Separation, that their rigorous course against Congregationalists in England, was justified by the process of the rulers here, against dissenters from themselves; and pray that the governors of New England would regard their brethren there, so much as to remit these proceedings. What was said in answer thereto, we shall see presently, after I have observed, that Elder Russell was taken from his beloved flock by death, December 21, 1680; upon which the church met the next day, and agreed that their brother Callender, should be helpful in carrying on their worship in Boston, on Lord's days in the forenoon, and brother Drinker in the afternoon, in the absence of Elder Hull. It is evident, that the gifts and graces of Elder Russell were not small; and his memory is precious. His grand-daughter Brooks, married in Swanzey, whose sons, Job,[1] Russell and John Mason have been, and the two latter still are, useful gospel preachers in the Second Baptist church in that town. Also Messrs. Joseph, William and Jonathan Russell, now noted traders in Providence, are of his posterity.

In 1681, a minister of the church of Boston, which was formed in a schismatical way in 1669, published an answer to the Baptist's Narrative; and though its author was deceased, yet he entitled it, " *Ne sutor ultra crepidam* :[2] or brief animadversions upon the New England Anabaptists' late fallacious Narrative; wherein the notorious mistakes and falsehoods by them published, are detected; by Samuel Willard, &c." To which he adds as a motto, Romans 16. 17, 18. Dr. Increase Mather wrote a preface to this work, wherein he says :—

> Many are of the mind, that it is not worth the while, to take notice of what is emitted by men so obscure and inconsiderable..... It seems to me that the reverend author of the following animadversions, hath shewed humility, in condescending to take persons in hand, between whom and himself there is such an *impar congressus*.....As for the brethren, that

[1] Elder Job Mason died since this history was in the press, aged 80.
[2] Cobbler, keep to your last.

have thought good to prefix an epistle to such a narrative, and therein declare that molestation is given and severity is exercised towards Antipædobaptists in New England, merely for a supposed error about the subject of baptism, controverted amongst learned and holy men, they are marvelously deceived in that their supposition. Protestants ought not to persecute any, yet, that protestants may punish protestants, and as the case may be circumstanced, a congregation of such as call themselves protestants, cannot rationally be denied. Those of the Congregational way, fully concur with the old puritan nonconformists, such as Cartwright, Rainold, Whitaker, Bains, Parker, &c., in whose writings Congregational principles about church government, are to be seen.[1] Now the old nonconformists (notwithstanding their sufferings from those that took delight to smite their fellow servants) did believe that disorders in whole congregations were liable to the civil magistrate's censure.····Our famous Cotton was another Moses, in respect of meekness and Christian forbearance, as to dissenters from his judgment in matters of a lesser concernment, yet would he sometimes make a zealous protestation, that if magistrates in New England should tolerate transgressors against the rules of godliness (as well as offences contrary to what the rules of honesty require) he believed that God would not long tolerate them.....I would entreat the brethren that have subscribed the epistles seriously to consider; 1. That the place may sometimes make a great alteration as to the indulgence to be expected. It is evident, that that toleration is in one place, not only lawful, but a necessary duty, which in another place would be destructive; and the expectation of it irrational. That which is needful to ballast a great ship, will sink a small boat.....2. Let them consider, that those of their persuasion in this place have acted with so much irregularity and profaneness, that should men of any persuasion whatsoever have done the like, the same severity would have been used towards them.

This hard sentence his son has propagated to posterity.[2]

But, search through all they have said against those people, and I am confident that the greatest real disorder they

---

[1] These are the men referred to in page 9, who opened a door for Mr. Robinson and his brethren, by which themselves entered not. Their first Admonition to the Parliament, was presented thereto by Mr. John Field and Mr. Wilcox; for which they were committed to Newgate Prison, on October 2, 1572. This caused Mr. Thomas Cartwright to write the Second Admonition to Parliament, quoted by Mr. Robinson, and also to answer what Dr. Whitgift had written against the first. And Mr. Neal says, the reason why they could not settle the controversy, was because Cartwright was for making his Bible the only standard of doctrine, discipline and government; but Whitgift held the latter of these to be changeable, to accommodate the civil governments we live under. History of the Puritans, Vol. I, pp. 190—197. [300—307.]

[2] Magnalia, B. 7, p. 28. [Vol. II, p. 461.]

have produced, was the church's receiving Farnum as they did; which, when they had proper knowledge of, they rectified. But is this comparable to the disorders at Hingham, twenty years before, where Lieut. Eames was regularly chosen their Captain, and presented to the Court for a commision; but soon upon it, a notion was started to choose another man, related to the minister, into that office, who accordingly was chosen and presented. And when the reason of it was asked for, they said Eames had resigned; but he said he had not. Hereupon the minister censured him for lying; and this cost three or four days' tedious labors of a council, without being able to settle it; and occasioned the petition of Dr. Child and others, with much trouble to Governor Winthrop and the Assembly.[1] Yet the issue of all was, that the minister of Hingham excommunicated Captain Eames, contrary to the minds of other ministers, and by their advice, "those that were without just cause cast out at Hingham, were received into the church of Weymouth, the next town, and the matter so continued through the stiffness of their minds, and their self-willed resolutions."[2]

In the piece upon infant baptism, which Dr. Mather had

[1] See page 116.
[2] Winthrop, [Vol. II, pp. 261, 278, 285—295, 321.] Hubbard, [pp. 417—419.] Neal, Vol. I, p. 233. How just also was it for both ministers and courts to accuse that Baptist church, of having excommunicated officers, in the plural, when they never had but one?—B.

This difficulty with Dr. Childs was followed by another on the question of "the enlargement of privileges," which was a long and grievous trouble to Governor Winthrop and the General Court. Finally Dr. Childs and his sympathizers carried their complaint to England, where their cause was presented in a pamphlet entitled "New England's Jonas cast up at London." It is reprinted in Massachusetts Historical Collections, Second series, Vol. IV. This was answered by Mr. Winslow, in a pamphlet, entitled, "The Salamander," intimating that the opposite party were never at rest except they were in the fires of contention. It is to this latter difficulty that the above-cited passages from Winthrop and Neal refer. Savage (Winthrop, Vol. II, p. 292,) charges Hutchinson (Vol. I. p. 138,) with being misled by Mather to confound the two controversies; and Backus, by the references he gives, might seem obnoxious to the same charge. But similar questions were agitated in both controversies, and the one was doubtless the outgrowth of the other.—ED.

published, he accused those Baptists of the sin of Jeroboam, who made priests of the lowest of the people;[1] in which, says Mr. Russell, " we easily understand what he means;" our evil in this respect, is our calling to office those who have not been bred up in colleges, and taught in other languages, but have been bred to other callings. It is not because we are against learning, for we esteem it, and honor it in its place; and if we had such among us who were together with that, otherways duly qualified for the work of the ministry, we should readily choose them. But we do not think the Spirit of God is locked up so in the narrow limits of college learning, that none are to be called to office in a church but such, nor that all such are fit for that work, be they never so great scholars; neither do we think that all those who have not that learning, are to be accounted the lowest of the people. Indeed, the priesthood was bounded to the tribe of Levi, by divine institution, but we cannot find that the Lord hath, by divine institution, given the work of the ministry to men of such learning only. Whom he will he fits and qualifies for that work; neither are we left without a plain rule in the New Testament to direct us in this matter.[2] In these plain gospel sentiments have the Baptists, on both sides of the Atlantic, persevered to this day. But his opponent said of the text referred to:—

The Belgic and others read it, "Of both ends of the people;" if a fit man would accept it, so; if not, to the other end, and take one unfit. The Anabaptists would have a learned man if they could get one of their mind; if not, John Russell the shoemaker.....Truly, if Goodman Russell was a fit man for a minister, we have but fooled ourselves in building colleges, and instructing children in learning.[3]

[1] The Divine Right of Infant Baptism asserted, and proved from Scripture and Antiquity, page 26.—ED.
[2] Russell, p. 14.
[3] Willard, p. 26.—B.
Cotton Mather repeats the argument of his father and Mr. Willard as follows:—
"They did seem to do what Jeroboam was taxed for, in making priests of the lowest of the people; or, as the Belgic and others do read it, Of both ends of the people; and as the learned Zepperus lamented the wrong done to religion in it, that

Here is a plain specimen of what many call learning, though the truly learned apostle Paul, renounced it with abhorrence; 2 Corinthians 4. 2. Either those who have a college education, are thereby made the head of the people, and the rest are to be ranked to the other end, or else this is a handling the word of God deceitfully; and God says, "*The prophet that teacheth lies, he is the tail.*"

Again, the Baptists had said in their confession of faith, that those who gladly receive the word and are baptized, are saints by calling, and fit matter of a visible church.[1] This Dr. Mather called a pernicious principle.[2] But says Mr. Russell :—

Who dare deny this to be a sound truth? as for the conclusion he draws from thence, viz., that there are no visible believers but those that are baptized, [it] is his own, not ours; the improvement he makes of it, not what we make of it. Far be it from us to judge all that are not baptized, not to be visible saints, for we judge that the Lord hath many precious people in the world that are not baptized, according to, or in the manner we baptize; and further we judge they should be visible saints, before baptized, or else they have no right to baptism, for it is not baptism that can make saints. And as for looking upon infant baptism as nothing, or a nullity,[3] that is true; and we can look on it no otherwise, till we see light to own it to be that which he thinks of it, viz., of divine right, which we cannot see ground from the word to do; and as for not owning their churches,.... we never yet denied them to be churches of Christ. It is enough for every one to prove his own work; but we have owned them as such; for where there is true matter

they make *ministros de extremitatibus populi, sartoribus, sutoribus, idiotis,* taylors and cobblers, and other mechanicks to be ministers, thus these people chose an honest shooemaker to be their pastor, and used other mechanicks in the constant preaching of the gospel; which caused some other people of a more liberal education to reflect that if Goodman such an one, and Gaffer such an one, were fit for ministers, we had befool'd ourselves in building of colleges." Magnalia, Book VII; Vol. II, p. 460.—ED.

[1] "Christ's commission to his disciples is to teach and baptize; and those who gladly receive the word and are baptized, are his by calling, and fit matter for a visible church; and a competent number of such, joined together in covenant and fellowship of the gospel, are a church of Christ." Articles of Faith of the First Baptist church, Boston; 1665.—ED.

[2] Divine Right of Infant Baptism; p. 26.—ED.

[3] In connection with what has already been quoted, Dr. Mather had said, "Now they look upon infant baptism as a mere nullity, or, as the apostle saith of an idol, that it is nothing in the world." Divine Right, &c., p. 26.—ED.

joined together in the bond of a holy covenant they may be looked at as a true church, though not in due order.¹

This was not enough for the other party, but their cry still was:—

They say baptized persons are true matter of a visible church, and they say those that were only sprinkled in their infancy, were never baptized; and will not this undermine the foundation of all the churches in the world but theirs? and what more pernicious! they had even as good cry with Edom's sons, Raze it, raze it to the foundation! .... Experience tells us that such a rough thing as a New England Anabaptist is not to be handled over tenderly; the spirit which they have at all times discovered under the greatest disadvantages (and God grant that they may never have more advantage over us) easily tells us what they would have been if circumstanced as those whom they accuse.²

Mr. Hubbard got the most out of temper upon this occasion that he ever did in a whole volume in folio, and said:—

One John Russell, a wedderdrop'd shoemaker, ... stitched up a small pamphlet, ... wherein he endeavors to clear the innocency of those commonly (though falsely he says) called Anabaptists. Surely he was not well aware of the old adage, *Ne sutor ultra crepidam*,³ or else he would not have made such botching work.

He goes on to recite what you may see of the Simple Cobbler, in page 154, which he calls Honest stitches used to much better purpose. But having taken the old round to Germany, he recovers his senses again, and then says:—

To return to what was in hand, and give this gospel-ordered church (as John Russell terms them) what is their due, from an historian; as for the persons of those seven [first males of the church] he apologizes for, it may

---

¹Russell, page 14.   ²Willard, pp. 10, 27.

³It was truly of some age; for after James I. had preached in the Star-Chamber, "that the mystery of the king's power is not lawful to be disputed; for that is to wade into the weakness of princes, and to take away the mystical reverence that belongs to those who sit in the *throne of God*; .... it is atheism and blasphemy to dispute what God can do; .... so is it presumption and high contempt in a subject to dispute what a king can do or say;" he, the year after our fathers first came to Plymouth, reprimanded his parliament for petitioning against his taking a popish wife for his son Charles, and said, "A small mistaking of matters of this nature, may produce more effects than can be imagined; therefore, *Ne sutor ultra crepidam*." Rapin, Vol. II, pp. 192, 211. [London, 1729, Vol. IX, pp. 393, 485.]

be more easily granted that they were good in the main, than that it was a good work for God, they were engaged in. .... Good men may be found to be ill employed; as Peter was, whom Christ rebukes and calls Satan, and bids him get behind him. Whether any of them did absolutely deserve to be delivered to Satan, for their obstinacy in their opinions, or rather miscarriages, which either through weakness of their judgments, or strength of their passions, which in defence of their opinions or practices they run into; or whether there were not more acrimony of the salt, than sweetness of the gospel spirit of peace, in those that managed the discipline of the church against some of them, ... must not be here discussed. .... Yet that can give no color to .... a few giddy sectaries, that fondly conceit themselves to be an orderly church, when their very constitution [coalition] is explicitly, not only without, but against, the consent of all the rest of the churches in the places, [place] as well as the order of the civil authority.[1]

I love to see honesty even if persons are erroneous; for then we have an advantage to judge for ourselves, and to know the better how to deal with them. And I must say that Governor Winthrop, from whom Mr. Hubbard took many things, exceeded him in that noble quality; and that Mr. Hubbard exceeded all the historians I have seen who have copied from him, except the pious Mr. Prince. Others have often given us hard names without explaining what they meant by them; but Mr. Hubbard plainly tells us that soon after Mr. Cotton's arrival at Boston,—

The ministers [about Boston ....] did use to meet once a fortnight at one of their houses in course, where some question of moment was debated. Mr. Skelton, pastor of Salem, and Mr. Williams (as yet not ordained an [any] officer there], out of a rigid separation jealousy, took exception at it; prognosticating that it might in time bring forth a presbytery, or superintendency, to the prejudice of the churches' liberties. (A spirit of rigid separation had, it seems, so early fly-blown their understandings) .... the venom of which spirit had soon after infected so many of that church and people at Salem, as will appear in the next chapter. But this fear was without cause; nor did it spring from a godly jealousy, but from the bitter root of pride, that venteth itself above order, and against love and peace. No such spirit was ever observed to appear in Mr. Cotton's days, but a spirit of love and meekness, nor since his time, to the present year.[2]

[1] Hubbard, pp. 624—627.—ED.
[2] Hubbard, pp. 189, 190.—ED.

And though the author of the Massachusetts History, approves of Mr. Williams's opinion about liberty of conscience, and fixes upon his moving Mr. Endicott to cut the cross out of the training colors, as the best plea he could make for their banishing of him;[1] yet Mr. Hubbard honestly says, " This essay did but tick at some of the upper branches, whereas Mr. Williams laid his axe at the very root of the magisterial power in matters of the first table, which he drove on at such a rate, that many agitations were occasioned thereby, that pulled down ruin upon himself, friends and his poor family."[2] Now if the reader will look back to pages 131, 148, and compare that with their actings down to this time, he will have a fair opportunity to know the meaning of the terms, Rigid separation, Turbulent Anabaptists, Giddy sectaries, &c., as they were often used by that party.

Mr. Williams closed his second plea for religious liberty, with an address to the popish, prelatical, Presbyterian and Independent clergy of the whole kingdom, wherein he makes use of the fable or similitude of a " wolf and a poor lamb coming down to drink at the same stream together."

The wolf, cruel and strong, drinks above and aloft; the lamb, innocent and weak, drinks upon the stream below; the wolf questions and quarrels the lamb for corrupting and defiling the waters; the lamb (not daring to plead how easily the wolf, drinking higher, might transfer defilement downward, but) pleads improbability and impossibility, that the waters descending could convey defilement upwards; this is the controversy, this the plea; but who shall judge? Be the lamb never so innocent, his plea never so just, his adversary, the wolf, will be his judge, and being so cruel and so strong, soon tears the lamb in pieces. Thus the cruel beast, armed with the power of the kings, Rev. 17, sits judge in his own quarrels against the lamb, about the drinking at the waters. And thus (saith Mr. Cotton) the judgments ought to pass upon the heretic, not for matter of conscience but for sinning against his conscience.

Objection. Methinks I hear, the great charge against the Independent party to be great pleaders for liberty of conscience, &c. Answer. Oh, the horrible deceit of the hearts of the sons of men! And what excellent physic can we prescribe to others, till, as Job said, our soul comes to be in

---

[1] Hutchinson, Vol. I, p. 41.—ED. [2] Hubbard, pp. 189, 190.—ED.

their souls' cases? What need have we to be more vile, with Job, before God, to walk in a holy sense of self-insufficiency, to cry for the blessed leadings of the Holy Spirit of God, to guide and lead our heads and hearts uprightly!

He then goes on to shew, that each of these denominations had been sufferers in their turns, and when so, had always complained of it, and pleaded for liberty to their own consciences; and then says:—

New England laws, lately published in Mr. Clarke's Narrative, tell how free it shall be for people to gather themselves into church estate, how free to choose their own ministers, how free to enjoy all the ordinances of Christ; but yet, provided (so and so) upon the point, that the civil state must judge of the spiritual, to wit, whether persons be fit for church estate, whether the gathering be right, whether the people's choice be right, doctrines right; and what is this in truth, but to swear that blasphemous oath of supremacy again, to the kings and queens and magistrates of this and other nations, instead of the pope! Into these prisons and cages, do those, otherwise excellent men, the Independents, put the children of God, and all the children of men, and then bid them fly and walk at liberty (to wit, within the conjured circle) so far as they please.[1]

Toward the close of this year Mr. Miles came again and ministered a while to his brethren in Boston. And Mr. Sprague, who in those times joined the Baptist church in Providence, in writing to the Massachusetts many years after, says:—

Why do you strive to persuade the rising generation, that you never persecuted nor hurt the Baptists, which is so apparently false? .... Did you not barbarously scourge Mr. Baker in Cambridge, the chief mate of a London ship? where also you imprisoned Mr. Thomas Gould, John Russell and Benjamin Sweetser, and many others, and fined them fifty pounds a man. .... And did you not nail up the Baptist meeting-house doors, and fine Mr. John Miles, Mr. James Brown and Mr. Nicholas Tanner? &c.

I find also that a number of people from Kittery, on Piscataqua River, in the province of Maine, were baptized this year, and in the beginning of the next, sent their most gifted brother to Boston with a letter of recommendation and re-

[1] Reply to Cotton, pp. 315—318.

quest;[1] in consequence of which the church there wrote thus on January 11, 1682:—

To ALL WHOM IT MAY CONCERN:—These are to certify, that our beloved brother William Screven is a member in communion with us, and having had trial of his gifts among us, and finding him to be a man whom God hath qualified and furnished with the gifts of his Holy Spirit and grace, enabling him to open and apply the word of God, which through the blessing of the Lord Jesus may be useful in his hand, for the begetting and

---

[1] A copy of this letter is preserved in the papers of Rev. Silas Hall, of Raynham, Massachusetts. Though not faultless in rhetoric, it is of sufficient interest to justify its publication, even aside from the consideration that it is probably the oldest document in existence relating to the history of the Baptists in the State of Maine.

"Humphrey, a servant of Jesus Christ to the church which is at Boston; grace be with you, and peace, from God, even the Father of our Lord Jesus Christ, the Father of mercies and the God of all comforts, who comforteth us in all our tribulations that we may be able to comfort them that are in any trouble, as we are comforted of God. Most dearly beloved brethren and friends, as I am, through free grace, a member of the same body and joined to the same Head, Christ Jesus, I thought it my special duty to inform you that the tender mercy of God in and through Jesus Christ, hath shined upon us by giving light to them that sit in darkness, and to guide our feet in the way of peace; for a great door, and effectual, is opened in these parts, and there are many adversaries, according to the 1st of Corinthians, 16. 9. Therefore, dearly beloved, having a desire to the service of Christ, which is perfect freedom, and the propagating his glorious gospel of peace and salvation, and eyeing that precious promise in Daniel the 12th, 3d, 'They that turn many to righteousness shall shine as the stars forever;' therefore I signify unto you, that here [are] a competent number of well established people whose hearts the Lord hath opened insomuch that they have gladly received the word and do seriously profess their hearty desire to the following of Christ and to partake of all his holy ordinances, according to his blessed institution and divine appointment; therefore I present my ardent desire to your serious consideration, which is, if the Lord see it fit, to have a gospel church planted here in this place; and in order hereunto, we think it meet that our beloved brother, William Screven, who is, through free grace, gifted and endued, with the spirit of veterans to preach the gospel; who, being called by us, who are visibly joined to the church. When our beloved brother is ordained according to the sacred rule of the Lord Jesus, our humble petition is to God that he will be pleased to carry on this good work to the glory of his holy name, and to the enlarging of the kingdom of his beloved Son, our dear Redeemer, who will add daily to his church such as shall be saved; and we desire you in the name of our Lord Jesus not to be slack in this good work, believing verily that you will not, and that you are always abounding in the work of the Lord, and we humbly crave your petitions for us to the throne of grace, and we commend you to God and the good word of his grace, which is able to build you up and to give you an inheritance among them that are sanctified.

"Written by mine own hand, this 3d of January, 1681.
HUMPHREY CHURCHWOOD."
The above date is in Old Style; in modern reckoning it should be 1682.—ED.

building up of souls in the knowledge of God, do therefore appoint, approve and encourage him, to exercise his gift in the place where he lives, or elsewhere, as the providence of God may cast him; and so the Lord help him to eye his glory in all things, and to walk humbly in the fear of his name.

Signed by us in behalf of the rest.

ISAAC HULL,
JOHN FARNUM.

But no sooner was this design heard of in their town, than Mr. Woodbridge the minister, and Hucke the magistrate, began to bestir themselves, and not only spread the slanders we have heard so much of against the Baptists at Boston, but the magistrate repeatedly summoned those people before him who had been to the Baptist meetings, and threatened them with a fine of five shillings for every such offence for the future. On January 23, he convented Humphrey Churchwood, a baptized member of Boston church, before him, where was the said minister, who, after casting those old stories upon him, said, "Behold your great doctor, Mr. Miles of Swanzey, for he now leaves his profession and is come away, and will not teach his people any more, because he is like to perish for want, and his gathered church and people will not help him." Churchwood told them it was a great untruth; and directly wrote to Boston upon it, which letter is now before me.[1] Several others from that place were

---

[1] "Humphrey, to the church of Christ at Boston: Grace be multiplied, and peace, from God our Father, and from the Lord Jesus Christ. Most dearly beloved brethren and Christian friends, I thought good to inform you that since our beloved brother Screven went from us, who, I trust is by God's mercy, now with you, by his long absence from us, has given great advantage to our adversaries to triumph and to endeavor to beat down that good beginning which God, by his poor instrument hath begun amongst us; and our magistrate, Mr. Hucke, is almost every day summoning and threatening the people by fines and other penalties, if they ever come to our meetings any more, five shillings for every such offence. And yesterday, being the twenty-third of this instant January, I was fetched before him by a summons, whither being come, he demanded of me how I spent my time; being informed, as I understood, that I made it my business to go from house to house as a seducer; but after I gave him to understand that I was joined to the baptized church of Boston, in covenant and fellowship, he told me that he was very sorry that I was deluded and misled; and our minister, Mr. Woodbridge, being present, he began to rail upon you, and especially of being built upon excommunicate persons, naming

baptized soon after; but to hinder their proceedings, their General Court took the matter in hand as follows, viz. :—

William Screven, appearing before this Court, and being convicted of the contempt of his Majesty's authority, and refusing to submit himself to the sentence of the Court, prohibiting his public preaching, and upon examination before the Court, declaring his resolution still to persist therein, the Court tendered him liberty to return home to his family, in case he would forbear such turbulent practices and amend for the future; but he refusing, the Court sentenced him to give bond for his good behavior, and to forbear such contentious behavior for the future, and the delinquent to stand committed until the judgment of this Court be fulfilled.

Vera copia, transcribed, and with the records compared, this 17th of August, 1682.

per EDWARD RISHWORTH, Recorder.

one John Farnum, who, he said was a grievous, censorious man; and would not let Mr. Mader, [Mather] alone till he had cast him out of his church. Then I gave him the book set forth by Elder John Russell, and told him, if he would impartially read that book, he would not speak so evilly of them. But Woodbridge told him that he would affirm that there were many palpable untruths in that book; but I said there were many grievous, false scandals and false insinuations in their book entitled The Divine Right of Infant Baptism, falsely laid upon those who professed believers' baptism, which had been fully answered by a letter from one Kiffin, of London, and confuted by all sober men, and taken to arise from a spirit of inveteracy and animosity. And having a long dispute concerning infant baptism and ordination of ministers, and that none might preach except called by men, I affirmed that it is written God's people shall all be taught of him, and therefore, as every man has received the gift of God, so let him administer the same as good stewards of the manifold grace of God. Then Mr. Hucke answered, saying, Behold your great Doctor, Mr. Miles of Swanzey, for he now leaves his profession and is come away, and will not teach his people any more, because he is like to perish for want, and his gathered church and people will not help him. I answered, it was a great untruth, but he said he could bring two sufficient men to testify that they had it from his own mouth at Boston. Dear brethren, I cannot harbor any such thing, but it is in every one's mouth, and it is a great stumbling block to many tender consciences; therefore I request you not to fail, as soon as you can possibly, if this letter come to your hand before brother Screven cometh from thence, that you would send an answer to this thing, for the satisfaction of our friends here, and I hope you will take that into serious consideration which I sent by brother Screven. And the good will of him that dwelt in the bush, be with you to guide you in all your undertakings. And so, humbly craving your prayers for us, and that you will dispatch brother Screven as soon as he cometh back from Swanzey, for his long tarrying maketh us conclude that he is gone thither. All our friends here are well, blessed be God! and we hope the same by you, which is the tenor of our prayers.

"Written by mine own hand this 25th day of January, 1681[2].

Rev. S. Hall's Collection of papers.

The reader will observe, in this letter, a discrepancy of one day in dates. It may have been commenced on the 24th and finished on the 25th.—ED.

To this is added a copy of the same date by the same hand, of an act of their Executive Court, which says :—

This Court having considered the offensive speeches of William Screven, viz., his rash and inconsiderate words tending to blasphemy, do adjudge the delinquent, for his offence, to pay ten pounds into the treasury of the county or province. And further, the Court doth forbid and discharge the said Screven, under any pretence, to keep any private exercise at his own house or elsewhere upon the Lord's days, either in Kittery or any other place within the limits of this province, and is for the future enjoined to observe the public worship of God in our public assemblies upon the Lord's days, according to the laws here established in this province, upon such penalties as the law requires upon such neglect of the premises.

But he was so far from yielding to such sentences, that on September 13, he with the rest sent a request to Boston that Elder Hull and others might visit and form them into a church,[1] which was granted; so that a covenant was

---

[1] "To Thomas Skinner, Boston, for the church: Dearly beloved brethren in the Lord Jesus Christ, the King of saints. I and my wife salute you with our Christian love in our Lord Jesus, hoping through grace these few lines will find you in health of body and mind. Blessed be God for Jesus Christ, in whom he is pleased to account his saints meet to be partakers of the blessed rest provided for them in his mansion-house eternally in the heavens. That will be a happy day when all the saints shall join together in sounding of his praise. The good Lord enable us to prepare for that blessed day. To that end, brethren, let us pray, every one himself, for himself, and for one another, that God would please to search our hearts and reins, so as that we may walk with God here, and hereafter dwell with him in glory.

"I had thought to have been with you last church-meeting, but my wife's condition was such I could not come, and this time by providence, I have taken some hurt, so that I cannot ride so far as yet. I hope to be with you next month, if the Lord will. And we have sent you our apprehensions about our present state. I hope we are conscientious in what we have said to you. I believe you will not judge otherwise. I am persuaded it will do much for the honor of God to have it done here. Besides, my mother-in-law hath desired to follow Christ in that ordinance. We all conceive it will be more honorable and expedient that it be done by the Elder Hull, that is so truly praised here. I pray you to consider these things. Both may be done when the messengers come up to us. My humble request to you is, that you will grant us what we have conscientiously treated you for. I conceive we are all agreed to leave our burdens, and you to agree on the time. No more at present; but rest, your unworthy brother in gospel relation.

WILLIAM SCREVEN.

"The 13th of the 7th month, [September, O. S.] 1682.
To Brother Tho. Skinner, Will. Squire, Elias Callender."
Rev. S. Hall's Collection of Papers.—Ed.

solemnly signed on September 25, 1682, by William Screven, Elder, Humphrey Churchwood, Deacon, Robert Williams, John Morgandy, Richard Cutt, Timothy Davis, Leonard Drown, William Adams, Humphrey Azell, and George Litten, and a number of sisters.[1] A Baptist church was also formed this year from that of Boston, at Newbury, by William and John Sayer, Benjamin Morse, Edward Woodman and others,[2] to whom I find Elder Hull and Elder Emblen writing as a sister church, on March 25, 1689; though how much longer they continued a distinct church I do not find.

Mr. Philip Edes, a member of the first Baptist church in Newport, died this year on March 16, of whom Mr. Samuel Hubbard says in a letter to Governor Leete, "This friend of yours and mine, one in office in Oliver's house, was for liberty of conscience; a merchant, a precious man, of a holy life and conversation, beloved of all sorts of men, his death much bewailed by all." Mr. Thomas Olney, senior, also died this year. He was next to Mr. Williams in the pastoral office at Providence, and continued so to his death, over that part of the church who were called Five Principle Baptists, in distinction from those who parted from their brethren about the year 1653, under the leading of Elder Wickenden, holding to the laying on of hands upon every church member. The greatest fault that I find Mr. Olney charged with is, that he was for extending the first deed of Providence up to the

---

[1]This church had but a brief existence. "As the result of a long cherished and well organized religious intolerance, venting itself in vehement and impassioned persecution, these humble Christians became disheartened and overcome. In less than one year from its recognition, the church was dissolved, and the members scattered like sheep upon the mountains." Millet's Maine Baptists, p. 27; Benedict, Vol. I, p. 309.—ED.

[2]"1682. Early this year, a small Baptist church was formed in Newbury, as appears from the following extract from the records of the First Baptist church in Boston:—'February 6th, 1681, [O. S.] Agreed, upon a church meeting, that we, the church at Boston, have assented unto the settling of the church at Newbury.' The persons who formed this church were probably George Little and Philip Squire, who united with the Baptist church in Boston in 1676, Nathaniel Cheney, William Sayer and wife, Mr. Edward Woodman and wife, John Sayer and Abel Merrill, all of whom became members in 1681." History of Newbury, p. 135.—ED.

head of the two great rivers it lay between, or at least as far as their charter reached, from the words *Without limits*, in page 72. In this he was opposed by our elders, Wickenden and Dexter, the latter of whom informs us that Mr. Williams said, the only intent of the expression was to prevent the Indians hurting their cattle if they wandered far into the woods. Their writings on both sides are yet extant in their town clerk's office. They tell me at Swanzey that Elder Miles permitted Mr. Brown's wife, who was not a Baptist, to commune with their church, till by Elder Olney's influence she was dismissed to Mr. Angier's church in Rehoboth. It is very evident that Mr. Olney was a capable and very useful man, both in church and state for forty-four years after he left the Massachusetts; as his son also was for many years; and his posterity are respectable in that town and State to this day. Mr. Holmes, of whom much has been said, who wrote the account of himself in 1675, that is given in pages 173—176, 206—209, and succeeded Mr. Clarke in the pastoral office at Newport, died there, October 15, 1682, aged seventy-six. He has a large posterity now remaining in New England and New Jersey.

The learned and pious Mr. Miles having returned to his flock in Swanzey, fell asleep in Jesus, on February 3, 1683; and his memory is still precious among us. We are told that being once brought before the magistrates he requested a Bible, and upon obtaining it, he turned to those words, "Ye should say, Why persecute we him, seeing the root of the matter is found in me;" Job 19. 28; which having read, he sat down; and the word had a good effect upon their minds, and moved them to treat him with moderation if not kindness. His son went back to England, and his grandson, Mr. Samuel Miles, was an Episcopal minister at Boston in 1724. Though Mr. Willard, and the Magnalia from him, accused the Baptists of Boston, of separating because they wanted to be teachers,[1] yet that was so far from truth, that

[1] Magnalia, Vol. II, p. 460.—ED.

on June 27, 1681, they wrote to London for a minister, giving this as one reason for it, that, "our minister is very aged and feeble, and often incapable of his ministerial work;" and as another motive they say, "We conceive there is a prospect of good encouragement for an able man to come over, in that there seems to be an apparent and general apostacy among the churches who have professed themselves Congregational in this land; whereby many have their eyes opened, by seeing the declension and confusion that is among them." A kind answer hereto was returned by eleven Baptist ministers, which is before me.[2]

[2] "London, the 13th of the 8th [?] month, 1681.

"BELOVED BRETHREN—For whom we pray that the Father of mercies may fill you with the knowledge of his will, in all wisdom and spiritual understanding in the knowledge of our Lord Jesus, that you may be to the praise, honor and glory of him that hath called you out of darkness into his marvelous light. We have received yours to us, wherein you acquaint us with the good hand of Providence towards you in having your liberty again to meet in your public place, and the hopes you have of a considerable increase; also the sense you have of the present want of a faithful, able man to go in and out before you in the work of the ministry, the Lord having deprived you of him that was formerly very useful to you therein, who is now fallen asleep in the Lord. We do assure you that there is nothing wanting, nor shall be, to help you herein, but at present cannot think of any, the Lord knowing the laborers are few amongst us, especially such as have the courage whereby they may have the more acceptance with you, and be able to maintain the truth against gainsayers. But you may be assured of the utmost we can do herein, and we trust and pray that the Lord will be pleased to spirit such amongst yourselves as may be a means to build you up in the ways of holiness. We have had experience that when such help hath been wanting amongst us as you desire, the Lord hath made it up with his special presence, and the assistance he hath given to poor, despised, unlearned men hath been so blessed that greater addition hath been to the churches than now; and we hope what may be wanting in the gifts you wait for, the Lord will help you to make up by that humble and gracious frame of spirit, shining in your love to Christ and to each other, as may put to silence those that may take an occasion to reproach you for want of having those abilities amongst you as they have amongst them. He that hath the abundance of the Spirit, is able to make supply to all your wants, according to the riches of his glory by Jesus Christ.

"And since the Lord hath abated the heats of some men's spirits amongst you, and you have now liberty to move more freer than formerly, you have need be very watchful over your own hearts and the great enemy of our peace, Satan, lest any occasion be given for any to stumble, that are now making inquiry after the farther manifestations of the mind and will of God amongst you; and we are persuaded that, as he hath opened a door amongst you, so he will furnish you with abilities and strength from himself, for your farther edification and comfort. We kindly thank you that you have the remembrance of us to God, in your prayers, and we desire

And now, as some singular and curious things are generally expected from a new country, I shall relate the closing part of one of the greatest curiosities I have met with in modern history; the sum whereof is this. A large number of people fled out of the old world into this wilderness for religious liberty; but had not been here long before some put in high claims for power, under the name of orthodoxy; to whom others made fierce opposition professedly from the light within; and their clashings were so great that several lives were lost in the fray. This made a terrible noise on the other side of the water. But as self-defence is a natural principle, each party wrote volume after volume to clear themselves from blame; and they both conspired to cast a great part of it upon one singular man, whom they called a weathercock and a windmill.[1] Now let the curious find out

the continuance thereof, not knowing what, nor how soon, troubles and sorrows may befall us. The cloud has been black a great while over us, and it is marvelous in our eyes that our peace hath been and is lengthened out as it is; but surely a very great storm is a-coming, and who shall be able to stand in that day, the Lord only knoweth. That indeed is our comfort, that we are under the promise of a faithful God, that as the day is, so our strength shall be. We are very glad to have some lines from you, and desire it may be continued as often as you have any opportunity; and we trust we shall not be wanting to return answers to them. With our prayers to the Lord to keep you faithful to the end, and our real love to you all, remain,

<table>
<tr><td>WM. KIFFEN,</td><td>WILLIAM DIX,</td></tr>
<tr><td>HAN. KNOLLYS,</td><td>ROBERT SCELLING,</td></tr>
<tr><td>DANIEL DYKE,</td><td>TOBIAS RUSSELL,</td></tr>
<tr><td>WM. COLLINS,</td><td>MAURICE KING,</td></tr>
<tr><td>NEH. COXE,</td><td>JNO. SKINER."</td></tr>
<tr><td>EDW. WILLIAMS,</td><td></td></tr>
</table>

The original of this letter, with the autograph signatures, is preserved among the Backus papers in the library of the Backus Historical Society.—ED.

[1] "Here is a lying, scandalous book of Roger Williams of Providence..... I have known him about fifty years, a mere *weathercock*, constant only in inconstancy..... They ought to have feared God and the king, that is to punish evil doers, and therefore not to meddle to their hurt with him that is given to change." Coddington's Letter. See pp. 353, 354.

"In the year 1654, a certain windmill in the Low Countries, whirling round with extraordinary violence, by reason of a violent storm then blowing; the stone, at length, by its rapid motion, became so intensely hot as to fire the mill, from whence the flames, being dispersed by the high winds, did set a whole town on fire. But I can tell my reader, that about twenty years before this, there was a whole country in America like to be set on fire by the rapid motion of a *windmill* in the head of one particular man. Know then that about the year 1630, arrived here, one Mr. Roger Williams," &c. Magnalia, Vol. II, p. 430.—ED.

if they can, first, how men of university learning, or of divine inspiration, came to write great volumes against a windmill and a weathercock? secondly, how such a strange creature came to be an overmatch for them all, and to carry his point against the arts of priestcraft, the intrigues of court, the flights of enthusiasm and the power of factions, so as after he had pulled down ruin upon himself and his friends, yet to be able, in the midst of heathen savages, to erect the best form of civil government that the world had seen in sixteen hundred years? thirdly, how he and his ruined friends came to lie under those reproaches for a hundred years, and yet that their plan should then be adopted by thirteen colonies, to whom these despised people could afford senators of principal note, as well as commanders by sea and land? The excellency of this scene above those which many are bewitched with, consists in its being founded upon facts and not fictions; being not the creature of distempered brains, but of an unerring Providence.

According to Mr. Williams's own testimony, his soul was renewed by divine grace when he was not more than ten or twelve years old.[1] And the mystery of his being rigidly set in his way, and yet " given to change," is to be explained thus. Neither frowns nor flatteries could move him to part with what he judged to be truth, or to assent to anything contrary thereto. As he scrupled the exactness of the calendar then in use, so he discovered it in all his dates. Even when dedicating his Quaker dispute to the king, he dated it March 10, 1672, 3, (*ut vulgo.*) On the other hand he was ever ready to change, when he could obtain light for it from any quarter. While he ministered to his brethren at Plymouth, he objected against their custom of giving their neighbors the title of *Goodman*, if they were not judged to be godly persons. When Governor Winthrop paid them a visit in 1632,[2] and his advice was asked upon it, he showed them that they ought to distinguish betwixt theological and

---

[1] See p. 118.   [2] See p. 43.

moral goodness, and observed that when trials by jury were first introduced in England, after the names of fit persons for the purpose were called over, the crier called them to attend, *Good men and true*, from whence proceeded the custom then in question; and he thought it a pity to make a stir about a custom so innocently introduced.[1] Mr. Williams readily embraced this advice, and made a very good use of it afterward, in exposing the mischiefs that arose from a confounding of those two sorts of goodness together, as Mr. Cotton and many others had done. And because he was earnestly looking for a better church establishment than he had then seen, they imposed the name of Seeker upon him. The great Mr. Baxter calls him The father of the Seekers in London.[2] When he went there in 1643, and published his testimony against the Bloody Tenet, Mr. Cotton, among other reflections, said, " Thus men that have time and leisure at will, will set up images of clouts, and then shoot at them."[3] In answer to which Mr. Williams appealed to the people of Plymouth, Salem and Providence, that he had not led such a life in this country; and as to the other, he says:—

> I can tell that when these discussions were prepared for the public in London, his time was eaten up in attendance upon the service of the parliament and city for the supply of the poor of the city with wood, during the stop of coal from Newcastle, and the mutinies of the poor for fireing. .... These meditations were fitted for public view in change of rooms and corners, yea, ... in a variety of strange houses, sometimes in the fields in the midst of travel.

For this service, through the hurry of the times, and the necessity of his departure, he lost his recompence to this day. He continues:—

> Well, notwithstanding Master Cotton's bitter censure, some persons of no contemptible note nor intelligence, have by letters from England, informed the discusser, that by these " images of clouts" it hath pleased God to stop no small leaks of persecution, that lately began to flow in

---

[1] Magnalia, B. 2, p. 14. [Vol. I, p. 117.]   [2] Crosby, Vol. I, p. 118.
[3] Tenet washed, p. 31.

upon dissenting consciences, and among others, to Master Cotton's own, and to the peace and quietness of the Independents, which they have so long, and so wonderfully enjoyed.[1]

As to his later services, he was so far from being meanly hired, as they said, for a piece of bread,[2] to write against the Quakers, that after he had done it, he wrote thus to Newport:—

MY DEAR FRIEND, SAMUEL HUBBARD: To yourself and aged companion, my loving respects in the Lord Jesus, who ought to be our hope of [and] glory, begun in this life and enjoyed to all eternity. I have herein returned your little, yet great, remembrance of the hand of the Lord to yourself and your son late departed. I praise the Lord for your humble kissing of the holy rod, and acknowledging his just and righteous, together with his gracious and merciful, dispensation to you. I rejoice also to read your heavenly desires and endeavors, that your trials may be gain to your own souls, and the souls of the youth of the place, and all of us. You are not unwilling, I judge, that I deal plainly and friendly with you. .... After all that I have seen and read and compared about the seventh day (and I have earnestly and carefully read and weighed all I could come at in God's holy presence,) I cannot be removed from Calvin's mind, and indeed Paul's mind, Col. 2, that all those sabbaths of seven days were figures, types and shadows, and forerunners of the Son of God, and that the change is made from the remembrance of the first creation, and that (figurative) rest on the seventh day, to the remembrance of the second creation on the first, on which our Lord arose conqueror from the dead. Accordingly I have read many, but see no satisfying answer to those three Scriptures chiefly, Acts 20, I Corinthians 16, Revelation 1, in conscience to which I make some poor conscience to God as to the rest day..... As for thoughts for England, I humbly hope the Lord hath hewed [shewed] me to write a large narrative of all those four days agitation between the Quakers and myself; if it please God I cannot get it printed in New England, I [yet] have great thoughts and purposes for Old..... Mine age, lameness, and many other weaknesses, and the dreadful hand of God at sea, calls for deep consideration. What God may please to bring forth in the spring his holy wisdom knows. If he please to bring to an absolute purpose I will send you word, and my dear friend Obediah Holmes, who sent me a message to the same purpose. At present I pray salute respectively Mr. John Clarke and his brothers, Mr. Tory, Mr. Edes, Edward Smith, William Hiscox, Stephen Mumford and other friends,

---

[1] Reply to Cotton. p. 38. See pp. 130, 146, 147, 157, &c.
[2] See p. 353.—ED.

whose preservation, [and] of the Island, and this country, I humbly beg of the Father of mercies, in whom I am yours, unworthy.

R. W.

If the reader reviews Dr. Chamberlain's first letter,[1] and is informed that he with the brethren he wrote to, took the whole of the ten commandments to be moral and immutable, and held that it was the little horn that changed the time from the seventh to the first day; but that Mr. Olney and his church observed to their brethren, that Paul speaks of a glory which was done away, that was written and engraven in stones; II Corinthians 3. 7; compared with this letter, he will then have a plain idea of the nature of that controversy on both sides, as it was managed in that day. And, to go on, it is to be remembered, that some persons in different parts of the colony had such a conceit of liberty, as that officers should manage the government without any reward from them; by which means Mr. Clarke received but part of his pay for procuring their charter as long as he lived; and this occasioned a remonstrance from his executors to the Assembly upon it soon after his death. A clause from Mr. Williams upon it, I have already recited;[2] to which I now add the following. In August, 1678, he was appointed to assist Mr. Daniel Abbot in setting their town records in order, the latter being then chosen their clerk. Three years after, Mr. Williams wrote to him thus:—

My Good Friend: Loving remembrance to you. It hath pleased the Most High and Only Wise, to stir up your spirit to be one of the chiefest stakes in our poor hedge. I therefore, not being well able to come to you, present you with a few thoughts about the great stumbling block, to them that are willing to stumble and trouble themselves,—our rates. James Matison had one copy of me, and Thomas Arnold another. This I send to yourself and the town (for it may be I shall not be able to be at meeting.) I am grieved that you do so much service for so bad recompence; but I am persuaded you shall find cause to say, The Most High God of recompence, who was Abraham's great reward, hath paid me.

[1] See pages 378, 379.   [2] See page 371.

CONSIDERATIONS PRESENTED, TOUCHING RATES.

1. Government and order in families, towns, &c., is the ordinance of the Most High, Romans 13, for the peace and good of mankind. 2. Six things are written in the hearts of all mankind, yea, even in Pagans. 1st. That there is a Deity; 2d. That some actions are naught; 3d. That the Deity will punish; 4th. That there is another life; 5th. That marriage is honorable; 6th. That mankind cannot keep together without some government. 3. There is no Englishman in his Majesty's dominions, or elsewhere, who is not forced to submit to government. 4. There is not a man in the world except robbers, pirates and rebels, but doth submit to government. 5. Even robbers, pirates and rebels themselves, cannot hold together but by some law among themselves, and government. 6. One of these two great laws in the world, must prevail; either that of judges and justices of peace in courts of peace, or the law of arms, the sword and blood. 7. If it comes from the courts of trials in peace, to the trial of the sword and blood, the conquered is forced to seek law and government. 8. Till matters come to a settled government no man is ordinarily sure of his house, goods, lands, cattle, wife, children, or life. 9. Hence is that ancient maxim, It is better to live under a tyrant in peace, than under the sword, or where every man is a tyrant. 10. His Majesty sends governors to Barbados, Virginia, &c., but to us he shows greater favor in our charter, to choose whom we please. 11. No charters are obtained without great suit, favor or charges. Our first cost an hundred pounds, (though I never received it all,) our second about a thousand, Connecticut about six thousand, &c. 12. No government is maintained without tribute, customs, rates, taxes, &c. 13. Our charter excels all in New England, or in the world, as to the souls of men. 14. It pleaseth God, Romans 13, to command tribute, custom and consequently rates, [&c.,] not only for fear, but for conscience sake. 15. Our rates are the least by far of any colony in New England. 16. There is no man that hath a vote in town or colony, but he hath a hand in making the rates by himself or his deputies. 17. In our colony the General Assembly, Governors, magistrates, deputies, towns, town clerks, raters, constables, &c., have done their duties; the failing lies upon particular persons. 18. It is but folly to resist, (one or more, and if one why not more?) God hath stirred up the spirit of the Governor, magistrates and officers, driven to it by necessity, to be unanimously resolved to see the matter finished; and it is the duty of every man to maintain, encourage and strengthen the hand of authority. 19. Black clouds (some years) have hung over Old and New England heads. God hath been wonderfully patient and long suffering to us; but who sees not changes and calamities hanging over us? 20. All men fear that this blazing herald from heaven denounceth from the Most High, wars, pesti-

lence, famines; is it not then our wisdom to make and keep peace with God and man?

Your old, unworthy servant,
ROGER WILLIAMS.[1]

Providence, 15th January, 1680,[1] (so called.)

The last act that I have found upon record, performed by this eminent peacemaker, was on January 16, 1683, when he, with Mr. Carpenter, and the heirs or assigns of the other eleven original proprietors, signed a full settlement of the long continued controversy about Pawtuxet lands. On the 10th of May following, Mr. John Thornton wrote to Mr. Hubbard and said:—

Dear brother, you gave me an account of the death of divers of our ancient friends; since that time the Lord hath arrested by death our ancient and approved friend Mr. ROGER WILLIAMS, with divers others here. The good Lord grant that we may be stirred up, with the wise virgins, to be trimming our lamps, and getting them full of the spiritual oil, and standing with wise Habakkuk upon our watch towers till our appointed change.

Thus lived and thus died the first Baptist minister in New England, and the first founder and supporter of any truly free civil government upon earth, since the rise of antichrist; "and he was buried with all the solemnity the colony was able to show."[2] This was in the eighty-fourth year

---

[1] These excellent observations are still extant in his own hand writing. The last article refers to a remarkable blazing star that appeared in those times.—B.

Professor Howell, who copied the above document for Backus, appended to the last sentence the following note: "Alluding to the very remarkable appearance of the comet of 1680, the tail of which was said to be eighty-two millions of miles long, its period five hundred and seventy-five years, and that it came so near the sun as to be heated two thousand times hotter than red hot iron." Many testimonies remain of the terror with which this comet was then regarded. Professor Howell had doubtless seen it at its reäppearance in 1758, after a period of a little more than seventy-five years, instead of five hundred and seventy-five; and its appearance in 1835, is still well remembered. It is the same comet which, in 1456, evoked the famous order of Pope Calixtus III, that all church bells should be rung each noon, an extra Ave Maria be repeated and the prayer added, "Lord, save us from the devil, the Turk, and the comet!"—the same which, according to the speculations of Whiston, successor of Newton in the professorship of mathematics at Cambridge, swept its tail over the earth in the days of Noah and produced the deluge!—ED.

[2] Callender, p. 93, [147]. In 1686 Mr. S. Hubbard wrote that Mr. Thornton, and Mr. Joseph Clarke, were all that were then living who were baptized in New England before him.

of his age, being fifty-two years after his arrival in this country.

His wife, whose name was Mary, came with him from England; their children were, 1. Mary, born at Plymouth the first week in August, 1633. 2. Freeborn, at Salem in October, 1635. 3. Providence, born at the place he so called, in September, 1638, said to be the first English male born there. 4. Marcy, born July 15, 1640. 5. Daniel, born February 13, 1642. 6. Joseph, born in December, 1643. The last of these, and a grandson of the same name, were magistrates in that colony, and some of great knowledge, compute his present posterity at near two thousand. Thomas Ward, Esq., who was a Baptist before he came out of Cromwell's army, and was a very useful man in this colony, was ancestor to two late governors, and to the present secretary of it, in the male line, as Mr. Williams was in the female; one of them was the Honorable Samuel Ward, Esq., who died a member of the Continental Congress at Philadelphia, on March 26, 1776, aged 52. The family of Hopkins in Providence, which has afforded an honorable member of that Assembly, and two commanders for the continental fleet, descended in the male line from Mr. Thomas Hopkins, who followed Mr. Williams from Plymouth, and in the female from Mr. Wickenden, an early member, and long a teacher of the Baptist church there. The noted family of Brown, in Providence, sprung from Mr. Chad Brown on the one side, and from Mr. Williams on the other. And our Generals, Greene and Arnold, sprung from two of the first twelve proprietors of those lands, which were given for a place of refuge for such as were distressed for conscience sake elsewhere. May that great design never be forgotten by us or ours? Some have been ready to make those religious contentions and oppressions an argument against all revealed religion, but if they duly consider the following things, compared with the foregoing, perhaps it may alter their minds. To guard against evil biases in our dealings, the great Author of our religion said, With what judgment ye judge, ye shall be judged; and with what measure ye mete, it shall be measured to you again. Was not his word verified in the following instances ?

1. The ruling party in the Massachusetts, had not only raked up the real faults of the Baptists, and exposed them in their worst colors, but also slandered them in many particulars. And now Edward Randolph went eight voyages to England in nine years, and treated them in the same manner at the British Court, on purpose to get away their charter.[1] 2. By a plea from the king's grant in that charter, they had cruelly oppressed their brethren and neighbors in many instances; now in 1684 the charter was vacated by a decree in chancery, without giving them opportunity to answer for themselves; and "those who were in confederacy with Sir Edmund Andros, for the enriching themselves on the spoils [ruins] of New England, did invade the property as well as liberty of the subject; .... and gave out, that now their charter was gone all their lands were the king's; that themselves did represent the king, and therefore men that would have any legal title to their lands must take patents of them, on such terms as they should see meet to impose. What people that had the spirits of Englishmen could endure this ?"[2] 3. Their charter never gave them any right to establish their mode of worship by force; but in order to do it they presumed to leave the word *lawful* out of their oaths;[3] and Ipswich gave an early example of seizing their neighbors' property in that illegal way, against the weighty arguments of Judge Symonds.[4] Now the scale was turned, so that an arbitrary Governor and Council made laws and imposed taxes upon all, without any House of Representatives; and for refusing to carry an order for such a tax into execution in Ipswich, Mr. John

---

[1] Massachusetts History, Vol.I, pp. 329, 335, [297, 301.] Vol. III, pp. 480, 490, &c.
[2] Revolution in New England Justified, printed 1691, and reprinted 1773, p. 17.
[3] See pp. 47, 49.   [4] See pp. 248, 249.—ED.

Wise, a minister, who spake upon it in their town meeting, was imprisoned, and denied the benefit of the Habeas Corpus Act; and when he upon his trial pleaded the Magna Charta, and laws of England, he was told by one of the judges, that "he must not think the laws of England followed them to the ends of the earth." "Mr. Wise," said he, "you have no more privilege left you, than not to be sold for slaves." The honorable John Appleton, Esq., was treated in the same manner; and both were put from office, fined fifty pounds apiece, and ordered to give bonds of one thousand pounds each, for their good behavior for one year. Four other men of that town received like sentences, only in less sums.[1] Was not this a teaching by cudgel instead of argument?[2] To justify or excuse their making the law against the Baptists in 1644, Mr. Hubbard said:—

> It were well if [all] those who cannot comply with the religion of the state or place where they live, yet had so much manners as not to jostle against nor openly practise that that is inconsistent therewith, as if they would bid a kind of defiance thereunto. Moses would not do that in Egypt, upon [the] account of religious worship, that might seem a matter of abomination to them who were lords of the place.[3]

And Dr. Mather had lately said:—

> If a considerable number of Antipædobaptists should (as our fathers here did) obtain liberty from the state, to transport themselves and families, into a waste American wilderness, that so they might be a peculiar people by themselves; practising all, and only the institutions of Christ; if now Pædobaptists should come after them, and intrude themselves upon them,.... surely they would desire such persons either to walk orderly with them, or return to the place from whence they came. Let them then do as they would be done by.[4]

Now John Palmer, one of Andros's council, to vindicate their conduct, said, "It is a fundamental point, consented to by all Christian nations, that the first discoverer of a country inhabited by infidels, gives [a] right and dominion of that country to the prince in whose service [and employ-

---

[1] Revolution in New England, Justified, p. 16.
[2] See page 80.
[3] Hubbard, pp. 373, 374.—ED.
[4] Preface to *Ne Sutor*, p. 5.

ment] the discoverers were sent." But they of Massachusetts say, "We affirm that this fundamental point, as he calls it, is not a Christian, but an unchristian principle."[1] Yes, and it was as much so when they banished Mr. Williams, as it is now. 4. We have seen how Dr. Mather treated the characters of the Baptists; now, a letter is forged in his name, full of ridiculous and treasonable expressions, which being pretendedly detected in its way to Holland, was laid before the British ministry, and then was printed and spread through the nation to expose him. When he came to know it he said, "That which troubled me was, that I was like to suffer as an evil doer, through the malice and falsehood of wicked men. Might I have suffered for any truth which I had borne witness to, I could have rejoiced in it."[2] Yes; but his persecutors were as little inclined to give him that honor, as he was the Baptists. 5. Governor Bradstreet who helped to banish Mr. Williams, for opposing an oath that was contrary to his conscience, lived to feel and see what such impositions meant upon themselves. For refusing to swear on the book, many were not only put by from serving on juries, but were fined and imprisoned; and, says the historian, "the faithful of New England chose rather to suffer affliction, than to use a rite in the worship of God, which they suspected sinful."[3] And Dr. Increase Mather took pains to publish a discourse upon "The unlawfulness of using common prayer; and of swearing on the book." 6. Andros carried his Episcopal worship into Mr. Willard's meeting-house, after their exercise was over, and threatened "to shut up their doors if he was refused, and to punish any man who gave two pence towards the support of Nonconformist ministers; and that public worship in the Congregational way, should not be tolerated." This felt so to them, that when King James sent over his proclamation, of indulgence and liberty of conscience, " the ministers of Bos-

---

[1] Revolution justified, p. 44. [2] His Life, pp. 93, 94.
[3] Magnalia B. 7, pp. 3, 12, 13, [Vol. II, pp. 434, 438, 439.]

ton proposed unto their congregations to keep a day of thanksgiving, to bless God for what they enjoyed; [but the Governor assured them] "that if they did, he would clap a guard on their persons and their churches too," and so prevented it. Hereupon they thought proper to send Dr. Mather as their agent to England. He had accused Randolph or his brother, of forging the aforesaid letter to expose him; upon which Randolph prosecuted him for defamaation; and though he was acquitted upon trial, yet, to prevent his going to England, Randolph designed by another writ to seize, and clap him up in prison; to avoid which, Dr. Mather escaped out of town in disguise, and was carried on board a ship in the night, April 7, 1688; and upon his arrival at London, he with others petitioned the king, "that there might be liberty of conscience in matters of religion, ... and that all their meeting-houses may be left free to them, according to the intention of the builders thereof; but this application met with no success."[1]

Do not these things verify the truth of the Christian revelation? They brought Dr. Mather over to acknowledge, that the parable of the tares was a declaration of our Saviour's will for a toleration; and "that a good neighbor and a good subject has a claim to all his temporal enjoyments before he is a Christian; and he thought it very odd, that the man should lose his claim, from his embracing of Christianity, because he does not happen to be a Christian of the uppermost party among the subdivisions. For an uppermost party of Christians to punish men, in their temporal enjoyments, because in some religious opinions they dissent from them, or with an exclusion from the temporal enjoyments which would justly belong unto them, is a robbery."[2] And how were the Baptists treated after this?

Their church at Boston had received Elder John Emblen from England, July 20, 1684. Mr. Richard Dingley was

[1] His Life, pp. 103—111. Massachusetts History, Vol. I, p. 368, [327.]
[2] His Life, pp. 58, 59. See Isaiah, 61. 8.

received a member there the same year, and soon after succeeded Mr. Holmes in the pastoral office at Newport, where he continued about ten years, and then went to Carolina. Mr. Samuel Luther succeeded Mr. Miles at Swanzey, where he was ordained by our elders, Hull and Emblen, on July 22, 1685, and he was continued a great blessing to them thirty-two years. But Elder Emblen dying about 1699, that church remained in destitute circumstances for some years, and then chose Mr. Callender in his room; to whom the following letter was directed, the original of which is now before me.

16d. 1m. 1714.

SIRS:—As in the distresses of the winter, we did, with the solemnities of humiliation, call upon our gracious God, so, since he has graciously recovered so many of our people, and sent in such seasonable provisions for our necessities, it has been proposed among the ministers of the [this][1] town, that our good people may acknowledge these favors of our prayer-hearing Lord, with the solemnity [solemnities] of a thanksgiving, in our several congregations; for which, also, we have had the encouragement of the government. The time we would propose for such a service is Thursday, the first of April, if the churches have no objection against it. And it was desired that you might be seasonably apprised of this proposal, because we are well assured of the welcome, which a motion of such a nature will find with you, and the people of God unto whom you stand nearly related. Having thus discharged the duty in this matter incumbent on me, I take leave to [and] subscribe,

Sir, your brother and servant,

COTTON MATHER.

To my worthy friend, Mr. Ellis Callender, elder of a church of Christ in Boston.

His son Elisha had joined that church the tenth of August preceding, and he gave him an education at Cambridge; and Dr. Increase Mather having signified his willingness for such a thing, the church called him, his son, and Mr. John Webb, to assist in ordaining the said Mr. Elisha Callender,

---

[1] The words in brackets, indicate the form of this letter according to the copy in Rev. S. Hall's Collection of papers.—ED.

their pastor[1] on May 21, 1718 ; and in the preface to that Ordination Sermon, the old gentleman says :—

It was a grateful surprise to me, when several of the brethren of the Antipædobaptist persuasion came to me, desiring that I would give them the Right Hand of Fellowship in ordaining one whom they had chosen to be their pastor. I did (as I believe it was my duty) readily consent to what they proposed ; considering the young man to be ordained is serious and pious, and of a candid spirit, and has been educated in the college at Cambridge ; and that all of the brethren of that church with whom I have any acquaintance, (I hope the like concerning others of them) are, in the judgment of rational charity, godly persons.

Two of them were old Elder Callender and Deacon Sweetser, who were principal members when their meetinghouse was formerly nailed up. Dr. Cotton Mather preached the Sermon, which he entitled Good Men United. After opening the nature and importance of such a union, he says :—

It is very sadly true, that many ecclesiastical communities, wherein piety has its votaries, yet are guilty of this evil, that they impose terms of communion which many that have the fear of God, are by just exceptions kept from complying withal. Now in this unhappy case what is to be done? Do this ; let good men go as far as they can without sin in holding communion with one another. But where sinful terms are imposed, there let them make their stops ; there a separation becomes a duty ; there the injunction of heaven upon them is, Be ye separate, saith the Lord, and touch not the unclean thing, and I will receive you. The imposers are

---

[1] "The following is the copy of the letter sent to the church under the care of Dr. Mather and Rev. Mr. Webb, on Mr. Callender's ordination :

"HONORED AND BELOVED IN THE LORD : Considering that there ought to be a holy fellowship maintained among godly Christians, and that it is a duty for us to receive one another as Christ also received us, to the glory of God, notwithstanding some differing persuasions in matters of doubtful disputation ; and although we have not so great latitude as to the subject of baptism as the churches of New England generally have; notwithstanding, as to the fundamental principles in your doctrine of Christ, both as to faith and order of the gospel, we concur with them; being also satisfied that particular churches have power from Christ to choose their own pastors, and that elders ought to be ordained in every church; and having chosen our well beloved brother, Elisha Callender, to be our pastor, we entreat you to send your elders and messengers to give the Right Hand of Fellowship in his ordination." Notes to Memoir of John Callender, R. I. Historical Collections, Vol. IV, p. 27. —ED.

the schismatics. .... The unity which beautifies the true people of God, is called The unity of the Spirit. Eph. 4. 3. The right basis for a union among us, is, the Holy Spirit inclining us to glorify God, with an obedience to his will revealed in his word; and to glorify our Saviour with a dependence on him for all the blessings of goodness; and to love our neighbor as ourselves. There have been many attempts to unite people in forms and terms, that are not the pure maxims of living unto God; and so to build the tower of Zion, on a foundation which is not the tried stone and the precious, and so not the sure foundation. There has hitherto been a blast from heaven upon all those attempts; they have miscarried, as being rather calculated for the tower of Babel. .... We are sometimes fearful of paying the respects which we really owe to a people of true piety, (such a people as we this day meet withal) forsooth, lest we confirm them in what we take to be an error, or mislead others into it. I hope it is needless fear. .... O, you who cannot but own yourselves brethren to one another, and bound up in one bundle of life; how is it possible for you to require of one another, submission to terms which, you cannot but think that men may be good men, and have the evident tokens of salvation upon them, without submitting to? And the terms which you have so pitched upon, how can you proceed so far, as not only to withdraw your fellowship from the good men to whom they do not appear so necessary, but also inflict uneasy circumstances upon them, under the wretched notion of *wholesome severities!* *Cursed the anger, for it is fierce; and the wrath, for it is cruel!* good for nothing but only to make divisions in Jacob, and dispersions in Israel. Good men, alas! good men have done such ill things as these; yea, few churches of the reformation have been wholly clear of these iniquities. New England also has, in some former times, done something of this aspect, which would not now be so well approved of; in which, if the brethren in whose house we are now convened, met with any thing too unbrotherly, they now with satisfaction hear us expressing our dislike of every thing that has looked like persecution in the days that have passed over us.[1]

I thought it best thus to collect these passages into one view, which may remind us of the apostle's words, "Happy is he that condemneth not himself in that thing which he alloweth." After the vacation of the Massachusetts charter, Mr. Joseph Dudley was appointed President of the colony, till Governor Andros arrived in December, 1686, who had all New England and New York included in his commission.

[1] Mather's Sermon at Callender's Ordination, pp. 18, 25, 34, 38, 39.

Randolph brought a *quo warranto* against Rhode Island charter, June 22, 1686, upon which the freemen met, and gave their opinion to the General Assembly, and then left the affair with them, who, on June 29, concluded not to stand suit with his Majesty, but sent a humble address to him, "to continue their privileges according to charter." Andros's commission was published among them the 12th of January following, and he, with a few mandamus counsellors, tyrannized over all these colonies, till John Winslow brought a copy of King William's proclamation to Boston, and Andros imprisoned him therefor; upon which the people arose, April 13, 1689, and seized him and his council, and resumed their former order of government; which being heard of in Rhode Island colony, their freemen met at Newport, May 1, and voted to resume their charter, and to have their former rulers take their places again. They met again February 20, 1690, and elected new rulers in the place of some who declined serving, and they, with Connecticut, have enjoyed their privileges to the present times.

I shall close this chapter with a list of New England rulers, and a few remarks thereon. Plymouth never had any charter but only from the Council for New England that was established at Plymouth in Devonshire. Their form of government was settled by voluntary agreement among themselves. At first they only chose a Governor; the next year, one Assistant with him; in 1624, they chose five, and in 1633, seven Assistants, and kept to that number to the end of their colony. Mr. Bradford was always an Assistant when he was not Governor, as long as he lived; his son was Assistant and then Deputy Governor till the revolution; and he and several of his posterity have been Counsellors in this province; and one of his descendants[1] is now Deputy Governor of the State of Rhode Island. In 1639, they began to have a House of Deputies in their General Court; and about 1662, they agreed that their eldest Assistant should

---

[1] William Bradford.—ED.

have the power of a Deputy Governor, to act in the Governor's place when he was absent. This continued till 1680, when, by reason of Mr. Alden's age, though they continued him an Assistant, they began to choose other Deputy Governors.

A LIST OF PLYMOUTH GOVERNORS, THE YEARS THEY RULED, AND THE TIME OF THEIR DEATHS.

1. John Carver, 1620; died, April, 1621.
2. William Bradford, 1621—33,[1] 35, 37, 39—44, 45—57; died May 9, 1657, æt. 69.[2]
3. Edward Winslow, 1633, 36, 44; died May 8, 1655, æt. 61.
4. Thomas Prince, 1634, 38, 57—73; died March 29, 1673, æt. 73.
5. Josiah Winslow, 1673—80;[3] died December 18, 1685, æt. 52.
6. Thomas Hinckley, 1681—86, 89—92; died 1705, æt. 74.[4]

DEPUTY GOVERNORS.

1. William Colliar, 1662—66.
2. John Alden, 1666—80.
3. Thomas Hinckley, 1680.
4. James Cudworth, 1681. He went their agent to England, and died there the same year.
5. William Bradford, 1682—86, 89—92.

ASSISTANTS; THE YEARS WHEN FIRST CHOSEN, AS FAR AS I CAN FIND FROM THEIR RECORDS.

Isaac Allerton,	1621	William Colliar,	1634
Edward Winslow,		Thomas Prince,	1635
Miles Standish,		Timothy Hatherly,	1636
John Howland,		John Brown,	1636
John Alden,		John Jenny,	1637
John Doane,		John Atwood,	1638
Stephen Hopkins,		Edmund Freeman,	1640
William Gilson,[5]	1633	William Thomas,	1642

[1] From the election in 1621 to the election of his successor in 1633. This explanation applies to the other terms of office, similarly indicated, in these tables.—ED.

[2] He was in his sixty-ninth year. Generally, in these tables, Backus seems to have given the ages in this manner.—ED.

[3] He was reëlected in 1680, and died in office.—ED.

[4] Allen's Biographical Dictionary gives his age, seventy-five.—ED.

[5] Here should be inserted the name of William Bradford. In 1633 he declined reëlection as Governor, and was made an Assistant. See Morton's Memorial, p. 115. —ED.

Thomas Willet,	1651	Nathaniel Bacon,	1667
Thomas Southworth,	1652	Const. Southworth,	1670
James Cudworth,	1656	Daniel Smith,	1679
Josiah Winslow,	1657	Barnabas Lothrop,	1681
William Bradford,	1658	John Thatcher,	1682
Thomas Hinckley,	1658	John Walley,	1684
James Brown,[1]	1665	John Cushing.	1690
John Freeman,	1666		

NOTE.—The Appendix to Morton, mistakes in placing the first choice of Cudworth and Brown after 1670; and the Magnalia sets Smith too early.

MASSACHUSETTS GOVERNORS.

1. Matthew Cradock, 1628.
2. John Winthrop, 1629—34, 37—40, 42—44, 46—49; died March 26, 1649, æt. 62.
3. Thomas Dudley, 1634, 40, 45, 50; died July 31, 1653,[2] æt. 77.
4. John Haines, 1635.
5. Henry Vane, 1636; died 1662, æt. 50.
6. Richard Bellingham, 1641, 54, 65—72;[3] died 1672, æt. 81.
7. John Endicott, 1644, 49, 51—53, 55—65; died March 23, 1665.
8. John Leverett, 1673—78; died March 16, 1678.
9. Simon Bradstreet, 1678—86, 89—92; died March 27, 1697, æt. 94.

DEPUTY GOVERNORS.

1. Thomas Goff, 1628.
2. John Humphrey, 1629.
3. John Endicott, 1629, 41—44, 50, 54.
4. Thomas Dudley, 1630—34, 37—40, 46—50, 51, 52.
5. Roger Ludlow, 1634.
6. Richard Bellingham, 1635, 40, 53, 55—65.
7. John Winthrop, 1636, 44, 45.
8. Francis Willoughby, 1665—71.
9. John Leverett, 1671—73.
10. Samuel Symonds, 1673—77.
11. Simon Bradstreet, 1677, 78.
12. Thomas Danforth, 1678—86, 89—92.

[1] In the first edition, this name is given, James Bawn. It is a typographical error, as the name is afterwards correctly given.—ED.

[2] Allen's Biographical Dictionary, usually the best authority in early New England biography, gives this date erroneously, 1652. The American Cyclopædia copies the error. See p. 228; Morton's Memorial, p. 166.—ED.

[3] He was reëlected in 1672, and died in office.—ED.

Assistants.

Sir Richard Saltonstall,		H. Atherton,	1654
Isaac Johnson,		Richard Russell,	1659
John Endicott,		Thomas Danforth,	1659
Increase Nowel,		William Hawthorn,	1662
William Vassel,		Eleazer Lusher,	1662
William Pinchon,		John Leverett,	1665
Edward Rossiter,		John Pinchon,	1665
Roger Ludlow,		Edward Tyng,	1668
Thomas Sharp,		William Stoughton,	1671
John Revel,		Thomas Clarke,	1673
William Coddington,		Joseph Dudley,	1676
Simon Bradstreet,[1]		Peter Bulkley,	1677
John Humphrey,	1632	N. Saltonstall,	1679
John Winthrop, jun.,	1632	Humphrey Davy,	1679
John Haines,	1634	James Russell,	1680
Atherton Hough,	1635	Samuel Nowel,	1680
Richard Dummer,	1635	Peter Tilton,	1680
Richard Bellingham,	1636	John Richards,	1680
Roger Harlakenden,	1636	John Hull,	1680
Israel Stoughton,	1637	B. Gidney,	1680
Richard Saltonstall,	1637	Thomas Savage,	1680
Thomas Flint,	1642	William Brown,	1680
Samuel Symonds,	1643	Samuel Appleton,	1681
Will. Hibbens,	1643	Robert Pike,	1682
Herbert Pelham,	1645	Daniel Fisher,	1683
Robert Bridges,	1647	John Woodbridge,	1683
Francis Willoughby,	1650	Elisha Cooke,	1684
Thomas Wiggan,	1650	William Johnson,	1684
Edward Gibbons,	1651	John Hawthorn,	1684
John Glover,	1652	Elisha Hutchinson,	1684
Daniel Gookin,	1652	Isaac Addington,	1686
Daniel Denison,	1653	John Smith.	1686
Simon Willard,	1654		

Their charter appointed eighteen Assistants, but they had scarce ever chosen above half so many, till by the King's order they chose the full number in 1680.

[1]These twelve were here in 1630, but Johnson and Rossiter died before the year was out. Saltonstall, Vassel, Sharp and Revel soon went back.—B.

Eighteen Assistants were chosen in 1628, only five of whom are here named. Others, not mentioned here, were chosen between 1629 and 1632.—ED.

RHODE ISLAND RULERS.

Roger Williams, was truly the founder of that Colony, and a principal ruler among them, as we have seen from the beginning. Those who began upon the Island had a different notion about government from him at first, and as their covenant on page 74, was printed from an imperfect copy, I shall here insert it exactly from their records as follows :—

We whose names are under-written do here solemnly, in the presence of Jehovah, incorporate ourselves into a body politic, and as he shall help, will submit our persons, lives and estates, unto our Lord Jesus Christ, the King of kings and Lord of lords, and to all those perfect and most absolute laws of his, given us in his Holy Word of truth, to be guided and judged thereby.

Exod. 34, 3, 4.[1]
2 Chron. 11, 3.
2 Kings 11, 17.

They then appointed Mr. Coddington as Judge, and Mr. Aspinwall Secretary, to rule them according to this covenant, till on January 2, 1639, an assembly of the freemen said :—

By the consent of the body it is agreed that such who shall be chosen to the place of Eldership, they are to assist the Judge in the execution of justice and judgment, for the regulating and ordering of all offences and offenders, and for the drawing up and determining of all such rules and laws as shall be according to God, which may conduce to the good and welfare of the commonweal; and to them is committed by the body the whole care and charge of all the affairs thereof; and that the Judge together with the Elders, shall rule and govern according to the general rules [rule] of the word of God, when they have no particular rule from God's word, by the body prescribed as a direction unto them in the case. And further, it is agreed and consented unto, that the Judge and [with the] Elders shall be accountable unto the body once every quarter of the year, (when as the body shall be assembled) of all such cases, actions or [and] rules which have passed through their hands, by them to be scanned and

---

[1] This reference is retained, as printed in the former edition, and as Backus gave it twenty-seven years later in his Abridgment, page 43. We are informed of a recent "letter from Hon. John R. Bartlett, Secretary of Rhode Island," which states "that the original manuscript of the covenant of the early settlers of Rhode Island has the marginal notes precisely as published by Mr. Backus." The published R. I. Colonial Records give the reference, Exodus 24. 3, 4; and Professor Elton, in an Appendix to Callender's Century Sermon, R. I. Historical Collections, Vol. IV, p. 213, gives it in the same form. This passage seems to have a plain significance and the one given above scarce any significance in connection with the covenant.—ED.

weighed by the word of Christ; and if by the body or any of them, the Lord shall be pleased to dispense light to the contrary of what by the Judge or [and] Elders hath been determined formerly, that then and there it shall be repealed as the act of the body; and if it be otherwise, that then it shall stand, (till further light concerning it) for the present, to be according to God, and the tender care of indulging [indulgent] fathers.

WILLIAM DYRE, Clerk."

They then chose the elders named in page 78, and went on as is there mentioned, till March 16, 1641, when they disfranchised Carder, Holden, Shatton and Potter, and suspended from voting George Parks,[1] John Briggs, and Mr. Lenthal, who was gone for England; and then said, " It is ordered by the authority of this present Court, that none be accounted a delinquent for doctrine, provided it be not directly repugnant to the government and laws established." In September following they said, " The law concerning liberty of conscience in point of doctrine is perpetuated." After they received their charter, their rulers were as follows:—

PRESIDENTS OR GOVERNORS.

John Coggshall, 1647.
Roger Williams, 1648[2], 54—57; died 1683, æt. 84.
John Smith, 1649, 52.
Nicholas Easton, 1650, 51, 72, 73; died 1675.
Gregory Dexter, 1653.
Benedict Arnold, 1657,—60, 62—66, 69—72, 77, 78; died June 19, 1678.
William Brenton, 1660—62, 66—69, died 1674.
William Coddington, 1774, 75, 78; died November 1, 1678, æt. 78.
Walter Clarke, 1676, 86, 96, 97; died June, 1714.
John Cranston, 1678—80; died March 12, 1680.
Peleg Sanford, 1680—83.
William Coddington, 1683—85; died 1688.

---

[1]This name should probably be *Parker*. It is several times given thus in the Rhode Island Colonial Records.—ED.

[2]William Coddington was elected President this year. As he did not appear at the Assembly, and charges arose against him, Jeremy Clarke was appointed to fill his place, with the title of President Regent. At a special Assembly in Warwick, in March, 1649, before the close of this legislative year, Roger Williams was chosen to act as President. See pp. 168—171; Rhode Island Colonial Records; Arnold's History of Rhode Island, Vol. I, pp. 219—225.—ED.

[1690.] OFFICERS IN RHODE ISLAND COLONY. 429

Henry Bull, 1685, 89.
John Easton, 1690—95; died 1705, æt. 85.
Caleb Carr, 1695.
Samuel Cranston, 1698—1727; died April 26, 1727.
Joseph Jencks, 1727—32; died June 15, 1740, aged 84.
William Wanton, 1732—34.
John Wanton, 1734—41.
Richard Ward, 1741—43.
William Greene, 1743—45, 46, 48—55, 57.
Gideon Wanton, 1745, 47.
Stephen Hopkins, 1755—57, 58—62, 64, 67—69.
Samuel Ward, 1762—64, 65—67.
Josias Lyndon, 1769.
Joseph Wanton, 1770—75.
Nich. Cooke, 1775—77.

Deputy Governors.

William Brenton, 1663—66.
Nicholas Easton, 1666—69, 70.
John Clarke, 1669, 71.
John Cranston, 1672, 76—78.
John Easton, 1674, 75.[1]
James Barker, 1678, 79.
Walter Clarke, 1679—85, 1701—14.
John Coggshall, 1690.
John Greene, 1690—1701.
Henry Tew, 1714.
Joseph Jencks, 1715—21, 23—27.
John Wanton, 1721—23, 29—34.
Jonathan Nichols, 1727.
Thomas Fry, 1727—29.
George Hazard, 1734—38.

Daniel Abbott, 1738—40.
Richard Ward, 1740.
William Greene, 1741—43.
Joseph Whipple, 1743—45, 46, 52—54.
William Robinson, 1745, 47.
William Ellery, 1748—50.
Robert Hazard, 1750—52.
J. Gardner, 1754, 56—64.
Jonathan Nichols, 1755.
Joseph Wanton, jun., 1764, 67—69.
Elisha Brown, 1765—67.
Nicholas Cooke, 1769, 75.
Darius Session, 1770—75.
William Bradford, 1775—77.

Assistants.

Roger Williams,	1647	Samuel Gorton,	1649
John Sanford,	1647	William Field,	1650
W. Coddington,	1647	John Porter,	1650
Randal Holden,	1647	John Wickes,	1650
Jeremiah Clarke,	1648	John Sayles,	1653
John Smith,	1648	Stukely Westcoat,	1653
Thomas Olney,	1649	Thomas Harris,	1654
John Clarke,	1649	John Roome,	1654

[1] The name of William Coddington should here be inserted, as Deputy Governor in 1678.—ED.

Benedict Arnold,	1654	John Albro,	1671
William Baulston,	1656	Richard Smith,	1672
John Coggshall,	1656	Francis Brinley,	1672
Arthur Venner,	1657	Henry Brown,	1672
Richard Tew,	1657	Walter Clarke,	1673
Joseph Clarke,	1658	Daniel Gould,	1673
John Greene,	1660	Job Almy,	1673
James Barker,[1]	1663	Henry Bull,	1674
Walter Todd,	1664	Benjamin Barton,	1674
John Gardner,	1665	Edward Thurston,	1675
Edward Smith,	1665	Thomas Barden,	1675
William Carpenter,	1665	William Codman,	1676
John Brown,	1665	Samuel Gorton, jun.,	1676
Samuel Wilbore,	1665	John Whipple,	1677
John Easton,	1666	Thomas Greene,	1678
William Harris,	1666	Caleb Carr,	1679
Richard Carder,	1666	Thomas Ward,	1679
Benjamin Smith,	1666	William Coddington,	1680
Peleg Sanford,	1667	Joseph Jenckes,	1680
William Reape,	1667	George Lawton,	1680
Stephen Arnold,	1667	Richard Arnold,	1681
John Cranston,	1668	John Potter,	1685
Thomas Olney, jun.,	1669	Walter Newbury,	1686
Joshua Coggshall,	1669	Benedict Arnold,	1990
John Tripp,	1670	Christopher Almy,	1690
James Greene,	1670		

CONNECTICUT GOVERNORS.

Edward Hopkins, 1636; died in England, 1657.
John Haines,
George Wyllys.
Thomas Wells.
John Webster.
J. Winthrop,[2] 1662—76; died April 5, 1676, æt. 71.
William Leete.
Robert Treat.

J. Winthrop,[3] died 1707.
G. Saltonstall, 1707—24.
J. Talcot, 1724—41; died October, 1741.
Jona. Law, 1741—50; died 1750.
R. Woolcot, 1750—54.
Thomas Fitch, 1754—66.
Wm. Pitkin, 1766—69; died 1769.
Jona. Trumbull, 1769—77.

[1]The above-named Messrs. Baulston, Porter, Williams, Olney, Smith, Greene, Coggshall, Barker, Field and Joseph Clarke, were the ten Assistants appointed in their last charter.

[2]John Winthrop son of John Winthrop of Massachusetts.—ED.

[3]John, otherwise called Fitz John, Winthrop, son of a previous Connecticut Governor.—ED.

New Haven Governors.

Theo. Eaton, 1637—57; died 1657.   Wm. Leete, 1660—62.
F. Newman, 1657—60; died 1660.

Brief Remarks.

1. These facts may teach us what to think of the exclamations that have often been made against a free government, where each freeman may have a voice in choosing their chief rulers. Plymouth had this liberty in its full extent; having full power to lay the plan of their government as they pleased, and to elect whom they would into office. Each freeman in that colony had his equal vote in the annual choice of their Governor; and had not Governor Bradford requested them sometimes to elect others into that office, it is probable that in the whole seventy-three years of their continuance as a distinct colony, they would never have changed it into any more hands than death obliged them to; and, in fact, they never did but five times in all those years; and New Haven made no such change while they remained a distinct government. And we have a good evidence that even a sergeant in Plymouth militia was treated with more honorable regards than captains have now been for these many years past. In Connecticut where their Governors have always been elected annually, by votes of the freemen sent in from every town in the colony, they have chosen but sixteen men in a hundred and forty years, and but ten in a hundred years, only two or three of whom were left out of office till they died. And the Massachusetts chose but eight Governors in sixty-three years. But since this fickle popularity (as some call such government) was taken away, and the power was vested in a crowned head, to fix Governors over us by a steady commission, in which the people had no voice, the province in eighty-two years has had a Phips, Stoughton, Bellamont, Dudley, Tailor, Shute, Dummer, Burnet, Belcher, Shirley, Phips, Pownal, Bernard, Hutchinson, and Gage, for commanders-in-

chief, who have each in their turns been invested with power, to negative our councillors when elected, and to negative any and every act that our Assembly could pass, and to dissolve them when they pleased. All these in a space when Connecticut had but about half so many governors, and in thirty-four years of the time Rhode Island had but two. And the evil effects afterward of a depreciating currency, and of party influence in elections, all need to beware of at this day. Hence, 2. Learn the importance of viewing persons and actions in their distinct light, so as not to confound good and evil, truth and falsehood, together. God says, Only by pride cometh contention; but with the well-advised is wisdom. Pride caused a contention about who should be greatest, even among the apostles, and made them think of calling for fire from heaven to consume such as would not receive them. And Dr. Owen well says, " Gospel constitutions, in the case of heresy or error, seem not to favor any course of violence, I mean of civil penalties. Foretold it is, that heresies must be; I Cor. 11. 19; but this for the manifesting of those who are approved, not the destroying of those that are not. .... Perhaps those who call for the sword on earth, are as unacquainted with their own spirits, as those that called for fire from heaven. Luke 11. And perhaps the parable of the tares gives in a positive rule as to this whole business."[1] These sentiments were inculcated upon our Plymouth fathers before they came to this country.[2] Governor Bradford was the owner of the book which contained them, that I am now favored with; and while he continued Governor, Mr. Williams could be comfortable at Plymouth; but when Mr. Winslow came into that office in 1633, he requested a dismission to Salem. And the second time Mr. Winslow was Governor, he wrote to Mr. Williams to remove out of that jurisdiction,[3] and a law was made that year to forbid the gathering of any

[1] See pp. 18, 22.   [2] Collection of his Tracts, 1721, p. 314.   [3] See p. 57.

church therein without the rulers' leave. He and Mr. Colliar were the Commissioners for Plymouth, who, on September 7, 1643, signed the articles of confederation that the other three colonies had entered into the May before; and who then concurred in the delivery of Miantinomo to Uncas to be slain, (though without torture,) and in advising the Massachusetts to send an armed force to Warwick. He was again a Commissioner in their meeting at Hartford, September 1, 1644, when they wrote to each colony, to enter upon a method of rating all persons by authority, that refused or neglected to give what the rulers judged to be their meet proportion toward ministers' maintenance; against which Mr. John Brown, the other Plymouth Commissioner, entered his dissent. In October, 1645, in a thin Assembly at Plymouth, Mr. Winslow propounded, " and after a whole day's agitation" got something of this nature allowed and entered upon their waste book; but when a full Assembly met the next week, Mr. Brown and other magistrates, " excepted the entry of that order, as pernicious and destructive to the weal of the government, and tendered a proposition, to allow and maintain full and free tolerance of religion, to all men that would preserve the civil peace, and submit to government."[1] But Mr. Winslow had influence enough to prevent the putting of that matter to vote. When the Commissioners met at New Haven, September 9, 1646, they said:—

> Upon information of what petitions have been lately put up in some of the colonies against the good and straight ways of Christ, both in the churches and in the Commonwealth, the Commissioners, remembering that these colonies, for themselves and their posterity, did unite [enter] into this form of [firm and] perpetual league, as for other respects, so for mutual advice, that the truth and liberties of the gospel might be preserved and perpetuated, [propagated] thought it their duty seriously to commend it to the care and jurisdiction [consideration] of each General Court within these United Colonies, that, as they have laid their foundations and measured the house [temple] of God, the worship and worshippers, by the rod [that straight reed] God hath put into their hands, so they would

[1] Massachusetts History, Vol. III, pp. 153, 154.

walk on, and build up (all discouragements and difficulties notwithstanding) with an undaunted heart and unwearied hand, according to the sure rules and patterns;....that anabaptism, familism, antinomianism, and generally all errors of like nature, which oppose, undermine and slight either the Scriptures, the Sabbath or other ordinances of God, and bring in and cry up unwarrantable revelations, inventions of men, or any carnal liberty, under a deceitful color of liberty of conscience, may be seasonably and duly suppressed; though they wish as much forbearance and respect may be had of tender consciences, seeking light, as may stand with the purity of religion and peace of the churches.

The commissioners for Plymouth, Brown and Hatherly, did not concur with this.[1]

Mr. Winslow was then gone to England, from whence he never returned; and not having his influence, all the ministers in Plymouth colony, and the Massachusetts Court to help them, could not prevail in 1650, with Governor Bradford and his Court, to inflict so much as a fine upon Mr. Holmes; who was most cruelly whipped at Boston, the next year.[2] Said ministers were not of the original planters of Plymouth colony, and because their Court would not be governed by them, the most of them left it, and carried their complaints to Boston, from whence fresh exertions were made, which then in a measure introduced a State-worship, and State-way of maintenance into Plymouth colony. Though the bloody work that followed at Boston, gave such a shock to it as turned them back again in a great measure. Mr. John Brown had been a magistrate seventeen years, and a Commissioner for his colony eleven years, even down to 1656. And we are told that he was, "well accomplished with abilities [in] both civil and religious [concernments] and attained, through [God's] grace, unto a comfortable persuasion of the love and favor of God to him; he, falling sick of a fever, with much serenity and spiritual comfort fell asleep in the Lord, at Wannamoiset near Rehoboth, in the spring of the year 1662."[3] His son James joined the next year in forming a Baptist church

[1]Records of the United Colonies. [2]See page 177, &c. [3]Morton, pp. 175, 176.

there, and both in 1665 and 1666, the freemen through the colony elected him for one of their magistrates, at the same time that the Massachusetts Court disfranchised two of their ancient freemen, for no worse crime than Mr. Brown then lived in.[1] Though he did not see cause then to accept of that office, yet being chosen again in 1673, he accepted it, and served his colony therein eleven years; in the midst of which time persecution was again revived at Boston, and Mr. Brown and his minister were fined for visiting their afflicted brethren there. With what face then can any man reproach New England in general, with the persecutions which its first founders, and many of its best members afterward abhorred? And of all men how inexcusable are Episcopalians in so doing, when it was the errors which Massachusetts brought out of their church that produced all those mischiefs, of which they were then, and have been ever since, much more guilty than those they complain of here! In England and Scotland they, in that day, destroyed more hundreds of lives, in trying to establish their supremacy over the consciences of men, than the Massachusetts hanged persons. And they have not only always taxed dissenters to their ministers wherever they could get power to do it, but also in Virginia, they have fined and imprisoned our ministers only for preaching without their license; and continued this cruel trade till the present rupture put a stop to it. 3. Hence, see the pernicious evil of using carnal weapons in religious affairs. Papists, Episcopalians, Presbyterians and Congregationalists, have all tried it in their turns; but, instead of giving up the root of this mischief, they have each of them tried to cast all the reproach of it, upon the bad dispositions of their neighbors; and so it has been a constant source of raillery and slander. But where can a better set of men be found upon earth, since Constantine first brought the carnal weapon into the church, who concurred in using of it there, than the fathers of the Mas-

[1] See pages 298, 303.—ED.

sachusetts? Look back to pages 114—116, and then tell me where you can find a more excellent ruler than Governor Winthrop, that ever traveled in that path? And Mr. Shepard of Cambridge, who died five months after him, said:—

Surely all the persons, whose hearts the Lord stirred up in this business, were not rash, weak-spirited, inconsiderate of what they left behind, or what it was to go into a wilderness. But if we were able to recount the singular workings of Divine Providence, for the bringing on this work to what it is come unto, it would stop the mouths of all. Whatever many may say or think, we believe after times will admire and adore the Lord herein, when all his holy ends, and the ways he has used to bring them about shall appear. .... What shall we say of the singular providence of God, in bringing so many ship-loads of his people through so many dangers, [as on eagles' wings] with so much safety from year to year?[1] the fatherly care of our God, in feeding and clothing so many in a wilderness, giving such healthiness and great increase of posterity? .... But above all, we must acknowledge the singular pity and mercies of our God, that hath done all this, and much more, for a people so unworthy, so sinful, that by murmurings of many, unfaithfulness in promises, oppressions, and other evils that are found among us, have so dishonored his Majesty, exposed his work here to much scandal and obloquy, for which we have cause forever to be ashamed; that the Lord should yet own us, and rather correct us in measure, [mercy] than cast us off in displeasure, and scatter us in this wilderness.[2]

We are informed that when Governor Winthrop lay on his death bed, Mr. Dudley requested him to sign a warrant to banish Mr. Mathews, a Welsh minister, but that he refused, saying, "I have had my hand too much in such things already."[3]

---

[1] It was computed that from 1628 to 1643, (when the times turned in England, and some went back,) the number of ships which brought them over were two hundred and ninety-eight; the men, women and children who came in them, twenty-one thousand two hundred, or thereabout. That the passage of the persons cost ninety-five thousand pounds, the live stock, twelve thousand pounds, beside the price of them in England; procuring food till they could raise it here, forty-five thousand; nails, glass and other material for building, eighteen thousand; arms and ammunition, twenty-two thousand; in all, one hundred and ninety-two thousand pounds, beside much more which the adventures laid out in England for their use. Johnson, pp. 28—31.

[2] Magnalia, B. 3, p. 89. [Vol. II, pp. 350, 351.]   [3] Bishop, p. 226.

[1690.] HARDSHIPS AND BLESSINGS OF THE FIRST SETTLERS.

Captain Roger Clap, one of the first planters of Dorchester, the commander of Castle William for twenty years, and who bore several other offices in the State with honor, and died in Boston in 1691, in such esteem that the whole General Assembly attended his funeral, wrote some memorials of those early times, with his fatherly advice to his children. And, observing that their straits were sometimes so great that the very crusts of his father's table in England would have been as a dainty in this wilderness, he says :—

> I took notice of it, as a great favor of God unto me, not only to preserve my life, but to give me contentedness in all these straits; insomuch that I do not remember that I ever wished in my heart that I had not come into this country, nor wished myself back again [to my father's house.] Yea, I was so far from that, that I wished and advised some of my dear brethren to come hither also; which accordingly one of my brothers, and those who married my two sisters, sold their means, and came hither. The Lord Jesus Christ was so plainly held out in the preaching of the gospel unto poor lost sinners, and the absolute necessity of the new birth, and God's Holy Spirit, in those days, accompanied [was pleased to accompany] the word with such efficacy upon the hearts of many, that our hearts were taken off from old England, and set upon heaven. .... Many were converted, and others established in believing. Many joined unto the several churches where they lived, confessing their faith publicly, and showing before all the assembly, their experiences of the workings of God's spirit in their hearts, to bring them to Christ; which many hearers found very much good by, to help them to try their own hearts, and to consider how it was with them. .... Oh, the many tears that have been shed in Dorchester meeting-house at such times, both by those that have declared God's work on their souls, and also by those who heard them! In those days God, even our own God, did bless New England.[1]

Another of their captains who came over in 1630, says :—

> Those honored persons who were now in place of government, having the propagation of the churches of Christ in their eye, labored by all means to make room for inhabitants, knowing well that where the carcass is, thither will the eagles resort. But herein they were opposed by certain persons, whose greedy desire for land, much hindered the work for a time; as indeed such persons do to this day; and let such take notice how these were cured of this distemper. Some were taken away by death, and then, be

---

[1] Prince's Christian History, Vol. I, pp. 70—72.

sure, they had land enough. Others, fearing poverty and banishment, supposing the present scarcity would never be turned into plenty, removed themselves away, and so never beheld the great good the Lord hath done for his people. But the valiant of the Lord waited with patience, and in the miss of beer, supplied themselves with water; even the most honored as well as others, contentedly rejoicing in a cup of cold water; blessing the Lord that had given them to taste of that living water, and that they had not the water that slakes the thirst of their natural bodies given them by measure, but might drink to the full; as also in the absence of bread, they pleased [feasted] themselves with fish. The women once a day, as the tide served, resorted to the muscles and clam-banks, where they daily gathered their families' food, with much heavenly discourse of the provisions Christ formerly made for many thousands of his followers in the wilderness. Quoth one, My husband hath travelled as far as Plymouth, [about forty miles] and hath with great toil brought a little corn home, and before that is spent the Lord will assuredly provide; quoth the other, Our last peck of meal is in the oven at home a-baking, and many of our godly neighbors have quite spent all, and we owe one loaf of that little we have. Then spake a third, My husband hath ventured himself among the Indians for corn, and can get none, as also our honored Governor hath distributed his so far, that a day or two more will put an end to his store and all the rest; and yet, methinks our children are as cheerful, fat and lusty, with feeding upon these muscles, clams [clam-banks] and other fish, as they were in England with their fill of bread, which makes me cheerful in the Lord's providing for us; being further confirmed by the exhortation of our pastor to trust in the Lord, whose is the earth, and the fullness thereof. As they were encouraging one another in Christ's careful providing for them, they lift up their eyes and saw two ships coming in, and presently this news comes to their ears, that they were come from Ireland full of victuals.[1]

Oh! how gloriously do they shine, and how manfully do they talk, when exercising themselves in the gospel armor, to what they do when they come down to the use of earthly weapons in heavenly concernments! In 1645 they compared the Baptists' opposition to such conduct, to what Amalek did to Israel when they were weak. And the erecting of a small Baptist church in 1665, was called a

---

[1] In one of those ships came Mr. Roger Williams. Johnson, pp. 48, 49; Prince's Annals, pp. 18, 47. [344, 377.] We are told that one of the fathers of that day, having dined with his friends on clams without bread, devoutly returned thanks, that God had caused them to *suck of the abundance of the sea, and of treasures hid in the sand.* Magnalia, B. 1, p. 22. [Vol. I, p. 72.]

strong attempt against them from the spirit of Anabaptism; the permission of which among them they said, manifestly tended to the destruction of their churches, though they had above forty of them then in their colony, in joint communion with about as many more in neighboring colonies.[1] And in 1781 they compared their ecclesiastical establishment to a small boat, and those few illiterate Baptists to the ballast of a great ship, which was like to sink it. Hence it was their weakness, and not their strength, that caused them to treat the Baptists so cruelly. The extending of the gospel ordinance of baptism to subjects who are in a state of nature; limiting the church of Christ to human schools for ministers, and compelling all to support such and only such, are points which had but a weak bottom to stand upon in that day, when the power of godliness was so well known in the country.[2]

[1] Christian History, Vol. I, p. 64.
[2] The seven foregoing chapters, with an Appendix which will be found at the close of this volume, constitute Volume I of the original edition. This will explain the character of the last few pages; and also, as Volume II was not published or written till several years later, will explain certain differences of style and method which the reader will notice in the chapters that follow, as compared with those that have preceded.--ED.

CHAPTER VIII.

A FIRST PRINCIPLE OF THESE CHURCHES.—OF WITCHCRAFT.—UNJUST ATTEMPTS TO TURN IT AGAINST THE BAPTISTS.—OPPRESSIVE LAWS.—EFFECTS THEREOF.—PLYMOUTH PROCLAMATION.—THEIR CHURCH ORDER.—EVILS OF DENYING IT.—FIRST MINISTERS OF MIDDLEBOROUGH AND DARTMOUTH—OF PLYMPTON.

The fathers of New England came much nearer to the apostolic order of the church, than most other reformers had done. Dr. Cotton Mather published a specimen thereof in the year 1690. Says he, " A church (as the Greek name for it allows us to think) is to consist of a people called out from the ways of sin, by the powerful and effectual work of God upon their souls. Regeneration is the thing without which a title unto sacraments is not to be pretended. Real regeneration is the thing which, before God, renders men capable of claiming sacraments ; and visible and expressed regeneration is that which, before men, enables us to make such a claim."[1] From the first planting of the country to 1662, none were allowed to come to the ordinance of the supper, nor to bring their infants to baptism, without such a profession. The synod of that year opened a door for the children of church members to bring their infants upon a lower profession ;[2] though in the Massachusetts a profession of regeneration was still held to be necessary, in order for coming to full communion, or having a vote in the government, either of church or State. This was essential to

[1] Companion for Communicants, pp. 29, 30, 37. [2] See page 267.—ED.

the nature of their plan of a holy government, in imitation of the church of Israel. And for the church to govern the world, for good men to govern bad ones, seemed much more rational and scriptural, than for the world to govern the church about soul-guides, as they have done since. Previous to this, the country was involved in most deplorable circumstances; their charter lost; their sea coasts infested with privateers and pirates, and their frontiers with savage enemies. An attempt to take Quebec in 1690, was defeated, which enraged the enemy the more against them, and also involved the country in a heavy debt; to discharge which, paper money was first made here, the effects whereof were very pernicious. Officers and people were greatly divided in their minds about the causes of these calamities, and about what was the best way to remove them. And in this juncture they were alarmed with an apprehension that the powers of hell were let loose upon them, which amazed and confounded them inexpressibly. The scene was introduced in the following manner:—

A variety of books concerning witchcraft, had been published in London and Boston, which were dispersed in New England. And near the close of 1691, a young daughter and a neice of Mr. Samuel Parris, minister of Salem Village, (now Danvers,) with two other girls in the neighborhood, made such complaints of distress and injuries upon their bodies, that a physician pronounced them bewitched. Hereupon an Indian woman from New Spain, that lived at the minister's house, tried some experiments to find out the witch, which she pretended to have been used in her own country. This coming to the knowledge of those children, they accused her of being the witch; of appearing to them and pinching, pricking and tormenting them. Teachers, rulers and people, were so much affected with this calamity, as to keep days of fasting and prayer for its removal; first at said minister's house, next in the village, and then through the colony. Such notice being taken of, and pity shown to, those children, they increased their complaints; and others advanced like accusations, not only against the Indian woman, but also against two other old women in the place, so that all the three were committed to prison on March 1, 1692. And this noise increased, and such accusations spread, till about an hundred persons were imprisoned on that account. In the midst of which distress, on May 14, Sir William Phips, the Governor, arrived at Boston with their new charter, in company with Dr. Increase Mather, who procured it. The Governor and Council were so much concerned to purge this growing evil from the land, that they did not wait for the meeting of the Legislature, to whom the constituting of Courts of Justice belonged, but constituted one themselves, whereof Lieutenant Governor Stoughton was President, and by their sentence one woman was hanged on June 10; and by September 22, they executed seven men and thirteen women; after which that Court was dissolved. And by the time that a Court of Oyer and Terminer was constituted according to charter, rulers and ministers were so far convinced that they had acted upon wrong principles, and had also admitted the testimony of accusers without sufficient care and caution, that all the rest of the accused were either acquitted upon trial, or pardoned by authority. A first principle that they acted upon in those condemnations was, that God, in his providence, would not suffer the devil to appear to and afflict any in the shape of an innocent person. And they admitted one accuser to one instance, and another to another, of those spectral appearances, to make up two witnesses. They also who would confess themselves to be witches, were admitted as witnesses against others. And, says a gentlemen who was a careful observer of those transactions, "These confessors, by their plausible confession and accusations of others, begetting credit, have been a great, if not the greatest engine of Satan to carry on the accusing and apprehending of others, until this matter came to such a height, that, if it had not been stopped, might have brought the best Christians in the country under the imputation of that abomination, and have involved all in confusion and blood.[1]" Deplorable indeed was the case of New England at that time; though we are assured, by men who have searched fully into the matter, that a greater number of persons were executed for witchcraft in only one county in England, even in the loose reign of Charles the Second, than all that were put to death here; and also that these executions were under the influence of laws and precedents from thence.[2] But this being a new country, it was more taken notice of, and was more severely felt than there.

We cannot find that the Baptists had any hand in those confused and bloody proceedings; yet much pains have been taken to turn the same against them. A late minister of Danvers, the place where those delusions began, says, "It is reported of witches, and those that hold unlawful commerce with evil spirits, that in order to their entering into confederacy with them, they are solicited to renounce their baptism, even though received in infancy; which shews that such a renunciation of baptism, which Dr. Gill pleads for and commends, is a matter of great impiety."[3] What Dr. Gill pleaded for, was the renouncing of infant sprinkling, and the practicing of believer's baptism, according to primitive institution. But how far was that from the witchcraft at Danvers or Salem! The plainest instances of any mention of baptism therein were as follows. In the examination of a woman before authority, July 21, 1692, were these questions and answers, viz.:—

<small>Question. Goody Lacey, how many years ago since they were baptized? Answer. Three or four years ago, I suppose. Q. Who baptized them? A. The old serpent. Q. How did he do it? A. He dipped their heads in</small>

---

[1] A Modest Inquiry into the Nature of Witchcraft; by John Hale, Minister of Beverly, 1697, p. 88.
[2] Hale, pp. 25, 26, 69. Hutchinson, Vol. II, pp. 22, 69. [22, 60.]
[3] Clark against Gill, 1752, p. 33.

the water, saying they were his, and that he had power over them. Q. Where was this? A. At Falls River. Q. How many were baptized that day? Some of the chief, I think there were six baptized. Q. Name them. A. I think they were of the higher powers.

Also Captain Osgood's wife, of Andover, was made to confess, that she with others, had been carried through the air to a certain pond, where the devil dipped her face in the water, and made her renounce her former baptism. But she with five others, in prison, gave in a retraction of their confessions to the Court, wherein they declared that they were amazed and affrighted out of their reason, by some gentlemen who told them they knew they were witches, and therefore they assented to what was suggested to them, as the only way they had left to save their lives; but when they came to be better composed, they professed that they were innocent and ignorant of such things. And fifty-three of their neighbors gave in a written testimony to the Court, that they believed this to be an honest retraction; one of whom was Dudley Bradstreet, Esq. Mr. Parris and other ministers were very officious in those examinations of persons accused of witchcraft;[1] and sixty years after, Mr. Clark must bring up the same, to prove that " renouncing of his early dedication must appear such an instance of impiety, as to a considerate person were enough to put a stop to his proceedings, how inclinable soever he might be to those principles on other accounts."[2] Such methods have they taken to frighten people from seeing with their own eyes, and from acting according to their own judgments, in the great concerns of the soul and eternity.

The second Massachusetts charter, which was dated October 7, 1691, allowed equal liberty of conscience to all Christians, except Papists. The first General Court under it met at Boston, June 9, 1692, to which Dr. Cotton Mather delivered a sermon, wherein he said, " The civil Magistrate

---

[1] Hutchinson's History, Vol. II, pp. 31, 36, 40—44. [31, 35, 39, 43, 44.]
[2] Against Gill, p. 33.

is most properly the officer of human society, and a Christian, by non-conformity to this or that imposed way of worship, does not break the terms on which he is to enjoy the benefits of human society." And ten years after, he published this and other passages, in his history of New England, and said he would thereby stop the noise about persecution therein. [1]But how could that be done? for he said, "The General Assembly may, by their acts, give a distinguishing encouragement unto the religion which is the general profession of the inhabitants;"[2] that is, may empower some to judge for others about worship, and to enforce their judgments with the sword; which is the root of the worst persecutions in the world. He knew that such acts as he spoke of could not take place here without the royal assent; yet said he, "I am verily persuaded, that the nearness of our dependence on the crown will be found one of our most glorious advantages." His reason therefor is, its giving them a greater security in future shaking times. But experience has now demonstrated, that it is better to trust in the Lord than to put confidence in princes. He, in that sermon, called Cambridge College "A river, the streams whereof made glad the city of God;"[3] which method of applying those words of divine revelation to human schools, is doubtless a perverting of them; and is a way which has done much hurt to mankind. Christians are required to withdraw from such as suppose that gain is godliness; yet now a freehold worth forty shillings a year, or other estate worth fifty pounds (which was soon after reduced to forty) gave every inhabitant a right to vote for legislators; and an Assembly so elected, in their session at Boston, October 12, 1692, enacted:—

That the inhabitants of each town within this Province shall take due care, from time to time, to be constantly provided of an able, learned and orthodox minister or ministers, of good conversation, to dispense the word

[1]Magnalia, B. 7, p. 28, 29. [Vol. II, p. 462.]
[2]Account of his father's life, p. 141.   [3]Sermon, pp. 57, 66, 87.

of God to them; which minister or ministers shall be suitably encouraged, and sufficiently supported and maintained by the inhabitants of such town. And all contracts, agreements and orders, heretofore made, or that shall hereafter be made, by the inhabitants of any town within this Province, respecting their ministers or school-masters as to their settlement or maintenance, shall remain good and valid, according to the true intent thereof, the whole time for which they were or shall be made, in all the particulars thereof, and shall accordingly be pursued, put in execution, and fulfilled. And where there is no contract and agreement made in any town, respecting the support and maintenance of the ministry, or when the same happens to be expired, and the inhabitants of such town shall neglect to make suitable provision therein, upon complaint thereof made unto the Quarter Sessions of the Peace for the county where such town lies, the said Court shall, and hereby are empowered to, order a competent allowance unto such minister, according to the estate and ability of the town, the same to be assessed upon the inhabitants, by warrant from the Court, directed to the Select Men, who are thereupon to proceed to make and apportion said assessment, in manner as is directed for other public charges, and to cause the same to be levied by the constables of such town, by warrant under the hands of the Select Men or of the town clerk by their order.

Be it further enacted, that where any town shall be destitute of a minister qualified as aforesaid, and shall so continue by the space of six months, not having taken due care for the procuring, settling and encouragement of such a minister, the same being made to appear upon complaint unto their Majesty's Justices of the General Sessions of the Peace of the county, the said Court shall, and hereby are empowered to, make an order upon every such defective town, speedily to provide themselves of such a minister as aforesaid, by the next sessions at the furthest; and in case such order be not complied with, then the said Court shall take effectual care to procure and settle a minister qualified as aforesaid, and order the charge thereof, and of such minister's maintenance, to be levied on the inhabitants of such town.

And it is further enacted, that the respective churches, in the several towns within this Province, shall at all times hereafter use, exercise and enjoy, all their privileges and freedoms respecting divine worship, church order and discipline; and shall be encouraged in the peaceable and regular profession and practice thereof.

And further it is enacted, that every minister, being a person of good conversation, able, learned and orthodox, that shall be chosen by the major part of the inhabitants of any town, at a town-meeting duly warned for that purpose, (notice being given to the inhabitants fifteen days before the time of such meeting) shall be the minister of such town; and the whole town shall be obliged to pay towards his settlement and maintenance, each man his several proportion thereof.

They had here entered upon a new and untried scene; and the glaring contradiction betwixt the last two paragraphs of this law, with their finding that some towns had more than one church therein, as also that Boston would not submit to it, caused the Assembly, in their next session of February 3, 1693, to repeal those two paragraphs, and in addition to the rest of that law to enact, "that each respective gathered church, in any town or place within this Province, that at any time shall be in want of a minister, such church shall have power, according to the directions given in the word of God, to choose their own minister;" yet not to settle him without the concurrence of the majority of voters in town affairs, who usually meet therewith for worship; but that being obtained, then "all the inhabitants and ratable estates lying within such town, or part of a town, or place limited by law for upholding the public worship of God, shall be obliged to pay in proportion towards the minister's settlement and support; provided, that nothing herein contained is intended, or shall be construed to extend, to abridge the inhabitants of Boston of their accustomed way and practice, as to the choice and maintenance of their ministers."

Here it is to be noted, that like causes may ever be expected to produce like effects. One of our most essential rights is that we shall not be taxed where we are not represented. And it is most certain, that a civil legislature are not our religious representatives; and in order then to tax the country to religious teachers, they were *abridged* of the rights which Boston would not part with. So when Governor Hutchinson was pursuing the scheme, in 1769, of having America taxed by Britain, he said, "there must be an abridgment of what are called English liberties." But the bloody effects of that attempt, are a loud warning to all after ages. The Assembly went on, in said law, to empower the ratable inhabitants of any town where no church was gathered, to call and settle a minister, by the advice and direction of three neighboring ordained ministers, who should be supported as others were; and also to enact, that if any town or place neglected to obey these laws, their Select-men, or other officers, should be convented before their county Court, and, upon conviction of such neglect, be fined forty shillings for the first offence, and four pounds for every after conviction. As a fruit of which, a warrant was sent from Bristol Court, "requiring the town of Swanzey to choose a minister according to law." The town met upon it August 28, and adjourned to October 17, 1693, when they concluded to report to the Court, that Elder Samuel Luther was their minister.[1] He was ordained pastor of the first church there, July 22, 1685, by the assistance of the Elders Hull and Emblen, of Boston. And the rulers of Plymouth Colony had publicly owned him in that office; one instance whereof take as follows:—

At a Court of Assistants held at Plymouth, the first Tuesday of August, 1690, it being manifest that the Lord our God calls his poor people in this wilderness to great humiliation and mourning, for those awful tokens of his displeasure that are upon us, and our manifold sins, the procuring cause thereof, the Governor and Council do therefore commend it to all the churches of God and people in this Colony, to set apart and observe the last day of this instant as a day of solemn fasting and prayer, wherein to deprecate those heavy judgments impending, and to entreat the Lord to take away all our iniquities, and receive us graciously: particularly that God would prosper the Agents of the country in their weighty negotiation in the other England; that our address may be accepted with our lord the king, and we may have a settled establishment of our ancient liberties and privileges, sacred and civil; that God would call back the commission he hath given to the sword of the enemy to be drawn among us, and direct and manage all the counsels of his servants in this dark and difficult day of war, and give success in the destruction of our adversaries, and restore peace to us; that contagious and afflictive distresses may be removed; that the necessities of the poor may be supplied, and the judgment of scarcity and famine prevented; and that God would bless the labors of our hands, and give both seed-time and harvest; and that, in a way of humiliation and reformation, we may be prepared to meet God, and wait for him in the way of his judgments, and that mercy may be the latter end of all his dispensations to us.

Per order of the above-said Court,   SAMUEL SPRAGUE, Recorder.
To Samuel Luther, Elder of the church of Swanzey, for him to communicate to the church and congregation there.

[1] Swanzey Town Records.

This I carefully copied from the original preserved in Elder Luther's family; and Bristol Court could not be ignorant of his being thus owned as the settled minister of Swanzey; yet this attempt must be made for the other denomination, though they have never been able to set up their worship in that town to this day. A second Baptist church was formed therein, and Mr. Thomas Barnes was ordained pastor of it in 1693. It may be serviceable to enquire into the reason of their being so much better treated when under Plymouth government, than they were after they were incorporated with the Massachusetts.

Plymouth people were taught in Holland, that the church was the school wherein Christ trained up his ministers; though they were far from despising human learning in its place. One of their proofs was the 14th chapter of the First Epistle to the Corinthians; upon which their learned pastor, Mr. Robinson, made the following remarks. Says he:—

That the apostle in this chapter directs the church in the use of extraordinary gifts, is most evident. Neither will I deny but that the officers are to guide and order this action of prophesying, as all other public business, [businesses] yea, even these wherein the brethren have greatest liberty: But that he intends the establishing of, and so takes order, and gives direction for an ordinary, constant exercise in the church, even by men out of office, I do manifest by these reasons. (1.) Because the apostle speaks of the ministration of a gift or grace, common to all persons, as well brethren as ministers, ordinary as extraordinary, and that at all times, which is *love;* as also of such fruits and effects of that grace, as are no less common to all than the grace itself, nor of less continuance in the churches of Christ, to wit, of edification, exhortation and comfort; verse 3, compared with I Thes. v. 11, 14. (2.) In verse 24 he permits all to prophesy, and speaks as largely of prophesying as of learning, and receiving comfort. But lest any should object, May women also prophesy? the apostle prevents that objection, and it may be reproves that disorder amongst the Corinthians, ver. 34, by a flat inhibition, enjoining them expressly to keep silence in the church, in the presence of men, to whom they ought to be subject, and to learn at home of their husbands, [ver. 35,] and not, by teaching [the] men, to usurp authority over them; I Tim. ii. 11, 12; which men in prophesying, do lawfully use. (3.) Now .... in that Paul forbids women, he gives liberty to all men, gifted accordingly, opposing women to men, sex to sex, and not women to officers, which were frivolous. And again, in restraining women, he shews his meaning to be of ordinary, not extraordinary prophesying; for women immediately and extraordinarily [and miraculously] inspired might speak without restraint; Exod. xv. 20; Judg. iv. 4; Luke ii. 36; [Acts xxi. 9]. (4.) The prophets here spoken of were not extraordinary, because their doctrines were to be judged by other prophets, and their spirits to be subject unto the spirits of others; ver. 29, 32; whereas the doctrines of the extraordinary prophets were neither subject to nor to be judged by any; but they, as the apostles, being immediately [and infallibly] inspired, were the foundation upon which the church was built, Jesus Christ himself, being the chief corner stone; Eph. ii. 20, and iii. 5. (5.) The apostle [ver. 37] makes a prophet and a man spiritual all one, whom he further describes, not by any extraordinary gift, but by that common Christian grace of submission unto the things he writes, as the commandments of the Lord: unto whom he opposeth a man wilfully ignorant, ver. 37, 38, teaching us, that he doth not measure a prophet, in this place, either by the office of ministry, or by any extraordinary prophetical gift, but by the common Christian gift of spiritual discerning. (6.) It is the commandment of the Lord by the apostle, that a bishop must be apt to teach, and that such elders or bishops be called as are able to exhort with sound doctrine, and to convince the gainsayers. Now, except men, before they be in office, may be permitted to manifest their gifts, in doctrine and prayer, [Tit. i. 9; Acts vi. 4,] which are the two main works requiring special qualification in the teaching elders, how shall the church (which is to choose them) take knowledge of their sufficiency, that with faith and good conscience they may call them, and submit unto them for their guides?[1]

Now, as the church of Plymouth had always acted upon these principles, it was easy for them to look upon Elder Luther as a minister of Christ, whose church was of the same mind about that point of gospel order. But a minister of chief note among the Massachusetts says:—

That custom, of the prophesying of private brethren, was not observed in any of the churches of New England besides themselves; the ministers of the respective churches there not being so well satisfied in the way thereof as Mr. Robinson was. The most judicious and leading elders among said churches, as Mr. Cotton, &c., that were not absolutely against the thing, were yet afraid that the wantonness of the present age would not

---

[1] Robinson against Bernard, pp. 236, 237. [Works of John Robinson, Congregational Board, London, 1851; Vol. II, pp. 247—249.]

well bear such a liberty as that great light of these churches expressed, to a person of great quality, to whom he bore no small respect, a few hours before he departed this life.[1]

Mr. Robinson says :—

It is apparent, both in the Scriptures and ecclesiastical writers, that not only pride and contention, but heresy, and almost all other evils, have sprung from the officers and governors of the church. And surely nothing hath more in former days advanced, nor doth it this day more uphold the throne of antichrist, than the people's discharging themselves of the care of public affairs in the church, on the one side, and the priests and prelates arrogating all to themselves on the other.[2]

Two brethren of Plymouth church were ordained pastors of other churches in 1694. One of them was Mr. Jonathan Donham, who was ordained at Edgarton, on Martha's Vineyard. The other was at Middleborough, fourteen miles west of Plymouth. About sixteen families began to plant here a little before Philip's war; who moved away when the war broke out, and returned again after it was over; and Mr. Samuel Fuller preached to them till a church was constituted among them this year, and he was ordained their pastor. The settlement of Dartmouth began about the same time with Middleborough, and their first teacher was also from Plymouth, but not in the same way. His name was John Cooke. He was a deacon in Plymouth church for some years; but was cast out of it in the latter part of Mr. Reyner's ministry there, who left them in November, 1654. It is said that Cooke was excommunicated for having been the author of much dissension and division, and for afterwards running into sectarian and anabaptistical principles; and also that Reyner's removal was partly occasioned by the unsettledness of the church, too many of the members being leavened with prejudices against a learned ministry, by means of sectaries then spreading through the land.[3] Some light

[1] Hubbard, [pp. 65, 66.]
[2] Robinson, p. 204. [Works of John Robinson, Vol. II, p. 213.]
[3] Plymouth Register, pp. 4, 12. [Massachusetts Historical Collections, Vol. IV, pp. 111, 118.]

concerning them may be gathered from the following facts. Plymouth church took much pains to obtain learned pastors, if they were otherwise well qualified; but they refused to be confined to human schools for ministers, or to compel the world to support them. They labored hard to get the learned Mr. Charles Chauncy to settle as a colleague with Mr. Reyner; but Mr. Chauncy could not consent to it, because gospel baptism appeared to him to be dipping, and that sprinkling for baptism was unlawful, as their church records witness. In 1650 a separation commenced at Rehoboth, because Mr. Newman, their minister, with six others, assumed all the power of church government to themselves, under the name of "The church representative."[1] For this usurpation a number of the church withdrew, and set up worship by themselves; and the ministers tried hard to move Plymouth Court to suppress them by force, but could not prevail therein. These people soon after became Baptists; and one of them was most shamefully and cruelly persecuted the next year at Boston.[2] By searching into these matters, Mr. Dunstar, President of Harvard College, was brought openly to renounce infant baptism; and seeing the temper which was discovered in the Massachusetts, he removed into Plymouth Colony, the very year that Reyner moved out of it; as several other ministers also did about that time, because they could not bring Plymouth rulers into the use of tax and compulsion for their support.[3] And though Reyner excommunicated Cooke, yet, not being able to bring the church into all his measures, he left them, and robbed them of their church records, which they never recovered; so that what records Plymouth church now has, were afterwards collected from memory and private writings. These facts may help the reader in forming a judgment of what Cooke's sectarian

---

[1] Clarke's Narrative, p. 24. [Massachusetts Historical Collection, Fourth Series, Vol. II, p. 54.]—B.

See also pages 176, 177, 204.—ED.   [2] See page 192.—ED.

[3] See pages 227—229, 256.

principles were, and also how he came by them. His posterity inform me, that he was a Baptist, and that he preached the doctrine of election, with the other doctrines of sovereign grace, in Dartmouth for a number of years. And it appears by Mr. Samuel Hubbard's letters, that a Baptist church was formed upon the west borders of Dartmouth, in the year 1685, wherein Hugh Mosier and Aaron Davis were principal leaders; which church is continued by succession to this day; though the Quakers are the most numerous of any one sect in that town.[1]

On August 24, 1695, the church of Middleborough was bereaved of their beloved pastor, aged 66; "a great loss to the place," said Mr. Cotton, "he being a sincere, godly man, and useful preacher." Mr. Isaac Cushman, another member of Plymouth church, was invited to succeed him; but having a call at Plympton (betwixt here and Plymouth) at the same time, he accepted it; and was ordained there in 1698;[2] and was continued a great blessing to them for about

[1] "Next to the Friends in numbers and influence, stood the Baptists. John Cooke, whose name we meet with on the first and on nearly every page of the early records of the town, as a deputy and a select-man, filling various offices of trust and honor, was a Baptist minister for many years. But this same town official, October 29, 1670, was fined ten shillings 'for breaking the Sabbath by unnecessary travel thereon.' If the record of the case had been preserved, it would have appeared, we think, that Elder John Cooke was not a Sabbath-breaker, but travelling upon his circuit as a Baptist preacher." Old Dartmouth Centennial, p. 86. Backus says in his Abridgment, page 135, "Cooke was a Baptist minister in Dartmouth many years, from whence sprung the Baptist church in the east borders of Tiverton." Benedict says of this church in Tiverton, that it "was formed in the adjoining town of Dartmouth about 1685; the members at first lived in Dartmouth, Tiverton and Little Compton. Their first minister was Hugh Mosier, and next to him Aaron Davis. This was the seventh Baptist church formed on the American continent. In process of time, its seat was removed from Dartmouth to Tiverton, where it continues to the present day." History of the Baptists, Vol. I, p. 503. The church will be subsequently noticed in this work, as the First Baptist church in Tiverton, R. I.—ED.

[2] Mr. John Cotton, above referred to, was son to the famous minister of that name in Boston. He was minister at Plymouth about thirty years, till contentions about the above points of church order occasioned his dismission, by advice of a council in 1697; and the next year he went and gathered a Congregational church in Charleston, South Carolina, where he died, much lamented, September 18, 1699. Plymouth Register, pp. 21. 22. [Massachusetts Historical Collections, Vol. IV, pp. 127, 128.]

forty years. But thirteen ministers, in and near Boston, published a letter of advice to the churches, dated December 28, 1699, in the eighth page of which they represent it to be a *jesuitical principle* for any to hold, "that *illiterate* men may be serviceable and admirable preachers." This with other things moved their churches to look only to colleges for ministers for a long time after. In the meanwhile, as the empowering the world to control the church in the choice of pastors was an untried path to them, it took them three years to find out what to do, when a parish did not concur with the church therein. But when the Assembly met at Boston, May 29, 1695, they enacted, that in such a case the church should call a council of three or five neighboring churches, who should decide the controversy thus.: If the council approved of the person elected, the parish must submit and support him, if not, then the church must give up their choice, and call another minister; and in this method they have proceeded ever since. And it may be serviceable to hear the judgment of a number of their most eminent men, about the state of religion in New England in those times.

CHAPTER IX.

DECLENSIONS DESCRIBED AND LAMENTED, BY MR. PRINCE.—WILLARD AND TORREY.—MITCHEL.—MATHER.—WILLARD.— STODDARD'S ERRORS.—EPISCOPAL SOCIETY INCORPORATED.—ARBITRARY LAWS AND PROPOSALS.—QUAKERS' ATTEMPTS AGAINST THEM.—SOME REVIVAL, AND SOME BAPTIST LETTERS.—OTHER CHURCHES CORRUPTED.—AND ENSLAVED.—OPPOSITION THERETO AT NORWICH.—A FEW THINGS CONCERNING THE BAPTISTS.

The learned and pious Mr. Thomas Prince, says:—

The second generation rising and growing thick on the stage, a little after 1660 there began to appear a decay, and this increased to 1670, when it grew [very] visible and threatening, and was generally complained of and bewailed bitterly by the pious among them; and yet much more to 1680, when but few of the first generation remained.

One of his proofs hereof is what Mr. William Stoughton delivered in an Election Sermon at Boston, April 29, 1668; when he said:—

The death and removal of the Lord's eminent servants in one rank and in another, hath manifested the *lie* in many of us. Whilst they lived, their piety and zeal, their light and life, their counsels and authority, their examples and awe, kept us right, and drew us on in the ways of God, to profess and practice the best things. But now [that] they are [dead and] gone, ah! how doth the unsoundness, the rottenness and hypocrisy of too many among us make itself known, as it was with Joash after the death of Jehoiada.![1]

Other of his proofs are in pages 320, 321.

---

[1] Christian History, Vol. I, pp. 94, 95. In 1671, Mr. Stoughton was elected into the Council, and he died there, Lieutenant Governor in 1702.

In 1680, Mr. Willard said :—

> Be sure, when the glory of God and the spiritual good of your brother requires it, that you carry on your reproofs to conviction. There are some things that arise only from sudden passion, and there a transient rebuke may be enough ; other things may be [more] deliberate, and men are led into them more gradually ; they may also be eminently reproachful to religion, and a dangerous snare to the souls of them that are [so] tempted ; our connivance in such cases may not only blemish our profession, but be a great hazard to it also. At such times, and in such [a] case, you break your covenant if you suffer sin in your brother, without using all the means which Christ hath prescribed, and in the order he hath prescribed them, till the end be obtained. If private admonition, followed with gentleness and patience will not gain, but they still persist in evil courses, or are not humbled for such faults, you must proceed by steps as far as Christ hath bid you. And I believe there is no one thing wherein the covenant is more universally broken, than in the neglect of this duty ; and if the use of these ordinances shall once come to cease among the churches, and the sins of church members be not regularly suppressed, by reason of the unfaithfulness of brethren, religion will languish, and the power of godliness fail. It is not the extending of the covenant to Christians, (as some dream) but [it is] the neglect of covenant duties towards them, that is like to be the bane of our profession, if any thing. Eli indulged his sons, and one professor indulgeth another ; and it is to be feared, that if this were searched to the [root and] bottom [of it,] it would be found that the original of it is self-indulgence, and that when men wink at scandals in their brethren, it is because they expect the like in way of retaliation. And if things once come to this pass, let any sober and prudent man conjecture whether this be not the way to cherish apostasy.[1]

Dr. Increase Mather, in the Preface, gave a special recommendation of this passage. Three years after, another of their fathers, who was minister at Weymouth, delivered a sermon before their Legislature, which he called " A plea for the life of dying religion ;" wherein he said :—

> There is already a great death upon religion, little more left than a name to live..... Consider we then how much it is dying respecting the [very] being of it, by the general failure of the work of conversion, whereby only it is that religion is propagated, continued and upheld in being, among any people. As converting work doth cease, so doth religion die away; though more insensibly, yet most irrecoverably..... How much is it dying,

---

[1] Willard on Covenant-keeping, pp. 110, 111.

respecting the visible profession and practice of it, partly by the formality of churches, but more by the hypocrisy and apostacy of formal hypocritical professors.[1]

The life of Mr. Jonathan Mitchel was published in 1697; and Dr. Increase Mather dedicated this work, which his son had compiled, to the church and college at Cambridge; to whom he said:—

A learned and renowned author, [Dr. Owen,] has evinced, that the letting go this principle, that particular churches ought to consist of regenerate persons, brought in the great apostasy of the Christian church. The way to prevent the like apostasy in these churches, is to require an account of those that offer themselves to communion therein, concerning the work of God on their souls, as well as concerning their knowledge and belief. .... Mr. Mitchell says, [in a manuscript of his which I have seen, has these weighty words:] The over-enlarging of full communion, or admission of persons thereto, upon slight qualifications, without insisting upon the practical and spiritual part of religion, will not only lose the power of godliness, but in a little time bring in profaneness, and ruin the churches, these two ways. 1. Election of ministers will soon be carried by a formal, looser sort. 2. The exercise of discipline will by this means be rendered impossible. Discipline failing, profaneness riseth like a flood; for the major part wanting zeal against sin, will foster licentiousness. It is not setting down good rules and directions, that will save it; for the specification of government is from men, not from laws. Let never so good a form of government be agreed upon, it will soon degenerate, if the instruments that manage it be not good.[2]

When Mr. Mitchel wrote this, about 1664, he had no idea of pastors being elected in New England by any others but communicants; and he gives these weighty reasons against admitting such upon slight qualifications, which Dr. Mather, then President of the College, endeavored to enforce.

In the year 1700, Mather published another book, which he dedicated to the churches of Christ in New England, to whom he said:—

The Congregational church discipline is not suited for a worldly interest, or a formal generation of professors. It will stand or fall as godliness, in

---

[1] Torrey's Election Sermon at Boston, May 16, 1683, p. 11.
[2] Dedication of the Life of Jonathan Mitchel, pp. 16, 17. [Magnalia, Vol. II, p. 59.]

the power of it, does prevail, or otherwise. That there is a great decay of the power of religion throughout all New England, is lamentably true; if that revive, there will be no fear of departing from the holy discipline of the churches of Christ. .... If the begun apostasy should proceed as fast, the next thirty years, as it has done these last, surely it will come to that in New England, (except the gospel itself depart with the order of it) that the most conscientious people therein will think themselves concerned to gather churches out of churches.

He goes on to caution and warn them against many evils; one of which is a dull formality in relations of experiences, in order for admission to communion. And he then says:—

There are reports, as if in some churches persons have brought *written* relations, first to the minister and then to the church, which were not of their own dictating, but devised by others for them. I hope these reports have nothing of truth in them; but if they have, I am sure that such *liars to the Holy Ghost* have exceedingly provoked the Lord.

Another evil which he warns the churches against, is admitting any but communicants to vote for pastors; and he cites Acts i. 26; vi. 2—5; xiv. 23, to prove that God has plainly given this privilege " to the brethren of particular churches;" and declares it to be " simonical to affirm, that this sacred privilege may be purchased with money.[1] This testimony was then given by one of the most eminent ministers in the land, who had been President of Harvard College about twenty years; but by unfair means he was removed from that office the next year.[2]

[1] Vindication of the Order of the Gospel in New England, pp. 11, 12, 38, 67, 68.
[2] His life, p. 173.—B.

"There were some disaffected men who, for some reasons, (God knows what they were,) were willing to have the College taken out of Dr. Mather's hands. To accomplish it, they obtained a vote of the General Assembly which appeared of a plausible aspect, that no man should act as President of the College who did not reside at Cambridge. The leaders in this vote knew very well that the Doctor would not remove his habitation from a loving people at Boston to reside at Cambridge, while the College was as it then was. But yet his abdication was after all brought about, I will but softly say, not so fairly as it should have been. I think there are thanks due to me for my forbearing to tell the story. This was in 1701, twenty years after his beginning to serve that society in quality of a President. And I think it will do no hurt for me to mention a passage which he wrote on this occasion. 'I have received more discouragement in the work of God, from those whom I have laid under the greatest obligations, than by all the world besides. Let not my

Mr. Willard also published a discourse in the year 1700, entitled, " The Perils of the Times Displayed;" in which he said:—

That there is a form of godliness among us is manifest; but the great inquiry is, whether there be not too much of a general denying of the power of it. Whence else is it, that there be such things as these that follow, to be observed? that there is such a prevalency of so many immoralities among professors? that there is so little success of the gospel? How few thorough conversions [are] to be observed, how scarce and seldom. ... It hath been a frequent observation, that if one generation begins to decline, the next that follows usually grows worse, and so on, until God pours out his Spirit again upon them. The decays which we do already languish under are sad; and what tokens are on our children, that it is like to be better hereafter? God be thanked that there are some among them that promise well; but alas, how doth vanity [and a fondness after new things] abound among them! How do young professors grow weary of the strict profession of their fathers, and become strong disputants for the [those] things which their progenitors forsook a pleasant land for the avoidance of.[1]

And forty years after, Mr. Prince said, " We have been generally growing worse and worse ever since."[2]

The greatest evils that our fathers came here to avoid, were the mixture of worthy and unworthy communicants in the churches, and the tyranny of secular and ministerial Courts over them; but these evils were now coming in like a flood upon New England. A church was formed in Brattle Street, Boston, in 1699, with a professed design of not requiring such a strict profession of communicants as their fathers did.[3] And Dr. Colman, their minister, was judged

children put too much confidence in men. It may be, such as they have laid under the greatest obligations of gratitude, will prove the most unkind unto them. I have often had experience of it.'" Parentator; Remarkables in the Life of Dr. Increase Mather, pp. 473, 174.—ED.

[1] Christian History, Vol. I, pp. 100, 101.   [2] Ibid, p. 108.

[3] "We only propose that the Holy Scriptures may be publicly read every Sabbath in the worship of God, which is not practised in other churches of New England at this time; and that we may lay aside the relation of experiences which are imposed in other churches, in order to the admission of persons to the Lord's table." Extract from the Letter of Invitation to Mr. Colman; Drake's History of Boston, p. 519. It is not surprising that this church in later years drifted still farther from orthodoxy. It is now the well known Brattle Street Unitarian Church.—ED.

to have the chief hand in publishing an anonymous answer to President Mather's vindication of their former order. And a discourse was printed in London, in 1700, written by Mr. Solomon Stoddard, of Northampton, wherein he blends the Jewish and Christian dispensations together, in such a manner as to hold, that as all who were circumcised were obliged to keep the passover, so all who have been baptized ought to come to the Lord's Supper, yea, "*though they know themselves to be in a natural condition.*" And by confounding the work of Jewish and Christian officers together, he asserted that the power of admitting, censuring, and restoring members, is wholly invested in the elders, so that, "the brethren of the church are not to intermeddle with it." When any of them were unjustly dealt with, they might appeal to a classical, provincial and national judicature. And says he, " A national synod is the highest ecclesiastical authority upon earth. . . . . Every man must stand to the judgment of the national synod ; Deut. xvii. 12."[1]

These are the words of a minister of great note in New England, whose doctrine has had an extensive spread therein ever since. Yet these are some of the main principles that formerly brought on the antichristian apostasy ; and no text in the bible could be more aptly turned to favor their bloody persecutions than the one here brought to prove his last point. For it says, " The man that will do presumptuously, and will not hearken unto the priest, or unto the judge, even that man shall die." The priest was to explain God's law, and the judge was to carry the same into execution. This is the very passage that the ministers brought in 1668, to prove that the Baptists in Boston ought to be banished.[2] But Dr. Owen, in his piece upon toleration in 1648, truly observed, that, as God was the head and lawgiver of that nation, idolatry, blasphemy, or seducing of others from his worship, were capital crimes ; and that applying of those

---

[1] Stoddard on Instituted Churches, pp. 12, 21, 29, 33.   [2] See p. 307.

laws to cases of worship or discipline in other nations, with the infliction of any other punishment than death, was nothing but arbitrary proceedings. To which I may add, that Jesus Christ, and souls who are born again, are all the priests that are named in the New Testament; 1 Pet. i. 23; ii. 5; and the name is never applied therein to officers, in distinction from other saints. Men who have tried to take the power of church government out of the hands of the saints, in particular churches, have never been able to fix any rational bounds to it elsewhere. A synod of each nation is the bounds that Mr. Stoddard proposed in this piece, but would exclude the English bishops therefrom, because they are not chosen by the church, but the State;[1] but they were for other measures.

When his book was published in London, a small Episcopal society in Boston was the only one of that denomination in all New England. But on June 16, 1701, a charter was procured, to incorporate a society to propagate (what they called) the gospel in foreign parts. And they sent over missionaries, and got their matters in such forwardness, in about twelve years, as to obtain an order from the Crown to bring a bill into Parliament, to establish Episcopacy in America; and its speedy accomplishment was expected, when Divine Providence prevented it by the sudden death of Queen Anne, August 1, 1714. And the two succeeding princes did not see cause to revive that scheme.[2] In 1701, the two eldest ministers in this province published their testimony for the ancient order of these churches, and against growing declensions and corruptions; namely, Mr. John Higginson, of Salem, aged 85; and Mr. William Hubbard,[3] of Ipswich, aged 80; wherein they give their particular approbation of President Mather's vindication of that order.[4] In 1702, Mather

---

[1] Stoddard on Instituted Churches, p. 30.
[2] Chandler's Appeal, 1767, pp. 50—54.   [3] The historian so often quoted.
[4] See Wise's works, [A vindication of the Government of New England Churches. By John Wise, A. M., Pastor of a church in Ipswich.] pp. 68—74.

published another book, entitled, "The Glory Departing from New England;" wherein he says:—

> Alas! what a change is there in that which hath been our glory! .... What a glorious presence of Christ was there in all his ordinances! Many were converted, and willingly declared what God had done for their souls; and there were added to the churches daily such as should be saved. .... There is sad cause to fear, that greater departures of the glory are hastening upon us. Neither our civil or ecclesiastical state is ever like to be what it once was.[1]

The Massachusetts Legislature, which met October 15, 1702, made a long preamble about some irreligious towns, that refused or neglected to receive and support orthodox ministers; upon which they added another law to empower the County Courts, after fining such assessors as did not fulfill their orders, to appoint others to do it, and then to procure a warrant from two Justices of the Quorum, requiring the constables of delinquent towns or districts to collect such taxes, upon the same penalty as for other taxes; and the fines imposed upon delinquent officers were to go to pay these new assessors for their service; and the ministers, who were thus supported, were then contriving to get a classical judicature established over the churches. They drew up proposals for associations to be formed in each county, who should have the power of licensing candidates for the ministry, and of directing particular societies, in the call and settlement of ministers; to which was to be added a Standing Council, whose sentence should be final and decisive, but not without the concurrence of the majority of the pastors present. A number of ministers signed these proposals November 5, 1705, a hundred years to a day after the gunpowder plot was to have blown up the Parliament in Westminster. They were sent round for others to sign, in order to their being presented to the Legislature. But Mr. John Wise had been so well taught, by the briers and thorns of tyranny,[2] that, instead of signing them, he wrote a sharp

---

[1] Christian History, Vol. I, pp. 102, 103. [2] See page 417.

answer to them;[1] and though he was forced to send into another colony to get it printed, yet their design was defeated thereby. The ancient church of Plymouth changed their way of receiving members, from verbal to written relations, in this month of November, 1705.[2]

Dartmouth and Tiverton, where the Quakers were the majority, were put to trouble, from time to time, because they did not receive and support such ministers as others called orthodox; and they also met with ill treatment elsewhere. An old law was in force in Connecticut, entitled, Heretics, which forbade any town or person to entertain any Quaker, upon penalty of five pounds a week, and required that they should be imprisoned and sent out of the Colony; that none should hold unnecessary discourse with them, upon penalty of twenty shillings; that none, except rulers and ministers, should keep any Quaker books, upon penalty of ten shillings, and that all such books should be suppressed; and that no master of any vessel should land any Quakers, without carrying them away again, under the penalty of twenty pounds. And though this law was not rigorously executed, yet it was not repealed; therefore their friends in London made application, in 1704, to the Presbyterian, Congregational, and Baptist ministers there, desiring that, as they would shew themselves friends to equal liberty, they would use their influence in their favor, and apply to the queen for a repeal of said law. This was thought not to be so agreeable, as to try for a reformation in New England; and therefore said ministers in London wrote, to some ministers of

---

[1] This treatise bore the following title:—" The Churches' Quarrel Espoused, or a Reply, in Satyr, to certain Proposals made in answer to this Question: What further steps are to be taken that the Councils may have due constitution and efficacy in supporting, preserving and well-ordering the interest of the Churches in the country? By John Wise, A. M., Pastor of a Church in Ipswich.

'Wherefore rebuke them sharply, that they may be sound in the faith.'

Abjiciendus pudor quoties urget necessitas?"—ED.

[2] Plymouth Register, p. 31. [Massachusetts Historical Collections, Vol. IV. p. 138.]

influence here, a letter to be communicated to others, wherein they said :—

> We cannot but judge it disagreeable with the spirit and principles of the gospel, and an encroachment upon the divine prerogative and the undoubted rights of mankind, to punish any for their conscientious and peaceable dissent from the established way of religion, while they are not justly chargeable with any immorality, or what is plainly destructive of civil society.[1]

But as that law was not repealed here, the queen and Council repealed it, October 11, 1705; a copy of which act was published by John Rogers, of New London, soon after; and the same is in a late history.[2]

In the beginning of the year 1705, such a revival of religion was granted in Taunton, in the county of Bristol, as turned the minds of the people there in general from vain companies, and many immoralities, to an earnest attention to religious worship and conversation.[3] Some things of like nature appeared in Boston, and in several other places. About the same time, Elder Valentine Wightman,[4] from North Kingstown, went and settled at Groton, seven miles north of New London, where he became pastor of the first Baptist church in Connecticut. For some years they were oppressed by the ruling party; but in his latter days they enjoyed liberty, and also much of a divine blessing. He ministered there to good purpose for more than forty years, and died June 9, 1747, as his son who succeeds him informs me. Their brethren at Boston, being destitute of a pastor, wrote again to England for help, from whence a number of ministers sent them the following answer :—

> To the church of Christ, baptized on profession of their faith, in Boston, New England:
>
> London, March 17, 1706-7.
>
> DEAR BRETHREN :—We are heartily concerned for you, since we have heard of your being destitute of a pastor; and are so much the more troubled, because we cannot think of a minister, who is at liberty, proper for you. We are glad to hear that you find so much kindness among the

---

[1] Calamy's Abridgment, p. 671.
[2] Douglas, Vol. II, pp. 389, 340.
[3] Christian History, Vol. II, pp. 108—112.
[4] See page 322, note.—ED.

ministers of another denomination, that they are willing to assist you, and should more rejoice to hear you had a minister well qualified of your own persuasion; but at present we can serve you no otherwise than to pray for you that you may have an agreeable settlement; that you may increase both in knowledge and grace, and may adorn the doctrine of our God and Saviour, by a holy conversation. So pray, dear brethren, your brethren and servants in the gospel of Jesus Christ,

NATHANIEL WYLES,	RICHARD ADAMS,
RICHARD PARKES,	JOHN PIGGOT,
JOSEPH STENNETT,	BENJAMIN STINTON,
NATHANIEL HODGES,	RICHARD ALLEN.
JOSEPH MASTERS,	

The Baptist church which was formed at Kittery, in 1682,[1] returned again to their connection with the church at Boston, and Mr. Drown moved there, whose son Shem was long serviceable in the office of deacon among them. Elder Screven went to South Carolina, to whom the church at Boston now wrote; and on June 2, 1707, he returned an answer, wherein he said:—

Dearly beloved, this may inform you, that I have many thoughts of heart about you, and am much concerned for you; and hope I may say, my prayers are to God for you, though I am not with you; nor can I come as I was inclined to do, our help being taken from us; for our minister who came from England is dead, and I can by no means be spared. I must say it is a great loss, and to me a great disappointment, but the will of the Lord is done. I have longed to hear that you was supplied with an able minister, who might break the bread of life among you; but if the Lord do not please to supply you in the way you expected, your way will be to improve the gifts you have in the church. Brother Callender and Joseph Russell, I know, have gifts that may tend to edification, if improved. I think you should call one or both of them to it.

They did so to Mr. Callender, as appears by a letter from Charleston, South Carolina, to him, of August 6, 1708, which mentions it;[2] and the letter closes thus:—

I have been brought very low by sickness; but I bless God I was helped to preach and administer the communion last Lord's day, but am still weak.

---

[1] See page 405.

[2] "I rejoice that you are inclined to, and employed in, the blessed work of the Lord for the support of his cause, and the comfort of his saints left of a poor, languish

Our society are for the most part in health, and I hope thriving in grace. We are about ninety in all. I rest your affectionate brother and fellow-laborer, in the best of services, for the best reward,

WILLIAM SCREVEN.

We must now consider how error had a further spread in this country. Mr. Stoddard published a sermon from Exod. xii. 47, 48, wherein he says, "A minister who knows himself unregenerate, may nevertheless lawfully administer baptism and the Lord's Supper. Men who are destitute of saving grace may preach the gospel, and therefore administer and so partake of the Lord's Supper." President Mather answered him in 1708, when he said of this passage, "I am mistaken if in this logic there is not sophistry." But the misery of both of them was, an entanglement in an inconsistent scheme. The advocates for the Half-way Covenant in 1662, said, we know of no stronger argument for infant baptism than this, that church members are to be baptized;[1] and now Stoddard says, "This sacrament is a converting ordinance to church members only, and not for other men. The children of God's people should be baptized, which are generally at that time in a natural condition." Upon which his opponent says, "We are to judge as charitably of the child as we do of the parent. We baptize them as being disciples and believers, and visibly belonging to the kingdom of heaven; Dr. Goodwin says, the infants of believers are the purest part of the church."[2]

How imperfect is human knowledge! Stoddard published a reply in 1709, wherein all his arguments turn upon these points, viz., that "if unsanctified persons might lawfully come to the passover, then such [they] may lawfully

---

ing church with you; as it must and will, with the blessing of God, be, if you have the blessed ordinances of the holy Jesus among you again. . . . . I pray God to be with your spirit and strengthen you to the great work to which you are called; and that the little vine may be flourishing under your hand." Extract from Screven's letter to Callender; Rev. S. Hall's Collection of Papers.—ED.

[1] See page 268.
[2] Stoddard's Sermon, pp. 13, 27; Mather's answer, pp. 67, 68.

come to the Lord's Supper; and they who [do] convey to their children a right to [the sacrament of] baptism, have a right themselves to the Lord's Supper, provided they carry inoffensively."[1] He could plainly see that there was no half-way in the Jewish church; and his opponent could see as plainly, that fruits meet for repentance were required in order for baptism, even of such as were in the covenant of circumcision. But as tradition had taught them both to build the Christian church upon that covenant, neither of them could act consistently thereon; though they were two of the most eminent ministers then in New England. Most of their successors have held fast their errors, but not their virtues. And as these things shew how the churches were corrupted, so what follows discovers how they were enslaved.

The third Governor Winthrop[2] died November 27, 1707, upon which a special meeting of the Assembly of Connecticut was called on December 17, to choose them another Governor. By a law then in force, he was to be elected out of a certain number of men in previous nomination; but they broke over those limits, and elected an ordained minister of New London for their Governor; who, when they sent an account of it to him, readily quitted the solemn charge of souls, for worldly promotion, and was sworn into his new office, January 1, 1708; after which they repealed the law that they had before broken, and enacted that for the future, the Governor might be chosen out of any of the freemen.[3] Mr. Gurdon Saltonstall, son to a Massachusetts magistrate, and a graduate of Harvard College, was the Governor thus chosen, and by annual elections he was continued in that office for sixteen years. He was a great politician, and he exerted all his influence to raise ministerial power as high as possible. He took the proposals of 1705, and pre-

[1] Appeal to the Learned, pp. 50, 89.
[2] Fitz John Winthrop. See p. 430.—Ed.
[3] Trumbull's History of Connecticut, Vol. I, Chapter XVIII, pp. 431, 432.—Ed.

sented them to their Legislature, where their unscriptural form was soon taken notice of; for there was not a text of Scripture in the whole scheme. Perceiving that it could not be received so, it was withdrawn without much noise, and the following method was taken to carry his point. An act was passed by the Assembly that met at Hartford, May 13, 1708, which says:—

> This Assembly, from their own observation, and from the complaint of [many] others, being made sensible of the defects of the discipline of the churches of this government, arising from the want of a more explicit asserting the rules given for that end in the holy Scriptures, from which would arise a firm [permanent] establishment amongst ourselves, a good and regular issue in cases subject to ecclesiastical discipline, glory to Christ our Head, and edification to his members;[1] hath seen fit to ordain and require, and it is by authority of the same ordained and required, that the ministers of the churches, in the several counties of this government, shall meet together at their respective county towns, with such messengers as the churches to which they belong shall see cause to send with them, on the last Monday in June next, there to consider and agree upon those methods and rules for the management of ecclesiastical discipline, which by them shall be judged agreeable and conformable to the word of God; and shall at the same meeting appoint two or more of their number to be their delegates, who shall all meet together at Saybrook at the next Commencement to be held there,[2] where they shall compare the results of the ministers of the several counties, and out of and from them to draw a form of ecclesiastical discipline.

This was to be presented to the Assembly for their acceptance, and the expense of those meetings was to be borne out of the Colony treasury. This order was obeyed; and the ministers who met at Saybrook, September 9, 1708, adopted the Confession of Faith that was composed at the Savoy in London, 1658,[3] and the heads of agreement en-

[1] Church and State are here confounded together; as if a being members of the civil community, made men members of Christ, and him their Head.

[2] This was the Commencement of the "Collegiate School of the Colony of Connecticut," afterwards Yale College, which was founded at Saybrook and continued there till 1716.—ED.

[3] The Savoy Confession of Faith was drawn up and adopted by an assembly of the ministers and messengers of Independent churches. It is a modification of the Westminster Confession, omitting from that the articles relating to church discipline, and adding instead a few articles affirming and explaining Independency. Neal's History of the Puritans, Toulmin's edition, Vol. IV, pp. 213—218.—ED.

tered into between Presbyterians and Independents in London, 1690, and then added fifteen articles concerning church discipline, which were the proposals of 1705 new modeled, with Scripture references annexed to each article; though a gentleman of that day observed, that the text which speaks of Balaam's saddling his ass would have been as much to the purpose as many they brought. Their second article, which contains a summary of the whole scheme, is in these words, viz.:—

> That the churches, which are neighboring each to other, shall consociate for mutual affording to each other such assistance as may be requisite, upon all occasions ecclesiastical; and that the particular pastors and churches, within the respective counties in this government, shall be one Consociation (or more if they shall judge meet) for the end aforesaid. Psalm cxxii. 3—5; cxxxiii. 1; Eccl. iv. 9—12; Acts xv. 2, 6, 22, 23; I Tim. iv. 14; I Cor. xvi. 1.[1]

The first of these texts speaks of princes on their thrones, and not of church officers. And when we come to the antetype of Aaron's and David's line, we find none therein but Jesus Christ, and regenerate souls. Officers, as distinguished from other saints in the Christian church, are never called priests nor kings in the New Testament. And, said an eminent father of New England, "The order of officers in the church is an order of servants, and the order of saints an order of kings (which is the highest order in the church) sitting upon the thrones of David for judgment, whom the ministers are to serve, in guiding and going before them in, and ministering of, their judgments."[2] Their second proof refers to the unity of brethren under our great High Priest, who most explicitly excludes all striving about who shall be the greatest from his kingdom. Neither is the third text any more to their purpose. The fourth gives an account of the meeting of one church, at the request of another two hundred miles off, upon a special occasion, and not of the

---

[1] Trumbull's History of Connecticut, Vol. I, Chapter XIX, pp. 481—483.—ED.
[2] Robinson against Bernard, p. 227. [Works of John Robinson, Vol. II, p. 238.]

meeting of neighboring churches upon all occasions ecclesiastical. The last two treat of gifts received by prophecy, and of orders given to the churches by apostolic authority; and until ordinary ministers can prove that they, as such, are princes on their thrones, and are endowed with apostolic authority over the churches, we may safely conclude that the above application of Scriptures was a perverting of them from their genuine meaning and design. Yet thereby two kinds of judicatures were set up over the churches. The one called Consociations, consisting of ministers meeting in their own persons, and churches by their messengers, whereof each church may send one or two, though the want of them is not to invalidate the acts of any council; but none of their acts are esteemed valid without the concurrence of the majority of the pastors present. They are the Standing Council within each circuit upon all occasions ecclesiastical, though in cases of special difficulty they may call the next Consociation to sit and act with them. They are to have a new choice of messengers and moderators once a year, if not oftener, and the last moderator is to call a new meeting when it is judged proper. Their sentence is to be final and decisive. Their other judicatures are called Associations, which are meetings of ministers by themselves in each circuit, as often as they think proper, to hear and answer questions of importance, to examine and license candidates for the ministry, to receive complaints from individuals or societies, and to direct to the calling of the Council to try the same, when they judge proper; to direct destitute churches in calling and settling of pastors, and to make complaint to their Legislature against such as they judge to be negligent of their duty in that respect. And each Association sends a delegate or two to a General Association once a year, from all parts of that government.

This scheme was not introduced without glaring deceit; for their Fourth Article says, "that according to the common practice of our churches, nothing shall be deemed an act or judgment of any council, which hath not the major part of the elders present, concurring, and such a number of the messengers present, as makes the majority of the council,"[1] whereas this practice was so far from being common, that it was an innovation then made, directly subversive of the fundamental principles of the New England churches;[2] as we are assured by Mr. Wise, Dr. Mather, and others. No man knew better what those principles were than Mr. Thomas Hooker, the first minister of Hartford; and he is full in it, that, though it is expedient on special occasions to call councils or synods, yet elders act therein as commissioners sent, and not as pastors; and that other messengers sent have equal power with them.[3] Says he, " God hath set officers in the church; I Cor. xii. 28 ; therefore the church is before officers." And from Matt. xviii. 15—18, and I Cor. v. 12, he concludes, " that each man and member of the society, in a just way, may be directed, censured, reformed or removed, by the power of the whole, and each may and should judge with the consent of the whole. This belongs to all the members, and therefore to any that shall be in office, if they be members. They are superior as officers, when they keep the rule ; but inferior as members, and in subjection to any when they break the rule. . . . . Christ gave some to be pastors, some to be teachers. He alone, out of his supreme and regal power, doth furnish them with graces and abilities, appoints the work, lays out the compass thereof, the manner of dispensing, and the order and bounds of their dispensation." And he observes, that to remove the power of censure from a particular church, leads into endless disputes ; because no General Council was called in the

---

[1] Trumbull's History of Connecticut, Vol. I, Chapter XIX, p. 483.—ED.

[2] Mr. Backus seems to have misapprehended the force of the above Article. It does not state that it had been the common practice of the churches, to hold ecclesiastical councils, or to allow them the authority which they afterwards exercised, but only that it had been the common practice of the churches to require a majority vote of both the elders and messengers in order to the validity of any act.—ED.

[3] Survey of Church Discipline, Part I, p. 119.

first three centuries, and no man can tell as there will ever be another.¹ Says he, " The truth is, a particular congregation is the highest tribunal, unto which the grieved party may appeal in the third place, if private council, or the witnesses of two, have seemed to proceed too [much] sharply. If difficulties arise in proceeding, the council of other churches should be sought to clearthe truth; but the power of censure rests in the congregation, where Christ placed it. . . . . The churches sent them, and therefore are above them."² Yet now the churches were not allowed the power to say whether their ministers should meet at Saybrook, or not; and the result of their meeting being laid before the Legislature of October 14, 1708, they said:—

> This Assembly do [doth] declare their great approbation of such a happy agreement, and do ordain that all the churches within this government, that are or shall be thus united, in doctrine, worship and discipline, be, and for the future shall be owned and acknowledged, established by law, provided always, that nothing herein shall be intended and construed to hinder or prevent any society or church, that is or shall be allowed by the laws of this government, who soberly differ or dissent from the united churches hereby established, from exercising worship and discipline in their own way, according to their consciences.³

Thus artfully was this new scheme established, and all others declared to be no more than allowed or tolerated.

Mr. John Woodward, another Cambridge scholar, was then minister of Norwich; and he soon got and read off to his congregation the first part of this act, but without the proviso. Richard Bushnel and Joseph Backus,⁴ Esquires, who had opposed that scheme in the Assembly, informed their church of the liberty that they had to dissent from it; but the minister carried a major vote against them; therefore those representatives, and other fathers of the town, withdrew from that tyranny, and held worship by themselves

---
¹Survey of Church Discipline, Part I, pp. 119, 188, 190, 232, 238.
²Ibid, Part IV, pp. 19, 47.
³Trumbull's History of Connecticut, Vol. I, Chapter XIX, p. 487.—ED.
⁴Joseph Backus was the author's grandfather.—ED.

for three months. For this, the minister and his party censured them; an account of which being sent to the next meeting of the Assembly, they were expelled therefrom. Hereby we may see how far corruption had prevailed in our land. For in 1641, three years after the first taxing law for ministers was made in New England, a law was made at Boston, which said, "·No church censure shall degrade or depose any man from any civil dignity, office or authority, he shall have in the Commonwealth."[1] How much more equitable was this, than another law in Connecticut, which said:—

Whatsoever persons shall on the Lord's day, under any pretence whatsoever, assemble themselves together in any of the public meeting-houses, provided in any town, parish or society, for the public worship of God, without leave or allowance of the minister and congregation for whose use it was provided, and be thereof convict, every such person shall incur the penalty of ten shillings for every such offence. Nor shall any persons neglect the public worship of God in some lawful congregation, and form themselves into separate companies in private houses, on penalty of ten shillings for every such offence.

This part concerning separate meetings caused sore exercises to many serious minds, and great difficulties in procuring civil officers; yet it was never repealed until October, 1770. But not long after the Norwich minister had censured their representatives, he consented to refer the matter to a council; and they followed it, with council after council, for about six years. Governor Saltonstall came there himself upon one of those occasions; and Mr. Stoddard of Northampton was Moderator of the last but one of those councils. My grandfather went a journey as far as Boston and Ipswich, a hundred and thirty miles, to consult with Mr. Wise and the two Mathers upon these affairs. At last, by advice of a council that met August 31, 1716, said minister was dismissed, and the church in Norwich determined to abide upon their ancient foundation. And it was known that when the church was constituted at Saybrook, in 1660,

---

[1] Massachusetts Law-book, printed 1672, p. 44.

with the approbation of other ministers, Mr. James Fitch was ordained their pastor, by the laying on of the hands only of their two deacons, as a token that the power of ordination is in the church as a body. They came and planted Norwich the same year; and Mr. Fitch was continued one of the most useful ministers in Connecticut for near fifty years. The church in East Windsor, under the care of Mr. Timothy Edwards, father of Mr. Jonathan, also refused to receive the Saybrook Platform. And the temper of those who introduced it farther appears by the incorporating act of the town of Killingly, passed in May, 1708; which says, "No person now inhabiting on said lands, or any other persons dwelling without this colony, who have purchased any lands within the said township, that shall not give due obedience to all the laws of this colony for the upholding the worship of God, and paying all public charges, shall have any benefit by this act." At the same time they gave their Governor two hundred acres of land therein. This account is carefully taken from the public records and laws, and other authentic vouchers.

A few things concerning baptism shall close this chapter. An aged and honorable gentleman near Piscataqua River informed me, that about the year 1710, a number of people in Dover[1] were so fully persuaded that they ought, in a literal sense, to be buried in baptism, that on a Lord's day and the day after, Mr. Pike, their minister, baptized nine persons in that way, in a branch of that river. But such a noise was made, and opposition raised against it, as prevented any further proceedings therein. About the same time a Baptist meeting was set up at Scituate, in the county of Plymouth, where President Dunstar spent his latter days to good purpose.[2] Mr. John Peirce preached to them for some time, until he and others removed to Swanzey, in or about 1711, and on October 19, 1715, he was ordained a pastor of

---

[1] Mr. Hansard Knollys was minister there, from the spring of 1638 to the fall of 1641. See pp. 81, 82.
[2] See pp. 255, 256.

the second church there, colleague with Elder Joseph Mason, who was ordained in July, 1709. And they continued in good esteem in their offices, until Elder Mason died, May 19, 1748, and Elder Peirce, September 8, 1750, being each of them near ninety years old. On March 16, 1714, Dr. Cotton Mather wrote the letter to the Baptist church in Boston, which is in page 420; subscribed thus, viz., "To my worthy friend, Mr. Ellis Callender, elder of a church of Christ in Boston." He joined it in 1669; was a leading member of it when the Court nailed up their meeting-house in 1680; and he was continued a great blessing to them until he died in a good old age, after the year 1726.

CHAPTER X.

ARBITRARY CLAIMS AND PROCEEDINGS.—MOODY AND WHITE AGAINST THEM.—A CRUEL LAW.—LIBERTY IN RHODE ISLAND.—MATHER FOR IT. IS FRIENDLY TO THE BAPTISTS.—JENNINGS JOINS THEM.—WALLIN'S LETTERS.—ARIAN HERESY.—HOLLIS'S DONATIONS.—SOME REVIVAL OF RELIGION.—COMER CONVERTED.

Governor Lyndon informed me, that when the Quakers were hanged at Boston, a view of the cruelty then exercised towards them, and of their behavior under their sufferings, moved Peter Wanton to join with that people. And his son Joseph was a teacher among them in Tiverton for many years; whose daughter Richardson told me, that, during Governor Dudley's administration, her father was frequently sent to Boston, to defend his town against the arbitrary claims of other ministers; and that the Governor privately favored him therein. Some extracts from the records of the Quaker society show, that in 1707, a cow worth three pounds, was taken from John Packom, of Little Compton, for a ministerial tax of six shillings and twopence; and that their monthly meeting on Rhode Island, in the seventh month, 1708, sent Joseph Wanton with an address to Governor Dudley, "desiring relief from sufferings for priests' rates, by a repeal of those laws;" informing him that if it was not done here, they thought it their duty to address the British Court upon it. A like application was afterwards made by the hand of Ebenezer Slocum, who reported to a meeting in 1709, that the Governor appeared kind and friendly; but as no relief was granted, they then sent to England upon those matters. By the same records we are informed, that in 1716, five cows and calves, worth twenty-five pounds, were taken from Peleg Slocum, and twenty-four sheep worth eight pounds, eight shillings, from John and Abraham Tucker, all upon Slocum's Island, and near all for " a demand of Priest Holmes, of Chilmark," to which town said island belonged, although the great channel betwixt the main and Martha's Vineyard must be crossed to get to it. However, ministers were far from being content with all the power they had yet obtained, and therefore presented a petition to their Legislature, that they would call a General Synod; doubtless to revise and carry into effect the proposals of 1705. The Council voted to grant their petition, but it was not concurred with by the other branches of the Legislature.[1] And two excellent ministers had such a sight of their danger, as to write the following letter to Mr. Wise.

Gloucester, March 25, 1715.

REVEREND SIR:—We have had the favor and satisfaction of reading, and, according to our measure, considering, the transcendent logic, as well as grammar and rhetoric, of your Reply to the Proposals, by which our eyes are open to see much more than ever before we saw of the value and glory of our invaded privileges; and are of opinion, that if your consent may be obtained to a new edition, it may be of wonderful service to our churches, if God shall please to go forth with it. However, it will be a testimony that all our watchmen were not asleep, nor the camp of Christ surprised and taken before they had warning. We are, Reverend Sir, full of dutiful respect and gratitude, your sons and servants,

SAMUEL MOODY,
JOHN WHITE.

It was reprinted accordingly; and, with Mr. Wise's other works, it had two editions more in 1773, upon an occasion which will then be mentioned. These two ministers lived to see and rejoice in the glorious work of divine grace,

[1] Douglas, Vol. II, p. 378.

which was granted in New England, in and after the year 1740. Mr. Moody was minister at York, beyond Piscataqua River. He preached without notes, and refused to be supported by tax and compulsion; and was the most powerful and successful preacher of almost any in the land in those days.

Such opposition was raised against Governor Dudley, that he was removed, and never acted with our Legislature after August, 1715; and when they met again November 23, with the pliant Lieutenant Governor Taylor in the chair, the following act was added to their other taxing laws, viz.:—

AN ACT FOR MAINTAINING AND PROPAGATING OF RELIGION.

Whereas the laws of this province have made good and wholesome provision, that every town within the same be continually supplied with an able, learned, orthodox minister or ministers, of good conversation, to dispense the word of God unto them; and that such minister or ministers be suitably encouraged, and sufficiently supported and maintained, by the inhabitants of such towns; for the rendering the said laws more effectual, and to prevent the growth of atheism, irreligion and profaneness: Be it enacted and ordained by the Lieutenant Governor, Council, and Representatives, in General Court assembled, and by the authority of the same, that the Justices of the Court of General Sessions of the Peace, within the several counties, at the opening of their Courts from time to time, do give in special charge to the Grand Jury, to make diligent inquiry and presentment of all towns and districts within such county, that are destitute of a minister, as by law is directed; and of such towns and districts that neglect to fulfill their contracts and agreements, and do not make suitable provision for the support and maintenance of their minister or ministers accordingly. And upon such presentment, complaint, or information in any other manner, the Court are directed and required vigorously to put the laws in execution, for the redressing of all defects and neglects of that kind,[1] and forthwith to make the necessary orders to that end, as by law they are empowered. And in case their orders, so made, be not duly observed, or by the contrivance and practice of ill men be eluded and rendered ineffectual; for the speedy remedying and reforming of so great an evil, the Justices of such Court are to represent and make report of their proceedings unto the next session of the General Court or Assembly.

[1] From Scripture and all experience it plainly appears, that ministers have been as often guilty of defects and neglects as the people; but they made no law to punish ministers therefor; which partiality promoted atheism and irreligion, instead of preventing it.

Upon this the Assembly were to send a minister, recommended by three others, to every such town or district, and to provide for his "honorable maintenance," by adding a sufficient sum for the purpose to the province tax upon such places; and were to do the like to each place that neglected to fulfill former contracts with ministers; as also to "supply and support a minister in places that are destitute, where the Justices neglect their duty." All which sums their ministers were to draw out of the province treasury. This act was made for seven years, and then was revived and continued till 1730; and that method of charging the Grand Jury has been continued ever since.

Rhode Island Colony was now ruled by Governor Cranston, and Deputy Governor Jencks, in conjunction with other worthy men, under whose administration they enjoyed the greatest peace, for above thirty years, that they ever did since they were a distinct government. And for the continuance of the same, and to prevent any society or sect from trying for any preëminence in the government, their Assembly of May 2, 1716, enacted, "that what maintenance or salary may be thought necessary by any of the churches, congregations, or societies of people, now inhabiting, or that hereafter shall or may inhabit, within the same, for the support of their respective minister or ministers, shall be raised by free contribution, and no otherways." This law is still in force; and we shall presently hear a number of ministers commending the good fruits of these measures, which yet they were very unwilling to come into.

President Mather published another piece in 1716, wherein he says:—

> For ministers to pretend to a negative voice in synods, or for councils to take upon them to determine what elders or messengers a church shall submit unto, without the choice of the church concerned, or for ministers to pretend to be members of a council without any mission from their churches, nay, although the church declares that they will not send them, is prelatical, and essentially differing not only from Congregational, but

from Presbyterian principles. And now that I am going out of the world, I could not die in peace, if I did not discharge my conscience, in bearing witness against such innovations and invasions on the rights and privileges belonging to particular congregations of Christ.[1]

Yet all these innovations and invasions were made in the Saybrook scheme. And to shew that brethren, when chosen by the church, have a right to equal votes in Councils with elders, he says :—

There are mechanics, who although they do not excel in that which is called human learning, are well versed and learned in the Scriptures, spending much time in consulting those oracles of God, and being men of great piety, and excellent natural accomplishments, they may be very useful in synods. Ecclesiastical historians give a remarkable account of what happened in the Nicene Synod. A pious old man, who was no clergyman, nor exercised philosophical notions, by his plain discourse did more towards the conviction of an heretical philosopher, than all the learned bishops in the Council could do.[2]

These things naturally led him and his brethren into another sort of behavior towards the Baptists, than when he was Scribe of the Synod of 1769, who declared that they were setting up their posts by God's posts; which moved the Court to nail up the doors of the Baptist meeting-house. For Elder Callender's son Elisha was added to the church under his father's care, August 10, 1713; after which[3] he was educated at Harvard College, and called into the gospel ministry; and, as President Mather had expressed his willingness for such a thing to Elder Callender, his church called the President, his son, and Mr. John Webb, to assist in ordaining Mr. Elisha Callender, as pastor of the Baptist

---

[1] Disquisition concerning Ecclesiastical Councils, Preface, p. 13.
[2] Ibid., p. 19.
[3] "His son, Elisha Callender, became his successor in the pastoral office. He had received a liberal education at Harvard College, and was one of the fourteen students who were graduated in the year 1710. He was baptized and received into the church August 10, 1713..... Mr. Backus observes, ... that Mr. Callender received his education at Harvard College *after* he had joined the church; but in this he must be mistaken. Historical Sketch of the First Baptist church in Boston; James M. Winchell; p. 21.—ED.

church in Boston, May 21, 1718. And Dr. Cotton Mather, in the Ordination Sermon, said:—

> It is very sadly true, that many ecclesiastical communities, wherein piety has its votaries, yet are guilty of this evil, that they impose terms of communion which many that have the fear of God, are, by just exceptions, kept from complying withal. Now in this unhappy case what is to be done? Do this; let good men go as far as they can without sin, in holding communion with one another. But where sinful terms are imposed, there let them make their stops; there a separation becomes a duty; there the injunction of heaven upon them is, "Be ye separate saith the Lord, and touch not the unclean thing, and I will receive you." The imposers are the schismatics. There have been many attempts to unite people in forms and terms, that are not the pure maxims of living unto God; and so to build the tower of Zion on a foundation which is not the tried stone and the precious, and so not the sure foundation. There has hitherto been a blast from heaven upon all these attempts; they have miscarried, as being rather calculated for the tower of Babel. New England also has, in some former times, done something of this aspect, which would not now be so well approved of; in which, if the brethren, in whose house we are now convened, met with any thing too unbrotherly, they now with satisfaction hear us expressing our dislike of every thing that looked like persecution in the days that have passed over us.[1]

The case of a member who soon after joined that church, I think proper here to mention. Samuel Jennings, Esq., was born in Sandwich, in the county of Barnstable, February 19, 1685, where he lived till he was above eighteen years old, and then went a voyage to sea, where he was pressed on board a man-of-war. But meeting with very ill treatment there for five months, he, in the evening of March 26, 1704, the ship being in a bay at Barbados, attempted to make his escape therefrom by swimming; but by the way he was seized and hauled under water by a shark. A terrible case indeed! Yet, as he cried to God for help, the venomous creature let him go, and his life was preserved, with the loss only of a part of a foot and an arm.[2] He returned, married,

---

[1] See pp. 420, 422.

[2] "I had not swum far before I saw a shark, just as he took hold of my left hand. He pulled me under water in a moment. .... I thought of a knife I used to carry in my pocket, but remembered I left it on board. Then I kicked him several times

and lived in good repute in his native town, which he represented several times in our Legislature. After he had served them two years in that office, he wrote as follows concerning his soul affairs. Says he:—

Though I had heard much preaching, and read many books, to support the baptizing of infants, and had never read any books, or discoursed on that head with any that were against it, yet I found so much in the Scripture to the contrary, that I could not believe it to be right. Notwithstanding I went to several ministers, and discoursed [with] them on that point to get light, and also prayed to God to direct me in the right way; yet still it appeared to me unscriptural and erroneous. Then I went to Mr. Callender, the Baptist minister at Boston, who not only discoursed with me, but lent me books set out by those of his persuasion, to support the truth thereof; which when I had read, I found so agreeable with the Scriptures, and with the apprehensions I before had from them, that I quickly sought to be admitted into the communion of that church at Boston. And having made a verbal profession, before the church and congregation, I was baptized (that is, dipped in the water) by Mr. Elisha Callender, minister of the gospel, on the 9th day of June, 1718, in the thirty-fourth year of my age. And truly I may say, as is said of the Ethiopian eunuch, that I came away rejoicing. In a short time after, I arrived to a considerable degree of bodily health, which I had lacked for eight years before.

He served his town afterwards as their Representative, and in other offices; and, without his seeking, a commission of Justice of the Peace was sent him, which, for some reasons, he chose not to accept. He continued a member of said church in Boston till his death in 1764.

Soon after Mr. Callender was ordained, he opened a correspondence with friends in London, which, with other means, had very great and extensive effects. Thomas Hollis,

with my right foot, but that proving ineffectual, I set my foot against his mouth, intending to haul my hand away or to haul it off. Then he opened his mouth a little and took part of my foot into his mouth with my hand and held them both. Then I cried to God mentally that he would have mercy on my soul, which I thought would soon be separated from my body, but still did not cease striving, but punched him with my right hand, though to little purpose. At last, being almost drowned, for I was all this while under water, I had almost left off striving, and, expecting nothing but present death, all at once my hand and foot came loose, and I got up to the top of the water, and, having cleared my stomach of water, I called out for help, and swam towards the nearest ship." Extract from "A Narrative of the Wonderful Escape of Samuel Jennings;" Rev. S. Hall's Collection of Papers.—ED.

Esq., one of the most liberal men upon earth, had some acquaintance with President Mather, when he was agent for this province in England;[1] and now, receiving accounts of the transactions and catholic sentiments that were delivered at the ordination of a Baptist minister in Boston, who was educated at Harvard College, he became the greatest benefactor thereto that they have ever had to this day.

> "Nor yet to Harvard all his views confin'd;
> His active soul still nobler work designed.
> A kingdom's welfare dwelt on ev'ry thought;
> For gen'ral good his heav'nly candor wrought;
> To public peace his prudent schemes invite,
> Faction to quell, and clashing sects unite."[2]

With or near his first donation to the College, came the following letter from a minister of his acquaintance to his friend in Boston:—

London, March 9, 1720.

MUCH ESTEEMED BROTHER CALLENDER:—I thank you kindly for the particular account you gave me in your last; and I cannot but lament the sad consequences of sin, and the great degrees of it which remain, even in God's own people; for surely the greatest part, if not all those who suffered so much for their religion at home, and at last left their native country, and run such great hazards as they did for the sake of their consciences, must, in the judgment of charity, be esteemed the faithful servants of Christ. But when I consider the methods which these took, or encouraged others to take, with those who differed from them in matters not fundamental, I cannot but wonder at the depth of folly which remains with us, that any body of men should so soon and so zealously pursue those very methods which they had so justly condemned, and so greatly suffered by! It is a consideration enough to check the towering thoughts of vain man, and to shew the reasonableness of the apostolical advice, "Let him that

---

[1] Increase Mather's Life, p. 170.—B.
The words here referred to in the Life of Mather, (Parentator, &c.,) are as follows:—"When he went over to England he carried his care of his beloved College with him. Among other expressions of it, he procured some valuable donations to it. Yea, it was his acquaintance with, and his proposal to, that good-spirited man and lover of all good men, Mr. Thomas Hollis, that introduced his benefactions unto that College, to which his incomparable bounty has anon flowed unto such a degree as to render him the greatest benefactor it ever had in the world."--ED.
[2] Rudd's Poem on Hollis's Death, p. 29.

thinketh he standeth take heed lest he fall;" for I think we are but too subject to the lesser degrees of this temper and carriage, in almost every station of life. For though there is so good an understanding among the three denominations of dissenters, viz., Presbyterians, Independents and Baptists; yet we have too many who are whisperers and backbiters, who, by magnifying the weaknesses, or diminishing the real worth and usefulness of those who differ from them, shew that this spirit, as much as it is destroyed, is yet too much alive, and, were it clothed with power, would soon be formidable. But our wise and gracious Governor makes the weaknesses and wrath of men to praise him, and the remainder thereof he doth restrain.

As I heartily rejoice that the Lord hath preserved the baptized church, at Boston, through so many difficulties, so I am glad he hath raised up to them one so able and willing to promote the public good among them. May the Lord succeed you, my dear brother, that so peace and truth may spread and flourish in your days! I am indeed troubled at the paucity[1] of those of our denomination, in New England; though I cannot wonder at it, considering the treatment they have generally met with. I am grieved that any who profess the plain Scripture baptism should bring it into contempt, by holding with it such wild and unscriptural opinions; but so it hath been with us, and yet remains; though I think the number of such is diminished, within a few years last past. But although we have but few Soul-sleepers or Sabbatarians, &c., yet the number of those that plead for general redemption, and some other of the distinctive notions of Arminius, seem to increase among us. However, they seem not quite so rigid and uncharitable as formerly, and there is, I hope, the greatest number of our denomination free from these things. As to the method of educating youth among you, it must be allowed, that the design seemed to be well laid for promoting useful knowledge; and I hope your college will be improved to a very great advantage; but I find you have to lament, what we are not strangers to, viz., that those things which in themselves are good, and tend to fit persons for more extensive usefulness, are made necessary for a person in order to the ministry, or should be thought, at any time, to be a sufficient qualification for so great a work. Surely a man blessed with a good natural genius, who has been brought to a true sense of sin, and the saving knowledge of Jesus Christ, though he should want the advantage of human literature, must be better capable than one that has it, and is destitute of the other, to guide souls into the ways of salvation; because, as he knows something of the deceitfulness of sin, and the wiles of Satan, so he is more capable to comfort poor souls in distress, with the comforts wherewith he himself has been comforted of God. Therefore, though I have a high esteem for human learning, and wish every minister had the advan-

---

[1] Fewness in number.

tage of a good degree of it, yet I conceive it is far from being necessary to a man's being employed in the public ministry, and much less do I think it, in itself, a qualification sufficient for so weighty an undertaking. You will excuse me for so freely declaring my mind upon this head.

Before this comes to hand, I hope you will have received a letter, subscribed, Thomas Hollis. This worthy gentleman is my very good friend, and one who, with his plentiful estate, has done much good among poor ministers and churches here; and I hope New England will find yet more happy effects of his liberality, and that, with your kind assistance in finding and procuring proper objects, something may be done by him for the particular encouragement of our denomination. For, in conversing with him upon this head, he desired me to intimate to you, that he shall be well pleased, if you can find a proper person of the Baptist persuasion, for him to recommend to the governors of the college; and I doubt not but he will give some further encouragement to such an one, who is desirous to be qualified for public usefulness. I entreat you therefore to turn your thoughts to this subject, and give me a line, so soon as you have found a fit person, that so good a work as this may be begun. I am ready to believe, that, besides Mr. Hollis's interest with the governors, in behalf of a hopeful young man, who is of our persuasion, he may be prevailed upon to allow ten pounds per annum, of your money,[1] towards defraying the charges of the college; which will be some encouragement for one, who, with promising natural parts, is desirous to devote himself to study, in order to fit himself for public usefulness, but is not well able to go through the charge. I leave this with you, and pray God to direct you. You will find a copy of Mr. Hollis's to you; to which I have added a catalogue of the chest of books therein mentioned; and if any are not disposed of to the college library, yourself, &c., that then you would use your interest to obtain some of them for Mr. Daniel White.[2] When you have read Mr. Neal's History of New England, I desire you to give me your thoughts of it in general; and if you find anything in it which deserves to be taken notice of, in order to be altered in a second edition, pray freely communicate it to me, and I will do the same to the author, who is a very honest gentleman, and will be glad to be set right, in any thing wherein he may have been mistaken. Just now a gentleman has been with me, whose name is Spurier, who hath brought some hundred tons of silver ore from New England, and desires me to assist him in presenting a petition to the government, for encouragement.[3] If you have heard any thing of any late dis-

---

[1] Mexican silver was then about thirteen shillings per ounce, in our money. Douglas, Vol. I, p. 494.

[2] Mr. White came over from Mr. Wallin's church two years before, and was then preaching at Newport. Mr. Neal's history first came over this year.

[3] Great fraud and iniquity was practised in the nation, about such things, in the year 1720.

coveries made of silver mines with you, or any thing of the character of the man, or what notion the people have of it, and will please to give me a line, it may be of use to me; for, as I would willingly serve any honest man, according to my ability, so I would gladly know the persons I move for. I am now obliged to conclude at present, and with all my heart commend you to God and the word of his grace, which is able and I hope will build you up in all things. May the Lord be with you, and the church of Christ under your care, causing all blessings to abound towards you in all things. So rests your cordial friend, and unworthy brother in the Lord's vineyard,

EDWARD WALLIN.

Before this came to hand, our friends here had sent a letter directed thus: "The church of Christ at Boston, in New England, of the faith and order of the gospel, baptizing visible believers upon the profession of their faith, and believing the principles of a particular election of a certain number, who shall continue in the perseverance in grace; unto the several churches of Christ that are in the same faith and order of the gospel, in London, do heartily desire your increase and growth in the knowledge of our Lord Jesus, and in all the graces of his Holy Spirit." They go on to give an account of the first rise of their church, which say they, "Several wise and learned men endeavored, but could not accomplish it; however, God was pleased to succeed the endeavors of our brethren, who were not so accomplished with acquired parts and abilities, by enduring, and to appear for them under all their troubles, so that we continue, through rich grace, a church unto this day."[1] By

---

[1] This letter is preserved, and, we judge, is of sufficient interest to warrant its publication.

"The church of Christ at Boston in New England, of the faith and order of the gospel, baptizing visible believers upon the profession of their faith, and believing the principles of a particular election of a certain number, who shall likewise continue in their perseverance in grace; unto the several churches of Christ that are in the same faith and order of the gospel in London, do heartily desire your increase and growth in the knowledge of our Lord Jesus, and in all the graces of his Holy Spirit.

"Honored and dearly beloved friends and brethren; we take this freedom of writing these few lines to acquaint you with the circumstances of our condition, whereby there may be a sympathy which the Holy Spirit of God promotes in Christians at a

those wise and learned men, I suppose they intended President Dunstar and some with him, who did not accomplish what Elder Gould and his brethren did. One design of this letter was to request some assistance in enlarging and repairing their meeting-house; and it occasioned the following answer:—

London, August 3, 1720.

DEAR AND HONORED BROTHER CALLENDER: I received the honor of the church's and your letter together, by Captain Lawrence. After I had a little considered the contents of both, I waited upon our honored friend, Mr. Thomas Hollis, with the case, with whom I left it; and some little time after, he told me, that himself and brother, Mr. John Hollis, would advance some money to repair your meeting-house, upon condition I would prevail with my brethren, concerned in our little fund, to make a present

distance. It pleased the Lord, by his divine and wise disposing providence, to spirit a small number of men who were very gracious and enlightened in the knowledge of his truth as it is in Jesus, and to appear for the vindication thereof, and to encourage them for their gathering into a church in the way and order of the gospel as above mentioned, which several wise and learned men endeavored but could not accomplish it. However, God was pleased to succeed the endeavors of our brethren who were not so accomplished with acquired parts and abilities by learning, and to appear for them under all the troubles and difficulties they were exposed unto; And when we were favored with our liberty by virtue of the King's letter to the government, it pleased the Lord to put it into our hearts and to encourage us to build a meeting-house for the worship of our God; which is now about forty years since. And when we lost our elders, such as were accomplished for the work of the ministry in so public a place, we made our application to the churches in London, and unto Mr. Gifford, in that, if it were possible, we might have had a man suitable for the work of the ministry sent over to us, but could never obtain any; so that we were forced or necessitated to make use of our brethren for the upholding of our church and meeting. And now, God hath been graciously pleased to raise up one amongst ourselves, viz., a son of one of our brethren whom he hath brought up to learning, and whom God hath been pleased so to succeed with his blessing, as to spirit him with grace and principles and also to accomplish him with not only acquired parts and abilities but, we hope we may truly say, also with gracious qualifications for the work and service of the Lord among us. And this is our present concernment, that, having, by the blessing of our God upon us, obtained this blessing of a minister to break the bread of life to us, our meeting-house which, by reason of so long standing, has gone much to decay, requires repairing, and, being but a small company here in this town, and some of our small number, by reason of age, requiring relief, and those few of our brethren that live in this town being such as God is pleased to make his choice amongst, as mentioned in the 2d of James, 5th verse, we take this boldness of acquainting you therewith, that if the Lord may be pleased to incline the hearts of our dear and well beloved brethren with you, in the several churches, to afford us a small matter of your assistance towards the repair-to Mr. Callender, as a token of our Christian respects to him. The motion pleased me well; I willingly undertook my part, and happily accomplished it, though it were out of the common way of our exhibitions; and by the time this comes to hand, I hope you will find remitted by Mr. Hollis what I hope will fully answer the church's request, together with a small present, which I hope will not be unacceptable, to my brother Callender himself, and show at least our concern for the good of the baptized interest in Boston, though we may not be capable to promote it in that measure we heartily desire.

Concerning the state of the Arian controversy with us, and our ministers' concern therein, I shall briefly relate the whole, as follows. Some few years ago one Dr. Clarke,[1] of the established church, a gentleman of deserved reputation, wrote a book, entitled, The Scripture doctrine of the Trinity; in which he endeavors (after very high expressions of the dignity of the Redeemer's person and nature) to deny him to be a necessary, self-existent being; which is construed by his adversaries as a consequential denying his proper divinity, and a degrading our Saviour into a subordinate God, notwithstanding all he hath offered in honor to this hope of a true Christian. This made a great stir, and set many pens to work; some for and some against the Doctor's notions, among several of note in the church of England, and others; some of whom I think carried the point much further than the Doctor appears to have designed. I wish the contest had always continued in the established church; but a little time carried it among the dissenters, and one Mr. Pierce, a Presbyterian minister, of ingenuity, and considerable note, among others, espoused Dr. Clarke's notions openly (if he went no further.) The debates, *pro* and *con*, began to be managed with warmth, not only in the city, but in divers parts of the country. But Mr. Pierce being a man of so much note, and a minister in the city of Exeter, where the Presbyterian interest is in much credit, he was the first person who was very publicly noted among the dissenters. His people (after some considerable time, and several methods used to accommodate matters) proposed parting with him, as a man not sound in the faith. This occasioned each party to advise with their friends in the ministry, and others, what to do in the case. Some of the persons

---

ing of our meeting-house, we conclude it would be a good work of charity and redound to your honor here and to your good account in the day of retribution. If amongst the several churches, it might be but to the value of twenty pounds and laid out there with what may be suitable for this place, it would be treble that money here, and would find a welcome and a thankful acceptance with us. This, with our prayers that God would direct and bless you in all your concerns, and multiply your numbers, and increase in you all the graces of his Holy Spirit; and desiring likewise your prayers, for the like mercies for us, we remain your brethren in gospel bonds." Rev. S. Hall's Collection of papers.—ED.

[1] Samuel Clarke, D. D.

wrote to upon this account, (which were not a few) thought that Mr. Pierce had given too much cause for his people to believe that he had departed from the orthodox faith, in relation to the doctrine of the Trinity. Others, though they did not deny this, yet apprehended his people had not dealt so kindly by him in this matter as they ought to have done, by a man of his character and usefulness.

The case was some time before a committee of ministers and gentlemen of the three denominations in London, to see if they could find a way to accommodate matters at Exeter, and prevent divisions upon the same account in other places; but they were not all of one mind. Then the whole body of ministers in and about London was called together, and a paper of advices, proposed to be considered of in order to sign, for accommodating matters at Exeter. Some of the ministers, who were zealously concerned for the doctrine of the Trinity, at the same time proposed, that a declaration of our faith, with respect to that important doctrine of the Christian religion, should be signed, and sent down with the advices; but, upon a division of the ministers, it was rejected by a majority of about five persons. It was then agreed at the next meeting to consider the paper of advices, paragraph by paragraph; at which meeting were about one hundred and thirty ministers of three denominations, who placed your poor friend in the chair. That part who were against signing a declaration of faith, as above, earnestly insisted upon proceeding directly to read the paper of advices, as supposing it to be the immediate work of the meeting; the other side proposed that article in the church of England which relates to the doctrine of the Trinity, and those answers in the Assembly's Catechism to the same purpose, to be subscribed by the London ministers, before they proceeded to consider the paper of advices. Warm debates there were indeed for two or three hours, when on a sudden those brethren who resolved to subscribe those articles withdrew into the gallery; which, however just their zeal might be for the truth contended for, was not looked upon as a sufficient reason for the breaking up the meeting at that time. So, after some messages sent from the one part to the other, those above proceeded to subscribe those articles, as containing their sentiments of the doctrine of the ever-blessed Trinity; and the other proceeded to consider the paper of advices, and drew up a general article of their faith as to that doctrine, which was signed by their moderator by appointment. This they sent to Exeter; while the others drew up another set of advices, and sent down with the articles they had subscribed, and henceforward we came under the distinguishing characters of subscribers and non-subscribers, which distinction I fear will be too long remembered by us, for the common benefit of true religion.

Some of the too warm among the non-subscribers would fain fix the odious charge of persecution on the other, while they again, with full as much warmth, would fix the charge of Arianism upon them. But this severity is not allowed by the greatest part of either side of the question; and I hope time will produce a better temper in both parties; but at present the matter is not accommodated, nor so good a harmony among the ministers as could be heartily wished. As I am satisfied that some among the non-subscribers are gone too far into some of the distinctive notions of Arius, so I think some of the subscribers have given too much ground of jealousy, that they intended to set up those forms as a test of orthodoxy, and the signing of them as necessary to persons being acceptable and useful in the ministry. But I dare say for the much greater part of both sides, that they intended no evil to their differing brethren; and that it was a zeal for the doctrine of the Trinity, and the real divinity of our Saviour, which made some subscribe the articles, and not any desire to impose upon others; and that those who refused the subscription, did it with a design to maintain Christian liberty, rather than any design to encourage or promote Arianism. There is no great difference in the number of either side; but I think there are not so many of our denomination among the non-subscribers as are on the other side; and though I cannot say that there are none of our ministers who too much favor the new scheme, yet I may venture to say in general, that our ministers, especially those of the Particular denomination,[1] are sound in the faith, as to the real divinity of Christ, and the true doctrine of the blessed Trinity. Therefore those who upbraid you with their being contrary, act either from prejudice or misinformation. But such have been the visible consequences of this difference, that brotherly love and charity, that indispensible ornament of the Christian religion, have been greatly lost in the debates. May the Lord increase light and love, as well as zeal and faithfulness, among all the disciples of our blessed Redeemer. So I must have done. The Lord be with you and yours.

EDWARD WALLIN.

Mr. James Peirce, above referred to, was ejected from his church, in March, 1719; but a party followed him, and built another meeting-house for him, in the city of Exeter; to encourage whom, he declared his expectation, that by what they suffered, " the spirit of imposition and persecution would be rendered more odious." And he accused that church of attempting to set up an Inquisition, only because they brought on such a trial as constrained him to own his new opinions, which caused his removal from a profitable

---

[1] Those who hold to particular election.

living.¹ Mr. Benjamin Wallin, son and successor in office to Mr. Edward, published an excellent little volume upon the Sonship of Christ, in 1771, wherein he informs us, that ever since the above-mentioned time, creeds and catechisms have been cried down, and a regular Christian education much neglected, under a pretence of reason and liberty. And America has been much infected with the same distemper. But it is not all traditions and human creeds that such men reject, as the following extract from Peirce plainly shews. Under an appearance of a great regard to the Scriptures, he published a catechism, wherein the answers were in Scripture words; part of which say:—

Question. How many Gods are there? Answer. There is one God. Q. Who is this God? A. Though there be that are called Gods, whether in heaven or in earth, (as there be gods many and lords many,) yet to us there is but one God, the Father, of whom are all things, and we for him. One God and Father of all, who is above all, and through all, and in you all. I Cor. viii. 5, 6; Eph. iv. 6.

This creed is so far from delivering any from the tyranny of human inventions, that where the Scripture puts no more than a semicolon between the mention of the Father and the Son, Peirce puts a period and three pages in his book. And when he comes to speak of the Son, he picks out words that speak of his subjection and obedience to the Father, excluding those which assert his equality with him, which are many.² Whereas, if we leave out the succession of time, and the mode or manner wherein earthly relations commence, which have no place in the Deity, it is easy to conceive of a Father and Son of equal capacity and excellency; with such a oneness in nature, and peculiarity of relation, as no others have; and also that one may, by voluntary contract, subject himself to another for wise purposes, and take upon him the form of a servant, and yet remain perfectly equal in nature. How unreasonable then are those great pretenders to reason, who profess to take the Scriptures as their rule, and yet re-

¹Pierce's Works, printed 1728, pp. 115, 136.   ²Ibid, pp. 352, 418—422.

ject all those truths therein, which cross their darling notions! Those who are convinced of the infinite evil of sin, see the necessity of infinite merit to remove their guilt, and infinite power to change their hearts and lives, and to guide them to glory. We are told, that by openly owning these doctrines, Mr. Hollis gave a check to some who had no great opinion of them.[1]

The Baptists in Boston received from him and his brother, one hundred and thirty-five pounds two shillings, for repairing their meeting-house, for which a letter of thanks was returned. And in Harvard College Mr. Thomas Hollis founded a professorship of theology, with a salary of eighty pounds per annum to the professor, and an exhibition of ten pounds apiece per annum to ten scholars of good character, four of whom should be Baptists, if any such were there; as also ten pounds a year to the college treasurer, for his trouble, and ten pounds more to supply accidental losses, or to increase the number of students.[2] And as by charter the ministers of Boston, for the time being, were constituted a part of the overseers of the college, Mr. Hollis moved that Mr. Callender might have a seat among them. And in a letter to Mr. Callender, of February 8, 1721-2, Mr. Wallin said, "I congratulate my friend upon his admitment to the honor of an overseer of the college. I pray God that truth and Christian love may more and more abound." But we are informed by the late Mr. Condy, that Dr. Sewall, at the head of other ministers, positively denied him a seat there. Yet how often have such men accused the Baptists of being much more rigid than themselves? and there was not a word in their charter to exclude him.

Declension and stupidity had long prevailed in the land, till a revival in several places was granted in 1721. Windham had so large a share of it, under the ministry of Mr. Samuel Whiting, as to add eighty communicants to their

[1] Rudd's Poem, p. 23.
[2] Neal's History of New England, Vol. II, pp. 220, 221.

church this year; for which they kept a special day of thanksgiving to God. One curious event then happened there which I shall mention. The word preached was such a looking-glass to one man, that he seriously went to Mr. Whiting, and told him he was very sorry that so good a minister as he was should so grossly transgress the divine rule, as to tell him his faults before all the congregation, instead of coming to labor with him in private. The minister smiled, and said he was glad that truth had found him out, for he had no particular thought of him in his sermon. Norwich, ten miles from thence, enjoyed a considerable measure of this blessing the same year, from whence my pious mother dated her conversion.[1] Many young people in Boston were turned to a serious regard for religion in 1721. The small-pox coming there in April, and prevailing most terribly through the year, had a deep effect upon many souls. It was thought that not more than a quarter of the inhabitants had passed through that distemper before, and none of them who were under eighteen years.[2] One of them deserves particular notice here.

John Comer was born in Boston, August 1, 1704, and sat under the ministry of the two Mathers. Having a great inclination for learning, he, by President Mather's influence, was taken from an apprenticeship to a trade, and put to

---

[1] Mrs. Elizabeth Backus, the mother of the author of this history, has already been incidentally noticed in connection with John Tracy, her father. See p. 331. In his sermon on her death, Mr. Backus says, "She has often mentioned to her children a work of conviction and conversion which she experienced about the year 1721." Gospel Comfort for Mourners, p. 19. Before her conversion she had united with the regular church in Norwich, and she remained a member there until 1745, when, together with her son, she joined the Separatists. Denison's Historical Notes, p. 44; Life and Times of Backus, pp. 27, 42. Her fidelity and her sufferings in the cause of religion will be noticed hereafter. Says the biographer of Mr. Backus, "The mother of Isaac Backus was, in the truest and highest sense of the expression, an excellent woman. Often does he speak of her in terms of deep respect and love. With special satisfaction does he dwell upon the fruits of genuine piety which appeared in her life. In a sermon occasioned by her death, he calls her 'My dear, godly mother,' and there is ample reason for the belief that she was worthy of such a designation." Life and Times of Backus, pp. 26, 27.—ED.

[2] Christian History, Vol. I, p. 130. Vol. II. p. 375.

school, in December, 1720. Serious turns of concern about his soul had been frequent with him for several years; which greatly increased for seventeen days after he had taken that infection. "Nothing," says he, "but the ghostly countenance of death unprepared for, was before me, and no sight of a reconciled God, nor any sense of the application of the soul-cleansing blood of Christ to my distressed soul. I remained in extreme terror until November 22. All the interval of time I spent in looking over the affairs of my soul; and on that day I was taken sick. As soon as it was told me that the distemper appeared, all my fears entirely vanished, and a beam of comfort darted into my soul, and with it satisfaction from those words, 'Thou shalt not die but live, and declare the works of the Lord.' Yea, so great was my satisfaction, that immediately I replied to my aunt who informed me, 'Then I know I shall not die now;' but gave no reason why I said so." He recovered, and afterwards became a Baptist minister; and his ingenious diary and papers have furnished many valuable materials for our history. Ephraim Crafts, one of his young brethren, was baptized and added to that church in Boston, January 27, 1723. John Dabney, from London, had been received by them December 4, 1720, and Richard Bevens, from Wales, the next August, who were members of Baptist churches before they came here. Other members from Europe were added to them, both before and since.

CHAPTER XI.

ILL TREATMENT ABOUT WORSHIP AT SWANZEY.—AT FREETOWN.—TIVERTON AND DARTMOUTH.—SOME RELIEF FROM ENGLAND.—MINISTERS' ATTEMPTS FOR MORE POWER DEFEATED.—HOLLIS'S AND WALLIN'S LETTERS.—FURTHER DONATIONS, AND SPRINGFIELD AFFAIRS.—FIRST EXEMPTING LAWS FROM MINISTERIAL TAXES.—SUFFERINGS AT REHOBOTH.—THE LYME DISPUTE.—CONNECTICUT LAWS, AND YALE COLLEGE.

Equal religious liberty, by virtue of a special act, was enjoyed in Boston; but was so much denied in the country, that most of the Baptists had no heart to send their sons to Harvard College; though a few of them did so, whereby they made some use of Mr. Hollis's donations there. Great pains were taken to compel every town to receive and support such ministers as the Court called orthodox. A law was also made at Boston, in the May session of 1718, to tax all to the building and repairing of parish meeting-houses. In 1717 the pious and judicious Elder Luther fell asleep, leaving the care of the first church in Swanzey to Elder Ephraim Wheaton, who had been a colleague with him about thirteen years. The second church in Swanzey had then two ordained pastors; yet in April, 1719, their Selectmen were convented before Bristol Court, "for not having a minister according to the law of the province." But upon proving that Elder Wheaton was their lawful minister, they were dismissed, "paying costs."[1] His meeting-house stood

[1] Bristol Court Records.—B.
A similar experience of this church is recorded on page 449.—ED.

near the borders of Rehoboth; and he and many of his people who lived therein were taxed to Pædobaptist ministers of that town, of which we shall hear more presently.

Freetown, which lies on the east side of Great River against Swanzey, met with worse treatment than they did. For on September 9, 1717, they made choice of Thomas Craghead, a minister from Ireland, for their pastor; and he accepted of their call. But instead of an amicable agreement with them about his support, he went in January, 1718, and procured an act of Bristol Court, to compel Freetown to pay him a salary of sixty-five pounds a year, to begin from the day he was chosen their minister. And for refusing to pay it, about fourteen of the inhabitants were seized and imprisoned at Bristol; one of whom was Benjamin Chase, a member of a Baptist church in Newport. In April, 1719, each party carried witnesses about these matters to Bristol Court; but the Court dismissed them all, and required the town to obey their former order. In 1720, Thomas Gage and George Winslow, their Select-men, were fined forty shillings apiece for not assessing Craghead's salary. At last he was defeated in a trial at law, and was forced to quit the town; but these broils produced great and lasting evils therein. Little Compton had settled a legal minister; and as Elder Tabor owned some land in that town, he was taxed to him; for which a riding-saddle was taken from Tabor, as a person informed me who saw it.

Tiverton and Dartmouth were the only remaining towns in the province[1] which had not yielded to the ruling party about worship. When orders for that purpose had come from their Courts, they had reported, that Joseph Wanton was the minister of Tiverton, and Elder Tabor the minister of the west part of Dartmouth, and another man for the east part. But as the Court did not esteem them to be orthodox, a complaint against those towns was presented to

---

[1] Tiverton was at that time included in the colony of Massachusetts Bay, but was afterwards set off to Rhode Island. See page 282.— ED.

their Legislature in 1722; which annexed such sums as they thought proper for the purpose to their province tax. This being heard of, their Selectmen refused to assess it; for which two of them out of each town were seized on May 25, 1723, and were imprisoned at Bristol. Hereupon Thomas Richardson, who married friend Wanton's daughter, was sent over to London; and with Richard Partridge, agent for Rhode Island Colony, presented a memorial to the king in Council; wherein they observed, that our charter allows equal liberty of conscience to all Christians except Papists; and that neither the charter nor any law had established any test of orthodoxy in this province, only as Presbyterians and Independents had set up their major votes as such; whereby dissenters from them were frequently brought under great sufferings; from which no redress could be obtained here, " the Assembly always opposing whatever the Governor and Council were at any time disposed to do on that behalf." And as the king, at his accession to the throne, promised protection and liberty of conscience to all his dissenting subjects without exception, they prayed that he would denounce his negative upon those laws or parts of laws among us, that interfered therewith, and also order those prisoners to be released.[1] A committee was appointed upon the case; whose report, with the act of Council thereon, is as follows:—

TO THE KING'S MOST EXCELLENT MAJESTY: May it please your Majesty, in obedience to an order in Council, from the late Lord's Justices, during your Majesty's absence abroad, bearing date the 24th day of October last, we did make a representation upon an act passed in the

---

[1] This Memorial shows the affairs of Baptists and other dissenters from the Standing Order at that time, in so clear and just a light, that, notwithstanding its length, we insert it in full.

"To GEORGE, KING OF GREAT BRITAIN, &c.: The humble petition of Thomas Richardson and Richard Partridge, in behalf of Joseph Anthony, John Sisson, John Akin and Philip Tabor, prisoners in the common jail at New Bristol, in the king's province of the Massachusetts Bay, in New England, as also their friends (called Quakers) in general, who are frequently under great sufferings for conscience sake in that government; Showeth:

"That William and Mary, late King and Queen of England, &c., by their royal

province of the Massachusetts Bay, in New England, in 1722, intituled, An act for apportioning and assessing a tax of £6,232, 13, 11; since which time another act, mentioned in the said order of reference, passed the 29th day of May, 1723, intituled, "An act for apportioning and assessing a tax of charter, bearing date the seventh day of October, in the third year of their reign, did (for the greater ease and encouragement of their loving subjects inhabiting the said province, and of such as should come to inhabit there) grant, establish and ordain, that forever thereafter, there should be a liberty of conscience allowed, in the worship of God, to all Christians except papists, inhabiting or which should inhabit or be resident within the said province, 'with power also to make laws for the government of the said province, and support of the same; and to impose taxes for the king's service, in the necessary defence and support of the said government, and protection and preservation of the inhabitants; and to dispose of matters and things whereby the king's subjects might be there, religiously, peaceably and civilly governed, protected and defended;' and, for the better securing and maintaining liberty of conscience, thereby granted,—commanded that all such laws, made and published by virtue of said charter, should be made and published under the seal of the said province, and should be carefully and duly observed, kept and performed; and put in execution, according to the true intent and meaning of the said charter:

"That those sorts of Protestants called Presbyterians and Independents, being more numerous in the said country than others, (to whom the said charter gives equal rights) they become makers of the laws by their superior numbers and votes, and ministers of the privileges of the said charter, so as, in great measure, to elude the same, and disappoint all others of the king's protestant subjects, of the good and just ends of transporting themselves and families at so great hazard and charges, our great encouragement and inducement thereto being liberty of conscience and ease from priestly impositions and burdens: That in the year 1692, they made a law in the said province, entitled, 'An Act for the settlement and support of Ministers and Schoolmasters,' wherein it is ordained 'that the inhabitants of each town within the said province, shall take due care, from time to time, to be constantly provided of an able, and learned orthodox minister or ministers, of a good conversation to dispense the word of God to them; which minister or ministers shall be suitably encouraged and sufficiently supported and maintained by the inhabitants of such towns;' That the said law was further enforced by another made in the year 1695, reciting its title aforesaid; as also by another made in the year 1715, entitled 'An Act for maintaining and propagating religion,' in which said last Act, the prevention of the growth of atheism, irreligion and profaneness, is suggested as one great reason of its being; and the power of determining who shall be ministers under the qualifications, is, by the said laws, assumed by the General Court or Assembly, with the recommendation of any three of the ministers of the said same sects, already in their orders, and settled and supported by virtue of the said laws; though it is not determined, (as the petitioners humbly presume) either by the said charter or by any act of parliament in Great Britain, or by any express law of the said province, who are orthodox and who are not, or who shall judge of such qualifications in such ministers: And in all which said several laws, no other care is had or taken of religion (even in their own sense) than only to appoint ministers of their own way, and impose their maintenance upon all the king's subjects conscientiously dissenting from them. By force of which said laws, or some of them,

£6,205, 15, 7½," is come to our hands; by which act a tax is laid in express terms upon the inhabitants of Dartmouth and Tiverton for the support of a Presbyterian, whom they call an orthodox minister, which falls almost entirely upon the Quakers, there being very few inhabitants of any other

several townships within the said province, have had Presbyterian or Independent preachers obtruded and imposed upon them for maintenance without their consent, and which they have not deemed able, learned or orthodox, and which, as such, they could not hear or receive: That by another law, made in the years 1722 and 1723, it is ordained that the town of Dartmouth and the town of Tiverton, in the said province, be assessed for the said years, the respective sums of one hundred pounds, and seventy-two pounds and eleven shillings over and beside the common taxes for support of government, which sums are for the maintenance of such ministers: That the said Joseph Anthony and John Sisson were appointed assessors of the taxes for the said town of Tiverton, and the said John Aikin and Philip Tabor for the town of Dartmouth; but some of the said assessors being of the people called Quakers, and others of them also dissenting from the Presbyterians and Independents and greatest part of the inhabitants of said towns being also Quakers or Anabaptists or of differing sentiments in religion from Independents, though the said assessors duly assessed the other taxes upon the people there, relating to the support of government, to the best of their knowledge, yet they could not in conscience assess any of the inhabitants of these towns anything for or towards the maintenance of any ministers; That they, the said Joseph Anthony, John Sisson, John Aikin and Philip Tabor, on pretence of their non-compliance with the said law, were, on the 25th of the month called May, 1723, committed to the jail aforesaid, where they still continue prisoners, under great sufferings and hardships, both to themselves and families, and where they must remain and die, if not relieved by the king's royal clemency and favor: That the people called Quakers in the said province, are, and generally have been, great sufferers by the said laws, in their cattle, horses, sheep, corn and household goods, which from time to time have been taken from them by violence of the said laws for the maintenance of ministers who call themselves able, learned and orthodox; which said laws, and the execution and consequences thereof, are not only, (as the petitioners humbly conceive) contrary to the liberty of conscience and the security of religion, civil liberty, and the rights and privileges granted in the said charter, to all the king's protestant subjects, there eluded and made null and precarious, but opposite also to the king's royal and gracious declaration at thy happy accession to the throne, promising protection and liberty of conscience to all thy dissenting subjects without exception to those of the said plantations: That after repeated application made to the said government there for redress in the premises, and no relief hitherto obtained, (the Assembly always opposing whatever the Governor and Council were at any time disposed to do on that behalf,) the king's loyal, suffering and distressed subjects, do now prostrate themselves at the steps of the throne, humbly imploring thy royal consideration, that it may please the king to denounce his negative upon the said laws or such part or parts of them or any of them as directly or consequently effect the lives, liberty, property, religion or conscience of thy protestant subjects in the said province, and their families and privileges granted and intended in the said royal charter, or such other relief as thy royal wisdom and goodness may please to provide."

Rev. S. Hall's Collection of papers.—ED.

persuasion in those two towns.¹ But as by the charter granted to this Province, a free and absolute liberty of conscience to all Christians (except papists) was intended to have been their foundation and support, and as by several laws passed there, it seems to have been laid down as a just and equitable rule, that the majority of each town congregation should have the choice of their own teachers, we cannot see why the Quakers should be refused this liberty, in the towns where they are so great a majority, and be obliged to maintain a teacher of a different persuasion. Wherefore we humbly propose to your Majesty, that this act may be repealed; which is most humbly submitted.

WESTMORELAND,
T. PELHAM,
M. BLADEN,
EDW. ASHE.

Whitehall, May 6, 1724.

At the Court at St. James's, 2d day of June, 1724.

Present, the King's most excellent Majesty, his Royal Highness the Prince of Wales, A. B. of Canterbury, Lord Chancellor, Lord President, Lord Privy-Seal, Lord Chamberlain, Duke of Roxbùrg, Duke of New Castle, Earl of Westmoreland, Lord Viscount Townsend, Lord Viscount Torrington, Mr. Speaker of the House of Commons, Mr. Vice-Chamberlain, William Pultney, Esq.

Upon reading this day at the Board a report from the Right Honorable the Lords of the Committee of Council, upon the petition of Thomas Richardson and Richard Partridge, on behalf of Joseph Anthony, John Sisson, John Akin and Philip Tabor, prisoners at the common goal at New Bristol, in his Majesty's Province of the Massachusetts Bay, in New England, for not assessing the inhabitants of the towns of Dartmouth and Tiverton the additional taxes of £172, 11, imposed upon them by an act passed there in the year 1722, which appears to be for the maintenance of Presbyterian ministers, who are not of their persuasion; and also in behalf of their friends called Quakers in general, who are frequently under great sufferings for conscience sake in that government: by which report it appears that their Lordships are of opinion, that it may be advisable for his Majesty to remit the said additional taxes, so imposed on the said two towns, and to discharge the said persons from goal: His Majesty in Council taking the said report into consideration, is graciously pleased to approve thereof, and hereby to remit the said additional taxes of one hundred pounds, and seventy-two pounds, eleven shillings, which were by the said act to be assessed on the said towns of Dartmouth and Tiverton. And

---

¹The Memorial says, "The greatest part of the inhabitants of the said towns being Quakers, or Anabaptists, or of differing sentiments in religion from Independents and Presbyterians. Quaker Records.

his Majesty is hereby further pleased to order, that the said Joseph Anthony, John Sisson, John Akin and Philip Tabor, be immediately released from their imprisonment on account thereof. And the Governor, Lieutenant Governor, and Commander in Chief, for the time being, of his Majesty's said Province of Massachusetts Bay, and all others whom it may concern, are to take notice, and yield due obedience hereunto.

TEMPLE STANYAN.

Before this, I find Mr. Wallin, in one of his letters, saying of king George the First, " Without any partiality to him as our reigning prince, I believe he is the greatest man, and the most fit for government, of any prince in the Christian world." And his son and successor, then Prince of Wales, was not inferior to him. By the above act our friends were released from a thirteen months' imprisonment. And as Jacob Tabor and Beriah Goddard, of Dartmouth, were imprisoned for not assessing said tax of 1723, Henry Howland, their other assessor, laid their case before the Assembly at Boston, who, on November 26, 1724, passed an act to release them, " to signify their ready and dutiful compliance with his Majesty's declared will and pleasure." Anthony and Sisson were of Tiverton, the rest were of Dartmouth, and Philip Tabor was a Baptist minister therein. These things were far from affording any satisfaction to the ministerial party here, as the following facts will shew. For at the annual convention of their ministers at Boston, May 26, 1725, they drew up an address to their Legislature, which says :—

Considering the great and visible decay of piety in the country, and the growth of many miscarriages, which we fear may have provoked the glorious Lord, in a series of various judgments, wonderfully to distress us; considering also the laudable example of our predecessors to recover and establish the faith and order of the gospel in the churches, and provide against what immoralities may threaten to impair them, in the way of General Synods convened for that purpose ; and considering that about forty-five years have now rolled away since these churches have seen any such conventions ; it is humbly desired, that the honorable General Court would express their concern for the interests of religion in the country, by calling the several churches in the province to meet by their pastors and messengers in a Synod, and from thence offer their advice upon that weighty case which the circumstances of the day do loudly call to be considered :[1] What are the miscarriages whereof we have reason to think the judgments of heaven upon us call us to be more generally sensible, and what may be the most evangelical and effectual expedients to put a stop unto those or the like miscarriages? This proposal we humbly make, in hopes that, if it be prosecuted, it may be followed with many desirable consequences, worthy the study of those whom God has made, and we are so happy to enjoy, as the nursing fathers of our churches.

COTTON MATHER.

In the name of the ministers assembled in their General Convention.[2]

On June 3, the Council voted to grant their petition; but the Representatives voted to defer the matter till their next session, which the Council concurred with, and Lieutenant Governor Dummer consented thereto. June 11th, a committee of the General Court, whereof Samuel Sewall, Esq., was chairman, appointed upon the affair of ministers' salaries, brought in a report, to have a law made to compel every parish to make up to their ministers their several salaries, equal to what they were when their contracts were made; and for the Judges of their County Courts to determine how much their currency had depreciated. This report was not accepted; but instead of it a resolve was passed, recommending it to every town, precinct and parish in the province, to make up to their respective ministers their salaries equal to what money was when their contracts were made; which resolve they ordered to be read to each congregation the next Lord's day after it was received, and also in their parish meetings the March after.[3] Episcopalians sent an account to the Bishop of London of the said petition for a synod, who laid the same before the Lords Justices of the Regency; from whom a sharp reprimand was written to Mr. Dummer, October 7, 1725, for giving any countenance to said petition,

---

[1] What they wanted was to *recover and establish* the power which ministers claimed; and, like the Synod of 1679, which they refer to, to represent to rulers and and people that the judgments of heaven would follow them, if that was not granted. See page 385.

[2] Hutchinson, Vol. II, p. 322. [292.]   [3] Massachusetts Records.

and for not sending over an account thereof immediately after it was presented and acted upon. They declared that inquiry had been made by proper authority, and they could not find that there was any regular establishment of a national or provincial church here, so as to warrant the holding synods of the clergy; but that if there were, it was the king's prerogative to call them, which therefore was invaded by the General Court when they intermeddled therewith. And if such a synod was called, and should be sitting when their letter arrived, they wrote to Dummer:—

Cause such their meeting to cease, acquainting them that their assembly is against law, and a contempt of his Majesty's prerogative, and that they are forbid to meet any more. But if, notwithstanding such signification, they shall continue to hold such an assembly, you are then to take care that the principal actors therein be prosecuted for a misdemeanor; but you are to avoid doing any formal act to dissolve them, lest it be construed to imply that they had a right to assemble.

CHARLES DELAFAYE.

Mr. Dummer, in a letter to the Board of Trade, endeavored to excuse himself, by observing, that a like vote of the Council upon a like petition was passed in 1715, which was never censured from home as he knew of.[1] But then it was not countenanced by the other branches of the Legislature, as this was. The minister who, in behalf of the rest, signed the above petition for a synod, published a book in 1726, wherein he promises a faithful account of the discipline of the New England churches. Much of it was written many years before, and an attestation was prefixed to it by Dr. Increase Mather, dated December 10, 1719. After sixty-six years' labor in the great work of the ministry, he fell asleep, August 23, 1723, aged eighty-five. Though he was a friend to councils and synods, yet he testified against giving them such power as his son and many more wanted. But he and others being removed, their children renewed their attempts for that power. His son had a strong affec-

[1] Douglas, Vol. II, pp. 337, 378.

tion for the proposals of 1705, and for Governor Saltonstall, who procured the establishment of that scheme in Connecticut; even so that when Saltonstall died in 1724, Mather preached a funeral sermon for him at Boston, a hundred miles off, and got it printed at New London. He also now discovered his resentment against Mr. Wise, for writing against said proposals.[1] And having declared that four synods had been called by authority in the Massachusetts, he says, "The synods of New England know no weapons, but what are purely spiritual. .... They have no secular arm to enforce any canons; they ask none; they want none. And they cannot believe, that any Protestant secular arm would, upon [a] due information, any more forbid their meetings, than they would any of the religious assemblies upheld in the country."[2] Had this been true, we have no reason to think that their meetings would have been forbidden. But plain facts shew, that the immediate effect of the first of those synods was the dissolving of a House of Representatives (who would not punish such as the synod had condemned) and the calling of another; who disfranchised, disarmed and banished a considerable number of persons. And their second synod declared it to be the duty of the magistrate to put forth his coercive power against schismatics, the effects whereof were the fining, imprisoning, scourging, banishing and hanging of those whom they so called. And the result of the fourth synod caused the nailing up of the Baptist meeting-house in Boston.[3] Are all these weapons *purely spiritual?* His meaning no doubt was, that their synods only informed rulers of what was their duty, which they were to do out of regard to God, and not to them. But the most horrid persecutions that ever were practiced were done under such pretences. And this author was in earnest to have their order of ministers supported by taxes,

---

[1] Ratio Disciplinæ Fratrum Nov. Anglorum, p. 184.
[2] Ibid, pp. 172, 173.
[3] See pages 66—69, 159, 180, 192, 262, 393, 328, 385.

imposed and collected "in the king's name." To justify which, he says, "If the most of the inhabitants in a plantation are Episcopalians, they will have a minister of their own persuasion; and the dissenters, if there be any in the place, must pay their proportion of the tax, for the support of this legal minister."[1] He knew that such an instance had not then taken place in New England; and we know that every thing of that nature has been earnestly opposed therein ever since. And he then commended some of his party, for involving a salary for their ministers in a general rate for all town charges, "where Quakerism was troublesome,"[2] which he might have said was likewise done to the Baptists in Rehoboth, if he had been willing the whole truth should be known.

Mr. Hollis's ideas of the nature of religion, and of the state of this country, appear in the following letter to Elder Wheaton:—

London, March 13, 1723.

DEAR SIR:—I have newly received, under covert of Mr. Elisha Callender, your long looked-for letter, dated the 25th of December, and give you thanks for the account you give me of the affairs of your church, your circumstances, and your neighbors'. I am glad the books sent you are of use unto you; by the same hand you will have another forwarded, which I value, and suppose you will. I rejoice in the success of your ministry, and increase of your church, which will naturally increase your cares with your joy. I mourn because of the ignorance of your sleeping Sabbatarians; let us be thankful for our light, pity them and pray for them, and endeavor in love to lead them into the light also. God, that hath shined into our hearts by his gospel, can lead them from the Sinai covenant and the law of ceremonies, into the light of the new covenant and the grace thereof. I pity to see professors drawing back to the law, and desire to remember that our standing is by grace; and therefore not to be high-minded over them, but fear, remembering our Lord's words, Watch and pray, lest ye enter into temptation. Every word of God is precious; the saints love it; and they that honor him he will honor; and in keeping of

---

[1] Ratio Disciplinæ, &c., p. 21.
[2] Ibid, p. 22.—B.
"Where Quakerism is troublesome, some towns are so wise to involve the salary of the ministry in the general rate for all town charges, and so the cavils of those who would else refuse to pay the rate for the ministry, are obviated."—ED.

it there is present peace, and a promise of future reward. We now live by faith and not by sight. He that endureth to the end shall be saved. Go on, sir, sowing the seed, looking up to him whose work alone it is to give the increase, whoever be the planter or waterer; and as you do abound in your labors, and do find him multiplying seed unto you, may you yet abound more and more to the end, which is my sincere wish. Let no man rob us of our comfortable hope, that when we cease to be here we shall be present with the Lord, in whose presence the saints believe is fullness of joy in a separate state, and expectation of greater in the resurrection, when it shall be fully manifested how he loved them. Let none jeer us out of our duty now to lisp forth his praises with our tongues, since we expect hereafter to sing in a better manner the song of the Lamb, with a much more noble chorus.

In reference to your poll-tax and other taxes, which are necessary for support of the government and society, [they] are not to be esteemed a burthen; it is giving tribute or tithes to whom tribute is due, unless the taxes do oppress you unequally, because you are Baptists and Separatists; if so, then let me know, (who profess myself a Baptist) and I will endeavor to have a word spoken for you to the Governor, that you may be eased. You know that our profession is not mody in your country nor ours; few if any of the great men submitting to plain institution; and as we profess ourselves disciples of Christ, it is our duty to take up our cross with patience, and pay parochial duties where we live, and voluntarily maintain our own charge, and be thankful for our liberty, as men and Christians, to our good God, who in his providence has inspired many magistrates and ministers in your province with a truer spirit of catholic charity than formerly. You have heard, or may be informed by Mr. Callender, of my foundation in Harvard College, and the provision I have made for Baptist youth to be educated for the ministry, and equally regarded with Pædobaptists. If you know any as may be duly qualified, inform me, and I shall be glad to recommend them for the first vacancy. And to close; while we profess to worship God nearer to the rule of primitive institution and practice of our great Prophet and Teacher, the Lord Jesus Christ, and his apostles, let our light so shine before men in all holy conversation, that such whose inclinations may be ready to speak evil of our way, may be ashamed. May serious religion and godliness in the power of it flourish among us; every thing that goes in to make up the true Christian. Where the image of Christ is formed in any, I call them the excellent of the earth; with such I delight to associate and worship, whatever particular denomination they may go by among men; and this I would do till we all come into the unity of the faith, &c. Acts xx. 32.

Your loving friend,

THOMAS HOLLIS.

This I copied from the original letter; and would just observe upon it, that the generality of parish rates here were only for the support of one way of worship, and not for the government, as he supposed. And further light about the conduct of that day may be gained from the following letter:—

London, February, 18, 1724–5.

DEAR BROTHER CALLENDER: I had the pleasure of yours by Captain Lawrence, and am glad to hear of your welfare. May the Lord preserve your health and usefulness. I rejoice at the increase of your members, and the good prospect you have of more being added to your church, even of such who shall be saved. It is sweet encouragement to a poor laborer in Christ's vineyard, to find the Lord works with him; and some visible instances of sovereign grace and love among his people make his drooping spirit revive and sing. May you have more of these, especially among the rising generation; for it is a particular pleasure to see young ones look Zionward, and truly remember their Creator in the days of their youth; though in this case we have always reason to rejoice with trembling, because so many who seemed to run well for a time, have been turned aside by youthful lusts, (which war against the soul) to the wounding the hearts of their ministers, and the dishonor of Christ. I am sorry you have so much cause to complain, with us, of the great decay of the power and purity of religion. I am afraid this inquisitive age of professors spend too much time, and almost all their zeal, about matters of speculation, and neglect the closet and inward experimental religion too much. I observe by some letters and papers, by Captain Lawrence, that there is a number of young men formed into a society at Boston, who have taken upon them the name of the Berean Society. It is a noble design to be wholly governed by Scripture, and [I] wish every professor had such a resolution. They seem to be in earnest about what they propose, and if any of their zeal, for any particular point in dispute among Christians, should flame too high, I am glad they are under your conduct, by which I hope they will be well directed for their mutual edification, and the honor of truth. They will have some books, contained in the catalogue, sent soon, when I hope to write more particularly on this head. I met Captain Lawrence at our honored friend Mr. Thomas Hollis's, where we had some particular discourse about your place and people, and how his bounty to your church was laid out. From the whole, I apprehend Mr. Hollis was not displeased, but approved of what you had done, and hath been so good as to order the remaining part of the money for your own use; besides which, he hath been pleased to send you a present of books. I have often, my dear friend, adored the divine goodness, in disposing this gentleman's mind to so much service for the interest of Christ in general, in New England as well as Old; but especially for the providence by which such a gentleman came to the knowledge of our small interest in those Colonies, who had such a love to despised truth, as to own and encourage it in the face of so many and powerful opposers. It is this good providence, I apprehend, hath occasioned some persons to look favorably towards the baptized interest in Boston, and gives an encouraging view of greater advantage in years to come. His favors to you and yours hath doubtless been ungrateful to some of your neighbors, and perhaps some have been unkind and weak enough to design you a prejudice by some accounts given; but be in no pain for that, for Mr. Hollis is no stranger to the weakness which good men are liable to; nor will he be easily persuaded into hard thoughts of any, notwithstanding their many weaknesses, who in their general conduct have acquitted themselves like Christians and honest men; nor do any who attempt to draw his displeasure upon another person without good reason, do himself the least service thereby with Mr. Hollis. That the good will of him that dwelt in the bush may be with you and yours, is the hearty desire of your sincere friend and unworthy brother,

EDWARD WALLIN.

In addition to his other donations, Mr. Hollis founded a professorship of the mathematics and experimental philosphy in Harvard College in 1726, with a salary of eighty pounds a year to the professor; and he sent over an apparatus for the purpose, which cost about one hundred and fifty pounds sterling, besides large additions to the college library.[1] And by a letter to Mr. Callender, from Gay Head, on Martha's Vineyard, of September 11, 1727, I find Jonas Horswet, an Indian minister, sending for some of the books he had received, and also mentioning Thomas Sekins, another Indian preacher at Nantucket.[2] About this time four Baptists were seized for ministerial taxes in the country, and were cast into prison at Boston; but were soon released again by the special order of Lieutenant Governor Dummer.[3] Near the same time there came a letter from Springfield, signed by thirty men, directed to the Baptist church in Boston, requesting that their pastor might be sent up to labor among them. He went accordingly, and on

---

[1] Neal, Vol. II, pp. 220, 221.   [2] See page 347.
[3] Proctor's Remonstrance, in 1754.

July 23, 1727, baptized John Leonard, Ebenezer Leonard, William Scott, Abel Leonard, and Thomas Lamb, of Springfield, and Victory Skyes and Marcy Lawton,[1] of Suffield. A letter to him dated July 19, signed Daniel Brewer, Ebenezer Devotion, Stephen Williams, Samuel Hopkins, Nehemiah Bull, blames him for not first coming to them, and says, " We cannot think that preaching to or treating with particular persons in a private manner, to instil into them doctrines that we think are not according to truth and godliness, to be so Christian-like; and we assure you is not what we expected from Mr. Callender, whatever we might have feared from some others." Mr. Devotion was minister in Suffield, and Bull in Westfield; the other three were of Springfield. When Mr. Callender went there again the next year, the three Springfield ministers wrote to inquire whether he came prepared for and expecting a public dispute about baptism.[2] His answer was in these words:—

Springfield, September 17, 1728.

REVEREND SIR: It is not my custom and manner to go about the country to dispute and debate and wrangle with those that differ from me in opinion. It is well known that I am for peace with all men, and for

---

[1] In addition to these names, a manuscript of John Comer gives the names of Jonathan Worthington, John Pullin, Richard Gardner, and Mary Worthington. Also in his Diary, Comer wrote under date of October, 1727, that on the 23d of the previous July, Elisha Callender had baptized eleven persons in Springfield; and a letter from Springfield, given in the succeeding note, states that eleven persons had been baptized there.—ED.

[2] The correspondence in connection with this important movement in Springfield, this spontaneous springing up of Baptist principles in a new field, seems to be of sufficient interest and value to justify giving it in full.

To the Church of Christ in Boston under the care of Elder Elisha Callender, the subscribers hereunto send greeting:

BELOVED: Although we are no church nor members of any church, yet we have formerly looked upon ourselves, at least some of us, to have been members of such church or churches whose faith and practice is to baptize, or rather sprinkle, infants; but through God's goodness, by searching the Scriptures, and such other helps as we have received from some of your church, have been made sensible that our former practise with relation to baptism, has been grounded too much upon the traditions of men. And as, through grace, we hope we have in some measure been made sensible of the error that the churches in this land in general are in, with respect to baptism, both as to manner and subject, the which, in times past, we have

Christians to live in love and charity, and for every man to act as he is fully persuaded in his own mind. But if you will not be quiet and easy, and will insist upon it that your people must hear what is to be said in opposition to what I think contrary to truth and godliness, you may inform, Sir, your humble servant, ELISHA CALLENDER.

To the Reverend Mr. Daniel Brewer.

too fondly imbibed and embraced, so we desire to renounce and forsake the same, as not in the least corresponding with the word of God. And understanding that the church at Boston practises and allows of no other but believers' baptism; we, the subscribers, do therefore spread our case before the church, humbly entreating your advice under our present circumstances; and if it agree with the pleasure and advice of the church, (in order for the attaining further knowledge in the ways of God) to grant that Elder Elisha Callender may give us a visit and preach some sermons among us, who as yet, the most of us, never heard a sermon preached by a Baptist. And if it may stand with the pleasure of the church to grant this the request of our souls, we entreat the favor of a line to inform us when it may be. And now, leaving our concern with God, desiring the prayers of the church to the throne of grace that God would carry on the work which we hope through grace he has begun, and that he would perfect it to the end, we desire to subscribe, though unworthy, your brethren in the bonds of the gospel,

JONATHAN WORTHINGTON,"

[and fifteen others.]

"We, the subscribers, are hesitating in the doctrine of infant sprinkling, and desire further instruction to understand the true institution of baptism according to the word of God, and to be in the use of all proper means to attain the same.

JOS. BEDURTHA, jr.,"

[and twelve others.]

REVEREND SIR: We had a desire to have seen you and discoursed with you in a Christian, moderate, and calm manner, respecting your visiting the people of our parts and charge, and to have known from you whether it can be that the kingdom and interest of our glorious Lord Jesus is likely to be advanced and the welfare of precious souls furthered, by the measures you are now pursuing; or whether the interest of pure and undefiled religion is not like to suffer. We are not fond of men's being called the followers of Paul or Apollos, but if the good of men's souls be furthered, we shall rejoice. But, Sir, if heats, debates and divisions do follow, (as we fear they will) to the wounding of religion and the danger of vital piety, we ask whether blame must not be at your door? If you esteem of us as ministers of Jesus Christ, and would have been pleased to have conferred with us, we would, any of us, have endeavored to have given you as true account as we were capable, of the circumstances of these people; and should be glad to join with you, or any good man, in doing anything for the revival of decayed piety, &c. But we cannot think that preaching to or treating with particular persons, in a private manner, to instil into them, doctrines which, we think, are not according to truth and godliness, to be so Christian-like, and we assure you, is not what we expected from Mr. Callender, whatever we might have feared from others; and we should have thought it more fair if you had desired to have preached in one of our pulpits where we might have heard you and have had an opportunity to have made our remarks and replies [if we thought it not according to truth.) See Matthew 10. 26, 27. As to the book you were pleased to send to Mr. Brewer and Mr. Williams, just now we shall make no remarks upon it. EBENEZER DEVOTION, &c.

Springfield, July 19, 1727."

I find no answer to this.

Upon the receipt of their second charter, Dr. Cotton Mather said, " Religion is forever secured ; a righteous and generous liberty of conscience established. And the General Assembly may, by their acts, give a distinguishing encouragement unto that religion which is the general profes-

A few weeks later, those who had been baptized in Springfield, still seeking for light and guidance, wrote as follows :—

Springfield, September 6, 1727.

"To the church of Christ in Newport, under the care of Elder Peckom and Elder Comer; we, the subscribers hereunto, in the name and in behalf of eleven persons lately baptized hereabouts, we being of the number also, all baptized upon the profession of faith; send greeting."

DEARLY BELOVED IN OUR LORD JESUS, THOUGH UNKNOWN TO US: Whereas it pleased God, in infinite mercy to discover to us his will in his holy word, and our indispensable duty to submit to him in his ordinances; the which (we hope in obedience) we have so far done as to submit to his holy ordinance of baptism; and now are like sheep without a shepherd: do therefore write to entreat and beseech your prayers at the throne of grace that God would please send a laborer into his harvest here, and add daily unto us, such as shall be saved. We are not only as sheep without a shepherd, and few in number, but we are environed round about with enemies, and such as sometimes prove potent. Indeed, we are not without fear that the clergy which we are surrounded with, are enemies to our cause. Do therefore crave your advice and assistance at this difficult juncture especially. The same we have requested of the church at Boston, and have had Elder Callender with us, and being now wholly destitute of such help, desire also that your Elder Comer might give us a visit, preach amongst us and administer the ordinance of baptism, if any should present to the same : and that God would enable and assist us to persevere to the end, and build us up into a church, that so we may live in the enjoyment of all his holy ordinances, the which our souls long for and thirst after. Thus hoping and entreating that both the church and Elder Comer will grant these our desires, which are not the desires of the persons above mentioned only, but of divers others also ; we subscribe, though unworthy, with our Christian love presented, your loving brethren in the bonds of the gospel,

WILLIAM SCOTT, &c.

Mr. Comer relates in his Diary that he set out for Springfield with two brethren, "arrived safe at the house of Mr. Jno. Devotion at Southfield," Thursday, September 19, and the next day "went over to Springfield and found all things agreeable." The following Lord's day he preached to about "seventy auditors." Two ministers of the Standing Order came to see him, one of whom, he says, "seemed much troubled about the affair I came upon."

In his visit to Springfield the next year, Mr. Callender baptized Thomas Durkee of Windham, and Daniel Blodget of Stafford. The letter above mentioned, which he received at this time from ministers of the Standing Order, is as follows :

REVEREND SIR: Our laboring to wait upon you together on last year, not being well received by some, we shall not now take pains after any such thing; but take this method to ask you whether you came prepared for and expecting of a

sion of the inhabitants."[1] And for thirty-six years they made no act to exempt either Baptists or Quakers from taxes to his party of ministers. The great earthquake was in the evening of October 29, 1727; and the Assembly that met the 22d of the next month passed the first act of exemption therefrom, that they ever did for any denomination. It was to empower every settled Episcopal minister to draw all the money which was assessed upon any of his society, who lived within five miles of his meeting, if they usually attended worship there; who were also to be exempted from taxes for building or repairing of meeting-houses for the established way. But it required each parish to make up to their ministers, within two months, all the money that might by their means be taken from them. The five-mile limitation was dropped afterwards; and by an act in 1742, the minister and church wardens were required to give certificates to each parish treasurer, where any of their society lived, in order for their drawing said money.

Nothing is more amazing among men, than the influence which the love of power and gain has to blind their minds. The admission of the houses both of Orange and Hanover to the British throne, was upon the principle that government is founded in compact. And the most essential article of the national compact was, that none should be taxed but by their own representatives. Yet because the representatives in this government refused to put it out of their power

---

public dispute concerning the subjects and modes of baptism. We ask your answer by the bearer. From, Sir, your humble servants,

DANIEL BREWER,
STEPHEN WILLIAMS,
Springfield, September 16, 1728.   SAM'L HOPKINS.

"Please, Sir, by a line or two, to favor us with a reply to this as soon as possible, directing it immediately to me, D. B., or, (if an opportunity offers convenient,) immediately to Mr. Williams at the Meadows."

The answer to this, Backus gives in full.

Ten years later the Baptists in Springfield secured stated preaching, and after two years more a Baptist church was formed there.—ED.

[1] Account of his father's life, p. 141. He himself died February 13, 1728, aged sixty-five.

to give or withhold the salary demanded by the Crown for governors that they could have no choice in appointing or removing, an attempt was made in England to bring the case before the Parliament, and to take away our second charter. But Mr. Jeremiah Dummer, brother to the Lieutenant Governor, published in London such a defence of our charter rights in 1721, as, with other things, prevented it. Though in 1725 an explanatory charter was added, which deprived the representatives of power to put their own Speaker into office, without the consent of the Governor. These things were justly complained of, by those who daily practised a like iniquity themselves. For it is not more certain that America is not represented in the British Parliament, than it is that a quantity of *money* does not give any men a right to judge for their neighbors about soul-guides, and to enforce their judgments with the sword. Yet this was daily practised, to support teachers, that many who were taxed to them had no more voice in choosing, than said representatives had in their governors. But as hot contentions still continued about the Governor's salary, and other dangers hung over them, when their Assembly met at Boston, in May, 1728, they made a law, as follows:—

That from and after the publication of this act, none of the persons commonly called Anabaptists, nor any of those called Quakers, that are or shall be enrolled or entered in their several societies as members thereof, and who allege a scruple of conscience as the reason of their refusal to pay any part or proportion of such taxes, as are from time to time assessed for the support of the minister or ministers of the churches established by the laws of this province, in the town or place where they dwell, shall have their polls taxed towards the support of such minister or ministers, nor shall their bodies be at any time taken in execution, to satisfy any such ministerial rate or tax, assessed upon their estates or faculty; provided, that such persons do usually attend the meetings of their respective societies, assembling upon the Lord's day for the worship of God, and that they live within five miles of the place of such meeting.

The way prescribed for their being known, was for each County Court, at their next session after the first of June annually, to appoint meet persons of those societies, "to bring in a list, upon oath or solemn affirmation, of all persons within their respective towns or precincts, that profess themselves to be Anabaptists or Quakers, and usually attend their meetings as aforesaid, after which the clerk of the peace of the county shall give in to the assessors of each town or precinct a list of their names."

Here we may see that arbitrary power is always the same in nature, in every age, and every country. "Go ye, serve the Lord; only let your flocks and your herds be stayed," said Pharaoh. Let their polls be exempted, but their estates and faculties be taxed, said the Massachusetts. Herein they imitated him; but in two other points they went beyond him. "Go not very far away," said Pharaoh; "Go but five miles," said the Massachusetts; though many of their own parishioners, from that day to this, must go much further than that to meeting. Neither did Pharaoh require a list of the people upon oath, as these did. Little did Mr. Hollis know how his brethren here were treated. His friend Wheaton, who, as was before observed, with many of his society, lived within the bounds of Rehoboth, now hoped for some relief; and for that end applied to their next County Court; but they were told by the judges that said law did not take place that year. And for refusing to pay that year's tax to John Greenwood and David Turner, ministers of that town, twenty-eight Baptists, two Quakers, and two Episcopalians,[1] were seized and imprisoned at Bristol, by Jonathan Bosworth and Jacob Ormsbee, constables of Rehoboth; the main of them on March 3, 1729. Hereupon

---

[1] Obadiah Bowen, Azriakim Peirce, Jonathan Thurber, Jeremiah Ormsbee, Squire Wheeler, Daniel Bullock, Samuel Goff, Joseph Bowen, James Hicks, Seth Guernsey, Edmund Ingalls, Benjamin Ingalls, Ephraim Martin, Miel Peirce, Samuel Thurber, William Wheeler, Philip Wheeler, Gideon Hammond, Jeremiah Ormsbee, jun., Ephraim Martin, jun., John Jones, James Lewis, Thomas Horton, Richard Round, Jotham Carpenter, Samuel Bullock, Richard Bullock, Ephraim Wheaton, jun., Baptists; Henry Finch and John Hicks, Quakers; Samuel Carpenter and John Bowen, Episcopalians. Philip Wheeler was Colonel of the militia in that county afterwards. Wheaton was son to their minister.

they sent a petition to Governor Burnet in Council; wherein they claimed charter rights, and mentioned the late declaration from England, that there was no national or provincial church established here, and the release of prisoners upon that footing; and that if relief was not granted to them, they soon expected the imprisonment of several Baptists and Quakers of Taunton and Norton, on the same score. The Governor and Council, on March 8, gave their opinion, that said law did take place the preceding year; and ordered Seth Williams, Esq., Chief Judge of that county, to convene a number of Justices at Bristol, and to do all they lawfully could for the release of those prisoners. He convened some of them, but gave no relief to those men. Mr. Comer came and preached to them March 11. And as no other way appeared of deliverance from a nauseous place which had injured their health, but paying said taxes and costs, this was soon after done by their friends. However, lest further complaints should be carried to England, the Assembly at Boston, November 19, 1729, added an act to exempt their estates and faculties also; but "under the same conditions and limitations that their polls were before." And it was not to exempt from any tax that was made, and then in collectors' hands, nor to continue in force any longer than their May session, 1733.

After the death of Governor Saltonstall, the Connecticut Assembly of October 8, 1724, elected Joseph Talcott, Esq., in his stead; under whose administration they enjoyed more liberty for seventeen years, than they had under his predecessor. Stephen Gorton was ordained, at New London, pastor of the second Baptist church in Connecticut, November 28, 1726, by the assistance of their elders, Wightman, of Groton, and Comer, of Newport. And as Wightman was called to preach in Lyme, Mr. John Bulkly, a learned minister of Colchester, came and held a public dispute with him at Lyme, June 7, 1727, upon baptism and ministers' support. The question concerning the latter point Wightman stated thus :—" Whether ministers of the gospel ought to be maintained, in the least, by goods taken away by force from men of contrary persuasions?" And he gave these reasons against that practice :—" 1. Because there is no precept nor precedent for so doing in the New Testament. 2. Because so to do is what we would not be done unto ourselves. 3. Because the Lord requires only volunteers, and not forced men in his service." But Bulkly refused to dispute upon this footing, and shifted the question, to whether their way was lawful or not? And, after going far about, he said, " Lawful authority have a right to determine the undetermined modes of moral duties." To which Wightman said, " 1. But they must always determine the mode in the order of morality, and so they may do to others, as they would they should do to them in like case. Now would you have the superior powers of England so to determine for you, that you may have liberty and only bear your own charges in this affair? 2. This point, I think, is not undetermined in Scripture, which shows us no other way for the support of the gospel ministry, but what is from the free-will offerings of the people." And as Bulkly raked together many scandalous things that had been published against the Baptists, and then said, " They are but of yesterday, and so consequently the truth cannot be with them, as being not known in the world till about two hundred years past;" Wightman replied and said, " I never read of a Presbyterian longer than the said term ; how then can the way of truth be with them? If you say there were men of your principles many years before, I answer, that there were men professing the doctrines maintained by us long before that time."[1]

The May session of Connecticut Legislature, in 1729, passed an act in favor of Quakers, to exempt all from ministerial taxes, " who do attend the worship of God in such way as is allowed, and shall produce a certificate from such society, of their having joined themselves to them, and that

[1] Bulkly, pp. 132, 176; Wightman, pp. 25, 28, 41.

they do belong unto their society." At an association of Baptist churches at North Kingstown, September 6, 1729, they drew a petition to the General Assembly of Connecticut, that their brethren who were scattered up and down in that Colony, might be exempted from taxes to ministers and meeting-houses that they dissented from; which was signed by Richard Sweet, Valentine Wightman, Samuel Fisk, John Comer, elders; Timothy Peckom, Joseph Holmes, Ebenezer Cook, Benjamin Herenden, and other brethren, to the number of eighteen, one of whom was Thomas Durkee of Windham; to which was afterward added these lines, viz.:—

We, the subscribers, do heartily concur with the memorial of our brethren on the other side, and do humbly request the same may be granted, which we think will much tend to Christian unity, and be serviceable to true religion, and will very much rejoice your honors' friends, and very humble servants,

JOSEPH JENCKS, Governor,
JAMES CLARK,
DANIEL WIGHTMAN, Elders.

Newport, September 10, 1729.

Hereupon the Assembly, who met at New Haven, October 9, 1729, passed an act to allow the Baptists the same privileges as were granted to the Quakers the May before; both of them being perpetual laws, and not such temporary acts as the Massachusetts have perplexed themselves and others with. President Stiles informs me, that the Baptists in Saybrook were the first who took the benefit of this act.

A concise account of the affairs of the college over which he presides shall close this chapter. Connecticut Legislature first granted a charter for it in 1701. It was then intended to be at Saybrook; but after hot contentions, wherein a large and valuable part of their library was lost, it was settled at New Haven in 1718. Elihu Yale, Esq., Governor of the East India Company in London, made large donations to it, upon which it was called Yale College. In 1719, Mr. Timothy Cutler, minister at Stratford, was chosen Rector of it. But in September, 1722, he resigned that office, and went to England for Episcopal ordination, from whence he also received the title of D. D., and was a missionary many years in Boston. After his departure, Mr. Samuel Andrew, minister at Milford, presided at their Commencements, until Mr. Elisha Williams, of Wethersfield, was chosen their Rector in 1725; which office he sustained with honor to himself, and advantage to others, till he resigned it on October 31, 1739, and removed back to Wethersfield. He often represented this town in their Assembly, and was serviceable in other offices, one of which was to go over as a special agent for his colony to England. Mr. Thomas Clap, of Windham, succeeded him in the college; the government of which, by their first charter, was in the Trustees, who chose the Rector and tutors. But by a more ample charter from their Legislature, dated May 9, 1745, their order was changed to that of, " The President and Fellows of Yale College, in New Haven," whose number is twelve. The eleven Fellows are all settled ministers, who elect the President, and also their own members, when any of them resign, die, or are displaced; seven of the Corporation being a quorum.[1]

[1] Douglas, Vol. II, pp. 183—188.

APPENDIX A.[1]

Having had several interviews with divers of the people called Quakers, on the subject of the first volume of my History, and finding I have not clearly expressed their sentiments and practices, and some facts appearing to me different from what they did when I wrote, I am desirous, with them, to have the History corrected, and matters put in such a light, that posterity may not misapprehend them. Let the reader therefore receive the following correction, as what appears to me most consistent with the truth, and in justice to that people ought to be transmitted to posterity.

In page 117, the following extract from John Tyso's letter, "There was nothing *in* him (i. e. Dr. Increase Mather, as he said) that he hoped to be saved by," having been made by me to manifest an error in Friends respecting Christ within; I would observe, that I do not look upon it as an error, provided Christ without be also acknowledged, and it be held agreeably to the true sense of John vi. 56, xvii. 26; I John iii. 24; in which sense I am informed it is held by Friends.

In pages 118, 119, I have quoted some of Roger Williams's arguments against Friends' sentiments of the grace of God having appeared, or being manifested to all mankind universally; for their answer to which arguments, I would refer to Fox, &c., Answer, pages 17—20, Second part.

In page 245, I mentioned that Quakers were so called from Fox and his companions trembling and quaking before Gervase Bennet, a Justice in Derby. I meant not to insinuate, that their trembling on that occasion, or others, was occasioned by the fear of man; neither do I on a review of proofs find sufficient grounds to reject Fox's account of their receiving said name, which follows in the same page; though it is allowed by Barclay, as well as Mosheim, that their quaking and trembling in other places occasioned their being commonly called by that name.

[1] In the former edition, this Appendix is at the close of Volume II. As the arrangement of volumes is changed in the present edition, and the Appendix refers entirely to Volume I, it is inserted here.—ED.

In page 256, I undertake to inform posterity how those Quakers behaved under their sufferings; upon a review of which it appears just to add, that I find, and that by other parts of Cudworth's uncontroverted letter, not quoted by me, that he was turned out of office, as he expressly says, "Because I had entertained some of the Quakers at my house, that thereby I might be the better acquainted with their principles; the Court professing they had nothing at all against me, only in that thing, of giving entertainment to the Quakers." And he informs us, "that when the Quakers were committed to prison, they must be kept on coarse bread and water; no Friend may bring them any thing, none permitted to speak with them, nay, if they have money of their own, they may not make use of that to relieve themselves; they have many adherents; and, a little to acquaint you with their sufferings, which is grievous unto and saddens the hearts of most of the precious saints of God, it lies down and rises up with them, and they cannot put it out of their minds, to see and hear of poor families deprived of their comforts, and brought into penury and want. As far as I am able to judge of the end, it is to force them from their homes and lawful habitations, and to drive them out of their coasts. As for the means by which they are impoverished, these in the first place were scrupulous of an oath." This does not appear to be confined to allegiance or fidelity to government, but oaths at large, which principle, I understand, they maintain from our Saviour's command; Matt. v. 34; I say unto you swear not all, &c. "Why then we must put in force an old law, that all may take the oath of fidelity; —they cannot—then a fine of five pounds. On this account thirty-five head of cattle, as I am credibly informed, hath been by the authority of the Court taken from them the latter part of this summer. A poor weaver that has seven or eight small children, himself lame in his body, had but two cows, and both taken from him. The marshal asked him what he would do? The man said, that God, who gave him them, he doubted not, would still provide for him. To fill up the measure yet more full, though to the further emptying of Sandwich men, the Court of Assistants, the first Tuesday of this instant, was pleased to determine fines upon them for meetings, one hundred and fifty pounds, and among others the poor weaver spoken of, twenty pounds, &c." And after his mentioning their not suffering their friends of Rhode Island to come and trade with them, proceeds, "So that unless the Lord steps in to their help and assistance, in some way beyond men's conceiving, their case is sad and to be pitied, and truly it moves bowels of compassion in all sorts except those in place, who carry it with a high hand towards them. Our bench now is Thomas Prince, Governor, &c." See the letter in Bishop's History, pages 168—177, or more at large in the second volume, folio, of the book of sufferings of the Quakers, pages 191—195, which last I did not see till since the publication of the first volume of my History.

APPENDIX A. 525

From the foregoing account, and what Bishop charges upon Governor Prince, viz., "That in thy conscience they were such a people as deserved to be destroyed, they, their wives, their children, their houses and lands, without pity or mercy;" which sentiment of his against the Quakers, I am told, is remembered in the family, being handed down to those of his posterity now living, it must therefore be acknowledged, he must have had too great a share in the persecutions mentioned; and as the persecuted Norton said, the strength of darkness must then have been too unhappily over him. And in justice to Humphry Norton's character (which is understood to be lessened by my manner of inserting his letter, and treating this subject, in pages 247, 257, of my History) I think further to manifest his and J. Rouse's behavior under their sufferings, by inserting a paragraph in Bishop's History, page 179, which would render my account more intelligible and full. Speaking of the number of lashes, which I mentioned, he adds, "Which as it drew store of blood, so it took much with the spectators, who beheld them in the stocks first praying, then saluting each other, and bidding the executioner have patience a little (when he came to take off their clothes) and he should see they could give their backs to the smiters." And Bishop adds, that "They gave in a paper assigning the grounds and reasons of their returning, when they were demanded wherefore they came in, which the magistrates would not suffer to be read; and so envious were they, that for taking John Rouse by the hand they put three of the inhabitants of Sandwich in the stocks." And it appears by the said Bishop's History, and the book of Friends' sufferings, that other whippings and persecutions followed in Plymouth Colony, and the said Humphry Norton, under whippings and other persecutions at New Haven, appears to have behaved in a Christian temper, when being loosed from the stocks after being whipped, having a great iron key tied athwart his mouth, and burnt deep in his hand with a red hot iron, "He kneeled down and prayed to the Lord, uttering his voice towards heaven, to the astonishment of them all." The reader is referred thereto for a more particular account.

In page 257, I intrepreted the figurative expressions of "Rending the rocks of wisdom and knowledge, and exalting that which is low," as directed against civil and ecclesiastical government, which I supposed they meant to subject to a supposed spiritual power in Christians without outward laws and rules: but on further inquiry and conversation with Friends, I am convinced that they thereby referred to the coming of the Lord, by his spiritual work, to level the wise and great, compared to mountains; and the literal knowledge and mere scholastic divinity, compared to rocks, as being hard to penetrate and break; for that which is meek and low to be exalted, even Christ within, the hope of glory. In which sense I perceive that passage is now understood by Friends.

In the same page I observed, on some preceding extracts from Fox's and

Williams's writings, " This opens the plain cause, why they (the Quakers) militated so hard against other magistrates and government." And in the form of an allegory, in page 408, it is said, " To whom others made fierce opposition professedly from the light within; and their clashings were so great that several lives were lost in the fray." The terms "militate," "fierce opposition," and "clashing" to the loss of lives, used to represent the conduct of Friends in those days, in respect to civil government, are too harsh to be justified by any authenticated facts. I conceive it to be essential to civil government, that the magistrate have a power to inflict corporal punishments, and also to arm his subjects to war against invaders of their rights, and therefore that the teaching of a contrary doctrine in either of these points, so far as it has influence, tends to obstruct or pull down government; and in no other sense did I ever mean to charge the Quakers with militating against or obstructing government.

I find they allow magistrates to inflict corporal punishments upon their subjects, who transgress the rules of equity;[1] but do not approve of arming their subjects to war against others. And in all States where they have been, I know nothing but that, as a society, they have been either actively obedient thereto, or have passively suffered what they were pleased to inflict upon them, without plotting against the government thereof, or using any forcible resistance against it. And I desire the reader to remember that I mean to correct every thing in my History that seemingly or really contradicts these ideas, and this character of the society.

In page 258, I speak of our Lord's direction to his disciples, Mat. x. 23, and of his own conduct towards the Gergesenes, Mat. viii. 34, as forming a general rule for us, thence charging some blame upon those Quakers who returned into the Massachusetts; whereas they now both appear to me to refer to special and peculiar cases.

As to the writings I referred to on page 260, I rather think my memory failed me in that respect; and as to not having light from Scripture, for actions, in the same page, I find that they suppose that Isaiah xx. 2, and Micah, i. 8, prove, that the women there mentioned might be moved by the divine Spirit to do those actions; of which the reader is left to judge for himself.

Upon a review of pages 259 and 367, compared with their own writings, I find that I had some mistaken ideas of what they held concerning the light within, and therefore freely refer the reader to their own authors for information in that respect.

I did not mean, in page 367, to charge them with calling darkness light, any further than wherein they appeared to be against allowing others the

[1] See Fox's Epistle to Friends at Nevis, in 1675. Also, Isaac Pennington's Works, folio, First part, p. 323.

free liberty of examining, and by arguments opposing sentiments which they judged to be erroneous; which, whether they were against or not, I freely submit to the reader's judgment.

William Harris is referred to in page 128, note 1, and in page 363, is named as a Quaker; I am now convinced that he was not one then, if he ever was; and the word *only*, as I twice used it in page 373, and once in page 375, in a way that seems to acquit Mr. Williams from any blame in his dispute with the Quakers, was more than I intended; for I really think there was a great deal of imperfection discovered by him, as well as his opponents, in the management of that dispute; and if he meant to punish any merely for their plain use of Thee and Thou (which I think he did not) I do not concur with any such thing.

In page 368, I have not so fully quoted Friends' answer to Roger Williams's objections as might be necessary to give an adequate view of both sides of the dispute; therefore I refer my reader to their writings on that subject, particularly George Fox's Answer to said objections, page 155, and Appendix, pages 117, 118.

Page 374, line 22, after the word "sentence" insert, "viz., blood will be given," which words are particularly marked, as referred to by Grove.

As by the "grapes of Sodom and clusters of Gommorah," in page 366, some might suppose I meant to charge the vices, that are couched under those expressions, upon the Quakers; I here declare that I meant no such thing.

Perhaps the partiality, in favor of Mr. Cotton, which I mention in page 374, was owing to Mr. Coddington's particular affection for him, rather than to the cause there assigned.

APPENDIX B.

CONTAINING A BRIEF SUMMARY OF THE ECCLESIASTICAL AFFAIRS OF THIS COUNTRY DOWN TO THE PRESENT TIME. [1777.][1]

Four principles have, in different ages and countries, been proposed to found government upon, viz., nature, grace, power and compact. James the First took much pains to persuade his people, that he was born to rule them; even so that the privileges he was pleased to allow them, were rather favors from him, than original rights in them. And his flattering courtiers, perceiving his humor, gave him the title of "Sacred Majesty," which the kingdom was very little acquainted with before. His high claims occasioned perpetual troubles to himself, and cost his son his crown and the head that wore it. And when facts are examined it appears, that Henry VII, from whom came their hereditary title, had as little right by birth to the crown of England, as any man that had worn it in five hundred years; and he made his way to it through blood and slaughter.[2] The pope has been the most notable advocate for founding dominion in grace; and by deceitful reasonings from the Jewish hand-writing, he has usurped the seat of him who is head of all principality and power. Henry VIII took offence at the pope's conduct, and rejecting his power assumed it to himself;. and many others, not holding the Head have subjected souls to slavish ordinances, after the doctrines and commandments of men. Col. 2. Cromwell was a notable actor upon the third principle, who, having gotten the power into his hands, pleaded that he ought to use it for the good of the nation; and his enemies acknowledge the excellency of his talents for government, if he had but obtained his power in a righteous way. But

---

[1]This Appendix closed Volume I of the former edition. Being the summary of the history of a period that is treated in full in the succeeding volumes, it is largely repeated in them. Parts of it will be recognized in the last four chapters, which were in Volume II of the former edition, and parts in Volume II of the present edition.—ED.

[2]Rapin, Vol. II, pp. 160, 161.

he, dying, left the nation in great confusion; to get relief from which they restored the second Charles, with good words and fair speeches, without settling any fixed and certain conditions with him. Soon after this, priestcraft was used to stir up tumults in different parts of the country, and then to cry, The church is in danger! which moved the parliament to make laws to exclude all persons from teaching either in churches or schools, who refused an assent and consent to their ordinances of men, and also to declare it to be unlawful to take up arms against the king, upon any pretence whatsoever. And, as Dr. Calamy observes, passive obedience and non-resistance, was the doctrine that for twenty-five years made their pulpits ring and presses groan. Yet, no sooner was this doctrine turned against the Episcopalians than, behold! they called in the prince of Orange with an armed force, to drive their king from his throne! And now the fourth principle is preferred, and a compact, containing a large Bill of Rights, is made with William before his coronation; and he and his queen were brought, " solemnly to promise and swear to govern the people of the kingdom of England, and the dominions thereto belonging, according to the statutes in parliament agreed on, and the laws and customs of the same; and, to their power, to cause law and justice to be executed in mercy, in all their judgments." They enacted that this oath should be taken by all their successors in that office.

Now the word of God plainly shows, that this way of mutual compact or covenant, is the only righteous foundation for civil government. For when Israel must needs have a king like the rest of the nations, and he indulged them in that request, yet neither Saul nor David, who were anointed by his immediate direction, ever assumed the regal power over the people, but by their free consent. And though the family of David had the clearest claim to hereditary succession that any family on earth ever had, yet, when ten of the twelve tribes revolted from his grandson, because he refused to comply with what they esteemed a reasonable proposal, and he had collected an army to bring them back by force, God warned him not to do it, and he obeyed him therein. Had these plain precedents been regarded in later times, what woes and miseries would they have prevented! But the history of all ages and nations shows, that when men have got the power into their hands, they often use it to gratify their own lusts, and recur to nature, religion or the constitution (as they think it will best serve) to carry, and yet cover, their wretched designs. A lamentable proof of this is now before us.

Dr. Mather, as a capable and faithful friend to his country, labored unweariedly to have the rights and privileges of it restored and enlarged; in order to which he prevailed with Archbishop Tillotson to tell the king that, "it would by no means do well for him to take any of those privileges from the people of New England, which king Charles the First had granted them." He likewise obtained a promise from Bishop Burnet that, "on the first opportunity he would declare openly in the House of Lords, that there was a greater sacredness in the charter of New England, than in those of the corporations in England; because those were only acts of grace, whereas the charter of New England was a contract between the king and the first patentees. They promised the king to enlarge his dominions on their own charges, provided they and their posterity might enjoy such and such privileges; they had performed their part; now for the king to deprive their posterity of the privileges therein granted unto them, would carry a face of injustice in it." This had some effect upon the king's mind, and caused a scruple whether he might lawfully take from us the privilege of choosing cur chief rulers or not. To this some of his arbitrary councillors said, "Whatever might be the merit of the cause, inasmuch as the charter of the Massachusetts stood vacated by a judgment against it, it was in his power to put them under what form of government he should think best for them."[1] This was so flattering and plausible that it took with William, who had often heard of their persecutions here, and thought that by reserving to himself a power to negative all their acts, he should prevent the like for the future.

Accordingly a new charter was drawn, dated October 7, 1691, which included Plymouth colony, consisting of the counties of Plymouth, Barnstable and Bristol; the Massachusetts colony, which contained the counties of Suffolk, Middlesex, Essex, Worcester, Hampshire and Berkshire; the Province of Maine, viz., the counties of York and Cumberland; and Sagadahoc, which, with lands annexed in the county of Lincoln, extends to Nova Scotia. The islands south of Cape Cod were included in this charter of The Province of the Massachusetts Bay in New England, which reserved an arbitrary power in the crown, to appoint our Governor, Lieutenant Governor and Secretary; but that the people might choose a House of Representatives annually, to meet upon the last Wednesday in May; when they were to elect twenty-eight Councillors, which was to be their Legislature; the Council and House to have a negative on each other's acts, and after both were agreed therein, yet the Governor, or in his absence the Lieutenant Governor, might negative any act they could pass, and also negative the election of as many Councillors as he pleased. Upon all times, except election day, he could call, adjourn, prorogue or dissolve the Assembly at pleasure. He had the sole power of appointing military officers; and was to appoint all officers of the courts of justice with the consent of the Council; other civil officers were elected by the two houses, where he had his negative; and no money could issue out of the treasury but by his warrant, by the advice and consent of the Council. And after

[1]Mather's Life, pp. 126, 127, 132.

all, the king in council could, at any time within three years, disannul any act or law that all three branches here could make. Now from whence came this arbitrary power in the crown of England over this country? Their plea founded upon the vacation of the former contract, would disannul any contract that could possibly be made with any distant people in the world; for a complaint against us was entered and judgment was passed, before we could possibly have opportunity to answer for ourselves. The charter of the city of London was vacated by the same court, where they had opportunity to answer; but they would not crown William and Mary till that judgment was reversed, and all the charters in England restored, and their privileges enlarged much beyond what they were when the contract was made with New England. And in that, the king engaged for himself, his heirs and successors, that we should hold our lands, " in free and common socage, and not *in capite*, nor by knights' service, we yielding and paying to him, his heirs and successors the fifth part only of all ore of gold and silver, which from time to time and at all times hereafter shall be gotten, had or obtained, for all services, exactions and demands whatsoever."[1] And let our oppressors show if they can that we ever violated this contract.

As to affairs here, the charter declared " liberty of conscience in the worship of God to all Christians, except Papists, inhabiting or which shall inhabit or be resident within our said province or territory." But this most important article was construed by the ministers, as meaning, " that the General Court might, by laws, encourage and protect that religion which is the general profession of the inhabitants."[2]

Accordingly they in October of this year began the practice, which a noted author described thirty-four years after, in the following manner. After reciting an old saying, that ministers of the gospel would have a poor time of it, if they must rely on a free contribution of the people for their maintenance, he says, " The laws of the province having had the royal approbation to ratify them, they are the king's laws. By these laws it is enacted, that there shall be a public worship of God in every plantation; that the person elected by the majority of the inhabitants to be so, shall be looked upon as the minister of the place; that the salary for him which they shall agree upon, shall be levied by a rate upon all the inhabitants. In consequence of this, the minister thus chosen by the people, is (not only Christ's, but also) in reality the king's minister; and the salary for him is raised in the king's name, and is the king's allowance unto him. If the most of the inhabitants in a plantation are Episcopalians, they will have a minister of their own persuasion; and the dissenters, if there be any in the place, must pay their proportion of the tax for the support of this legal

[1] Massachusetts History, Vol. III, pp. 8, 9.
[2] Massachusetts History, Vol. II, p. 10. [17.]

minister. In a few of the towns, a few of the people, in hope of being released from the tax for the legal minister, sometimes profess themselves Episcopalians; but when they plead this for their exemption, their neighbors tell them, they know in their consciences, they do not as they would be done unto. And if a Governor go by his arbitrary power to supersede the execution of the law, and require the justices and constables to leave the Episcopalians out of the tax, the people wonder he is not aware that he is all this while forbidding that the king should have his dues paid unto him; and forbidding the king's minister to receive what the king has given him. .... Sometimes the Quakers also have given some occasion for uneasiness; but where Quakerism is troublesome, some towns are so wise as to involve the salary for the ministry in a general rate for all town charges, and so the cavils of those, who would else refuse to pay the rate for the ministry, are obviated."[1]

A few facts may help to explain this, and to show how much greater liberty of conscience we have enjoyed since the Revolution[2] than before. Before that memorable event, no man in the Massachusetts colony was allowed a vote, in choosing either minister or ruler, but members in full communion in their churches. And the skill of knowing that those who dissented from their judgments, sinned against their own consciences, was then limited to such good men; but now, having forty pounds worth of personal estate, or a freehold worth forty shillings a year, entitles every inhabitant to a vote in all such affairs, and to a power of judging that their neighbors sin against the golden rule, if they will not put into the mouths of him whom the majority has declared to be the legal minister. From that day to this, it is made a doubt among our lawyers and judges, whether a church of Christ be a society known in law, so as to be capable of holding a meeting-house or other estates, without having other persons to be trustees or guardians for them. The honorable Edward Goddard, Esq., of Framingham, who had been a member both of the Lower and Upper House, in our Legislature, described this matter to the life, in a piece he published in 1753, wherein he says:

> "Good conscience men allow, (they say)
> But must be understood,
> To say as they say themselves do say,
> Or else it can't be good."

For thirty-six years after the Massachusetts received their last charter, they exerted all their power, both in their legislative and executive courts, with every art that ministers could help them to, in attempts to compel every town to receive and support such ministers as they called orthodox.

[1] Mather's Ratio Disciplinæ, pp. 20--22.
[2] The abdication of James II, and the accession of William and Mary.—ED.

They made two attempts of this nature upon Swanzey; and in 1722, they added the sum of one hundred and seventy-two pounds eleven shillings, to the province taxes upon Dartmouth and Tiverton, for such ministers, intending that they should draw it out of the province treasury. For refusing to assess the same, Joseph Anthony, John Sisson, John Akin, Quakers, and Philip Tabor, a Baptist minister, Select-men of those towns, were seized and confined in Bristol jail, till the case was carried to England, and those taxes were disannulled by the king in council, and an express order was sent over to release them.

The first act that was made in our province, to exempt either Baptists or Quakers from taxes to Pædobaptist ministers was in 1728; which says, "that from and after the publication of this act, none of the persons commonly called Anabaptists, nor any of those called Quakers, that are or shall be enrolled or entered in their several societies as members thereof, and who allege a scruple of conscience as the reason of their refusal to pay any part or proportion of such taxes as are from time to time assessed for the support of the minister or ministers of the churches established by the laws of this province, in the town or place where they dwell, shall have their polls taxed toward the support of such minister or ministers, nor shall their bodies be at any time taken in execution, to satisfy any such ministerial rate or tax, assessed upon their estates or faculties; provided, that such persons do usually attend the meetings of their respective societies, assembling upon the Lord's day for the worship of God, and that they live within five miles of the place of such meeting." Here we may see that tyranny is always the same. "*Go ye serve the Lord ; only let your flocks and your herds be stayed,*" said Pharaoh. Let their bodies be exempted, but their estates and faculties be taxed, said the Massachusetts. "*I will let you go, that ye may sacrifice to the Lord your God in the wilderness ; only you shall not go very far away,*" said Pharaoh. Go but five miles, said the Massachusetts. Mr. Thomas Hollis, of London, had received such accounts of their catholic temper at Harvard College, confirmed by the ordination of a pious youth in Boston who was educated there,[1] that he became the greatest benefactor to that college that they ever had. I have a letter which he wrote to Mr. Ephriam Wheaton, pastor of the first church in Swanzey, dated March 23, 1723, wherein he says, " You have heard, or may be informed by Mr. Callender, of my foundation in Harvard College, and the provision I have made for Baptist youth to be educated for the ministry, and equally regarded with Pædobaptists. If you know any as may be duly qualified, inform me, and I shall be glad to recommend them for first vacancy." But what heart could he have to send any youths there, while a large number of his brethren, who, with himself, lived within the bounds of Rehoboth, were taxed from year to year to

---

[1] See pp. 420, 421.

Presbyterian ministers! After the above exempting act was made, they were told by their County Court, that it did not take place that year. For refusing to pay such taxes any longer, Elder Wheaton's son, and twenty-seven more of his people were seized on March 3, 1729, and confined in Bristol jail. More or less of such things, which by their eminent fathers are called tyranny and robbery,[1] have been practised to this day, under the mask of religion.

My dear countrymen, I must here solemnly call you to review the text which has often been cast upon us, viz., "Mark them who cause divisions and offences, contrary to the doctrine which ye have learned, and avoid them: for they that are such, serve not our Lord Jesus Christ, but their own belly; and by good words and fair speeches deceive the hearts of the simple." The uppermost party in every state has always been ready to apply this word to those who refuse a submission and conformity to them in religious matters. But the mark is set upon them who *cause* divisions, not merely upon such as are divided. Joseph was separated from his brethren, without his being the faulty cause of it. Again the mark is put upon such as cause divisions, *contrary to Christ's doctrine;* otherwise he declares himself, that he came to send divisions upon earth, and even betwixt near relations. This matter is justly stated in pages 421, 422. The inspired apostle commands us in the name of Christ to withdraw from every brother that walketh disorderly:—for we behaved not ourselves disorderly among you, neither did we *eat any man's bread for naught;* yet this great disorder has long been practised under good words and fair speeches. A pagan minister who loved the wages of unrighteousness once cudgelled his beast most cruelly for not carrying him forward against a drawn sword, whereby he would have been slain: and though the dumb ass, speaking with man's voice, forbade the madness of the prophet, yet the above practice which never had any better support than the cudgel,[2] is madly pursued by many who call themselves Christians to this day.

A convention of ministers published a discourse among us five years ago, entitled Catholicism, or Christian Charity; wherein, after saying many excellent things about charity, they, in page 38, accuse those who separated from their constitution in 1744, of zeal, yea rather fury against "giving and receiving ministerial support;" and with a want of "consistency and honesty," for now coming into that practice themselves. It is well known that this censure is leveled against many of my brethren and myself with them. I readily confess that I separated from their constitution about the close of that year; but positively deny that ever I appeared against giving and receiving ministerial support, and know not that any of my brethren in the ministry who separated from them ever did so. Had they said that we were zealous against assessing and forcing in such cases,

[1] See pp. 248, 419. [2] See pp. 80, 81.

they would not have wronged the truth and their neighbors, as they have now done. The constitution that we separated from, was formed in Saybrook in 1708, which says, "that the churches which are neighboring to each other, shall consociate for mutual affording to each other such assistance as may be requisite, *upon all occasions ecclesiastical.*" Their first proof to support this article is Psalm 122. 3—5, which speaks of the thrones of judgment that were set in Jerusalem for the house of David. A crafty ministerial Governor,[1] son to a Massachusetts magistrate, prevailed with the Connecticut legislature to approbate this platform the next year. Another Cambridge scholar[2] was then minister of Norwich, and was resolute to introduce the scheme there. The law whereby it was approbated said, "Provided, that nothing herein shall be intended or construed to hinder any society or church that is, or shall be, allowed by the laws of this government, from exercising worship and discipline in their own way, according to their consciences." Yet, because Richard Bushnel and Joseph Backus, Esquires, representatives for Norwich, (with other fathers of the town,) withdrew from the minister's party, rather than come under that yoke, they laid them under church censure, and by that means procured their expulsion out of the next Assembly when they met. About the same time, Mr. Stoddard publicly advanced his scheme of the Lord's Supper being a converting ordinance.[3] And though with much labor Norwich got rid of said minister, and settled another upon their former principles, yet, before I left this latter minister, he not only plainly discovered his fondness for Saybrook Platform, but actually procured a vote of the church to receive members without so much as a written account of any inward change; and they practise so to this day. A few months before I separated, Mr. Elisha Williams, a former President of Yale College, published A Seasonable Plea for the Rights of Conscience, wherein he says, "The fountain and original of all civil power is from the people, and is certainly instituted for their sakes; the great end of civil government, is the preservation of their persons, their liberties, and their property. A Christian is to receive his Christianity from Christ alone; for what is it which is necessarily implied and supposed in the very notion of a Christian but this, that he is a follower and disciple of Christ! As Christ's officers have authority to teach men his mind in things pertaining to his kingdom; so they have no authority to teach men anything but the mind and will of Christ. It is a truth that shines with a meridian brightness, that whatever is not contained in a commission, is out of it, and excluded by it; and the teaching his laws only being contained in the commission, what is not his

---

[1] Gurdon Saltonstall, minister in New London, before his election as Governor. See p. 469.—ED.

[2] John Woodward. See p. 474.—ED.

[3] See p. 385, note.—B.   See also pp. 462, 468.—ED.

law is out of it, and by that commission they are excluded from teaching it, or forbid by it."

But what can be more contrary hereto than for a civil legislature to form every town and parish into religious societies, and to force every inhabitant therein either to support the minister which the majority have chosen, or else to pay a yearly acknowledgment to that usurped power over their consciences? And this is as real a breach of public faith in our charter, as ever it was for the British Court to take from us the right of choosing our own Governors, and then to burn our towns and cut our throats for not paying them as much money as they demanded. I have the express testimony of the elders and brethren of seventeen of our Baptist churches, who met last year at Grafton, that they entirely agree with the sentiments and principles recited in our history, pages 10—22,[1] excepting that of infant baptism; yet great numbers of them have been taxed to Pædobaptist ministers since that time, only because we refuse to pay any further acknowledgment to the above-said usurped power over our consciences. And, since it is abundantly evident that our former sufferings would have been greater from the ruling party here than they were, if it had not been for restraints from the British Court; and as it is also certain that attempts have been made from thence to prevent our uniting now with our country against their invasions, how can those who still incline to oppress us ever expect to prosper, if they view the matter either in a natural, or a judicial light? Considered in a natural light; when we know and can prove that several thousand dollars' worth of estates have been wrested from us on religious accounts, since the present contest for civil liberty commenced, with what heart can we obey or support the power which still denies us equal liberty of conscience with themselves? And considering things judicially, let such read the warnings their fathers had, with their effects, on pages 209—212, 311—313, 416—418, and then venture on further in that way if they dare.

It is to be noted, that a very large number of our countrymen of various denominations are for the equal liberty we speak of; and I desire all to act in the case by the rule Mr. Robinson prescribes, pages 8, 9. I shall close with the words of the aforesaid Mr. Goddard, viz. :—

"In ancient ages, when the English realm
And popish zealots, placed at the helm
To 'stablish that religion; tithes were fix'd

---

[1] "Our Agent having given an account of his and the Committee's proceedings in the year past, in presenting our memorial to the Assembly, &c., and having read a state of the difference betwixt our churches and those who oppress us, to be inserted in our history, it was voted, unanimously, That the account Elder Backus has drawn up, of the sentiments and practices of the Baptist societies, is entirely agreeable to the minds of this Association.

JAMES MANNING, Moderator."

Minutes of the Warren Association, Grafton, September 10, 11, 1776, p. 6.—ED.

By canon laws; with civil intermix'd,
Which form'd the English constitution so,
That after ages can't the tithes forego;
And hence dissenters are obliged there,
To pay incumbents, whom they never hear,
Which some condemn, as a prelatic game,
Who yet, by MAJOR VOTE would play the same;
And LORD MAJORITY would claim the purse
For his incumbents; than which nothing worse,
LORDLY diocesan, himself, can claim;
So these two LORDS do differ, but in name,
One pleading English laws, for his support;
The other feigning acts of our own Court;
Alleging law, in a perverted sense,
To render CHARTER grant, a mere pretence;
And as if law and charter both intend
To crush one church, another to befriend;
They'd make them mean, the same that Pharaoh said,
' *Go serve the Lord, but let your flocks be stay'd.*'
But if one church be tax'd, to serve another,
No matter whether, done by this or t'other."

END OF VOLUME I.

General Index
to both Volumes 1 and 2
are in the back of
Volume 2.

THE BAPTIST STANDARD BEARER, INC.
A non-profit, tax-exempt corporation
committed to the Publication & Preservation
of The Baptist Heritage.

SAMPLE TITLES FOR PUBLICATIONS AVAILABLE IN OUR VARIOUS SERIES:

THE BAPTIST *COMMENTARY* SERIES
Sample of authors/works in or near republication:
John Gill - *Exposition of the Old & New Testaments (9 & 18 Vol. Sets)*
  (Volumes from the 18 vol. set can be purchased individually)

THE BAPTIST *FAITH* SERIES:
Sample of authors/works in or near republication:
Abraham Booth - *The Reign of Grace*
Abraham Booth - *Paedobaptism Examined (3 Vols.)*
John Gill - *A Complete Body of Doctrinal Divinity*

THE BAPTIST *HISTORY* SERIES:
Sample of authors/works in or near republication:
Thomas Armitage - *A History of the Baptists (2 Vols.)*
Isaac Backus - *History of the New England Baptists (2 Vols.)*
William Cathcart - *The Baptist Encyclopaedia (3 Vols.)*
J. M. Cramp - *Baptist History*

THE BAPTIST *DISTINCTIVES* SERIES:
Sample of authors/works in or near republication:
Alexander Carson - *Ecclesiastical Polity of the New Testament Churches*
E.C. Dargan - *Ecclesiology: A Study of the Churches*
J. M. Frost - *Paedobaptism: Is It From Heaven?*
R. B. C. Howell - *The Evils of Infant Baptism*

THE *DISSENT & NONCONFORMITY* SERIES:
Sample of authors/works in or near republication:
Champlin Burrage - *The Early English Dissenters (2 Vols.)*
Franklin H. Littell - *The Anabaptist View of the Church*
Albert H. Newman - *History of Anti-Paedobaptism*
Walter Wilson - *History & Antiquities of the Dissenting Churches (4 Vols.)*

For a complete list of current authors/titles, visit our internet site at
www.standardbearer.com or write us at:

The Baptist Standard Bearer, Inc.
No. 1 Iron Oaks Drive • Paris, Arkansas 72855
Telephone: (501) 963-3831   Fax: (501) 963-8083
E-mail: baptist@arkansas.net
Internet: http://www.standardbearer.com

Specialists in Baptist Reprints and Rare Books

Thou hast given a *standard* to them that fear thee; that it may be displayed because of the truth. -- *Psalm 60:4*

www.ingramcontent.com/pod-product-compliance
Lightning Source LLC
Chambersburg PA
CBHW020911020526
44114CB00039B/134